NUMBER FOUR IN THE

Amerind Foundation
New World Studies Series
Anne I. Woosley
Series Editor

Salado

Salado

EDITED BY
Jeffrey S. Dean

An Amerind Foundation Publication, DRAGOON, ARIZONA
University of New Mexico Press, ALBUQUERQUE

Library of Congress Cataloging-in-Publication Data

Salado / edited by Jeffrey S. Dean.—1st ed.
p.   cm.—(Amerind foundation new world studies series ; no. 4)
Includes bibliographical references and index.
1. Salado culture. I. Dean, Jeffrey S., 1939–   II. Series.
E99.S547 S23 2000
306´.09791—dc21   99-006792

Contents

Figures

Tables

Foreword

THE DETAIL IN WHICH WE CURRENTLY RECONSTRUCT Southwest prehistory is largely the product of federally funded archaeological projects responding to legislative directive and preservation concerns. In desert southern Arizona, one of the nation's fastest growing regions, development often means the construction of mechanisms that manage and distribute water with the Bureau of Reclamation playing a particularly active role in funding related archaeological mitigation. *Salado* marks the culmination of the Roosevelt Archaeological Project, an effort to preserve our knowledge of Salado sites and material remains in advance of major physical expansion to not only the dam and reservoir, but the construction of new roadways and recreational facilities.

Salado also marks a stage in the institutional history of the Amerind Foundation. During the mid 1980s Foundation personnel discussed the feasibility of establishing an advanced seminar program modeled on the popularly termed "think-tank" idea whereby a small group of researchers could involve themselves in intellectual exchange. Subsequent collaborative volumes based on seminar topics would follow. At about the same time, the Central Arizona Aqueduct Project had come to a close and Thomas R. Lincoln of the Bureau of Reclamation was considering a possible meeting place in which key CAP archaeologists might participate in a seminar setting. Tom Lincoln arrived at Amerind where we talked about our respective goals and, taking us at our word that we would actually have the seminar house renovated by the proposed meeting date, Tom and I shook hands on an agreement: Amerind would provide the seminar facility and some support and the Bureau would furnish principal funding, invite the archaeologist participants, and determine the specific subject matter to be addressed. Our mutual respect and common goal to better disseminate knowledge gained from monumental proj-

ects in synthetic fashion resulted in *Exploring the Hohokam*, the first Amerind seminar and published volume. The success of this endeavor and the quality of the collaborative book that followed could not have been a more auspicious beginning to what has become an established seminar publication series contributing significantly to anthropological studies.

Salado picks up where *Exploring the Hohokam* leaves off. It takes us into the so-called heartland of Salado culture—where ironically little work had previously been conducted—and investigates exactly what is meant by the term; does it have integrity and convey a cohesive, meaningful set of cultural data; does it represent a people; what is its geographic distribution and sphere of influence; how precisely does it relate to other regions of the U.S. Southwest and northern Mexico? As is often the case with complex subjects, more questions are raised than answered and the Salado seminar was no exception. No ultimate definition of Salado was forthcoming. A lack of consensus about what is Salado in no way detracts from the usefulness of this volume which presents the results of extensive field research that produced enormous quantities of data and thereby reshaped our thinking about the phenomenon known as Salado.

ACKNOWLEDGMENTS

The Amerind Foundation Seminar Series benefits from the gracious and generous support of its Board of Directors. We thank Wm. Duncan Fulton, Peter L. Formo, Michael W. Hard, Elizabeth F. Husband, Marilyn Fulton, George J. Gumerman, Peter Johnson, Sharline Reedy, and Lawrence Shiever.

ANNE I. WOOSLEY
THE AMERIND FOUNDATION, INC.

Preface

Jeffrey S. Dean

OVER THE LAST FEW DECADES SOUTHERN ARIZONA has experienced an immense population explosion. The voracious growth of Phoenix and its satellite cities in particular has strained the resources of the state, none more so than the scarce water supply of this arid region. The utter dependence of the desert megalopolis on a sufficient supply of water has been evident since territorial days, and the struggle to acquire and hold adequate water supplies has been the major theme in Arizona history (Fradkin 1984). It is no accident that the Salt River Basin saw the first large-scale federal water reclamation project in the United States, involving the construction of Theodore Roosevelt Dam and Lake in Tonto Basin between 1903 and 1911 and the subsequent construction of six additional dams and reservoirs on the Salt and Verde Rivers (Rogge et al. 1995:Figure 1.3) to provide water for the fields, businesses, and people of the Valley of the Sun. When it became apparent that growing demand would exceed the water capacity of the Salt River drainage, the monumental Central Arizona Project was built to bring water across the desert from the Colorado River to Phoenix and beyond. Together, the massive Salt River and Central Arizona Projects have kept southern Arizona from running out of this precious resource—for now.

Paradoxically, as Phoenix and neighboring communities encroached on the Salt River floodplain, the specter of *too much* water raised its head. In rare years when heavy precipitation in the mountain headwaters of the Salt drainage exceeds the water management system's capacity, torrents of water are released to rush through the Phoenix urban area, gouging out huge chunks of real estate, washing away bridges, disrupting traffic, and endangering property and lives. Disastrous flooding in the 1980s, coupled with the elimination of other planned components of the Central Arizona Project, inspired the Bureau of Reclamation to increase the capacity of Lake Roosevelt to better control the flow of water through the

Salt River system, especially during episodes of extremely high runoff, and thereby reduce the flood danger to the Phoenix metropolitan area.

THE ROOSEVELT ARCHAEOLOGY PROJECT

Raising the maximum water level of Lake Roosevelt impacted the archaeological resources of Tonto Basin in many ways in addition to the obvious one of inundating sites. Large-scale construction activities—raising a higher dam over the original structure, erecting a bridge over the lake, rerouting existing highways and secondary roads, acquiring construction materials, and building haul roads—impinged directly on the landscape and its archaeological remains. Furthermore, the planned addition of several thousand Forest Service camping spots around the lake threatened archaeological resources through the construction of new roads and campgrounds, many in hitherto inaccessible places rich in archaeological remains, and through the intentional or inadvertent acts of the vastly increased number of campers. Clearly, large-scale action was required, by law and by reason, to offset the massive potential loss of archaeological information occasioned by these activities.

The threat to Tonto Basin's archaeological riches also created an unparalleled opportunity to add significantly to knowledge of the Basin's prehistory and of its place in the larger context of Southwestern archaeology. Despite the controversy that had surrounded the Salado concept, surprisingly little focused archaeological research had been done in the geographical core of this complex of traits, inferences, and speculations. Here was a chance to answer the question of what, really, was Salado, and, perhaps more important, to systematically address a number of significant issues that concerned Southwestern archaeology.

The two federal agencies most closely involved in the Roosevelt augmentation project, the Department of the Interior's Bureau of Reclamation and the Department of Agriculture's Forest Service, rose to the challenge of mitigating the archaeological impact of this massive undertaking. As the agency directly responsible for the Roosevelt project, the Bureau of Reclamation accepted responsibility for the work's archaeological consequences and funded the mitigation. Archaeologists of the Bureau's Arizona Projects Office (now Phoenix Area Office) exercised primary oversight of the archaeological work, while archaeologists of the Tonto National Forest (TNF) represented the Forest Service's interests as custodian of the land on which most of the work occurred. Together with Arizona State Historic Preservation Office (SHPO) archaeologists, these individuals worked diligently to develop a large-scale research program that would effectively mitigate the physical impact of the Roosevelt project and, at the same time, produce the maximum amount of information pertinent to research questions of current concern in Southwestern and American archaeology (Rice 1998:1–2).

These objectives required an overall approach centered on one or more important general issues, each comprising many related specific problems, that prevailing archaeological knowledge indicated could be profitably confronted in Tonto Basin. Reclamation, TNF, and SHPO archaeologists identified three major problem domains that could be effectively addressed in Tonto Basin. Rather than mount one enormous mitigation effort to deal comprehensively with all these issues, it was decided to support three separate, more easily managed projects, each focused on one problem domain. A fourth project was added at a later date. The largest component of the project would be charged with tracking the activities, collating the data, and combining the results of all three into a comprehensive synthesis of the projects, the prehistory of Tonto Basin, and its relationships to the Southwest as a whole. Oversight by Reclamation and TNF archaeologists would assure that legal requirements were satisfied and the goals of the integrated mitigation effort were met. Thus were born the Roosevelt Platform Mound Study (RPMS), the Roosevelt Community Development Study (RCDS), the Roosevelt Rural Sites Study (RRSS), and the Roosevelt Bajada Survey (RBS).

The largest component of the Roosevelt Archaeology Project, RPMS, was awarded to the Office of Cultural Resource Management in the Department of Anthropology at Arizona State University (ASU) in Tempe. The principal objectives of RPMS were to investigate several platform mound sites in order to illuminate the structural and functional attributes of these somewhat enigmatic features, characterize the communities of which they were parts, and assess their relationships to the better known Hohokam platform mounds and communities in the Phoenix and Tucson Basins. RPMS undertook intensive and extensive investigations in five platform mound communities along both sides of the Salt and Tonto Arms of the Basin. In a change that reflects the flexibility of the Reclamation, TNF, and ASU programs, an investigation of Upland sites, based on the RBS project, was added to RPMS when it became necessary to further explicate the relationships between Upland and Lowland communities. In addition to research on platform mound communities, ASU was charged with integrating the results of all three studies into a final summary and synthesis of the Project's accomplishments.

Desert Archaeology, Inc., in Tucson, Arizona, was awarded RCDS to investigate the origin and development of platform mounds and platform mound communities in the Basin. This effort involved excavating sites ranging from Early Ceramic period pithouse villages to Roosevelt phase platform mound communities and representing a span of more than 1000 years (ca. 300–1325) along the right bank of the Salt River downstream from where it debouches from its canyon into Tonto Basin. In addition, RCDS undertook demographic studies involving population estimation and identifying immigration into the Basin.

RRSS—focused on small "rural" sites, their socioeconomic roles, and their relationships to the larger site complexes—was awarded to Statistical Research, Inc., in Tucson. RRSS examined three small-site complexes along either side of the Salt Arm and three complexes on the west side of Tonto Creek. In addition, RRSS was charged with characterizing past environmental variability and prehistoric farming practices. These studies involved assessing existing paleoenvironmental reconstructions, reconstructing other variables, and assessing the effects of fluctuations in these factors on the economies of the prehistoric residents of Tonto Basin.

RBS, a sample survey of upland localities on the northern flanks of the Basin, was undertaken by the Tucson office of SWCA, Inc. The results of this work subsequently were incorporated into the Uplands component of RPMS and used to select upland sites for more intensive investigation.

From the beginning, Reclamation and Tonto National Forest personnel were determined to see the widest possible dissemination of the data, analyses, and results produced by the Roosevelt Archaeology Project. So far, the outcome of this commitment includes 17 massive descriptive reports (comprising 29 volumes) that are cited repeatedly throughout this book, planned books on pertinent topics, and numerous symposia and papers at local, regional, and national professional meetings. Mindful of the responsibility to inform the American public, the ultimate supporters and beneficiaries of the research, Project archaeologists provided information to local and national print and broadcast media, held open houses for the public to observe work in progress, collaborated in the video taping of their activities, delivered numerous talks to civic and avocational groups, crafted fixed and traveling displays, and produced popular books and articles.

The Amerind Foundation Seminar

Built into the Roosevelt Archaeology Project were plans for a concluding conference modeled on the highly productive Amerind Foundation seminar that wrapped up Reclamation's Central Arizona Project Hohokam research and produced the hugely successful book *Exploring the Hohokam: Prehistoric Desert Peoples of the American Southwest* (Gumerman 1991). The "Prehistoric Salado Culture of the American Southwest," convened at the Amerind Foundation in Dragoon, Arizona, in May 1995, allowed senior participants in RPMS, RCDS, and RRSS to synthesize and discuss their research while the data and their implications were fresh in their minds. Experts on other parts of the Southwest attended to help place Salado within the broader context of what was happening throughout the region in the thirteenth to fifteenth centuries. Two discussants were present to evaluate the deliberations in terms of current theoretical frameworks in American and world archaeology and of possible connections between the Southwest and Mesoamerica.

Rather than address the individual research of each project, the conference was organized around several themes and the Project's contributions to elucidating them. Some of these matters were foreseen in developing the original Roosevelt Project research designs. Others became apparent during the course of the field work and had to be incorporated into revised research designs. Still others arose when the research contradicted initial work-

ing hypotheses and required the construction of replacement formulations. Finally, some new themes emerged from the seminar itself.

Each participant, often with the help of coauthors, prepared a paper that was circulated to the attendees prior to the seminar, thus obviating the need for time consuming presentations. Instead, each author's precis of his or her paper was followed by a group discussion of the topic in general and the author(s) position on it. This approach sharpened the focus on particular problems, often altered the group's perception of them, and sometimes indicated other problems that had not been anticipated. On the last day, the discussants reviewed the papers, evaluated the discussions, and inaugurated additional exchanges on important matters. This procedure stimulated substantial postconference revision of most papers; consequently, the papers in this volume are quite different from the versions presented at Amerind.

The Book

This book includes the revised versions of the papers presented at the Amerind Foundation seminar plus that of one invitee, E. Charles Adams, who was not able to attend the meeting but whose paper was available to the participants. Although space limitations prohibited attendance by additional individuals, many coauthors made valuable contributions to the chapters, before and/or after the meeting.

In general, the style of the volume closely follows the American Antiquity Style Guide with a few minor exceptions that will be evident only to former and current editors of that journal. Other usages conform to University of New Mexico Press specifications. Numerous conventions were adopted to save space and ensure consistency of allusion and definitions of terms among the chapters. Most of these represent punctuation, spelling, capitalization, and italicization standards that need no specific notice. A couple others, however, require some elaboration. First, because nearly all the calendar dates that appear in the book fall in the A.D. period, A.D. dates are designated solely by the number (e.g., 1377 rather than A.D. 1377) except for a few cases in which clarity demands the modifier. Thus, unless otherwise indicated, all dates are A.D. dates. B.C. dates are labeled as such. Second, numerical site designations are abbreviated from the conventional form adopted by the Roosevelt Project and used in the publications resulting from that work. Under this convention, site numbers consisted of the standard Arizona State Museum (ASM) designation (Wasley 1957) followed by the Tonto National Forest inventory number. Thus, a typical site number would be AZ V:6:1/1372, in which AZ stands for Arizona, V for the local "quadrangle" (one degree of latitude and longitude on a side), 6 for the appropriate rectangle (15 minutes on a side) within the quadrangle, 1 for the first site numbered within that rectangle, and /1372 for the 1372nd site recorded on the Tonto National Forest. Since all the sites with this type of number mentioned in this book are in Arizona, the state designation is superfluous and is dropped. Because the ASM component of the number provides a unique designation for the site, the TNF number is redundant, and it, too, is dropped. Thus, the original site number AZ V:6:1/1372 appears here simply as V:6:1. All numbers are ASM unless otherwise designated, for example V:6:1 (ASU).

ACKNOWLEDGMENTS

A product such as this book involves the input of numerous individuals and institutions. It is our distinct pleasure to acknowledge as many of these contributions as can be recalled at this late stage in the production process.

First and foremost, we thank the American people who, through their representatives in Congress and the Executive Branch, recognize the importance of archaeological resources to the nation and its citizens. Without the incentive and support provided by pertinent statutes, directives, and procedures, the vast majority of the research reported in this book, and the book itself, would have been neither conceivable nor possible. The immediate instruments of these national policies, the Bureau of Reclamation and the Forest Service provided funding, broad direction, and general overview of the Roosevelt research. The local arms of these Departments, Reclamation's Arizona Projects Office and the Tonto National Forest, administered the funding, developed the general conception and organization of the projects, and provided on-the-spot direction and administration of the research. Reclamation personnel who merit special recognition include: the late Ward Weakly who, as Bureau Senior Archeologist, fought to establish high standards for the mitigation of damage to archaeological resources by Bureau activities; Gene Rogge who articulated the integrated, scientific, hypothesis-testing approach to large-scale mitigation activities that was so successfully implemented by the Roosevelt Archaeology Project; Tom Lincoln who provided the continuity of oversight, constancy of purpose, and high-level diplomacy necessary to see the Project through from beginning to end; Kathy Pedrick, Jon Czaplicki, and Theresa Hoffman, who managed various aspects of the work. Scott Wood, Tonto National Forest Archeologist, contributed significantly to all aspects of the project (from research design to oversight of field operations to manuscript evaluation), insisted on high research performance standards, and saw that they were met. Finally, Shereen Lerner and Ann Howard of the State Historic Preservation Office provided valuable insights into project design and review and compliance of results. Without the interest and guidance of these institutions and individuals none of what appears here would have been possible.

Contract archaeology institutions and individuals associated with the Roosevelt Archaeology Project were, of course, instrumental in the conduct and final results of the work and in the organization and content of this volume. It is impossible to list the hundreds of people who worked so diligently and effectively on these projects. Noting the institutions involved must be taken as acknowledging the vital contributions of these dedicated individuals to the research and the book. To the Office of Cultural Resource Management of the Department of Anthropology at Arizona State University, Desert Archaeology, Inc., Statistical Research, Inc., and SWCA, Inc. (Tucson Office) go thanks for many jobs well done. Ably led by, respectively Chuck Redman and Glen Rice, Bill Doelle, Jeff Altschul, and Tom Euler, these organizations accomplished remarkable feats of field and laboratory logistics, personnel management, research performance, and report production, all while displaying an extraordinary degree of equanimity and interproject communication under a great deal of pressure.

The Amerind Foundation deserves special thanks for hosting the seminar on Salado. The discussions, debates, and occasional polite disagreements were fostered by the congenial ambiance of this oasis of learning in the Arizona desert. Anne Woosley and her capable staff made the group's stay most pleasant, stimulating, and productive.

Several people and institutions worked diligently on this book. We are grateful to the Laboratory of Tree-Ring Research at The University of Arizona and its Director, Malcolm Hughes, for providing Dean with the opportunity to undertake this editing venture. The authors of the individual chapters have graced the book with the latest thinking, backed up by vast quantities of new data and analyses, on the Salado "phenomenon." Many people who contributed editing, computer, illustrative, and other skills to the book are acknowledged in the individual chapters. A few people aided immensely in the production of the volume as a whole. Allan McIntyre of the Amerind Foundation did the final editing of the manuscript for submission to the University of New Mexico Press. Andrea Ondreyco of the Bureau of Reclamation

Phoenix Area Office produced many of the illustrations in both digital and paper formats. Carrie Dean of the Tree-Ring Laboratory spent untold hours reading proofs, entering innumerable editorial changes into the manuscripts, and reducing text and tables to computer files.

To all these people and many, many more who cannot be individually acknowledged we extend our heartfelt thanks for countless jobs well done. It would not have been possible without you.

Salado

Introduction:

The Salado Phenomenon

Jeffrey S. Dean

SALADO IS A TERM THAT EVOKES NEARLY AS MANY different responses from Southwestern archaeologists as there are Southwestern archaeologists. Reactions range from affirmations of the respondents' knowing exactly what the word means to vehement denials that it means anything at all. It has been the unhappy fate of this term to be enveloped in ambiguity and controversy since its introduction by Gladwin and Gladwin in 1930. Acceptance and use of the Salado concept has waxed and waned over the intervening years depending on changing emphases in Southwestern archaeology and on perceptions of the idea's descriptive or explanatory power. A recent rekindling of interest in Salado, occasioned by modern flood control activities on the Salt River, has done little to alleviate disagreement over the term.

In the 1980s and 1990s, a Bureau of Reclamation project to raise the maximum water level of Lake Theodore Roosevelt necessitated large-scale cultural resource mitigation in Tonto Basin, the supposed "heartland" of the Salado phenomenon. Not unexpectedly, it was hoped that the Roosevelt Archaeology Project would resolve the Salado issue once and for all (Pedrick 1992; Rice 1998). Wide ranging surveys and the complete or partial excavation of 155 sites produced a vast data base and innovative analyses ranging across the archaeological spectrum. Toward the end of this work, the Bureau sponsored the Amerind Foundation New World Study Seminar to synthesize the Roosevelt research, place it into the broader context of Southwestern archaeology, and provide the definitive statement on Salado. The seminar brought together senior Roosevelt Archaeology Project personnel, Bureau of Reclamation and Forest Service archaeologists, and authorities on areas around Tonto Basin to discuss and summarize the knowledge gained from the massive research effort and assess its impact on ideas about Southwestern prehistory. As the outcome of those deliberations, this book attempts to synthesize archaeological and environmental data on Tonto Basin in particular and the Salado phenomenon in general within the framework of several topics pertinent to the prehistory of Tonto Basin and the Salado phenomenon writ both small (local) and large (regional).

Several issues were deemed by the seminar to be especially important to understanding Salado and its place in Southwestern prehistory. Among these are the concept of Salado, the environment's effects on local and regional Salado developments, the place of irrigation in Salado economic and social development, the role of demographic factors on local and regional levels, economic productivity and specialization, modeling social processes and social dynamics on local and regional scales, political relations (complexity), the local and regional effects of migration and ethnic relationships, ideological and religious aspects of Salado, and the geographic scale of the Salado expression. Some ideas raised about these topics at the seminar are discussed below.

THE SALADO CONCEPT

Thanks to Lincoln's (this volume) and Rice's (1990b) excellent reviews of the Salado concept, I can skip the origin, development, and intellectual substance of this formulation and move on to particular points raised in the seminar and book.

Gladwin and Gladwin's definition indicates what initially was meant by the term Salado. "Salado is the name suggested to cover the remains of the people who colonized the Upper Salt River drainage, and who developed various specialized features in the region adjacent to Roosevelt Lake" (Gladwin and Gladwin 1930:3). The rest of the Gladwins' monograph is devoted to describing ceramics, later assigned to the Roosevelt Red Ware (Colton 1965), that they thought were "characteristic of this culture" (Gladwin and Gladwin 1930:3).

Embedded in these brief statements are five of six elements that individually or in various combinations have been the focus of six decades of debate over Salado. These elements are: 1) a characteristic assemblage of archaeological remains (particularly ceramics, architecture, and burials); 2) a group of people; 3) a culture; 4) a bounded spatial distribution (the upper Salt drainage, especially Tonto Basin); and 5) migration. Later, a specific temporal range was added to complete the set of six elements most commonly used to characterize Salado. Through time, Salado came to be considered equivalent to other distinctive archaeological patterns such as the Kayenta, Mesa Verde, and Chaco "branches" of the Anasazi tradition (Haury 1976c:125). Yet there always has been a degree of debate over whether Salado is the same sort of expression as these branches or something different and more restricted or more expansive.

Archaeologically, Salado has been recognized by the occurrence, singly or in combination, of a relatively few material attributes that have a limited distribution in time and space. The chief criterion always has been Roosevelt Red Ware ceramics, primarily the Salado polychromes: Pinto, Gila, and Tonto. On occasion, pottery alone has been used to assign sites to the Salado category. A few minor artifact types also are thought to

typify Salado assemblages. Commonly, settlement, architectural, and burial traits also are factored into the mix. A distinctive type of site—the *compound* characterized by above-ground rooms and considerable unroofed space enclosed by a rectilinear wall (see Wood, Chapter 5:Figure 5.4)—has been thought to characterize Salado. In terms of ceremonial architecture, Salado is distinguished by the presence of platform mounds and special rooms and the absence of ball courts, kivas, and great kivas. Extended supine inhumation, usually with Salado ceramic vessels (Loendorf 1998; Ravesloot and Regan, this volume), is the final major component of the complete Salado diagnostic package. Often, the Salado pattern occurs with preexisting local configurations, particularly in late Classic Hohokam sites in the Phoenix Basin (Gladwin 1928; Haury 1945; Schmidt 1928; see Lincoln, Chapter 1 this volume), which gave rise to the idea of Salado people as migrants intrusive into established communities.

The Salado pattern commonly was seen to have fairly definite spatial and temporal boundaries. The distribution of the full panoply of Salado traits led archaeologists to define Tonto Basin as the "homeland" out of which Salado people and/or ideas expanded into other areas. Tonto Basin (Figures 1 and 2) is a bounded lowland zone in central Arizona above the confluence of the Salt River and Tonto Creek. Environmentally, the Basin represents an extension of the Lower Sonoran Desert into the mountainous Transition Zone between the desert to the south and the Mogollon Highlands to the north. The range of Salado traits extends well beyond Tonto Basin, but the associations among these attributes become increasingly attenuated with distance from the heartland. The purely ceramic version of Salado eventually occupied much of southern Arizona and New Mexico and part of northern Sonora and Chihuahua (Crown 1994:Figure 1.1; Rice 1998: Figure 1.3; see Lincoln, Chapter 1). Much of the controversy over Salado grew out of the fact that the diagnostic trait complex as a whole is localized in only a small area and elsewhere is disaggregated and represented by some, but not all, of the elements.

The temporal dimensions of Salado always have been well understood. Even before the advent of calendric dating, the relative position of Salado at the beginning of the Anasazi Pueblo IV period and the Hohokam late Classic period was clear. Subsequently, ceramic and tree-ring dating placed the Salado pattern within the 1150 to 1450 interval (Crown 1994:12). A major accomplishment of the Roosevelt Archaeology Project was the adoption, at

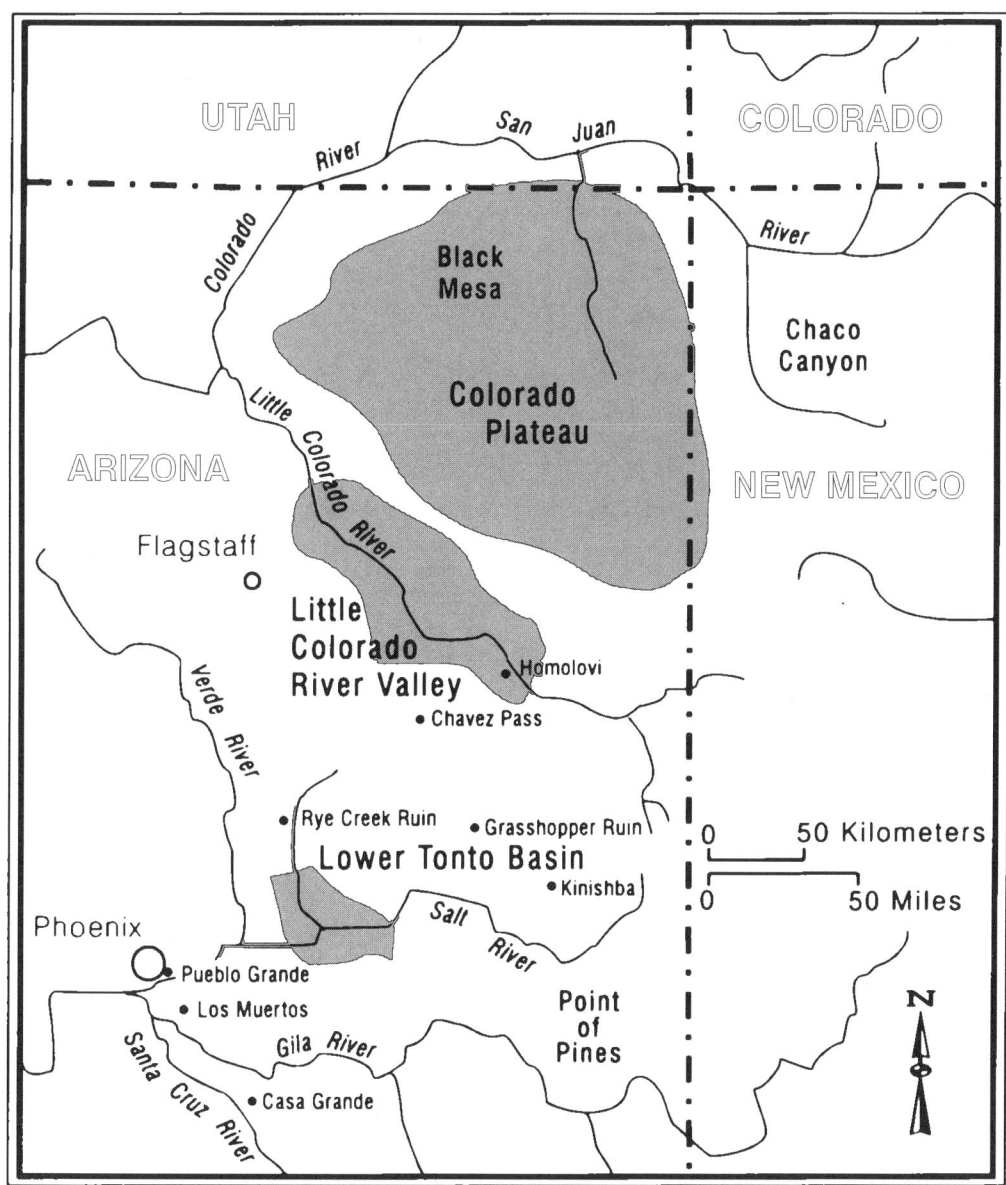

Figure 1.   The northern Southwest showing the location of Tonto Basin relative to other areas occupied during the fourth through fifteenth centuries.

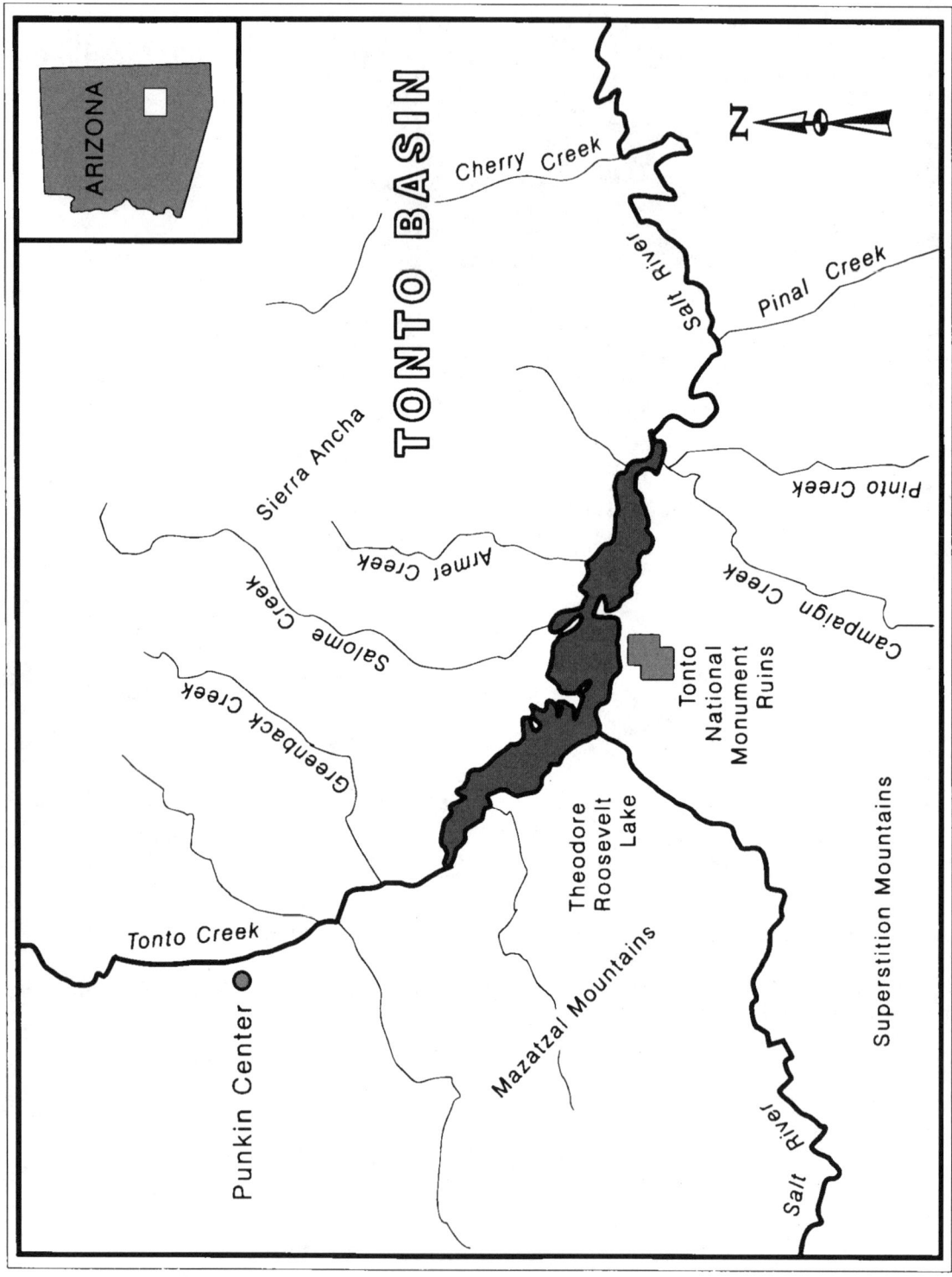

Figure 2. Tonto Basin.

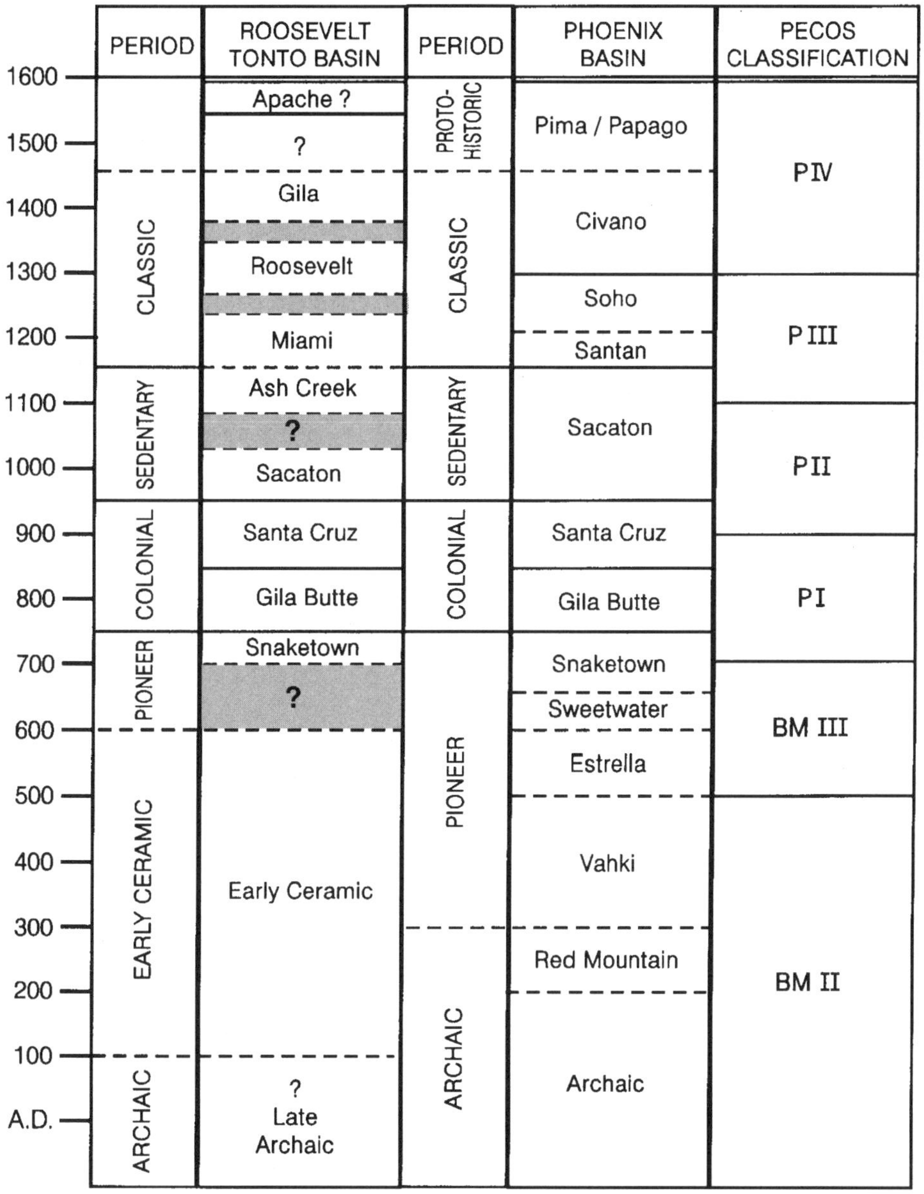

	PERIOD	ROOSEVELT TONTO BASIN	PERIOD	PHOENIX BASIN	PECOS CLASSIFICATION
1600	CLASSIC	Apache ?	PROTO-HISTORIC	Pima / Papago	PIV
1500		?			
1400		Gila	CLASSIC	Civano	
1300		Roosevelt		Soho	PIII
1200		Miami		Santan	
1100	SEDENTARY	Ash Creek	SEDENTARY	Sacaton	PII
1000		?			
		Sacaton			
900	COLONIAL	Santa Cruz	COLONIAL	Santa Cruz	PI
800		Gila Butte		Gila Butte	
700	PIONEER	Snaketown	PIONEER	Snaketown	BM III
600		?		Sweetwater	
	EARLY CERAMIC			Estrella	
500					
400		Early Ceramic		Vahki	BM II
300			ARCHAIC	Red Mountain	
200					
100	ARCHAIC	?		Archaic	
A.D.		Late Archaic			

Figure 3. Chronologies and phase sequences for Tonto Basin, the Phoenix Basin, and the southern Colorado Plateau (Pecos Classification). The Tonto Basin sequence is that adopted in 1994 by the Roosevelt Research Teams (Elson 1996b).

a meeting of the Roosevelt Research Teams at Arizona State University in January, 1994, of a standard chronology and phase system for Tonto Basin (Figure 3; Elson 1996b:Table 1, Figure 4; Rice 1998:Figure 1.2), which places Salado between 1250 and 1450. This example of scientific cooperation, based on abundant well controlled archaeological and chronometric data, places future considerations of Salado on firm chronological footing.

A great deal of contention has arisen over what the Salado archaeological pattern(s) means in human terms. Salado originally was thought to represent a people and a culture, which implied an organized social group or groups that shared a common cultural "template" and behaved in patterned ways that produced the Salado archaeological configuration. In addition, these people were seen as militant migrants who transported their culture into foreign communities and eventually spread across a huge area of the southern Southwest. Salado also was comprehended as the elite component, either home grown or imposed from outside, of stratified late Classic Hohokam communities in the Phoenix and Tucson Basins in which the elites occupied elevated platform mounds and displayed Salado items as symbols of rank while the "commoners" occupied surrounding rooms or pithouses and made do with more mundane items (Rice 1990c). Salado also was thought to represent a macroregional interaction system in which economic relationships among expansive elites united societies across the southern Southwest and northern Mexico. Commonly, this proposed polity was considered to emanate from Casas Grandes (Wilcox 1995). More recently, Salado has been perceived as an ideology or cult, exemplified by a distinctive ceramic iconography, that encompassed many different peoples and cultures (Crown 1994).

In contrast to the attempts to assign meaning to Salado, some scholars viewed the concept as a chimera that forever eluded attempts to come to grips with its archaeological expressions and sociocultural concomitants. Still others, frustrated by the ambiguities of the concept, declared that it represents nothing real either archaeologically or culturally and should be expunged from the scientific lexicon.

Such was the situation in the 1980s when the Bureau of Reclamation launched its Lake Roosevelt project in Tonto Basin. Mitigation of the project's impact on the "cultural resources" of the storied Salado "heartland" provided a unique opportunity for an intensive archaeological examination of the questions that had swirled for decades around the Salado concept. One goal of the Amerind Foundation seminar was to use the Roosevelt data to produce a consensus definition of Salado that could be applied in most archaeological contexts. Readers searching this book for such a definition will be disappointed. Salado remains as murky a concept after the Roosevelt Archaeology Project and the seminar as it was before.

Seminar participants thoroughly dissected and rejected the "classic" archaeological definitions of Salado. They could isolate no consistent association or spatial distribution of archaeological attributes that could be invariably labeled Salado. Tonto Basin still comes closest to exhibiting such a pattern, but only in the context of considerable variability. The group affirmed the traditional belief that the distribution of Salado polychromes marks some sort of archaeologically visible prehistoric behavioral pattern that could be called Salado but agreed that the cooccurrence of a few pottery types hardly justified assigning a congeries of otherwise disparate sites to a single category. These considerations gave rise to the idea of recognizing two kinds of Salado based on the geographic scale of the archaeological attributes involved. Local Salado refers to the distinct configuration in and around Tonto Basin that conforms closely to the "classic" definition of the term. Regional Salado describes the archaeological pattern represented primarily by the far flung distribution of the Salado polychromes.

Considerable support was evinced for versions of Crown's (1994) idea that the widespread occurrence of locally made Salado polychromes and the common iconography embedded in their decoration (regional Salado) represent an ideological or religious movement, the Southwestern Cult. Another idea that received serious consideration is that Salado is an expression of the many and varied demographic, and sociocultural changes that occurred throughout the Southwest between 1250 and 1450 (Nelson and LeBlanc 1986).

The wide variety of contexts in which Salado diagnostics, especially ceramics, occur is incompatible with the idea that Salado represents a single sociocultural entity. Thus, the term seems not to be prescriptively applicable to a particular group of people, an archaeologically recognizable culture (however that may be defined), an ethnic group, ethnic enclaves within other groups, or a unified socioreligious movement. The facts that Salado polychromes seem to be locally made and not distributed from a few manufacturing centers weaken the idea that Salado represents a centralized trading system or a macroregional polity controlled by interacting elites in stratified communities. This pottery's occurrence in a wide variety of site, architectural, and burial contexts also militates against its reflecting elite components of hierarchical political systems or a single religious system.

In the end, no agreement was achieved as to exactly what Salado signifies in any sort of "universal" sense. Some participants argued that the word carried too much historical baggage and should be abandoned because it confused rather than clarified things. Others maintained that the thirteenth to fourteenth century archaeological pattern of the Tonto and Phoenix Basins deserved a name and that Salado was as good as any. Still others conceded that Salado was not a particularly useful technical term but thought that the familiar label was needed for communicating with the public. Finally, a few clung to the hope that an all-inclusive definition could yet be formulated. Clearly, Salado means different things in different places and contexts and cannot be pinned to a single local or regional pattern. Since the work of the Roosevelt Archaeology Project and the deliberations of the seminar failed to resolve the Salado issue, Southwestern archaeologists are left, as before, on their own in deciding whether and how to use the term.

ENVIRONMENTAL CONSIDERATIONS

The Roosevelt Archaeology Project reconstructed several aspects of Tonto Basin environment over the past 2,000 years (Ciolek-Torrello and Welch 1994; Van West et al., Chapter 2 this volume), including annual drought (Rose 1994), annual agricultural productivity (Altschul and Van West 1992; Van West and Altschul 1994), and long term changes in floodplain deposition, erosion, and hydrology (Waters 1997). These retrodictions combined with extant reconstructions of annual streamflow in the Salt River and Tonto Creek (Graybill 1989; Waters 1997) and of regional scale environmental fluctuations in annual dendroclimate (Dean 1988b, 1996b), annual spatial and temporal climatic variability (Dean 1988b, 1996b), spatial coherence in dendroclimate (Dean 1996b; Dean and Funkhouser 1995), low frequency climatic variations (Grissino-Mayer 1994), and low frequency fluctuations in alluvial processes (Dean 1988b, 1996b) characterize a broad spectrum of past environmental conditions, variations, and changes that affected the prehistoric human populations of the region in general and Tonto Basin in particular.

As Van West et al. (Chapter 2 this volume) show, precipitation alone is too variable to support subsistence agriculture in Tonto Basin. By itself, dry farming would have been dependable only in the higher flanks of the Basin where there was too little land to support many people. Therefore, water augmentation techniques, such as irrigation and terracing, usually would have been necessary to ensure satisfactory crop production. In fact, suitable farming strategies, ranging from dry farming to irrigation, would have varied with fluctuating climatic and hydrologic conditions (Waters 1997; Van West et al., Chapter 2:Table 2.3 this volume). It probably is no coincidence that the major occupation of Tonto Basin came during a period of relative climatic and hydrologic stability extending from around 950 to 1375 (Van West et al., Chapter 2:Figure 2.6 this volume) and that the Salado fluorescence peaked at about the same time the stable interval ended. Indeed, it is tempting to infer that the post-1375 change to a more variable streamflow regime characterized by much higher annual flows (as in 1382 and 1384) may have hastened the end of Salado in Tonto Basin.

Another significant aspect of the Tonto Basin environment is the major difference in salinity between the Salt River and Tonto Creek, the former averaging four times the amount of dissolved solids as the latter (Van West et al., Chapter 2:Figure 2.1 this volume). Thus, the Salt River is the more suitable for growing salt tolerant crops such as cotton, which appeared in the Basin by the fourth century A.D. (Elson and Lindeman 1994:112). Given the post-1300 importance of cotton fabrics in ritual and the extensive trade in cotton and cotton cloth (Adams, Chapter 11 this volume), the Salt Arm likely was an important center of cotton production and export between 1250 and 1450. Salado developments in Tonto Basin and the geographic dispersal of Salado traits may have been fostered by large-scale production of these commodities along the Salt River. Clearly, more work needs to be done on cotton production and trade (Teague 1992a; Van West and Altschul 1997) as well as the intriguing matter of relationships and possible competition between the Tonto Basin and Middle Little Colorado River centers of post-1300 cotton production (Adams, Chapter 11 this volume).

Van West et al.'s (Chapter 2 this volume) analyses show that the Salado occupation of Tonto Basin exemplifies the ecological rule that, in the long run, generalized adaptive strategies are more resilient than specialized ones. While irrigation agriculture and cotton export supported a degree of social complexity involving moderate social stratification and intercommunity organization, this level of attainment could not be sustained for long, especially in the face of changed climatic and hydrologic regimes. On the other hand, generalized economic strategies that spread subsistence risk over a variety of habitats and resources probably could have carried less complex groups in Tonto Basin through the environmental transition, just as they did Puebloan societies on the Colorado Plateau. It seems likely that when the specialized Salado economic system could not adapt to changed conditions and could not be translocated to another suitable area, the sociopolitical system "collapsed," and the Basin was largely abandoned. Moving complex social systems, rather than simplifying them, occurred more than once in the Southwest (Dean 1969: 195–196) and may be a general response to socioeconomic stress and a common stimulus of migration as long as suitable destinations are available.

Finally, prehistoric human events in Tonto Basin exemplify regularities in behavior-environment interaction observed elsewhere in the Southwest. First, low frequency environmental variability appears to have influenced human behavior more regularly than high frequency variations did. This probably is due to human adaptive behavior being more finely attuned to and more capable of dealing with high frequency variation (Dean 1988a), low frequency changes being more likely to alter the environmental thresholds of adaptive configurations, and low frequency transformations being beyond a group's recent experience and thereby taxing their reservoir of potential responses to changed adaptive conditions. Second, it is becoming increasingly apparent that regional scale environmental variations and change affect human behavior more than local fluctuations do. Even when detailed, high resolution paleoenvironmental reconstructions are available, it is difficult to directly link human behavior to environmental variability in specific localities. This could be due either to the subtlety of such behavioral adjustments or to the archaeological record's lacking the temporal resolution of the paleoenvironmental record. On the other hand, local responses to regional scale environmental changes abound, probably because regional changes affect more people at one time and the responses of one group of people are likely to impinge on other groups in a sort of domino effect. No better examples of these phenomena could be advanced than the events of the late thirteenth and early fourteenth centuries in the Southwest. Large spatial and temporal scale environmental disruptions—including falling alluvial groundwater levels, the inception of widespread arroyo cutting, the Great Drought, and the breakdown in climatic spatial coherence—triggered population movements, intergroup contacts and conflicts, and social splits and amalgamations that ramified throughout the Southwest and heavily impacted Tonto Basin. These regional events and their local consequences deserve additional attention in order to better understand Southwestern prehistory and increase knowledge of the general adaptive and sociocultural processes involved.

IRRIGATION IN TONTO BASIN

A major interest of the seminar was the practice of irrigation and its effects on Salado society in Tonto Basin. The presence of cotton at the Eagle Ridge site (Elson and Lindeman 1994:112) implies that irrigation may have been practiced along the Salt Arm as early as the fourth century. Traces of prehistoric canals and ditches along the Salt River (Waters 1997) and Tonto Creek (Jacobs 1997b:213–14) establish irrigation as an important component of Salado crop production. Wood's (Chapter 5:Figure 5.8 this volume) division of the Basin into eight irrigation districts on the basis of maximum possible main canal lengths indicates the degree to which settlement was controlled by reliance on this technique. Constructing and maintaining these labor-expensive water management systems, establishing and defending ownership of these works, allocating access to land and water, distributing agricultural products, and growing and processing cotton for export would have fostered the development of fairly high levels of social organization and control (Craig 1995). The resulting sociocultural complexity is indicated by the hierarchical structure of the settlements in each irrigation district (Elson et al., Chapter 7 and Wood, Chapter 5 this volume) and the structured relationships among these groups (Rice, Chapter 6 this volume).

SALADO SOCIAL DYNAMICS

A major concern of the seminar was how to understand Salado social processes on both local and regional scales. As became increasingly clear during the meeting, these scales presuppose quite different sets of processes that cannot be encompassed by a single model. Therefore, understanding Tonto Basin social organization and process is not likely to yield a satisfactory explanation of the regional attributes of the Salado phenomenon.

Applying current anthropological and archaeological theory and modern field, laboratory, and analytical methods to an enormous, high quality data base, the Roosevelt Archaeology Project substantially increased knowledge of social stasis, variation, and change in Tonto Basin (see the chapters in this volume by Elson et al., Lindauer, Rice, Simon and Jacobs, Whittlesey et al., and Wood). The research clearly showed that, rather than being unitary structural-functional entities, platform mounds took different forms and functions in different contexts and were generated by different growth processes. Functions range from supporting structures that housed people and activities representing the communities' social, political, and religious leadership (Rice, Chapter 6 this volume) to supporting elevated surfaces for viewing the countryside (Elson 1994a). Most platform mounds are incorporated into compounds (Craig and Clark 1994; Jacobs 1997a; Lindauer 1995a; Wood, Chapter 5:Figure 5.4 this volume), but some occur in pueblo-like sites (Elson and Craig 1992b; Lindauer 1996a; Wood, Chapter 5:Figure 5.4 this volume). Some mounds were built in a single operation, some grew by accretion, some originated as platform mounds, and some were produced by filling and capping the ground floor spaces of preexisting rooms. These differences have yet to be satisfactorily explained.

Platform mound communities clearly were stratified into elites and nonelites. Differential burial treatments and the distribution of inherited skeletal anomalies reveal social and genetic relationships among individuals that suggest the presence of ranked unilineal descent groups whose members occupied hereditary leadership positions (Loendorf 1998; see Lindauer, Chapter 9 and Nelson, Chapter 15 this volume). The small populations involved (Doelle, Chapter 4 this volume) and the lack of evidence for elites' accumulating great wealth and amassing large quantities of trade goods (Rice, Chapter 6 this volume) suggest that, as among the Western Pueblos (Whittlesey et al., Chapter 10 this volume), the power differential between elites and subordinates was neither great nor immutable.

More inclusive organization probably involved "confederacies" of irrigation communities allied by connections among elites. The sizes of such confederations probably varied situationally, probably in the segmentary fashion

outlined by Rice (Chapter 6 this volume). The surprisingly low population estimates for Tonto Basin and surrounding areas (Doelle, Chapter 3 this volume) indicate that fewer people than generally thought can sustain hierarchical communities as complex as those of the Basin, maintain regional scale socioeconomic interaction systems, and construct, maintain, and operate moderately sized irrigation systems.

A major implication of most conceptions of Tonto Basin platform mound communities is that elites controlled the production, accumulation, internal distribution, and trade of items manufactured by artisans specializing in particular products. Except for localized production and Basinwide distribution of some plainware ceramics (Miksa 1998:96), however, precious little evidence for the specialized manufacture of trade items was recovered by the Roosevelt Archaeology Project, nor were large stores of artifacts, amassed as if for exchange, found (Rice, Chapter 6 this volume). The production of cotton and cotton textiles for export may be an exception to this generalization, but little evidence for large-scale manufacture, such as looms and other weaving tools, has been recovered in Tonto Basin sites.

A major focus of the Roosevelt research was the relationships between Lowland and Upland communities in Tonto Basin. The original RPMS research design hypothesized that Upland and Lowland communities were reciprocally linked in a system in which Lowland communities, in exchange for Upland resources, provided agricultural products to subordinate Upland communities that could not produce enough food for themselves (Rice 1990a). This hypothesis was rejected when it was discovered that Upland communities were self sufficient (Oliver 1994b:469). As a result, the mechanisms by which Upland resources made their way into the Lowlands and the connections between Upland and Lowland communities remain obscure.

Several models of Salado community organization have been advanced. Primary among these are constructs based on prevailing models of stratified Hohokam platform mound communities involving powerful elite leadership and strong intercommunity ties (Rice 1990c; Gregory 1987), Western Pueblo (primarily Hopi) hierarchical organization in which little material reward accrues to the leaders who exercise power (Whittlesey and Ciolek-Torrello 1992; Whittlesey et al., Chapter 10 this volume), the global ethnography of mound building societies, which vary widely in the concentration of political power and wealth in ruling descent units (Elson

1996a), and the concept of segmentary organization advanced by African ethnologists (Rice, Chapter 6 this volume). All these models illuminate aspects of Salado community organization, and testing them against the Roosevelt data has materially advanced understanding of Salado social organization in Tonto Basin. Nevertheless, to a greater or lesser degree, each falls short of capturing the full range of variability exhibited by the Tonto Basin communities. Undoubtedly combinations of these and other potential models eventually will more closely approach the explanatory ideal.

The social correlates of regional Salado, spread as it is over a vast territory, present problems quite different and more intractable than those of Tonto Basin. The wide variety of contexts in which these manifestations appear (see the chapters by Adams, Doyel, and Lekson) suggests that the social processes by which the elements of regional Salado were integrated into disparate cultures, a process dubbed "Saladoization" by Ben Nelson, differed from one area to another. It seems unlikely, for example, that the strong Salado components of Late Classic Hohokam sites represents the same social processes as the Salado ceramic veneer on sites in southwestern New Mexico or the mercantile context of Salado pottery at Casas Grandes. Therefore, understanding regional Salado requires detailed examination and comparison of the individual contexts in which its markers occur and the development of explanatory constructs that encompass the full rage of variability involved.

Currently, the main contender as a general explanation of Saladoization is the idea that Salado represents an ideological system, the Southwestern Cult (Crown 1994), that spread across a large area probably in response to the social turmoil of the 1250–1450 period. Regional and local environmental crises would have increased the uncertainty of food production thereby exacerbating existing social inequalities and schisms, differential access to resources, and unequal distribution of wealth. Widespread population movements would have brought previously separate groups into contact and even conflict, created ethnically mixed communities (Elson et al., Chapter 7 this volume; Whittlesey et al., Chapter 10 this volume), and dislodged established groups. The social destabilization resulting from these economic and demographic changes would have required the development of new ways of interacting with other social groups, handling internal and external disputes, integrating immigrants into established communities, and

organizing "multiethnic" communities. An overarching ideological system (cult) that could be adapted to local conditions could prove attractive as a means of solving or at least mitigating these problems. The existence of such a system, with its iconography expressed on portable or easily replicated items (pots), could well explain the rapid geographical spread of the ceramic styles emblematic of regional Salado and the different local contexts in which these items occur. This contextual variation (see Doyel, Chapter 13 and Lekson, Chapter 12 this volume), however, is inconsistent with the spread of a homogeneous cult across many societies. Rather, it appears more likely that the societies involved adopted elements of the Southwestern Cult and adapted them to their particular configurations and needs. If this hypothesis is correct, it will be difficult to isolate the diagnostic elements of the Southwestern Cult and determine how they were organized into a system.

The general instability of the 1250–1450 period probably spawned an alternative religious system to the Southwestern Cult as represented by the Salado polychromes. The ascension of the Katsina Cult (Adams 1991) and the spread of Jeddito Yellow Ware ceramics and design styles across the southern Colorado Plateau, the northern Rio Grande Valley, and even into the Tonto Arm of Tonto Basin could represent a similar northern response to the same general disruptions. Thus, the period could have been characterized by two opposed Cults, Katsina in the north and Southwestern in the south, that served similar general functions in dissimilar ways. The Jeddito Yellow Ware and Salado polychrome markers of these religious systems have discrete distributions except where they overlap along both sides of the Mogollon Rim. Unlike the Salado polychromes, which were manufactured in many places, the Jeddito Yellow Ware were produced in and distributed from a single locus in the Hopi Mesas. The greater homogeneity of the Katsina Cult may explain why it outlived the Southwestern Cult and persists into the present among most Puebloan groups.

EXTERNAL RELATIONS, MIGRATION, AND ETHNICITY

That the residents of Tonto Basin were never isolated from contemporaneous populations is demonstrated by local participation in regional patterns (such as the Early Ceramic horizon), movement of people into and out of the area, involvement in wide ranging exchange networks that brought nonlocal items (such as shell and pottery) into the area (see the chapters by Adams, Doyel, Elson et al., Lekson, Whittlesey et al., and Wood) and sent local items (cotton and pottery) out of the Basin. Wood's (Chapter 5:Figure 5.7) study of potential routes of travel provides information on trails, interactions between Tonto Basin and other peoples, trade relationships, potential clients in the cotton commodities trade, sources of immigrants and destinations of emigrants, and the dispersal of the material attributes that define regional Salado.

Aggressive migration, often thought to involve the domination of other groups, long has been an integral component of the Salado concept. It is not surprising, therefore, that migration appears to have played a large role in the prehistory of Tonto Basin. Somewhat surprising, however, is the probability that the Basin commonly was the destination rather than the source of migrants (Stark, Clark, and Elson 1995a; Elson et al., Chapter 7 this volume). The first major immigration appears to have involved Hohokam colonists who established communities at several places in the Basin beginning around 700. The second major influx occurred between 1150 and 1350 when Anasazi immigrants from the Colorado Plateau apparently took up residence in established communities in the Salt Arm. Unlike the Hohokam, who moved in community-sized groups, the Anasazi appear to have moved in smaller groups such as households. It was hoped that morphological attributes of human teeth recovered by the Roosevelt Archaeology Project would illuminate the genetic affiliations of Tonto Basin populations and perhaps even identify immigrants' points of origin (Turner et al. 1990b:133). Analyses of dental attributes were inconclusive, however, and the genetic sources of these people remain unresolved (Turner 1998; Ravesloot and Regan, Chapter 3 this volume). It has become clear that there was no militant movement out of the Basin to impose Saladoan elites on Hohokam societies of the Phoenix and Tucson Basins and to spread Saladoan influence even farther. Rather, the major emigration occurred when Salado ended, and few archaeological effects of this diaspora have been observed. These migrations reflect many of the processes specified by migration theory (Anthony 1990; Clark 1995b; Stark, Clark, and Elson 1995a), including premigration between-group contact as indicated by ceramic exchange, movement in small groups, migrants' leap-

frogging or dislodging intervening groups, immigrants' forming enclaves within established local communities, and the reorganization of recipient communities to adjust to the presence of erstwhile foreigners.

Recognizing prehistoric immigration is predicated on archaeological evidence for immigrants; that is, groups of foreigners who differed from indigenous groups, ethnic groups in current parlance. Colonial-to-Sedentary period Hohokam occupants of Tonto Basin apparently coexisted, primarily in separate communities, with local groups before 1100. Later, immigrants from the Colorado Plateau lived as enclaves in sites along the Salt Arm. Such enclaves, similar to those inferred for Point of Pines (Haury 1958) and Grasshopper (Reid 1989), probably represent intact social units dislodged by the social upheavals and population movements of the period. Clearly, the presence of ethnically distinct immigrants and indigines together in the same community would have created unprecedented, complicated, and fragile social arrangements to define and maintain relationships between the groups and to preserve the communities against the strong fissive pressures inherent in such situations. Although it has been inferred that the immigrants provided a handy labor pool for operating irrigation systems, the exact nature of the between group social arrangements in these sites is as yet unclear. More attention needs to be given to the theoretical, methodological, and organizational ramifications of this intriguing issue.

CASAS GRANDES

Looming over the seminar, like the proverbial 600 pound gorilla, was the gargantuan presence of Casas Grandes, the fourteenth and fifteenth century northern Chihuahuan metropolis that contains large quantities of Salado polychrome pottery. Surprisingly little overt attention was directed at this colossus, probably because it has been relegated to the Salado back burner by the demonstration that it does not predate local Salado (Dean and Ravesloot 1993) and therefore cannot be the progenitor of local and regional Salado and the source of Salado polychromes as maintained by Di Peso (1976a). Nevertheless, the relationship between Casas Grandes and Salado remains a key to understanding the late prehistory of the Southwest and northern Mexico. While the site is part of the regional Salado phenomenon, it appears to differ qualitatively from most other elements of

this pattern. Outside Tonto Basin most Salado polychrome vessels occur in ceremonial contexts, primarily
burials (Crown 1994), while at Casas Grandes they are
virtually absent from burials (Ravesloot 1988) and appear to have been warehoused (Lekson, Chapter 12 this
volume), perhaps for transshipment to some other locality. The ultimate destination, if other than Casas
Grandes, of these vessels is not clear, but it probably was
not to the north where such pottery was abundant. No
southern terminus of Casas Grandes trade in Salado
polychromes has yet been identified.

Numerous hypotheses have been advanced to explain
Casas Grandes' role in the late prehistoric Southwest.
Several place it at the center of a vast regional political or
economic system, affiliation with which was marked by
Salado polychromes and other items (Di Peso 1974a;
Wilcox 1995, 1998; Doyel, Chapter 13 this volume; Lekson,
Chapter 12 this volume). Minnis and Whalen (1993;
Whalen and Minnis 1996), on the other hand, consider
it to be a local polity of considerably less magnitude.
Others view it as a participant in, but not the master of,
regional Salado (Crown 1994; Douglas 1995). Still others
consider it to be a Southwestern outpost on the Mesoamerican frontier that adopted numerous Mexican traits
and controlled for a time much of the north-south flow
of exotic goods across the "border." Clearly, much more
work is necessary to evaluate these and other ideas. The
Roosevelt Archaeology Project has clarified this process,
however, by demonstrating that events in Tonto Basin
during the Salado period were independent of Casas
Grandes and cannot be explained by rule or influence
from northern Chihuahua.

CONCLUSIONS

By any measures (except an absolute definition of
Salado) the Roosevelt Archaeology Project must be considered a resounding success. It is probable that no other
large Southwestern contract archaeology operation has
increased knowledge as much as the Roosevelt Project.
To be sure, the magnitude of the Project's accomplishment is due in part to the fact that it started from an
information base near zero in terms of studies equipped
with modern research designs and methods. Apart from
a few other investigations, exhaustive site inventories
assembled by the Tonto National Forest and surveys
done in connection with the Central Arizona Project

provided most of the modern data for characterizing the
prehistory of Tonto Basin. Furthermore, Salado was
"blessed" by an accumulation of outdated, often poorly
informed speculation that was ripe for correction and
amplification. These initial conditions, however, provided but a small, fortuitous boost that the Project exploited to the fullest with well conceived research
designs, inventive and flexible field implementation, sophisticated and comprehensive data analyses, careful
evaluations of the results, and well reasoned conclusions
and hypotheses drawn from the totality of the research.
As a result, we now know far more than before about the
paleoenvironment and prehistory of Tonto Basin; the
Basin's place in Southwestern archaeology; human population sizes, biological relationships, and health; the
Salado phenomenon in its local and regional guises; and
important general aspects of culture including hierarchical settlement systems, segmentary social organization,
specialized economic production and exchange, migration,
ethnicity, the composition and maintenance of multiethnic
communities, regional scale religious systems, local consequences of regional scale social instability, and behavioral
adaptation to environmental variability and change.

All three major components of the Roosevelt Archaeology Project—RPMS, RRSS, and RCDS—achieved
most of the goals outlined in their research designs and,
in addition, made important discoveries about the prehistoric human occupation of Tonto Basin that had not
been anticipated. The Amerind Foundation seminar
expanded on many of the issues addressed by the Roosevelt Project research and attempted to integrate them
into the larger regional context of the Southwest and
northern Mexico and the theoretical concerns of contemporary archaeology. A few examples indicate the
magnitude of the changes wrought in prevailing ideas by
the Roosevelt research. In one particularly good example
of the application of the scientific method, the demonstration that Upland communities were self sufficient
forced the rejection of one of the primary hypotheses of
the RPMS research design—that Upland communities,
lacking the ability to support themselves, depended on
platform mound communities in the more productive
Lowlands for sustenance—and the formulation of alternative hypotheses about Salado community organization in Tonto Basin. The discovery that platform
mounds exhibited considerable formal, functional, contextual, and developmental variability required modification of prevailing ideas about the nature of these

structures, their roles in their settlements, and the organization of hierarchical societies in the Basin. The recognition of at least two major types of large site, platform mound sites (compounds) and syncretic platform mound sites (blocks of contiguous rooms) required revision of ideas about community development and organization, particularly in the Gila phase. The identification of immigrant groups illuminated the general processes of migration and aspects of ethnicity. The surprisingly early appearance and continued cultivation of cotton identified the Salt Arm as a probable center of cotton production and the Tonto Basin Salado as major participants, for a time, in the post-1300 cotton commodities trade. Sophisticated paleoenvironmental reconstructions illuminated the role of local and regional scale environmental variations in the turbulent history of Tonto Basin and the Southwest between 1250 and 1450. Finally, the Roosevelt Archaeology Project tested, rejected, and/or refined several models of Salado settlement and social organization. In addition to synthesizing Tonto Basin Salado, the seminar clarified the fundamental difference between local and regional Salado; examined the nature, local contexts, and geographical range of the archaeological markers of regional Salado; considered the local and regional roles of environmental variability and demographic factors in the development of both levels of Salado; evaluated various models advanced to explain regional Salado; and produced some explanations of its own.

One goal that neither the Project nor the seminar could achieve was the development of an unconditional, universally applicable definition of Salado. It was obvious, however, that the application of the term to at least two categorically different archaeological phenomena had been a major source of confusion. Local Salado was recognized as a fairly strong archaeological pattern that occurs in and around Tonto Basin and includes the "classical" elements: Salado polychrome pottery, compound architecture, platform mounds, and other, minor traits. Unfortunately, the associations among the elements of this pattern deteriorate rapidly with distance from the center, and the local definition becomes irrelevant. Regional Salado simply denotes the presence of Salado polychrome pottery, which occurs in so wide a variety of contexts that no more specific definition is possible.

The seminar favored two overlapping models that have been advanced to explain regional Salado. Crown's (1994) Southwestern Cult model accounts for many attributes of regional Salado. Except for Casas Grandes, the apparent variances from the expectations of a homogeneous cult model can be attributed to the selective adoption of elements of the cult and adapting them to local conditions and needs. The second formulation is based on Nelson and LeBlanc's (1986) observation that the Salado polychromes nearly always occur in the context of significant local sociocultural change. Thus, this pottery appears to mark a horizon of culture change that spanned much of the southern Southwest but was expressed differently in different localities. This idea is consistent with the selective acceptance of a cult as a means of coping with the environmental and social upheavals that characterized the Salado period across the entire region.

A major outcome of the Roosevelt Project, as of most archaeological endeavors, was the generation of many new research questions. Generally, these relate either to local or regional Salado with little overlap. Despite being a major focus of the RPMS research design, the relationship between Upland and Lowland communities in Tonto Basin remains unclear. Although the former can no longer be considered as dependents of the latter, the interactions between these communities and the mechanisms by which Upland resources made their way to Lowland sites remain to be determined. The behavioral correlates of the formal differences between platform mound (compound) and syncretic (room block) sites are not obvious. Do these dissimilarities reflect differences in social organization, ethnicity, or the historical circumstances involved in the founding and growth of each type of site? How did the inhabitants of one kind of platform mound site interact with residents of the other? Was platform mound community leadership based on inherited privilege or personal achievement? The likely presence of immigrant groups at some sites gives rise to questions about migrants' decisions to move and their choices of destination, why they were accepted by the local populations, how they were integrated into the local communities, and their ultimate fate (moved on as at Point of Pines, totally assimilated so as to disappear from the archaeological record, departed when the site was abandoned). Elucidation of the role of Tonto Basin in the post-1300 cotton trade, particularly its relationship to the Middle Little Colorado production center, would enhance understanding of the interaction networks that connected the late prehistoric populations of the southern Colorado Plateau, the Sonoran Desert, and northern Mexico. More work needs to be done to establish how far beyond Tonto Basin the local version of Salado extends. Although the range usually is given as the Tonto Basin-Globe-Miami area, recent work indicates that the diagnostic archaeological pattern also extends into the Gila and lower San Pedro River Valleys. The actual range of the pattern is crucial to understanding local Salado and its relations with surrounding areas. Finally, the various models of local Salado society need further refinement. Till now, explanatory models have reflected the geographic backgrounds of their promulgators; for example, the Phoenix Basin perspective of RPMS and the Mogollon-Plateau outlook of RRSS. The time is ripe to integrate the best features of extant models with new ideas to create closer approximations of the true situation.

The seminar isolated a number of questions relating to regional Salado. The most obvious issue is what, exactly, the wide distribution of Salado polychromes across many different societies means in terms of human behavior. Linked to this are the issues of how the manufacture and use of the Salado polychromes spread and how the ideas and behaviors associated with them were integrated into many disparate societies. An intriguing question, but one that may never be answered, is whether the spread of Salado polychromes is related to the trade in cotton and cotton fabrics inferred to have taken place after 1300. The idea that regional Salado reflects the expansion of a religious cult adopted and adapted to help allay the distress caused by the environmental crises, social upheavals, and cultural changes of the period has great appeal and deserves further investigation. Such an examination would have to cover the entire affected area and take into account the many local variations encompassed by the phenomenon. Finally, many questions remain about the place of Casas Grandes in the regional Salado context. It probably was not the center of a Salado regional system from which Salado polychromes were distributed, although the possibility remains that it was

the center of a regional system that encompassed aspects of regional Salado. The apparently secular context of Salado polychrome vessels at Casas Grandes contrasts markedly with their probable ritual associations at other sites and suggests that these vessels performed functions at Casas Grandes different from elsewhere. If Casas Grandes was the center of a mercantile system that moved goods between the Southwest and northern Mexico, the destinations of the warehoused Salado polychrome vessels have yet to be identified. Finally, knowing more about the relationship between the collapse of Casas Grandes and the disappearance of regional Salado would vastly increase understanding of late prehistoric sociocultural dynamics and the conditions encountered by the sixteenth century Spanish entradas into northern Mexico and the Southwest.

The Roosevelt Archaeology Project, the Amerind Foundation seminar, and this book have materially advanced understanding of the archaeology of Tonto Basin, the Salado concept, local and regional manifestations of Salado, the prehistory of the Southwest and northern Mexico, numerous general sociocultural processes, and many more topics. But, as usual, this progress created as many questions as it answered. These questions, informed by the Roosevelt results, are much more refined and specific than the comparatively crude and general problems that structured the original Roosevelt research. The profound differences between the initial Project research questions and those that can now be asked are a measure of the magnitude of the Project's contributions to Southwestern prehistory in particular and archaeology in general. Decades of fruitful research can, and will, be built on the firm conceptual and procedural foundations laid by the Roosevelt research. In a real sense, the Roosevelt Archaeology Project has elevated a scientific platform from which to launch future, more advanced investigations of Salado and all its ramifications.

CHAPTER ONE

A Brief History of Salado Archaeology

Thomas R. Lincoln

If we say that Salado is a fiction, then we had better begin to ask ourselves whether Kayenta or Mesa Verde or Chaco are not fictions also.

Emil Haury, 1976

As unlikely, unpalatable, and unprecedented as it may seem, recent research into the Salado Culture, in particular the work of Patricia Crown (1994) in her broad analysis of Salado polychrome ceramics and of researchers conducting large-scale investigations in the Salado "heartland" of Tonto Basin, seems to support the idea that the Salado as a culture group can no longer be supported (Ciolek-Torrello and Welch 1994; Doelle, Wallace, and Craig 1992; Rice, ed. 1990, 1992). Doing away with a long held tradition in North American archaeology, as in any discipline, is nasty business. History and tradition will always argue for retention of ideas and concepts that have standing; however, with evidence and convincing arguments, new alternatives to understand human behavior are possible. While it is not my intent to argue for the demise or even reduced status of the Salado Culture concept, I discuss trends in Southwestern archaeology that allow a richer and fuller understanding of the prehistoric inhabitants of east-central, southeastern, and southern Arizona, southwestern New Mexico, and northern Sonora and Chihuahua—the Salado (Figure 1).

In 1987, a team consisting of archaeologists from the Bureau of Reclamation, U.S. Forest Service, and Arizona State Historic Preservation Office, designed a mitigative data recovery program for impacts to archaeological sites caused by the reconstruction of Theodore Roosevelt Dam, in Tonto Basin of central Arizona. Many affected sites were attributed to the Salado, while others showed relationship to the earlier Hohokam culture. Questions of complexity, architectural patterning, ideology, settlement history, subsistence practices, external relationships, technology, etc. were considered by the team and eventually included in the research designs developed by the three organizations charged with conducting the mitigative research studies. A recurring theme centered on just who were the Salado. How did they come to be in Tonto Basin? Where did they go after 1450? Is Tonto Basin the Salado homeland from which Saladoness spread? All of the players in Reclamation's Roosevelt Dam Archaeology project participated in the Amerind Foundation New World Studies Seminar, from which the papers in this volume derive. Mostly these primary researchers grappled with these problems and offered ideas and solutions to these questions. My task is to place the Salado within the landscape of Southwest prehistory, and to provide a historical perspective on Salado research. Were the Salado aliens, indigenous, or conquerors of Tonto Basin?

As one would expect, the history of Salado archaeology has tracked along the path of North American archaeology. Interpretations promoted about the inhabitants of Tonto Basin have always reflected the dominant trends in cultural definitions and history. They are reflective of the archaeological techniques used by modern shadow catchers—archaeologists. Adolph Bandelier was the first to conduct archaeological research at "Salado" sites in Tonto Basin. His ramblings through central Arizona (Bandelier 1892) make for a lively and interesting story and have been well documented and discussed (Hohmann 1992a; Hohmann and Kelley 1988; Lange and Riley ed. 1971; Wood and Kelley 1988). Bandelier's reconnaissance recorded many of the well known and outstanding ruins of Tonto Basin. As can be expected and appreciated, in interpreting his findings Bandelier employed the direct historical approach championed by John Wesley Powell of the Bureau of American Ethnology. Like Powell's underlings, Bandelier concerned himself with establishing direct ties between the observed archaeological record and the anthropological knowledge of "living" Native American cultures. Prehistoric material items, the remains of past cultures, were collected and catalogued to explain perceived extant cultural ties to the past in what Trigger (1989:125) has termed a "flat" view of native history that, "unified ethnology and prehistoric archaeology as closely related branches of anthropology." While there is not much in the way of printed material by Bandelier about his reconnaissance of Tonto Basin, his observations of platform mound centered and compound enclosed villages, polychrome pottery, and irrigation systems certainly influenced the understanding and interpretation of Casa Grande, the large Hohokam village and ceremonial center that Jesse Walter Fewkes visited and investigated (Fewkes 1912).

Walter Hough, also of the Bureau of American Ethnology, visited Tonto Basin in the late 1890s and coupled observations on the ruins of Tonto Basin with those he made at sites along the upper Gila and Salt River valleys in Arizona and New Mexico (Hough 1907). Hough (1907:9) first suggested the possibility that what was later called Salado in Tonto Basin was the result of an "original" local source; a theory that was later discarded when the Salado were first defined.

More than thirty years after Bandelier visited the area, Erich Schmidt conducted the first investigations of the modern archaeological era in Tonto Basin; conducting excavations and infield analyses at some of the very ruins visited by Bandelier. As Director of the Mrs. William

Boyce Thompson Expedition, Schmidt, following a decidedly cultural historical approach, again, tracking with the theoretical tradition of the day, conducted limited excavations at five "Salado" villages on the banks of Lake Roosevelt (Hohmann and Kelley 1988:9). He also investigated other "Salado" sites southeast of Tonto Basin in the Globe/Miami area, one being Togetzoge Pueblo, a large 120 (estimate) room pueblo-style village. Schmidt excavated 52 rooms at Togetzoge Pueblo, and it served him as a major interpretive vehicle, as did the Classic period Hohokam platform mound village sites of Pueblo Grande and La Ciudad in the Salt River Valley.

Hohmann and Kelley (1988) published an excellent summary of Schmidt's work in Tonto Basin and the Globe/Miami area, and this document should be referenced for more detailed information. Schmidt's purpose was to investigate, "the Lower Gila region, an archaeological subarea that extends over the greater part of southern Arizona, including the Giant Cactus Desert in the west and a mountainous country in the east" (Hohmann and Kelley 1988:5). Schmidt's goals were typical of the time, chronological and spatial, reflective of his interest in determining which prehistoric peoples occupied this broad area, and documenting the relative chronology of those inhabitants. Results of Schmidt's work significantly contributed to subsequent debates about both Salado, and Hohokam archaeology. Schmidt's excavations of trash mounds at La Ciudad and Pueblo Grande clearly established his intimacy with Hohokam data and provided empirical support for Harold S. Gladwin's later definition of Salado. Schmidt (1928:281) noted, "It may be assumed that the appearance of the Gila ware [Salado polychromes] in the Lower Salt region was accompanied by a new, though short lived cultural epoch. At the present time it would be premature to suggest whether this new era was due to an actual invasion of the eastern neighbors or to close culture exchange between the Lower Salt and Central Gila populations, and whether there exists evolutionary relations."

Hohmann and Kelley (1988:149) also remind us that Schmidt recognized the link between south-central Arizona and Mesoamerica, and in particular the relationship between the "Salado" populations and Casas Grandes in northern Chihuahua, Mexico.

The 1930s mark a critical time for Tonto Basin and Salado archaeology because it was then that the Salado Culture was defined. Harold and Winifred Gladwin are credited with creating the "Salado" to describe the polychrome producing inhabitants of Tonto Basin (Gladwin and Gladwin 1930). However, Hohmann and Kelley (1988:31), Hohmann (1992a:7), and Reid and Whittlesey (1997) suggest that the Gladwins were strongly influenced by Erich Schmidt's observations, and really owe a debt to Schmidt and his insights. This does not erode the contribution made by the Gladwins (Gladwin 1957; Gladwin and Gladwin 1935), but it does remind us of the necessity of detailed and tenacious scholarship that is required when reproducing the history of archaeological research. As a result of excavations sponsored by the Gladwins' Gila Pueblo Research Foundation at Roosevelt 9:6 in Tonto Basin and at Snaketown on the Gila River, combined with Emil Haury's reanalysis of the Classic period occupation at Los Muertos (Haury 1932, 1945, 1976), a picture emerged that sudden cultural changes occurred in the Hohokam region, including Tonto Basin, beginning about 1100. These changes were seen as the result of an invasion by a group the Gladwins called the Salado (Gladwin and Gladwin 1930). The invasion concept, which first appeared in 1928 (Gladwin 1928) but not as a "Salado" invasion, was more specifically defined in 1935 (Gladwin and Gladwin 1935). The Gladwins championed a model where Tonto Basin was initially populated by immigrants from the Little Colorado River region to the northwest, beginning about 1100. The Salado, they argued, were recognized by distinctive traits including masonry compounds, trough metates, three-quarter grooved axes, inhumation burials, and Pinto Polychrome pottery. About 1300, a new round of population movement brought new immigrants from the Kayenta area to the Basin, bringing with them pueblo architecture with enclosed plazas, another distinctive Salado trait.

At about the same time, Florence Hawley formulated a theory that the Salado originated in the Upper Gila River drainage, and that by 950 these mountain people were migrating into the Tonto Basin/Globe-Miami regions (Hawley 1932). She also recognized a second migration of Little Colorado River peoples about 1100, and the merging of these two culture groups—ceramic technology from the eastern mountains and decorative styles from the Colorado Plateau—led to the development of the distinctive Salado polychrome pottery.

Migration theories abounded at this time, and Haury posted his own thoughts in his dissertation (Haury 1945:204–208), a reanalysis of the Hemenway Southwestern Archaeological Expedition material from Los Muertos. Haury, drawing on his seminal work at Snaketown, Roose-velt 9:6, ongoing excavations in the Forestdale Valley, and his analysis of the Hemenway Expedition material from Los Muertos and other nearby ruins, developed an encompassing and elegant Salado hypothesis. He believed that Tonto Basin was colonized relatively early (Colonial period) by a Hohokam population that originated in the Salt-Gila Basin. These people later abandoned Tonto Basin, during the Hohokam Sedentary period, creating an occupational hiatus that was later filled by movement of people from the Little Colorado River drainage, about 1100. To Haury (1945:205), "It appears that the culture [Salado] emerged from a combined Mogollon-Anasazi base—stamped most heavily by the latter—in the area below the Mogollon Rim." Haury (1945:208) went on to conclude that, "As part of [a] general expansion, the Salado people, obviously related to those of the Little Colorado, gave way and moved into the Gila Basin to share that area with the Hohokam, and even still farther south as far as the international line." This later Salado migration occurred in the late thirteenth century, coincidentally with chaotic shifts in cultural influence and population density across the Colorado Plateau (Pueblo), the central mountains of Arizona and New Mexico (Mogollon), and southern Arizona (Hohokam). As the Salado expanded over the greater Southwest, traits associated with them and their "heartland" in Tonto Basin dominated the landscape and left a telltale presence for archaeologists to decipher. Haury expanded the Salado trait list to include brachycephalism, multistoried great houses, animal figurines, disc-type spindle whorls, turquoise overlay shell jewelry, pahos, and protokachina iconography (Haury 1945:207).

Migration theories came to dominate archaeological ideas about the Salado; who they were, how they influenced other culture groups, how they developed as a culture, etc. From the mid-1930s until the mid-1970s the Salado were seen as a distinct culture group; or at least archaeologists wanted to view the Salado that way. Cultural historicism was the paradigm of the day as archaeology grappled with chronological ordering, cultural classification (e.g., Hohokam phases as developed by Gladwin), and description. Migration, diffusion, and consideration of cultural traits shared with extant Native American cultures were how prehistoric populations were ordered and defined. Interpretation relative to patterned behavior and comparative relationships were secondary considerations, and rare in the archaeological literature.

Other voices of the day, Reed (1950), Schroeder (1953), Steen (1962), Pierson (1962), and Di Peso (1974b, 1976) promoted migration hypotheses to account for various models of Salado origins. All of these competing migration models have been important to the conceptual development of the Salado Culture concept and to what has become the "Salado Problem" (Nelson and LeBlanc 1986:1). All have been promoted within the conceptual paradigms that shaped and dominated North American archaeology during the last 60 years. They cannot, nor should they be ignored.

Erik Reed saw Salado as a Western Pueblo phenomenon, having been derived from the Cibola Branch (Reed 1950:130). Albert Schroeder (1953:82) championed a model of Salado development that stemmed from influences blended from the Sinagua and Hohokam to the west and northwest. These groups aggregated in Tonto Basin as the Salado, according to Schroeder. After excavations at Tonto National Monument ruins, Charlie Steen (1962) postulated migration from both the east (middle Gila River) and north (Little Colorado River); while in the same publication, Pierson (1962) suggested that an amalgamation of Anasazi, Mogollon, and Hohokam occurred to produce a Salado that migrated from the Forestdale region, thus agreeing with Haury (1945:205).

Di Peso's argument of Salado origins was radically different from others. He postulated that Salado origins were evident at Casas Grandes in Chihuahua, Mexico, and that it was the result of a Mesoamerican influenced and controlled *puchteca* trading system joined with the indigenous population of northern Chihuahua (Di Peso 1974b:290–95). Evidence for this argument came from Salado polychromes manufactured at Casas Grandes. Di Peso (1974b:531) dated the context of these ceramics as early as 1060, significantly earlier than appearance of Salado polychromes from other sites in its range—generally agreed as late thirteenth century. However, Dean and Ravesloot (1993:96) reexamined the dating of Casas Grandes and concluded that this early date is incorrect because of the use of tree-ring dates from shaped and weathered beams that have many outside rings removed, thus obscuring the cutting date. They show that the Salado polychromes date between 1200 and 1450–1500, dates agreeable with Salado occupations to the north. As Crown (1994:15) states, "A southern origin for the Salado polychromes seems unlikely...." Di Peso's work at Casas Grandes stimulated much discussion about trade networks, political hierarchy, population movement, and social boundaries. He maneuvered Southwestern archaeologists into thinking anew about the Salado origin

question; he set the stage for a Southwestern case study that might test the development and evolution of economic relationships between the "core" at Paquimé and the "peripheral" areas surrounding and supporting its grandeur and regionally dominant position. Despite negative reviews and comments about his thoughts on Salado origins, a key finding from Di Peso's work documented the local manufacture of Gila Polychrome at Casas Grandes, "pottery made in the Gila Polychrome tradition was independently made at a number of widely separated villages rather than being an export of, or even a cultural diagnostic of, a single hearth area. As a ceramic tradition, the conceptual designs and ceramic forms that identify this school may have been transmitted by a number of devices including itinerant potters, small migrant groups, or perhaps as a widespread fad inspiration that led local potters to produce imitations in addition to their own styles, as at Casas Grandes in the Medio period (about 1060)" (Di Peso 1976b:59).

As others have investigated Salado polychrome technology, it has become irrefutable that Salado polychromes were locally manufactured throughout the Salado area, a fact that bears importantly on recent Salado and Classic period syntheses (Crown 1994:209).

Prior to the mid-1970s the intent had been to define Salado as a separate culture with its own distinct set of traits; a culture that relates to its neighbors but is clearly distinct from them; a culture that has a beginning and an end. At this time, however, significant changes in archaeological method and theory were occurring. The multilinear materialist views of cultural ecology (Steward 1955) and the cultural evolutionary models of the neoevolutionists (Fried 1967; Sahlins 1968; Service 1962, 1975; White 1949, 1959) came to Arizona and flourished as students trained in the 1960s and 1970s began their professional careers. The archaeological renderings of Lewis Binford (1962, 1965, 1968, 1977) were at the fore of what has been called "New Archaeology," or processual archaeology, because of its heavy reliance on scientific analysis to organize and manipulate data. Significant contributions to New Archaeology were also made by Watson et al. (1971) and Flannery (1972), among others, in their promotion of systems theory and the principles of homeostasis as critical forces in human behavior.

Research into the Salado culture grew in intensity beginning in the 1970s. The Miami Wash Project (Doyel 1978), excavations at Ushklish Ruin (Haas 1971), the Reno-Park Creek Project (Jeter 1978), the Ord Mine

Project (Ciolek-Torrello 1984), and the Ash Creek Project (Rice 1985) represent significant investigations under the auspices of cultural resource management and a body of Federal legislation that requires consideration of impacts to archaeological sites affected by Federal development projects. In addition to these highway construction projects, important work was begun by the Tonto National Forest as it initiated a permanent program of archaeological resource management, including a healthy dose of inventory surveys. The 1970s saw the beginnings of surveys for the development of Plan 6, the Central Arizona Project water storage alternative that would have the most dramatic effect upon Salado research in Tonto Basin (Rice and Most 1984). Importantly, just as this work and renewed interest was beginning, Doyel and Haury sponsored the 1976 Salado Conference.

The first Salado Conference focused on the "Salado phenomenon" (Doyel and Haury 1976:1), and the invited attendees were requested to center their papers on cultural historical reconstruction, chronology, and the process of evaluation of Salado material. The outcome was a "working statement" (Doyel and Haury 1976:2) that brought attention to Salado prehistory, and served as a research design for much of the field efforts that followed. For the current team of Tonto Basin researchers, the *Kiva* publication of the conference is a well-worn document. Included in it are then current perspectives on the competing migration theories (Di Peso 1976a; Doyel 1976b, 1976c; Franklin and Masse 1976; Haury 1976b; Mayro et al. 1976; Pilles 1976) and relevant commentary by Emil Haury (1976c), Charles Di Peso (1976b), and Ed Dittert (1976), all senior researchers with considerable experience in southern Arizona's Classic period. Some more interesting observations include:

> Perhaps one of the problems inherent in the Salado definition resides in the development of its classificatory system, wherein the final result is a compiled and somewhat contrived trait list. We must begin to think in terms of multiple occupancy in so-called specific culture areas and we must do this in terms of not only space but also time (Di Peso 1976b:126).

> I am increasingly persuaded that one of the reasons why we have had so much trouble with the Salado concept stems from the intellectual environment of the time when it was first defined. The trait-list was the way to do it in those days. Today, the trait-list approach has been drawn-and-quartered (Haury 1976c:125).

These various positions were presented as ideas for investigators to consider, and all participants agreed that little specific information is known about the complexes represented in all of the aforementioned areas. It was also pointed out that little systematic survey has been accomplished upon which to base statements regarding population movements (Dittert 1976:134).

It is important to remember that revitalization of work in Tonto Basin has been conducted by archaeologists trained in the principles of processual archaeology. Though not much had changed about the Salado in the published works before 1976, a young generation of archaeologists was poised to take to the field and question previous interpretive models about the Salado.

This group brought scientific rigor in the form of multidisciplinary ecological analysis to Salado research. Identification of settlement patterns and establishment of chronological control, all under the principle of evolution and ecological determinism, became paramount issues, as did functionalist analyses of artifacts. Hill (1968, 1970a, 1970b) and Longacre (1970), in particular, contributed much to a functionalist method that would help focus attention on defining social behavior. Many younger scholars were trained at the University of Arizona and by a faculty that not only included the powerful mind and energy of Emil Haury, but the newer thinking of William Longacre and the influential University of Chicago school. The stage was set for serious work on the Salado "phenomenon" by a group of young, energetic scholars fresh from the rigors of a university. The Salado ruins were also primed as huge construction projects would begin to exert their destructive influences on Tonto Basin. In 1976, Salado archaeology was in a state of confusion; the Salado were poorly understood both areally and temporally, the definitive work having been done in the 1920s and 1930s and much of that in the Salt-Gila River Valleys. Huge construction projects were on the horizon that would allow an opportunity to encompass the Salado "heartland" within a new archaeological paradigm.

I have stated that the Salado cannot be intellectually separated from the Hohokam. The Hohokam were the essential prehistoric group of northern Sonora. They are clearly defined geographically, they possessed a consistent set of traits that are identifiable in the archaeological record, they can be explored with confidence because they had a beginning and an end that are defined. In the 1970s, a group of important contributors began to publish their ideas about the Hohokam; views that began to expand and question earlier conclusions. In a series of seminal publications, Wilcox (Wilcox et al. 1981; Wilcox and Shenk 1977; Wilcox and Sternberg 1981, 1983) explored Hohokam social organization by detailing community structure. This coupled with the subsistence, architectural, and material analyses by field practitioners (Ciolek-Torrello and Wilcox 1988; Czaplicki and Ravesloot 1989; Doyel 1978; Fish et al. eds. 1992; Henderson 1987a, 1987b, 1993; Rice 1987a, 1987b; Teague and Crown 1984) led to the development of models of Hohokam social complexity, social interaction, and economics; and these then facilitated new views on Hohokam social organization, social behavior, and religion. The expansion of Hohokam research to include these topics, again, tracks with general trends in North American archaeology as the isolationism of neoevolutionary processual approaches began to be questioned. Wallerstein (1974, 1980) and Wolf (1982) present cogent arguments for large-scale social change brought about by economic forces. Although their focus was on the development of capitalism, Wallerstein's "world system" concept is useful as a way to integrate developmental factors into a coherent intellectual process (McGuire 1986, 1991, 1992; McGuire et al. 1994; Trigger 1989:332–33; Upham 1986; Whitecotton and Pailes 1986). With new theoretical models to rely on, the Hohokam began to be viewed in terms of "interaction spheres" (Doyel 1976c:35), "macro regional relationships" (McGuire 1986), "exchange networks" (Wood and McAllister 1982), and as a "regional system" (Wilcox et al. 1981); concepts adopted from, and adapted to world systems theory.

As early as 1972, Doyel (1972) hinted that broader scaled analyses were necessary to clearly define the Salado. Although Doyel speaks of the "Salado cultural tradition" (Doyel 1978:213), he later quotes Hill (1971) and supports the process of looking into cultural behavior causes of social development. This approach is mirrored by Wood and McAllister (1982:85) who saw Salado as, "a unique historical development resulting from the modification of local adaptive patterns by such local and regional processes as territorial, political, and trade expansion." Further, Wood and McAllister went on to state that research into Salado archaeology, "must attempt to understand local adaptations and internal developments, *as well as the effects of such regional events as colonization, acculturation, mercantilism, and trade alliance.*" (Wood and McAllister 1982:85; emphasis added). Clearly, a major research emphasis today focuses on eco-

nomic relations and how they might affect social organization. Religion, ideology, and symbolism can have just as large an effect on social organization (Hodder 1982, 1986; Leone et al. 1987; Trigger 1989:340–411). Hodder (1979) has demonstrated that material culture is not solely a reflection of ecological adaptations and resultant social political organization. Thus, he rejects materialist functionalism as well, but he argues that it (material culture) is an active component of group and individual relations that can mask as well as reflect social relations. The recent trend in North American archaeology is the recognition of an imperative to view social phenomena in their totality (Trigger 1989:354), rather than the singular stark coldness of science at the obfuscation, or even rejection, of human pageantry.

POSTPROCESSUALISM AND SALADO ARCHAEOLOGY

Postprocessualism in archaeology evolved during critical debates concerning what some believe to be the disregard by neoevolutionist processualists for human-centered cultural influences. Dunnell (1982:521) has observed that evolutionary and ecological approaches, first developed in the biological sciences and applied to archaeology, are not designed to explain idiosyncratic behavior or motivational and symbolic structures within societies. Leone (1986:422) admirably describes the issue, "culture is a level of meaning or thought that includes values, cosmology, patterns held unawares, or structures composed of oppositions. Such a reality exists alongside and is independent of social organization. Culture facilitates social reality."

Postprocessualism has been grasped by world systems advocates because it embraces the necessity of a broader regional coverage as a prerequisite for meaningful interpretation: "World systems theory (Wallerstein 1974) avoids conceiving of societies as bounded entities and allows for the simultaneous possibilities of autonomy and relatedness" (McGuire et al. 1994:250).

Marxist archaeology is one component of the many-headed postprocessualist movement in archaeology, sometimes labeled "alternative" archaeology. It can be argued that much of today's "new" archaeology has a great deal in common with Marxist archaeology. However, it is lacking the political rhetoric that follows hand in hand with Marxist philosophy. Marxist archaeology is very compatible with cultural ecology, cultural materialist theory, and cultural evolution. It does distinguish differences between unilinear cultural evolution as promoted by White (1949, 1975) and multilinear evolution (Steward 1955), and thus aligns itself more closely with cultural ecological models (McGuire 1992). In addition, current research trends often include ideological symbology in interpreting the past; an idea compatible with Marxist archaeology. Where Marxist archaeology differs from North American processual archaeology is in the political agenda promoted by Marxists; that archaeologists should actively engage in social engineering to fight and end economic disparity and exploitation. By staying politically neutral, processual archaeologists who combine the best scientific principles of Marxist archaeology and the symbolic and ideological tenants of postprocessual archaeology allow themselves the opportunity to identify empirical approaches to the less well defined area of human behavior—its motivational and symbolic systems. Baker et al. (1990:2) point out a serious problem with many of the "alternative" archaeologies: "Below each 'ism' is a real issue, and a committed archaeology is doomed to failure if it mistakes the two. Behind feminism is the problem of sexism, (read sexual inequality), behind Marxism is the problem of poverty (read economic inequality). Which real issue does postprocessualism address?"

The "new" archaeology (read traditional processual archaeology) will succeed in promoting better explanations of prehistoric behavior if it avoids entrapment in political posturing and assistance to present-day social issues.

Given that the theoretical landscape today has many more explanatory alternatives than it did a generation ago, what is the trend in Salado archaeology? Looking at Bureau of Reclamation sponsored work in Tonto Basin, I believe we can see implementation of explanatory models that employ postprocessual explanatory techniques within an evolutionary and cultural ecological context. Rice, ed. (1990) approaches Salado research from a strong perspective of materialist data analysis and manipulation. However, he does not stop there. Included in the Arizona State University (ASU) approach is reference to issues important to cultural historicism (Rice 1990c:31), cultural ecology (1990c:32), and evolutionary, or developmental processes leading to social complexity derived from economic determinants (1990c:36). In addition, Rice (1990c:37) is not ignorant of the potential for an ideological basis of Salado complexity, and preliminary results show that approaching the issue from this perspective will bear fruit (Jacobs 1992).

Statistical Research, Inc. (SRI), with a research team headed by Richard Ciolek-Torrello investigated "rural" sites in Tonto Basin and developed appropriate theoretical models, stating that:

The relationship between food production strategies and settlement systems is part of a much broader theoretical issue that has emerged in recent years. This issue concerns whether the emergence of complex systems and, presumably, intensive food production strategies in the Tonto Basin and adjacent Hohokam areas of south-central Arizona were associated with the development of social complexity and economic specialization [Ciolek-Torrello et al. 1990:21].

Thus, Ciolek-Torrello sets up an alternative approach to Rice and the ASU team on the issue of Tonto Basin complexity. Ciolek-Torrello et al. (1990:27) focus on a set of research questions that include a functionalist perspective as well as cultural historicism (ethnographic analogy) and economic determinism. The result is an eclectic brand of archaeological research that includes multiple analytical and theoretical approaches.

SRI has had the first word on the Roosevelt Dam research program (Ciolek-Torrello and Welch 1994) and present a stimulating treatise on "rural" sites archaeology and the agricultural and subsistence economy potential of Tonto Basin. They present compelling arguments about Tonto Basin cultural evolution using both the archaeological data and ethnographic analogy. Their results are not without criticism (Wood 1992), and the result sets the stage for future reports that will be prepared by ASU and Desert Archaeology. However, the results are thought provoking because they were derived from detailed analyses of alternative models of Salado/Tonto Basin cultural development. The ideas are fresh and challenging:

The view of the evolution of prehistoric land-use systems and sociopolitical organization presented in these volumes is preliminary, representing a first attempt to synthesize the results of our research with the rapidly growing body of data from the Tonto Basin region. This perspective requires considerable refinement and evaluation, but it is much more consistent with the archaeological and historical record of the Southwest than the core-periphery paradigm, which suggests that socioeconomic and political developments in the Tonto Basin primarily represent an outgrowth of relations with the Phoenix Basin or an elite model that involves the development of complex and sophisticated sociopolitical systems [Ciolek-Torrello and Welch 1994:492].

Doelle, Wallace, and Craig (1992) reflect this opinion when they caution that a core-periphery model may become overly mechanistic, and researchers may assume that core areas are dominant over the entirety of prehistoric social phenomena (a direct criticism of world systems theory): "As long as researchers acknowledge fully that peripheral areas represent subsystems that must be considered in their own right, then such models provide useful framework for conceptualizing regional diversity (Doelle, Wallace, and Craig 1992:135)." As does Rice, Doelle, Wallace, and Craig (1992) invoke ideology and "ritual" behavior as a factor critical to interpreting Salado, and really Southwestern, prehistory. In their final statement, Elson et al. (1995:477) acknowledge that identification of ritual behavior is critical to a complete understanding of Tonto Basin prehistory.

These studies have in common an approach to archaeological interpretation that differs significantly from the paradigm within which the principle investigators were trained. Aspects of post-processualism are now common in Southwestern archaeology, though the researchers might not be aware that their traditional processual methods have been augmented by alternative theoretical paradigms. Crown (1994) presents an exhaustively researched review of Salado polychrome ceramics, their place in interpretive models of Salado development, and their role as an integrative mechanism. She convincingly concludes that the Salado phenomenon was a regional cult rather than a culture, and she bases this conclusion to a great extent on ideological components of social functioning.

Crown's "Southwestern Cult" (1994) has its development in similar ideas recognized by other researchers, although it was Crown who clearly argued and articulated the concept. Nelson and LeBlanc (1986:13) proposed "Southern Pueblo" as a companion to the previously defined Western Pueblo tradition. They correctly argue that post-1300 occupations in the Southwest cannot be categorized as Anasazi, Mogollon, or Hohokam, and continue that, "it is time to throw out simplistic conceptions of the Salado as a group that developed in a single 'heartland' and later migrated en masse to other locations" (Nelson and LeBlanc 1986:14).

J. Scott Wood and Martin McAllister have promulgated the Central Arizona Tradition (Wood and McAllister 1984b) based on more than two decades of experience in Tonto Basin and the Tonto National Forest. Wood has consistently argued that the "Salado" represent entrepreneurial Hohokam who blended traits from throughout central Arizona, including the Mogollon area of east-central Arizona and the Little Colorado River drainage (Wood 1983, 1985, 1986, 1989; Wood and McAllister 1980, 1982, 1984b). Wood's is an economic deterministic model that incorporates world systems interpretive methodology.

Mark Elson has similarly defined the sub-Mogollon Rim Cultural Tradition (Elson 1992a:151–53; 1992b:6) based on recent excavations at the Rye Creek Ruin. Because of data restrictions, Elson limits the geography of his tradition to a stretch from the Verde River east into western New Mexico. Obviously, Wood sees the Central Arizona Tradition in central Arizona. Nelson and LeBlanc (1986) view the Southern Pueblo "group" as encompassing the range defined by Salado polychromes.

The common thread in these definitions of Salado is that Salado is not a culture as defined by traditional North American cultural historicism. Instead, these authors believe that Salado should be more appropriately viewed, and redefined, as a tradition (Willey and Phillips 1958:37). In *Dynamics of Southwestern Prehistory*, Cordell and Gumerman (1989:2) chose not to include the Salado as a group, though they were discussed in the book. On their map, Tonto Basin is included within the sphere of the Hohokam.

SALADO ORIGINS

Migration models dominated Salado origin concepts from their inception until the mid-1970s. At the first Salado Conference in 1976, despite arguments against all migration models, none were rejected, and all were afforded a degree of sympathy. The invited participants seemed uncertain as to what the Salado phenomenon was though they desperately wanted a new definition. The conference attendees did conclude that the one common thread in defining the Salado was Salado polychrome pottery (Doyel and Haury 1976).

Recent excavations in Tonto Basin suggest a strong Hohokam presence and development by an indigenous population into Salado (Elson and Craig 1992a; Elson et al., Chapter 7). These data support many of Wood's long held beliefs about Salado development; that they were shaped by a strong and dominant Hohokam presence in Tonto Basin, established at least by the Colonial period. However, Elson et al. (Chapter 7) and Stark, Clark, and Elson (1995a) demonstrate a population increase in the early Classic period Roosevelt phase (ca. 1280) and show that some residents of Tonto Basin were migrants from the north. Based primarily on spatial configurations of room blocks, evidence from three sites, Griffin Wash, Saguaro Muerto, and Meddler Point, suggests coresidence by indigenous and nonindigenous folk, the latter possibly from the Cibola area (Stark, Clark, and Elson 1995a:236–37).

These conclusions paint a picture that is not as simple as earlier models of Basin development, but one that is based on reliable evidence. That Tonto Basin provided a significant opportunity for residential success is evident by the Early Ceramic period materials found at the Eagle Ridge site. This site suggests that a robust group of agriculturalists occupied the Basin's Salt River Arm as early as 100. Later, a significant Colonial and Sedentary period Hohokam occupation is also evident, documenting more than 1,000 years of unbroken occupation in the Basin with the last 400–450 years of that sequence being Hohokam. Occupation in the Ash Creek phase (1050–1150) and the Miami phase (1150–1250), arguably precursors to the recognizable Salado, fill the gap between the Hohokam presence and full-blown Salado in the Roosevelt phase. Clearly, Tonto Basin population dynamics cannot be separated from influences derived from the

Phoenix Basin, Little Colorado River, and Central Mountain areas. Tonto Basin was a crossroads that provided subsistence security for its inhabitants and access to economic and social markets. The local geography and archaeological evidence describe Tonto Basin as a place to prosper and thrive. In the Classic period a people known as Salado inhabited the Basin. They had relationships with the identified culture groups that were located adjacent to the Basin; however, all of the recent research in the Basin suggests that they cannot be identified as a separate group, like the Hohokam or Mogollon. Crown's (1994) arguments for the Southwestern Cult are cogent, showing that Tonto Basin is not the Salado "heartland"; no place can be so labeled. Salado is a regional phenomenon unique to the Southwest United States and portions of extreme northern Mexico.

Much remains to be written about the people who participated in the Salado phenomenon, or Southwestern Cult, or Southern Pueblo; however it is labeled. Southwestern archaeology has a continuing challenge to identify, isolate, and investigate the prehistoric Classic period. This was a very complex time, ripe with population movement, environmental disruption, economic expansion, religious institutionalism, and intense political interaction. The theory, method, and practice of American archaeology is positioning itself to render meaningful explanation to these social phenomena, and the Theodore Roosevelt Dam Archaeology Project is but one of many recent examples of archaeological research that will contribute to this effort.

CHAPTER TWO

Subsistence and Environmental Interactions

Carla R. Van West, Richard S. Ciolek-Torrello, John R. Welch, Jeffrey H. Altschul,
Karen R. Adams, Steven D. Shelley, and Jeffrey A. Homburg

In the closing decades of the thirteenth century, a remarkable reorganization of human communities occurred in the Greater Southwest. The dramatic developments of the fourteenth and fifteenth centuries took a variety of forms, but everywhere seem to entail population aggregation, agricultural intensification, and attempts to integrate human communities through religious revitalization. Populations in Tonto Basin of east-central Arizona were caught up in these processes and were influenced by powerful forces that strongly conditioned where they lived, what they did, and to whom they were connected.

Some of these forces were social and related to historical developments both within and beyond the confines of the Basin. Certainly, the evolution of new religious cults in the upper Little Colorado River region, the political preeminence of Casas Grandes, and the growing economic power of irrigation communities along the lower Salt and Gila Rivers are examples of contemporary, sociocultural elaborations that influenced human behavior in the late prehistoric period. Other forces that affected human endeavors, however, were natural. Floods, droughts, and the changing distributions of important subsistence resources (e.g., flowing water, arable soil, plants, and animals) acted singly or in concert to affect landscapes already altered by humans through their economic adaptations.

TONTO BASIN: ENVIRONMENTAL OPPORTUNITIES AND CONSTRAINTS IN THE TRANSITION ZONE

Physiography

Tonto Basin is one of several finger-like intrusions of the Sonoran Desert into the rugged and heavily forested upland belt of central Arizona referred to as the Transition Zone. The Transition Zone separates the lower Sonoran deserts of the Basin and Range province to the south from the upper Sonoran deserts of the Colorado Plateau province to the north. Mountains and upland features delimit the perimeter of the Basin: the Mogollon Rim to the north, the Sierra Ancha to the east, the Salt and Superstition Mountains to the south, and the Mazatzal Mountains to the west.

Although small (60 by 15 km), Tonto Basin is characterized by marked environmental diversity. In a day's walk (less than 20 km), one can ascend 2,000 m from valley floor (ca. 580 m or 1,900 feet) to the summits of the Mazatzal Mountains (ca. 2,400 m or 7,875 feet) or the Sierra Ancha (ca. 2,350 m or 7,700 feet) and pass through most of the Southwest's biotic life zones: Lower Sonoran, Upper Sonoran, Transition, and Canadian (Merriam 1890, 1898).

The Basin is divided into three geographic units: 1) the Upper Tonto Basin, consisting of the middle reaches of Tonto Creek and its major tributary, Rye Creek; 2) the

Tonto Creek Arm of the Lower Basin; 3) the Salt River Arm of the Lower Basin, that extends from its entrance into the Basin on the east to its confluence with Tonto Creek on the west.

Each geographic unit contains three topographic subdivisions: the riverine, bajada-piedmont, and mountain zones. The riverine zone consists of the floodplains and lower terraces of the two primary drainages and their largest tributaries, places where canal irrigation, floodwater, and other forms of farming could have been practiced. Holocene soils of the riverine zone are generally, but not uniformly fertile (Broderick 1974; Homburg 1994). Mesic habitats along floodplains, drainages, springs, and ditches provide the best agricultural opportunities as well as a variety of grasses, ruderals, and water-loving trees.

The bajada-piedmont zone is the more rugged and heavily dissected upland area between the riverine zone and mountains. Bajada-piedmont settings support a distinct suite of useful wild resources as well as small-scale opportunities for irrigation (from small streams, springs, and seeps), floodwater farming, and in higher areas, dry-farming.

The mountain zone is the steepest and most rugged portion of the Basin with a low potential for agriculture due to sparse and rocky soils. Although Wood (1989; Wood and McAllister 1984:287–88) suggests that Tonto Basin's upland soils are generally thin and infertile and that their overexploitation resulted in a pattern of transient settlement, Homburg's (1994) soil productivity study indicates that soils on the Pleistocene terraces of the uplands are generally quite fertile and exhibit few signs of nutrient depletion. Soil moisture, rather than fertility, is the most significant factor limiting sustainable upland food production (Homburg 1994:295). Mountain slopes and high-elevation valleys also sustain useful upland plant species and provide deer hunting grounds.

Hydrology

Tonto Basin has perennially flowing water in its two major streams, the Salt River and Tonto Creek. Of the two, the Salt is by far the larger. With its headwaters in the White Mountains of the Colorado Plateau, the Salt is second in size only to the Colorado River in Arizona. Its watershed incorporates 11,153 km^2, and it produces an average annual flow of 647,453 acre feet of water per year at the gauging station 27 km above Roosevelt Lake (M. R. Waters 1996:Draft 2.12). In contrast, Tonto Creek, with

headwaters in the highlands above the Mogollon Rim, has a watershed of 1,750 km^2 and an average annual streamflow of 110,579 acre-feet per year at the gauging station above Gun Creek (M. R. Waters 1996:Draft 2.11).

Although more drought-sensitive than the Salt, the gentler hydrological regime of Tonto Creek is more easily managed by farmers who are able to divert its waters onto arable soils of the lowest river terraces (Welch 1992, 1994a; J. S. Wood et al. 1992). Further, Tonto Creek is superior to the Salt in at least two other respects; it is less prone to flooding because of its wider valley profile, and it is significantly less saline (Figure 2.1). As a consequence, more irrigable land is located adjacent to Tonto Creek, agricultural features and fields are easier to maintain, and crops that are moderately sensitive to salt uptake, such as corn and beans, may be grown more productively. Similar crops may be grown along the Salt River, but additional water must be applied to fields before and during the growing season to leach potentially damaging salts from the root zone. Cultivation of relatively salt-tolerant crops, such as cotton, present fewer problems for Salt River irrigation farmers.

M. R. Waters (1996) estimates that some 627 ha (1,550 acres) of irrigable land were available to Tonto Creek farmers, whereas only 300 ha (740 acres) of comparable land could potentially be irrigated on the Salt River arm of Tonto Basin. These values, however, do not include floodplain soils; they consider only those alluvial terrace sediments (i.e., the modern T2 Holocene terrace) that were accessible prehistorically.

Climate

Semiarid overall, Tonto Basin combines an upland precipitation regime with a growing season nearly as long as those of the desert areas to the south and west (Welch 1992, 1994a). Annual precipitation is distributed in a bimodal pattern (Figure 2.2). The majority of the Basin's precipitation is delivered during the winter storm season (56 percent from November through March) in the form of widespread and prolonged but gentle storms. Snow above 900 m is common at this time. The remainder is delivered chiefly in the form of violent thunderstorms during the summer monsoon period (July through September). A small and quite irregular component of annual moisture occurs in October. When these storms occur, they frequently bring heavy rain and often result in floods and property damage.

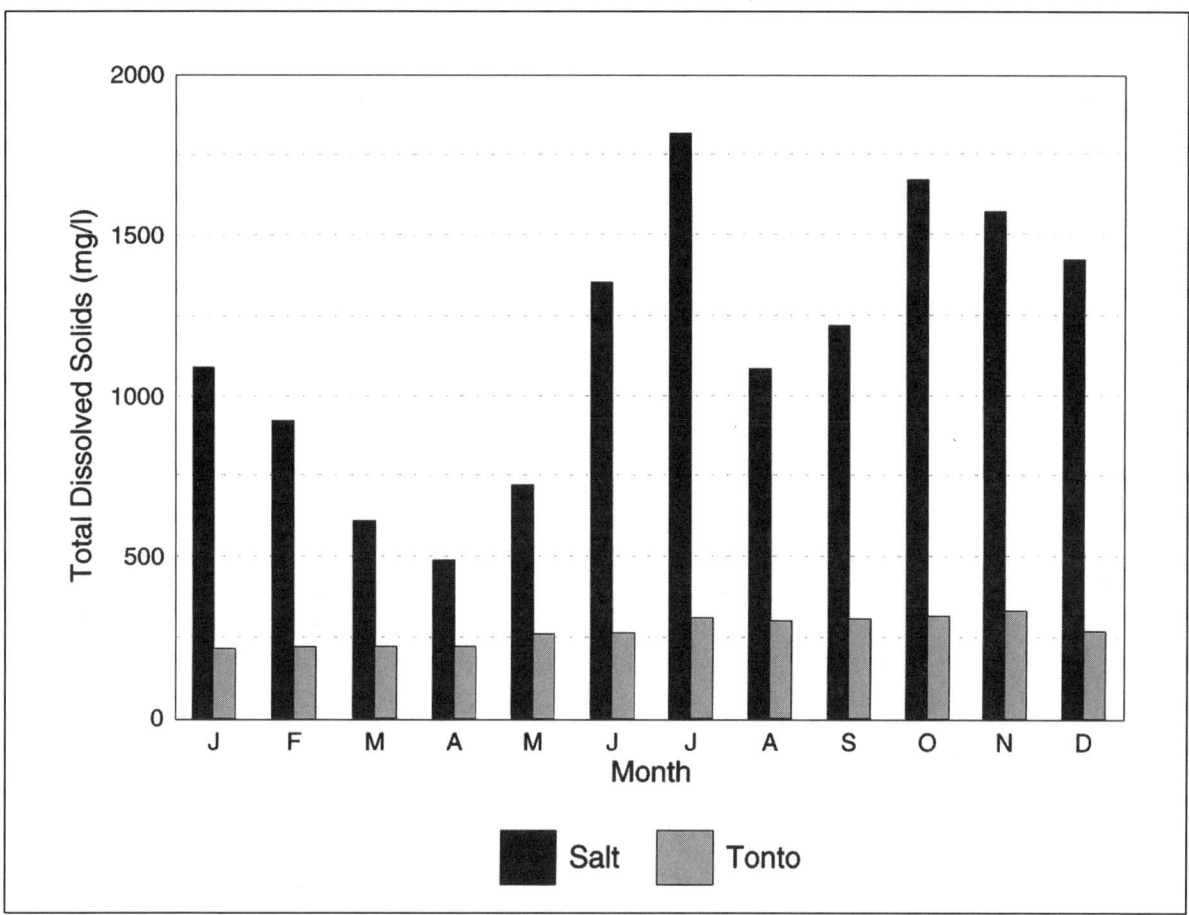

Figure 2.1.   Mean monthly salinity levels for the Salt River (1934-1995) and Tonto Creek (1987-1991).

Precipitation and temperature are highly variable within the Basin. Spatially, both vary with elevation, landform, and aspect. Temporally, they vary greatly from season-to-season and year-to-year. Average annual precipitation ranges from about 380 mm (15 inches) in the valley floor at Roosevelt Dam to a high of about 523 mm (20.6 inches) in Payson (Welch 1994a:28). Although winter moisture generally contributes slightly more than half of the total annual precipitation, its occurrence and timing diverge greatly from one year to the next, signifying that it is less predictable than the summer moisture. Nevertheless, fall and winter moisture largely determine streamflow and soil moisture characteristics of the following growing season.

Temperature (Figure 2.3) ranges from highs over 38 C (>100 F) at the lower elevations in the summer to lows below 0 C (<32 F) at elevations above 1,524 m (5,000 feet) in the winter. Evapotranspiration is high throughout, particularly in the lower, drier locations. The length of growing season (the period between killing frosts) varies from a mean of 300 days at 670 m (2,200 feet) to a mean of about 130 days at 1478 m (4,850 feet)—ample time for the maturation of at least one crop of all indigenous Southwestern cultigens.

Floral and Faunal Resources

The biotic communities of Tonto Basin are numerous and varied (Adams and Welch 1994a, 1994b; Baker 1996). Their location and richness are determined by physical factors, primarily landform, aspect, elevation, soil, and cold air drainage. Most of the Basin below 1,050 m (ca.

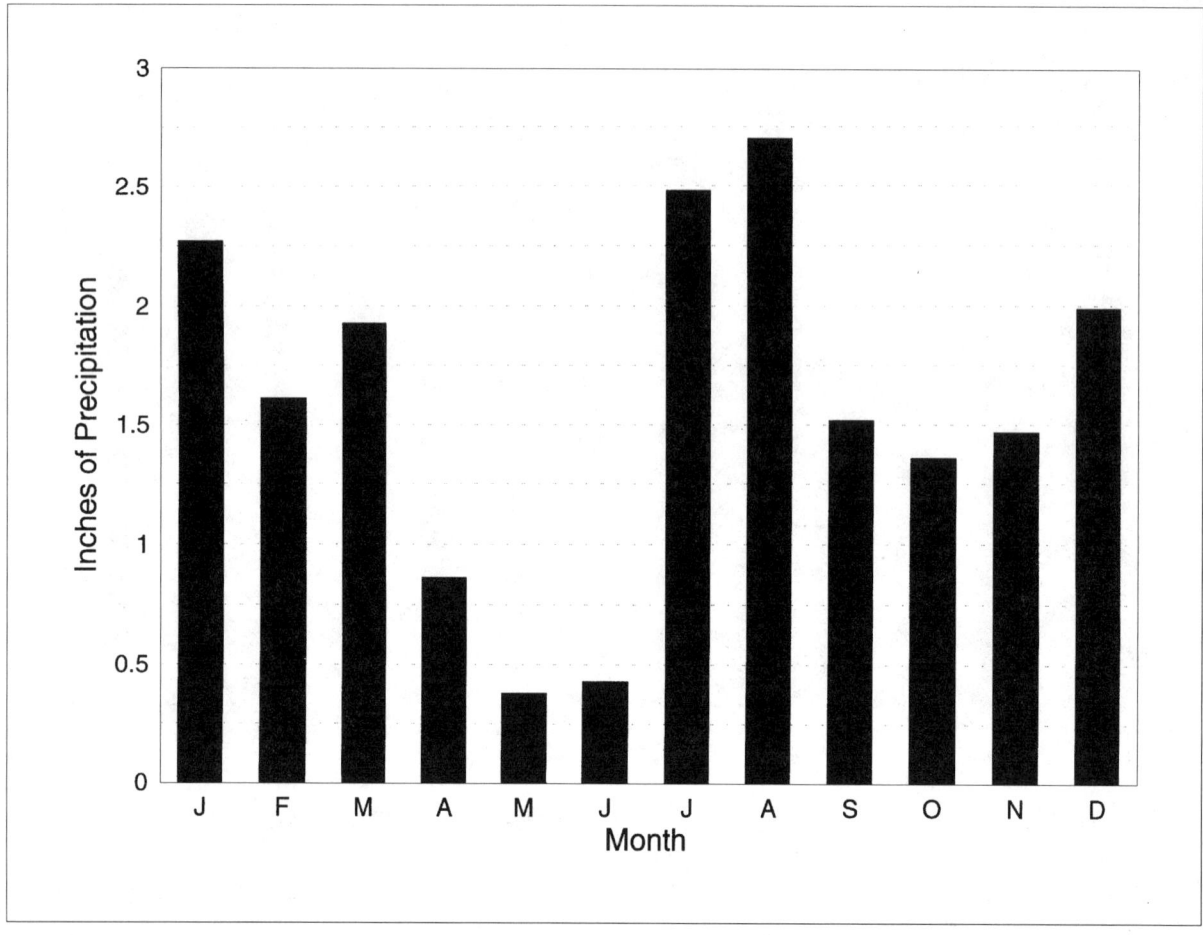

Figure 2.2.   Mean monthly precipitation (inches) for east-central Arizona, Climatic Division 4, 1895-1987.

3,450 feet) is best described as belonging to the Arizona Upland subdivision of the Sonoran Desertscrub and Semidesert Grassland biomes (Brown 1994). Desertscrub communities often include mesquite, paloverde, acacia, desert hackberry, jojoba, creosote, bursage, saguaro, hedgehog, cholla, prickly pear, and a variety of grasses and shrubby species. Riparian vegetation typically includes cottonwood, willow, and a variety of weeds and grasses. Secondary components of grassland communities include many economically important forbs, weeds, and succulents such as amaranth, mallow, spiderling, filaree, buckwheat, devil's claw, agave, yucca, and sotol.

Between 1,050 m and 2,000 m (ca. 3,450 feet and 6,500 feet), Interior Chaparral and Madrean Evergreen Woodland communities predominate (Brown 1994). Chaparral environments are dominated by shrub oak; other woody plants include mountain mahogany, buckbrush, velvet ash, bear grass, silk-tassel, and other oaks. Woodland communities commonly include Emory and Gambel's oak, manzanita, several forms of juniper, and pinyon.

Above 2,000 m occurs the Montane Conifer Forest (Brown 1994). Associated with the dominant ponderosa pine are Douglas-fir, white fir, quaking aspen, and a few understory shrubs and grasses.

Indigenous animals of Tonto Basin include the economically important jackrabbit, desert cottontail, muledeer, white-tailed deer, and bighorn sheep. In addition, a wide variety of fish, amphibians, reptiles, rodents, carnivores, and birds inhabits the Basin (J. L. Cameron 1996b).

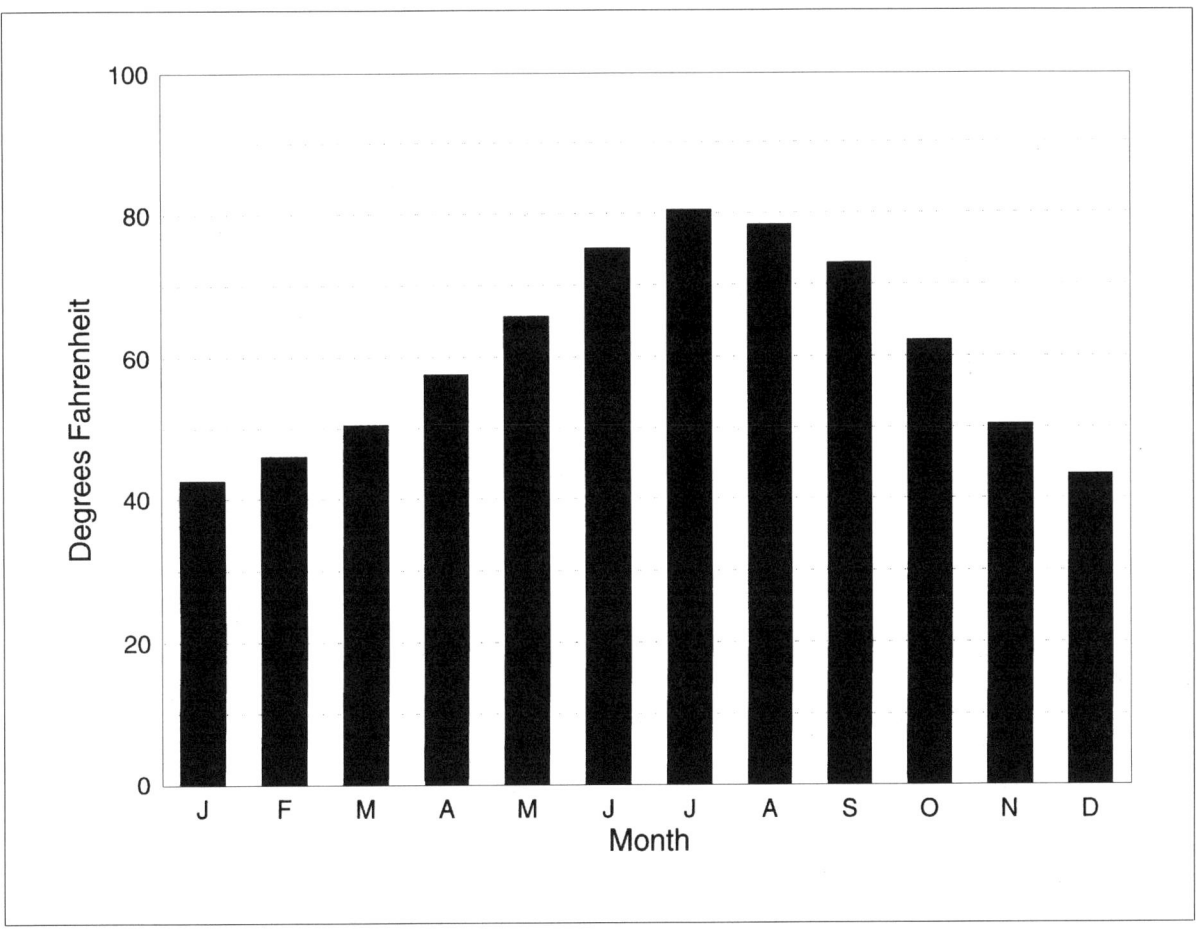

Figure 2.3.   Mean monthly temperature (°F) for east-central Arizona, Climatic Division 4, 1895-1987.

Summary

The floodplains, terraces, slopes, and mountains of Tonto Basin offer diverse combinations of plant, animal, and geological resources in a relatively small area. Possessing a long growing season and permanent water, the Basin appears at first glance to offer all that any human population needs to sustain itself. A closer inspection, however, reveals that the Basin and its economic resources are not entirely dependable. The variability inherent in the timing, duration, and magnitude of precipitation events, the high evapotranspiration rate, the interseasonal and interannual differences in streamflow and water quality, the limited areas available for irrigated and floodwater fields, and the susceptibility of biotic communities to human impact independently, or collectively, present substantial challenges to survival for those whose technological capabilities and residential mobility are limited. In short, Tonto Basin offers many economic opportunities, but its endowment is neither constant nor entirely predictable.

Environmental Variability and Economic Vulnerability in Tonto Basin: A Reconstruction for the Prehistoric Period

As the twentieth century draws to a close, we are able to document much about the prehistoric environment of Tonto Basin, both prior to and during the Salado period.

Theoretical models (Dean 1988a, 1996b; Dean et al. 1994; Halstead and O'Shea 1989; Kohler and Van West 1996; Minc and Smith 1989; Minnis 1996; Plog et al. 1988); reconstructions of climate, soil moisture, and streamflow (Dean 1988b; Graybill 1989; Rose 1994; Van West 1996; Van West and Altschul 1994; M. R. Waters 1996); geological studies of floods, water table variation, river terrace development, and soil fertility (Ely et al. 1988; Homburg 1994; Partridge and Baker 1987; M. R. Waters 1996); and special analyses of botanical and faunal materials from excavated sites (Adams 1994a, 1994b; Bohrer 1962; Bozarth 1994; Cairns 1994; J. L. Cameron 1994, 1995a, 1996a, 1996b, 1997a, 1997b 1997c; Dering 1994, 1995a, 1996a, 1996b, 1997a, 1997b, 1997c; Donaldson 1996; Elson, Fish, James, and Miksicek 1995; Elson, Gregory, and Stark 1995; Fish 1994, 1995a, 1995b, 1996a, 1996b, 1997a, 1997b, 1997c; James 1995; Miksicek 1995; Spielmann 1994, 1996, 1997; J. A. Waters 1996) allow us to infer considerable detail about past conditions. These investigations, in conjunction with studies of nonindustrial agroecology, archaeological studies of settlement patterns and economic adaptations in the Transition Zone, and ethnographic and historic analyses of land use in east-central Arizona, enable us to make a number of inferences about prehistoric ecology in Tonto Basin (Ciolek-Torrello and Welch 1994; Welch 1994b; Welch and Ciolek-Torrello 1994).

Our approach to this topic has been influenced considerably by the "Anasazi adaptive systems model" developed by Dean (1988a:25–88) for explaining aspects of cultural change in the northern Southwest. Although it was applied first to research in the Anasazi cultural area, its conceptual scheme and method of investigation are relevant to Tonto Basin. The model identifies three general classes of variables—environment, demography, and behavior—and specifies that it is the interaction of these classes, as they are related to each other through the concept of carrying capacity, that defines an adaptive system at any given time. Each of the three domains is characterized by considerable temporal and spatial variability, and it is the interplay of these variable factors that results in cultural stability or cultural change. Of the three factors, Dean suggests that environment and demography act most often as independent variables in analyses of cultural change. However, each is capable of being either a dependent or independent variable, given certain circumstances.

As a result of these studies, we are now able to address the following questions. What biotic resources were of human economic importance, and of these, which taxa were particularly emphasized? How did humans alter their surroundings? Why were certain subsistence and settlement strategies favored or disfavored during particular periods in the past? Which inherently variable environmental conditions would have been most stressful and when? What combination of environmental, demographic, and behavioral conditions would have promoted the collapse of the Saladoan system in the fifteenth century?

In our investigation of these issues, we have found that climatic variation and its effects on environmental resources did not determine human behavior in Tonto Basin. Rather, they placed constraints upon the choices that could be made at any particular time. Subsequent choices were then further limited by these past choices. The palimpsest of social, environmental, and historic constraints over time resulted in a complicated subsistence, settlement, and social organizational framework that could not be unraveled or devolved into its earlier and more flexible structure.

Tables 2.1 and 2.2 list the plant and animal taxa from excavated sites in Lower Tonto Basin. Figures 2.4a-c and 2.5 depict the presence (biotic "ubiquity") of select taxa in the samples examined from the 27-site sample[1] used in this paper to track diachronic trends, comparing their representation in the Preclassic pre-Salado period with that in the Salado period Roosevelt and Gila phases. Figure 2.6a-d depicts annual streamflow variability along the three most important streams of east-central Arizona—the Salt, the Verde, and Tonto Creek—for the eight centuries prior to the demise of the Salado phenomenon when we have sufficient tree-ring data to build a chronology (see Van West 1996 for data, methods, and assumptions; also see Graybill 1989). Table 2.3 describes each period statistically and correlates it with the agricultural strategy (either irrigation agriculture, runoff farming, or both) that would have been favored from the perspective of reconstructed climate.

Summary

The environment of Tonto Basin during its occupation by prehistoric agriculturalists was quite similar to that of the present. Landforms, climate, biotic communities, and streamflow characteristics were fundamentally the same. Apart from the presence of the Roosevelt Dam and its artificial reservoir, what has changed is the vertical location of the river, the erosion of formerly arable surfaces on the margins of the floodplain and the adjacent river terraces, and, in some locations, the distribution and density of plants and animals from historic disturbance and overgrazing.

Table 2.1. Occurrence of Economic Plants from Prehistoric Sites in Tonto Basin Excavated by the Roosevelt Rural Sites Study, Roosevelt Community Development Study, Roosevelt Platform Mound Study, and Tonto National Monument.

Taxon and Parts Recovered	Common Name	Preclassic		Classic	
		Macro	Pollen	Macro	Pollen
Domesticated Plants					
Agave heart, fiber, epidermis, leaf, stalk, thorn	Agave	X		X	X
Amaranthus hypochrondriacus or leucocarpus seed	Grain Amaranth	X		X	
Canavalia ensiforma, C. maritima, C. mexicana, C. fendleri seed	Jack Bean	X		X	
Cucurbita moschata, C. pepo, C. mixta Monocot tissue, seeds, rind, fiber bundles	Cushaw, Pumpkin, Squash	X	X	X	X
Gossypium hirsutum var. punctata seed	Cotton	X		X	
Lagenaria siceraria seed, rind	Bottle Gourd			X	
Phaseolus vulgaris, P. acutifolius, P. lunatus seed	Common Bean, Tepary, and Lima	X		X	
Zea mays kernel, cob, cupule, stalk, shank, husk, tassel frag, leaf	Corn	X	X	X	X
Wild Plants					
Acacia greggii seeds, miscellaneous plant parts	Catclaw Acacia	X	X	X	X
Amaranthus seeds	Pigweed			X	
Arctostaphylos seed	Manzanita			X	
Argemone seed	Prickly Poppy			X	
Artemisia leaf, stem, flowers	Sagebrush			X	
Avena fatua seeds, spikelets, awns	Wild Oats			X	
Boerhaavia seed	Spiderling	X	X	X	X
Boraginaceae seed	Borage			X	
Celtis seed	Hackberry, Desert Hackberry			X	
Cercidium microphyllum, C. floridum seed	Yellow Paloverde, Blue Paloverde		X	X	X
Cereus-type seed	Saguaro, Hedgehog, and related cacti	X	X	X	X

(table continues)

Table 2.1. *(Continued)*

Taxon and Parts Recovered	Common Name	Preclassic Macro	Preclassic Pollen	Classic Macro	Classic Pollen
Cheno-am seed	Chenopodium and Amaranth	X	X	X	X
Chenopodium seed	Goosefoot			X	
Cirsium seed	Thistle			X	
Cleome serrulata seed	Beeweed			X	
Compositae, low spine type	Bursage		X		X
Compositae, high spine type	Sunflower Family		X		X
Cruciferae	Mustard Family		X		X
Cucurbita foetidissima rind	Buffalo Gourd or Coyote Melon				X
Cylindropuntia seed, buds	Cholla	X	X	X	X
Cyperaceae	Sedge				X
Dasylirion wheeleri leaf fiber	Sotol				X
Descurainia seed	Tansy Mustard		X		X
Echinocereus seed, spine	Hedgehog Cactus			X	
Ephedra	Morman Tea		X		X
Eriogonum seed	Wild Buckwheat		X		X
Erodium seed	Filaree or Heron Bill		X		X
Euphorbia seed	Spurge		X	X	X
Ferrocactus seeds	Barrel Cactus			X	
Garrya wrightii twig	Silk Tassel			X	
Gramineae grains, stems	Grass Family	X	X	X	X
Helianthus/Viguiera achene, seed	Sunflower/ Goldeneye	X		X	
Hoffmanseggia	Hog Potato		X		X
Hordeum pusillum seed, rachis	Little Barley	X		X	
Juglans major seed (nut)	Walnut			X	
Juniperus seed	Juniper			X	X

(table continues)

Table 2.1. *(Continued)*

Taxon and Parts Recovered	Common Name	Preclassic Macro	Preclassic Pollen	Classic Macro	Classic Pollen
Kallstroemia	Arizona Poppy		X		X
Larrea tridentata stem, flower	Creosote Bush			X	
Leguminosae seed, cotyledon fragment	Pea Family	X	X		X
Leptochloa seed	Sprangletop			X	
Liguliflorae	Dandelion type, Sunflower Family			X	X
Liliaceae	Lily Family				X
Malvaceae	Mallow Family	X		X	
Mammillaria spine	Fishhook Cactus			X	
Sphaeralcea -type seed	Globe Mallow	X	X	X	X
Sporobolus seed	Sacaton Grass			X	
Nicotiana seed	Tobacco			X	
Nolina macrocarpa	Beargrass			X	
Olneya tesota seed	Ironwood			X	
Onagraceae	Evening Pprimrose Family		X		X
Opuntia englemanii, O. vivipara, O. versicolor seed, miscellaneous plant parts	Prickly Pear, Cholla, Pencil Cholla	X	X	X	
Oryzopsis hymenoides grain	Indian Rice Grass	X			
Panicum seed	Panic Grass			X	
Phragmites communis stems	Reedgrass			X	
Physalis seed	Groundcherry, Tomatillo			X	
Pinus edulis seed (nut)	Pinyon			X	X
Plantago seed	Indian Wheat			X	X
Platyopuntia	Prickly Pear		X	X	X
Polanisia seed	Clammy Weed			X	
Portulaca seed	Purslane	X		X	
Proboscidea seed, devilclaw	Devil's Claw			X	

(table continues)

Table 2.1. *(Continued)*

Taxon and Parts Recovered	Common Name	Preclassic		Classic	
		Macro	Pollen	Macro	Pollen
Prosopis juliflora, P. pubescens seed, pod, miscellaneous plant parts	Mesquite	X	X	X	X
Quercus seed (acorn)	Oak			X	X
Rhus seed	Sumac			X	
Rumex seed	Canaigre			X	
Salix	Willow				X
Salvia seed	Chia	X			
Scirpus seed	Bulrush, Sedge			X	
Simmondsia chinensis seed, husk	Jojoba		X	X	X
Solanaceae	Potato Family				X
Sporobolus seed	Dropseed			X	
Tidestromia	Tidestromia		X		X
Trianthema seed	Carpetweed, False Purslane	X		X	
Typha	Cattail		X		X
Umbelliferae	Parsley Family		X		X
Vitis arizonica fruit	Wild Grape			X	
Yucca miscellaneous plant parts, seeds	Yucca	X		X	X

Note: When no plant part is listed under a given taxon, it signifies that only pollen was recovered.

Table 2.2. Occurrence of Archaeofauna from Prehistoric Sites in Tonto Basin Excavated by the Roosevelt Rural Sites Study, Roosevelt Community Development Study, Roosevelt Platform Mound Study, and Tonto National Monument.

Taxon	Common Name	Preclassic	Classic
Class Mammalia			
Order Lagomorpha			
Lepus californicus	Black-tailed Jackrabbit	X	X
Sylvilagus auduboni	Desert Cottontail	X	X
Sylvilagus	Cottontails	X	X
Order Rodentia			
Ammospermophilus harrisi	Harris' Antelope Squirrel		X
Castor canadensis	Beaver		X
Dipodomys merriami	Merriam's Kanagroo Rat		X
Neotoma albigula	White-throated Woodrat	X	
Neotoma	Woodrats	X	X
Ondatra zibethicus	Muskrat	X	X
Perognathus	Pocket Mice		X
Peromyscus	White-footed Mice		X
Sciurus	Squirrels		X
Sigmodon hispidus	Hispid Cotton Rat		X
Spermophilus tereticaudus	Round-tailed Ground Squirrel		X
Spermophilus tridecemlineatus	Thirteen-lined Ground Squirrel		X
Spermophilus variegatus	Rock Squirrel	X	X
Thomomys bottae	Botta's Pocket Gopher	X	X
Order Carnivora			
Bassariscus astutus	Ringtail		X
Canis familiaris	Domestic Dog		X
Canis latrans	Coyote	X	X
Canis lupus	Gray Wolf		X
Canis	Canines	X	X
Felis rufus	Bobcat		X
Lutra canadensis	River Otter		X
Procyon lotor	Raccoon	X	X
Taxidea taxus	Badger		X
Urocyon cinereoargenteus	Gray Fox	X	X
Order Artiodactyla			
Bison bison	Bison	X	
Bos taurus	Domestic Cow		X
Odocoileus hemionus	Mule Deer	X	X
Odocoileus virginianus	White-tailed Deer		X
Odocoileus	Deer	X	X
Ovis canadensis	Bighorn Sheep		X
Class Osteichthyes			
Family Catostomidae	Sucker Family	X	X
Catostomus insignis	Gila Coarse-scaled Sucker	X	
Catostomus clarki	Desert-Mountain Sucker	X	X
Catostomus latipinnis	Flannelmouth Sucker		X
Xyrauchen texanus	Razorback Sucker	X	X
Family Centrarchidae	Sunfishes, Black Basses, Crappies		X
Family Cyprinidae	Minnow Family		X

(table continues)

Table 2.2. *(Continued)*

Taxon	Common Name	Preclassic	Classic
Gila elegans	Bony Chub		X
Gila robusta	Roundtail Chub	X	
Gila	Chubs		X
Ptychocheilus lucius	Colorado Squawfish		X
Class Amphibia			
Bufo alvarius	Colorado River Toad	X	
Bufo cognatus	Great Plains Toad	X	
Bufo	Toads		X
Rana	Frogs		X
Class Reptilia			
Order Testudinata	Turtles	X	X
Kinosternon sonoriense	Sonoran Mud Turtle	X	X
Gopherus agassizi	Desert Tortoise	X	X
Order Squamata	Lizards and Snakes	X	X
Crotapytus collaris	Collared Lizard		X
Dipsosaurus dorsalis	Desert Iguana		X
Phrynosoma solare	Regal Horned Lizard		X
Pitousphis melanoleucus	Gopher Snake		X
Crotalus	Rattlesnakes		X
Class Aves			
Accipiter cooperii	Cooper's Hawk		X
Anas platyrhynchos	Mallard Duck		X
Aphelocoma coerulescens	Scrub jay		X
Aquila chrysaetos	Golden Eagle		X
Anas	Ducks	X	X
Ara	Macaws		X
Ardea herodias	Great Blue Heron		X
Branta canadensis	Canada Goose		X
Bubo virginianus	Great Horned Owl		X
Buteo jamaicensis	Red-tailed Hawk		X
Callipepla squamata	Scaled Quail		X
Callipepla gambelii	Gambel's Quail		X
Callipepla	Quails	X	X
Chordeiles minor	Nighthawk	X	
Circus cyaneus	Marsh Hawk		X
Colaptes auratus	Red-shafted Flicker		X
Corvus brachyrhynchos	Common Crow		X
Corvus corax	Common Raven		X
Falco sparverius	Sparrow Hawk		X
Falco	Hawks		X
Geococcyx californianus	Roadrunner		X
Haliaeetus leucocephalus	Bald Eagle		X
Meleagris gallopavo	Wild Turkey	X	
Micrathene whitneyi	Elf Owl		X
Family Picidae	Woodpeckers		X
Podilymbus podiceps	Pied-billed Grebe	X	
Toxostoma	Thrashers		X
Zenaida asiatica	White-winged Dove	X	
Zenaidura macroura	Mourning Dove		X

Figure 2.4a. Ubiquity of selected plant taxa from macrobotanical.

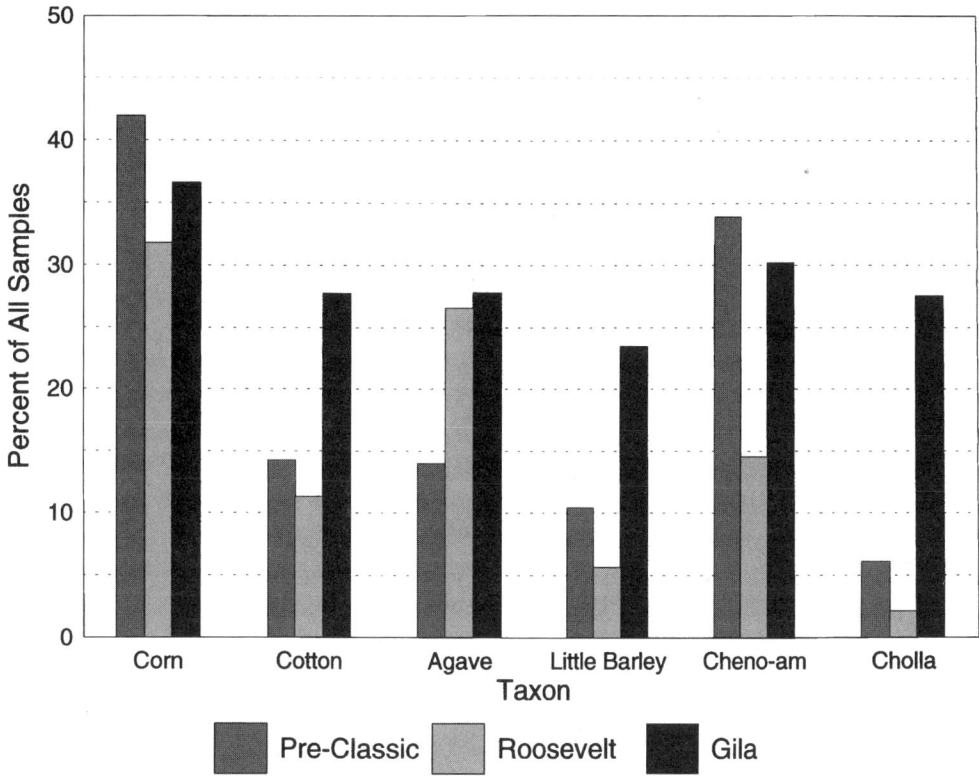

Figure 2.4b. Ubiquity of selected plant taxa from pollen samples.

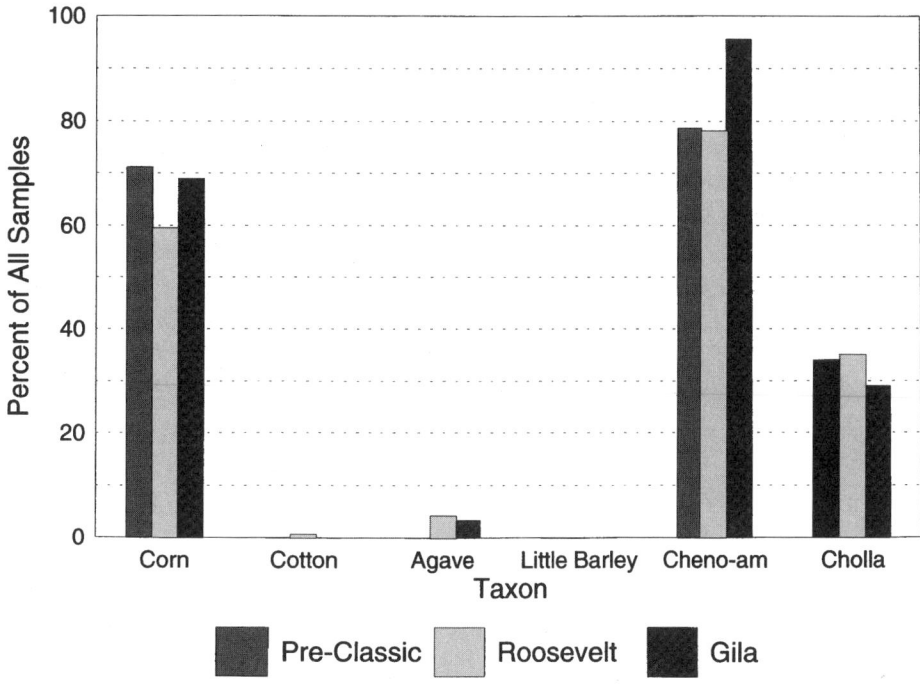

(figure continues on overleaf)

Figure 2.4c.
Ubiquity of
selected animal
taxa.

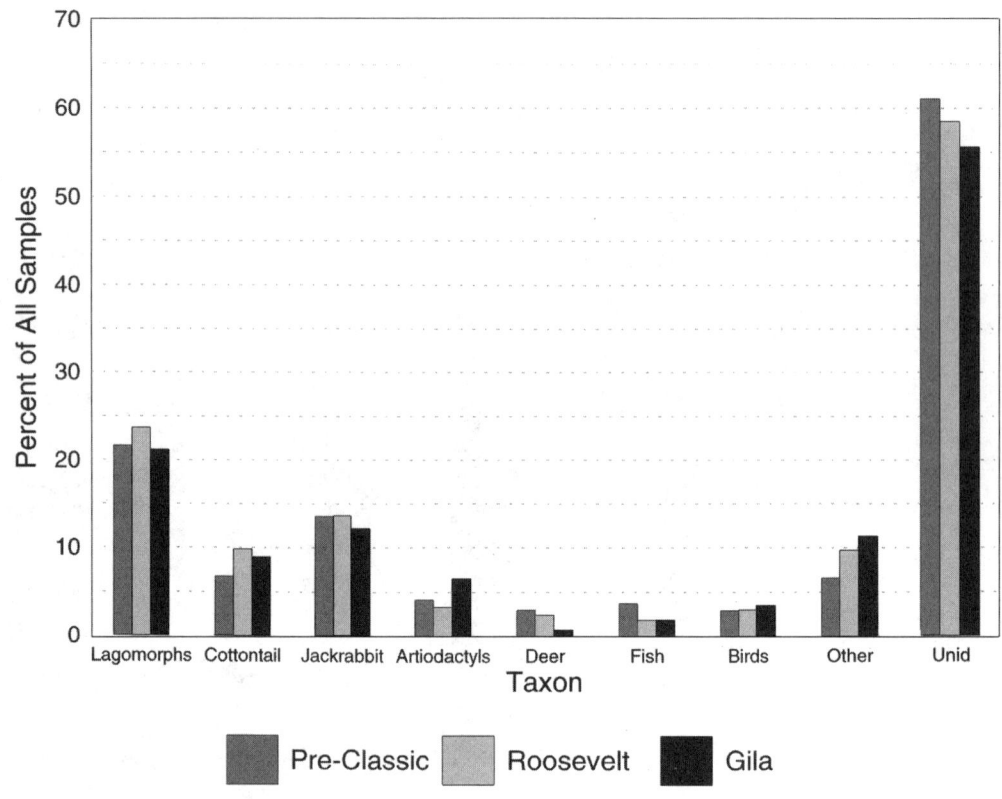

SETTING THE STAGE:
PRE-SALADOAN SUBSISTENCE,
SETTLEMENT, AND ANTHROPOGENICALLY
ALTERED LANDSCAPES

Recent investigations reveal that the first agricultural settlements in Tonto Basin date to the Early Ceramic period (100–600; Elson 1996b). Subsistence remains from the Early Ceramic component of the Eagle Ridge site (V:5:104, Locus B) are associated with bean-shaped pithouses and a larger, circular communal structure dated between 200 and 400 and with basin-shaped pit structures dated between 350 and 550 (Elson 1996b; Elson and Lindeman 1994). These data suggest that subsistence was based on a variety of cultivated and wild plants and in-

digenous animal species mainly from lowland and riverine environments (Fish 1995b; James 1995; Miksicek 1995). The ubiquity value for corn and the presence of at least two other cultigens, cotton and beans, suggest that occupation at the Eagle Ridge site extended from at least spring through autumn and that much of the diet was derived from cultivated products at this early time. Radiocarbon dates on cotton seeds from a hearth in a bean-shaped structure fall within a one standard deviation calibrated range of 240–390 and a two standard deviation range of 130–430, making this the earliest securely dated cotton in the Southwest (Elson and Lindeman 1994:112; Elson, Gregory, and Stark 1995:4–9).

It is important to note that cotton was an ideal crop for Tonto Basin farmers, and agricultural groups may have

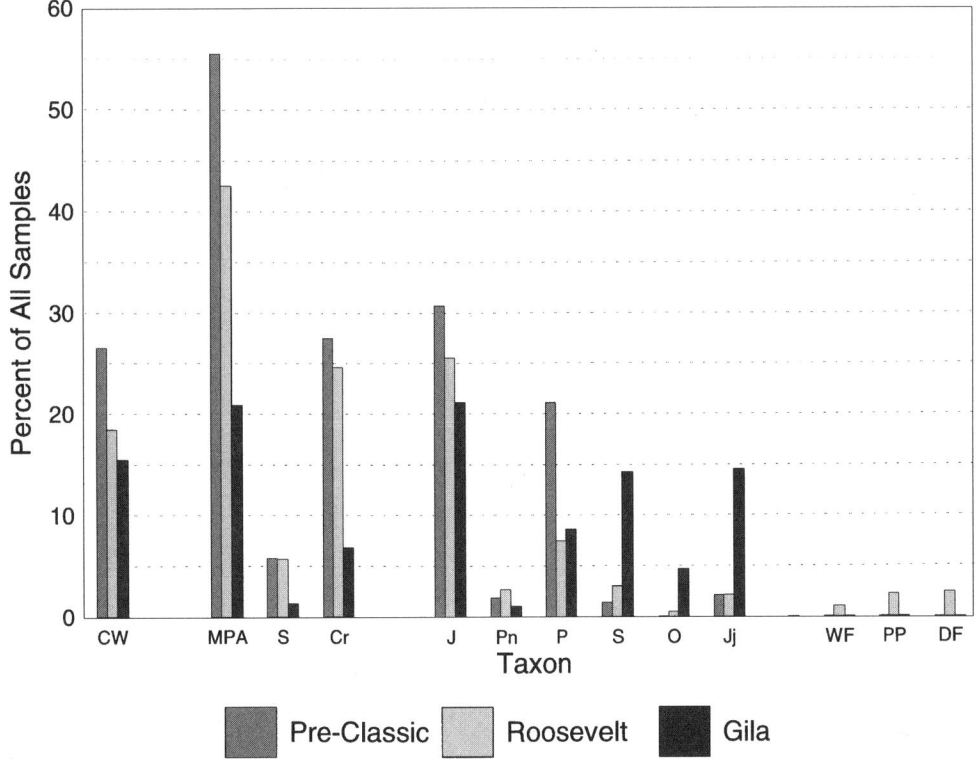

Figure 2.5. Ubiquity of selected wood taxa, fuelwood, and construction wood (CW=cottonwood-willow, MPA=mesquite-paloverde-acacia, S=sahuaro, C=creosote, J=juniper, Pn=pinyon, P=pine, O=oak, Jj=jojoba, WF=white fir, PP=ponderosa pine, DF=Douglas-fir).

sought out the Basin and other similar settings expressly for the purpose of growing this highly valued plant, perhaps even at the expense of growing food crops. Requiring consistent warmth and a significant amount of water throughout its long growing period (ca. 200 days), cotton could tolerate the saline waters of the Salt River, that could be predictably carried to fields through irrigation ditches and canals. That cotton seeds were recovered from a securely dated Early Formative period structure is significant in that their presence seems to foreshadow important developments surrounding the cultivation of cotton in Classic period times.

In short, the subsistence evidence from Eagle Ridge suggests that the pattern of small residentially stable, agricultural settlements that characterized most of the Formative

period in Tonto Basin was established at this early date. As such, this adaptation is unusual. In surrounding regions at the same time, localities were characterized by a pattern of seasonal habitation and part-time farming (Ciolek-Torrello 1994, 1995; Deaver and Ciolek-Torrello 1995).

Although the number of agricultural settlements appears to have increased during the following Snaketown phase of the Pioneer period (675/700 to 750) and the Colonial period (750 to 950), populations were small and widely scattered. Subsistence practices remained largely unchanged from the preceding period and apparently involved a broad spectrum of wild and domestic plants with an emphasis on small-scale farming in the riverine zones of the Basin. Farming appears to have been restricted to the margins of the Salt River and Tonto Creek floodplains and the floodplains and stream-side terraces of tributaries, locations more easily managed by the small resident populations. Utilization of the uplands was extremely limited at this time.

Squash first appears in the record during the Colonial period, although no evidence of beans was found. An increase in agave, especially agave hearts, suggests the greater reliance on this useful plant (Elson, Gregory, and Stark 1995:4–12; Elson 1996b:127). High ubiquity values for wild plants and faunal resources, including aquatic species, reveal the importance of hunting, gathering, trapping, and fishing in Colonial period times (Fish 1995b; James 1995; Miksicek 1995; Vokes 1995). Important wild plant species include cholla, prickly pear, saguaro, tansy mustard, amaranth, chenopodium, and little barley. The increase in lagomorphs, especially jackrabbits, suggests that additional land with mature trees was being cleared for agricultural fields, an inference supported by high percentages of riparian charcoal samples (Elson, Fish, James, and Miksicek 1995).

Beginning with the Colonial period, we have confidence that the data presented in Figure 2.6a-d and Table 2.3 are reasonably good indicators of local climate and streamflow. Perhaps the most important variability in the Colonial period is that of the regional water table. From about 750 to 925, regional water tables dip to their 550-year minimum (Dean 1988b:156, Figure 5.7). As water tables lowered, opportunities for agriculture and native plant collection in the uplands would have become more limited, possibly confined to only the wettest periods when precipitation temporarily offset low ground water levels and minimal surface flows. Save for two short but epic-level wet intervals—one at the beginning (803–806) and one at end of the ninth century (897–899)—the Colonial period was moderate to moderately dry. The small and scattered populations of Tonto Basin would have succeeded more years than not by cultivating the floodplains and low terraces of the Salt River and Tonto Creek.

Numerous farmsteads and small hamlets are dated to the following Sedentary period (950 to 1150), but only a small number produced enough subsistence remains to afford a detailed reconstruction of food resources (Adams 1994a, 1994b; Bozarth 1994; Elson, Fish, James, and Miksicek 1995; Fish 1995b; James 1995; Miksicek 1995; Vokes 1995). These data indicate that populations of Tonto Basin were fully committed to the intensive cultivation of corn and cotton. They also raised a variety of

squashes, jack beans, and common beans and possibly grew grain amaranth and little barley. Increased agave use may indicate that the deliberate cultivation of these plants for food, fiber, and possibly drink had begun in the late Preclassic period. Wild plant food remained important; cheno-ams, sunflower family plants, prickly pear fruit and pads, cholla buds, saguaro fruit, wild legumes, cattail, grasses, and certain weedy plants were emphasized. Lagomorphs—both cottontail and jackrabbits—were choice game, as were deer, fish, and selected species of rodents, birds, and reptiles[2].

The Sedentary period represents a time of expanding settlement and diversification of agricultural strategies into the lower and middle sections of the uplands (Ciolek-Torrello, Whittlesey, and Welch 1994:444; Wood and McAllister 1984:282). Many of these settlements appear to have been farmsteads or small hamlets occupied on a recurrent seasonal basis or for relatively short periods (Doyel 1978; Elson 1992a; Rice 1985). In contrast, Sedentary period settlements in riverine locations, particularly on the Salt arm, appear to represent more permanent, year-round settlements (Ciolek-Torrello and Whittlesey 1994; Ciolek-Torrello, Whittlesey, and Welch 1994; Elson, Gregory, and Stark 1995).

Climatic conditions during much of this period were variable but moderate, although tending toward dry (especially 951–1032). The beginning of this period corresponds with an extended period of very high water tables that continued throughout the early Classic period (Dean 1988b:156, Figure 5.7). These environmental conditions would have favored a mixed strategy of farming both riverine and nonriverine settings with a combination of high water table, irrigation, and floodwater methods. In selected upland locations, water-harvesting and possibly true dry farming techniques were used. It is probably not coincidental that an expansion of upland exploitation and habitation began precisely at the time when high water tables would have made surface water in the uplands most abundant. By the middle 1000s, conditions became moderately moist and more consistent from year to year. After 1087 and until 1151, local conditions returned to a more variable regime with low year-to-year persistence, when conditions were moderate or moderately dry, again favoring use and settlement of floodplain and near-floodplain settings. In general, the Sedentary period was more moderate and less variable than the Colonial period. Use of nonriverine settings in the uplands would have proved a successful

Figure 2.6a.
Reconstructed
streamflow:
750–950.

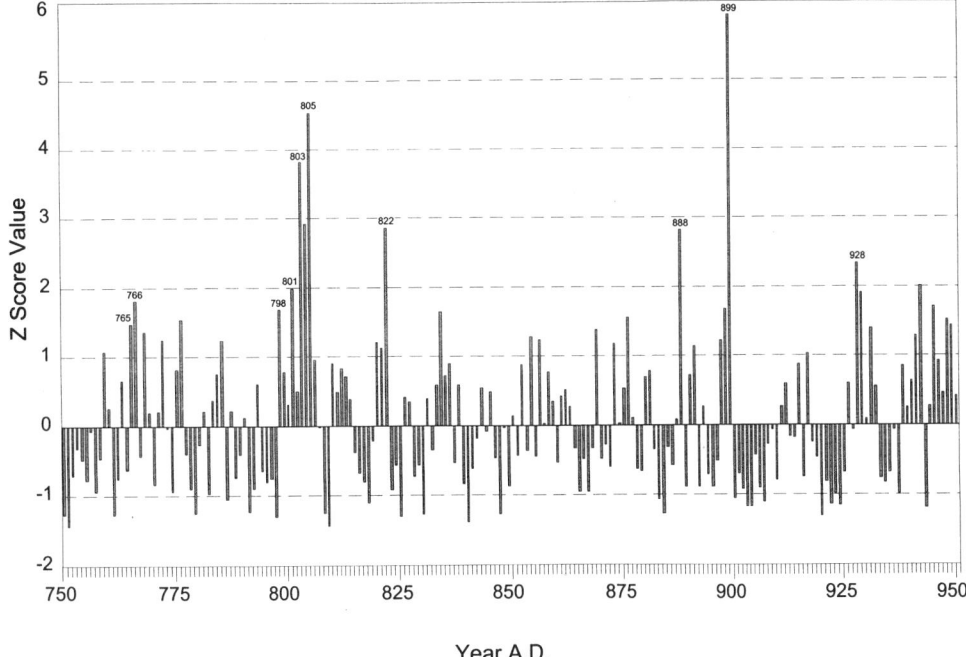

Figure 2.6b.
Reconstructed
streamflow:
950–1150.

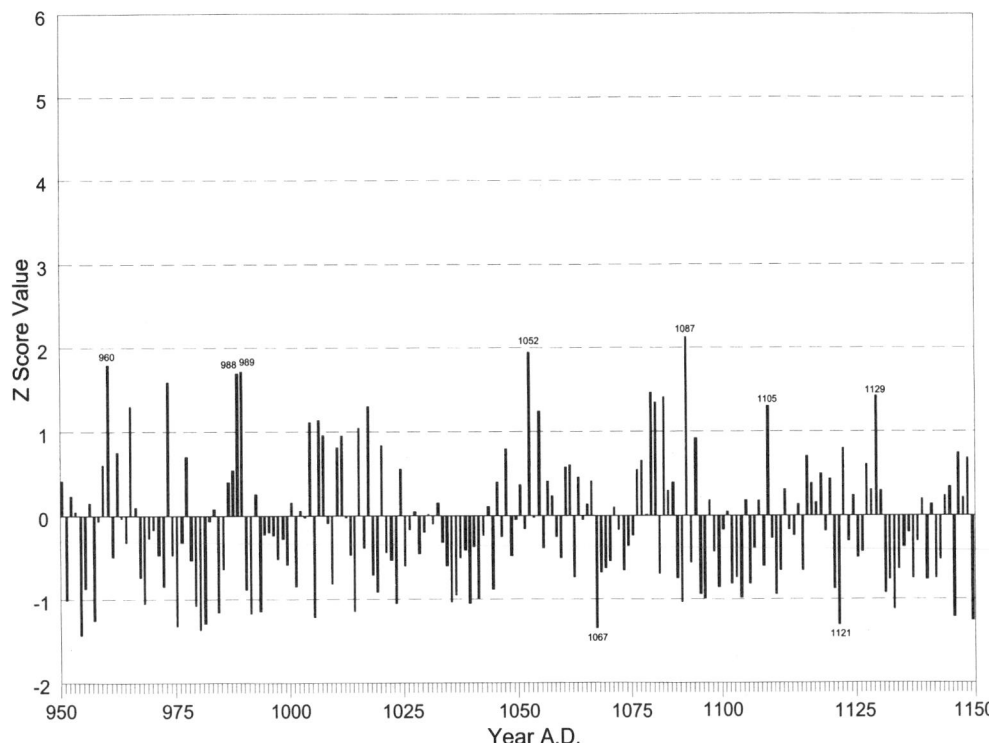

(figure continues on overleaf)

Figure 2.6c.
Reconstructed
streamflow:
1150–1350.

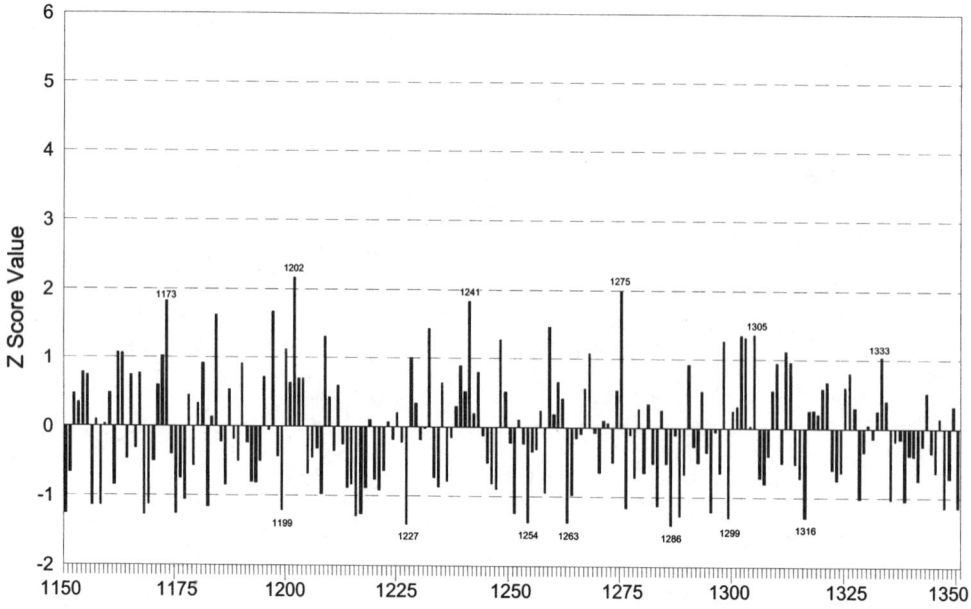

Figure 2.6d.
Reconstructed
streamflow:
1350–1550.

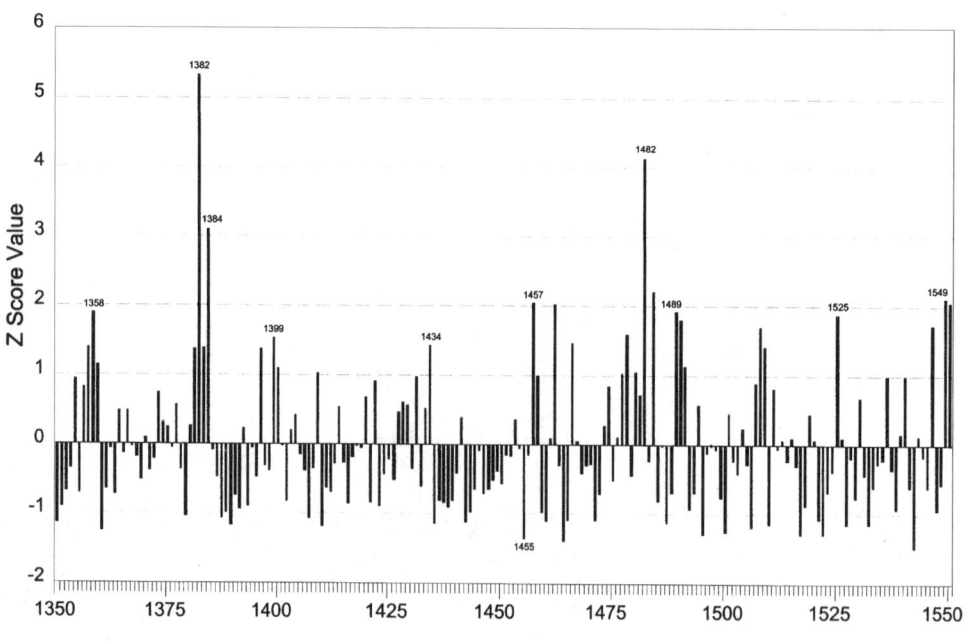

Table 2.3. Dendrohydrologic Streamflow Reconstruction and Favored Agricultural Strategies in Tonto Basin, A.D. 750-1500.

Start Date	End Date	Number of Years	Period Mean	Period Stand. Dev.	Period C.V.	C.V. Rank	Period Z Score	Yrs. > 1 Stand. Dev.	Yrs. < 1 Stand. Dev.	% of Period Extreme	Climatic Assessment	Favored Agricultural Strategy	Water Table	Regional Variability Spatial Variability	Temporal Variability
737	797	61	995,268	533,141	53.6	30	-0.21	8	10	30	variable, mod-dry	mixed, floodplain	H/M	L	H
798	807	10	2,233,383	986,646	44.2	16	1.73	5	0	50	consistent, wet	dry farm	M	L	H
808	896	89	1,128,661	556,640	49.3	23	-0.00	11	9	22	variable, moderate	mixed	M/L	L	H
897	899	3	2,994,920	1,653,022	55.2	31	2.93	3	0	100	consistent, wet	dry farm	L	L	H
900	925	26	804,313	404,993	50.4	26	-0.51	1	7	31	consistent, dry	flooplain	L	L	H
926	950	25	1,485,590	620,487	41.8	12	0.56	8	1	36	consistent, wet	dry farm	M	L	H
951	1003	53	999,109	518,886	51.9	28	-0.21	5	11	30	variable, mod-dry	mixed, floodplain	M/H	L	H
1004	1032	29	1,122,716	478,561	42.6	14	-0.01	4	3	24	variable, moderate	mixed	H	L	L
1033	1044	12	750,870	238,087	31.7	3	-0.60	0	2	17	consistent, dry	floodplain	H	H	L
1045	1087	43	1,217,932	489,042	40.2	10	0.14	6	2	19	consistent, mod-wet	mixed, dry farm	H	H	L
1088	1151	64	998,564	402,417	40.3	11	-0.21	2	4	9	variable, mod-dry	mixed, floodplain	H	H	L
1152	1182	31	1,125,046	545,771	48.5	21	-0.01	4	7	35	variable, moderate	mixed	H/M	L	L
1183	1204	22	1,278,963	570,754	44.6	18	0.23	4	1	23	variable, mod-wet	mixed, dry farm	M/H	L	L
1205	1227	23	871,884	411,803	47.2	20	-0.41	1	3	17	consistent, dry	floodplain	H	L	L
1228	1249	22	1,265,481	497,226	39.3	6	0.21	3	0	14	consistent, mod-wet	dry farm	H	L	L
1250	1275	26	1,105,898	512,172	46.3	19	-0.04	3	3	23	variable, moderate	mixed	H	L	L
1276	1299	24	900,135	446,622	49.6	24	-0.36	1	6	29	consistent, dry	floodplain	H	L	L
1300	1334	35	1,223,171	453,491	37.1	5	0.15	5	1	17	variable, mod-wet	mixed, dry farm	H/M	L	L
1335	1355	21	867,818	346,917	40.0	8	-0.19	0	4	19	consistent, dry	floodplain	M	L	L
1356	1359	4	1,950,865	288,356	14.8	1	1.29	3	0	75	consistent, wet	dry farm	M	H	H
1360	1379	20	1,046,241	329,002	31.4	2	-0.13	0	2	10	consistent, moderate	mixed	M	H	H
1380	1384	5	2,573,532	1,258,223	48.9	22	2.27	3	0	60	consistent, wet	dry farm	L	H	H
1385	1395	11	750,876	295,835	39.4	7	-0.60	0	2	18	consistent, dry	floodplain	L	H	H
1396	1434	39	1,143,833	458,374	40.1	9	0.02	5	2	18	variable, moderate	mixed	L	H	H
1435	1456	22	798,964	292,442	36.6	4	-0.52	0	3	14	consistent, dry	floodplain	L	H	H
1457	1472	16	1,091,306	701,075	64.2	33	-0.06	3	4	44	variable, moderate	mixed	L	H	H
1473	1491	19	1,557,875	816,402	52.4	29	0.67	8	1	47	consistent, wet	dry farm	L	H	H
1492	1506	15	882,768	378,259	42.8	15	-0.39	0	3	20	consistent, dry	floodplain	M	H	H

Notes: These data are derived from Van West (1996: Table 2.1). Mean and standard deviation for full-period series (A.D. 572–1985) is 1,130,731 ± 636,052 acre feet per year. C.V. is the Coefficient of Variation, the ratio of the standard deviation to the mean multiplied by 100. It is a measure of variability. The lower this value, the less variable a given range of values. C.V. Rank is the rank order of the Coefficients of Variation. The period identified as Rank 1 is the least variable of the 28 periods; the period identified as Rank 33 is the most variable. Pd. Z Score is the Z Score equivalent of the period mean. Yrs.> or < 1 S.D. is the number of years in the period when the annual value exceeds or falls below 1 standard deviation. % Extreme is the proportion of the period when climatic conditions are beyond what was considered normal variation. Assessment is the verbal interpretation of the data presented in the columns to the left. Favored Strategy is inferred agricultural strategy (or strategies) that is predicted to have realized successful harvests most of the time during the period. Regional Variability is proxied by the level of the regional water table and the spatial and temporal variability in dendroclimate (Dean 1988b: Figure 5.7).

agricultural strategy in most years of this particularly salubrious period. Archaeological evidence of more frequent use of nonriverine settings, then, is not surprising.

The Miami phase (1150 to 1250), which represents the first century of the Classic period, is perhaps the most poorly understood of all the Formative-level archaeological periods in Tonto Basin. Evidence for this Early Classic occupation takes the form of post-reinforced and upright cobble architecture, roasting pits, pit structures, and ceramics that date to the late twelfth and early thirteenth centuries. Unfortunately, these early deposits are obscured by later cultural deposits, and few conclusions have been reached about Miami phase remains (Elson 1996b:134–37).

The evidence for subsistence pursuits in the Miami phase is slim, but the following is suggested. A mixed subsistence strategy that included hunting, gathering, and small-scale agriculture was still in effect. The pattern along the Salt River stands in marked contrast with data from contemporary sites in the uplands of Upper Tonto Basin where ubiquity measures of corn are high in small permanently inhabited settlements and evidence for hunting is minimal, suggesting that these settlements were focused on small-scale farming (Ciolek-Torrello 1987; Halbirt and Gasser 1987; Wright 1991). Special use sites devoted to wild plant gathering also appear to have been present (Halbirt and Gasser 1987). Ciolek-Torrello, Whittlesey, and Welch (1994:447–50) suggest that the Miami phase represents a time of increased population dispersal without a significant increase in population size. Early Classic populations exploited both riverine and upland settings, continued small-scale agricultural efforts, and opportunistically deployed a diverse set of agricultural strategies. In the riverine areas, agricultural techniques were likely limited to high water table and nonintensive irrigation; in the uplands, a variety of floodwater, run-off control, and dry farming techniques was used.

From the perspective of climate, the 100 years of the Miami phase were moderate to moderately wet. Conditions were quite variable from 1152–1204, but greater year-to-year persistence occurred between 1205 and 1249. A higher percentage of years with extreme conditions (drought or floods) distinguishes this period from the preceding Sedentary period. Water tables remained high throughout most of the Miami phase (Dean 1988b:156, Figure 5.7). Consistently high water tables and moderate climatic conditions probably meant that upland springs and seeps were abundant and generally productive. In addition, it is likely that the smaller upland drainages contained surface water as well, at least during the spring runoff and summer monsoon seasons. Thus, nonriverine farming of the uplands would have been favorable in all but the 1205–1227 period, and farming of the primary floodplain would have been successful in most years between 1152–1227.

These environmental conditions seem to fit the settlement patterns observed for this Early Classic period. It was during this time that permanent or long-term seasonal habitation occurred in the middle and upper portions of the bajada. Agricultural terraces, rock pile fields, check dams, and numerous field houses suggest intensive farming of diverse locales in the uplands. Riverine settlement also expanded, but it remains unclear whether the size or density of settlements increased at this time. The correspondence of these climatic and settlement trends support our assumption that the early Classic settlement-subsistence system was a highly flexible and opportunistic system that employed a diverse set of food production and procurement strategies on a small-scale rather than one that was larger in scale and focused on intensifying one particular strategy.

Summary

Archaeological evidence for sedentary living and the regular cultivation and storage of domestic crops dates to the first half of the first millennium. Corn was always the most important domesticate, but several species of bean and squash, grain amaranth, and little barley were also grown in Tonto Basin during the Preclassic period. Cotton was a fungible commodity by the Sedentary period, if not earlier. Agaves were important food and fiber resources and may have been transported from their native habitat to fields closer to settlements in the lower elevations of the Basin where they could be tended more easily. Fuelwood and construction timber were obtained from sources close to residences and field houses, which meant that most wood came from riparian and low desert settings. At least 40 economically important plant taxa and 30 animal taxa have been recovered from excavated sites dating to 100–1250 period (Tables 2.1 and 2.2).

Biotic resources were used for a wide variety of subsistence purposes, including food, clothing, medicine, tools, utensils, and containers. Charring, age-altered surface condition, skeletal representation, butchering, and deliberate modification of bone, turtle carapaces, artiodactyl antlers, animal hide, and other soft tissue constitute the evidence for the use of animal resources. Recovery of hearth and roasting pit charcoal, structural timbers and roof closing materials, plant parts preserved in storage contexts, middens, and thermal features, pollen aggregates of historically documented economic plants incorporated into structural floors and other culturally meaningful contexts supply evidence for the use of plant resources.

By the beginning of the Salado period, agricultural populations had lived in Tonto Basin for at least 1200 years. They were well acquainted with the bounty of the Transition Zone and had slowly but surely left their mark on the landscape. Areas near their homes, fields, and trails were altered by human occupation; various surfaces had been compacted, loosened, leveled or filled, contoured with rock alignments, covered with rock features and structural features, and denuded of native vegetation. Weedy species[3] thrived in disturbed areas, and formerly dispersed insect and animal populations were attracted to cultivated fields. Once-dense bosques of mesquite were thinned or removed for construction wood, fuel, and fields. Useful wood and plants close to residential districts were diminished considerably from their pristine state (Kohler 1992; Kohler and Matthews 1988). Not all the impacts were negative, however (Kohler 1992). Irrigation practices created additional farmland and increased the edible biomass (both plants and animals) from irrigated land. Such practices have been documented elsewhere to increase soil productivity, improve microclimate in the vicinity of fields, and regulate excess ground water (Erickson 1992; Fish and Fish 1992).

Although detectable, the overall impact of humans on the natural environment was small.[4] No taxa were depleted; only local stands near habitations areas were affected. The total population of Lower Tonto Basin probably never exceeded 1,200 people prior to the Roosevelt phase (Van West and Altschul 1994). Despite extended periods of flood, drought, or low water tables, small-scale agriculturalists in Tonto Basin had survived for more than a millennium. Their limited numbers, relative mobility, and highly opportunistic strategies permitted them to thrive in the remarkably diverse, productive, and predictably variable Tonto Basin environment.

SUBSISTENCE, SETTLEMENT, AND ENVIRONMENTAL INTERACTIONS DURING THE SALADO PERIOD

Roosevelt Phase (1250 to 1350)

The emergence of the Salado phenomenon in Tonto Basin is signaled by the appearance of Roosevelt Red Ware and platform mound architecture at about 1280. Internal population growth, augmented by immigration from the highlands below the Mogollon Rim, the Colorado Plateau, and perhaps northern Mexico, resulted in at least a doubling of the Preclassic population during the Roosevelt phase. It is at this time, especially after 1280, that we see important subsistence and settlement changes in the Basin (Ciolek-Torrello and Whittlesey 1996; Ciolek-Torrello, Whittlesey, and Welch 1994; Elson, Gregory, and Stark 1995).

During the Roosevelt phase, populations expanded upland settlement to the perimeter of Tonto Basin and reached their maximum geographic limit (Ciolek-Torrello, Whittlesey, and Welch 1994:450). At the same time, cliff dwellings in Tonto Basin (Tonto National Monument) and the nearby Sierra Ancha were established (Ciolek-Torrello and Lange 1990:145, Table 6; Steen et al. 1962). Formerly dispersed populations gathered around platform mounds to form the first village-sized habitations in the Basin. And it was here that most Roosevelt populations lived, ultimately making this period the most heavily occupied of any time in the history of the Basin (Ciolek-Torrello, Whittlesey, and Welch 1994:450–51; Doelle 1995a, 1995b). Nevertheless, village populations were low. Estimates range from fewer than 67 people at Bass Mound (Lindauer 1995a:435) to no more than 150 at Meddler (Craig 1995:235). Recent estimates of total (average) population during the Roosevelt phase in Lower Tonto Basin range from a low of about 2400 (Van West and Altschul 1994) to a high of more than 3550 (Doelle 1995b). Earlier estimates projected 5000 people or more (Wood 1989:21).

However large or small, Roosevelt populations made a greater commitment to agricultural production than ever before. We presume that their goal was the steady production of cotton fiber and various agave products. To assure predictable yields of cotton, they expanded the irrigation system and laid claim to the irrigable terraces along the Salt River and Tonto Creek (Craig 1995; M. R. Waters 1996). Irrigation systems were expanded, and communities responsible for their use and maintenance likely formed the "irrigation districts" described by J. S. Wood et al. (1992).

We are not certain when irrigation started in Tonto Basin or when the first canals were constructed. We assume that at least by the Colonial period, ditches and small canals were built to irrigate the stream-side terraces of secondary drainages and perhaps the margin of major floodplains. At least one canal and an associated pithouse east of Meddler Point have been dated to the Preclassic period (M. R. Waters 1996); however, the association of these dates with their contexts is questionable. Most of the known or suspected canals apparently date to the Classic period, and many archaeologists consider them one of the hallmarks of the Salado phenomenon in Tonto Basin (Mills and Mills 1975; Van West and Altschul 1994; M. R. Waters 1996; Wood 1989).

Unlike the domesticated cotton, agave (also known as mescal, maguey, or century plant) is native to the Transition Zone; it occurs naturally at elevations above 2,400 m but can survive as a transplant at lower, drier elevations. Once established, it is relatively drought and cold tolerant and can thrive in impoverished soils (Parsons and Parsons 1990:335). Agave fiber can be twisted into strong twine and used for cordage, basketry, and woven textiles, agave sap can be made into fermented beverages like pulque, and agave hearts can be roasted and preserved as a sweet and nutritious food, with a caloric content equal to corn. Agave products were widely traded in early historic times and were commonly supplied to Plateau and desert groups like the Hopi, Zuni, Navajo, and Pima by the Havasupai, Walapai, and White Mountain Apache (Ford 1983:715). Accessible, low maintenance, and widely desired, agave products were clearly an important part of Salado period economic endeavors (Fish, Fish, Miksicek, and Madsen 1985; Fish et al. 1992b).

More subsistence information is currently available for the Roosevelt phase than for any other time period in the area. Over half the sites in our Tonto Basin sample date to the Roosevelt phase. Subsistence information is drawn from riverine platform mound communities such as Meddler Point, Pinto, and Bass (Elson, Fish, James, and Miksicek 1995; Elson, Gregory, and Stark 1995; Jacobs 1994a; Lindauer 1995a; Oliver 1997a); nonresidential platform mounds (e.g., Livingston and Pyramid Point; Elson 1994a; Jacobs 1994a); villages without platform mounds (e.g., Griffin Wash; Swartz and Randolph 1994b); as well as hamlets, farmsteads, and field houses in both lowland and upland settings (Ciolek-Torrello and Welch 1994; Ciolek-

Torrello et al., eds. 1994; Elson and Clark 1994; Elson and Swartz 1994; Elson, Gregory, and Stark 1995b; Oliver 1997a). These data augment earlier studies that provided significant subsistence information for the Mazatzal piedmont in the western Tonto Basin, the Rye Creek and Ash Creek area of the Upper Basin, and the cliff dwellings of Tonto National Monument on the south side of the Lower Basin (e.g., Ciolek-Torrello 1987; Elson and Craig 1992a; Fox 1996; Rice 1985; Steen et al. 1962).

With the exception of the cliff dwellings, the riverine sites, where the greatest amount of research has taken place, produce the widest variety of cultigens and economically important plants. Beans, squash, and grain amaranth are reported for these platform mound communities. In contrast, beans and squash have not yet been recovered from nonriverine sites, and cotton and agave are represented by significantly lesser quantities. Overall, sites on the lower and middle bajada (the "upland sites"), where less intense work has been conducted, tend to have more limited subsistence assemblages. Differential preservation, site function, seasonality of use, site permanence, occupational intensity, as well as variable data recovery and analytic methods, all potentially contribute to the problem of comparability.

Subsistence data indicate that the number of plant and animal species exploited in the Roosevelt phase increases over Preclassic levels (Figures 2.7a-c). Bottle gourd, a few species of squash, and tepary bean are added to the list of domesticates. But by far, the most abundant new taxa are wild plants (Table 2.1). Roosevelt phase populations continued to collect the same set of resources as their predecessors, but analyzed samples reveal the presence of more than 30 new species of potentially useful wild plants. The ubiquity value for corn falls from Preclassic levels, but still it remains the primary cultigen recovered in botanical samples. Similarly, the ubiquity value for cotton and little barley decreases slightly, but the presence of agave parts increases dramatically, indicating intensification of production and use of this highly valuable plant. The recovery of all parts of the cotton plant—lint, seed, boll parts, pollen—signify the continuing, if not growing, importance of raising cotton in Tonto Basin.

Emphasis on riparian, low desert, and lower bajada resources continues; mesquite remains the fuelwood of choice, but higher ubiquity values for middle elevation species, such as juniper, pinyon, jojoba, sycamore, and oak are indicated (Figure 2.5). Of special interest is the presence of upper elevation wood taxa in the assem-

Figure 2.7a.
Plant species
diversity through
time from
flotation and
macrobotanical.

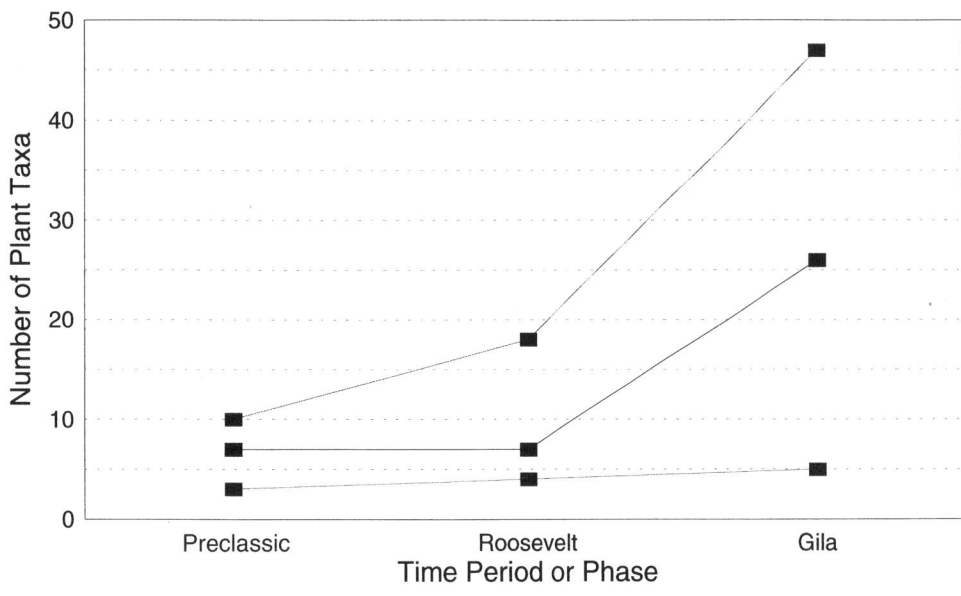

Figure 2.7b.
Plant species
diversity through
time from pollen
samples.

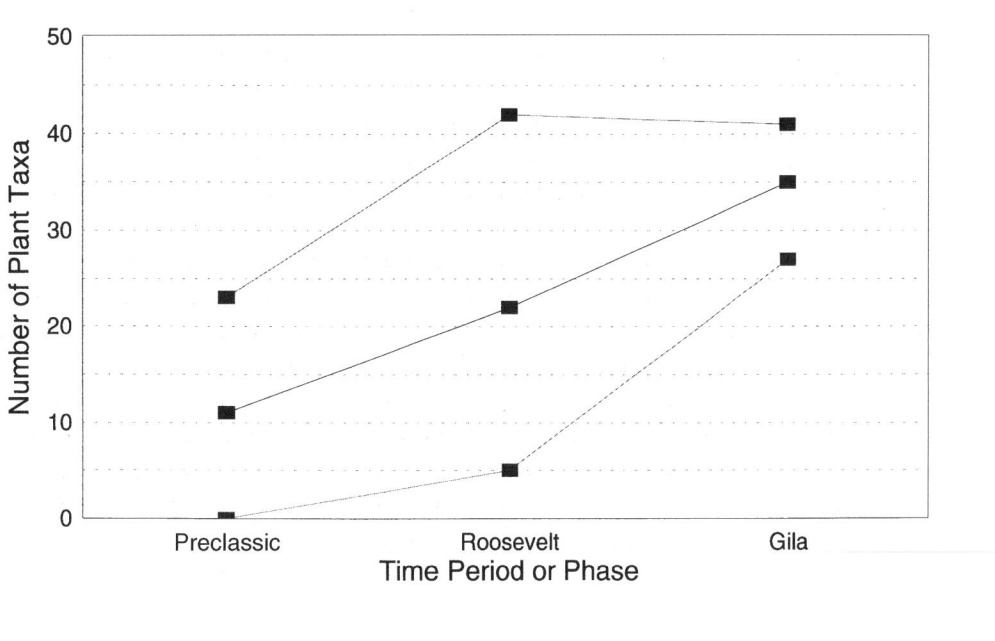

(figure continues on overleaf)

Figure 2.7c.
Faunal species
diversity through
time: nonhuman
bone.

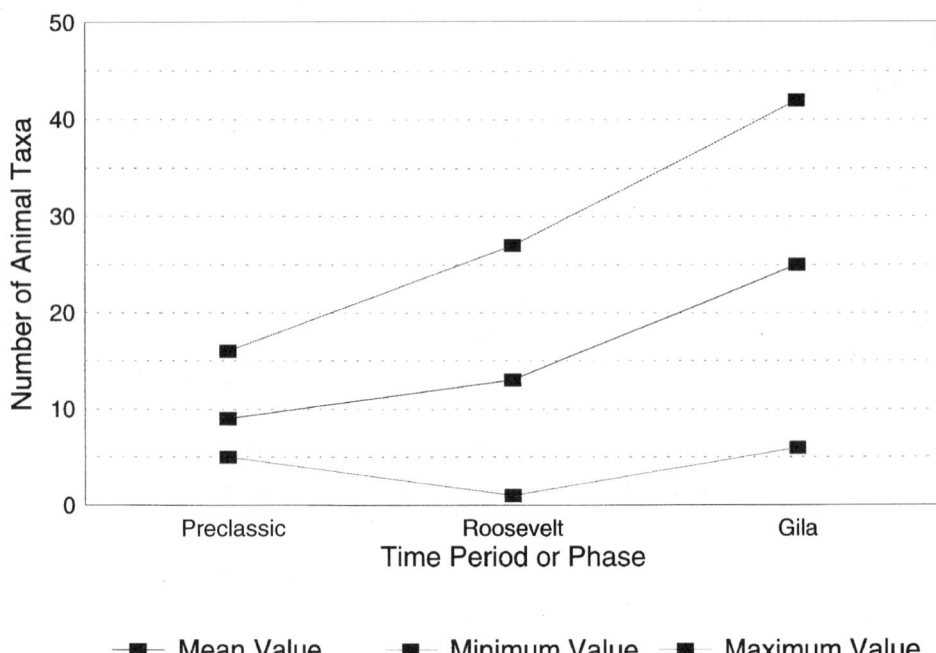

blages of two Roosevelt-phase sites: Griffin Wash Pueblo and the Meddler Point site. Ponderosa pine, Douglas-fir, and white fir, that are identified as structural timber rather than driftwood used as fuel, were recovered from only these two habitation sites. Elson, Fish, James, and Miksicek (1995) surmise that the increase in upper elevation wood types may have been due to one or more factors, including a cultural preference for higher elevation trees and their symbolic importance, the technical requirements for roofing rectangular masonry rooms rather than oval or round pit structures, and the depletion of lower elevation taxa. After reviewing data from other contemporary and later time period sites, we suggest that cultural preference and the greater familiarity of immigrant Pueblo populations with these wood types best explains the highly selective appearance of these upper elevation timbers in these two sites. Elsewhere, architectural requirements and local wood shortages may have promoted the use of higher elevation wood types.

Comparable trends occur in faunal data sets (Figures 2.4c and 2.7c). Ubiquity values indicate that lagomorphs (especially jackrabbits) and artiodactyls (primarily deer) maintain their lead over all other animal taxa. Nonetheless, there is an increase in species diversity from the Preclassic, with a decrease in the presence of artiodactyls and fish remains and an increase in bird taxa. This in-

crease in bird taxa likely represents the capture of avian species not only for field pest reduction and meat, but also the capture of special birds for their plumage and ritual significance (Crown 1994). The greater ubiquity values for rodent, reptile, amphibian, carnivore, and certain bird taxa in both the Roosevelt and Gila phases are interpreted here to represent increased opportunity for natural deposition. Longer occupations, unoccupied and abandoned structures, deeper middens, and larger areas of disturbed ground undoubtedly attracted rodents, especially mice, and their predators. Nevertheless, some of these taxa were edible or otherwise useful, and they do appear in contexts that suggest deliberate human capture.

Not surprisingly, the recovery of plant and animal species is closely correlated with specific environmental settings; lowland sites produced greater quantities of lowland resources and high elevation sites exhibited greater quantities of middle elevational plants. Regardless of setting, all settlements appear to have had regular access to lowland, middle elevation, and upper elevation resources. Some trends in resource use are evident, however. Riverine sites, where the greatest number of people were located, seem to have been dominated by jackrabbits, whereas upland sites seem to have been dominated by cottontails. Some analysts (Bayham and Hatch 1985; J. L. Cameron 1996b; Szuter 1989) assume that the ratio of cottontails to jackrabbits measures vegetative cover; cottontails generally prefer brushy cover and jackrabbits generally prefer open settings. If true, we might infer that the catchment areas surrounding riverine sites were more heavily disturbed by human occupation than those of upland sites.

The Roosevelt phase (1250 to 1350) encompassed four distinct periods of climatic variation. The first 26 years (1250–1275) were quite variable but predominantly moderate. A risk-minimizing strategy of simultaneously planting both upland and lowland fields would have produced successful harvests in most years.

The next 24 years, equivalent to the "Great Drought" of 1276–1299 (Douglass 1929), were rather consistently dry, with only one year of excessive moisture (1298) and six years of greater-than-normal drought (1276, 1283, 1286, 1288, 1295, 1299). At the same time, regional water tables began to drop (Dean 1988b:156, Figure 5.7). Such widespread conditions would have been inimical to upland water sources, and settlement would have been favored along watercourses with the most dependable flows (Van West 1994, 1996; M. R. Waters 1996). In addition, wild resource productivity, especially for annuals dependent on soil moisture and direct precipitation, may have suffered both in upland and lowland zones.

In contrast, the interval between 1300 and 1334 was quite variable and moderately wet. Five years of greater-than-average moisture and only one year of greater-than-average aridity occurred. Regional water tables, although dropping, were still reasonably high and were offset by generally wetter conditions that recharged upland springs, improved yields of wild plants, and favored nonriverine agriculture. Of all four Roosevelt phase regimes, this 35-year interval would have been the time most likely to have encouraged upland settlement. We suggest that most of the upland sites examined by the recent investigations date to this period. Available evidence appears to support this inference.

Finally, the interval from 1335 to 1355, that may either be the terminal years of the Roosevelt phase or the beginning of the Gila phase, experienced consistently dry climatic conditions. Once again, riverine settings would have been favored for settlement and agriculture over upland settings. No extremely wet years are documented for this 21-year interval, whereas four years of greater-than-normal dryness are documented. Falling regional water tables would have exacerbated this condition and rendered upland settings everywhere less attractive.

Gila Phase (1350 to circa 1450)

A Gila phase assignment is generally given to a site or site component producing Gila Polychrome, Gila Black-on-red, and Tonto Polychrome from the Roosevelt Red Ware, Fourmile or Showlow Polychrome from the White Mountain Red Ware, or any types in the Jeddito Yellow Ware.

Subsistence and settlement data for the Gila phase derive primarily from riverine villages of Schoolhouse Point and Cline Terrace Mounds, a few sites in the Upland Complex, and the extremely well-preserved, mostly Gila phase, cliff dwellings in Tonto National Monument (Bohrer 1962; Donaldson 1996; Jacobs 1997; Lindauer 1996a; Oliver 1997a; J. A. Waters 1996). Additional data on a Gila phase settlement also are available from the surface investigation of the large and long-lived Tuzigoot-on-Salome site (Germick and Crary 1990).

Doelle (1995b) suggests that the population of the Gila phase was smaller than that of the Roosevelt phase and in the vicinity of about 2,900 people. M. R. Waters (1996) suggests that Gila phase population may have been even larger; irrigated fields alone could have supported some 2,750 people. Recently, however, Jacobs and Rice (1997:577) suggest that 80 to 120 people could have lived at the Cline Terrace Mound, and Lindauer (1996c:849–50) suggests that a maximum of 150 people could have lived at Schoolhouse Point Mound during the Gila phase. These data suggest that the aggregate population of the Basin was smaller than in Roosevelt times. Settlement data indicate that fewer habitation sites were occupied in the Gila phase, although some of these may have been larger than the largest Roosevelt phase villages.

Gila phase subsistence is characterized by the continuation of a strong dependence on agricultural products (Dering 1996b; Fish 1996b) with seemingly less reliance on wild plant and animal foods. Corn and cotton continue to be the major cultigens (Figure 2.4a and 2.4b). The increase in the ubiquity values for cholla, agave, and cheno-ams, suggests deliberate cultivation and intensified use of these native species. The diversity of faunal and economic plants in the Gila phase increases markedly from those of earlier phases and seems to indicate the broadening of the subsistence base to include an even wider variety (if not quantity) of native plants and animals than in the Roosevelt phase (Figure 2.7a-c). Ubiquity values indicate that fewer samples contained lagomorphs (both cottontails and jackrabbits), deer, and fish, whereas other artiodactyl taxa and birds increase. Still, rabbits and deer continued to be the most commonly hunted animals, with other mammals and fish making small but steady contributions to the diet of Gila phase populations (J. L. Cameron 1996b).

The ubiquity of woody taxa from riparian, low desert, and low bajada settings continues to decrease, whereas ubiquity for upper bajada and middle elevation species increases (Figure 2.5). Importantly, no clearly upland wood species—ponderosa pine, Douglas-fir, or white fir—appear in the sample of Gila phase sites. Apparently, there was no basin-wide depletion of choice construction or fuelwood species; populations were not harvesting high elevation trees because all usable low elevation trees were gone. Rather, the shortage of specific wood types was a local occurrence and was most pronounced near inhabited districts. People simply had to travel farther to procure what they wanted.

Environmentally, the final 100 years of the Tonto Basin sequence were characterized by constantly falling water tables (Dean 1988b:156, Figure 5.7) and six periods of alternating wetness and aridity. More years were dry than wet, but relatively few of them varied considerably outside of the normal range. But when they did, they were notable, especially the wet years. Two episodes incorporating extremely high streamflows occurred: one four-year interval from 1356–1359 with significant discharge in 1357 and 1358 (Nials et al. 1989:69) and another five-year "event" with four consecutive years of exceptionally high magnitude discharge between 1381 and 1384 (Table 2.3; Nials et al. 1989:75). Many researchers have interpreted these unusually high reconstructed discharge values as proxy evidence for the occurrence of major floods or when water-caused damage to irrigation systems was great (e.g., Ackerly 1989; Howard 1992b). From the middle to late 1300s, regional environmental conditions were unpredictable from year to year and place to place, while local conditions were fairly persistent within variable-length periods (1360–1379 and 1385–1395). From about the turn-of-the-century through the middle 1400s, however, local climatic conditions and streamflow were again inconsistent and persistently arid. Nevertheless, M. R. Waters (1996:Draft 2:37) suggests that the period between 1384 and 1457 would have been the best years for canal irrigation in Tonto Basin during the Classic period because streamflow discharge was predictable and only three moderate droughts and four episodes of minor floods took place.

Tree-ring data reconstructs 1382 as the second most extreme flood year in the entire prehistoric sequence of Tonto Basin, exceeded only by the flood of 899. The 1382 flood, which was truly of epic proportions, was preceded and followed by greater-than-normal wet years also with floods. Immediately thereafter, a long dry spell lasting until 1456 set in and was initiated by a persistent eleven-year drought (1385–1395) that took place when regional water levels were already low and dropping. The 72-year dry spell terminated with another 22-year drought (1435–1456) that was potentially more disastrous by virtue of its length, sequencing, and cooccurrence with severely depressed water tables (also see M. R. Waters 1996). It is at this time that the Gila phase draws to a close.

CONCLUSIONS: UNAVOIDABLE DISSOLUTION OR UNMET CHALLENGES TO REFORMATION?

We return now to our questions as they apply to the Salado period in Tonto Basin. What emerges is a complicated picture of opportunities realized, limitations reached, and decision-making occurring on a spatial scale that encompasses much of the Greater Southwest. We consider the role that natural variability and anthropogenic factors may have played in the environmental "pulls" that helped create the Salado Phenomenon and the environmental "pushes" that resulted in its disappearance (Cameron, ed. 1995). We also consider the notion that an "environmental gradient" or "differential" existed during the period of interest and that events in east-central Arizona reflected the productive potential of regions to its north and south (Ahlstrom et al. 1995; Dean and Funkhouser 1995). Finally, we speculate as to what combination of environmental and social factors might have been responsible for the changes during two centuries between 1250 and 1450.

Environmental Variability and Adaptation in Tonto Basin

For more than 1,000 years, populations in Tonto Basin managed to survive in a richly varied but highly unpredictable environment by practicing a sustainable subsistence strategy that could be maintained by low population densities, small and relatively mobile settlement, and a subsistence system that emphasized generalization as opposed to specialization (Welch 1994b). When regional climate and demographic patterns changed in the late 1200s, Tonto Basin became an attractive refuge for displaced migrants because of its productive potential and its dependable water supply. In response to greater numbers of people, newly available labor, and external demand for its products, multiethnic populations developed an economy that focused on the production of corn and cotton through irrigation and the cultivation of agave through dryland techniques. It is likely that the potential to grow cotton in Tonto Basin, with its long growing season, normally abundant water supply, and irrigable soils, was the prime attraction to immigrants. And given its moderate tolerance for saline water and soil conditions, cotton was an especially appropriate crop for fields irrigated by the well-named Salt River. Despite the agricultural emphasis, human populations of the Roosevelt phase still exploited the rich and varied biotic communities of the Transition Zone. In fact, more taxa of plants and animals were gathered, trapped, and hunted than ever before (Tables 2.1 and 2.2, Figures 2.7a–c), and no signs of serious resource depletion can be cited.

The intensified agricultural strategy of the Roosevelt phase was successful in the short-term. It was particularly effective at the end of the thirteenth century (1276–1299, the so called "Great Drought" of the Colorado Plateau) when dryland farming opportunities both within and outside Tonto Basin were relatively limited. Various populations coalesced as local multisettlement communities organized around one or several platform mounds at the edge of the Basin's most dependable water sources. It was at those places that irrigation agriculture made crop production sufficiently predictable to sustain the larger populations of the Roosevelt phase (Craig 1995; Van West 1996; Van West and Altschul 1994).

In the early fourteenth century (1300–1334), variable but moister conditions prevailed. The cyclical trend toward channel entrenchment and falling water tables (Dean 1988b; Plog et al. 1988) was temporarily offset by predictable and widespread biseasonal moisture, an environmental condition that would have encourage diversified food procurement strategies, including upland farming, to reduce the risk of crop shortfalls. This more diversified subsistence strategy probably involved seasonal or temporary moves to upland locations by members of the riverine communities (Whittlesey et al., Chapter 10) or relocation of settlements to locations with access to upland and riverine farmlands. This inference is supported by archaeological data that suggest most habitation sites in the uplands, including the cliff dwellings of the nearby Sierra Ancha, were established after 1300.

By the 1330s, however, environmental and social conditions were sufficiently different in the region as a whole (Dean and Funkhouser 1995) that local populations had to respond to survive. A condition of general aridity returned, accompanied by further entrenchment of river channels, lower water tables, lower year-to-year persistence in climate, and greater differences in productivity throughout the Southwest. Of the many potential reactions, the ones that affect economic practices, including settlement patterns, subsistence choices, storage behavior, and extralocal exchange, are easiest to examine. These are the conditions and behavioral responses that terminated the Roosevelt phase and initiated the Gila phase.

The responses of late Roosevelt and early Gila phase populations were varied. Some people apparently moved away, others stayed. The overall affect, however, was population reduction (Doelle 1995b), abandonment of all but the most optimal of upland settings, further aggregation along the banks of the Salt River and Tonto Creek, dietary additions, renewed emphasis on cotton and agave production, and continued reorganization of the sociopolitical structure (Whittlesey et al., Chapter 10). Surviving Gila phase riverine settlements were located in the best locations for managing the largest expanses of irrigable land (J. S. Wood et al. 1992). The few remaining upland sites were near the most dependable water sources and the largest patches of arable land. In both settings, the diversity of plant and animal species increased from previous periods, and the number of facilities and settings associated with storage appears to have increased markedly (Lindauer 1996a; Spielmann 1996). Ubiquity values for all domesticated and encouraged plants rose modestly for already abundant corn and agave but increased dramatically for cholla, little barley, and cotton.

The climatic and environmental conditions of the Gila phase were not static. The two episodes of great wetness and probable flood (1356–1359 and 1380–1384) were so extreme that we suspect they further exacerbated the difficulties of making a living in east-central Arizona. Extreme discharge in combination with the low water tables may very well have caused the severe post-1000 slackwater deposits, channel incision, and terrace erosion documented by Ely et al. (1988) and M. R. Waters (1996). Should this have been the case, loss of irrigable farmland within the claimed use areas of particular communities could have been very serious. The exceptional floods of the 1380s could have initiated rapid soil loss along the irrigable terraces of Tonto Creek and the Salt River. Thereafter, even modest floods that in other times would have not been considered unusually destructive could have caused problems, including major downcutting, additional soil loss, and stranding or destruction of water intake features, that would have resulted in inoperable irrigation systems. Similarly, low water tables would have resulted in the desiccation of the smaller springs and seeps not fed by melting winter snows, as well as reduced ground cover. Erosion and arroyo cutting under similar circumstances have been well documented in the Southwest (Bryan 1925, 1928, 1940; Cooke and Reeves 1976; Dean 1969; Hastings and Turner 1965).

Farmers who diverted water from the Salt River would have been particularly at risk for salinization problems. Low flows of the normally saline water would have concentrated salts even further. Without sufficient streamflow to flush salts from irrigated soils, salt enrichment in the rooting zone of plants could easily have made the cultivation of salt-sensitive plants, such as corn and beans, difficult if not impossible (Ayres and Westcot 1989).

We suspect that few locations existed that could support groups larger than three or four households. And what arable land existed must have been devoted largely to food crops and personal subsistence rather than products for exchange. Emphasis on the production of agricultural surplus would have been strong; archaeologically the increase in the number and size of storage facilities is particularly evident (Lindauer 1996a; Spielmann 1996). Without access to additional farmland or the water technology to remedy this situation, the adaptive responses of Gila phase populations would have been limited to those that required significant dietary changes, local dispersal, or relocation to more favorable settings outside the Basin. Seemingly, some people did leave by the 1380s, but others remained or dispersed within the Basin and managed to survive for a few more generations. Ultimately, they too left, and Tonto Basin was abandoned by agricultural groups by 1500, if not earlier.

ENVIRONMENTAL GRADIENT: WAS THE GRASS GREENER ON THE OTHER SIDE?

In a volume on migration and movement of people in the prehistoric Southwest (Cameron, ed. 1995), various authors describe the essential attributes of long-distance migration and its complement, abandonment. At a minimum, there must be a population at a point of origin, a destination, a directed movement across an ecological or cultural boundary, and a perception that environmental and/or social conditions are more attractive in the target zone. Ahlstrom et al. (1995) describe the prerequisites for this type of population movement as an "environmental gradient," where a measurable differential exists between source and target areas during some period of time. Stark, Clark, and Elson (1995a) marshall compelling evidence for a migration into Tonto Basin during the late thirteenth century. What remains now is a consideration of migration out of Tonto Basin in the fourteenth and fifteenth centuries.

Dean and Funkhouser (Dean 1994, Dean 1996b; Dean and Funkhouser 1995) have recently reported the startling results of a quantitative study that reconstructs regional scale patterns in dendroclimatic variability. They identify a 200-year period from about 1250–1450 when long-term patterns in the distribution of annual precipitation broke down and became highly erratic for portions of the northern Southwest. Ahlstrom et al. (1995) suggest that this climatic disruption contributed to an adaptive crisis for the thirteenth century populations of the Four Corners area and promoted their migration to areas unaffected or less affected by the chaotic precipitation regime.

We suggest that similar principles operated at the end of the 200-year anomaly, as well as the beginning. The immediate destinations of emigrants from Tonto Basin are not certain (but see Adams, Chapter 11), although former homelands, unoccupied new lands, and locations with similar characteristics to Tonto Basin were potential targets. Clearly, the degree of familiarity and connectedness that migrating populations had with other regions and other populations would largely determine their movements. Prior trade and marriage relations, as well as regular expeditions to secure special resources (e.g., salt, obsidian, medicinal plants, ritual or game animals) and pilgrimages to ancestral sacred places, would have been important. In short, we suggest that environmental "pushes" and "pulls" operating from areas of lesser to greater opportunity and security existed at the end of the Gila phase.

Where did these people go? The answer to this question is not clear. Intuitively, one would suspect the immediate surrounding regions, such as the Phoenix Basin, the lower Verde River Valley, the middle Gila River region, or the lower San Pedro River Valley. The problem with these candidates is that they too experienced population decline at precisely this time. Farther south, we can examine possibilities in the upper river valleys of the Santa Cruz and San Pedro Rivers. Although the data are poor, these areas appear to have maintained populations into the late fourteenth and early fifteenth centuries. But as Altschul and his colleagues point out for the upper San Pedro, these areas were never incorporated into the Classic period Hohokam or Salado cultural spheres, maintaining a southerly orientation (Altschul 1996; Altschul and Quijada 1996; Altschul et al. 1996).

To the north, the picture is also murky. Fourteenth and fifteenth century aggregations are found at Homol'ovi along the Little Colorado River, at Hopi, near Zuni and Acoma, and farther east along the Rio Grande. But these communities supposedly were composed of dispersed Plateau populations; could they support an influx of people from the Transition Zone as well? We propose that for much of the migrant population the answer is "yes." The Salado Phenomenon was born out of economic necessity. Dry farming populations from the Colorado Plateau and the Mogollon highlands moved into the river valleys of the Transition Zone because they offered a seemingly viable livelihood that was environmentally prohibited to the north. Here, they mixed with local populations to create multiethnic communities that ranged in form from the platform mounds of Tonto Basin to the pueblos of the middle Gila and lower Verde to the mixed trait compounds of the lower San Pedro. This marriage of necessity was short lived. There are probably many reasons for the demise of these systems. Environmentally, these river valleys may not have been able to sustain the unprecedented population densities. Economically, dry farmers used to "spreading risk over the landscape," may never have felt comfortable with putting their trust in intensive irrigation. Ideologically and socially, the systems' blend of Hohokam, Mogollon, and Anasazi features may not have worked. Regardless, we suspect that when environmental and social conditions to the north ameliorated, families whose ancestors had migrated into Tonto Basin became, in turn, migrants themselves and returned to former homelands.

CONCLUSION

The pumped up social, economic, and political systems of the Salado period were highly vulnerable to regional environmental perturbations. The interacting environmental, demographic, and technological realities of the late thirteenth, fourteenth, and early fifteenth centuries resulted in a complicated set of conditions that continu-

ally forced local populations and their leaders to respond. The sustainability of the specialized Roosevelt phase adaptations depended on three conditions: 1) a sufficiently large population to provide the labor and carry out the social roles that the economic, religious, and political systems required; 2) regional environmental conditions that made certain well-watered river valleys like Tonto Basin attractive for agriculture, and by contrast, made other places far less attractive, and; 3) a compelling ideological climate that fostered intergroup cooperation and participation in institutional activities. It succeeded in its most elaborate form when environmental and social conditions promoted localized pockets of abundance and prosperity in a larger scale setting of resource scarcity and hardship. When environmental or social conditions changed, the economy changed as well. What *is* predictable is that the cultural system would change, but what *is not* predictable are the forms those changes would take.

Why the Gila phase populations of Tonto Basin failed to meet the challenge of adaptation to new social and economic conditions, we can only guess. Contemporary systems elsewhere did survive. The continued existence of puebloan populations at Hopi, Zuni, and Acoma, for example, proves that other groups did find solutions that enabled them to survive in place as cultural entities. We suspect that political and religious leaders of the late Roosevelt phase and early Gila phase failed to offer sufficient practical solutions to keep the diverse populations of Tonto Basin from defecting (compare Adams 1991). What resulted then, was depopulation, reorganization, discontent, and eventually diaspora. Not an event but a process, it transpired over the course of more than 150 years, time enough to see the comings and goings of seven or eight generations. By the end, their sparse numbers, technological limitations, weakly integrated social system, and possibly their economic marginality to ongoing systems elsewhere worked against them. By 1500 or perhaps earlier, the Salado Phenomenon was a thing of the past, and descendant populations likely retained only the most resilient of their ancestral traditions in their new sixteenth century homes.

ENDNOTES

1. The 27 sites used in this paper to monitor synchronic and diachronic change in subsistence patterns include

the following. Four sites were excavated by Statistical Research, Inc. during the Roosevelt Rural Site Study (RRSS; Sedentary period sites Grapevine Vista Locus B and Riser and Roosevelt phase sites Porter Springs and Grapevine Springs). Six sites with eight temporal components were excavated by Desert Archaeology, Inc. during the Roosevelt Community Development Study (RCDS; Early Ceramic period Eagle Ridge Locus B; Colonial period Hedge Apple and Meddler Point Locus A; Sedentary period Eagle Ridge Locus A; and Roosevelt phase Meddler Point Mound, Pyramid Point, Griffin, and Porcupine). Fourteen sites were excavated by Arizona State University during the Roosevelt Platform Mound Study (RPMS; Sedentary period U:8:304 and U:8:577 on Schoolhouse Mesa; Roosevelt phase Bass Mound in the Rock Island area, Pinto Mound, Livingston Mound, Sand Dune, Saguaro Muerto, V:5:119 and V:5:121 in the Livingston area, and U:8:25 and U:8:454 on Schoolhouse Mesa; and Gila phase Cline Terrace Mound, Schoolhouse Mound, and U:8:530 in Upland Unit 27). The 1995 excavations at the Upper Ruin of Tonto National Monument (TNM) by the National Park Service contribute the final samples. These data are on file at Statistical Research, Inc., POB 31865, Tucson, Arizona, 85751 and can be obtained on computer disk or as hard-copy.

2. Rodents considered regular sources of food include rock squirrels, Botta's pocket gopher, white-throated woodrat, muskrat, beaver. Birds regularly considered food items include quails, mourning doves, roadrunner, and thrashers. Edible fish include desert-mountain suckers, chubs, and Colorado squawfish.

3. Plants in the family that contains chenopodium and amaranth (generally referred to as "cheno-ams"), wild buckwheat, and filaree, as well as some of the common agricultural weeds, such as spiderling, globemallow, and Arizona poppy, typically are used as disturbance indicators by archaeobotanists (Bozarth 1994; Dering 1996b; Donaldson 1996; Fish 1995b; Miksicek 1995). The results, however, are not always unambiguous. Ethnographers of Native American populations record that many of these taxa were used for food, spices, and medicines. Therefore, their presence in archaeological contexts may be cultural as well as natural (Adams 1994a, 1994b).

4. Evidence for anthropogenic alteration of the Tonto Basin environment exists, of course, but no data indicate that the changes were widespread, irreversible, or limit-

ing to human subsistence. Impacts are inferred from the changing proportion of various plants and animals identified in samples from excavated sites. Impacts also can be monitored through soil studies that measure nutrients known to be altered by agriculture and by geological methods that document topsoil loss and erosion. Studies of soil quality in Tonto Basin have so far been unable to document detrimental, human induced change (Homburg 1994), but biological studies offer several lines of evidence.

Elevated levels of pollen from weedy plants known to thrive in disturbed soil start to appear in the Colonial period, continue to rise, and remain high through the Gila phase. Their increasing representation in archaeological contexts is generally interpreted as reflecting additional land being brought under cultivation or habitat conducive for weedy plant growth existing close to the residential and farming areas.

Change in the types and volume of fuelwood brought into a habitation site and in the woody taxa harvested for construction is also used to monitor human impacts to specific geographic zones. Long-term trends in wood use suggest that riparian zones, lowland dry washes, and areas on the low and middle bajada were most regularly used for gathering driftwood and downed wood for fires. Similarly, these were the same zones where building material was found. By the end of the Gila phase, a smaller proportion of wood for fuel and timber came from the lowlands and a greater proportion came from middle elevation plant communities. Although never depleted, lowland vegetation communities were affected by human land use. Agricultural fields, irrigation ditches, earthworks, activity areas, riverside trails, and other human handiwork displaced, thinned, or altered previous vegetation, modified landscapes, and created new opportunities or constraints on the animal life that formerly inhabited the area.

Similarly, the changing proportions of key faunal taxa in the assemblages of excavated sites monitor the effects of land clearance and human presence in a locality or the long-term impact of hunting on local game. Jackrabbits, who prefer more open environments, increased relative to cottontails, who prefer more heavily vegetated areas. Fewer deer and other large game appear in the faunal assemblages examined, and smaller mammals and birds appear more frequently. These changes suggest resource depletion or scarcity to some analysts.

CHAPTER THREE

Demographic, Health, Genetic, and Mortuary:

Characteristics of Late Prehistoric Central Arizona Populations

John C. Ravesloot and Marcia H. Regan

Tʜᴇ ᴄᴏɴᴄᴇᴘᴛ ᴏꜰ ᴛʜᴇ Sᴀʟᴀᴅᴏ ᴀs ᴏʀɪɢɪɴᴀʟʟʏ ᴘʀᴏ-posed by Gladwin and Gladwin (1935) defined a constellation of traits that was markedly different from the earlier Hohokam tradition of the Gila-Salt Basin. The distinguishing characteristics of the Salado as outlined by the Gladwins were massive adobe-walled architecture with compound enclosures, polychrome pottery, and extended inhumations. The Gladwins explained the contrast between the remains of the Hohokam and Salado in the Gila-Salt Basin as evidence for the arrival of a new ethnic group. This new ethnic group was proposed to have originated in the upper Little Colorado River area, subsequently appearing in the Tonto Basin area, and eventually moving to the Gila-Salt Basin.

Over the last 60 years, the Gladwinian model has been criticized and debated, as new archaeological sites were excavated and classified as Salado. The debate has primarily focused on questions relating to the cultural identity and origins of the Salado (Cordell 1984; Doyel 1976b; Nelson and LeBlanc 1986; Rice 1990b; Whittlesey and Reid 1982;), although more recently the social complexity of the Salado has taken center stage (Crown 1994; Rice 1990b; Whittlesey and Ciolek-Torrello 1992).

Regrettably, the acquisition of new excavation data from Salado sites appears only to confuse the picture, since a consistent definition of the Salado concept has not been applied (Doyel and Haury 1976; Nelson and LeBlanc 1986). The only distinguishing characteristic of Salado that has been consistently applied is the presence of Gila Polychrome pottery (Crown 1994; Doyel 1972; Nelson and LeBlanc 1986; Rice 1990b).

For years, archaeologists have argued that confusion surrounding the concept of the Salado could be adequately addressed only when large-scale excavations were conducted in the so-called heartland, the Tonto Basin region of central Arizona. Now that this long-awaited work has been done, what have we learned? When we compare the architecture and material culture of the Tonto Basin Salado with Salado sites from other areas, it is obvious that there is considerable variability in the archaeological record. This is particularly true of "Salado" burial practices, but what about the physical remains of the people themselves? At no time in the history of the Salado debate has a high quality and systematically collected burial population been available to test hypotheses related to origins, immigration and emigration of populations, adaptation to local environmental conditions, and the evolution of social organization.

In this paper, we focus on a comparative interpretation of available demographic, health, genetic, and mortuary data from Tonto Basin Salado sites. Bioarchaeological data are applied to questions such as: How does the overall health of Tonto Basin populations compare with other contemporaneous (1250 to 1450) Southwestern populations? What evidence (biological or cultural) is there for immigration of populations into Tonto Basin around the time of the Great Drought, 1276–1399? Are the Tonto Basin populations more closely related to the Mogollon, Hohokam, or Anasazi, or is this an intractable problem as suggested by Turner (1993)? What do the biological and mortuary data suggest with regard to the organizational complexity of central Arizona populations during the Classic period?

BIOARCHAEOLOGICAL DATABASE

More than 480 burial features were excavated from 39 sites by Arizona State University's (ASU) Roosevelt Platform Mound Study (RPMS) (Table 3.1). Burial feature types included mainly inhumations, some cremations, and a few atypical deposits such as secondary burials. Although many burial features were excavated, our data recovery was limited by two uncontrollable factors: poor preservation and extensive pothunting. Because the soil in Tonto Basin generally causes poor bone preservation, many of the skeletons were already fragmented or reduced to dust before excavations began. Pothunting caused bone breakage, destruction, removal, and commingling of individuals from different burial episodes, further reducing the amount of recoverable information.

Historic vandalism was not the only cause of bone commingling; large burials pits were often reused by the prehistoric inhabitants. When graves were reopened, the preceding occupant's bones were gathered up or pushed aside, thus destroyed the original context of the bones. Finally, rodent activity was so extensive at some sites that Regan et al. (1996) suggested that Tonto Basin be renamed Gopher Gulch.

Archival research (Ravesloot 1990, 1994a) and mapping of pothunter holes suggests that there originally were many more graves than those identified. With the exception of several Roosevelt phase (1250 to 1350) residential compounds, the burial collections recovered from the Tonto Basin sites are probably not representative of the range of mortuary treatments utilized; this is particularly true of the Gila phase (1350 to 1450) burials (Loendorf 1996a; Ravesloot 1990).

Comparative bioarchaeological data come from other Classic period Southwestern sites, in particular, Casas

Grandes (Benfer 1968; Corruccini 1983; Di Peso 1974a; Ravesloot 1988; Weaver 1985); Casa Buena (Barnes 1988; Howard 1988), Grand Canal Ruins (Fink 1989; Mitchell et al. 1989); Grasshopper Pueblo (Berry 1985a, 1985b; Ezzo 1993; Hinkes 1983; Whittlesey 1978), and Pueblo Grande (Mitchell 1992, 1994; Van Gerven and Sheridan 1994).

DEMOGRAPHY

Age and sex are among the most basic but most informative types of information gathered from skeletal remains. The frequency distributions of ages and sexes in a cemetery population can both answer old questions and provoke new ones about prehistoric life and health. Age at death distributions provide insight into adult age-specific mortality risks and relative fertility; changes in these distributions over time or space prompt questions about lifestyle differences that lead to better or worse health. Sex distributions in the adult age categories indicate differences between men's and women's lives, often related to warfare and childbirth. Because age and sex are the primary criteria of social differentiation in many societies, we can infer much about prehistoric social organization from age- and sex-based mortuary treatments. Skewness in these distributions can inform about differential burial practices from which we can infer social distinctions (Binford 1971; Brown 1971; O'Shea 1984).

Age and sex distributions (Table 3.2) were developed for a combined Tonto Basin sample using data from all RPMS sites. Age and sex determination standards are given in Turner et al. (1990) and Regan et al. (1996).

In order to better understand what the age and sex distributions mean and to compare the data to other populations, life tables were constructed. Subadults were placed into five-year age categories. Adults were grouped in ten-year age categories, to accommodate errors in age estimation. For the life table calculations, adults who could not be specifically aged were divided evenly among the five adult ten-year age categories. The fetal individuals and the six individuals for whom age was uncertain were not included in the life table calculations. Calculations were made according to directions given in Ubelaker (1989).

The life table data for the combined RPMS sample (Table 3.3) indicate that overall life expectancy was good for a prehistoric population. Life expectancy at birth was greater than 22 years and remained high throughout the

Table 3.1. Tonto Basin Sites with Burials

Site Number	Site Type	Phase[a]	Number of Burial Features	Number of Individuals
U:3:128	Compound	R/G	13	16
U:3:133	Cobble masonry room block	G	8	6
U:3:139				1
U:3:214	Compound	R	1	2
U:4:07	Compound	R/G	20	17
U:4:09	Cobble masonry room block	R/G	29	22
U:4:10	Cobble masonry room block	G	14	21
U:4:11	Compound	G	1	2
U:4:12				1
U:4:13	Compound	R	4	2
U:4:29	Compound	R	3	2
U:4:32	Compound	R	9	8
U:4:33	Platform mound	G(R?)	34	52
U:4:60				1
U:4:62	Cobble masonry room block	R/G?	5	1
U:4:75	Compound	P/R	14	10
U:4:77	Compound	P/R	1	2
U:8:23	Platform mound	R	7	19
U:8:24	Platform mound	R/G	158	239
U:8:25	Compound	R	23	21
U:8:385	Field house	S	3	1
U:8:450	Compound	R/G	66	78
U:8:451	Compound	R	8	8
U:8:453	Compound	R	1	1
U:8:454	Cobble masonry room block	R	2	1
U:8:456	Compound	R	9	4
U:8:458	Compound	P/R	5	2
U:8:514				1
U:8:530	Cobble masonry room block		3	2
U:8:577	Pithouse	S	2	1
V:5:61	Compound	R	9	3
V:5:66	Platform mound	R/G?	5	22
V:5:112	Compound	R/G?	4	6
V:5:119	Compound	R	12	15
V:5:121	Compound	R	4	6
V:5:128	Cobble masonry room block	R	3	5
V:5:137				3
V:5:138	Compound	R	1	1
V:5:139	Compound	R/G?	6	11
		TOTALS	487	616

[a]P=Postclassic G=Gila
R=Roosevelt S=Sacaton

Table 3.2 Age and Sex Distributions and Life Table for RPMS Samples*

Age	M	F	?	N	%	x	Dx	dx	lx	qx	Lx	Tx	ex
Fetal			17	17	2.76	0–5.5	209.0	35.60	100.00	0.3560	452.09	2530.11	25.30
Newborn			50	50	8.12	5.5–10.5	31.0	5.28	64.40	0.0820	308.77	2078.02	32.27
0.0–0.5			77	77	12.50	10.5–14.99	6.0	1.02	59.11	0.0173	263.71	1769.25	29.93
0.5–1.5			37	37	6.01	15–19.99	15.0	2.56	58.09	0.0440	284.07	1505.24	25.92
1.5–2.5			18	18	2.92	20–29.99	80.2	13.66	55.54	0.2460	487.05	1221.47	21.99
2.5–3.5			9	9	1.46	30–39.99	83.2	14.17	41.87	0.3385	347.87	734.41	17.54
3.5–4.5			13	13	2.11	40–49.99	65.2	11.11	27.70	0.4010	221.47	386.54	13.95
4.5–5.5			5	5	0.81	50–59.99	49.2	8.38	16.59	0.5051	124.02	165.08	9.95
5.5–6.5			8	8	1.30	60–69.99	48.2	8.21	8.21	1.0000	41.06	41.06	5.00
6.5–7.5			13	13	2.11	Total	587.0	100.00			2530.11		
7.5–8.5			2	2	0.32								
8.5–9.5			3	3	0.49								
9.5–10.5			5	5	0.81								
10.5–14.99	1	0	5	6	0.97								
15.0–20.99	3	3	9	15	2.44								
20.0–29.99	21	12	2	35	5.68								
30.0–39.99	21	15	2	38	6.17								
40.0–49.99	8	12	0	20	3.25								
50.0–59.99	2	2	0	4	0.65								
60+	0	3	0	3	0.49								
Adult	48	44	134	226	36.69								
Unknown	0	0	12	12	1.95								
Total	104	91	421	616	100.00								

x: age interval
Dx: # of deaths
dx: % of deaths
lx: % survivors entering
qx: probability of death
Lx: total years lived between x and (x+5)
Tx: total years lived after lifetime
ex: life expectancy

*All sites included.

age ranges. Subadults including fetal individuals comprised 41.9 percent of the population, a figure that is well within the "normal" range of 30 to 50 percent for preindustrial anthropological populations (Howells 1960; Weiss 1973). The producing sector of the population, that is, adults between 15 and 50 years of age, totaled 41.5 percent of the population, while 16.6 percent of the population was old adults.

Although the observed age and sex distributions constitute a reasonable prehistoric sample, it must be noted that the recovered skeletons do not represent the entire burial population. Lindauer (1996a) estimates, based on architectural features, that the population of Schoolhouse Point Mound at any given time was probably 150 individuals. We can evaluate the representativeness of the burial population

two ways: by estimating the size of the donor population, based on the number of recovered individuals; and by estimating the potential burial population based on architectural estimates of population size. Acsadi and Nemeskeri (1970) give the following formula for estimating both donor populations and cemetery size:

$$P = \frac{k + (De_0^0)}{t}$$

where:

P = population size
D = cemetery size
e_0^0 = estimated life expectancy at birth
t = duration of cemetery use
k = a correction factor, usually ten percent of t

Table 3.3 Life Table Statistics for Selected Comparative Populations

a. RPMS, all sites combined

x	Dx	dx	lx	qx	Lx	Tx	ex
0–5.5	209	35.60	100.00	0.36	452.09	2530.11	25.30
5.5–10.5	31	5.28	64.40	0.08	308.77	2078.02	32.27
10.5–14.99	6	1.02	59.11	0.02	263.71	1769.25	29.93
15–19.99	15	2.56	58.09	0.04	284.07	1505.54	25.92
20–29.99	80.2	13.66	55.54	0.25	487.05	1221.47	21.99
30–39.99	83.2	14.17	41.87	0.34	347.87	734.41	17.54
40–49.99	65.2	11.11	27.70	0.40	221.47	386.54	13.95
50–59.99	49.2	8.38	16.59	0.51	124.02	165.08	9.95
60–69.99	48.2	8.21	8.21	1.00	41.06	41.06	5.00
Total	587	100.00			2530.11		

b. Ash Creek (recalculated from Bassett and Atwell 1985)

x	Dx	dx	lx	qx	Lx	Tx	ex
0–4.99	13	22.41	100.00	0.22	443.97	2702.59	27.03
5–9.99	6	10.34	77.59	0.13	362.07	2258.62	29.11
10–14.99	1	1.72	67.24	0.03	331.90	1896.55	28.21
15–19.99	3	5.17	65.52	0.08	314.66	1564.66	23.88
20–29.99	8	13.79	60.34	0.23	534.48	1250.00	20.71
30–39.99	5	8.62	46.55	0.19	422.41	715.52	15.37
40–49.99	16	27.59	37.93	0.73	241.38	293.10	7.73
50–59.99	6	10.34	10.34	1.00	51.72	51.72	5.00
60–69.99	0	0.00	0.00	0.00	0.00	0.00	0.00
Total	58	100.00			2702.59		

c. Hohokam: Casa Buena and Grand Canal (Fink 1989)

x	Dx	dx	lx	qx	Lx	Tx	ex
0–4.99	15	8.93	100.00	0.09	477.68	3254.46	32.54
5–9.99	6	3.57	91.07	0.04	446.43	2776.79	30.49
10–14.99	1	0.60	87.50	0.01	436.01	2330.36	26.63
15–19.99	5	2.98	86.90	0.03	427.08	1894.35	21.80
20–29.99	36	21.43	83.93	0.26	732.14	1467.26	17.48
30–39.99	51	30.36	62.50	0.49	473.21	735.12	11.76
40–49.99	37	22.02	32.14	0.69	211.31	261.90	8.15
50–59.99	17	10.12	10.12	1.00	50.60	50.60	5.00
60–69.99	0	0.00	0.00	0.00	0.00	0.00	0.00
Total	168	100.00			3254.46		

d. Grasshopper (recalculated from Berry 1985a:46)

x	Dx	dx	lx	qx	Lx	Tx	ex
0–4.99	334	54.40	100.00	0.54	364.01	1494.30	14.94
5–9.99	58	9.45	45.60	0.21	204.40	1130.29	24.79
10–14.99	16	2.61	36.16	0.07	174.27	925.90	25.61
15–19.99	14	2.28	33.55	0.07	162.05	751.63	22.40
20–29.99	48	7.82	31.27	0.25	273.62	589.58	18.85
30–39.99	50	8.14	23.45	0.35	193.81	315.96	13.47
40–49.99	66	10.75	15.31	0.70	99.35	122.15	7.98
50–59.99	28	4.56	4.56	1.00	22.80	22.80	5.00
60–69.99	0	0.00	0.00	0.00	0.00	0.00	0.00
Total	614	100.00			1494.30		

e. AZ:T:16:88 (Regan n.d.)

x	Dx	dx	lx	qx	Lx	Tx	ex
0–4.99	27	42.86	100.00	0.43	392.86	2301.59	23.02
5–9.99	2	3.17	57.14	0.06	277.78	1908.73	33.40
10–14.99	0	0.00	53.97	0.00	269.84	1630.95	30.22
15–19.99	3	4.76	53.97	0.09	257.94	1361.11	25.22
20–29.99	7	11.11	49.21	0.23	436.51	1103.17	22.42
30–39.99	4	6.35	38.10	0.17	349.21	666.67	17.50
40–49.99	12	19.05	31.75	0.60	222.22	317.46	10.00
50–59.99	6	9.52	12.70	0.75	79.37	95.24	7.50
60–69.99	2	3.17	3.17	1.00	15.87	15.87	5.00
Total	63	100.00			2301.59		

Table 3.4. Demographic Profiles for the Roosevelt (U:8:24 and U:8:450) and Gila (U:8:24) Phases in Tonto Basin

a. *Roosevelt phase*						b. *Gila phase*					
Age	M	F	?	N	%	Age	M	F	?	N	%
Fetal	0	0	3	3	1.97	Fetal	0	0	7	7	4.79
Newborn	0	0	6	6	3.95	Newborn	0	0	18	18	12.33
0.0–0.5	0	0	12	12	7.89	0.0–0.5	0	0	37	37	25.34
0.5–1.5	0	0	10	10	6.58	0.5–1.5	0	0	13	13	8.90
1.5–2.5	0	0	6	6	3.95	1.5–2.5	0	0	4	4	2.74
2.5–3.5	0	0	5	5	3.29	2.5–3.5	0	0	3	3	2.05
3.5–4.5	0	0	4	4	2.63	3.5–4.5	0	0	3	3	2.05
4.5–5.5	0	0	1	1	0.66	4.5–5.5	0	0	0	0	0.00
5.5–6.5	0	0	4	4	2.63	5.5–6.5	0	0	2	2	1.37
6.5–7.5	0	0	2	2	1.32	6.5–7.5	0	0	4	4	2.74
7.5–8.5	0	0	0	0	0.00	7.5–8.5	0	0	0	0	0.00
8.5–9.5	0	0	2	2	1.32	8.5–9.5	0	0	0	0	0.00
9.5–10.5	0	0	2	2	1.32	9.5–10.5	0	0	1	1	0.68
10.5–14.99	1	0	0	1	0.66	10.5–14.99	0	0	3	3	2.05
15.0–19.99	2	2	3	7	4.61	15.0–19.99	0	0	3	3	2.05
20.0–29.99	11	3	1	15	9.87	20.0–29.99	3	1	0	4	2.74
30.0–39.99	8	5	0	13	8.55	30.0–39.99	4	2	0	6	4.11
40.0–49.99	0	7	0	7	4.61	40.0–49.99	2	2	0	4	2.74
50.0–59.99	0	0	0	0	0.00	50.0–59.99	1	1	0	2	1.37
60+	0	1	0	1	0.66	60+	0	0	0	0	0.00
Adult	14	14	20	48	31.58	Adult	9	8	15	32	21.92
Unknown	0	0	3	3	1.97	Unknown	0	0	0	0	0.00
Total	36	32	84	152	100.00	Total	19	14	113	146	100.00

In both calculations, the Roosevelt and Gila phase samples from Schoolhouse Point Mound and U:8:450 were combined. To determine P, let D = 285, $e_0^0 = 21.59$, t = 150 years (Glen E. Rice and Owen Lindauer, personal communication 1995), and k = 15. Solving the equation yields a P of *42.67*, much smaller than the architectural estimate for Schoolhouse Point Mound. Turning the equation around to estimate D with P set at 150 and all other variables the same yields an estimated cemetery size (D) of *1,049.23* individuals. The excavated sample (*298*) is only about *28* percent of what should be there.

It must be stressed that these solutions are estimates. If t is reduced from 150 to 100, P = *64.01*, and D = *699.25*. However, these solutions still indicate that the excavated sample is only *43* percent of what should have been

found, if the architectural estimate is correct. It would be unreasonable to assume that archaeology has recovered a 100 percent sample. At Schoolhouse Point Mound, burials most likely remain within the mound itself (Glen E. Rice, personal communication 1995). Erich F. Schmidt excavated burials from trash mounds in the 1920s that are not part of this analysis (Hohmann and Kelley 1988), nor are those acquired by Gila Pueblo (actually, artifact collections were purchased, the whereabouts of the skeletal remains is unknown). Vandalization of graves creates uncertainty in the counting of individuals. The age structure and apparent sex ratios, however, are not out of the ordinary for a prehistoric population. It is unlikely that one segment of the population was sampled more heavily than another when the phases and sites are combined.

To explore differences within the Tonto Basin samples, specifically between the earlier and later phases, the burial sample was divided into Roosevelt and Gila phases on the basis of stratigraphic relationships of burials and decorated ceramic associations. The Gila phase sample consists only of individuals from Schoolhouse Point Mound, while the early sample contains individuals from Schoolhouse and U:8:450, a residential compound. Separate demographic profiles and life tables were constructed for each sample (Tables 3.4 and 3.5). Comparative population and survivorship curves are presented in Figures 3.1 and 3.2.

The most striking differences between the Roosevelt and Gila phases are in life expectancy at birth. For the Roosevelt phase, life expectancy at birth is 25.25 years, while for the Gila sample it is only 17.75 years. Does this indicate such a severe decline in living conditions that infant and young childhood mortality rates doubled? Perhaps, but more likely explanations can be found by examining the nature of the archaeological samples. All Roosevelt phase skeletal series from Tonto Basin appear to have fewer subadults than the Gila phase series. This is true of the samples from the Livingston sites (Turner et al. 1994a), U:8:450, and Schoolhouse Point Mound. Gila phase samples from Schoolhouse Point Mound have an overabundance of infants and children. The severe decline in estimates of life expectancy at birth from the Roosevelt to the Gila phases is due to the substantial difference in proportion of infants and young children in the two subsamples (Table 3.4; Figure 3.2). The questions then arise, does this shift reflect actual life history differences between the earlier and later phases, or did something else happen to produce the appearance of increased subadult mortality? And where are the earlier phase subadults?

A shift in burial practices could account for the differential recovery of the youngest cohorts. Most of the Gila phase infants were recovered from beneath room floors, while Roosevelt phase infants and children were buried in extramural locations (Loendorf 1996a). Because the area around the Schoolhouse Point Mound site was extensively tested, it is unlikely that any cemeteries went undetected. Therefore, the uneven numbers of subadults between the two phases at Schoolhouse Point Mound is an artifact of sampling.

The RPMS life expectancies are compared (Table 3.3) to those from other Southwestern prehistoric sites (Bassett and Atwell 1985; Benfer 1968; Bennett 1973a; Berry 1985a; Fink 1989; Van Gerven and Sheridan 1994) and one

Table 3.5 Life Table Statistics for the Roosevelt and Gila Phase Populations in Tonto Basin

a. *Roosevelt Phase (U:8:24 and U:8:450, combined)*

x	Dx	dx	lx	qx	Lx	Tx	ex
0–5.5	44.0	30.14	100.00	0.30	467.12	2538.53	25.39
5.5–10.5	10.0	6.85	69.86	0.10	332.19	2071.40	29.65
10.5–14.99	1.0	0.68	63.01	0.01	282.02	1739.21	27.60
15–19.99	7.0	4.79	62.33	0.08	299.66	1457.19	23.38
20–29.99	24.6	16.85	57.53	0.29	491.10	1157.53	20.12
30–39.99	22.6	15.48	40.68	0.38	329.45	666.44	16.38
40–49.99	16.6	11.37	25.21	0.45	195.21	336.99	13.37
50–59.99	9.6	6.58	13.84	0.48	105.48	141.78	10.25
60–69.99	10.6	7.26	7.26	1.00	36.30	36.30	5.00
Total	146.0	100.00			2538.53		

b. *Gila phase population (U:8:24 only)*

x	Dx	dx	lx	qx	Lx	Tx	ex
0–5.5	78.0	56.12	100.00	0.56	395.68	1727.52	17.28
5.5–10.5	7.0	5.04	43.88	0.11	206.83	1331.83	30.35
10.5–14.99	3.0	2.16	38.85	0.06	169.96	1125.00	28.96
15–19.99	3.0	2.16	36.69	0.06	178.06	955.04	26.03
20–29.99	10.4	7.48	34.53	0.22	307.91	776.98	22.50
30–39.99	12.4	8.92	27.05	0.33	225.90	469.06	17.34
40–49.99	10.4	7.48	18.13	0.41	143.88	243.17	13.41
50–59.99	8.4	6.04	10.65	0.57	76.26	99.28	9.32
60–69.99	6.4	4.60	4.60	1.00	23.02	23.02	5.00
Total	139.0	100.00			1727.52		

c. *Combined Roosevelt and Gila phase populations*

x	Dx	dx	lx	qx	Lx	Tx	ex
0–5.5	122	42.81	100.00	0.43	432.28	2142.98	21.43
5.5–10.5	17	5.96	57.19	0.10	271.05	1710.70	29.91
10.5–14.99	4	1.40	51.23	0.03	227.37	1439.65	28.10
15–19.99	10	3.51	49.82	0.07	240.35	1212.28	24.33
20–29.99	35	12.28	46.32	0.27	401.75	971.93	20.98
30–39.99	35	12.28	34.04	0.36	278.95	570.18	16.75
40–49.99	27	9.47	21.75	0.44	170.18	291.23	13.39
50–59.99	18	6.32	12.28	0.51	91.23	121.05	9.86
60–69.99	17	5.96	5.96	1.00	29.82	29.82	5.00
Total	285	100.00			2142.98		

x: age interval
Dx: # of deaths
dx: % of deaths
lx: % survivors entering
qx: probability of death
Lx: total years lived between x and (x+5)
Tx: total years lived after lifetime
ex: life expectancy

Figure 3.1.
Comparative
population profile.

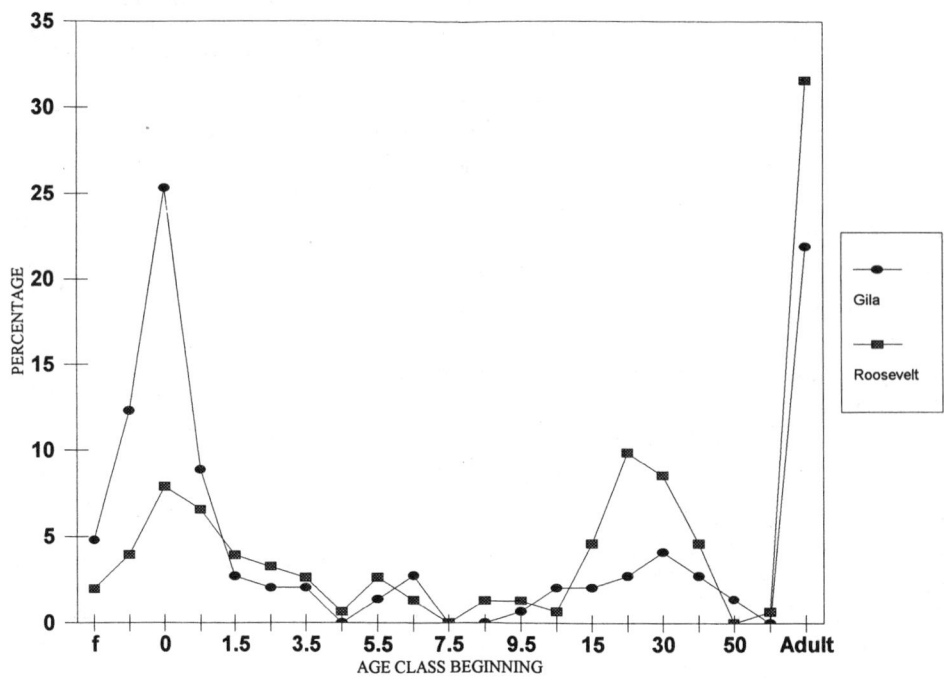

Figure 3.2.
Comparative
survivorship curves.

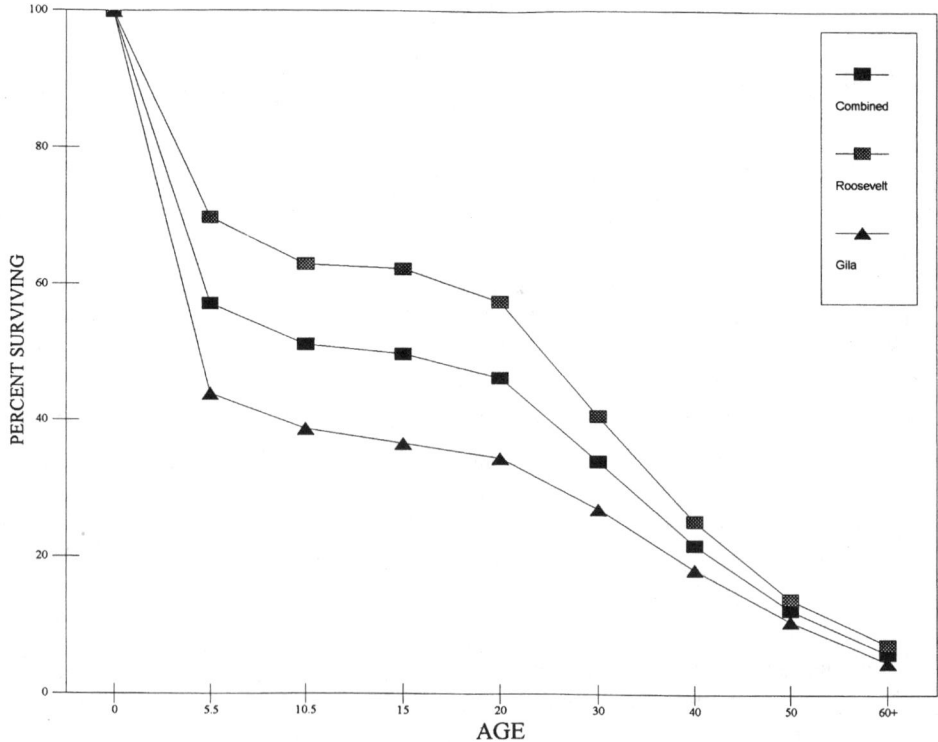

historic Pima cemetery from the Gila River Indian Community (Ravesloot 1992; Regan n.d.). Life expectancies for adult age categories are generally comparable and illustrate that similar forces affected all the populations. Except for the Casas Grandes sample, the greatest among-sample variation is in life expectancies at birth. These variations can be explained by examining the actual numbers of individuals within the youngest age categories and appreciating how life tables work. The composite abridged life tables that are routinely calculated for prehistoric populations only accurately reflect the true underlying population dynamics if the donor population was stable and stationary; that is, if the population was neither growing nor declining. Populations that are growing or declining generate mortality samples that do not reflect existing population dynamics. Prehistoric populations that were increasing, whether from increased fertility or immigration, generate mortality profiles that underestimate life expectancy at birth, while population decline overestimates life expectancy at birth (Noss 1986; Paine 1994; Sattenspiel and Harpending 1983).

It is unlikely that any of the Southwestern prehistoric skeletal samples meet the criteria for a stable, stationary population. Therefore, the differences in the estimated life expectancies at birth should not be taken primarily to indicate health or mortality differences in the youngest age classes. The adult age classes, however, are fairly insensitive to fluctuations in the numbers of infants and children (Moore et al. 1975) and provide relatively good comparative data. With these points in mind, let us consider the major variations in life tables from the Southwestern comparative samples.

First, the Hohokam series from Grand Canal and Casa Buena exhibits an exceptionally high life expectancy in the youngest age group. Examination of the age structure of the samples, though, reveals that subadults are highly under represented—only 13 percent of the population was under the age of 15 years, a percentage that falls outside what is considered normal and should lead to rejection of this life expectancy estimation (based on criteria in Weiss 1973). But because infant and child under enumeration only affects life table calculations in the younger age categories, the adult life expectancy estimates are probably still valid. This Hohokam life table begs an explanation of why there are so few in the youngest age categories. It is so often assumed that infants and young children are underrepresented due to preservational differences (Brothwell 1971; Genoves 1970) that this assumption risks becoming a truism. However, the large numbers of fetal, neonatal, and infant remains recovered from large sites such as Grasshopper (Ezzo 1993; Hinkes 1983;) and Schoolhouse Point Mound (Regan et al. 1996) indicate that the vagaries of preservation cannot always be invoked. More telling still is the Hohokam series from Pueblo Grande, in which over 28 percent of the sample was under the age of four years (Van Gerven and Sheridan 1994). The underrepresentation of subadults at Grand Canal and Casa Buena may be the result of excavation practices, or it may signal demographic nonstationarity, specifically emigration.

Second, the Casas Grandes series (Medio period, 1200 to 1450) reveals very low adult life expectancies, due to a clustering of adults in the 20–29.9 year age category. Without redistribution of the unaged adults, the Casas Grandes sample has as many individuals in the 20–29.9 year age groups as there are in the 0–4.9 age group. With redistribution, there are more individuals in this young adult category than in the youngest subadult category. Such a pattern is unlike any patterns commonly seen in either prehistoric or historic populations. Explanations for this pattern could involve sampling and/or warfare deaths (Ravesloot 1988).

Finally, the Grasshopper sample exhibits the lowest life expectancy in the youngest age categories, but comparable life expectancies in the adult age groups. Questions have been raised about the representativeness of the Grasshopper skeletons (Cordell et al. 1987), but further analysis has shown that, while there are significant deviations from model predictions, the overall representativeness is good (Paine 1989). The observed low life expectancies have three possible explanations. One, there truly were more infant and childhood deaths, possibly indicating poorer health for the infants; Hinkes (1983) demonstrated that subadult skeletons from Grasshopper present numerous pathologies. Two, archaeological sampling may have preferentially targeted areas in which infants and young children were buried and bypassed the areas in which the adults were interred. Three, the increased numbers of infants and young children could indicate increased immigration to the pueblo, because in the skeletal record, immigration mimics increased childhood mortality (Johanson and Horowitz 1986; Paine 1994). Given the explosive growth of the pueblo (Graves et al. 1982; Longacre 1976), immigration is a likely explanation for the demographic picture.

On a regional scale, adult life history forces were similar among all the comparative populations, with the possible exception of Casas Grandes. The largest variations among samples are in the life expectancies for the youngest age group, but this is also the age group that is most affected by demographic nonstationarity. The variances among the samples raise more questions than they answer, questions about population movements, fertility, or decreasing health.

The demographic picture for Tonto Basin does not differentiate it from other Southwestern populations. Adult and subadult life expectancies for all populations are broadly similar, with those of the older Tonto Basin children slightly better than in the comparative samples. The overall good life expectancies and lower childhood mortality levels for Tonto Basin are reflected in the dental and skeletal data, which show lower levels of indicators of childhood disease and nutritional stress.

HEALTH

Disease and poor nutrition were significant stress factors in the prehistoric Southwest (Martin 1994; Palkovich 1985). Surprisingly, evidence from Tonto Basin indicates that health, while far from perfect, was better than in that of contemporaneous populations elsewhere. Relatively lower levels of hard tissue pathology suggest fewer and less severe disease episodes or nutritional insults than elsewhere in the Southwest. This is not to say that Tonto Basin populations were pictures of good health. Far from it, they displayed a wide variety of diseases, most of which were found throughout the prehistoric Southwest. It is the reduced frequency and severity of the disease expression, coupled with other skeletal and dental evidence, that suggests the disease experience of the Tonto Basin populations was less severe.

Dental Pathology

Dental health is assessed through wear, caries, antemortem tooth loss, enamel hypoplasia formation, and calculus buildup. Because the permanent dentition develops throughout childhood and remains (more or less) throughout adulthood, it provides a longitudinal record of individual health during childhood. Metabolic insults are recorded in the enamel and are lost only through dental wear or tooth loss. Dental caries reflect both the cariogenic quality of the posteruption diet and the nutritional quality of the diet during tooth formation. Similarly, dental wear reflects the abrasiveness of the diet (caused by tough or gritty foods) and the hardness of the

teeth, which is influenced by childhood nutrition. Unhealthy teeth are more than just an aesthetic problem. Rotting teeth can allow oral bacteria to enter the bloodstream (Hillson 1986), leading to abscesses and tooth loss (Scott and Turner 1988). Missing teeth can alter the chewing efficiency of the dentition, resulting in reduced food and nutritional intakes.

Dental wear scores for the Tonto Basin populations, based on the ASU scale of zero to four (Turner et al. 1991), show that dental occlusal wear can be classified as moderate (Grade 2). In comparison, a Classic period Hohokam sample from the Grand Canal site in Phoenix frequently exhibited severe grades of wear (Fink 1989). Dental wear results from chewing tough, fibrous foods or foods with a high grit content. Low wear in the Tonto Basin samples may be due to either less abrasive diets or shorter life spans (since wear is age cumulative) or both. The demographic structure of the population does not indicate that they died earlier than adults in other Southwest populations. Thus, it is likely that diets were less abrasive.

Dental caries frequencies were also lower in Tonto Basin than elsewhere in the Southwest. Less than 41 percent of the observed adults had carious lesions, affecting less than 13 percent of the erupted permanent teeth. Although these frequencies place the Tonto Basin peoples firmly in the range of caries frequencies exhibited by agricultural peoples (Turner 1979), they are lower than the frequencies exhibited by contemporaneous Southwestern populations. For example, at the Hohokam site of Grand Canal, 74 percent of the adults had carious lesions (Fink 1989). Berry (1985b) found that 48 percent of adults at Turkey Creek Pueblo had cingular caries (at the junction of the tooth crown and root). At the Sundown site, three of seven (42.9 percent) adults had carious teeth, but three of the four without caries also had extensive (even total) antemortem tooth loss, some of which was most likely due to carious activity (Merbs and Vestergaard 1985). At Casas Grandes, the "teeth are very worn, attrition being heavy throughout the sample" (Benfer 1968:9). Caries, like dental wear, is age dependent; however, the age structure of the Tonto Basin skeletal sample contains numerous middle-aged and older adults, indicating that age alone does not explain the lower caries frequencies.

Enamel hypoplasias are developmental defects occurring during enamel matrix production, before the tooth is erupted. They have a wide variety of causes including nutritional deficiencies, infectious diseases, and enteropathies such as diarrhea (Pindborg 1982). Enamel hypoplasias were present in 54 percent of observed individuals but in only 22 percent of all recovered permanent teeth. The hypoplasias are slight, and the majority occurred between the third to sixth years of life. In comparison, at Grand Canal Ruins, 87 percent of observed teeth exhibited one or more hypoplastic defect (Fink 1989). All adults at the Carter Ranch Pueblo site exhibited enamel hypoplasias (Danforth et al. 1994). The Pueblo Grande Hohokam exhibited hypoplastic enamel on 99 percent of 216 individuals and on 94 percent of teeth (Karhu and Amon 1994; Karhu et al. 1992).

Tonto Basin teeth, then show lower frequencies of several different pathologies related to diet and disease stress. The evidence indicates that prehistoric Tonto Basin children suffered fewer disease and nutritional insults and that adults had fewer caries than the comparative populations. From a dental perspective, prehistoric Tonto Basin was a relatively healthy place to live.

Skeletal Pathology

Pathological abnormalities of the skeleton indicate chronic health problems. Bone is relatively slow to respond to disease, so that insults of short duration generally leave no marks on the skeleton. Skeletal pathological changes only occur after the individual has been able to mount some resistance to disease or nutritional stress; thus, skeletal pathologies indicate survival beyond the critical initial stress episode. Individuals whose immune systems produce no or only a limited response to infection die quickly and appear in the skeletal record as "healthy" skeletons, i.e., those without pathological abnormalities. Individuals who show skeletal lesions survived for some time after onset of the disease

(were "healthier"), while individuals without skeletal pathology may have succumbed more quickly to the same disease (were less "healthy"). Thus, absence of pathology cannot be interpreted as absence of disease. Similarly, an increase in skeletal pathology over time or space can indicate either an increased incidence of infection or nutritional stress and generally better immune system responses in the more "pathological" group (allowing skeletal pathological responses time to develop) or a shift in disease load toward more chronic diseases. This characteristic of the skeleton has been referred to as "the osteological paradox" (J. W. Wood et al. 1992) and presents a confounding variable in paleopathological interpretation.

Among the most common skeletal pathologies reported for the Southwest are cribra orbitalia and porotic hyperostosis, both of which are considered to be markers of iron deficiency anemia. At Schoolhouse Point Mound, eleven of 33 observable individuals (33.3 percent) had some expression of active or healed cribra orbitalia, porotic hyperostosis, or both. The sample includes adults and children dating to both the Roosevelt and Gila phases (Regan et al. 1996). Expression was scored on a ranked scale with five grades (none, very slight, mild, moderate, severe; Regan et al. 1996). The majority exhibited mild or very slight degrees of expression. Table 3.6 presents comparative data.

The ASU physical anthropology studies are not the first to suggest that the inhabitants of Tonto Basin were healthier than their contemporaries elsewhere in the Southwest. Bassett and Atwell (1985) found few skeletal or dental indications of nutritional stress in their sample from the Ash Creek area. However, estimations of "health" in prehistory are elusive, confounded by the fact

Table 3.6.   Comparison of Frequencies of Porotic Hyperostosis and Cribra Orbitalia

Site	Culture	Ages	Frequencies[1]	Reference
Anasazi (Canyon Bottom)	Anasazi	all	54% (a, h)	El-Najjar et al. 1976
Anasazi (Sage Plain)	Anasazi	all	14.5% (a, h)	El-Najjar et al. 1976
Arroyo Hondo Pueblo		> 5 years	23%	Palkovich 1980
Kechipawan		all	54.7% (a, h)	Lahr and Bowman 1992
Carter Ranch Pueblo	Mogollon	> 2 years	80% (a)	Danforth et al. 1994
Carter Ranch Pueblo	Mogollon	adult (>35 y)	30% (h)	Danforth et al. 1994
Casas Grandes Medio period		all	48%	Weaver (1985)
Grand Canal	Hohokam	adult	43% (h)	Fink and Merbs 1991
La Ciudad	Hohokam	adult	54% (h)	Fink and Merbs 1991
Casa Buena	Hohokam	adult	50% (h)	Fink and Merbs 1991
Pueblo Grande	Hohokam	adult	54% (h)	Mittler and Van Gerven 1994
Schoolhouse Point Mound	Salado	all	33% (a, h)	Regan et al. 1996

[1]a, h: active, healed

Table 3.7. Tuberculosis in the Prehistoric Southwest

Site	Culture	Dates	Reference
Pueblo Bonito, NM	Anasazi	A.D. 828–1130	El-Najjar (1979)
Tocito, NM	Anasazi	A.D. 900–1300	Fink (1985)
Chavez Pass, AZ	Sinagua	A.D. 900–1100	El-Najjar (1979)
Los Muertos, AZ	Hohokam	?	Matthews et al. (1893)
Point of Pines, AZ	Mogollon	A.D. 1282–1450	Micozzi and Kelley (1985)
AZ J:54:9	Kayenta	A.D. 875–975	Sumner (1985)
Schoolhouse Point Mound	Salado	A.D. 1250–1450	Regan et al. (1996)

that, generally, only chronic conditions appear in the skeletal record. If skeletal pathology indicates survival well into disease, and healed porotic hyperostosis in adults indicates survival of childhood anemia, perhaps all afflicted Tonto Basin individuals died before they could develop skeletal evidence of anemia. If this were the case, subadult mortality would be higher for the Salado, thus lowering life expectancy estimates. This is not the case. Thus, the relatively low levels of anemia-related skeletal pathology must indicate sufficient dietary iron, low incidence of anemia-causing gastrointestinal infections, or both.

Tuberculosis was also, in all probability, present in prehistoric Tonto Basin by the Roosevelt phase and possibly earlier. A child (ten years ± 30 months) from Schoolhouse Point Mound had bony pathology suggestive of a long-standing tuberculous infection (Regan et al. 1994). Burial treatment suggests that this child may have belonged to a ceremonially important family, or one of the wealthier families that inhabited Schoolhouse Point Mound. The presence of tuberculosis in Tonto Basin is interesting because of what it implies about regional interaction. Tuberculosis is spread through human-to-human contact (Daniel 1981; Keck et al. 1973) and depends somewhat on social conditions for its maintenance, flourishing under conditions of crowding and less-than-optimal nutrition. The fact that the disease was widespread in the prehistoric Southwest (Table 3.7) suggests significant contact between different groups. Because skeletal tuberculosis develops in only a small percentage of individuals who have had primary tuberculosis, its presence possibly indicates more widespread infection (both active and inactive cases) in the population as a whole.

Subadult Long Bone Lengths

Child health in living populations is a sensitive indicator of a community's nutritional quality and disease load (Eveleth and Tanner 1976; Jenkins 1981; Malina and Himes 1971). Population statistics such as height-for-age, weight-for-height, and weight-for-age summarize the nutritional status of the population (Billewicz and McGregor 1982; Martorell 1989). The corresponding statistic in prehistoric populations is long bone length for dental age. Under the assumption that taller equals healthier, as it does in living populations, prehistoric skeletal samples showing greater subadult long bone lengths are inferred to be generally healthier.

The rather sparse long bone data for Tonto Basin appear to create a conundrum within the generally favorable picture of Salado health. Average long bone lengths for the youngest three age groups, (.0–.5, .5–1.5, and 1.5–2.5 years), which are the only ones with sufficient data, indicate that the Salado subadults were of similar size to the comparative group in the youngest age category but were generally shorter in the .5–1.5 and 1.5–2.5 year age groups (Table 3.8, Figure 3.3a–c; Merchant and Ubelaker 1977; Regan 1988). The easy interpretation would be that the shorter long bones indicate decreased growth and generally poorer health among the Salado than among the comparative groups, especially the Plains Arikara who have much longer average lengths. This interpretation, however, is tough to reconcile with the other physical anthropological information indicating generally better health with fewer childhood metabolic insults.

Examining the nature of a cemetery sample and how individual children become members of that sample shows that the easy and obvious interpretation is not necessarily correct. Subadults in cemetery samples are nature's failures, the ones who, for whatever reason, did not make it to adulthood. They are not representative of their living subadult cohorts. Therefore, subadult skeletons represent only the frailer portion of the population (i.e., those with greater chances of dying). How, then, can average long bone lengths inform us about the health of the subadults, especially about those who did not die?

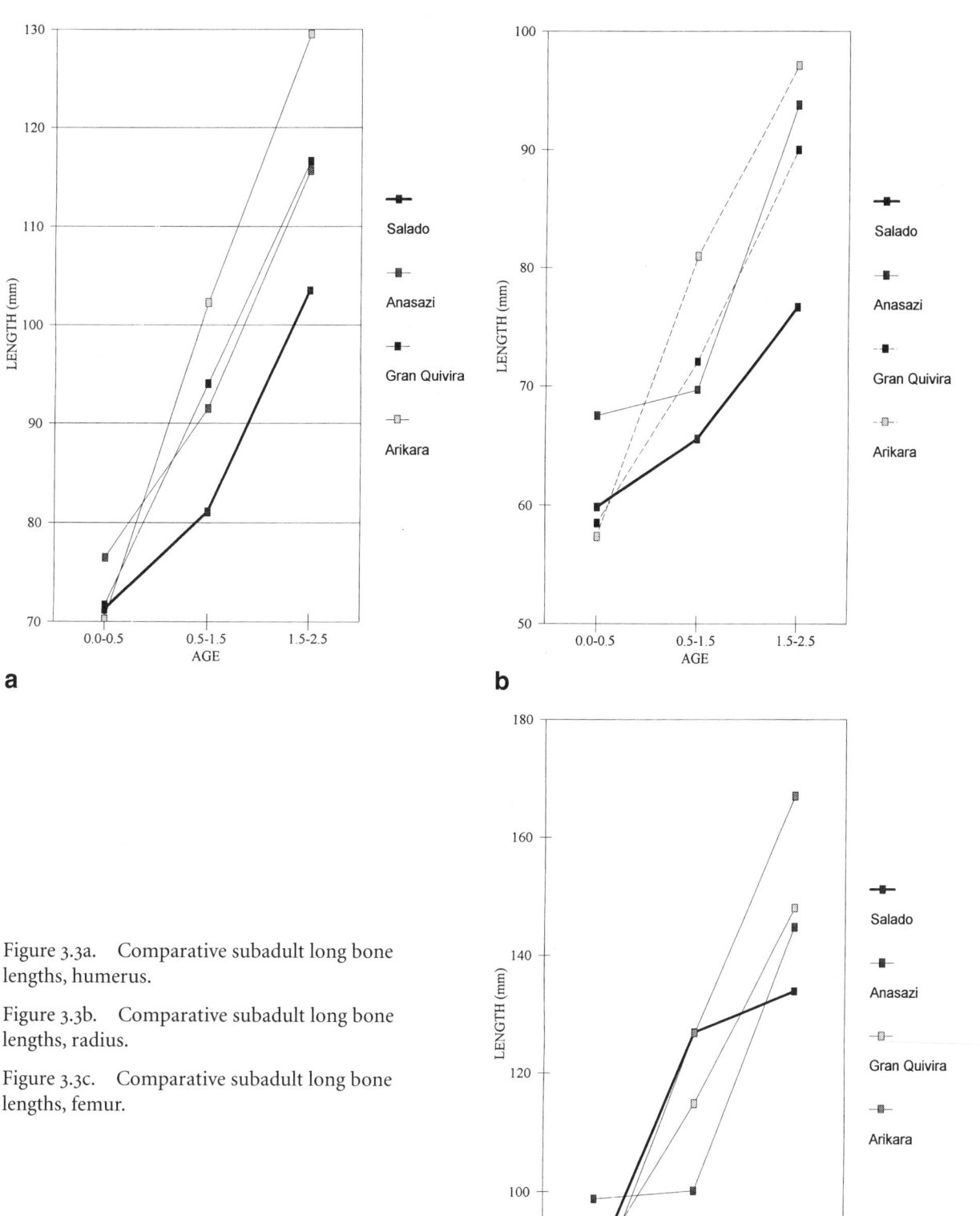

Figure 3.3a.   Comparative subadult long bone lengths, humerus.

Figure 3.3b.   Comparative subadult long bone lengths, radius.

Figure 3.3c.   Comparative subadult long bone lengths, femur.

Table 3.8. Subadult Long Bone Length Averages, in Millimeters

	Age Class	Salado	Anasazi[a]	Gran Quivira[a]	Arikara[b]
Humerus	0.0–0.5	71.29	76.5	71.7	70.25
	0.5–1.5	81.13	91.5	94	102.3
	1.5–2.5	103.5	115.7	116.6	129.5
Radius	0.0–0.5	59.82	67.5	58.5	57.4
	0.5–1.5	65.58	69.7	72.1	81
	1.5–2.5	76.7	93.8	90	97.1
Ulna	0.0–0.5	66.41	65.1	66.2	66.1
	0.5–1.5	74.2	80.3	81.3	92.1
	1.5–2.5	92.3	98	99	108.5
Femur	0.0–0.5	86.47	98.8	87.2	82.2
	0.5–1.5	127	100.2	114.9	126.9
	1.5–2.5	134	144.9	148.1	167.1
Tibia	0.0–0.5	69.59	82.8	74.1	71.6
	0.5–1.5	85.75	84.5	94.8	104.8
	1.5–2.5	120.15	119.6	122.1	138.6
Fibula	0.0–0.5	64.79	—	69.7	68.9
	0.5–1.5	93.7	88.6	93.3	103
	1.5–2.5	116.7	122	119.3	133.2

[a]Comparative data from Regan (1988).
[b]Comparative data from Merchant and Ubelaker (1977).

Undernourished and sickly children are at the most risk of dying, and these individuals also tend to be the shortest. If the smallest individuals are at most risk of dying, these individuals are most likely to enter the cemetery sample. If we imagine that stature within each age group is a relatively normally distributed within each age group, and under "normal" conditions only the shortest members at the small tail of the distribution die, a cemetery sample with greater average long bone lengths indicates that the sample was drawn from a greater portion of the short end of the curve; that is, more of the taller (and supposedly less frail) individuals died. In the "short" sample from Tonto Basin, however, only the shortest (and frailest, we assume) children died, while taller children with long bones lived. Thus, rather than

taller equaling healthier, taller actually indicates that health was poorer for a larger segment of the subadult population. J. W. Wood et al. (1992) explain how higher mortality in an age group increases stature in the cemetery sample. Thus, what at first appeared to indicate poorer health in the Salado really indicates that conditions beyond the first six months of life were relatively good, which caused fewer individuals to enter the cemetery sample. This interpretation fits well with the dental pathological indications of relatively fewer childhood stressors than in other Southwestern populations and with the adult stature estimates.

Adult Stature

Adult stature is one of the better measures of a community's overall nutritional quality. Although final adult stature is due to both genetics and environment, taller adults usually indicate better childhood nutrition with fewer episodes of growth interruption or slowdown. To minimize the influence of genetic differences, Salado statures are compared only to other contemporaneous Southwestern populations (Table 3.9). Stature estimates from eight living populations and one historical skeletal sample are also included.

Male and female stature estimates for Tonto Basin and all comparative samples were calculated according to the formulae of Genoves (1967) using maximum lengths of either the femur or the tibia. The Salado males are taller than any of the other prehistoric samples, and are surpassed only by the historic Pima skeletal series. The Salado females are fourth tallest.

While the evidence points toward better childhood nutrition as the cause of taller adult stature, genetics cannot be totally ruled out. The range of statures among living Southwestern Native Americans is great, as indicated by Scott's (1981) data (Table 3.9), and it may be possible that the Salado are tall because of genetic ties to taller prehistoric Amerindians. Possible genetic influences on stature are discussed in the following section.

BIOLOGICAL AFFINITY

The biological relationships among and between historic and prehistoric Southwestern populations have been extensively studied. Blood groups, anthropometric data, and skeletal and dental metric and nonmetric traits have been used to determine genetic relationships, often with

Table 3.9.   Adult Stature Comparisons

Males(skeletal)

Group	Stature (cm)[l]
Pima (historic)[m]	168.20
Salado[n]	167.02
Grand Canal[b]	165.30
Anasazi[c]	165.04
La Ciudad[d]	164.20
Arroyo Hondo[e]	163.87
Black Mesa[f]	163.40
Casas Grandes[g]	163.11
Carter Ranch[h]	162.20
Gran Quivira[l]	162.20
Casa Buena[i]	162.00
Point of Pines[l]	162.00
Pecos[l]	161.40
Tijeras Canyon[j]	160.13
Puerco Valley[k]	159.60

Females(skeletal)

Group	Stature (cm)[l]
Grand Canal[b]	160.20
La Ciudad[d]	156.40
Arroyo Hondo[e]	156.24
Salado[n]	155.85
Casas Grandes[g]	154.00
Anasazi[c]	154.00
Black Mesa[f]	153.50
Casa Buena[i]	153.00
Puerco Valley[k]	152.81
Tijeras Canyon[j]	150.35
Carter Ranch[h]	147.70

Males (living)[l]

Group	Stature (cm)
Maricopa	174.9
Pima	171.8
Navajo	171.3
Papago	170.9
Taos	164.1
Hopi	163.8
Laguna	163.7
Zuni	163.5

[a]All statures calculated according to Genoves (1967)
[b]Fink (1989)
[c]Regan (1988)
[d]Fink and Merbs (1991)
[e]Palkovich (1980)
[f]Martin et al. (1991)
[g]Benfer (1968)
[h]Danforth et al. (1994)
[i]Barnes (1988)
[j]Ferguson (1980)
[k]Wade (1970)
[l]Scott (1981)
[m]Regan (nd)
[n]Regan et al. (1994)

conflicting results (Bennett 1973b; Corrunccini 1972; El-Najjar 1974, 1978; Hanna 1962; Hooton 1930; Hrdlicka 1931; McWilliams 1974; Merbs 1992; Miller 1981; Scott 1973; Seltzer 1944; Shipman 1982; Spuhler 1954). Data on historic groups indicate biological distances that correspond to linguistic and geographical separations. Studies on living populations may be sampling the effects of historical processes involving reduced interregional contact following Spanish and American incursions.

Data on prehistoric groups may be more ambiguous. While Hooton (1930) found increasing homogeneity through time at Pecos Pueblo, Hrdlicka (1931), using more broadly distributed samples from the Southwest, determined that there were two distinct Pueblo strains. Seltzer (1944), who studied many of the same samples as Hrdlicka, found enough similarity to consider them a homogenous population. Corruccini (1972) found that Puebloan groups formed a distinct population when compared to non-Southwestern samples, but when compared to each other there were significant differences. McWilliams (1974) found significant differences between Gran Quiviran skeletons and some of the other eleven populations that he tested. El-Najjar (1974) found increasing homogeneity over time at Canyon de Chelly. In a later paper, El-Najjar (1978) found further evidence of biological similarities among an expanded comparative sample; within and between group differences were relatively small. Bennett (1973b) found extensive similarities between the earlier and later populations at Point of Pines. Miller (1981) and Shipman (1982) found patterns of biological similarity among their study populations, focusing on central and east-central Arizona, respectively.

There does not appear to be a coherent opinion regarding the biological relationships of the prehistoric populations in the Southwest, except that workers utilizing skeletal series from central and southern Arizona seem to find greater homogeneity than those using skeletons from the Rio Grande or Four Corners regions. Much of the lack of agreement may be due to differences in types of data. What does this mean for how the prehistoric residents of Tonto Basin were related to their contemporaries in the Southwest? Christy Turner's studies of Southwestern Native American dental morphology provides interesting clues to regional genetic relationships (Regan et al. 1996; Turner 1987, 1993; Turner et al. 1994a). In the broadest analysis of prehistoric Southwest teeth to date, Turner (1993) found that the Tonto Basin samples behaved as outliers compared to other Southwest groups. He interpreted this to mean that the Tonto Basin people were a rather mixed population, which he found, "not unreasonable given their rather central geographic location in the Greater Southwest" (1993:52). Turner (1993:52) goes on to say:

> In fact, the Salado are dentally a 'bridging' population between the prehistoric groups of the southern deserts and northern plateau country, through which or aided by; the Hohokam may have moved in among the Hopi.

His sample size was small, consisting of 75 individuals, most from Togetzoge south of Tonto Basin between Superior and Miami. Dental data from the RPMS excavations (Rice et al. 1992) confirm the admixed nature of this population. The earlier Roosevelt phase populations were genetically closer to the Sinagua and Western Anasazi from northern Arizona while the later Gila phase people were more closely related to the Hohokam of southern Arizona. Interestingly, the Mogollon populations from Grasshopper and Point of Pines in eastern Arizona were only distantly related to Tonto Basin populations. Much more closely related were Mimbres and northern Mexican populations.

The statures presented in Table 3.9, when interpreted in the context of Turner's dental findings, suggest that there is a strong genetic component to the taller Tonto Basin statures. Tall stature may be due to better nutrition in childhood, fewer disease episodes, or genetics, or a combination of all three. Because the Salado have genetic ties to the Ho-

hokam and taller desert peoples, we cannot say for sure that increased stature was due solely to environment.

The possibly mixed nature of the Tonto Basin population does not contradict the findings of previous skeletal biological distance studies. The findings of morphological homogeneity (Miller 1981) within broad geographical regions suggests significant gene flow. It is not unreasonable to assume that the Tonto Basin people were in contact with other areas. In fact, the contacts may have extended into Mexico, as suggested by Ramos Polychrome pottery reported at Togetzoge (Schmidt 1928) and modified human teeth found at Schoolhouse Point Mound. These teeth, as described by Turner (Regan et al. 1996), came from two individuals and were modified in different ways. The first individual had longitudinal flakes intentionally removed from the labial (outer) surface of his upper incisors a practice recognized in teeth found in west Mexico (Gill 1985:202). The second individual had minute vertical striations on the upper right first and second incisors, which Turner attributes to tooth polishing. Tooth polishing has been recognized in New World skeletal series only in sacrificial and other burials and skull racks at the Aztec site of Tlatelolco (Christy G. Turner II, unpublished observations). Because of the fragmentary and historically disturbed nature of the burial from which these teeth came, it is impossible to determine whether the teeth were from Mesoamericans or from Tonto Basin individuals imitating Mesoamericans. Either way, it speaks for wide-ranging contacts between the Basin and the rest of the Southwest.

Mortuary Practices

There is no single burial practice that characterizes sites with Salado polychrome pottery, nor do burial practices change dramatically in most areas when the Salado polychrome appear. If anything, the period in which Salado pottery occurs in the Southwest is characterized by a dizzying variety of burial practices, with multiple practices within single sites (Crown 1994:201).

The variability in mortuary practices described by Crown has led some archaeologists (Hohmann 1985a, 1985b, 1992b; Hohmann and Kelley 1988; Rice 1990b) to argue that the Salado were characterized by regional integration and social hierarchies, where recruitment to the most important social positions in the society was based on ascription rather than achievement. Rice (1992) has proposed that the people who made and occupied the Tonto Basin platform mounds were organized on the basis of a system of ranked segmentary lineages. Turquoise-mosaic pendants with frog or bird motifs are believed by Hohmann and Kelley (1988:34) to represent symbols or badges of status and authority within a regional social hierarchy. Others have rejected the elite paradigm and argued that the variability in mortuary treatments observed in Salado cemeteries reflects an organizational structure that is more consistent with the sacred and ceremonial nature of clan, sodality, and kin-based memberships (Reid 1989; Whittlesey 1978; Whittlesey and Ciolek-Torrello 1992). Whittlesey and Ciolek-Torrello (1992:321) argue that clan and kin-based organizational structures and elaborate ritual systems fashioned after the Hopi model functioned to integrate Salado populations during times of stress and uncertainty. In contrast to the elite model, Salado social organization is viewed as most closely resembling an egalitarian form where differential recruitment to social positions can be explained by an individual's personal abilities and the simple biological parameters of age and sex.

How did the "Salado" socially differentiate their dead through mortuary treatments? Is this mortuary variability attributable to the age, sex, and/or personal abilities of the deceased, or were other criteria employed to differentiate the dead? General trends in the mortuary practices of the prehistoric Tonto Basin Salado and other late prehistoric central Arizona populations illuminate alternative perspectives on social complexity and the question of Salado ethnic identity.

Form of Interment

Primary inhumation in an extended supine position was the standard mortuary treatment observed at Roosevelt and Gila phase sites in Tonto Basin. Thirty (91 percent) burials from the Livingston area sites on the south side of the Salt River were found to have been interred in such a manner (Ravesloot 1994b). Other forms included cremations and secondary burials (true secondary or disturbed primary?).

Cremation, a common mortuary treatment prior to 1250, appears to have been restricted to a small portion of most communities during the Roosevelt phase. Loendorf (1996a) reports that only 17 (seven percent) of the Roosevelt phase burials from Schoolhouse Point Mound were cremations. This low frequency of cremat-

ing the dead during the Roosevelt phase also compares favorably on a regional scale (Hohmann 1992b; Ravesloot 1990). By the Gila phase this treatment was virtually nonexistent.

The shift from predominately cremation to inhumation burials across a broad area at roughly the same time has intrigued archaeologists since the change was first observed. Over a century ago, the discovery of both cremations and primary inhumations at the Classic period Hohokam site of Los Muertos led Cushing to conclude that the differences in burial treatment reflected a two-class society: priests and commoners. Some fifty years later, this variability was attributed by Haury (1945) to ethnic differences in the Los Muertos population. Doyel (1981:51–52) has argued that these distinctive treatments represent different ideological traditions. More recently, Loendorf (1996a) suggested that a scarcity of fuel may have precipitated the change from one form to the other.

Orientation

Orientation does not appear to differentiate males from females or adults from subadults. Nevertheless, a preference for an eastern orientation of the head has been documented at Salado sites (Haury 1930; Hohmann 1985b, 1992; Loendorf 1996a; Ravesloot 1990, 1994b). A similar pattern has been observed at Classic period Hohokam sites in the Phoenix Basin (Effland 1988; Mitchell 1992; Mitchell et al. 1989). This practice parallels modern Pueblo mortuary rites, in which head orientation to the east reflects the direction in which the deceased individual's journey to the underworld begins (Ellis 1968:65; Parsons 1939:70). Alternatively, Merbs (Merbs and Brunson 1987) suggested that the prehistoric Hohokam practice of eastern orientation may represent an attempt to bury their dead towards the sunrise.

Location of Cemetery

Previous studies have noted that Salado dead were most often buried in formal extramural disposal areas such as courtyards, plazas, and trash mounds, although some individuals were interred in the fill of earlier pithouses or in the fill or below the floors of habitation rooms (Doyel 1978; Hartman 1987; Hohmann 1985a; Ravesloot 1990). Hohmann (1985a:219) suggested that burial in formal disposal areas reflected a social organization that was characterized by "a limited form of social differentiation with an achieved ranking system founded on age distinctions." Burial in formal extramural cemeteries was practiced during both the Roosevelt and Gila phases; however, burial, particularly of infants, below the floors of living rooms, appears to have been more prevalent during the Gila phase.

Following the argument of others (Goldstein 1981; Mitchell 1992; Saxe 1970) that corporate groups maintain formal burial areas for the exclusive use of their dead, Loendorf (1996a) proposes that multiple corporate groups may have occupied Schoolhouse Point Mound during the Roosevelt and Gila phases.

What direct evidence is there for kin groups' utilizing discrete burial areas at Schoolhouse Point Mound? We suspect that a multiple grave represents a family tomb containing more than one generation, since there is skeletal evidence for a genetic relationship among four of the six individuals interred there. The four individuals (24 and 36 year-old males, and 40 to 50 and 48 to 50 year-old females) had fused middle and distal toe phalanges, which is genetic in origin (Sarrafian 1983:102). A 17 to 22 year-old female from the same grave lacked fused phalanges but did have various other developmental deviations of the foot (Regan et al. 1996).

Cemeteries may have also been established and maintained by social groups who abandoned Roosevelt phase(?) residential compounds during the Gila phase (Loendorf 1996a; Ravesloot 1990). Several sites in Tonto Basin (i.e., U:8:450 [Loendorf 1996a] and Ash Creek [Hohmann 1985a]) exhibit extensive evidence of long-term use as cemeteries, since the number of burials recovered from them far exceeds the size of the population that could have lived there at any one time. For example, 66 burial features containing 78 individuals were unearthed at U:8:450, a residential compound south of Schoolhouse Point Mound.

Form of Grave Facility

Salado burials, especially those associated with Roosevelt phase compounds, commonly are described as being interred in simple earthen pits (Doyel 1978; Hohmann and Kelley 1988; Ravesloot 1990). While many Saladoans were buried in this fashion, others were afforded more labor intensive grave facilities. In Tonto Basin, graves other than simple pits have been found at residential compounds and platform mounds occupied during the Roosevelt and Gila phases. Some pits had been lined with clay or stone slabs, while others were constructed with ledges and/or benches and roofed with timbers and/or stone caps (Haury 1930; Hohmann 1985a; Loendorf 1996a; Loendorf et al. 1995; Ravesloot 1990, 1994b). In many of these graves, a small crypt large enough to accommodate a body or bodies was excavated on one side of the shaft. The interment of multiple individuals does not appear to have been restricted to any particular age group or sex, since adults and subadults and males and females are represented.

Variability in grave construction has been studied by Hohmann (1985a, 1992b; Hohmann and Kelley 1988) to measure the relative levels of energy expended in Salado mortuary ritual. This categorization of burials follows the energy expenditure approach proposed by Tainter (1975, 1978) to investigate ascriptive social ranking with mortuary data. Hohmann (1985a) suggests that graves requiring more energy to construct were restricted to small segments of Salado burial populations. Although not all Salado corpses were interred in benched, roofed, crypt-like graves, no evidence supports the proposition that the level of energy expended in grave construction is a direct measure of social status. At least in the Salado heartland, similar grave facilities have been documented at both residential compounds and platform mounds. The vandalized condition of most Tonto Basin cemeteries, particularly those at platform mounds, makes it impossible to determine if the construction of crypt-like graves was restricted to a small segment of the society.

The construction of benched and crypt-like graves with roofs was not restricted solely to populations that inhabited Tonto Basin. Log roofs on graves have also been reported for Kinishba Pueblo (Cummings 1940), Grasshopper Pueblo (Whittlesey 1978), and Rye Creek Ruin (Haury 1930). Cummings (1940:95) reports that, at Kinishba, "In two instances the body had been covered with a roof of poles and bark before the covering of earth was added." At Grasshopper Pueblo, the cribbing rested on a ledge on one or both sides of the grave pit (Whittlesey 1978). Pit and chamber graves, similar to crypt-vaults found in Tonto Basin, have also been observed at Grasshopper Pueblo. Log cribbing to enclose the grave pit or cover the body has also been reported for Pueblo Grande (Mitchell 1992) and other Classic period Hohokam sites in the Phoenix Basin (Effland 1988; Mitchell et al. 1989). Crypt-like or niche graves similar to those in Tonto Basin and Pueblo Grande, commonly referred to as undercut burials, are reported for Tuzigoot (Caywood and Spicer 1935), and Montezuma Castle (Jackson and Van Valkenburg 1954; Schroeder 1947; Wells and Anderson 1988). However, in these cases, the openings of artificially constructed caves or tombs usually were covered with one or more slabs of limestone prior to filling the shaft of the grave (Wells and Anderson 1988).

Historical and modern analogies for crypt or niche graves are reported for the Hopi (Simmons 1942) and the Pima (Grossman 1873; Ravesloot 1992; Russell 1908).

What does the widespread occurrence of crypt-like and bench graves among diverse groups suggest with regard mortuary ritual and world view? We speculate that the construction of "houses" for the dead was related to the belief in life after death. There is no evidence from either the prehistoric or historic record to support the proposition that bench and crypt-like graves were elaborate tombs constructed only for "elite" families or socially prominent individuals.

Postmortem Body Treatments

Red ocher on burials has been observed at many so-called Salado sites (Hohmann 1985a; Hohmann and Kelley 1988; Loendorf 1996a; Loendorf et al. 1995; Ravesloot 1990, 1994a) but never in very high frequencies. Body painting crosscuts all age and sex categories, although it appears to have been more frequently associated with adults than subadults.

Pueblo ethnographies and body and face painting from other prehistoric burials provide potential insights into the cultural significance of this practice for Tonto Basin populations. Whittlesey (1978) has summarized ethnographic references (Eggan 1950; Parsons 1923, 1939:70; White 1942, 1962) to special postmortem face painting of the deceased by Pueblo groups who use face painting to identify membership in clans and ceremonial societies. Eggan (1950:266–67) states:

> The faces of the deceased are painted "to show who it is to our mother." According to some of Parsons's informants, there are special paintings for each clan; the medicine men have special facial paintings regardless of their clan. The facial paintings resemble those of Katsina impersonators, and some of the songs sung over the corpse imply an association with the storm clouds. Some, at least, of the dead go to Wenimatse, the home of the Katsinas in the west [east] near Zuni.

While facial painting has not been reported for Grasshopper Pueblo, Whittlesey (1978:187) observes that 97 percent (n=401) of the burials had pigment, presumably red ocher, on their bodies.

Face and body painting is also reported from Arroyo Hondo, a prehistoric Pueblo, in the northern Rio Grande region (Palkovich 1980). A 44 year-old male's face, arms

and legs had been painted with yellow and white pigment. An adult female had red ocher staining on her feet and legs. Palkovich (1980:60) argues that, "The practice is also strikingly similar to the painting of the corpses of 'Made People' mentioned by Ortiz (1969:96), a parallel that implies a ritual basis for the status distinction." Tewa distinguish between the "Made People" who are the religious leaders and the "Dry Food People" or the ordinary people.

Painting the face of the dead to differentiate priests from commoners is also reported for the protohistoric Zuni Pueblo of Hawikuh. Smith et al. (1966:254) report that the skull of an adult female was painted in, " black under left eye, across nose and upper and lower lips." Black paint was significant, according to Zuni workers, because only priests were given such treatment.

Mitchell (1992, 1994) reports that body painting with red, blue-green, and yellow pigments was observed on bodies of a few (n=37 or 4.3 percent of 850) of the burials from Pueblo Grande. Within this small number of burials, painting was observed most often on the head, although it was also noted on the middle and lower portions of the body.

Based on these prehistoric examples and ethnographic analogies, it is not unreasonable to speculate that the postmortem body painting observed on Salado burials may signify membership in clans and ceremonial societies. The rarity of this postmortem body treatment indicates that it may have been used to differentiate priests from commoners signifying an important ritual status distinction. Another possible explanation for why some individuals were painted with red ocher may be related to ideology or world view. Huntington and Metcalf (1982) note that red is commonly associated among Native American groups with death. Historically red winding cloths and/or red colored clothing were used by the Gila River Pima to wrap the bodies of subadults and adults prior to burial (Ravesloot 1992).

Funerary Accompaniments

Modern Southwestern Puebloan groups are known to have buried their dead with their personal possessions (Ellis 1968; Fewkes 1895; Ortiz 1969). This practice has also been documented for the historic Pima (Ravesloot 1992; Russell 1908) and continues to this day. Among the Pima, variability in funerary accompaniments was related primarily to an individual's gender.

Tonto Basin and other so-called Salado populations apparently held a similar world view and thoughts about death, since the dead were almost always buried with one or more funerary offerings (Hohmann 1985b, 1992b; Loendorf 1996a, 1996c; Ravesloot 1990, 1994b). Pottery was by far the most common item buried with the dead, although the number of types and the range of forms varied considerably. Items of personal adornment such as hair ornaments, *Glycymeris* shell bracelets, and composite necklaces (e.g., beads and pendants fashioned from shell, turquoise, steatite, and argillite) were the second most commonly observed artifact class. Funerary accompaniments other than personal adornment included bone awls, projectile points, bifaces, ground stone, pigments, tabular knives, copper bells, crystals, fossils, concretions, painted sticks, wooden bows, and unworked raw materials (turquoise, azurite). Although funerary accompaniments were not associated with any specific age category or sex, the largest quantity and diversity of funerary objects appears to be associated primarily with adults, both males and females.

Pottery was usually placed along either side of the body from the shoulders to the feet, however, it has also been placed above the head. Most vessels were whole, although some were fragmented and may have been intentionally broken or ritually killed. The purposeful destruction of pottery vessels used to wash the deceased is reported for Pueblo mortuary rituals (Whittlesey 1978; cf. Parsons 1936; Tyler 1964).

The pottery probably held offerings of food and water that were buried with the deceased for the journey of death to the future world. Some of the ceramic vessels may have been personal possessions of the deceased; however, most probably represent offerings of food made by the group(s) recognizing social obligations to the deceased (Whittlesey 1978; Simon and Ravesloot 1995). Compositional analyses of ceramic vessel accompaniments "strongly supports the interpretation that burial pots and their placements may reflect the social relationships of the deceased within the larger community" (Simon and Ravesloot 1995:122).

SALADO POLYCHROMES

Earlier in this paper, we noted that one of the defining characteristics of the Salado, Gila, and Tonto Polychrome pottery, is actually found in extremely low frequencies at most sites. What do we know about the distribution of Gila Polychrome in mortuary contexts? How does it compare to nonmortuary contexts? Was Gila Polychrome commonly interred with the dead, or was it a rare occurrence? Is there any evidence that it was restricted to selected segments of the population? Was it produced primarily as a symbol of "membership in an elite kin group" (Wilcox 1987:172)?

Crown (1994:7) argues that the large-scale spatial distribution of these pottery vessels during the thirteenth–fifteenth centuries reflects the presence of a regional cult or ideology that helped stabilize social relationships. She further argues that the icons portrayed on Salado vessels, "reflect a belief system involving the earth, sun, weather phenomena, impersonations of deities, and fertility" (Crown 1994:7). Salado polychrome vessels, according to Crown, were not associated with a single burial practice and do not appear to have been made exclusively as mortuary accompaniments (Crown 1994:101). Furthermore, in her opinion, no evidence supports the proposition that Salado polychromes were produced as symbols of elite authority or membership in kin groups. Crown (1994:191–92) states: "They occurred with primary and secondary cremations, and with flexed, extended, and multiple inhumations. There was no single rule for head orientation, burial pit construction, alteration of the body prior to burial, placement of the pottery in relation to the body, or placement of the burial pit within the site. The pottery occurred with all age groups and sexes in individual sites." Crown's conclusions, while intriguing, are based to a large extent on museum collections lacking contextual data. Therefore, another look at the Salado polychrome question appears to be warranted. A preliminary review of the distribution of Salado polychromes, specifically Gila and Tonto, from burial contexts is presented in Table 3.10.

About 121 Gila phase burial features at Schoolhouse Point Mound yielded only 13 Salado polychrome vessels (Table 3.10). Gila and Tonto Polychrome account for about six percent of the whole vessels from mortuary contexts. While the sample of Gila and Tonto Polychrome vessels is extremely small, their distribution in burial contexts provides at least limited support for several of Crown's conclusions. Salado polychromes are associated with both adults and subadults, and do not occur more frequently with males or females. This pattern is similar to that at Los Muertos (Brunson 1989) and differs from that at Grasshopper Pueblo (Whittlesey 1978) where polychrome vessels are associated more often with males than females.

Table 3.10. Distribution of Salado Polychrome Pottery from Burials

Site	Percent of Total	Percent of Decor.	Number of Burials	Poly Assoc.
Escalante (Doyel 1974:138–145)	10.2	87.8	20	0
University Indian Ruin (Hayden 1957:122)	4.1	13.5	4	0
Pueblo Grande (Peterson 1995:375, 399)	3.3	90.0	600 460 dated	14
AZ U:3:49 (Hohmann 1985a:243–266)			73	3
Schoolhouse Point Mound (Ravesloot and Loendorf 1996; Simon 1996a)	10.6	67.6 40.2 Gila 16.6 Tonto 10.0 Gila-Tonto	121	10
Togetzoge (Hohmann and Kelley 1988:174–175)			70	15/2.1%
Cline Terrace** (ASM Collections; Simon 1997)	36.4 12.7	75.1 91.3 42.0 Gila 25.3 Tonto 22.5 Gila-Tonto	67	118/56.7%
Grasshopper Pueblo*				
Rye Creek Ruin** (ASM Collections)	1.9	7.9	190	8/4.2%
Casas Grandes (Di Peso 1974a; Ravesloot 1988)	2.9	51.7 of intrusives	576	0

*Reid and Whittlesey (1992:223–229) state that Gila Polychrome as traditionally defined is actually scarce; mostly Pinto.
**Data from burial contexts

At the northern end of Tonto Basin, along Tonto Creek, the Cline Terrace Mound shows a somewhat different distribution of Salado polychromes in burial contexts. Seventy-four burial features excavated in the 1930s produced an assemblage of 324 ceramic vessel accompaniments (Arizona State Museum collections and archives). This assemblage is interesting from a number of perspectives, not the least of which is the large number of Salado polychrome vessels in burial contexts. Salado polychromes account for 121 (77 percent) of the decorated mortuary vessels. Of this total, Gila Polychrome (n=97) was more abundant than Tonto Polychrome (n=21). The number of Gila Polychrome vessels interred with a single burial varies from one to 13. Regrettably, we have no information on the skeletal remains themselves,

nor the placement of the vessels in relation to the body.

In contrast to previously discussed sites, such as Schoolhouse Point Mound, the frequency of Salado polychromes in mortuary contexts at Cline Terrace is striking. Was Cline Terrace simply occupied later than Schoolhouse Point Mound? Was Gila Polychrome produced on a larger scale than at other Tonto Basin sites?

As we move north, the frequency of Salado (Gila) polychromes in burials decreases substantially, while yellow wares become more prevalent. Craig and Doelle (1990) argue that the Rye Creek Ruin, a fourteenth to fifteenth century platform mound village of about 150 rooms, at the junction of Deer and Rye Creeks (Gladwin 1957; Haury 1930), coincides with the northern boundary of the platform mound system.

One hundred and ninety burials were excavated from Rye Creek Ruin in 1929 and 1930, 160 by two Roosevelt Lake area residents in 1929, and 30 by Gila Pueblo archaeologists in 1930 (Haury 1930, personal communication 1989). The Rye Creek Ruin burial ceramic collection consists of 417 vessels, 316 (75 percent) of which are plain, red, and corrugated wares. Eight Gila Polychrome vessels account for 10.5 percent of the decorated assemblage. Contextual information is available for only one of the Gila Polychrome vessels, which was interred with an infant (Haury 1930:26). What do the low frequencies of Gila Polychrome in mortuary contexts at Rye Creek Ruin indicate? Was Gila Polychrome in short supply or rare at Rye Creek? Or do the low frequencies simply indicate that the site is located on the northern boundary of the distribution of Gila Polychrome.

In contrast, yellow wares such as Jeddito and Awatovi Black-on-yellow and Bidahochi, Fourmile, Homolovi, and Sikyatki Polychrome comprise over half of the decorated vessels from burials. The large percentage of Hopi yellow ware may be partially explained by the site's proximity to the Colorado Plateau. Bishop and Canouts's compositional study of several of these vessels indicates that they may have originated in the Awatovi area (Valetta Canouts, personal communication 1995).

To the extreme south, at Casas Grandes, a completely different pattern of Gila Polychrome pottery as a burial accompaniment emerges. Despite being recovered in large quantities from architectural contexts, Gila Polychrome was not utilized as a burial accompaniment (Ravesloot 1988). On the other hand, Escondida Polychrome, considered by some to be an imitation of Gila Polychrome (Brand 1943; Crown 1994; Kidder 1916) was found in burials, but only with individuals with elaborate mortuary treatments (Ravesloot 1988). This and other examples suggests that our understanding of the use of Gila Polychrome as an elite type is far from complete.

CONCLUSIONS

While the skeletal and dental evidence indicates broad similarities among the Salado and other Southwestern populations, it also points up some intriguing differences that indicate possible better health in the Tonto Basin populations. Pathologies of the teeth testify to fewer childhood nutritional or metabolic insults and to better dental health in the adults. Skeletal pathologies show relatively low levels of porotic hyperostosis and cribra orbitalia, and those cases that are present are relatively minor. Even individuals with special mortuary treatments such as postmortem body painting do not exhibit evidence of better skeletal and dental health, which indicates their diets were no better or worse than the majority of the population.

The statistical dental morphological evidence indicates that the Salado are neither more like nor more different from other Southwestern populations, although qualitative comparisons of the Roosevelt Platform Mound Study data suggest greater similarity to the Mogollon than to the Hohokam. These data raise more questions about the Salado than they answer. If genetically they are equidistant from other populations, does "Salado" culture have biological reality? We argue that it does not.

Tonto Basin mortuary patterns exhibit considerable variability but also reveal broad similarities among Salado populations and other late prehistoric and historic Southwestern populations. Variability in mortuary treatment does not necessary equal social status distinctions, nor do similarities signal ethnic ties. The considerable variability among so-called Salado populations, regionally and site-specific, can be explained by the age, sex and personal abilities of the deceased rather than by ascriptive social hierarchies. Mortuary treatments, at least those reported for Tonto Basin, probably reflect an organizational structure that was integrated on the basis of clans, sodalities, kin-based memberships, and roles within ritual systems, with a belief system revolving around water, fertility, and death. Some practices, such as body painting and the inclusion of painted sticks with the deceased, may have differentiated those individuals who held important ceremonial and/or ritual positions in life. Whether these treatments reflect distinctions between priests and commoners and the presence of a religious hierarchy where one's position(s) in life and social status were tied to control of ceremonial knowledge is impossible to assess with the available mortuary data.

Finally, we are not convinced that the concept of the Salado as originally proposed is still a viable and useful construct. In our opinion, the term Salado, like other cultural area concepts devised by archaeologists to classify data and facilitate description, is outdated and to a large extent has outlived its usefulness (see Speth 1988 for a similar view). The concept of the Salado is simply a label for a material culture phenomena, as is the prevailing view of the term Hohokam (Gumerman 1991:6–7). It refers to a time period (1250 to 1450) when Gila Polychrome was being produced and exchanged among prehistoric Southwestern societies.

Judging from the biological and cultural data at hand, we agree with Turner's (1993:52) conclusion that "The Salado identity and affinity remains an intractable problem."

ACKNOWLEDGMENTS

We would like to thank Christy G. Turner II and Joel D. Irish for their contributions to the human biology section and Jeffrey Dean and Patricia Spoerl for their comments on the manuscript. Our thanks also to Brian Ravesloot for help with the reference section of the paper.

CHAPTER FOUR

Tonto Basin Demography in a Regional Perspective

William H. Doelle

THE STUDY OF PREHISTORIC DEMOGRAPHY IS COMPLI-cated greatly by the difficult measurement problems that must be confronted. For this reason, this paper addresses only an essential core set of issues. The primary intent is to place the demographic trajectory of Tonto Basin into a broader regional context. This involves characterizing population magnitude for a large study region at roughly 100-year intervals. The maps that display this information provide a view of regional population structure and scale and how these two variables change over time. The term *scale* refers to an estimate of absolute population size. Small differences are not considered relevant, but it is very important to know whether a particular subarea such as Tonto Basin reached a peak population in the 2,500 to 5,000, 5,000 to 10,000, or 10,000 to 20,000 range. In addition, it is important to know whether an area such as Tonto Basin had a population similar to that of sur-rounding areas, or if it was appreciably different. Popu-lation *structure* relates to how population density varied over space, and the goal here is to characterize the rela-tive differences between areas. Thus, establishing that population was roughly three times greater in one area than in another provides a basis for weighing the relative importance of demographic variables in those two areas. In summary, the goals of this paper are ambitious in that population size is being estimated for a relatively large region. On the other hand, the many problems of measure-ment are clearly recognized, and the inferences drawn from the regional numbers are kept relatively modest.

Due to recent research in Tonto Basin, it has been possible to set detailed goals in this subarea. Scale is still important, and is examined on the levels of the house-hold, the settlement, the local community, and the basin. Of particular interest is population change over the more than 1,000 years that are represented by sites excavated as part of the Bureau of Reclamation's Roosevelt Lake projects. The population estimates that have been devel-oped allow the calculation of rates of change on a phase level, measures that can provide insights into issues of population movement that are important topics in the Roosevelt Community Development Study (RCD) re-search program (Doelle, Wallace, Elson, and Craig 1992).

Multiple scenarios of population size are considered for both Tonto Basin and the regional study area. For the Tonto Basin, a "preferred" estimate is suggested, but two other estimates that display variability in the data are also presented. On the regional level, an "unadjusted" estimate is developed directly from the archaeological data base, and an "adjusted" estimate is presented in which several potential sources of error are considered. The presentation of several options underscores that this chapter is not intended to come up with numbers that represent final answers. The goal is to provide a better understanding of demographic scale and the role that demographic variables may have played in the 1,000-year trajectory of Tonto Basin prehistory considered here.

THE STUDY AREA

This study is conducted on three spatial scales. The first is Tonto Basin, an area that includes both the Upper and Lower Tonto Basins. Second, a region that is centered on the distribution of platform mounds in southern Arizona is used to conduct a large-site study. For this study, site information was gathered for an area of roughly 75,000 km² (Figure 4.1). Third, to provide regional context, this study uses data from adjacent areas that were compiled by Dean et al. (1994). The study area is subdivided into smaller units through a combined consideration of natural hydrological basins as well as cultural criteria.

CHRONOLOGICAL FRAMEWORK

Because of the large area under consideration, there is a crosscutting of numerous local phase systems. Furthermore, data quality and the reliability of dating vary dramatically over the study region. Slightly different approaches are taken for Tonto Basin and the regional study areas. For Tonto Basin, the revised phase system presented in this volume (Elson et al., Chapter 7) is employed. For the large-site study area, population estimates are labeled with absolute dates. These dates represent the currently understood correlations of the various Arizona phase systems with the modern calendar. There also has been an attempt to estimate population at approximate 100-year intervals, but there are some periods where this is not feasible. The initial three estimation points are 700 (650–750), 800 (750–850), and 900 (850–950), which represent midpoints of 100-year intervals. As midpoints, they also convey a sort of "average" of the developments that took place in a particular interval.

The later periods require slightly different approaches. Rather than "averages," they are viewed more as "snapshots" that characterize relatively limited periods. The next period is labeled 1000 to 1050 because major social changes, such as the reorganization of the Hohokam ball court system, may have occurred at slightly different times in different subareas. Thus, the population con-

figuration represented under this label includes sites that may not have been absolutely contemporaneous for the entire period. This penalty must be paid when dealing with regional data under our current degree of chronological resolution. However, it is not believed to be a major source of error in the population estimates developed here. The period between 1050 and 1150 is estimated only with tabular data, and estimates are presented as the average of the population for the phases immediately preceding and immediately following this period. This period is very poorly understood throughout the study region, and adequate criteria for identifying sites on a regional scale are not currently available. The subsequent early Classic period suffers from some of the same problems in its early years, and the next time population can be reasonably represented is during roughly the 1250 to 1275 interval. The final estimates are for the period around 1350, a time of very rapid change. Although it is possible that some sites were not absolutely contemporaneous, it is believed that most were. Unresolved issues related to the collapse of the Phoenix Basin platform mound system and the dating of the Polvorón phase make this a difficult time to characterize. Thus, 1350 seems to be about the latest time for which one can assemble a regional data set that can be considered roughly contemporaneous.

For the data set that encompasses the entire Southwest, it has been necessary to force all data into 100-year intervals for the sake of presentation. Thus, these data are presented as values that represent an entire century. For an area such as Chaco Canyon where a major transition is believed to have occurred at 1150, for example, the maximum population of the area at 1150 would represent the entire 1100s. The fact of a population decline would not be displayed until the 1200s. Furthermore, for many areas the time range has been extended beyond the points where population estimates existed. Thus for southern Arizona and the San Juan Basin, population was projected back to 200 in order to provide a somewhat more realistic perspective on the growth of population in the Greater Southwest. For this a growth rate of 0.1 percent was considered to have characterized the area in earlier centuries. In addition, it was necessary to provide projections into the 1400s for several areas. The results are clearly not "hard" numbers, but they do serve to fill in some of the critical pieces of missing data in the regional population curve that was presented by Dean et al. (1994).

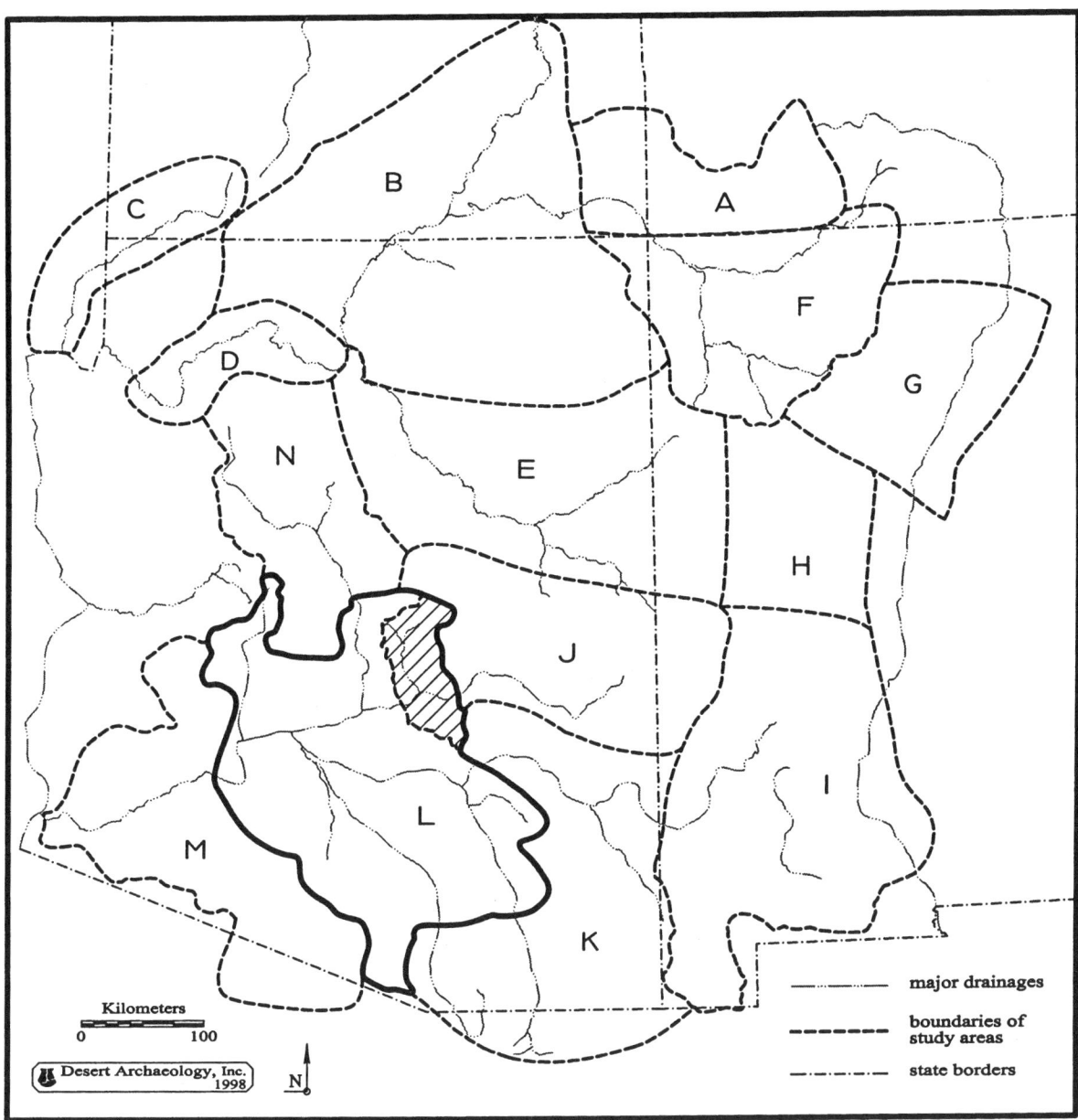

Figure 4.1. The regional study and its subdivisions.

TONTO BASIN POPULATION

The data quality for the RCD study allows a much more intensive assessment of population for the four mile length of the project area than for the rest of Tonto Basin. The combination of mapping, testing, and intensive excavation allows estimation of total numbers of houses and households for both the Preclassic period, when pithouses were the residential norm, and for the Classic period, when masonry rooms were the standard residential structure. For Tonto Basin as a whole, the substantially greater visibility of Classic period structures results in a reasonably complete inventory of medium and large sites dating to this time. For Preclassic times, however, the existing data inventory cannot be considered representative and is very likely misleading.

Due to the possible impact of nonlocal populations on the residents of Tonto Basin (Clark 1995b; Elson, Gregory, and Stark 1995; Stark, Clark, and Elson 1995a, 1995b), special effort is made to examine possible changes in the scale of population inflow or outflow from the Basin. Because of the regional approach to population adopted here, the Tonto Basin study area examined here includes both the Upper and Lower Tonto Basin. Other Roosevelt researchers have considered only the Lower Basin in their discussions of population (e.g., Van West and Altschul 1994; M. R. Waters 1996).

Methods

In the RCD research design, Doelle and Craig (1992:85) point out that corporate groups, which often maintain continuity over several generations, are preferred units on which to base population estimates because their persistence lessens the likelihood of the same unit being counted more than once due to the limits of temporal resolution. Gregory (1995b) argues that courtyard groups and compounds in the RCD sample tend to reflect a size and spatial patterning representing the residential locus of one or more households. The data that Gregory developed are the basis for Table 4.1, which summarizes the numbers of households believed to be present at all RCD Study area habitation sites by period. Estimates for Miami and Roosevelt phase households are derived from Gregory (1995b) and from a study by Wallace (1995b) and are discussed in greater detail with the presentation of results.

The household estimates that have been developed are the basis for three population estimates. A "preferred"

Table 4.1. Estimated Numbers of Households at RCD Preclassic Habitation Sites by Time Period

Zone	Site	Early Gila Butte	Gila Butte and Santa Cruz	Sacaton	Ash Creek
East	Meddler A	3	5	5	3
	Meddler B	—	—	1	2
	AZ V:5:176	—	4	1	—
	Hedge Apple	5	—	—	—
	AZ V:5:92	—	2	2	—
	Porcupine B	—	1	1	1
Central	Eagle Ridge A	—	—	2	2
	AZ V:5:100	—	—	—	2
	Las Manos D	—	2	2	—
	AZ V:5:178	—	—	2	—
	Pyramid A	—	1	1	1
	Pyramid D	—	2	2	—
	AZ V:5:98	—	—	—	1
	AZ V:5:99	—	—	2	—
West	AZ V:5:177	—	—	2	2
	Griffin D	—	1	1	2
	Griffin A	2	2	2	2
Summary: Households by Zone					
	East	8	12	10	6
	Central	0	4	10	6
	West	2	3	5	6
	Total	10	19	25	18

estimate is based on the application of a number of assumptions that appear to be justified by current understanding of Tonto Basin archaeology. The other estimates, labeled the "midpoint" and "high" estimates, minimize these assumptions and provide insights into the implications of both the midpoint and the maximum population sizes suggested by the household data. Consideration of these three estimates ensures that the population issue is not narrowed to a single scenario too quickly. The many unresolved issues of estimation argue for maintaining a multiple model approach.

Household estimates are possible only for the RCD Study area at present. A major issue is how to generalize this detailed information to the much larger, less intensively studied remainder of Tonto Basin where survey data are simply not reliable for the Preclassic period. The approach taken is to consider the RCD Study area, a continuous four-mile segment of the Salt River, as a representative unit, and to use those data to extrapolate demographic processes in other stretches of the drainage system. In this manner, Tonto Basin was subdivided into 21 four-mile zones. Gregory (1995b) points out the uniqueness of the RCD Study area along a large and very stable meander of the Salt River. If the RCD area was a preferred location, it may have had a higher population level than other areas. This presents a problem because the method of estimating population assumes that all other four-mile segments of the river were equivalent to the RCD area. To correct for this possible over representation, the RCD data were reduced to roughly 80 percent of their estimated population values. This is simply a best guess.

The nature of the archaeological record in Tonto Basin creates very different visibility issues for the Preclassic and Classic periods. The pithouse architecture that characterized the entire Preclassic occupation results in archaeological sites with very low visibility. In contrast, the Classic period is characterized by masonry architecture that is usually easily visible on the ground surface. This sharp contrast in the archaeological record means that Preclassic sites are dramatically under represented in the available archaeological surveys. This was the principal reason that the method of projecting the RCD data to the other zones of the Basin had to be developed. However, there is a very good inventory of Classic period sites for Tonto Basin. Because of this, it is possible to use the actual site distribution data when making the preferred population estimate for the entire Basin for the Roosevelt and Gila phases. However, even for the Classic period, the projection of RCD data to the 21 zones is used to derive the maximum and midpoint estimates.

Tonto Basin Population Estimates

Before making estimates, it is important to review the data by period so that any bridging assumptions are identified and discussed. Population size can then be estimated, and the implications of those estimates considered.

Phase-Specific Considerations

A major and unanticipated outcome of the RCD fieldwork is the documentation of an Early Ceramic period occupation at the Eagle Ridge site (V:5:104; Elson and Lindeman 1994). Gregory (1995b) reviews the hypothesis that there may be temporal continuity between the Early Ceramic period and early sites in Upper Tonto Basin, such as Deer Creek (Swartz 1992) and Ushklish (Haas 1971), where Snaketown phase ceramics were present in very low frequencies. The alternate hypothesis—that there was a hiatus in occupation between the Early Ceramic period and the Snaketown phase, at least in the Salt Arm of Tonto Basin—is also considered (Elson, Gregory, and Stark 1995; Gregory 1995b). These researchers favor the idea of continuous occupation, but more survey and excavation are required to resolve this issue.

Because there are no good survey or excavation data for the Snaketown phase in Tonto Basin, the few known early sites are discussed in order to gain insights into the possible scale of population in the Snaketown phase. At the Early Ceramic period Eagle Ridge site (Elson and Lindeman 1994), long continuity, relatively large size, and the presence of probable integrative architecture suggest an occupation of reasonable size, perhaps 25 to 50 persons at its peak. Sites such as Deer Creek (Swartz 1992) and Ushklish (Haas 1971) may provide support for a model for the Snaketown phase of several households living adjacent to favorable agricultural localities throughout Tonto Basin. It seems likely that a population size of 20 to 25 would be a maximum number for a site such as Deer Creek.

From these "known" points, a relatively gross estimate of the Snaketown phase population of Tonto Basin has been made. It assumes that population was evenly distributed over the entire Basin (all 21 four-mile zones), and it assumes a population of 35 persons per zone (the midpoint between the 20 to 50 range that might be expected of early sites). The resulting figure of 735 persons is rounded to 750 for the sake of convenience. This number is intentionally higher than what the survey data can support. Its use is justified by two considerations. First, Early Ceramic period and Snaketown phase sites are difficult to recognize archaeologically. Second, a low starting population would essentially force acceptance of immigration to account for subsequent population sizes achieved in Tonto Basin. Even with this relatively high initial population, it will be argued later that significant immigration into Tonto Basin was likely.

The other Preclassic population estimates can be derived more directly from Table 4.1. This table lists sites from the east end of the RCD project area to the west, and it groups them into eastern, central, and western clusters (zones). Obvious spatial patterns show up on Gregory's (1995b) settlement pattern maps. The summary figures for households by zone in Table 4.1 illustrate that the early settlement distribution was highly clustered but tended to become more even over time. Household estimates are considered to be the average number of households occupied during the phase, and they are used to generate momentary population estimates at the approximate midpoint of each period. Because there are at least minor issues unique to each time period, it is useful to briefly review phase-specific variations in the estimation process.

The intensity of investigation of the Gila Butte occupation in the RCD project area makes it likely that these data are reliable. However, the RCD data also underscore the extent to which this period is likely to be under represented elsewhere. The Hedge Apple site (V:5:189) had an extremely low surface visibility (Swartz and Randolph 1994), and similar sites elsewhere in Tonto Basin could easily be obscured by sedimentation and modern land use, or Roosevelt Lake. Furthermore, in areas such as the Tonto Creek Arm of the Basin, immigration from the Phoenix Basin possibly occurred at a lower rate or did not occur at all, similar perhaps to what has been suggested for the Upper Basin (Elson, Gregory, and Stark 1995; Elson et al. 1992). Thus, the frequencies of diagnostic buff ware ceramics may be much lower at other sites than what was observed at the RCD sites.

Meddler Point (V:5:4) is the largest Gila Butte and Santa Cruz phase occupation in the RCD Study area. However, because temporally mixed Colonial period trash deposits provide the basis for the estimation of households, it has been necessary to lump the latter portion of the Gila Butte phase and the entire Santa Cruz phase into a single category.

There is a substantial increase in the number of households during the Sacaton phase. This increase is especially notable for the central zone, where the number of households more than doubles, from four to ten. Heidke and Stark (1995) argue on the basis of temporally diagnostic ceramics that the sites in this portion of the RCD Study area represent a series of sequential occupations, rather than being long-term throughout both the Sacaton and Ash Creek phases. For this reason, a correction factor, which assumes that only half of the central zone households were contemporaneous, is used in making the preferred population estimate for the Sacaton phase.

The Ash Creek phase presents particular visibility problems. The intensive excavation of Locus A at Eagle Ridge has shown that northern white wares replaced Phoenix Basin buff wares around 1050. This change marks the transition between the Sacaton and Ash Creek phases, though it is known from Eagle Ridge that the occupation of that settlement did not appear to be directly affected by the ceramic shift (Elson, Gregory, and Stark 1995). Only a few relatively rare white ware types serve as diagnostic markers for the Ash Creek phase (see Elson 1996a; Elson and Gregory 1995; and the calibration data sets used by Craig and Clark 1994:169 and Wallace 1995). Because of these identification problems, an undercount of households from this phase is assumed, and the preferred population option is based on a projection that population grew at an average of 0.1 percent per year from the Sacaton phase.

Incomplete visibility continues into the Miami phase. Wallace (1995b) used the midpoint of his estimated range of Miami and Roosevelt phase households and obtained a similar count of nine households for each phase. However, his data on rates of sherd deposition indicate a dramatic increase in the rate for the Roosevelt phase. If this figure is taken as a rough indicator of variation in population size between the two phases, the Miami phase population would be roughly two-thirds of the Roosevelt phase population. This correction factor was used in establishing the Miami phase household count that is used to develop population estimates.

The Roosevelt phase data are by far the strongest in the RCD data set, and no adjustments were made to them. The issue of the transition from the Roosevelt to the Gila phase is less clear, however. All of the RCD sites were abandoned by the end of the Roosevelt phase, as were most of the Livingston sites. Except for Schoolhouse Point, only the Pinto Point Mound shows a significant, but brief, extension into the Gila phase (Jacobs 1994b). Maps of Schoolhouse Point (Lindauer 1996; Rice and Redman 1993) suggest that an estimate of 25 households would be generous for all settlements on Schoolhouse Mesa during the Gila phase. Since this area is the only portion of the eastern end of Tonto Basin that continued to be occupied in the Gila phase, a decline in the local population appears to have taken place.

Estimating Population

The data from Table 4.1 must be converted to population numbers for the RCD Study area. As usual, this path is not a simple one. Table 4.2 presents data for several population options. The number of households comes directly from Table 4.1. Two methods of converting household counts to population estimates are employed. The first uses a range of five to eight persons per household as a constant for each period. The second uses indicators of changing house and household size discussed by Gregory (1995b) as a means to adjust the estimate of household size to better fit the archaeological data. Application of either method indicates a general trend of increasing population size over time, with the possible exception of the Ash Creek and Miami phases. Population estimates generated by the second option result in a narrower range and are used in making the preferred estimate. The midpoint and upper end of the broad ranges provided by the first method are the sources for the "midpoint estimate" and "high estimate," respectively. The midpoint and high options are taken directly from the corresponding population ranges in Table 4.2. The preferred option, however, requires additional explanation.

Early Gila Butte Phase

The higher end of the range was selected due to the concern that there may be sites like Hedge Apple, which was not visible on the surface, in other portions of Tonto Basin. It is also possible that in some areas, intensive later occupations may partially mask early Gila Butte occupations, even in the intensively studied RCD project area.

Gila Butte/Santa Cruz Phase

No obvious adjustments are needed to fit the archaeological record. Selection was made from the lower half of Population Range 2 (Table 4.2), a choice that reduces the rate of change from the previous phase and therefore structures the data to not force a conclusion that immigration occurred.

Sacaton Phase

The number of households in the central section of the RCD Study area occupied at any one time is assumed to be only five instead of ten. This derives from the argument by Heidke and Stark (1995) for sequential occupation of these sites. It also explains why the number (120) is less than those in Population Range 2 (138–63).

Table 4.2. Household Counts and Population Estimates for the RCD Study Area

	Early Gila Butte	Gila Butte & Santa Cruz	Sacaton	Ash Creek	Miami	Roosevelt	Gila
Population Range 1:							
Household Size Range = 5 to 8							
Households	10	19	25	18	24	36	25
Population Range	50–80	95–152	125–200	90–144	120–192	180–288	125–200
Population Range 2:							
Variable household size over time							
Household size	5–6	5–6	5.5–6.5	5–6	5–6	6–7	8
Population Range	50-60	95–114	138–163	90–108	120–144	216–252	200
Three Population Estimates							
Preferred	60	100	120	133	160	216	200
Mid-Point	65	124	162	117	156	234	162
High	80	152	200	144	192	288	200

Ash Creek Phase

Because archaeological visibility is low for this period, it is suspected that the apparent decline in households is not valid. Furthermore, because settlement pattern data suggest that this was not a time of major disruption, it seems possible that population may have continued the gradual upward trend that it had shown in previous phases. Therefore, the preferred option simply assumes a 0.1 percent annual rate of increase over the corrected Sacaton phase figure.

Miami Phase

As noted earlier, based on Wallace's (1995b) information on ceramic deposition rates, Miami phase households are calculated as two-thirds the number of Roosevelt phase households.

Roosevelt Phase

The low end of the range was selected because contemporaneity problems are suspected with at least some sites. For example, some of the compounds are believed to represent sequential, short-term occupations and were not all absolutely contemporaneous (Gregory 1995b).

Gila Phase

The high end of the range was chosen to minimize the contrast with the previous phase.

Demographic estimates from the RCD Study area were extrapolated to Tonto Basin as a whole by taking the three population estimates in Table 4.2 and multiplying them by 16.8. This represents the 21 four-mile segments along the Salt River and Tonto Creek with the application of the 80 percent correction factor discussed earlier (21 x 0.8 = 16.8). For

the Roosevelt and Gila phases, Tonto Basin settlement pattern data are the source of the population estimates for the preferred estimate only. The results of this process are displayed in Table 4.3 and Figure 4.2.

Discussion

Figure 4.2 provides a framework for comparing these three population estimates. Inspection of this figure indicates that each option follows the same general trend of increase from the Snaketown through Roosevelt phases, which is followed by a Gila phase decline. The preferred option is generally lower than the other two, and it is always more gradual in its rate of change. The concurrent display of these options helps maintain an awareness of those periods in which abrupt changes *may* have occurred, and which are being masked by the assumptions inherent in the preferred option estimates.

Before considering the meaning of these population scenarios, it is useful to provide some context for the issue of population change. Hassan (1981:234) suggests that a growth rate of 0.1 percent per year is reasonable to expect for an agricultural population over an extended period of time. Therefore, that rate has been used as a baseline to model what would happen if an initial population of 750 were allowed to grow on its own for 600 years (Figure 4.3). Even after 600 years, the population size would not exceed 1,500 persons. Blake et al. (1986) use a rate of 0.3 percent per year in their study of Mimbres valley population, and if applied here, it does reach the preferred estimate figure of 3,000 by roughly 1300. A third alternative is plotted in Figure 4.3. This maintains a constant internal growth rate of 0.1 percent

Table 4.3. Three Population Estimates by Phase for Tonto Basin

Population Option	Snaketown	Early Gila Butte	Gila Butte & Santa Cruz	Sacaton	Ash Creek	Miami	Roosevelt	Gila
Preferred	750	1,008	1,680	2,016	2,234	2,688	3,150[a]	2,900[a]
Midpoint	750	1,092	2,083	2,721	1,966	2,621	3,931	2,722
Maximum	750	1,344	2,554	3,360	2,419	3,226	4,838	3,360

[a]Roosevelt and Gila phase figures for the preferred option are developed from actual site distribution data for the Tonto Basin.

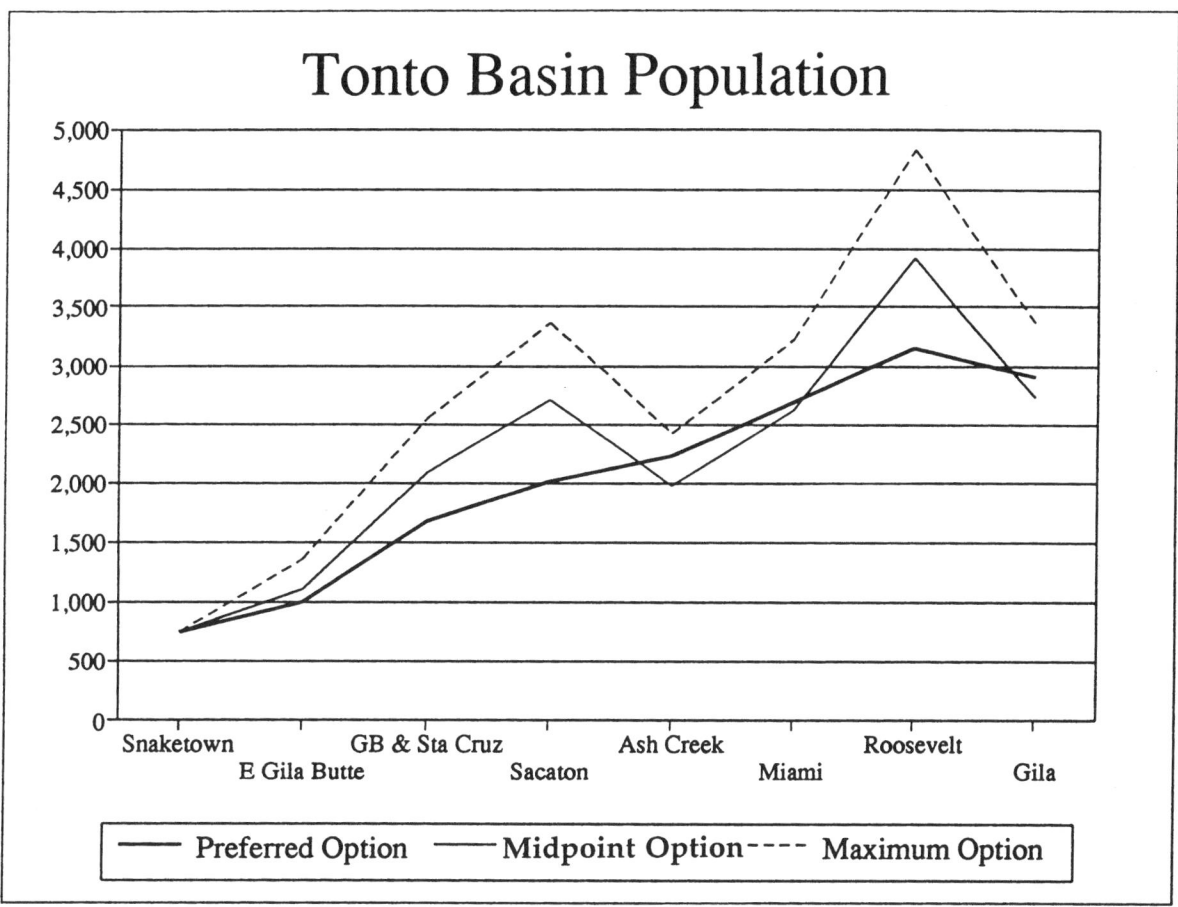

Figure 4.2.   Comparison of three population estimates for Tonto Basin.

annually and also assumes a net immigration of 2.5 persons per year. If household size is assumed to range between 5 and 8, this would average out to an immigration rate of one household every two or three years over the 600-year time span displayed in Figure 4.3. This achieves a population size of 3,000 during the early 1300s, which is suggested by the preferred option in Figure 4.2. This exercise cannot resolve issues regarding migration or internal growth, but it does provide a basis for expecting that a relatively rapid growth rate must have been the case for at least portions of Tonto Basin prehistory. Because the population estimates do not indicate a growth pattern as constant as that shown in Figure 4.3, it is appropriate to return to those estimates to consider further implications.

Table 4.4 presents average annual growth and migration rates derived from the preferred population estimate. The rate estimates begin with early Gila Butte because the table displays the rate of change that took place between the Snaketown phase and early Gila Butte times. This table shows a clear trend. There is an early period (early Gila Butte and Gila Butte/Santa Cruz) when the rate of population increase is very high, between 0.51 and 0.60 percent per year. These rates are significantly higher than the 0.1 percent or the 0.3 percent average growth rate that Hassan (1981) and Blake et al. (1986) deem reasonable for a farming population over the long term, and they are suggestive of immigration into Tonto Basin. The rate decreases during the Sacaton phase to 0.18, and a rate of 0.1 percent was built in as an

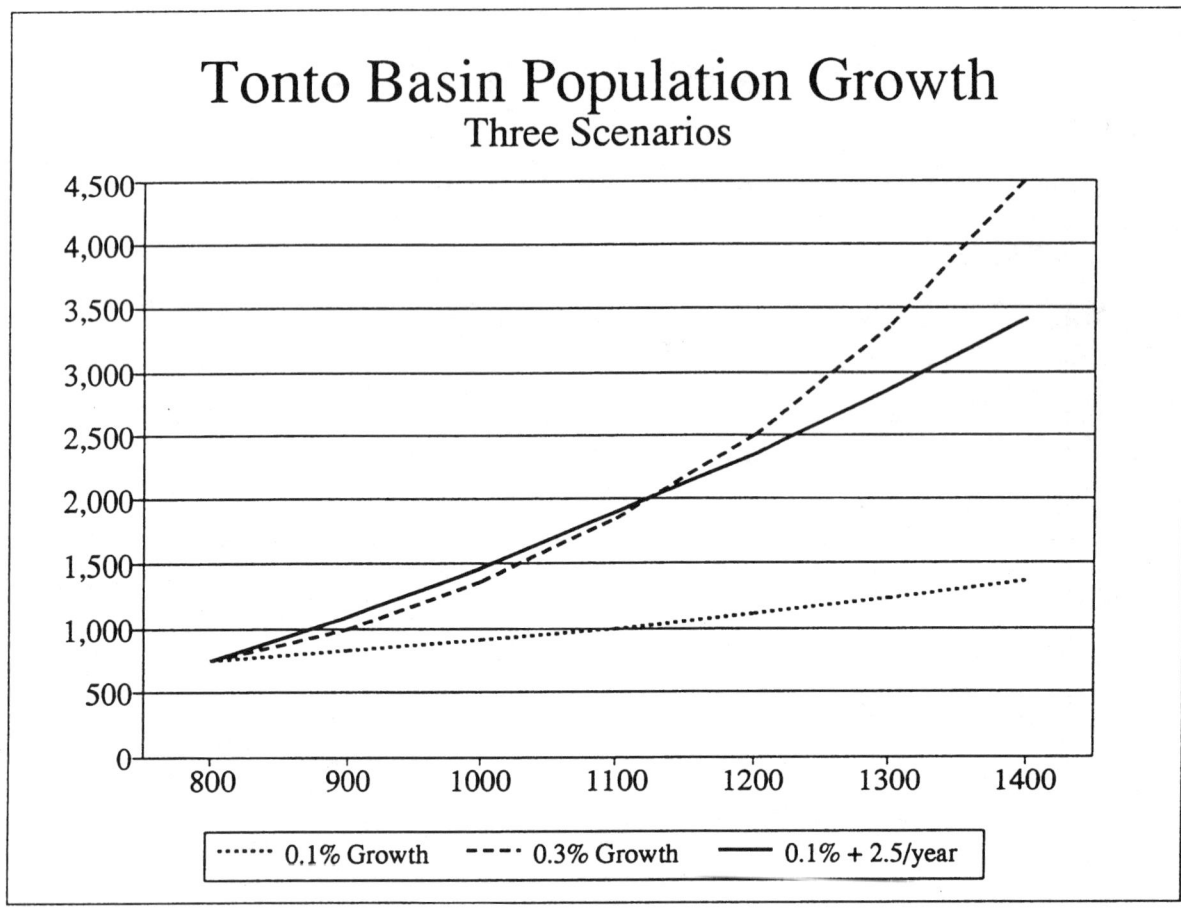

Figure 4.3.   Three hypothetical population growth scenarios for Tonto Basin.

assumption for the following Ash Creek phase. These rates increase to 0.18 and 0.16 for the Miami and Roosevelt phases, respectively. By themselves, rates of change cannot be considered definitive evidence to help distinguish between internal growth and migration for the Sacaton through Roosevelt phases. The negative rate for the Gila phase suggests a final period of emigration.

These data fit reasonably well with the reconstruction of eastern Tonto Basin settlement presented by Elson, Gregory, and Stark (1995) and Gregory (1995b). The archaeological data were used to suggest two periods of immigration: one during the early Colonial period (primarily Gila Butte phase) by Hohokam groups and one during the early Classic period (primarily Roosevelt phase) by pueblo groups. Emigration from Tonto Basin

during the Gila phase is also supported by the settlement data; almost all sites in the eastern Tonto Basin were abandoned at that time.

To put these rate changes into more human terms, Table 4.4 also calculates two possible migration rates. The maximum migration rate is the number of persons per year that would have to move into or out of Tonto Basin if there were no internal population growth. The second rate is how many persons per year would be required to migrate in or out if there were a constant internal growth rate of 0.1 percent per year. Using the latter rate, these data suggest that the early and late periods of immigration would have averaged roughly one household each 1 and 2.5 years, respectively. If household size averaged five persons, this would represent an immigra-

Table 4.4. Using the Preferred Tonto Basin Population Estimate to Calculate Growth Rates and Migration Rates

Tonto Basin Phase	Estimated Population	Population Date (A.D.)	Elapsed Years	Annual Growth Rate (%)	Maximum Migration Rate[a]	Migration Rate[a] with 0.1% Growth
Snaketown	750	750	0	—	—	—
Early Gila Butte	1,008	800	50	+0.60	+5.2	+4.0
Gila Butte & Santa Cruz	1,680	900	100	+0.51	+6.7	+5.4
Sacaton	2,016	1000	100	+0.18	+3.4	+1.4
Ash Creek	2,234	1100	100	+0.10	+2.2	+0.1
Miami	2,688	1200	100	+0.18	+4.5	+2.1
Roosevelt	3,150	1300	100	+0.16	+4.6	+1.7
Gila	2,900	1350	50	−0.17	−5.0	-8.0

[a]Migration rate is expressed as persons per year.

tion of some 148 households over 150 years for the early Gila Butte through Santa Cruz phases and some 76 households over 200 years during the Miami and Roosevelt phases (calculated by multiplying the migration rate by the number of years, then dividing by 5 persons per household).

These numbers are averages for periods of 100 to 150 years. It is expected that actual immigration would have been more episodic than can be modeled here (Clark 1995b). For example, if migration events averaged three households moving at one time, the Gila Butte and Santa Cruz phase immigration could have been accomplished in as few as 50 events, an average of only three per decade. When all of these factors are considered, the scale of population movement does not appear to be great. Furthermore, it seems to fit well with the archaeological data, which suggest that the Colonial period migration from the Phoenix Basin occurred primarily into a few sites. In the later period, there is evidence of relatively small social units (one to a few households) moving into the peripheries of established settlements (Elson, Gregory, and Stark 1995).

Rather than go through the same detail for the other two population options, Figures 4.4 and 4.5 present data for all three options in a comparative framework. Figure 4.4 displays information on the average annual rate of population change, and Figure 4.5 shows the maximum migration rate data. The other options are similar in identifying the same periods of change, though there are variations in magnitude among the options. Generally, the preferred option is smaller in magnitude than the other options. The Gila phase population decline is also highlighted by all options. To place this discussion in a broader context, population estimates for the larger regional setting are developed.

REGIONAL POPULATION

Several approaches are necessary to place Tonto Basin within the context of the entire Southwest. For the area where platform mounds are distributed in southern Arizona, site-level data were assembled. The methods and assumptions used for this study area are presented in greater detail in Doelle (1995a, 1995b) and are briefly summarized here. To expand this data set, the data assembled by Dean et al. (1994) for the entire Southwest were incorporated into this study. Finally, some areas that were not included in either of the above studies were incorporated in at least a preliminary fashion. As a result, data for the subareas shown in Figure 4.1 were compiled. They are presented in aggregated form in later figures and tables.

Figure 4.4.
Comparison of
average annual
growth rates for the
three Tonto Basin
population estimates
(three options).

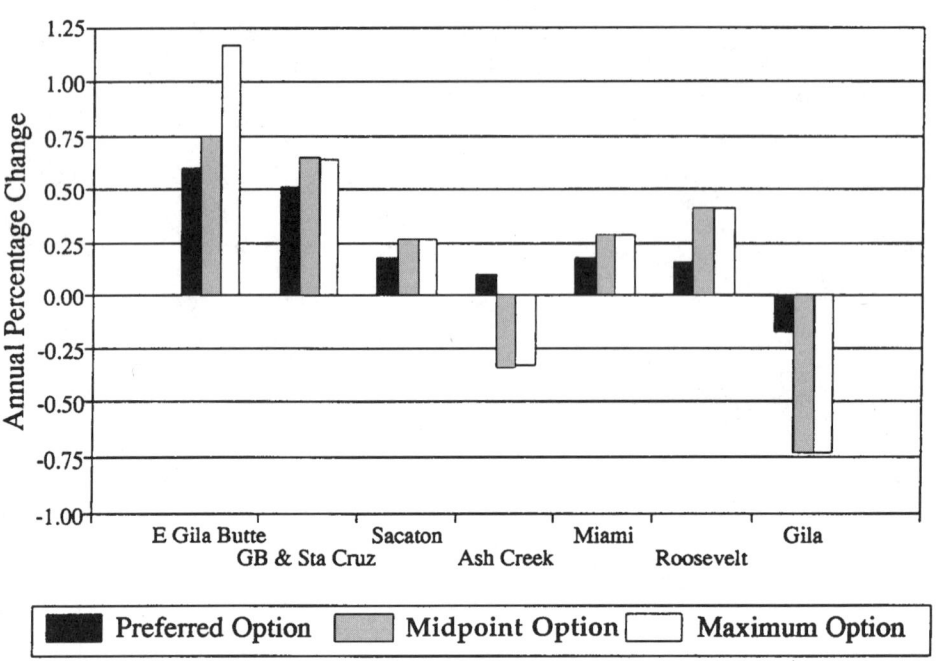

Figure 4.5.
Comparison of
maximum annual
migration rates for
the three Tonto Basin
population estimates
(three options).

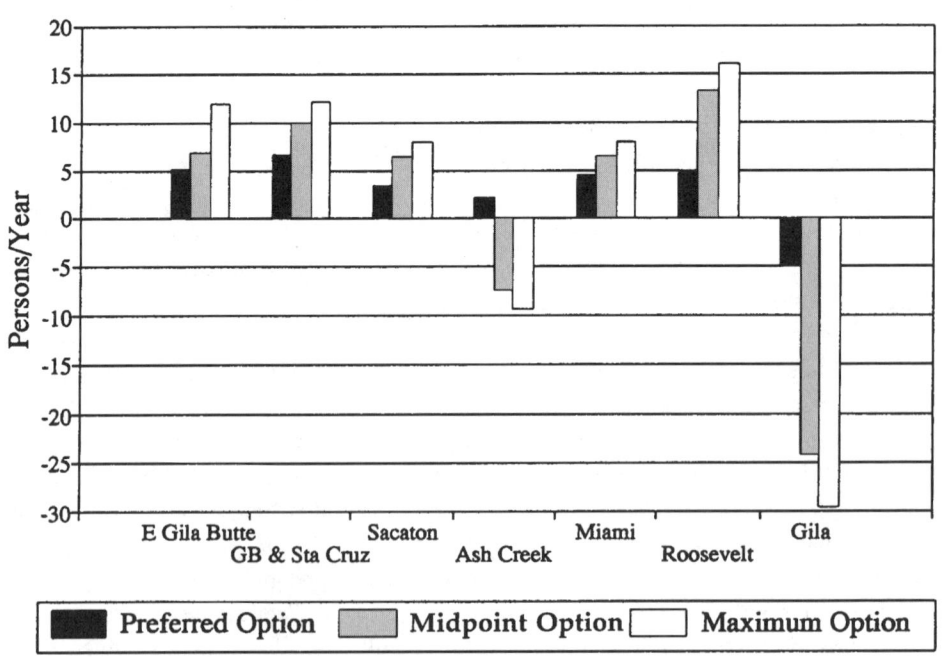

Methods for Using Large-Site Data for a Regional-Scale Population Estimate

Because the area and periods under study in this analysis include both pithouse and masonry house types, an approach depending on numbers of rooms would have little chance of success. Furthermore, much variability exists in the quantity and quality of archaeological surveys that have been completed over the entire region. In the face of these nearly overwhelming obstacles, a "large-site study" was undertaken. By focusing on large sites, the problems of variable survey coverage are greatly reduced. Villages and many of the larger hamlets are often reasonably well known, even in areas that have not received intensive survey. An inventory of large-scale reconnaissance surveys that have taken place over the past century, along with more recent surveys and reassessments of previous work, is provided in Doelle (1995b). For example, the Center for Desert Archaeology recently completed a moderate-intensity survey of nearly 75 miles along the lower San Pedro River (Wallace et al. 1998). There are no published large-scale surveys for the lower San Pedro area, but reconnaissance work by Gila Pueblo, the Arizona State Museum, the Amerind Foundation, Alice Carpenter, and Bruce Masse identified all 14 of the large Classic period habitation sites, 10 of which have platform mounds. Desert Archaeology's survey found no new platform mound sites and only a single ball court that was previously unrecorded. This does not mean that a perfect data set can be compiled from existing records, but it does suggest that a very good data set can be derived from such sources.

Review of a high quality data set from documentary sources provides insight into this large-site method. In a series of papers (Doelle 1981, 1984, 1992; Doelle and Wallace 1990), late seventeenth century documentary sources were employed to address issues of population size and distribution in Pimería Alta. At that time, the population of the area between the Magdalena-Altar Rivers in Sonora on the south, the Gila River on the north, the San Pedro River on the east, and a line between Gila Bend and the Gulf of California on the west was estimated at roughly 15,000 by observers such as Father Kino and his military escort Juan Mateo Manje (Bolton 1948; Burrus 1971). The documents provide counts for individual settlements that total to roughly 13,000. Given that settlements as small as 20 persons were tallied, this set of figures illustrates very well how population was distributed in settlements of differing sizes at

that time. Figure 4.6 shows the actual counts of settlements by population size ranges. It is clear that small settlements dominate this distribution. However, Figure 4.7 shows that when population is the focus, these small settlements represent only a minor portion of the total population. For example, the two smallest categories represent just over 60 percent of the total number of settlements, yet they have only 22 percent of the regional population. These data underscore the fact that the methods employed here, which focus on sites believed to have had 100 or more persons living in them, have a reasonable likelihood of identifying the vast majority of the regional population. They also provide a partial rationale for applying up to a 20 percent correction factor to the population estimate that is derived from the large-site approach. Doelle (1995b) also considers site size, settlement pattern, and archaeological visibility as additional elements to incorporate into a correction factor.

For this study, a total of 471 sites, which represent 1,270 temporal components, has been compiled. While 471 sites may seem to be a small number when several tens of thousands of sites have been recorded within this large-site study region, this really just underscores the great advantage (and practical necessity) of the large-site approach. Small sites not only represent a very small percentage of the total population (Figure 4.7), but they often represent short-term or seasonal occupations. Such sites accumulate in very large numbers on the landscape, and they comprise a very high percentage of the sites that are in the regional site files. For many of the periods under consideration and over much of the study region, the predominant mode of settlement probably was in villages or large hamlets. For example, most sites with ball courts and platform mounds exhibit village- or hamlet-level site structure. The distribution of these forms of public architecture was one of the criteria used to define the "large-site" study area. However, there are subareas and time periods for which the approach is not as applicable. For that reason, an alternate approach to population estimation had to be employed for the Preclassic Tonto Basin in the first part of this chapter. The Papaguería is another such area because a seasonal settlement pattern may have prevailed for much of prehistory. Fortunately, in the Papaguería, the presence of sites with reservoirs provides a basis for identifying population aggregates that are likely to have been larger and more permanent. The focus on "large sites" should yield a comfortable *minimum* population estimate. To

Figure 4.6.
Frequency of
settlements by
population size
(n = 87 settle-
ments).

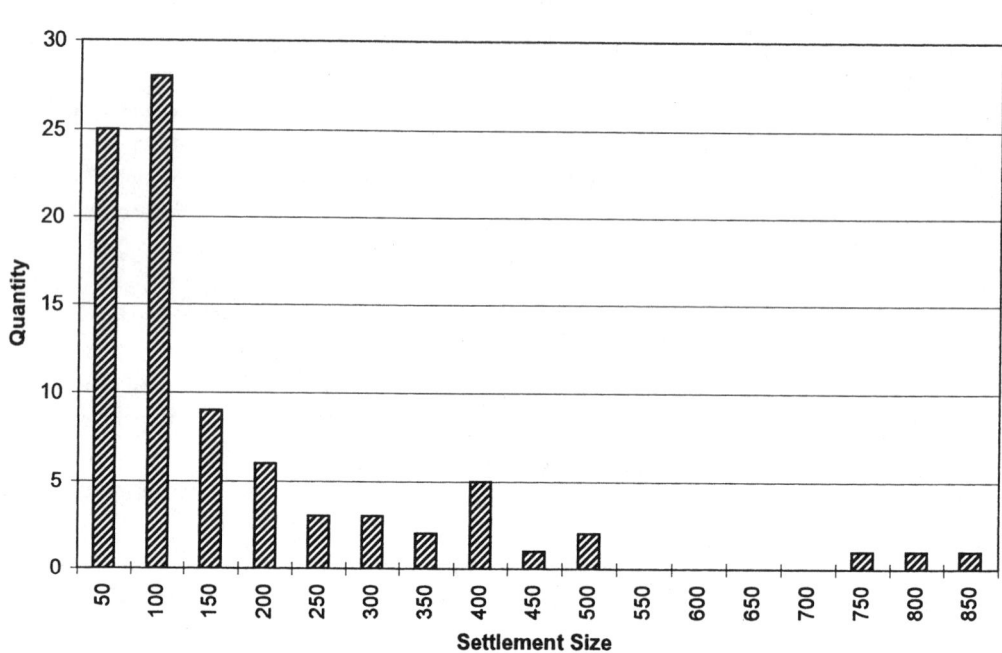

Figure 4.7.
Cumulative site
frequency and
population in late
seventeenth century
Pimeria Alta.

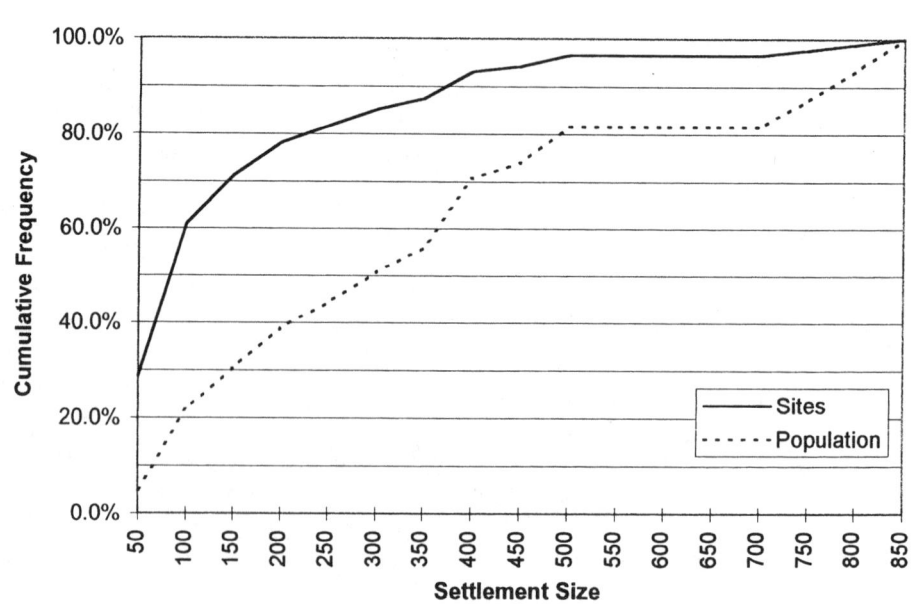

provide some consideration of the population that may have been living at smaller settlements, a correction factor is applied to the regional totals to provide an "adjusted" population estimate.

Available information on site size, number of trash mounds, number of rooms, spatial extent, temporal periods represented, public architecture (e.g., ball courts, platform mounds, kivas) present, and any other available relevant items was used to assess the "intensity of occupation" for each known site on an eight-part scale (see also Doelle 1995a, 1995b). For present purposes, it is a framework in which all available information about a site is reviewed, and the site is then judgmentally ranked in a manner that should be correlated with past population. Table 4.5 presents the conversion of the "intensity of occupation" rankings into population estimates.

There is simply nothing so basic to setting the scale for a research domain than the number of persons that are believed to have occupied a given site, valley, or region. In addition, all researchers carry hidden at some level within themselves "gut feelings" about these issues. These unstated assumptions do a great deal to structure specific approaches to research problems. By trying to clarify one approach to putting population numbers onto specific sites and regional maps, it is hoped that more researchers will address this topic in future studies.

Integrating Additional Population Data

The large-site study described above represents a methodological refinement and spatial expansion of the population estimate for the area labeled "Hohokam" in the study of population for the entire Southwest that was undertaken by Dean et al. (1994). It has not been possible

to reassess the entire data set from Dean et al.; however, a few areas have been updated. The first is the Mimbres area. The initial Mimbres figures came from an excellent review of the Mimbres valley by Blake et al. (1986). Fortunately, Lekson (1992b) has summarized a great deal of additional data for all of southwestern New Mexico that allows population to be estimated for a larger area. Lekson's article does not attempt to provide actual population figures, in fact he raises a number of thorny methodological issues that stand in the way of that process. By using the data sets from both of these studies, it has been possible to apply corrections to the Blake et al. (1986) study and to expand the geographic coverage for the Mimbres regional population.

The San Juan Basin data from Dean et al. (1994) were also reconsidered. When the many subareas that are reviewed in that study are compiled into a single table, the San Juan Basin represents well over half of the total population of the Southwest. It also displays particularly high rates of population increase. It is possible that these figures are indeed correct, but, at a minimum, they appear to represent a less conservative method of population estimation than was applied elsewhere. Lacking the expertise to revise these data in a detailed way, a relatively high population growth rate of .3 percent per year was applied to the data for the period from 700 through 1000. At the point where population began to decline in 1100, the same rates of decline that characterized the original figures were applied to these revised numbers. The overall effect is still a large population in the San Juan Basin, with a peak at just under 40,000. However, these revised figures are somewhat more in balance with their regional context than was the case with the earlier figures.

Finally, even with the entire data set from Dean et al. (1994) incorporated, some key areas were still missing. In particular, southeastern Arizona was poorly represented, but the southwestern and northwestern margins of the study area shown in Figure 4.1 were also gaps. Therefore, an attempt was made to incorporate at least an approximation of population for these areas. Methodologically the approach used for this area is the weakest. It involved talking with persons who have worked in these areas to find out how they saw population changing over time and what they felt was the maximum population for the area. This information was used in conjunction with the population density and growth rate data that were compiled for the large-site study area in order to "calibrate" the informed opinions of these experts. While less than

Table 4.5. Converting Intensity of Occupation Ranks to Population Estimates for Sites in the Large-Site Study Area

Intensity of Occupation	Population Range	Population Value
1	50	50
2	50–100	100
3	100–150	150
4	150–200	200
5	200–300	250
6	300–400	350
7	400–500	450
8	500–750	625

Table 4.6. Two Estimates of Population Size and Growth Rates for the Study Region

	A.D. 700	A.D. 800	A.D. 900	A.D. 1000–1050	A.D. 1150	A.D. 1250–1275	A.D. 1350
Unadjusted Estimates							
Population	9,350	19,198	26,740	30,896	32,438	33,800	31,200
Annual Growth Rate (%)	—	0.72	0.33	0.14	0.05	0.04	−0.08
Adjusted Estimates							
Population	18,700	21,120	32,090	33,990	35,580	37,180	37,440
Annual Growth Rate (%)	—	0.12	0.42	0.06	0.05	0.04	0.00

satisfactory as an approach, it succeeded in filling in these gaps.

Overview of Population at the Regional Level

The population estimates for the large-site study area are first examined at the aggregated level (Table 4.6, Figure 4.8) and then are considered in a comparative framework for the different subareas that have been defined for this study (Figure 4.1). Figure 4.8 displays unadjusted and adjusted population estimates for the region. The adjustments represent the application of correction fac-

tors of up to 20 percent as discussed above (see Doelle 1995a, 1995b for a more complete discussion). In the case of the 700 period, extreme problems with consistent identification of sites from this time was the basis for applying a correction factor of 100 percent. Figure 4.8 makes it clear that the adjustments do not greatly affect the general trajectory of demographic change in the study region. Because a central concern of this chapter lies in defining the scale of demographic issues, adjusted figures are considered to be better indicators of probable population growth rates for the region.

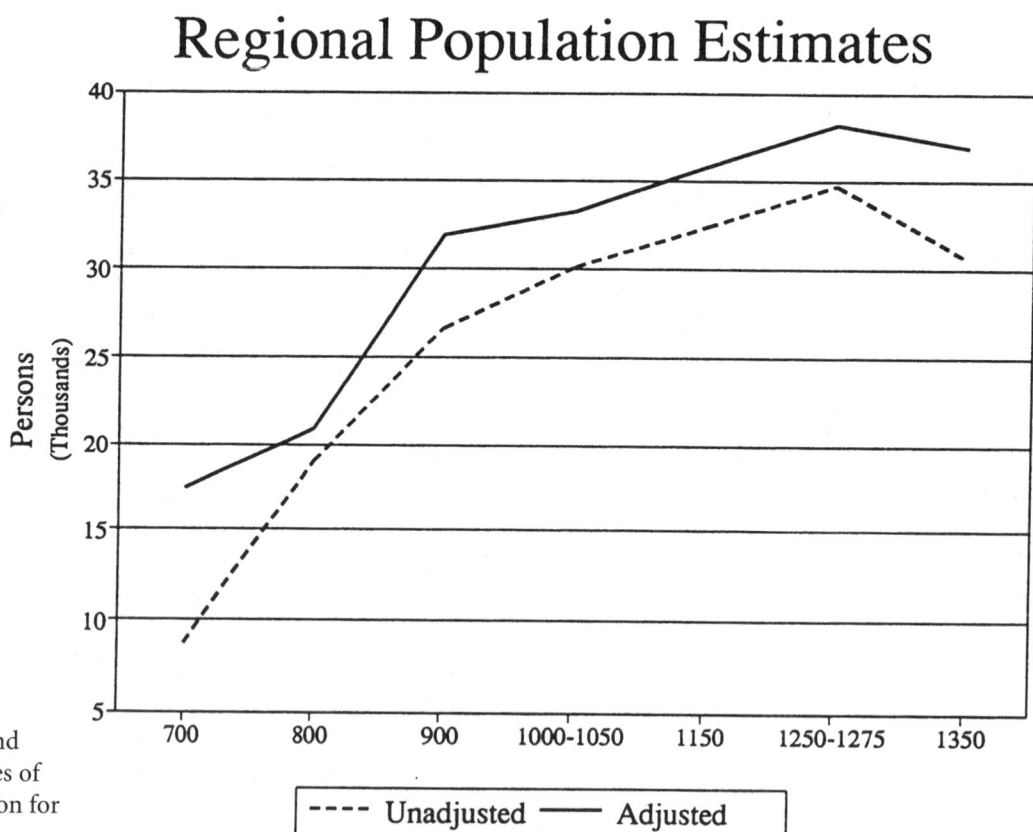

Figure 4.8. Unadjusted and adjusted values of total population for the study region.

Regional population growth rates were very high between 700 and 900 (Table 4.6). This rapid growth led to an approximate doubling of the regional population between 700 and 1050/1100. From about 950 to 1350, the average rate of population change was much more gradual at 0.04 to 0.06 percent per year, and the final phase of occupation may have seen a slight drop in overall population.

The maps in Figure 4.9 use contour lines to show how population distribution changed over time. The population contours were created by the Spatial Analyst module of the ArcView program using the population estimates for the individual sites by time period. The following discussion highlights key changes by time period and subarea.

A.D. 700

There are serious problems in recognizing sites of this period due to the low frequency of the decorated type Snaketown Red-on-gray (or buff). Furthermore, no public architecture has been observed on the surfaces of these sites, and it is likely that many are small and therefore not accounted for by this method. Thus, there is good reason to believe that the regional population may be substantially under represented at this time. However, the available information shows a broad distribution of sites that lie in the same general locations where sizable populations are documented for later periods. Of particular note is the degree of continuity in site occupations along major riverine settings from 700 onward. In the Salt and Gila river areas, this includes the establishment of a high percentage of settlements located at regular 3- to 5-km intervals along the rivers or canals (Gregory 1991, 1995b; Gregory and Huckleberry 1994).

The Gila Bend area is an interesting one to follow through this series of maps. No evidence of Snaketown phase occupation has been documented along this stretch of the Lower Gila River. It is not clear whether this represents a deficiency in the survey data, whether diagnostic ceramics were not present in this area during the Snaketown phase, or whether the area was actually vacant. Given that the nearby Papaguería was receiving at least some Snaketown phase pottery, and the level of field study is roughly comparable to the Gila Bend area, the data may accurately represent an area of very low population.

A.D. 800

The population increase that is evident in this period may, in part, reflect increased archaeological visibility. However,

there is every reason to believe that the Gila Butte phase was a time of major regional population increase. Improved varieties of maize may have contributed to the demographic surge. It seems that the rapid development and spread of the ideology associated with ball courts and the Hohokam mortuary complex also contributed to increased sedentism and intensified interaction over a very broad region. The importance of the Lower Salt, Lower Verde, and Middle Gila Rivers, and the secondary population center in the Tucson Basin, is very clear.

Gila Bend shows a population presence for the first time. The Rock Ball Court site (Wasley and Johnson 1965; Dart et al. 1989) was occupied only during the Gila Butte phase. It is the westernmost of the ball courts along the Gila River, and it probably represents an attempt to expand a canal-based agricultural strategy into a somewhat marginal area. The attempt was apparently unsuccessful, though settlements only slightly farther east flourished for several more centuries (Dart et al. 1989; Wasley and Johnson 1965).

A.D. 900

For the most part, this period exhibits internal growth of extant local populations. The one probable exception to this is the continued expansion into the New River area north of the Lower Salt (Doyel and Elson 1985). In the Tucson Basin, there are suggestions that all of the best agricultural lands had been settled during the previous phase, for ball court sites such as Waterworld (Czaplicki and Ravesloot 1989) and Honeybee Village (Craig and Wallace 1987; Craig 1989) were established in areas that lack permanent water. Like Rock Ball Court, the Waterworld site was not able to sustain a population for an extended period, though Honeybee Village was successful, and another site was founded roughly a mile away in a setting with even less access to permanent water.

The ball court system achieved its fullest extent during this period. Sites with courts tend to be spaced at regular intervals along major drainage systems, and there are ball courts in the Superstition Mountains foothills between the Salt and Gila Rivers and in the foothills of the Black Hills between the Tucson Basin and the Florence area on the Gila River. This apparent linking of riverine areas, where the ball court system was already well established, with adjacent nonriverine areas is probably best conceptualized as an infilling within the broad region that participated in the ball court system.

The San Pedro River area presents problems throughout the Preclassic period. Ball courts were present from

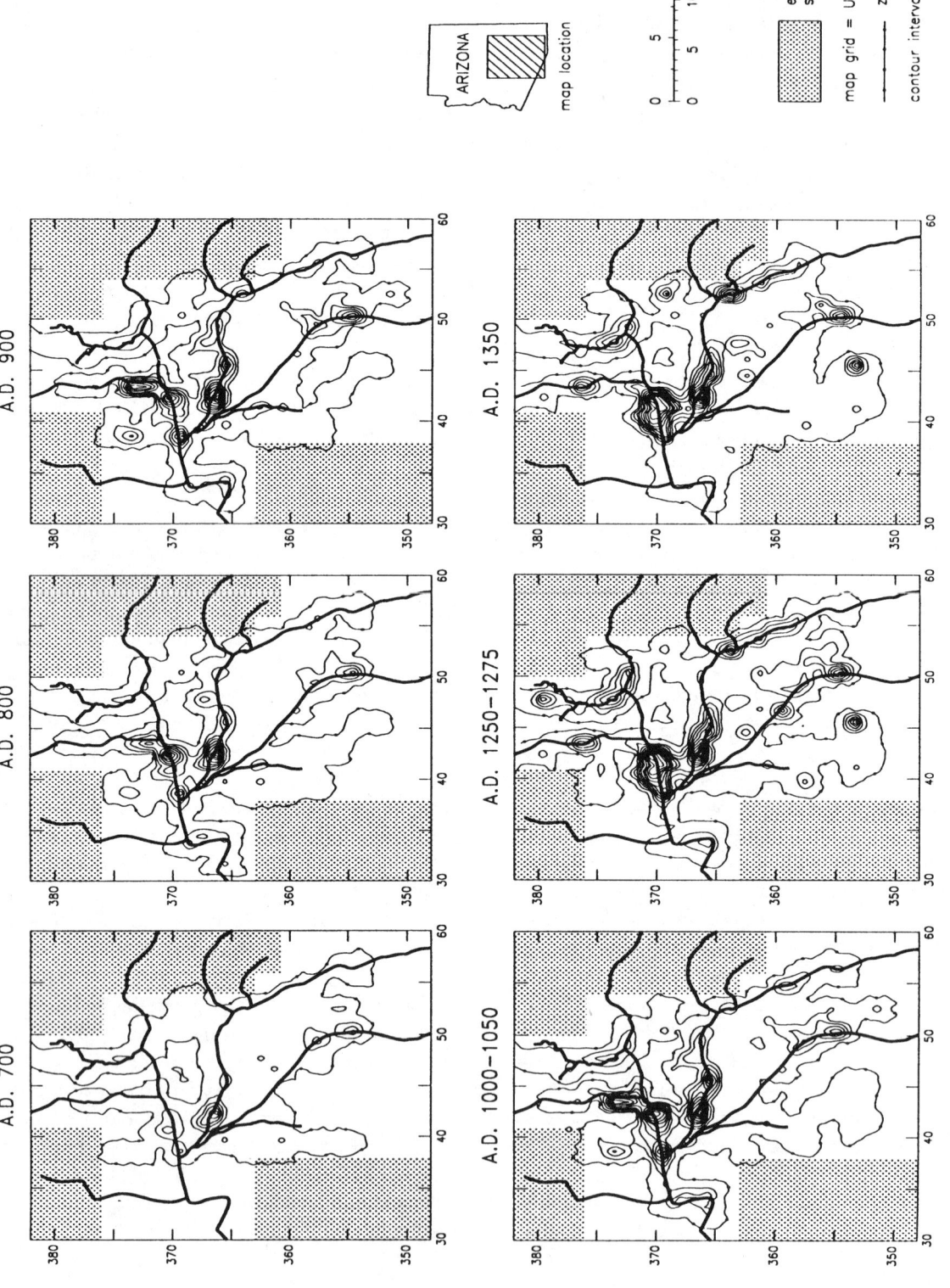

Figure 4.9. Regional population change from A.D. 700-1350.

very early on at three large sites spaced widely along the river. From north to south, these sites are Big Ditch, Redington, and Tres Alamos. The sites are spaced at intervals of 45 km and 37 km along the river, respectively. Those distances exceed the 36-km rule of thumb as to what constituted a day's walk (Drennan 1984; Elson, Gregory, and Stark 1995; Gregory 1995b); thus, they probably do not represent ball court settlements that were in close interaction. Each of these large courts has at least one other court within 8 km or less, but Desert Archaeology's Lower San Pedro survey did not document an evenly spaced distribution of ball courts that would have linked these three local systems (Wallace et al. 1998). Because the survey strategy could have missed some such sites, it is still possible that a more integrated network was once present. However, for the purposes of population estimation, it has been assumed that the San Pedro was characterized by three settlement clusters containing ball courts and denser populations with only lightly populated intervening areas. This issue merits further investigation.

A.D. 1000 to 1050

Population increased steadily in the densest population centers along the Lower Salt, Lower Verde, and Middle Gila Rivers. Major changes in the ball court system were initiated because ball courts probably had been abandoned by 1000 in the Tucson Basin (Doelle and Wallace 1991). The process is poorly understood, but the ball court system was probably in serious decline by 1050 or soon thereafter in the Phoenix Basin.

Several trends merit mention for the Gila Bend area. During this period, there is evidence of actual movement of groups that made pottery of the Patayan (Lower Colorado Buff Ware) tradition into the lower Gila (Stein 1977) and even into the Phoenix Basin at sites such as Las Colinas (Beckwith 1988). This population movement may have had multiple effects worth noting. First, the development of the platform mound at the Gatlin site (Wasley 1960) probably was initiated by 1050 and continued for another century thereafter. Whether there was a causal relation between platform mound development and the increasing presence of groups of different cultural affiliation is not currently understood. Second, the movement of new groups into the area may have encouraged, or at least coincided with, a retraction of Hohokam groups toward the Phoenix Basin. Thus, immigration may have been offset by, or even exceeded by, emigration

in the Gila Bend area. Third, the settlement pattern of the Patayan groups contrasted with the earlier Hohokam pattern. The less visible sites of the Patayan immigrants (Greenleaf 1975; Schroeder 1961; Vivian 1965; Wasley and Johnson 1965) may mean that population in the Gila Bend area is being underestimated in this and later phases. Note that the trends summarized here are initiated during this period, and they continued at least into the early Classic period.

The Lower Verde is of strong interest, for throughout Preclassic times, it maintained a high population and had numerous ball court sites. With the collapse of the ball court system, there was apparently a significant loss of population in the lowermost Verde River area. The effects of this are shown on the 1250 to 1275 map.

A.D. 1050 to 1150

This period is not covered in the maps because of the lack of a data base that breaks out this critical interval. This was a time of reorganization or substantial areal contraction of the Hohokam ball court system. Some canal systems along the Salt and Gila Rivers were consolidated, and platform mounds continued to develop as a form of public architecture in the Phoenix Basin.

A.D. 1250 to 1275

A new regional structure for population emerged at this time. The Gila Bend area has evidence of mixed cultural affiliations and a strong concern with defense at the Fortified Hill site (Greenleaf 1975). There was a substantial concentration of population in the Phoenix area along the Lower Salt and Gila Rivers. By the end of this period, platform mounds were being established in Tonto Basin, Lower San Pedro, Picacho Mountain, Tucson Basin, and eastern Papaguería. Population clusters generally corresponded with the distribution of platform mounds. The major exceptions to this pattern are at Gila Bend and along the Lower Verde, both of which lack platform mounds. Note that population had dropped sharply since the preceding period on the lowermost Verde River, although a significant population in the Horseshoe Reservoir area still thrived during the 1200s.

Tonto Basin and the Payson area require additional discussion. The Payson area had seen a population buildup in the 1150 to 1250 interval, and it was largely abandoned by 1250 or soon thereafter (Redman 1993). Thus, despite the attempt here to provide a single "snapshot" of this 25-year interval, the Payson area was declining, whereas the nearby Tonto Basin was growing. This is the first time that Tonto Basin shows a relatively high population density. Even so, the Lower Salt and Middle Gila areas strongly overshadow Tonto Basin. Tonto Basin is more on a level with other secondary areas, such as Santa Rosa Valley in the Papaguería, the Tucson Basin, the Lower San Pedro, and the Lower Verde. The New River area underwent a major drop in population.

A.D. 1350

The aggregation process continued, and population density reached its maximum in the Phoenix area. In some areas, there is evidence of population decline, such as the abandonment of the Marana and Los Robles platform mounds north of the Tucson Basin. As previously discussed, Tonto Basin also underwent population decline at this time. The site of Grasshopper, located approximately 60 km east of Tonto Basin, had undergone a major growth process during the prior 50 years but was already experiencing a population decline that extended over the ensuing 50-year interval. The Globe area, however, witnessed a substantial population increase at this time. Sites in the Sierra Ancha also underwent a rapid growth phase. Thus, although there is some evidence of population decline in Tonto Basin, nearby areas appear to have been growing at approximately the same time.

The issue of abandonment of the entire platform mound system is not addressed here. The recognition of late sites (for example, Polvorón phase sites in the Phoenix Basin) is not possible without excavation data, and there is not enough information as yet to deal with this period on a regional scale.

DISCUSSION

The Colonial Expansion

Having argued initially against an expansion of Phoenix Basin population into Tonto Basin during the Colonial period (Doelle and Craig 1992), I think it important to reopen this issue in light of the demographic data developed in this chapter and data presented elsewhere in this volume (Elson et al., Chapter 7). The primary issue is: How was the Phoenix Basin able to "export" population at this early time?

The goal is to consider how a Colonial period expansion could have taken place because the Lower Salt and Middle Gila cannot be said to have had huge populations during the Snaketown phase. Two factors seem important to consider. First, settlement size for the agricultural populations who lived along the Lower Salt and Middle Gila Rivers was probably relatively small—most likely around 50 persons and certainly no greater than 100 persons. Small settlements of this magnitude were apparently distributed at regular intervals along the margins of relatively short canals. These canals brought water from the Salt or Gila for both domestic and agricultural use (Gregory and Huckleberry 1994; Howard 1993). Second, it seems likely that under conditions of rapid population growth, the availability of new lands that were not yet under cultivation by others would have encouraged fissioning of these early settlements while village size was relatively small. Even more important, social controls to resolve conflicts that arise under conditions of population growth may not have been in place in these small settlements. While open land was still available, group fissioning may have been a common occurrence, with groups as small as 25 to 30 persons breaking away from their parent village to form viable new settlements.

For this process to work, either a rapid growth rate or a relatively long time is required. For example, at a very rapid growth rate of 0.5 percent per year, a settlement of 50 persons would take 100 years to increase to 80 persons. This growth rate could have achieved a substantial territorial expansion and a doubling of the number of settlements within a century. Alternatively, if a process of gradual growth (e.g., 0.1 percent per year) had been underway in the Phoenix Basin since the first century A.D. or so, and if settlements tended to fission whenever they reached the 50 to 80 range, all of the most desirable areas along the available floodplain could have been filled by the Snaketown phase, as suggested by settlement data for that time (Gregory and Huckleberry 1994; Howard 1993). Furthermore, much of the Lower Verde, the Tucson Basin, and even some areas along the San Pedro probably had been claimed by *local* agriculturalists by the Snaketown phase. As a result, areas such as Gila Bend and Tonto Basin were available (and suitable) for further expansion. The limited evidence from places such as the Rock Ball Court site (Wasley and Johnson 1965) and the Hedge Apple (Swartz and Randolph 1994b) and Roosevelt 9:6 (Haury 1932) sites in Tonto Basin support such a model.

The critical elements of this model are a relatively long time frame and a regular process of settlement fissioning at relatively low population levels. These processes could account for the observed settlement pattern data for the period around 700.

Potential problems with this model are that available settlement pattern data do not provide strong support for a very sizable Phoenix Basin population around A.D. 1, particularly along the Salt River. Excavations have shown that settlements are small, dispersed, and confined to the geological floodplain during the Red Mountain phase (Cable and Doyel 1985; others). It is post 300 or 400 that there is evidence of increased intensity of occupation along the Salt River (Doyel 1991a; Henderson 1989, 1995). Furthermore, the powerful flows of the Salt River would have regularly damaged the floodplain canal systems, and it was not until investment of sufficient labor to extend the canals out of the floodplain was accomplished that the productive potential of the area could be tapped. Thus it may be appropriate to consider a demographic model that involves a substantial movement of population into the Phoenix Basin, particularly the Salt River area, but perhaps to a lesser extent to the Gila River as well. The evidence for substantial Early Agricultural period and Early Ceramic period occupations in the Tucson Basin (Gregory 1998; Mabry 1998; Mabry et al. 1997, 1998), as well as the San Pedro (Huckell 1990), Cienega valley (Huckell 1995), San Simon (Sayles 1945), and San Carlos areas (Gregory 1995a) suggest that one or more of these areas could well have contributed population to the Phoenix Basin as that area underwent a substantial expansion in the late Pioneer period.

Neither internal growth nor immigration scenarios can be confirmed at present. However, it is possible to consider how population would increase under different assumptions. Examining options where population grew at a constant rate of .1 percent or .15 percent per year showed that the Salt River would require a population of roughly 1600 or 1200, respectively at A.D. 1 in order to reach the estimated population of nearly 3,850 by 800. These population figures seem relatively large for the known archaeological record, but the limits on data quality make a firm conclusion impossible at present.

Two migration scenarios were also reviewed that considered both the Salt and Gila river portions of the Phoenix Basin. One model assumed a long term growth rate of .1 percent per year, and it used populations from surrounding areas as the source for Phoenix Basin immigrants. It required some 2,000 immigrants to achieve the populations of 4,200 and 3,850 in the Gila and Salt, re-

spectively, that the regional data base documents for 800. Given the large number of immigrants relative to the local population, this scenario would be expected to result in the immigrants having a substantial effect on the social and cultural system of the Phoenix Basin. A second alternative used slightly higher initial populations at A.D. 1 (400 in the Salt, 1200 in the Gila) and a long-term growth rate of .15 percent per year. In this case 750 migrants to the Gila in the first several centuries A.D. were enough to achieve the 800 population of 4,200 *and* to provide more than 1,000 emigrants to help increase Salt River population in the 300 to 600 time range. In this scenario, the local Phoenix Basin population is always numerically dominant, and it is likely that the immigrants would have had a much more limited effect on the local cultural content than would be predicted for the first migration scenario.

Such exercises as this cannot resolve these issues. What they do provide is a way to tangibly specify a range of alternatives that can be tested with archaeological data.

The Scale of Local and Regional Population

The abundance of platform mound sites has led to the perception that Tonto Basin was the home of very large populations during late prehistoric times. The work of all three Roosevelt Lake project research teams has resulted in a dramatic realignment of that perception. Instead, relatively small populations are now envisioned as having occupied Tonto Basin from late Archaic times onward, with a peak population in the Classic period that was fewer than 5,000 persons and may have reached only the 3,000 to 3,500 range. Interestingly, Adolph Bandelier, who saw the ruins of Tonto Basin when they were in much better condition and who prepared remarkable maps of many of the major ruins (Hohmann and Kelly 1988), was not overly impressed with the numbers of people that once occupied them. In his description of Armer Ruin, Bandelier (1892:421) states: "I doubt whether this village, which is one of the most important in the Upper Salt River valley, could accommodate more than one hundred and fifty inhabitants." Bandelier (1892:420) also offered an assessment on a larger scale: "Thus the south side of Salt River valley [in Tonto Basin] was at one time dotted with a number of Indian settlements, erected at intervals of from a quarter to half a mile. Whether, in case they were all simultaneously occupied, their aggregate population amounted to over one thousand souls, appears to me to be doubtful."

Prior to the Roosevelt projects, Wood (1989) estimated that Tonto Basin population was in a range between 5,000 and 10,000. The present study yields a population figure that is less than half Wood's maximum estimate and is below his minimum by more than 1,000.

Phoenix Basin researchers have been particularly bold in committing population numbers to paper. Figure 4.10 displays some of those estimates. Thus, Turney (1929) quotes a number of early observers who felt that 100,000 and even double that number could once have lived in the Salt River Valley alone. This graph ignores the more outlandish of those early estimates and assumes that Turney and his contemporaries would not have been at all uncomfortable with an estimate of 100,000 persons inhabiting the combined Lower Salt and Middle Gila river areas. Haury's (1976a) estimate of 50,000 to 60,000 persons cut that number roughly in half. Doyel (1991a:266) estimated 45,000 Phoenix Basin residents during the Classic period, and Wilcox (1991a:262) argued that there were only 24,000. The present discussion drops that number to roughly 15,000. If the same correction factor (20 percent) that was used for the regional population were used on the Phoenix Basin data, it would raise the total to 18,000. That is just 36 percent of Haury's 50,000 figure, 40 percent of Doyel's number, and 75 percent of Wilcox's recent estimate. This is dramatically different from the assumptions of previous researchers. Some of this drop is due to an improved understanding of issues such as the use-life of houses. Better ceramic typologies that allow for finer time scales and the accumulation of information on more sites also have helped. Obviously, there is not yet consensus on how to measure prehistoric population size. However, the trend conveyed in Figure 4.10 does appear to be a general one. Thus, the accumulation of more information is leading researchers to conclude that population sizes of individual settlements, as well as local settlement systems, were smaller than had been originally estimated (though see Fish et al., eds. 1992:100 for an argument that 53,000 to 133,000 persons could have been supported in the Phoenix Basin).

Finally, as Wilcox (1998) has pointed out, the *relative* differences between areas such as the Phoenix Basin and any other subarea remain significant. By 1350, aggregation resulted in relatively high population densities in

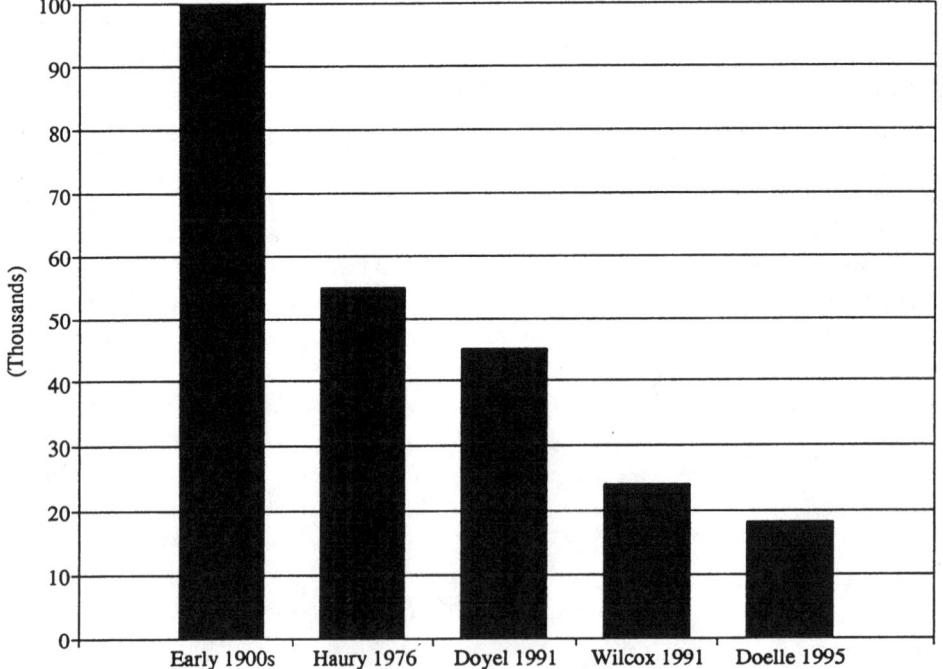

Figure 4.10.   Changing perspectives on the peak population size for the Phoenix Basin.

Table 4.7. Revised and Expanded Population Estimates from A.D. 1 to 1500 for the Entire Southwest, Developed from Data in Dean et al. (1994)

Map Key	Subregion	A.D. 1	100	200	300	400	500	600	700	800	900	1000	1100	1200	1300	1400	1500
A	SW Colo/SE UT		0	0	800	0	0	200	2,400	2,200	3,100	3,100	3,900	5,500	0	0	0
B	Kayenta		0	950	950	1,000	1,100	2,600	2,700	2,800	3,600	3,900	5,500	6,500	800	200	0
C	Virgin Branch	50	50	50	50	50	60	80	100	150	300	500	900	20	0	0	0
D	Grand Canyon		0	0	0	0	50	80	160	250	480	700	950	0	0	0	0
E	Little Colorado		0	0	0	0	200	500	600	1,000	1,200	1,600	8,500	12,000	18,000	8,000	11,000
F	San Juan Basin	4,550	5,650	6,550	7,600	8,850	10,300	12,000	16,200	21,900	29,500	39,800	29,500	13,200	0	0	0
G	Northern Rio Grande		0	0	0	0	0	0	0	500	500	500	1,000	7,000	28,000	23,000	16,000
H	Cebolleta		0	0	0	0	0	0	200	500	800	700	400	2,100	100	0	0
I	SW New Mexico*		0	830	1,120	1,520	2,050	2,760	3,720	5,020	6,770	9,150	12,350	10,000	10,000	2,500	0
J	Mogollon Highlands		0	700	800	1,100	1,400	1,700	2,100	2,400	3,300	4,000	3,500	4,000	3,400	2,000	0
K	SE Arizona*	1,500	1,500	1,500	2,000	2,000	2,000	2,500	4,000	5,000	5,650	6,600	7,380	8,200	9,700	9,840	0
L	Hohokam	8,000	8,000	8,800	9,700	10,700	11,800	13,000	18,700	21,120	32,090	33,990	35,580	37,180	37,440	30,000	25,000
M	SW Arizona*	400	400	400	500	600	700	800	900	1,300	1,750	2,050	2,050	2,050	2,050	1,800	0
N	Upper Verde/Agua Fria*	500	500	600	600	600	600	700	800	1,580	2,470	3,360	3,600	4,000	4,300	3,700	0
	Southwest Total	15,000	16,100	20,380	24,120	26,420	30,260	36,920	52,580	65,720	91,510	109,950	115,110	111,750	113,790	81,040	52,000
	Average Annual Growth Rate		0.10	0.24	0.17	0.09	0.14	0.20	0.35	0.22	0.33	0.18	0.05	-0.03	0.02	-0.34	-0.44

*Areas that were not included in the population estimates of Dean et al. (1994).

some subareas, but those areas are very limited in their spatial extent. Thus, the population map for 1350 clearly shows that the Phoenix Basin achieved not only the highest population values, but also that the population was distributed over a larger area than any other local system. The "intensity of occupation" scale that is at the base of these population estimates is ultimately a relative scale, so it is hoped that the present data set conveys a generally accurate picture of the *relative* scale of population differences over the region. Future work should refine these values by providing better data with which to estimate the intensity of occupation and to relate it to past population values.

The regional data are useful for considering the issue of long-term population growth rates. Table 4.7 displays the average annual percentage increase or decrease for each century for the Southwest study area. Growth rates for some centuries exceed .3 percent per year. This is more than three times the long-term rate that Hassan (1981) has noted. On a local scale, such high rates are certainly possible through combinations of higher fertility, lowered mortality, and immigration. It was argued earlier that when rates exceed .1 percent per year by very much, immigration is probably a factor. By expanding the spatial scale to the entire Southwest, however, the likelihood increases that positive and negative migration rates on local scales will tend to balance out, leaving the interaction of fertility and mortality as the major factors determining the population growth rate (which can be either positive or negative).

If this is accepted, a useful exercise can be conducted using variable long-term growth rates to consider how a population maximum might have been achieved around 1100, or alternatively, what the population may have been around A.D. 1. Table 4.8 takes the maximum population of 115,000 persons at 1100 and uses different average rates of growth to assess what the population would have been for this region at A.D. 1. The dramatic range in these figures underscores the effect of even small differences in average rates if they are maintained over a long period of time. Even with the strong differences between current researchers, it seems likely that most would find the two extremes in Table 4.8 at strong odds with the archaeological record. It seems likely that most researchers would find a "comfort zone" within the range of the .1 percent and .2 percent average annual rates.

Table 4.9 takes the figure of 15,000 people for the entire Southwest, the number shown in Table 4.7 for A.D. 1, as its point of departure. Again there is a dramatic range in the final population sizes achieved at 1100, and the .15 percent to .2 percent range seems to yield the "most reasonable" numbers. The "best fit" with the current data set is the .15 percent long-term rate. It is certainly possible that the population figure of 15,000 is low, given that data are very limited for this time period. An increase of just a few thousand people at the outset would make a big difference in the ultimate population sizes achieved.

The regional data that have been assembled for the entire Southwest serve to place Tonto Basin in a broad context. Figure 4.11 shows Tonto Basin plotted at a scale that is enlarged 10-fold over the regional data. The shape of the curve for the entire Southwest is not quite as steep in its ascent and decline as is the similar graph in Dean et al. (1994:74). This is largely due to the addition of estimated population for some areas that extend earlier and later than the Dean et al. data. I hope that this curve

Table 4.8.   The Relationship Between Population Growth Rate and the Initial Population Size Needed at A.D. 1 to Reach a Maximum Population of 115,000 at A.D. 1100

Growth Rate (%)	Initial Population (A.D. 1)
.05	66,400
.10	38,300
.15	22,100
.20	12,800
.25	7,400
.30	4,300

Table 4.9.   The Relationship between Population Growth Rate and the Maximum Population Size Achieved at A.D. 1100 Beginning with a Population of 15,000 at A.D. 1

Growth Rate (%)	Maximum Population (A.D. 1100)
.05	26,000
.10	45,000
.15	78,000
.20	135,100
.25	233,800
.30	404,700

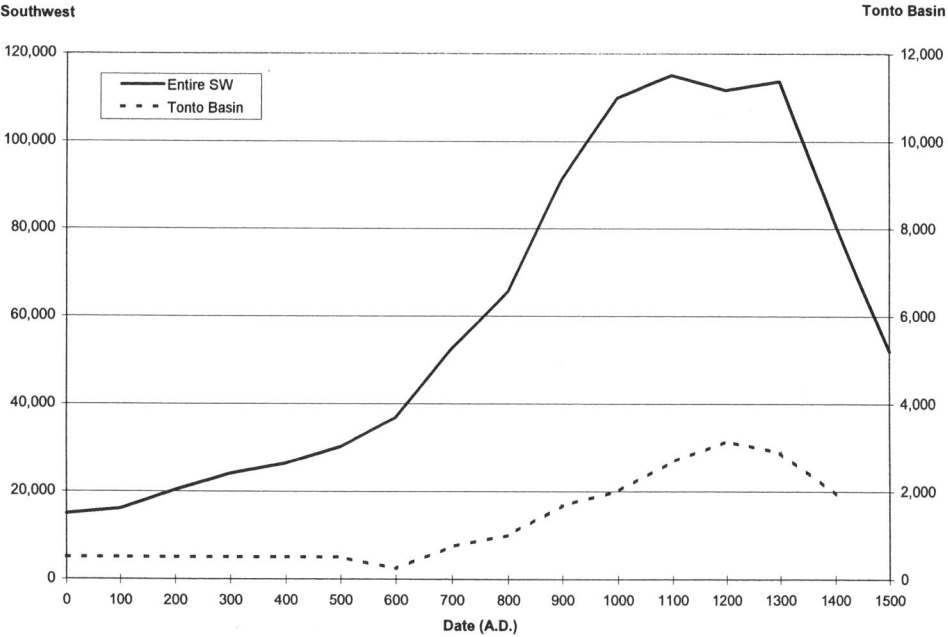

Figure 4.11. Comparison of population trends for Tonto Basin and the entire Southwest.

will stimulate other researchers to the extent that it does me. The dramatic rate of population increase, leveling, and collapse that is illustrated here inspires hundreds of questions. It underscores the incredible laboratory that the Southwest represents for the study of demographic issues and how they relate to other aspects of human culture and adaptation. It is satisfying to have contributed to clarifying somewhat how Tonto Basin fits into this larger whole, but it is frustrating that even the combined three projects have done little to explain the 15th century collapse in population.

Conclusions

This chapter has used several different approaches to estimate past population sizes for Tonto Basin and a much larger surrounding region. The data from Tonto Basin have led to two significant conclusions: First, population in Tonto Basin was never very large; second,

to achieve even its modest population size, the Basin very likely required a low level of immigration.

The regional data provide a context for comparing Tonto Basin with other subareas. Even in the thirteenth and fourteenth centuries when Tonto Basin population was at its peak, it was one of the smaller of several secondary population centers. Prior to the Classic period, Tonto Basin population was at a tertiary level, along with other areas that were outside the ball court system, such as the Santa Rosa Valley in the Papaguería.

This chapter has flirted with the potential of demographic studies. However, significant progress has been made in data base development and in addressing some of the more intractable methodological issues. The present study has given priority to establishing an empirical basis for assessing population history in a large portion of prehistoric southern Arizona, which can be expanded in the future. Also important for the future is a more extensive use of demographic theory to explore the mechanisms that lie behind the demographic trends being documented.

CHAPTER FIVE

Vale of Tiers Palimpsest:

Salado Settlement and Internal Relationships in the Tonto Basin Area

J. Scott Wood

Over the past 20 years I have presented various models of social and economic development to explain the archaeology of Tonto Basin (in particular, Wood 1989, 1992; Wood and McAllister 1984a). I will not repeat previous published discussion of these models (but see Van West et al., Chapter 2, for discussions of at least one of them) since the purpose of this chapter is to provide a generalized look at settlement patterning in and around Tonto Basin (Figure 5.1). Given the complexity of the problem much of the primary data is not presented here. It is available, however, in the Heritage Inventory for Tonto National Forest, which, combined with the Roosevelt Project excavations discussed in this volume, form the basis for this synthesis.

The "A" problem of Tonto Basin has been known for some time. Said to have been everything from the homeland for a group of people we call Salado to merely a stopping place on their wanderings through the Southwest, it became obvious early on that it was heavily occupied in prehistoric times and that there were at least two if not three basic temporal divisions in the occupation, each characterized by a different mode of residential architecture and a different constellation of decorated pottery types. In its simplest form, the temporal pattern was seen as beginning with Hohokam-style pithouse villages having Red-on-buff pottery (the "Preclassic" or Formative period) giving way to

surface-built cobble masonry and adobe compounds with Black-on-white pottery (the early Classic period) which in turn gave way to large "pueblos" and what we now know as platform mounds with the enigmatic Salado polychromes during the late Classic period.

As a result of the Roosevelt Projects' work and other recent projects in and around Tonto Basin we are able to refine this occupational history quite a bit. The first permanent residential occupation known so far was a rather nondescript pithouse village in the eastern part of the Salt Arm dating to the Early Ceramic horizon sometime between 100 and 600 (Elson and Lindeman 1994). The architecture of this site reflects contemporary patterns seen throughout central and southern Arizona, as does the meager, seed-jar dominated ceramic assemblage.

Hohokam influence begins to appear shortly after the occupation of this earliest settlement. An aceramic burial containing textiles described as Hohokam in style if not origin has been radiocarbon dated to ca. 600 (Adovasio and Andrews 1987), and Snaketown Red-on-buff pottery has been found at several sites in the Upper Basin, although no residential structures have been clearly dated to this time period. A number of settlements dating to the Gila Butte and Santa Cruz phases have been found in the Upper and Lower Basins. Hohokam influence appears to have been stronger in the Lower Basin, where

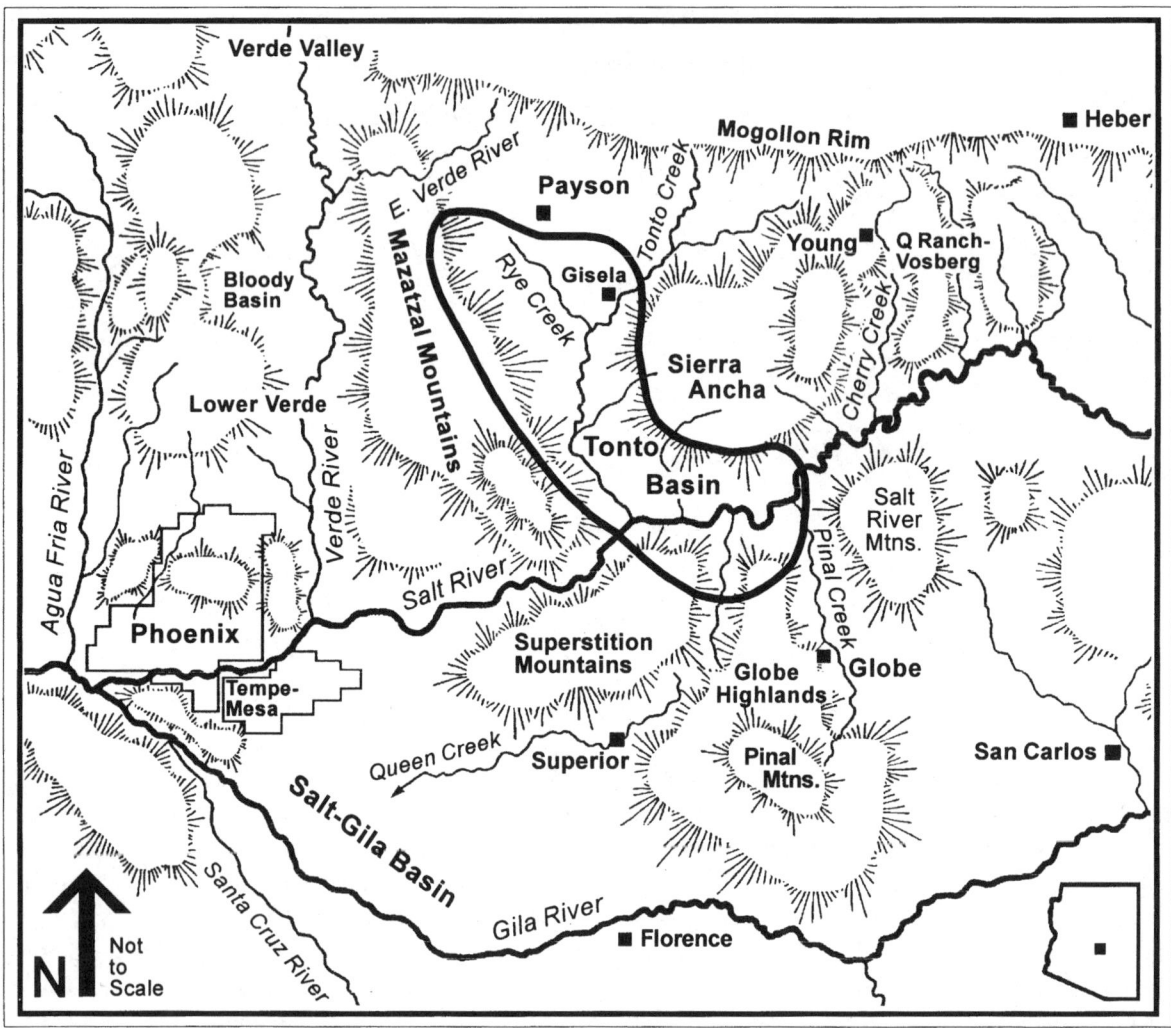

Figure 5.1.   Tonto Basin and its environs in central Arizona.

several sites having the appearance of having been transplanted into Tonto Basin from the Phoenix Basin, suggesting the actual immigration of Hohokam from the south (Elson et al., Chapter 7). Many more settlements can be dated to the subsequent Sacaton phase. About halfway through this phase surface architecture begins to replace pithouses, and the importation of Hohokam decorated pottery drops off rather quickly, being replaced by white wares from the Little Colorado and Cibola areas. While this largely reflects trends seen in and around the Phoenix Basin itself, these changes have prompted the introduction of the Ash Creek phase, as representing something of a transition between the Preclassic and Classic period patterns.

At first, archaeological work in the Basin followed the main roads that concentrate along the Salt River and Tonto Creek, and these were assumed to be the major foci of prehistoric occupation. Today the general opinion is still that the rivers provided the main focus for settlement, but we also recognize that a substantial population lived, at least for a time, in the surrounding uplands and neighboring mountainous areas. This almost dichotomous distribution of residence in the later part of the Basin's occupation is a major focus of this chapter, since it may provide insight into several important aspects of Salado culture history, not the least of which are the reasons for its organizational development and the nature of its so-called "ethnic" characteristics.

TONTO BASIN GEOGRAPHY

Tonto Basin is one of the defining features of central Arizona geography. A pocket of Sonoran Desert tucked away in the mountainous heart of the Transition Zone below the Mogollon Rim, the Basin is formed by two of the major drainages coming off the Rim, the Salt River, that heads well to the east of the Basin, and Tonto Creek, that falls off the Rim just to the north of it. Its southern and western boundaries are the Superstition and Mazatzal Mountains, respectively, while its northern and eastern boundaries are formed by the Sierra Ancha.

The interior geography of Tonto Basin can be seen in two primary orientations—horizontal and vertical. Horizontally, it can be broken into two major divisions each with two subdivisions, together covering about 750 square miles (Figure 5.2). The roughly L-shaped Lower Basin is formed by the confluence of the Salt River and Tonto Creek. Along the rivers, it extends from the confluence of the Salt River and Pinal Creek in the east to the confluence of Tonto Creek and Gun Creek in the north. It is divided into a Salt Arm and Tonto Arm at the confluence of those two drainages. The lower portion of both arms, especially the Salt Arm, is inundated by Roosevelt Lake, a circumstance that frustrates a full understanding of the archaeology.

The Upper Basin is an extension of Tonto Creek and several of its tributaries. The Rye Creek section is centered on a major tributary that runs against the foot of the Mazatzals up to its divide with the East Verde River. The Gisela Valley section is centered on a stretch of Tonto Creek that runs along the foot of the Sierra Ancha and continues up to a physical constriction a few miles north of the town of Gisela at a place called Houston Pocket. These two sections are separated by the divide between Rye Creek and Tonto Creek.

Vertically, the Lower Basin is a complex topography made up of valley fills between mountain ranges that are carved up into a series of Pleistocene and Holocene terraces (approximately twelve), outlying mesa like extensions from the mountain fronts, landlocked elevated basins, piedmonts, and bajadas (Anderson and Piety 1987; Barsch and Royse 1971; Royse et al. 1971). For this discussion, the area can be characterized as containing a series of "tiers" stepping up from the rivers to the crests of the mountain ranges (Figure 5.3; Van West et al., Chapter 2).

The first of these tiers consists of the irrigable floodplains and lower alluvial terraces (mostly Holocene) along Tonto Creek and the Salt River. Typically characterized by a combination of riparian gallery forest and mesquite bosque vegetation, these areas are known to have been used from the earliest to the latest phases of the prehistoric occupation. Unfortunately, most of these critical areas have been lost to either inundation or lateral channel erosion in the last century. There are still remnants along some stretches of Tonto Creek and Rye Creek, but these are generally privately owned and have not had much archaeological investigation.

The second tier consists of the Pleistocene upper terraces of Tonto Creek and the Salt River, prominent landforms that generally provide a sharp vertical edge to the riparian zone along the rivers. Broad, flat, and dry, these are very stable surfaces that have supported a Lower Sonoran vegetation (creosote bush to saguaro-paloverde) for millennia, though they have recently been invaded by mesquite and cat-claw at the lower elevations

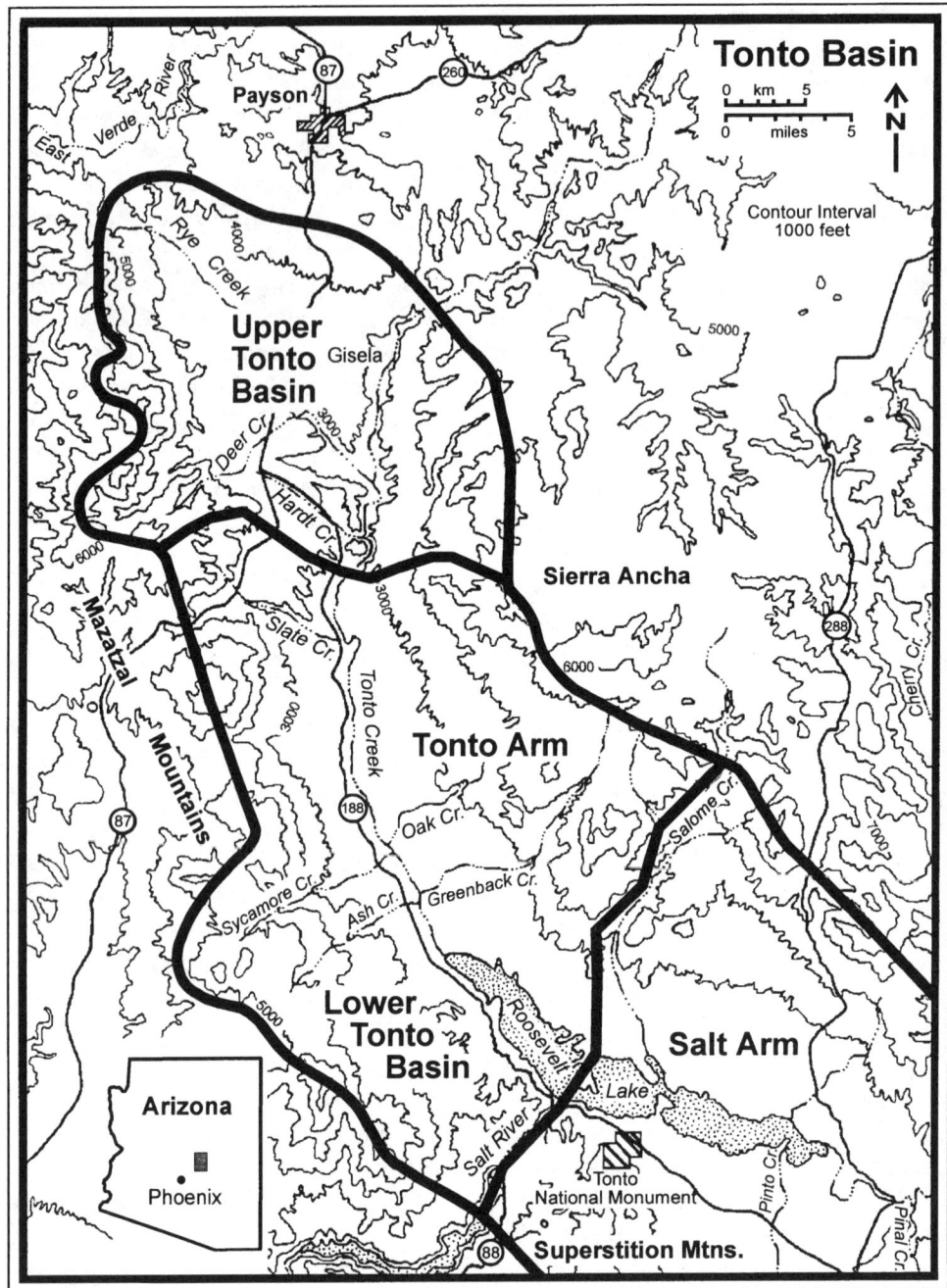

Figure 5.2.   Primary divisions of Tonto Basin geography.

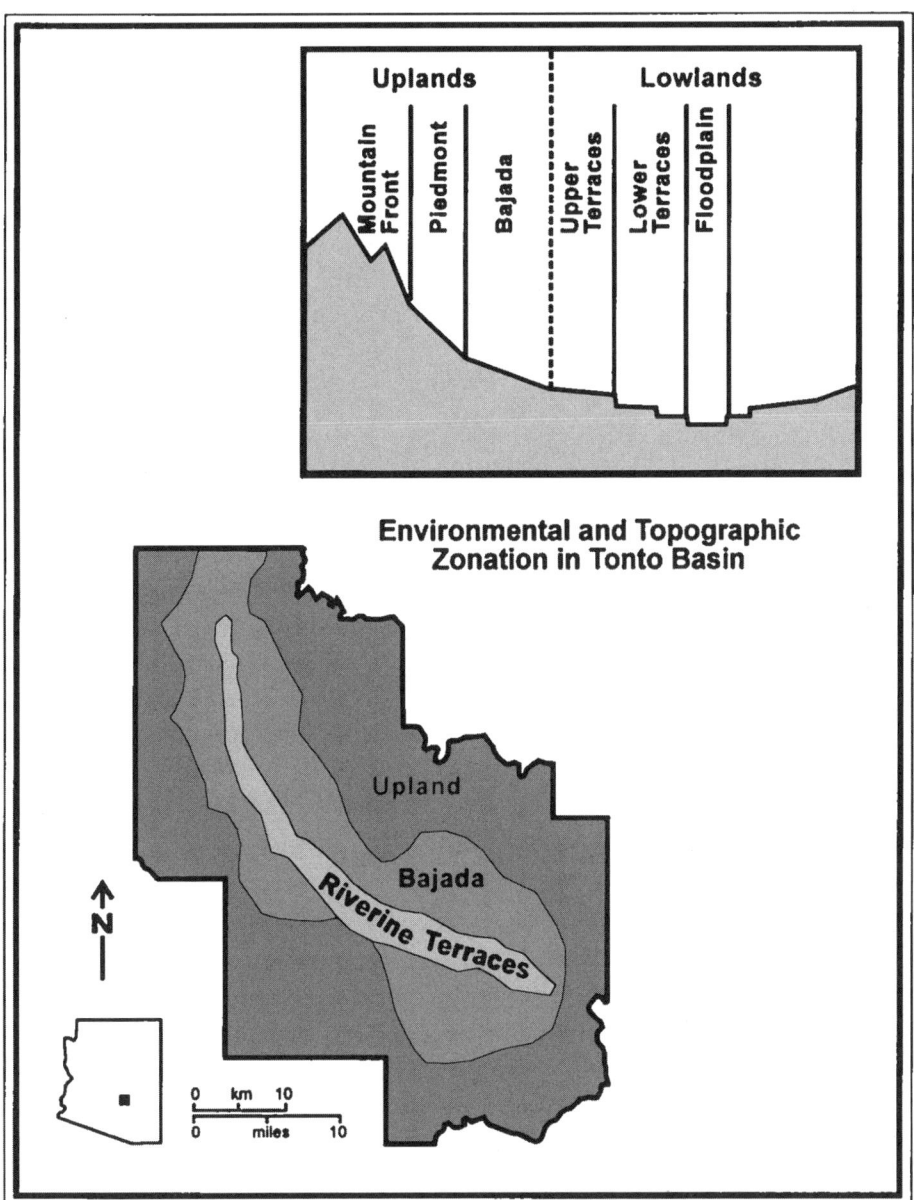

Figure 5.3. Environmental and topographic zonation in Tonto Basin.

and by juniper at the upper. Most of the archaeology of Tonto Basin is known from sites in this tier.

The third tier is the bajada at the feet of the surrounding mountain ranges. Primarily detrital in nature, at its upper end the slopes are fairly steep, but the lower bajada often merges imperceptibly into the back sides of the second tier terraces, often distinguishable only by the nature and grain size of the surface sediments.

The fourth tier is the piedmont of the mountain ranges—broken areas of steeper, rockier slopes, isolated mountainous features and mesa-like projections from the mountains themselves, often with secluded small valleys high above the Basin floor. At the boundary between the piedmont and bajada of both the east face of the Mazatzals and the south face of the Sierra Ancha is a spring line. Along these lines are a number of oases in an otherwise dry desert scrub/chaparral/juniper savannah environment.

The fifth tier is the face of the mountains themselves, steep, rocky, rugged areas that are essentially uninhabitable but for the occasional small interior basins that they conceal. Above this tier lie the mountain crest regions, thick with pinyon-juniper woodland and stringers of pine forest. For the purposes of this analysis, they lie outside the Basin, but we come back to them later since at least some of them appear to have played a significant role in the development of the Tonto Basin Salado.

There is also a sort of "sixth tier" around the edges of the Basin. While not strictly an elevation zone, it consists of broad, flat-bottomed and often spring-fed tributary drainages that contain their own miniature terrace systems: Park Creek, Sycamore Creek, Greenback Creek, Salome Creek, Armer Gulch, Cottonwood Creek, Campaign Creek, and Pinto Creek. This "tier" extends the floodplain and terrace environment of the Basin floor into upland settings. The junction of these "sixth tier" drainages with the piedmont spring line creates the upland oases mentioned above.

The Upper Basin is both similar to and different from the Lower. In the Rye Creek section, the west side reflects the same patterns as the Lower Basin. On the east side, however, the tiers are reduced essentially to a large bajada/piedmont zone below Oxbow Hill, the edge of the sub-Mogollon Rim plateau that contains the Payson Basin to the north. The Gisela Valley section is quite different, consisting primarily of a small flat-bottomed valley sandwiched between two steep mountain fronts with a bajada only on the west side.

The six tiers of Tonto Basin can be reduced to two occupation zones during the prehistoric period: upland and lowland (Figure 5.3). The Lowland consists of the first two tiers and the lower edge of the third, the toe of the bajada where it grades into the back side of the upper terraces. The Upland is everything else except the "sixth tier" drainages and oases.

While all six tiers in both upland and lowland settings were occupied at one time or another, the bulk of the population appears to have always favored the lowland settings, places with easy access to the rivers. Here settlements, while not necessarily permanent (e.g., 1000 years at the same address), were relatively stable and often occupied for the duration of several archaeological phases, frequently right across the temporal boundaries that are used to distinguish the different occupational periods and "ethnic" groups said to characterize Tonto Basin. Overall, the Lowland Zone was occupied continuously from the time of the first arrival or development of agricultural villagers in the Basin until the last prehistoric straggler finally gave up and walked away in search of more prosperous relatives.

The Upland Zone was apparently far less desirable, which is not surprising given its general lack of water and its thin, rocky soils. As the "frontier" of Tonto Basin, it was a very unstable occupation zone (Wood and McAllister 1984a; Van West et al., Chapter 2). During the earliest known occurrence of residential populations in the Basin, this area seems to have been only lightly used, though there are frequent finds of early projectile points throughout the Uplands. During the subsequent development of an agriculturally based sedentary village life during the Preclassic period, the Upland Zone appears rarely to have even been visited until very near the end of that period, when a few small settlements began to encroach on its lower extremities and spring locations. It is not until the early to middle Classic that the Upland Zone was seen as a viable location for residence, though this was a fleeting thing for the most part. By the late Classic, the Upland Zone was again empty of people except for a few oasis-like situations.

This dynamic occupational use of the Uplands, the periodic movement of large numbers of people up and down the tiers of the Basin, may hold some key to explaining some of the more puzzling aspects of Tonto Basin prehistory. In many ways the prehistoric occupation of Tonto Basin follows the "boom and bust" model of settlement common to the arid Southwest during the last century.

Site Types and Settlement Patterns in Tonto Basin

Since the focus of this chapter is on questions of occupation and relationship rather than subsistence, per se, we can limit our study of Tonto Basin site types to residential types. Since we are also focusing on the Classic period or Salado occupation, we can dispense with earlier forms, other than to note that the Preclassic occupation of Tonto Basin was characterized by variable sized settlements (mostly small, but abundant) made up of individual pithouses that were virtually identical to contemporary Hohokam pithouses in the Phoenix Basin to the south (Ciolek-Torrello et al. 1994; Craig and Clark 1994; Elson and Lindeman 1994; Haury 1932). Given that, however, there are many ways to look at the Classic period sites. The most descriptively basic way to look at them would be simply as site types; sites as architecture (Figure 5.4). We can even sort them by size, starting with the largest and working our way down.

Complex Platform Mound Sites

This site type represents an eclectic form of conglomerated residential structure involving the construction of both Hohokam-style platform mounds and compounds and "pueblo-like" buildings with interior courtyards defined by walls and plazas defined by massed or linear room blocks. They range in size from about 75 rooms to 150 or more rooms. Only three such sites are known with certainty: Rye Creek Ruin (150-plus rooms) and Gisela Mound (ca. 75 rooms) in the Upper Basin and Armer Ranch Ruin (150-plus rooms) in the Lower Basin. None have been extensively excavated, but the larger two, Rye and Armer, each appears to contain two platform mounds. Several other sites are suspected of having this configuration, including the Oak Creek Mound on Tonto Creek and the Wheatfields Mound on lower Pinal Creek (just outside what we have defined here as Tonto Basin). Unfortunately, the Oak Creek Mound has been very extensively damaged by erosion, pothunting, and road construction, so we may never know for sure.

These sites, in this configuration at least, appear to have been a late Classic development; all appear to have started out earlier as more or less typical platform mound compounds. Two of these sites—Oak Creek and Wheatfields—are situated in the midst of an assortment of contemporary settlements. The others—Rye, Armer, and Gisela—appear to have been the only substantial occupied structures in their respective areas during much of the late Classic.

Platform Mound Compounds

This site type is essentially identical with the type known from the Phoenix Basin: a traditional rectangular Hohokam style compound enclosing a relatively small number of rooms along with one or more purposefully built platform mounds that, in turn, supported their own small number of rooms. There is some variability in layout in Tonto Basin, and the mounds themselves tend to be small, but overall there is little variance from contemporary Hohokam architectural traditions other than in the greater use of rocks in construction. There are 17 of these in the Tonto Basin Lowland Zone (Figure 5.5). From northwest to southeast they are: Gisela Mound, Gisela Schoolhouse (mostly bulldozed away), Rye Creek Ruin, VIV Ruin (also mostly bulldozed away), Park Creek Mound, Oak Creek Mound, Encinito, Cline Terrace, Horse Pasture, Bourke's Teocalli, Rock Island Mound, Bass Point Mound, Armer Ranch Ruin, Pinto Point Mound, Livingston Mound, Meddler Point Mound, and the Wheatfields Mound. All but two of these—Park Creek and Livingston, neither of which appear to have been occupied after they were built—are in settings that overlook the main drainages from or near the terrace edges.

In addition to the lowland mounds, there are at least three in the uplands: Las Sierras, in the northern edge of the Superstitions (Crary et al. 1992), the Turkey Creek Mound in the Sierra Ancha, and the Ellison Ranch Mound on the east side of the Sierra Ancha in an upland environment but overlooking Cherry Creek. We might also include the Park Creek Mound in this group, since it was along a tributary drainage halfway up the Mazatzal bajada in the midst of an extensive, if low density, upland occupation (Germick and Crary 1990).

Based on the Roosevelt Projects excavations, construction of nearly every platform mound in Tonto Basin appears to have been initiated during a very brief horizon in the middle Classic period, sometime around 1280. All but two of the 17 Lowland Zone platform mound sites were built in the middle of extensive and relatively densely occupied residential complexes (three of them, however, are either under the reservoir most of the time or surrounded by it to the point where we have little information about their associated settlements). Building dates for the Upland mounds are less well known, as are their surrounding settlements, but at least one, Las Sierras, was in the midst of a cluster of apparently contemporary settlements.

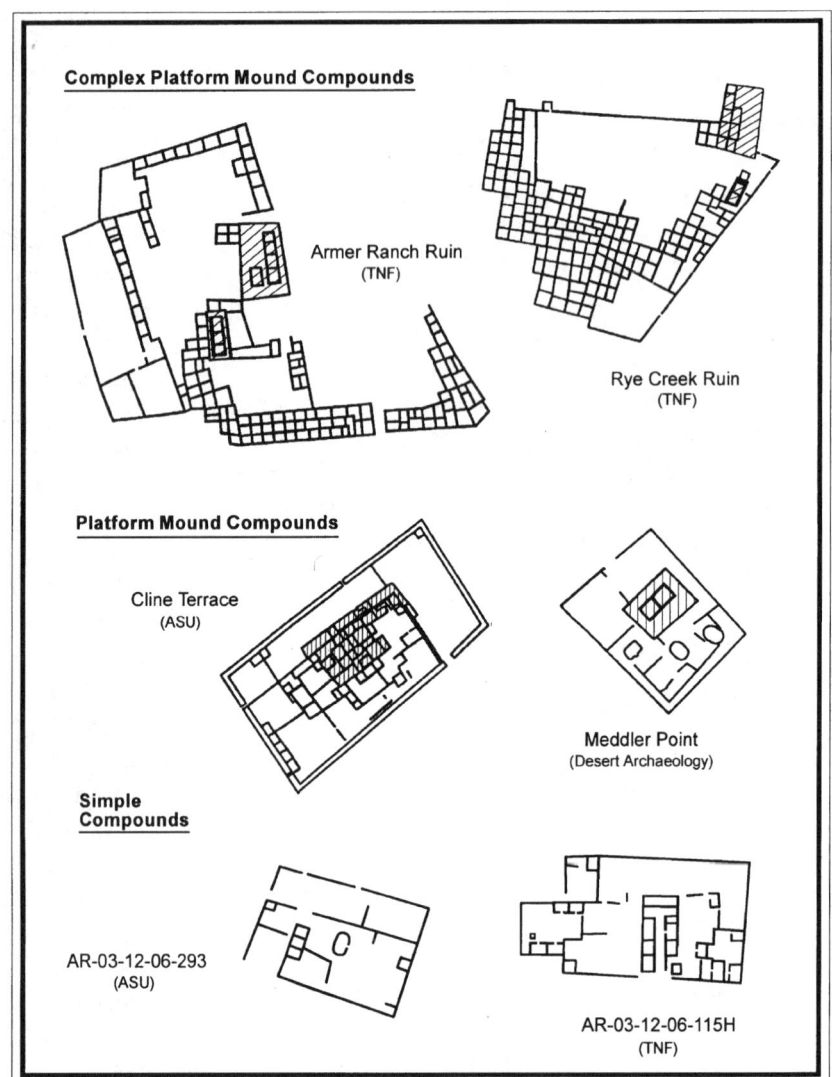

Figure 5.4a.
Site types in Tonto Basin.

Another site type present in the Tonto Basin area may be related to the platform mounds but has yet to be studied. This type has the same plan form as a platform mound compound only without the actual platform mound. Instead, it contains a central room block that is architecturally differentiated from other structures in the compound, often by the use of selected construction material (e.g., red scoria as opposed to local basalt) or by mass, usually by means of full-height masonry walls surrounded by walls and rooms of primarily adobe or jacal construction. Most of these sites are in the Upland Zone around the edges of the Basin.

Most of the platform mound sites continued to be occupied well into the late Classic period with several surviving right up to the time of the regional abandonment.

Some, as we saw above, changed form slightly with the addition of additional residential structures. Others, however, particularly in the eastern end of the Salt Arm, were abandoned right around the beginning of the late Classic, along with their associated residential clusters.

Compounds

With the regional difference in construction materials noted above, this site type is essentially the same as those in the Phoenix Basin and reflects the same architectural conventions. Generally rectangular in outline or made up of a series of abutted rectangular outlines in irregular but still rectilinear shapes, these sites consist primarily of enclosing walls and wall-divided interior courtyards containing a relatively small number of rooms. The rooms themselves can be

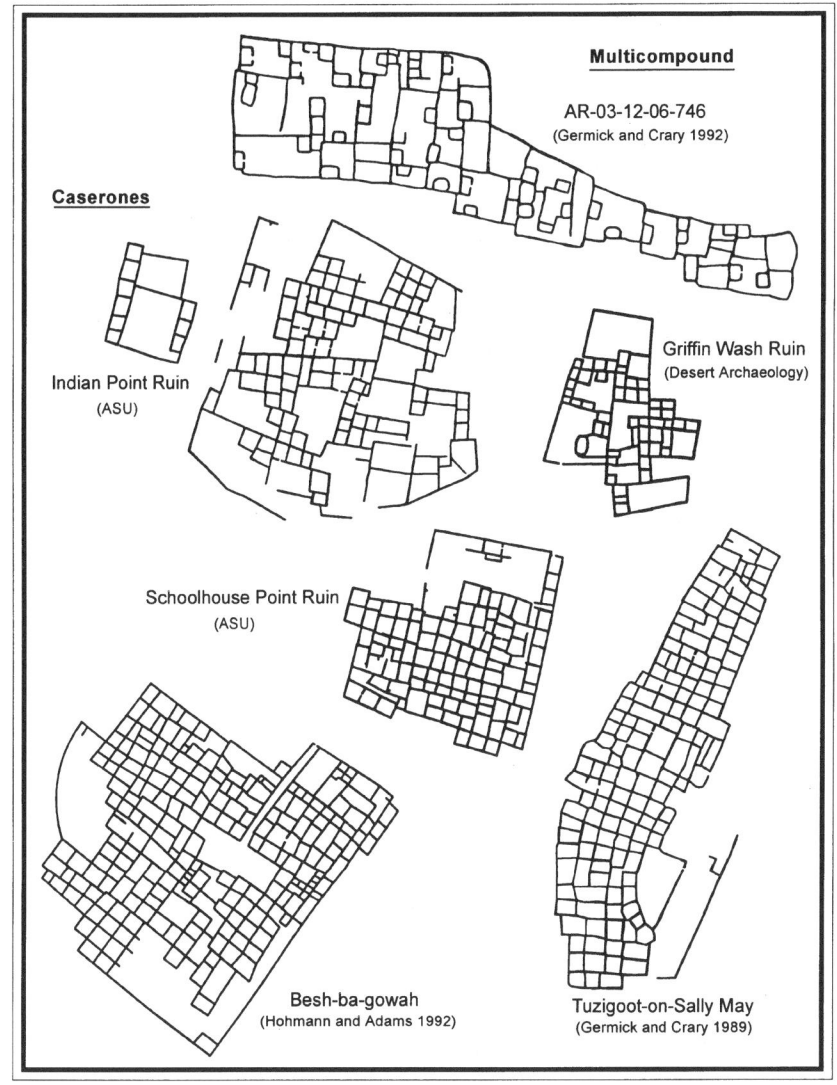

Figure 5.4b.
Site types in Tonto Basin.

either freestanding or abutted to the enclosing walls and may be detached from each other or grouped in small contiguous units. Compounds range from as few as one or two rooms to as many as 75 or more. Thus, taken by themselves, they cover the full range of settlement sizes, from single family homesteads to village. Frequently, however, they are found in contemporary clusters of variously sized units, suggesting that in some cases they represented household, lineage, or other corporate elements within a larger composite settlement not unlike what is commonly called a town.

In recent years we have seen a fairly clear developmental sequence in this site type in Tonto Basin—basically the same sequence seen in Hohokam settlements. The earliest attempts at architectural enclosure of the com-

mon areas amidst house clusters appear to have been in the form of wing walls attached to some houses. This seems to represent the beginning of a transition from plazas, where open space is freely accessible and public, defined by the arrangement of buildings, to courtyards, where open spaces are more commonly private than public, defined by enclosing walls within or attached to buildings that effectively restrict or control access even to public areas. Compounds as such appear to have originated by building enclosing walls around existing settlements made up of individual detached houses. This sometimes resulted in very irregular outlines, often with some houses being only partially enclosed as the compound walls abutted them at odd angles, perhaps as a result of connecting with earlier wing walls. Later, the

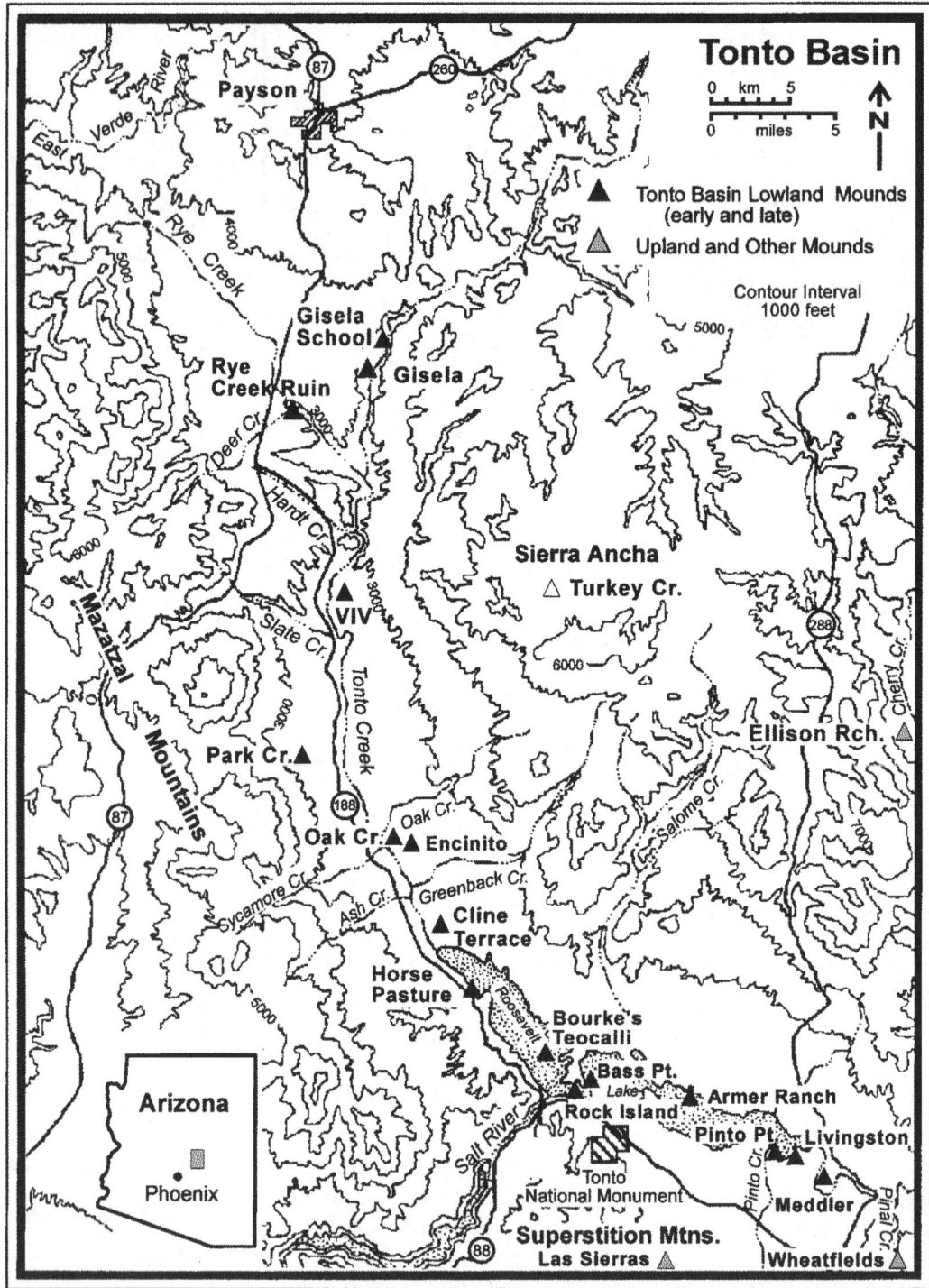

Figure 5.5.   Distribution of platform mounds in and around Tonto Basin.

compounds appear to have been more purpose-built and regular in outline, though it appears that a common mode of expansion was simply to tack another enclosure on the outside so that the larger ones again take on an irregular overall shape. Just to add to the confusion, we might refer to these as "multicompounds."

It can also be seen that these compounds grew almost directly out of the Preclassic idea of the pithouse cluster, as it is common to see early compounds that simply enclosed a group of pit rooms and jacals having a common focus on a shared activity area. The earliest compound rooms as well bespeak a pithouse heritage, being originally nothing more than adobe lined oval and rectangular pit rooms with vertical walls of pole-reinforced adobe or jacal, sometimes being built by modifying existing pithouses. Later, the rooms tend to become more commonly rectangular and used masonry for everything from simply bracing wall posts to wainscoting to full wall construction using various ratios of rock and adobe (Craig, Elson, and Jacobs 1992). As rooms tended to become rectangular, they were more often built in contiguous blocks rather than as standalone structures. Nevertheless, the old tradition of jacal walled oval houses appears to have hung on at least through the end of the middle Classic period such that one or more such rooms may frequently be found in compounds surrounded by rectangular houses and room blocks and yet filled with contemporary artifacts and used for the same residential purposes.

The temporal sequence in all of this is interesting. It seems from the evidence of both survey and excavation, particularly recent excavations along Tonto Creek sponsored by the Arizona Department of Transportation (Jeffery Clark, personal communication 1995), that the transition from pithouse to pit room took place sometime in the mid- to late-twelfth century. In the early part of the thirteenth century, both oval and rectangular forms remained in use, as did excavated floors, though the surface built, rectangular, pole-reinforced room type became increasingly common. Masonry was relatively rare outside the Uplands, and it was primarily used only as foundations for jacal walls. The first compounds, those built to enclose existing house clusters, are probably no earlier than the 1220s, but by 1250 or so they had become a common, if not yet dominant architectural type. Full cobble masonry wall construction began to come into common use sometime after that—perhaps as much as a century after its introduction in the nearby Lower Verde (Spoerl and Gumerman 1984; see below).

Why house clusters should have been enclosed by walls is a debate that has continued for generations, here and in the Hohokam country. The walls may have simply been a social convention for group identification, a way to keep the kids from running off, or they may have been defensive as such structures are commonly interpreted in most other parts of the world not hampered by the romantic notions of prehistoric pacifism that characterize American archaeology. If the final configuration of the compound wall at Cline Terrace—box rampart construction with an outer palisade—is any indication, a defensive origin may not be too unlikely.

Caserones

This type of residential structure, the name for which I adopted some years ago to avoid any "ethnic" connotations, represents a continuation of the conglomerate trend seen in the development of the later, larger compounds. The term caseron is Spanish and refers essentially to a large house (casa) with implications of a large resident population. They appear to have been most common in the later Classic period, apparently showing up on a small scale in the latter part of the thirteenth century.

These sites, characterized by more use of contiguous room construction than might be typical for a Hohokam style compound, vary in configuration and room density on a continuum from the multi compound type with a mixture of room blocks and small interior and exterior courtyards, to solid blocks of contiguous rooms with no exterior entries and no enclosed or otherwise defined open space of any kind. They were originally called checkerboards by Bandelier and are commonly, though I would argue, erroneously, referred to as "pueblos," despite the fact that they do not have the central room block defined plaza orientation typical of sites from the Colorado Plateau. There may, however, be some similarities with sites elsewhere below the Mogollon Rim to the east (e.g., Grasshopper or Kinishba), in that one site just outside Tonto Basin—Besh-Ba-Gowah in Globe—appears in its last configuration to have had a small internal plaza connected to the outside by a long hallway (Hohmann and Adams 1992). A similar configuration may be found at the unexcavated primary settlement on Polles Mesa southwest of Payson. Schoolhouse Point Ruin in Tonto Basin may also have had a similar appearance, but its elevated central interior common area was made up of the rooftops of a group of storage rooms and would have been broken up by many entryways (Lindauer 1996a), making the similarity more coincidental than functional. Rye Creek Ruin in the Upper Basin has a large common area in the middle of the site, but it is more of an irregular courtyard formed by building a wall across the open end of an unbroken arc of rooms. It is even possible that Armer Ranch Ruin was beginning to take on such a form before it was abandoned, with the construction of a partial hollow square of room blocks on the east side of the original platform mound compound. This pattern is seen in completed form at the Gisela Mound site. These, however, are the exceptions; most such sites in and around Tonto Basin do not contain large central interior plazas.

The larger caserones in Tonto Basin are often surrounded by abandoned earlier compounds, giving the impression that they represent the absorption of the previous population at a given site (see Lindauer, Chapter 9). In such cases these sites appear to represent a clear change in settlement organization from the compound; in others they appear simply to represent the growth of population within a single settlement. It has often been said that the caserones reflect the introduction of an architectural tradition into Tonto Basin that had an origin other than Hohokam, which is to say, Mogollon or Anasazi or something else "puebloan." However, given the continuous distribution of site structure from partially in-filled compound to solid room blocks, the close association between solid room blocks and topographic settings which would allow no other choices, and the fact that the same site types and developmental sequence can be seen to the west in the Lower Verde—Bloody Basin—Perry Mesa area, far removed from "puebloan" associations, the explanation for their adoption and/or development in Tonto Basin is probably not that simple. Nevertheless, their increasing dominance of residential patterns in the late Classic suggests changing notions about how social organization should be expressed by architecture.

There are three types of caseron: 1) sites like Griffin Wash or Indian Point that apparently originated as compounds or multicompounds (i.e., having an obvious retention of one or more original compound walls) but have been essentially filled in with contiguous rooms (a process I have called "tenementing") to make an irregular pattern of contiguous and detached rooms interspersed by multiple small interior courtyards and attached exterior courtyards; 2) sites that originated as contiguous room blocks without any enclosing compound wall or any interior open spaces, and often without even any attached exterior courtyards; and 3) a unique form we might call a house mound. All of them are relatively irregular in overall plan and rarely have any sort of surface entry through the outer walls. A fourth type might consist of those room block structures constructed in overhanging rockshelters, what we usually call cliff dwellings, but, aside from the area inside Tonto National Monument, such sites are quite rare in Tonto Basin itself. Curiously enough, just as Salado compounds parallel those of the Hohokam, there were also compounds in the Salt River Valley that appear to have undergone the same patterns of growth by abutment and tenementing that are seen in Tonto Basin, though without the same intensity and density (e.g., Haury 1945).

The Salado house mound, an architectural form so far only known from Tonto Basin, is a peculiar type of site. A variation of the other types of caseron, the house mound sites borrowed certain construction techniques from the platform mounds in that various blocks of rooms are elevated above the rest on raised foundations similar in construction to platform mounds. These elevated room blocks, however, do not follow the architectural conventions of platform mounds and tend to be simply portions of what would otherwise be contiguous room blocks. The use of these elevated areas also appears to be relatively diverse; at the Schoolhouse Point Ruin, the elevated blocks were arranged to create a protected storage area in the middle of the site, while at Indian Point they appear to have been used to terrace the slope of the ridge where the site is located. At the Armer Gulch Ruin, the elevation of a few rooms at the center of the site (Oliver 1997a) gives the impression of a terraced multistory structure while the single elevated room at Pyramid Point (Elson 1994a) gives the impression of a small platform mound (though it may have served more as a watchtower). In any case, such construction certainly exaggerated the vertical profile of what would otherwise be characterized as single story buildings (true multistory construction appears to have been relatively rare in Tonto Basin outside the protected context of large rockshelters). The house mounds appear to have been a very late development in Tonto Basin architecture and may, if Schoolhouse is any indication, have represented at least as much a change in defensive strategy as they did social organization.

Homesteads

Typically small (i.e., fewer than ten rooms), this residential type is characterized by a closely proximate cluster of detached and/or semidetached (two-three rooms stuck together) houses and storage structures. In layout, these sites appear to continue patterns established in the Preclassic with pithouses. Both oval and rectangular room forms are seen, and many sites contain both. While the oval forms are generally assumed to be earlier, say before 1250, they continued to be used throughout most of the thirteenth century. While assessing the duration of occupation of such sites is notoriously difficult, they can at least be generally assumed to have been residential in purpose; the mere fact that they represent some investment in capital and labor in a single location suggests that they were usually meant to be "permanent" rather than seasonal, though this is not a certainty. Such sites are found from the beginning to the end of the Classic period.

Field Houses

Typically isolated and usually no more than one or two rooms, these are insubstantial structures assumed to have been seasonal or otherwise temporary in purpose. Often they are associated with some type of agricultural facility—check dams, terraces, rockpile fields, and the like. This is, by far, the most common single site type in Tonto Basin.

Other Site Types

As noted above, the focus here is on Classic period residential sites, but there are many other types in Tonto Basin, including simple activity area artifact scatters, rock shelters, and a few walled hilltop forts, not to mention the various and sundry pithouse and pit room settlements that frequently (in some areas invariably) underlie the Classic period structures.

Ceremonial, Ritual, and Public Architecture

While not strictly a residential site type, there has been so much made over the last few years regarding the ceremonial or ritual nature of Salado settlements, that discussing this controversial topic would not be untoward.

While "kivas" are known from "Salado" contexts to the east and south, so far, the inventory of thousands of sites and the excavation of hundreds of them has revealed nothing resembling a kiva in or around Tonto Basin. The closest thing to a "ceremonial room" from the area is a single example from Besh-Ba-Gowah (Hohmann et al.

1992), but this example is hardly certain, and it has not been replicated anywhere else in the area. Likewise, there are no Classic period ball courts (or Preclassic ones either, for that matter, though the jury may still be out on that one). In fact, the only candidates for any form of public or ceremonial/ritual architecture are the platform mounds. Even this identification, however, is not without controversy. Platform mounds first appeared in the Preclassic period in the Phoenix Basin giving them a much greater time depth than in Tonto Basin. These early mounds might be considered "ceremonial" in that they were activity focused and clearly nonresidential, but by the time the Tonto Basin mounds were built, platform mounds in the Phoenix Basin were overtly residential (Gregory 1987). If the Tonto Basin mounds were derived from those in the Phoenix or Tucson Basins, as seems most probable, it is reasonable to assume that they would have followed the residential then current rather than the older (and possibly forgotten) ceremonial model. Of the five excavated platform mounds (not including Pyramid Point since it appears to have been something else), only the Meddler Mound even remotely conforms to any expectations of ceremonial use (Craig and Clark 1994) and much of the argument supporting this contention is equivocal. All the rest are clearly residential and are frequently isolated spatially, architecturally, and elevationally from the other residential units in their compounds. While the mounds may have served to focus some ceremonial activities and were almost certainly occupied by people having such social status as would probably require ceremonial obligations and leadership roles, it is difficult to understand how a structure dedicated to the residence of a small subset of a site's population and inaccessible to the rest could be considered "public."

The site types described above represent the building blocks of Salado settlement patterning in Tonto Basin. Several trends can be seen in the Basin, however, related to how these building blocks may have been used to create communities.

During the Preclassic, settlement distribution in Tonto Basin can be characterized as disaggregated. Small residential clusters of (so far) no more than a dozen or so pithouses at any one time are scattered all along the terraces overlooking the rivers in what amounts to an almost continuous linear distribution of people from one end of the Basin to the other, like a string of pearls.

This pattern appears to continue throughout the Classic period but by the mid-1200s the population along the rivers, at least, began aggregating into fewer but larger concentrations, a trend that continued to the end of the prehistoric occupation. Thus, by the end of the Classic we can find a wide variety of both disaggregated and aggregated settlements. The disaggregated settlements can further be divided into distributed and dispersed forms. The aggregated settlements can also be characterized as being of two basic types, agglomerated and conglomerated. We can look at these four forms as tiers within a hierarchy of settlement size and population density.

Conglomerated Settlements

These are the large, sometimes multilevel and occasionally (though rarely) multistory caserones and house mounds. Their definitive characteristic is that they are made up of a cohering mass of rooms and appear to have served as the single communal residence for a settlement. We might even include the larger multicompounds like the Sycamore Creek and Tilley Mesa sites in this category.

Agglomerated Settlements

This type of settlement seems almost unique to the Hohokam-related traditions of the southern part of Arizona. They typically consist of a noncohering cluster of closely proximate multiple compounds. While these clusters can involve as few as two to four compounds often, the larger ones, centering around platform mound compounds, can contain dozens. The platform mound aggregated settlements, in fact, can be quite large, encompassing as many as 500 rooms. There are at least seven such settlement complexes in Tonto Basin, only two of which, Cline Terrace and Armer Ranch (Figure 5.6), are known well enough to characterize. These two, with allowances for differences in topography, appear to be laid out in much the same manner as contemporary Hohokam towns in the Salt River Valley in that they consist of concentric "rings" of compounds and ranchería form residences around the central platform mound with an outer "ring" of temporary or seasonal structures and agricultural and processing facilities (Crary et al. 1992; Wood 1989). Given their size and differentiated organization, these settlements have something of an "urban" feel to them, particularly in the case of Armer Ranch. This type of settlement appears to have reached its peak in the late thirteenth and early fourteenth centuries, afterward being essentially replaced by settlements of the conglomerated type.

Distributed Settlements

This class of settlement represents the typical rural pattern of residence over most of the Basin. It consists of the smaller compounds and caserones that probably housed no more than a few households at any given time. These units are the same as those forming the residential elements of the aggregated settlements. The only difference is that these are distributed across the landscape in a variety of settings, often being quite isolated from other settlements (or as isolated as one could be in the narrow confines of Tonto Basin). Quite frequently these settings show a regard for defense capabilities, as they are often on top of hills, at the edges of mesas, and other places where there is a strategic view of the surrounding countryside.

Dispersed Settlements

As noted above, sites of this class are the most common in the area. Made up of no more than a few rooms, most have the appearance of having been only briefly occupied. While some of them may have been intended as the nuclei for permanent settlement, most, especially the so-called field houses were probably only used on a seasonal or temporary basis. Such sites are most common in the Uplands, but occur along the rivers as well. In some cases, they are associated with the later house mounds and may, as they appear to at Schoolhouse Point, represent the last effective use of the Basin by stragglers or people from outside venturing in only seasonally.

Unlike the distributed settlements that, at least along the rivers, frequently show considerable stability, many of them having been built on top of or even out of previous pithouse settlements, the dispersed settlements appear to reflect a tradition of mobility oriented adaptive flexibility. Even so, finding such small sites along the rivers sitting on top of a Hohokam pithouse or two is common.

THE TONTO BASIN UPLANDS

Most of what was discussed above pertains to Tonto Basin as a whole, but most particularly to the valley floor. Stability and continuity, sustained population growth and the development of large and complex settlements with internal hierarchical organization are the characteristics of the Lowlands. The Salado occupation of Tonto Basin, however, was not confined to the riverside. At various times is spread over nearly every elevational tier in the Basin.

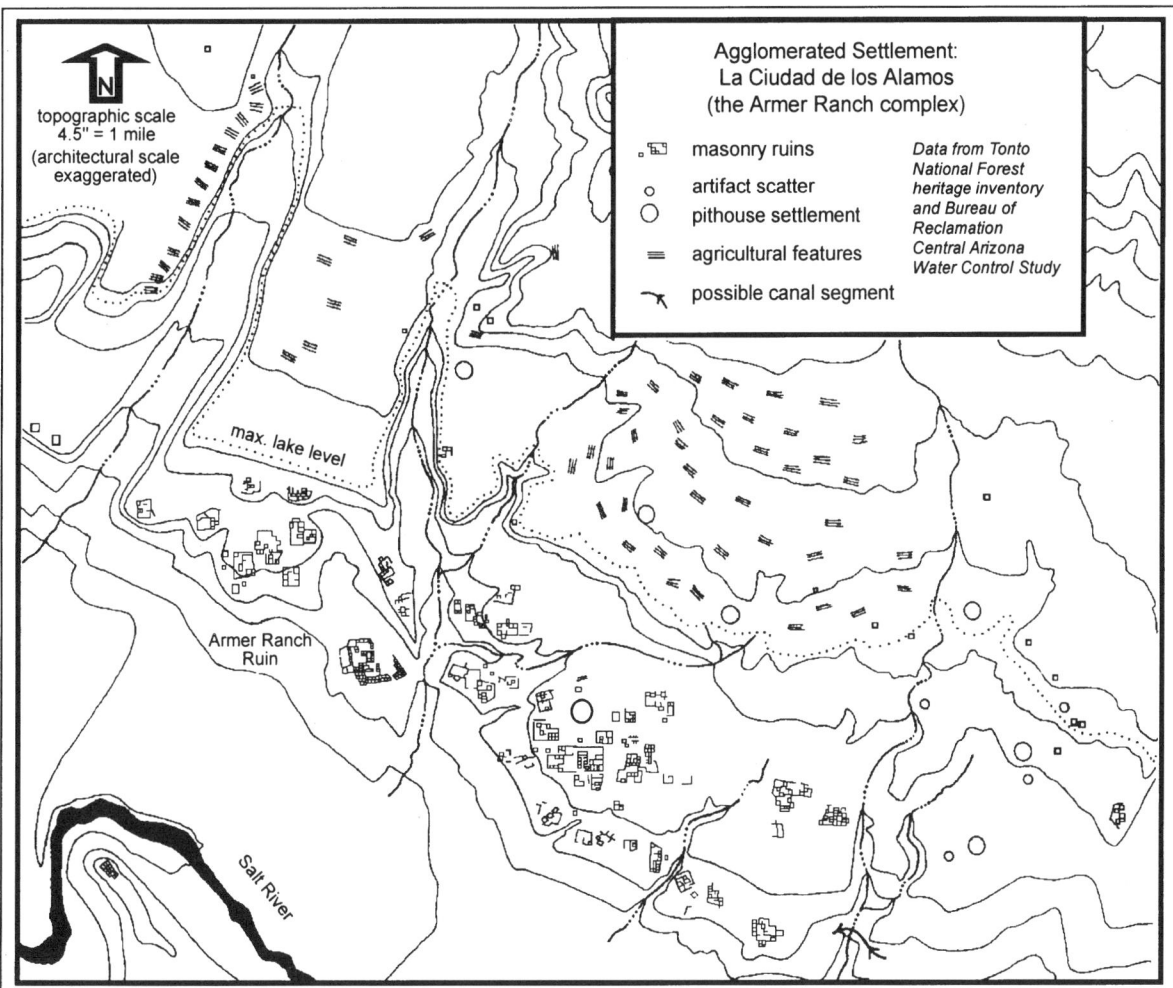

Figure 5.6.   Agglomerated settlement: La Ciudad de los Alamos (the Armer Ranch Complex).

We can preface this discussion by noting that, while survey coverage in the Uplands is quite extensive, temporal controls are limited to surface finds of decorated ceramics and so are subject to change. It should also be noted that decorated ceramics are not found on most Upland sites, further compounding the problem.

Upland settlements in the Basin took on as many different forms as there were environmental settings and time periods. They ranged from simple procurement and processing areas used seasonally or temporarily by means of field houses or camps to large, long lived conglomerated villages along the Sierra Ancha spring line that rivaled anything along the riverside (Germick and Crary 1989, 1990; Oliver 1997a; Wood and McAllister 1984a). Unfortunately, there is not enough space here to

cover the full range of variation; we must make do with some general patterns.

Overall, the first real occupation of the Uplands came late in the prehistory of Tonto Basin. While there are occasional Archaic sites in the Uplands, most Preclassic period occupation focused on the riverside and ignored the Uplands altogether. It is not until the Sacaton phase that we even begin to see small settlements, probably seasonal, showing up at favored, often spring-fed locations on the bajada. While some of these settlements exhibit enough trash accumulation to suggest that they were occupied for some time, most do not appear to have been viable and may have represented little more than explorations of agricultural and other economic opportunities.

It is not until the Hardt/Miami phase that any substantial population began to move away from the riverside. This appears to have taken place in the latter part of that phase, probably after about 1230 or so. While many of these sites are probably nothing more than field houses used by riverside folk to expand their agricultural possibilities, many are of homestead size and appear to have been more or less permanent. By Roosevelt phase, every form of settlement imaginable was present in the Uplands, from field houses to large compound villages. Most of these, however, were abandoned before the introduction of Pinto Polychrome, with the vast majority not lasting much past about 1280 or so. The survivors appear to have been those settlements situated along the spring lines. Sometime after the introduction of Gila Polychrome, new settlements were started again in the Uplands, and those oasis survivors from Roosevelt phase appear to have begun growing in size. Most of these new settlements, however, also failed or were consolidated into the larger conglomerated settlements like Tuzigoot-on-Sally May, many of which appear to have continued operations until the Basin as a whole was abandoned toward the end of the fourteenth century.

Within this overall pattern are several variations that appear largely to have been adapted to different local environments. As noted above, for the most part, the Uplands are an area of thin, rocky, and easily eroded soils of limited agricultural potential. Only the "sixth tier" tributaries and spring line localities offer any potential for long term agricultural use, even with the elaborate water harvesting technology evident in many parts of the Basin. In these areas, such as Salome Creek and Campaign Creek, settlement complexes rival those of the riverside in size and complexity. Tuzigoot-on-Sally May (Germick and Crary 1989) is one of the largest settlements in the entire Basin, despite location. The Las Sierras area of the Campaign Creek drainage appears to have supported an aggregated village similar to those at Armer Ranch or Cline Terrace, even having its own small platform mound compound (Crary et al. 1992). As we continue to refine our characterizations of Tonto Basin settlement patterns, we will need to differentiate these upland settlement systems with irrigation potential from those without such potential since they represent something quite different from the more expedient and unstable runoff exploitation farming systems commonly associated with upland settlement.

These larger settlements and population concentrations were the exceptions. In most places throughout the Uplands, the occupation was almost ephemeral. Even where there is a high density of multiple household compounds, most appear not to have been lived in for very long, suggesting that a large part of the occupation was based on entrepreneurial and opportunistic use of agricultural resources and that when the soils played out in one Upland valley, the occupants simply moved to another one. Unlike those within most of the Roosevelt Projects area, the Upland soils in Tonto Basin are topographically and climatically limited in their capability for regeneration, and water tables there are highly susceptible to drainage once eroded. Add to this the sustained demand for fuel wood and edible wild plants in an era before the spread of juniper and mesquite by cattle, and it becomes understandable why many upland settlements would have to change locations periodically. Given these problems, it is not surprising that even the larger Upland sites contain few decorated ceramics; with the exception of the "sixth tier" oases, Upland farming in Tonto Basin would have been difficult and probably offered few opportunities to accumulate disposable income. Nevertheless, even poverty may have advantages if it offers independence and access to resources not already claimed by others.

Nevertheless, the principal resource limiting Upland settlement was probably water. Most of that country is dry and very few drainages, even then, would have carried surface water year round. It is probably no coincidence, then, that the periods in which population moved either into or out of the Uplands correspond closely with the streamflow reconstructions of periods with or without sufficient water to carry out runoff-based farming (Van West et al., Chapter 2).

FRIENDS AND NEIGHBORS: SETTLEMENT AREAS AROUND THE EDGES OF TONTO BASIN

Estimates for the prehistoric population of Tonto Basin have varied widely over the years, but have always included an assumption of low population density in the Preclassic followed by striking growth during the Classic period. While recent excavations have revealed more late Preclassic settlements than most researchers had previously expected—nearly every Classic period compound excavated along Tonto Creek, for example, has an underlying Preclassic component—there does appear to have been population growth of some kind, especially since the Classic period sites tend to be larger. Yet was this growth natural and local or did other people begin streaming into the Basin during Roosevelt phase?

The short answer is that both mechanisms probably contributed to the "boom" phase of Tonto Basin prehistory. Since natural increase might be expected in a place with as much to offer as Tonto Basin, the focus shifts to the origins of these potential immigrants. Much has been made over the years of slight variations in architecture and ceramics, providing "evidence" of long distance migration by substantial numbers of people from the Colorado Plateau or "the north and east." While an intriguing and romantic notion, there is little if any unequivocal evidence of any substantial long distance immigration. There is evidence, however, that the Salado of Tonto Basin were not alone in central Arizona and that they took full advantage of their many social and economic contacts to develop their own distinctive way of life.

While this chapter may not the best place to address the "ethnicity" of the Tonto Basin Salado, I have always taken it as given that they were, to one degree or another, "multiethnic" in the sense of having come from at least two basic traditions (e.g., Wood 1989). Evidence from the Roosevelt Projects has finally, after decades of searching, located a settlement that appears to represent an indigenous population during the Early Ceramic horizon (Elson and Lindeman 1994). Further evidence discussed by Elson et al. (Chapter 7) has essentially confirmed Haury's (1932) and Gladwin and Gladwin's (1935) notions of a Hohokam colonization of the area, at least in the Lower Basin, followed by a period of strong acculturation to Hohokam traditions in architecture and material culture. This combination of indigenous and Hohokam derived traditions, then, forms the basis for what we call Salado.

It can also be assumed that the indigenous folk and the Hohokam were not the only people to find their way to the Basin; the frequency of traded goods in Salado sites alone is evidence enough for strong and persistent contacts with other groups that would have provided mechanisms and avenues for individual immigration at least and probably for whole families and possibly even lineages. Small scale migrations arising from trade relationships and marriage alliances, however, were undoubtedly a common occurrence throughout the prehistoric South-

west and, as such, would have made little splash as they were dropped into the local cultural soup. The general patterns of Salado life in Tonto Basin followed those of the Hohokam in the Phoenix Basin (up to the middle fourteenth century, anyway), and yet there are several distinctly "non-Hohokam" elements within what is called Salado. Not the least of these is the relatively extensive use of plain corrugated and Salado Red corrugated pottery and the development of the distinctly non-Hohokam conglomerated residential structures. If this was the result of immigration, and not simply the result of social, religious, and even technological trends spreading across the entire Southwest in the thirteenth and fourteenth centuries, we might first want to look at the folks living closest at hand for explanations.

While limitations do not permit us to look at the full range of relationships the Tonto Basin populations may have enjoyed with their neighbors, several areas stand out as potentially critical to understanding developments in the Basin: the Lower Verde River, the Payson Basin, the Globe Highlands, and last, but not least, the Sierra Ancha. We might also want to look at the increasingly critical area between San Carlos and the Salt River Canyon, but we will make do with those areas having inventory data.

The Lower Verde

The Lower Verde area, encompasses a broad swath across central Arizona from the Mazatzals west to the Agua Fria River north of the Salt River Valley, is important to Tonto Basin for what it does not contain. Its culture history and settlement development are similar, the only difference being that the indigenous population was probably more interactive with competing Hohokam. It is known to have had a sedentary Late Archaic population, at least at the southern end, and early Red-on-buff pottery, such as Snaketown and Gila Butte, is commonly found on the larger sites, one of which, Azatlan, is one of the largest extant and undisturbed Hohokam sites. As well, the Lower Verde contains one of the highest concentrations of ball courts anywhere in the Hohokam area.

Classic period settlement patterning in the Lower Verde developed in very much the same way as in Tonto Basin (Crary 1991). Typical Sacaton style pithouse settlements gave way to masonry founded oval-room settlements that were in turn incorporated into and replaced by the same types of compound settlements. By the late Classic, these settlements were phased out in favor of very large conglomerated caseron villages. In fact, the single largest structure known on the Tonto National Forest—Mercer Ruin, said to contain as many as 300 rooms—is located on the Verde. Similar sites containing 50 to 150 rooms are common throughout the rest of the area, particularly in Bloody Basin and on Perry Mesa. A small extension of the Verde tradition through the Mazatzals along the East Verde River even carries this pattern into direct contact with Upper Tonto Basin. The ceramic traditions of Tonto Basin and the Lower Verde are very similar, particularly in the use of the same striated-polish red wares typical of Classic period Hohokam.

What the Lower Verde does not have is corrugated pottery, whether of the plain or the Salado Red variety; not surprising, since the southern and western distribution of Salado Red is essentially the mountain ranges bordering Tonto Basin. It also does not appear to have any platform mounds except at the extreme southern end, though this may be an artifact of the nature of survey coverage and the fact that we have precious little excavation data from any of the larger, later sites; it has been suggested that there is a platform mound in the Horseshoe Basin, embedded in the later construction of Mercer Ruin (Crary 1991), though this may be nothing more than an example of the same sort of "house mound" construction seen in Tonto Basin. In essence, then, the Lower Verde area shows almost the same developmental patterns and histories seen in Tonto Basin but without any "eastern" influence in its ceramics and with less organizational development or differentiation.

The Payson Basin

The Payson Basin shares many characteristics with the upper portion of Tonto Basin in terms of its settlement history. Hohokam influence shows up early in both areas but without much strong evidence (so far) of an extensive Hohokam presence (Elson and Craig 1992c; Redman 1993). There appears to have been a sedentary Late Archaic occupation in the area, though it is known exclusively from rockshelter sites, no architectural manifestations having yet been identified. Ceramics dating to the Snaketown phase have been excavated around Payson, but the earliest documented ceramic period residential occupation does not appear to have been established until sometime around 850, during the Union Park phase, when there is a strong influx of Hohokam-style architecture and material culture. Substantial occupation, however, does not appear to occur until the subsequent Star Valley phase, ca. 1000–1150, during which surface architecture, mostly in the form of oval rooms, is introduced, and the frequency of Hohokam Buff Ware begins to drop off. Preclassic settlement patterns, at least in terms of the architecture and layout of settlements, pretty much follows the standard Preclassic Hohokam conventions, as does the local plain ware ceramic tradition (there are no locally produced decorated types). These early settlements were generally small, the largest known having no more than 15 pithouses. During the Payson phase, ca. 1150–1300, equivalent to the early Classic period in Tonto Basin, Payson underwent the same transition from oval house clusters to rectangular room compounds seen in the south, even to the point of single sites incorporating everything from oval rooms through courtyard focused compound subdivisions to caseron-style room blocks. Although the typical Payson phase residential site was still quite small, small farming villages of up to 30 rooms in a single multicompound or cluster of compounds are common and several villages, such as Shoofly or Round Valley contain three times that many rooms.

The ceramic tradition of the Payson Basin follows the trends seen in both Tonto Basin and the Lower Verde in that it focused on Hohokam-style plain wares in the Preclassic and adopted the manufacture of striated-polish red ware in the Classic period, closely paralleling trends and trajectories seen in the Phoenix Basin. There appears to have been very little in the way of local manufacture of decorated wares with the possible exception of the white painted red ware common to most parts of central Arizona. As buff ware from the Phoenix Basin stopped arriving, their place was taken by Little Colorado and Cibola White Wares, a pattern shared by the Upper Basin and to a certain extent, all along Tonto Creek. Eventually, however, the Little Colorado Ware dropped out in favor of the Cibola types.

Unfortunately, we know little beyond this, since the area was essentially abandoned early on. By the time platform mounds were being built in Tonto Basin, the large villages like Shoofly, Round Valley, and Risser Ranch had been abandoned, and by 1300, there was nobody living in the Payson area. Thus, given the many archaeological similarities between the Payson and Tonto Basins, this area becomes a potential candidate for causing some population growth in Tonto Basin, though such movement would have entailed adapting to the lower elevation environment.

The Globe Highlands

Although several of the largest sites in the Globe Highlands have been excavated, not to mention the presence of the Gila Pueblo Archaeological Foundation there in the 1930s and 1940s, this important area is less well known than Tonto Basin. Although no Late Archaic or Early Ceramic occupation has yet been identified, Snaketown Red-on-buff pottery has been found in the area, again without any clearly associated residential remains. From Gila Butte phase on, however, the area was heavily occupied, at least along the valleys of Pinal Creek and Miami Wash. There is even a small number of Sacaton phase settlements in the upland valleys of Pinto Creek and Powers Gulch and around the Pinal Ranch headwaters of Queen Creek. Surprisingly, there is also a strong Preclassic presence in the granite colluvial outwash on the eastern flanks of the Pinal Mountains just east of Globe in the outer fringe of the Chihuahuan Desert. The only confirmed ball court in the region is found on a mesa overlooking Ranch Creek on the San Carlos Reservation.

As in Tonto Basin, there appears to have been a transition from pithouses to surface architecture toward the end of the Sacaton phase, resulting in the early Classic Miami phase. By Roosevelt phase, the uplands surrounding Pinal Creek between Globe and Wheatfields were heavily encumbered with compound villages. In this area, settlement seems to have concentrated in four major clusters, one at the foot of the Pinals in a place called the Gap, a second around Six-Shooter Canyon centered on the sites of Besh-Ba-Gowah and Gila Pueblo, a third at the Pinal Creek-Miami Wash confluence in the form of a tight and very dense cluster of compounds on and around Bead Mountain, and a fourth lower down on Pinal Creek at Wheatfields (Crary and Germick 1992). More isolated settlements are also scattered throughout the upland areas to the west, particularly in the Pinto Creek-Powers Gulch-Pinal Ranch area. Several of these, such as Togetzoge (Hohmann and Kelley 1988), are quite large.

This same patterning held during the Late Classic as well, though many of the compounds were abandoned in favor of conglomerated settlements with small satellites, mostly field houses. This concentration of population into large, conglomerated caserones appears to have been the primary settlement pattern of the late Classic here, such that many areas previously characterized by an abundance of small distributed settlements were replaced by single, central structures. These caserones are very similar to those

in Tonto Basin, being made up of massive blocks of contiguous rooms with occasional attached courtyards or even compound walls, as at Togetzoge, but no central interior plazas and no kivas (with allowances for whatever was going on at Besh-Ba-Gowah).

While most of the apparent conglomeration seems to have taken place very locally (in other words, clusters of sites are replaced by expanded versions of selected sites within those clusters), some areas, like Powers Gulch, appear to have been abandoned in favor of large nearby sites in different valleys, as appears to be the case with Togetzoge, just across the watershed divide at the head of Powers Gulch. Still, most of the arable upland valleys, at least those with reliable water, remained occupied. In other areas, notably around Superior and along the middle reach of Pinal Creek, there are variations on this theme. Near Superior is a single relatively large Gila phase caseron, but the surrounding countryside is dotted with one room sites (Wood 1979). Some of these were probably field houses, but many, upon excavation, were found to be substantial structures that probably served as permanent single family homesteads; nearly all of them contained Gila Polychrome. Taken overall, the small sites around Superior are found in a series of clusters with each individual house separated from its neighbors by a considerable distance in a pattern reminiscent of O'odham rancherías. Unfortunately, chronological controls on the small sites are not sufficient to tell if they were contemporary with the caseron or represent some later reorganization of a reduced population.

On middle Pinal Creek, between the massive caserones at Bead Mountain and Murphy's Mesa (Wheatfields), is another variation. The small, late, single room homesteads are there as well but are joined by a few small Gila phase compounds and caserones. Again, dating controls are not yet sufficient to sharpen the temporal perspective.

Ceramically, the Globe Highlands began as something very close to the Queen Creek section of the Phoenix Basin and in fact, the Queen Creek variety of Gila Plain is quite common in the western half, as is Wingfield Plain. The buff ware trajectory here follows the same line seen in Tonto Basin and Payson, being replaced almost exclusively by Cibola White Ware. On the other hand, the Safford variety of Sacaton Red-on-buff is not entirely uncommon here, suggesting two different source areas. Strong eastern connections continued into the Classic period as well. A considerable amount of locally made corrugated pottery here may be related not so much to the Vosberg derived material seen in Tonto Basin but to the poorly known potteries of San Carlos and the middle Gila. For that matter, while Salado White-on-red is found around Globe, there is very little Salado Red corrugated relative to the Basin. There also seems to be more Gila Polychrome around Globe than in the Basin and the local assemblages appear to have a noticeably higher percentage of White Mountain Red Ware as well—even including such relatively rare types as Kinishba Polychrome, which does not show up in the Basin at all. Another type found in Globe but not in the Basin is Ramos Polychrome from Mexico—Globe appears to represent the northwestern boundary for its distribution (Wood 1987). Overall, while the architectural history of the two areas appears to differ primarily in the presence of platform mounds in Tonto Basin, the ceramic relationships seen around Globe show a much stronger connection to the middle Gila and Safford areas than do those of Tonto Basin.

The Sierra Ancha

The Sierra Ancha, home to an enigmatic group of people known for lack of a better term as Anchans, may be one of those special places in the Southwest that holds a key to understanding the developmental history of a broad area, in this case, the central sub-Mogollon Rim region. Unfortunately, after more than 20 years of survey and two field schools, it remains largely unknown and enigmatic, with solid data on only a few localities. Nevertheless, we do know a few things—one of which is that the eastern and western sides appear to have different developmental histories. The eastern side, the only area with any excavation data, appears to have become increasingly aligned with the Mogollon centers to the east. Most of what is known for this section comes from two areas, the Q Ranch/Vosberg valleys in the north and middle Cherry Creek to the south, famous for its many middle Classic period cliff dwellings. The western side on the other hand appears to have become increasingly associated with the Salado along Tonto Creek.

Q Ranch/Vosberg

Most of this area is forested with pine or at least pinyonjuniper woodland, and nearly all of its potentially arable locations consist of diabase derived soils. It generally lies several thousand feet higher than Tonto Basin and is wetter. It is also rich with certain minerals known to have been important trade commodities prehistorically, most notably steatite and specular hematite. The area seems to have been occupied very early on; there is a remarkable density of Late Archaic materials, and at least one Late Archaic camp site has been excavated in the Vosberg Valley (Chenhall 1972). No Late Archaic or Early Ceramic settlements are known so far, but there is solid evidence for a residential agricultural population by the time of Gila Butte phase, the same pattern as in Globe and Payson. The earliest documented residential sites are a couple of middle to late Preclassic pithouse settlements in the Vosberg Valley. One of them seems to reflect local developments but the other, characterized by an eclectic assortment of pithouse architecture, is often cited as evidencing a "joint occupation" by both Hohokam and "Anasazi" people (Morris 1970). Several houses at this site are similar to those used in the more eastern parts of Arizona, but all of the house forms at that site also have equally similar Hohokam counterparts, making for an intriguing puzzle.

Through the rest of the Preclassic, the area is characterized by small pithouse settlements made up of nondescript square to rectangular pithouses with architectural conventions that relate both to the Hohokam tradition and to contemporary forms from the Point of Pines area. Based on the small sample of excavated sites, it was apparently common for these forms to have been associated with Hohokam style houses that look like they were lifted right out of the Phoenix Basin. Sometime around 1050 or so, the pithouses began to give way to surface structures, that, as in Payson or Tonto Basin, included both oval and rectangular forms, though the oval form is less prevalent (Cartledge 1977; Morris 1967, 1969b; Simonis 1976). For the most part these involved relatively little masonry, even in the wall foundations; thick chunks of burned daub from jacal walls are typical of sites in this area. Most of these sites are arranged as loose clusters of individual houses, but many were laid out in a very characteristic "row house" pattern, linear blocks of three to six rooms, often with very light partition walls with no masonry foundations. In many cases, even where the houses are separate, they are arranged in rows and set very close together. This pattern can even be seen in some later pithouse sites. Some larger examples of these sites consist of a series of parallel rows separated by "streets" not much wider than the houses themselves. By 1200 or so, these had evolved into small room blocks, but the row house pattern appears to have persisted up to the fourteenth century.

After about 1275 or 1300, most of the previously scattered population of the Q Ranch/Vosberg area appears to have been concentrated into very few sites—one at Q Ranch and another at the south end of Vosberg Valley. Elsewhere in the area, many local populations appear to have taken refuge in large fortified hilltop locations; even the late village at Vosberg was built not on the valley floor like all its predecessors but on a prominent ridge forming the south edge of the valley. The Q Ranch site, the only one of these late settlements ever to have been excavated, is quite impressive; it contains several hundred rooms, making it the largest in the entire region, and is arranged in blocks of rooms that define a central plaza, much like Grasshopper (that is, after all, only ten miles away) or Kinishba (John Hohmann, personal communication 1995). It is even divided into two halves by a spring-fed drainage that has since eroded into a deep gully, just like Grasshopper or Kinishba. Because of the character of this late settlement, it is often said that the Q Ranch/Vosberg area was Mogollon. After 1300, it may have been acculturated to that tradition, but it did not start that way.

The two pithouse villages excavated in Q Ranch/Vosberg were each found to contain round structures that were interpreted as kivas and offered as evidence of Anasazi or Mogollon residence. One of these, dating probably to the late Santa Cruz and early Sacaton phases, contained one of the "floor drum" features now known as having been common in Sacaton style Hohokam pithouses from the Lower Basin (Jeffery Clark, personal communication 1995). As luck would have it, more of these features are now known from Tonto Basin than from the Anchas and sometimes may even predate the lone Vosberg example, making it equivocal who was borrowing from whom. That same site contained both the best examples of Hohokam architecture in the region and a relative wealth of imported Hohokam ceramics (both decorated and plain ware) and other items, like slate palettes. In fact, there was much more Hohokam pottery at this site than there was Anasazi, even in the kiva.

Whatever these early kivas may represent, the idea apparently did not persist in the Anchan region. Despite a considerable amount of excavation at Q Ranch in recent years, no kivas have been identified there. For that matter, few other Mogollon or Anasazi architectural ideas caught on either; even in the latest sites there are very few (if any) mealing bins and most of the hearths remained the same Hohokam style clay basin form that they had been from the time of the first pithouse, though a few slab lined hearths are known from the Q Ranch Ruin itself (John Hohmann, personal communication 1995).

The ceramic tradition of the Q Ranch/Vosberg area presents another enigma. Throughout its history the plain ware of the Sierra Anchas was a distinctive paddle and anvil made product tempered primarily with diabase (Wood 1987). It has a red ware component early on, as with both the Hohokam and Mogollon ceramic traditions, but this early red ware disappears quickly and no new red ware forms are introduced until about 1050 or so, following the Hohokam rather than the Mogollon red ware trajectory. Corrugated pottery was also introduced into the assemblage at about 1050 or so and quickly grew into a major component of the assemblage. After about 1200 or so, much of this material was obliterated corrugated, a pattern that increased to the point that, by 1300, most of it was so heavily obliterated as to obscure its original configuration altogether. Curiously enough, even the corrugated pottery appears to have been made using a variation on the paddle and anvil technique as some obliterated types show evidence of having been obliterated by paddling.

And then there is the probably misnamed but nevertheless famous Salado Red. The origins of this distinctive pottery are obscure, but given its distribution and densities, it appears to have originated somewhere in the Sierra Ancha, possibly as early as 1100. Even its distinctive raspberry color may be derived from a specific source of specular hematite found just north of the Q Ranch/Vosberg area.

The decorated potteries of this area have another story to tell. The earliest assemblages are dominated by Hohokam Buff Ware (often accompanied by schist tempered Gila Plain), and white ware from the Tusayan and Little Colorado traditions. There is little in the way of Cibola White Ware. This is in contrast to patterns just a few miles east on the Salt River Draw Plateau, where the early decorated material was almost exclusively Cibola White Ware. After about 1050, however, the Hohokam materials drop out of the Q Ranch/Vosberg assemblages and are "replaced" by Cibola White Ware, that remain the dominant imports from that time onwards. It is also at this point that the Anchans began decorating their red wares with white paint in the shared white-on-red tradition that extends across all across central Arizona. It was not until the introduction of Gila Polychrome, however, that there was any substantial production of local decorated pottery in the area, and even that awaits analytical confirmation.

While this is not the place to analyze Anchan culture history, its origins, potential for having been colonized by either Hohokam or Mogollon, its potential role in regional trade, or even its possible developmental relationships to Hohokam, Mogollon, Sinagua, or the distinctive developments atop the Mogollon Rim around Heber, this area clearly gave rise to a distinctive local tradition, neither Hohokam nor Mogollon, which underlies the later developments from the Salt Draw Plateau to Pleasant Valley and probably the rest of the Sierra Ancha and other surrounding areas as well, perhaps even Tonto Basin itself.

The Canyons of Cherry Creek

Possibly the most famous part of the Sierra Ancha, the eastern face fronting along Cherry Creek is well known for its many cliff dwellings hidden away in deep, rugged canyons far from any arable land. Unfortunately, little else is known about these sites owing to their having been thoroughly looted in the past.

The one good thing about these sites is that they are well dated. As a result, we know that the bulk of the cliff dwelling episode began around 1280 and, after a reorganization that appears to have concentrated most of the scattered populations into a few large sites shortly after 1300, was over by no later than 1330 and the area abandoned (Ciolek-Torrello and Lange 1979, 1990).

For the most part, these sites appear to be related to the rest of the Anchan population to the north and west, but they also show strong connections to the east, evidenced by high percentages of White Mountain Red Ware. However, since the cliff dwellings are such an aberrant form, we need not take up much space with them here, other than to make a few observations from their architecture. In keeping with local area traditions, the cliff dwellings do not contain mealing bins, slab lined hearths, or, so far as anyone has been able to identify, kivas. As for their plan and layout, those seem more an effect of their setting than any internal architectural tradition.

Just to the south of the cliff dwelling area, Cherry Creek opens up as it drops into a more desert environment on its way to the Salt River just east of Tonto Basin. From this point south, the occupation of Cherry Creek parallels both the compound architecture and distributed settlement patterning of Tonto Basin, at least until the late 1200s. The major difference is that there is only one identified platform mound known from this area,

the Ellison Ranch Mound, at the north end of the desert section of the creek, only a couple of miles from the southernmost cliff dwelling.

The later occupation of Cherry Creek is characterized by a concentration of population into a relative few conglomerated villages that were founded or grew from earlier settlements after folks came down from the cliffs. One of these, like those of Tonto Basin, is right along the creek and is associated with a historic irrigation system. Unlike the situation in Tonto Basin, most of the late settlements are located at some distance from the creek, either on prominent landforms or in hidden valleys well away from any significant amounts of flowing water. The best example of this is the Granite Basin Ruin. One of the largest settlements in the area, it features a very non-Salado like central plaza surrounded by dense blocks of relatively small rooms (most of which have been severely vandalized). One of these rooms has been noted as having a kiva-like bench at one end, but, given the condition of the room, it is hardly clear if this represents a kiva or if the vandals had merely dug through the floor into some underlying structure. The height of the rubble mound at this site suggests either two story construction or, possibly, that it represents something akin to a Tonto Basin house mound. One thing is certain—this site has a higher percentage of White Mountain Red Ware than anything in the Basin itself.

The Western Sierra Ancha

Possibly the least visited area in all of central Arizona, the western part of the Sierra Ancha, between Pleasant Valley and Tonto Basin, nevertheless contains thousands of sites and apparently supported a fairly large prehistoric population. Its earliest residential occupation appears to have been focused on Pleasant Valley itself, a broad alluvial basin similar to the Q Ranch/Vosberg locality, and on the Spring Creek drainage, a north flowing tributary of Tonto Creek. Unfortunately, very little is known of this early period, though survey data suggest that it was probably quite similar to that in the Q Ranch/Vosberg area, though perhaps without the same degree of Hohokam involvement, since there is little in the way of potential trade commodities in this area other than, perhaps, timber.

By the middle Classic period, however, a number of large villages are known along Spring Creek; while most of these have not been recorded, at least some of them are very Salado-like rectangular compounds. There are also small villages scattered throughout the forested area to the west, along the crest of the mountains overlooking Tonto Basin. By the late Classic, population had aggregated following the same trends seen elsewhere in the region. There is only one large settlement left at this time in Pleasant Valley, though it is relatively small, possibly no more than 40 rooms. Others are known from hilltop locations throughout the area, but too little information is available to characterize population levels.

The one portion of this region for which we have sufficient inventory data to begin characterizing the culture history of the western Sierra Ancha is the Picture Mountain locality, which straddles the crest near the Greenback Creek headwater.

Below the crest, in Greenback Valley—a well watered, diabase-filled upland oasis and the first place homesteaded in the area during the historic period—the prehistoric occupation appears to begin sometime during the late Preclassic. The earliest recorded residential sites are small clusters of pithouses and masonry founded jacal pit rooms that appear to date to the later part of the eleventh century. Shortly afterward, we see sites very much like those from Vosberg, with row houses and detached square to rectangular masonry-founded single room jacal houses in tight but not necessarily commonly focused clusters. By the mid 1200s or so, this pattern was supplemented by the construction of two typical Salado-style compounds at the southern end of the valley and possibly a third on a hilltop in the center. By the fourteenth century the entire population of the valley had apparently moved into this central site that became a 50-plus room caseron with both attached outer courtyards and a possible interior plaza (possible because the middle of the site has been dug out with a backhoe to provide the fill to build a dam for a nearby stock tank).

Above the crest in the pine forested area around Bearhead Mountain, we have a different occupational history that does not appear to have begun until perhaps as late as the middle thirteenth century. The residential settlements in this area are most commonly small house clusters of the Vosberg type, though there appear to be very few row houses. There are also several small to medium sized compounds containing anywhere from a couple of rooms to as many as 15 or 20. All of the larger settlements are associated with pockets of arable soil. The sites in the western part of the area are characterized by Vosberg Plain and Corrugated pottery with a small percentage of Tonto Plain—not surprising, since there is a lot of diabase in the area. Salado Red, while present, does not seem to have been a large component of the assemblage for these small sites. A few miles to the east, however, around Lookout Mountain, are several compounds, including one on a prominent and defensible hilltop, that contain more Salado Red than anything else.

Although the lack of datable ceramics on most of these sites makes it difficult to tell, it appears that the later part of the occupation in this area was focused on aggregated residences served by scattered field houses. Of the two known larger sites, one is a compound that incorporates a row house type room block, while the other is an irregular room block caseron with a couple of small attached courtyards. The compound is almost certainly Roosevelt phase in age; the caseron may be later, but its vandalized condition makes it difficult to tell. Neither contains more than 30 rooms.

Two other sites near Bearhead may also figure prominently in the developmental history of the Picture Mountain locality. One is a cave extending several hundred feet into a limestone hillside. Above its entrance is a small compound containing ten to 15 rooms, vandalized beyond all redemption. Inside the cave are nine masonry rooms, all built beyond the point where light can enter the cave. If there was ever a dedicated ceremonial/ritual site constructed in or around Tonto Basin, this would be it. The other site is the small platform mound compound mentioned above near Turkey Creek. While this is clearly a platform mound, it is unlike any in Tonto Basin. For one thing, the compound containing it is more or less oval rather than rectangular. Unfortunately, very little is known about the surrounding countryside other than that there is a small patch of arable on the creek below and field houses in all directions.

ACCESS:
POPULATION AND
COMMODITY MOVEMENT
IN AND OUT OF TONTO BASIN

So far, we have seen that Tonto Basin is situated in the midst of an interesting, if motley, assortment of peoples and cultural traditions. It is also located in a strategic position in central Arizona relative to transportation between the southern cultures and their trading partners north of the Rim. There has been discussion over many years regarding the "arrival" of this group or that trait into the Basin, but what are the potential travel routes in and out of Tonto Basin that may have helped shape its economic and cultural history? After all, travel routes often influence settlement patterns, and certainly influence the range of contacts available to any given settlement.

Analyzing the topography, site distributions, historic trails, wagon roads, sheep driveways, and historic descriptions of the area—especially those in military scouting reports, which describe and in some cases map the trails used by Pima and Maricopa guides and by the Apache—has made possible the reconstruction of a fairly credible "transportation plan" for Tonto Basin. There are seven major travel corridors in and out of the Basin, several of which can be combined into through routes (Figure 5.7). Clockwise from the east, these corridors are as follows:

(1). The Pinal Creek corridor has one route out of the Basin to the southeast down to Globe. This route basically followed the original eastern Apache Trail, out of the Basin via the Poison Springs Wash pass, down Devore Wash to Wheatfields and from there along the Bixby Road to Globe. From Globe, there are several trails to points south and east, the major ones being over the Pinal Mountains through Pioneer Pass to the San Pedro River, along Ranch Creek to the Gila River, and east of Cutter along Gilson Wash to San Carlos and Safford.

(2). The Superstition corridor has two routes roughly following Pinto and Campaign Creeks. The Pinto Creek route probably split near Haunted Canyon, one track heading west to Happy Camp Canyon and then south to Queen Creek and the Superior volcanic fields and obsidian "quarries." The other track would have followed Powers Gulch up to Togetzoge where it may have dead ended, unless they used the same alignment as the later military trail that ran west through Camp Surprise at the Queen Creek headwater and then down along the Stoneman Grade to Silver King and Superior. The Campaign Creek route was probably less well defined, as there are many different overland routes through the eastern Superstitions, though they all end at about the same place on Queen Creek as the Pinto Creek routes. Once at Queen Creek, which disappears into an inland delta near Snaketown, there were many options to any place in either the Salt or the Gila River Valleys.

(3). The Monument corridor has one route, up Cave Canyon, across Two Bar Mountain to Burnt Corral, and from there more or less along the Apache Trail to the foot of Fish Creek Hill. This was probably not a major route, since it peters out just beyond the Yavapai seasonal gathering place called Amanyika and essentially dead ends at Fish Creek.

(4). The Mazatzal corridor has three routes. The first one leaves Tonto Creek near Punkin Center to parallel Reno Creek up and over the Mazatzals at Reno Pass and then down to Sunflower. From there it essentially follows the general course of the Sycamore Creek that runs into the Lower Verde at Fort McDowell; this is essentially the route of the Reno Military Road. The other two start up from Tonto Creek along the Sycamore Creek south of the Butcher Hook, one splitting north to Sunflower through Boulder Canyon, the other, more directly, down Ballantine Canyon to Pine Creek, after which all three routes converge. Once down to Fort McDowell on the Lower Verde River, you are in the Phoenix Basin for all intents and purposes.

(5). The Rye Creek corridor has two routes. The Rye Creek route probably left the Lower Basin at or near the Gun Creek box, going north through a low pass east of Gold Creek to Hardt Creek and then north again across a series of long ridges to join Rye Creek, probably just above the Iron Bridge. From there it simply followed Rye Creek to its head, crossed the divide, and dropped into the East Verde through Pole Hollow to the Doll Baby Ranch. At the Doll Baby it split, one trail going west to the Verde River and Bloody Basin, another going north and then east through American Gulch into the Payson Basin, and a third continuing north to the Hardscrabble basalt quarries and from there to Camp Verde. This last trail may not have been heavily traveled, owing to the difficulties in crossing Fossil Creek, which, incidentally, forms the northern boundary of Gila Polychrome distribution on both sides of the Verde River. The other route, splits from the Rye Creek trail and runs up Tonto Creek a few miles to the Gisela Valley where it made connections to both the Payson Basin and the Sierra Ancha.

(6). The Sierra Ancha corridor has three or four routes. On the Tonto Creek side, trails along Oak Creek and Greenback Creek converge in Greenback Valley; from there, the trail climbs the crest of the Anchas and crosses Buckaroo Flats to Board Tree Saddle overlooking Cherry Creek. There was another connection between the interior of the Sierra Ancha and Upper Tonto Basin along the general route of the mail trail between Young and Gisela. On the Salt River side a single trail leaves the Basin along Armer Gulch, crosses the crest near Tanner Peak, and turns northeast to join the present alignment of the Young highway near Reynolds Creek, from which point it continues north to meet the Greenback trails at Board Tree Saddle. For many years Salome Creek has

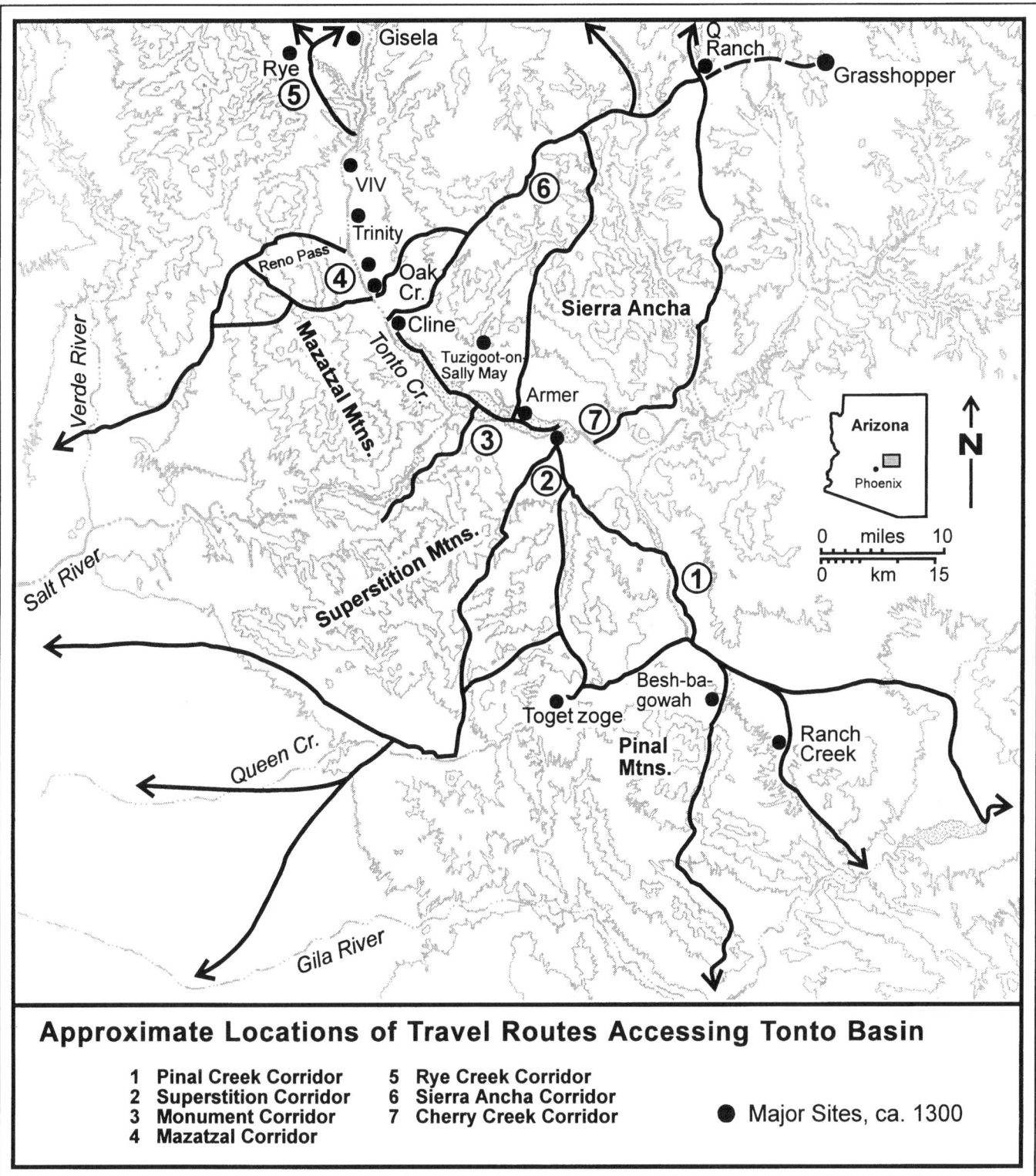

Approximate Locations of Travel Routes Accessing Tonto Basin

1 Pinal Creek Corridor
2 Superstition Corridor
3 Monument Corridor
4 Mazatzal Corridor
5 Rye Creek Corridor
6 Sierra Ancha Corridor
7 Cherry Creek Corridor

● Major Sites, ca. 1300

Figure 5.7.   Approximate locations of travel routes accessing Tonto Basin (base map from Elson, Gregory, and Stark 1994).

been touted as a major way out of the Basin. However, this seems unlikely given how it deepens and constricts north of Tuzigoot-on-Sally May; if it was used, it would have joined the other trails at Board Tree Saddle. From Board Tree Saddle the combined route drops down into Cherry Creek near Cow Flat Mountain and heads north. Near Vosberg Mesa, there is another split, with one branch continuing north between Vosberg and Pleasant Valley across Crouch Mesa and over the Mogollon Rim, probably headed for Heber. The other branch turns east into the Vosberg and Q Ranch valleys. So far, however, this branch seems to dead end; there is no known direct route from Q Ranch to Grasshopper or any of the other population centers to the east, though it seems likely that such a route did exist.

(7). The Cherry Creek corridor has one route that essentially follows the course of Forest Road 203 from the vicinity of Meddler Point east to Cherry Creek, which it follows north up to Oak Creek, at which point it heads overland roughly along Forest Road 202, which takes it through the heart of the asbestos and steatite country and into Q Ranch.

These seven access corridors can be combined into several regional travel routes as well. The Pinal Creek and Rye Creek corridors, when connected with the trail system that ran along the floor of the Basin, are part of a system that would have connected the Gila and San Pedro River Valleys with places as far west as the Agua Fria River and even Prescott. The Superstition and Cherry Creek corridors provided a direct link between the Phoenix Basin and the Mogollon Rim near Heber, with handy stopovers at the Superior obsidian source and the Cherry Creek steatite quarries. The Mazatzal and Sierra Ancha corridors would have provided similar access to the Rim from the Lower Verde and the Phoenix Basin.

While it is not possible here to explore the implications of these routes for the social and economic development of Tonto Basin and the rest of central Arizona fully, it can at least be pointed out that any modeling of population movements into (or out of) the Basin should consider these routes. Such consideration would, of course, also have to take into account the people already living along these routes at the time of any migration. Another consideration is how the location of these access corridors might have affected the placement of larger settlements, particularly regarding strategic trading geography.

There has been considerable speculation over the years as to the "ethnic" makeup of the Tonto Basin Salado. It

seems clear from the Roosevelt Projects' data that the Preclassic occupation was overtly Hohokam in its cultural traditions and was probably made up primarily of both indigenous people and actual Hohokam who entered the Basin from the south and established small but apparently influential colonies like Roosevelt 9:6 and the Hedge Apple site. The large increase in population during the Classic period is often seen as population influx. Based on the transition to surface architecture and a shift in the sources of decorated pottery, this influx has typically been characterized as "puebloan" from the "north and east."

Evaluating this assertion in light of research outside Tonto Basin might be useful at this point. The case in point: the short-lived Maverick Mountain phase of east-central Arizona. This distinctive and easily recognized archaeological complex is said to have resulted from the migration of considerable numbers of western Anasazi from the Tusayan or Kayenta areas into the Point of Pines-Safford region; similar developments are also recognized along the San Pedro River. This migration has been largely identified on the strength of finding substantially complete Anasazi architectural sets, involving such things as kivas, stone lined entry boxes in doorways, and Anasazi derived ceramics. Without reviewing the entire argument, these sites would appear to represent a substantial migration of people into an area east of Tonto Basin during the later part of Roosevelt phase (Woodson 1995).

The critical aspect of this example is that no such complex of architecture and ceramics as characterizes the Maverick Mountain phase has ever been found in Tonto Basin. A case might be made for Besh-Ba-Gowah representing such a settlement in the Globe area; its central plaza and hallway and "ceremonial room" may indicate some relationship with sites such as Grasshopper, though it shares little else. As an aside, it might even be important that Besh-Ba-Gowah was burned out and destroyed in much the same way as the Maverick Mountain enclave at Point of Pines. In any case, the best arguments to date for northern and eastern migration into Tonto Basin itself have so far hinged not on the presence or absence of recognizable cultural traditions but on mathematical models involving ratios of corrugated pottery and contiguous room indices (Elson et al., Chapter 7). Despite the systematic excavation of hundreds of sites in Tonto Basin—far more than in all of the Point of Pines-Safford area—we have found no kivas, no entry boxes, no mealing bins, no Anasazi-derived locally made decorated pottery. While there was clearly a substantial movement of people southward from the Colorado Plateau across the Mogollon Rim and down into the Gila Valley during the later Classic period, this corridor, and the people clearly using it, stayed well east of Tonto Basin. If there are aspects of Classic period settlement patterns, architecture, and material culture in Tonto Basin that depart from the expected, we need to begin exploring mechanisms other than long distance migration for their explanation (e.g., changes in ideology that might affect perceptions of appropriate behavior) or look closer to the Basin for their origins. Ideally, of course, we should do both.

Irrigation Districts: An Organizational Heuristic for Tonto Basin Settlement Patterns

So far we have considered just about every aspect of prehistoric settlement in Tonto Basin except the distribution of population along the rivers and the relationships between platform mounds and other foci of population concentration. A potentially promising way to look at the position of platform mounds in the settlement pattern is to look at irrigation potential within the Basin. Although only fragments remain today, Tonto Basin apparently once contained a number of prehistoric canals associated with both Preclassic and Classic period sites. Apparently, irrigation in the Basin operated under a unique set of topographic and hydrological constraints created by the very nature of the valley floor and its adjacent uplands (J. S. Wood et al. 1992).

Some years ago I proposed a model of settlement development in Tonto Basin that assumed an association between platform mounds and the organization and allocation of irrigation resources (Wood 1989; Wood and Hohmann 1985). This model had platform mounds distributed at three mile intervals along Tonto Creek and the Salt River in emulation of the canal-based distribution of platform mound communities in the Phoenix Basin. While intriguing and satisfying, given an apparent close fit between the model and the real distribution of mounds in the Basin, there were several problems, including gaps in the sequence along Tonto Creek and doubts about the nature of several sites classified as platform mounds. And, after all, the three-mile interval only

works in the Salt River Valley; it certainly does not work in either the Gila Valley or the Tucson Basin. Assuming that the three-mile interval between platform mounds was invalid and purely coincidental, I began to look at the association between the mounds and irrigation in terms of topographic segments in the Basin that might be defined as "irrigation districts." The idea that districts, rather than a specific canal system, as in the Phoenix Basin, may have served as the basis for local "irrigation communities" (Doyel 1981) and provided the geographic structure underlying mound placement in Tonto Basin appears to have considerable explanatory power (Elson, Gregory, and Stark 1995; J. S. Wood et al. 1992). Eliminating the expectation of a three-mile interval between mounds explains the absence of a platform mound along Tonto Creek between Oak Creek and the VIV Ranch.

Given the environmental constraints on agriculture derived from temperature, rainfall, and transpiration rates in the Basin, and the scarcity of high quality soils, it can be assumed that irrigation agriculture would have been required to sustain stable populations and allow for growth (see Van West et al., Chapter 2). Given the assumptions that the Salado of Tonto Basin depended to one degree or another on irrigation and that this technology may have affected the distribution and organization of population, we can further refine irrigation district boundaries previously defined by J. S. Wood et al. (1992) and by Elson, Gregory, and Stark (1995) and reassess several alleged platform mounds.

Both Tonto Creek and the Salt River are suitable for irrigation throughout most of the Basin in terms of streamflow, gradient, and riverside topography. So, too, are some reaches of Rye Creek, Salome Creek, and probably several other larger tributaries. Nevertheless, topographic limits to that irrigability restrict the number of diversion points, the amount of floodplain and terrace that can be subjugated, and the lengths of individual canal systems. Because flooding or heavy erosion throughout the Basin severely limits our ability to identify specific diversion points or characterize the suitability of particular terraces for efficient water distribution, we must concentrate on those factors that limit canal length. Basically, these amount to topographic constrictions of the valley floor and high volume tributary drainages.

Limitations placed on canal length by topographic constriction include insufficient room for both a canal and the stream or for fields. The effects of tributary drainages are less clear. That not all tributaries would necessarily disrupt canal construction or maintenance is shown by two aqueducts in the Horseshoe Basin on the Verde River that carried its main canal across two tributary drainages. However, a combination of high peak streamflow, steep gradient and high water velocities, "flashiness" of discharge (i.e., the rapid generation of high flows from brief rainfall events), and deep erosion relative to the irrigated terraces or floodplains may have prevented Tonto Basin irrigators from using this engineering solution to any great extent.

Given these considerations, we can identify eight or nine distinct irrigation districts in Lower Tonto Basin (Figure 5.8) Meddler, Livingston, Armer, Rock Island, Vinyard, Horse Pasture and/or Cline Terrace, Punkin Center, and Watkins' Ranch. At least three more may be identified in the Upper Basin: one along Rye Creek and two in the Gisela Valley on either side of Sand Wash.

The Meddler District runs from the box at the east end of the Basin to the east side of Meddler Point. The high topographic barrier presented by Meddler Point combined with the speed of flow coming out of the box effectively limits this district to the same fields cultivated today on the north side of the river east of the point (the Braddock Place). On the west side of Meddler Point, the area between the river and the point would have been unirrigable most of the time except by short, low volume ditches, and the next reliable canal head would have been just downstream from the site of Saguaro Muerto on the south side of the river. The limited arable land and historic susceptibility of the Braddock Place to heavy flood damage may help explain why the Meddler Point platform mound community was one of the first to be abandoned right around 1300. Water rights conflicts between this small, but unstable district and the larger ones downstream may also have contributed to its demise.

The Livingston District encompasses the area along the south bank of the Salt between the Saguaro Muerto take-out and Pinto Creek, which would have created a constant erosion hazard with flashy, high volume seasonal flows. It also creates a huge alluvial fan that would have directed canal grades back toward the river. There is a platform mound in this district at the Pinto Creek site. There are two other similar structures, but one of them, Pyramid Point, while eventually looking much like a platform mound, began as a tower and ended up looking more like the Armer Gulch Ruin, a cross between a compound and a caseron with a couple of elevated rooms. The other potential candidate is the Livingston

platform mound, but given its nearly invisible pottery signature and incomplete compound wall, it does not appear to have ever been occupied.

The Armer District, from Pinto Creek to the Windy Hill/Salome Creek constriction, is the largest district on the Salt Arm and the first to allow irrigation on both sides of the river. It is also the location of the largest and most complex late Roosevelt phase community in the Basin, centered on the platform mound at the Armer Ranch site. The south side contains an additional series of large and small villages distributed along the terrace edges between Grapevine Point and Windy Hill, with another high density settlement at Schoolhouse Point. The only platform mound, however, is the one (or two) at Armer Ranch.

The Rock Island District encompasses the entire area between Salome Creek and the Salt-Tonto confluence. Earlier analyses have broken this into two districts, one for Rock Island and another for Porter Springs, but no substantial natural barrier would necessitate this division. Doing away with it requires a second look at the Porter Springs site as a platform mound. Review of the inventory data, shows that it is not a platform mound, an initial determination that was based on its compact and contiguous room layout. Though the Gila Pueblo and J. W. Simmons descriptions in the 1930s, and Schmidt's description in the 1920s (Hohmann and Kelley 1988) make it sound mound-like, the only platforms for this district are clearly the two on Rock Island and that the presence of Gila Polychrome (contra Schmidt) provides at least the possibility that the Rock Island Mound succeeded the Bass Point Mound, going perhaps into middle Gila phases. Unfortunately, nearly constant inundation prevents our having much information on the size and extent of settlement in the district.

The Vinyard District is the first one up Tonto Creek, from the confluence with the Salt River upstream to the opposing entry of two major tributaries, Rock Creek and Methodist Creek, both of which built large alluvial fans. Bourke's Teocalli, despite having been visited only twice in the last 120 years, is clearly a platform mound in the middle of the district opposite a major caseron known as Hotel Ruin. As with the Rock Island District, very little else is known, owing to near constant inundation.

The Cline district is the next one going up Tonto Creek and runs between Rock Creek and Greenback Creek. It had been broken previously into two parts to accommodate apparently contemporary occupations at two differ-

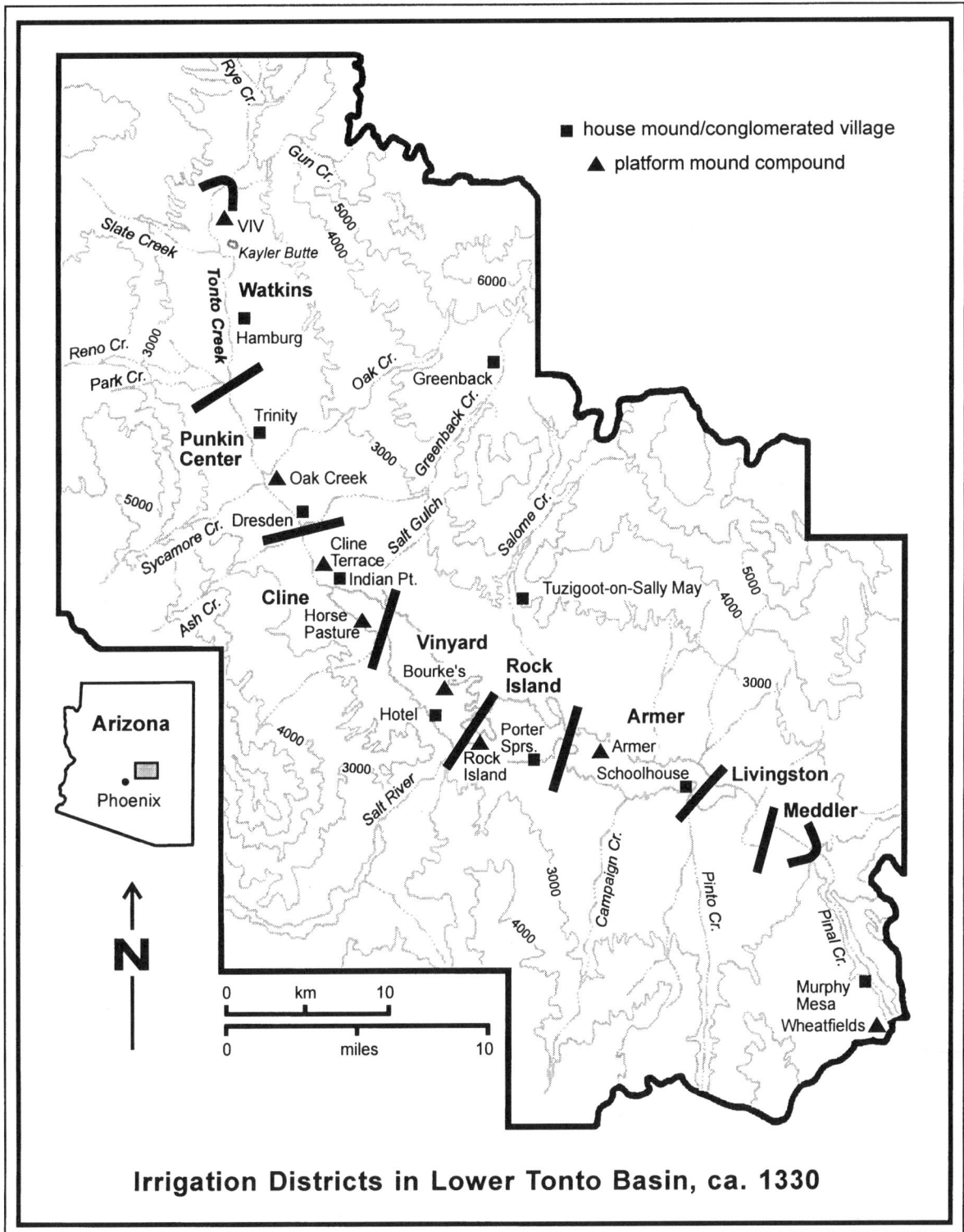

Figure 5.8.   Irrigation districts in lower Tonto Basin, ca. 1330 (base map from Altschul and Van West 1992).

ent platform mound sites, Horse Pasture and Cline Terrace, but there is no clear topographic or hydrological division nor any apparent break in the irrigation potential between the two mounds. It is possible that Salt Gulch, which dumps an extremely heavy plume of gypsum-laden silt into the reservoir, created an effective barrier to canal construction between the upper and lower portions of this district, but inundation makes this difficult to assess. This leads to a question of relationship between the two sites. Cline Terrace is obviously a platform mound and was occupied for most of the fourteenth century and was probably one of the last platform mounds in the Basin to be abandoned or replaced. Horse Pasture, despite its current eroded condition, is also a platform mound. However, inventory data indicate that it has no fourteenth century pottery, raising the possibility that it was superseded by Cline. Horse Pasture, like Meddler Point, is situated in the midst of a lot of earlier settlement. Cline appears to have been built on a new site without any underlying predecessor or adjacent compounds. Unfortunately, Young (1967) complicated the picture by assigning a number of Gila Polychrome vessels in the Gila Pueblo collections to Horse Pasture, which suggests that the two mounds are at least partially contemporary. Until we can learn more about the Horse Pasture Mound and its local hydrology, we have the apparent problem of a single irrigation district with two platform mounds that at least partly overlap in time.

The Punkin Center District is larger than the Cline District, running from the opposed confluences of Greenback Creek and Ash Creek to Punkin Center, where three high volume, high velocity drainages—Sycamore Creek, Reno Creek, and Park Creek—come together, funneling the runoff from a large Mazatzal watershed into Tonto Creek. There is a possible division at the area where Oak Creek comes in on the east side opposite another, much larger, Sycamore Creek, but there is survey evidence of a canal that crossed the mouth of Oak Creek. On the other hand, Forest Service inventory and recent excavations (Jeffery Clark, personal communication 1995) suggest that the west side of Tonto Creek from Ash Creek to the box at Gun Creek was for all intents and purposes abandoned shortly after 1300 following at least 500 years of occupation. The east bank, however, continued to be heavily occupied. In any case, the only platform mounds in this section are the two near the mouth of Oak Creek, a large, later one occupied into the fourteenth century and a very small one found

nearby that is similar to the initial stages of the Meddler Point Mound and was apparently abandoned prior to 1300. Another platform mound that might be included in the Punkin Center District is the Park Creek Mound, found more than a mile from Tonto Creek at the toe of the Mazatzal bajada. This mound, like that at Livingston, has no trash mounds and is all but devoid of artifacts, suggesting that it, too, was built but never operationalized. The purpose of this mound is unknown, but it may have analogs with the upland platform mounds and platform mound-like sites where integration and organization could not have had any strong focus on shared irrigation systems.

The Watkins' Ranch District runs from Punkin Center to the box at Gun Creek. It too has been divided in previous analyses at the Kayler Butte meander. However, a historic canal that headed upstream of the meander and delivered water to fields downstream of it suggests that this low relief meander, unlike the one at Meddler, presented no topographic barrier to irrigation. Another historic canal heads just below Gun Creek on the east side and was probably built in the 1880s along the alignment of a prehistoric canal. The platform mound in this district, at the VIV site, is near the head of this canal. Like the Cline Terrace mound, it appears to have been occupied into the later part of the fourteenth century.

All these potential districts appear to be quite equal in size of arable land, given the differences in streamflow between the Salt and Tonto Arms, a factor in how much of the available land could have been irrigated. The Tonto Creek districts tend to be larger, averaging a little more than 2,000 acres, with those on the Salt River averaging a little more than 1,500 acres. Actually, the Salt Arm average is probably more like 1,200 acres, since most estimates in the Livingston District include areas that were probably not irrigable although they may have been arable. Based on estimated production and consumption figures (Craig 1995), if only half of the average acreage was farmed, each irrigation district should have been able to support at least 500 people on corn agriculture alone; a baseline potential population of some 3,500 people. The Meddler District, however, is an exception to all of this. It probably never had much more than 300 acres of irrigable land, the smallest agricultural base in the Lower Basin, and it is also one of the most susceptible to flood damage and channel shifting. This district is one of the least densely occupied in Tonto Basin and one of the first to be abandoned, followed shortly by the Livingston District.

Moving to the Upper Basin, there are two small irrigation districts in Gisela, separated by Sand Wash. There are also two platform mounds in Gisela, located on either side of Sand Wash, almost within shouting distance of each other. While this is highly suggestive of a division, we may never know the temporal relationship between the two mounds, since the mound on the north side has been all but totally destroyed.

There is a third potential irrigation district on Tonto Creek near Gisela, between The Box and Rye Creek, the so-called Indian Farms area. It is not well known, but there is at least one large settlement at the south end and several smaller ones between there and The Box.

Rye Creek appears to have been irrigable only below its confluence with Rock Creek, and there are no large settlements above this point. It has a couple of potential natural divisions at Deer Creek and perhaps Barnhardt Creek, but neither of these served to break up the historic homesteads along the creek. There is only one known platform mound on Rye Creek, the magnificent Rye Creek Ruin at the Deer Creek confluence. Based on what we know at present, this entire drainage (which is much smaller than Tonto Creek) may have operated as a single irrigation district.

It may be possible to define other irrigation districts in and around Tonto Basin. There is certainly a small one associated with the settlement at Tuzigoot-on-Sally May, complete with a historic ditch. There may be others, perhaps along Armer Gulch or Cottonwood Creek, although none of the Upland tributary districts would have had anywhere near the production potential of those along the rivers. All of them have large late settlements, but none have platform mounds. In fact, only two of the four known upland mounds—Park Creek and Cherry Creek—are located in places that are even marginally irrigable and then only on a very small scale.

There is also the problem of the Wheatfields Mound on Pinal Creek. It is in an area used historically for small scale ditch irrigated farms, first by the Apache and later by truck gardeners feeding the mining communities around Globe (hence the name). The prehistoric settlement history of the area closely conforms to the patterns seen in Tonto Basin, even to the point of the platform mound and compound community being replaced by a massive caseron. However, there are no other platform mounds associated with Pinal Creek or any other drainage closer to Globe. Assuming a close connection between platform mounds and the development of sophisticated or large-scale irrigation systems,

this might be explained by the nature of the Pinal Creek drainage itself. From the confluence of Russell Gulch and Miami Wash down, the valley is characterized by unconsolidated terraces and constantly shifting channels filled with coarse gravels that drain so quickly that there is rarely any surface water in the creek until the reef just above Wheatfields near the confluence with Hicks Wash. It may be that building an efficient and stable irrigation system of any size on Pinal Creek was simply not possible except at Wheatfields so that farming here would have been small scale, uncoordinated, shifting in location, and opportunistic.

The association between the irrigation districts and the platform mounds is not the only association between population centers and irrigation districts in the prehistory of Tonto Basin. These same district divisions may also define the distribution of house mound and caseron villages following the collapse of the platform mound communities. There are very few Gila phase sites of any kind in the Basin compared with the number of settlements that came and went during Roosevelt phase. There are only eight large conglomerated villages. The same number as there were platform mound communities just after 1300: Hamburg, Trinity, Dresden, Indian Point, Hotel Ruin, Porter Springs (most of which fell into the Salt River before it was inundated), Armer Ranch, and Schoolhouse Point (Figure 5.6). For the most part there is only one such site per irrigation district. Only the Punkin Center and Armer Districts have more (two each). The two easternmost districts, Livingston and Meddler, were abandoned earlier than the rest and contain no such settlements.

The biggest problem so far in this reconstruction is the relationship between Cline Terrace and Horse Pasture. If Horse Pasture was succeeded by Cline, it could be said that the move was successful, at least for a time, given the apparent late occupation of Cline behind its massive rampart wall. Taking this one step further, many Tonto Basin platform mound compounds with fourteenth century ceramics—VIV, Oak Creek, Cline, Armer, Livingston—are relatively isolated from the residential compounds that surround them. This disjunction suggests that whatever the organizational structure expressed by the mounds may have been, it came to be operated to some degree independently from "traditional" settlement organizational institutions. Or, it could mean nothing more than that the mound builders chose to build in locations not already occupied. The "succession" of mounds may reflect nothing more than the consolidation of smaller irrigation districts whose boundaries are not obvious due to the effects of the reservoir. This would make the most sense for the Horse Pasture/Cline area, but seems less applicable to Pinto/Livingston and does not explain the succession from Encinito to Oak Creek. The idea that sites like Schoolhouse and Trinity succeeded platform mound communities like Pinto Point and Oak Creek needs the same kinds and quality of data. Focusing on the relationships between both the platform mounds and the late caserones and irrigation districts may provide an alternative way to look at the role of irrigation in settlement and sociopolitical-economic development in the Basin.

One thing, however, is obvious from this perspective. Since the conglomerated house mound and caseron villages and the platform mound villages were distributed in the same way relative to the potential irrigation districts, and thus were probably equally dependent on irrigation agriculture, we can infer that platform mounds were not absolutely necessary to organize, develop, or maintain irrigation systems. As a result, any assumptions that platform mounds developed, arose, or were adopted solely for irrigation management can be questioned, though it is still possible that the organizational structure they represent was somehow related to the scale of irrigation systems.

Internal Relationships

Over the years, I have attempted to view and portray the occupants of Tonto Basin as a dynamic, flexible, and entrepreneurial group with both strong contacts to the outside world and a stubborn insularity that allowed them to develop and maintain their own unique identity even when they were borrowing various social and economic institutions from others.

More than a decade ago, Martin McAllister, John Hohmann, and I proposed several models for the development and organization for the people of Tonto Basin. These models proposed that a relatively complex social organization and economy had developed there out of an occupation that was largely made up of folks who were culturally (if not always genetically) Hohokam and that followed settlement and organizational models similar to those of the Phoenix Basin.

The society we envisioned was made up of entrepreneurial farmers who knew their environment well enough to take the fullest advantage of it with the tech-

nology they had on hand and who developed or adopted organizational structures appropriate for an economic context that included a mixture of irrigated riverine agriculture and runoff-harvesting upland farming as its base. One of the primary engines driving Salado development was seen as the occasional need to deal with population expansion and contraction within the Basin. Other factors included climatic fluctuation (closely tied to population distribution), resource exhaustion, and extensive relations with other groups in central and southern Arizona, most particularly those of the nearby Phoenix Basin and the Sierra Ancha. The people in other areas that provided such transportable aspects of material culture to the Basin as decorated pottery were seen as trading partners more than cohabitants. A common thread running through all of this was our feeling that the platform mound system there represented the culmination of development just prior to a sudden and very thorough collapse.

Now, ten years, hundreds of excavated sites, and thousands of surveyed acres later, two things stand out as having changed our understanding of the sequence of events in Tonto Basin: 1) confirmation of our contention that there was an indigenous population, and 2) the realization that the large caserones, which we had assumed to have been contemporaneous with the platform mounds right up to the end, in fact overlapped and eventually replaced the platform mound settlement system, which collapsed some years before the final abandonment of the area. Additional surveys have refined our understanding of the sequencing and distribution of Upland occupation, which now appears to have involved two primary episodes, one that probably started in the late twelfth or early thirteenth century but was strongest and most widespread between about 1225–1230 and 1280 and another, more limited episode focused on fewer but more productive locations between about 1300 and 1330–1350.

It may, therefore, be useful to look at Salado internal relations in Tonto Basin in terms of the relationship between Upland and riverine settlements and the effects these relations had on organizational and other social developments during the Classic period.

We know from extensive surveys that small numbers of entrepreneurial farmers had been making sporadic and short-lived forays into the Uplands from about 1000 or so. Ameliorating climatic conditions in the late 1220s and early 1230s, following a drought that began in 1205, combined with the increasing circumscription of arable land as a result of population growth along the rivers to facilitate expanded use of the Uplands, both seasonally and permanently. Population growth continued throughout the middle 1200s, especially as expansion into the Uplands opened new economic opportunities, but the onset of drought in 1275 brought about the conditions for drastic change. Between 1275 and 1280, right around the time that Pinto Polychrome was introduced into the area (Crary et al. 1995), the Uplands were largely abandoned except for a few favored spring oases. While some of these folk may have left the area entirely, it seems reasonable that the majority merely gravitated toward the existing settlements along the rivers, where they would have had the strongest kin ties and best hope for assistance.

This concentration of population, combined with the prevailing climatic conditions of the time, would have led to intensification of the irrigation system as the primary viable agricultural strategy during this period. Landless labor from the Uplands around Tonto Basin (and perhaps from other drought stricken parts of central Arizona) would have contributed to this effort greatly without necessarily making any incursions into the extant system of tenure, increasing both social differentiation and dependence on agricultural surplus to support the displaced uplanders.

The platform mounds, therefore, can be seen as having arisen (or having been adopted from the Phoenix Basin Hohokam) in response to a variety of systemic needs for logistical organization, leadership, and adjudication including: 1) stress on access to arable land created by displaced uplanders moving into established riverine settlements and forcing local organizations to accommodate people either having no claim to land or claiming ancestral, kin based use rights, thus disrupting established patterns by then several generations old (the "Dust Bowl" model of Wood and McAllister 1984a), 2) production stress on riverine arable land due to the loss of upland agricultural production, and 3) irrigation expansion, intensification, and management needs arising both from the first two factors and from a variety of drought related problems (silt maintenance and field topography alteration due to increased erosion, lowered average streamflow, lowered water tables, and periodic flooding). The platform mound system in Tonto Basin was created shortly after the beginning of the generation-long drought at the end of the thirteenth century at about the same time that people began abandoning the Uplands for the more reliable water in the rivers. The system began to break

down and be gradually replaced by more communally oriented organization and settlement shortly after people began returning to the Uplands in the fourteenth century. The mounds may have served primarily to manage land tenure and access to water, with irrigation simply a means to that end, an opportunity to use additional labor to expand production to meet increased subsistence needs or move into trade commodity production with crops such as cotton. As a focus of economic decision making, the mounds would also have provided an excellent opportunity for the social and political aggrandizement of established founder lineages with the economic wherewithal (and accumulated debt obligation) to sponsor their construction.

Stated differently, the platform mounds and their organizational system probably served to reduce scalar stress arising from circumscription by increasing intervillage cooperation, establishing tenure over arable land and adjudicating water rights and allocation, and directing the construction and maintenance of the canal systems. Thus, the mounds were associated with irrigation, and their inhabitants probably used irrigation management as part of their leadership mandate; however, they were probably built in response to many different organizational needs and were not, as we have seen, required for the operation of irrigation systems. We might even speculate that with the rise of a new, integration oriented communal ideology (represented by the conglomerated villages), failures to respond adequately to destructive floods in the fourteenth century may have eroded confidence in the ceremonial/political establishment of the platform mounds and the leadership oriented and more individualistic ideology that they and their associated agglomerated compound villages represented. We could further speculate that reduction of intergroup conflict within each irrigation district as a result of mound-based organizational leadership would not have precluded—and in fact may have exacerbated—competition and conflict between districts, particularly as regards downstream water rights. There may even have been conflicts between the new centralized logistical organization of the platform mounds and the lower level traditional social and religious institutions that served to structure social and economic integration of different status or ethnic groups. No matter how the system broke down, given population levels before, during, and after the platform mound period, the organizational structure that the mounds represent may have been more efficient and productive than anything that preceded or followed it.

As we have seen, the settlement system that developed manifested itself into about eight or nine irrigation districts in Lower Tonto Basin—Meddler, Livingston, Armer, Rock Island, Vinyard, Horse Pasture and/or Cline Terrace, Punkin Center, and Watkins' Ranch—with several more in the Upper Basin. Each of these districts can be seen as having its own particular developmental history with minor variations in settlement, architecture, trade relationships, and material culture preferences, implying that each was essentially autonomous within the larger general patterns that characterize Tonto Basin.

The platform mound system appears to have operated with varying levels of success and stability up to about 1300. Once the drought had ended, the agricultural circumscriptions along the rivers, now accentuated by the overlay of a relatively complex managerial authority and even more restrictive access to arable land, would have tended to recreate the conditions prevalent in the middle 1200s. It is about this time, shortly after the introduction of Gila Polychrome (Crary et al. 1995), that we see new settlements in the Uplands and the growth of communities at the spring line oases (Germick and Crary 1989). As people began moving away again, the effectiveness of the labor intensive irrigation system along the rivers would have been reduced, though this may have been at least partially offset by the creation of new economic opportunities on the terraces and lower bajadas above the riverine zone, as the apparent increase in agave production during the fourteenth century might indicate (see Van West et al., Chapter 2). Even with the addition of such alternative sources of production, or perhaps as a result of it, confidence in the ceremonial authority might have broken down rather rapidly. Some parts of the riverine area (Meddler, for instance) were abandoned during this time, probably adding to the scalar stress of the areas where those people ended up. As a result, there was probably increased conflict between competing irrigation districts over water rights. One way or another, the established organizational institutions failed in response to the loss of labor due to upland resettlement and their resultant inability to respond to climatic variability. There may even have been, as some have suggested, an ideological response to the increasing development of social hierarchy and unequal distribution of wealth that resulted in a violent social leveling such as that recounted in Piman oral histories of the overthrow of the platform mound tyrants of the Phoenix Basin (Bahr et al. 1994).

This may account for the condition of the Cline Terrace platform mound compound at its abandonment: burned all at once with dead people missing vital parts left in the courtyards (Glen Rice, personal communication 1995). In any case, as the managerial hierarchy of the mounds collapsed, other segments of society may have taken over the organizational structure even to the point of physically appropriating the symbols of the old hierarchy by moving into and tenementing the platform mound compounds as appears to have happened at Armer (and perhaps also at Wheatfields, Oak Creek, Rye Creek, and Gisela). Other platform mound compound communities appear to have simply been abandoned in favor of new centers like Trinity, Dresden, or Schoolhouse, which reflects a different value system regarding individualism and communalism in settlement (agglomeration vs. conglomeration). By this time, ideological and economic conflict and emigration (possibly to the Superstition-Pinal highlands and the Globe-Miami area) may have depleted the population enough to reduce stress on the arable land and allow forms of agriculture with lower requirements for labor and facilities. The regional floods of the early 1380s (Van West et al., Chapter 2), followed by another severe drought, may have been too much for this system as well, since there seem to be few reliable dates for much occupation into the 1400s. By this time the technological, organizational, and resource potentials of the area and its people may have been too depleted (or too thinly distributed by the wealth dissipating leveling mechanisms typical of communal ideologies) to make it worth anyone's while to stay on.

Whatever happened, by 1350–1380 the platform mounds and their associated towns and villages made up of closely proximate clusters of compounds had been all but totally replaced by a different settlement system. Before the end of the fourteenth century, nearly the entire population of the Basin was housed in no more than a dozen fairly large structures strung along the rivers or tucked away in upland oases.

This chapter has covered a very wide range of topics; however, for every word describing these topics at least as much has not been said. Obviously I have greatly simplified the whole scenario, and many specific points need further research. The relationship between the upland and riverine parts of Tonto Basin, while potentially extremely important, is only one aspect of Salado developmental history. Other equally important aspects have not even been touched on. Foremost among these are the relationships between the Tonto and Salt Arms (which have recognizable differences in architecture and material culture) and between the Upper and Lower Basins. There is also the question of Tonto Basin's role in the regional cotton trade, given the recent evidence of extensive cotton production and the known economic and political importance of textiles among the historic tribes of the Southwest (Adams, Chapter 11; Van West et al., Chapter 2). Last, but not least, there is the question of population movement between Tonto Basin and the outside world, particularly the Sierra Ancha, and its effects on settlement and other aspects of Salado development. Perhaps these questions will drive the next generation of research into the Salado of Tonto Basin.

ACKNOWLEDGMENTS

As the title suggests, this paper is largely derived from a previous work of the same name, updated with the findings of Roosevelt Projects research. However, given the near legendary tendencies for differences of opinion regarding Tonto Basin archaeology, it is not intended to present a recitation of Projects reports or previous models. The essence of archaeology as I see it is not to dwell on the past but to learn from it, even our own. It is also the case that I see scholarship as a process of assimilation and not of mere citation.

Much of the settlement data used in the production of this paper can be found in the Cultural Resources Overview for the Tonto National Forest (Macnider and Effland 1989), which remains the best available source for detailed site distribution data in central Arizona. Though not extensively cited, the work of all the Roosevelt Projects contractors forms another primary basis for many of the interpretations presented here. In particular, the climatic and streamflow information, along with assessments of suitability for particular agricultural strategies or susceptibility of those strategies to flooding or drought, comes largely from the work of Van West et al. (Chapter 2). My specific interpretation of Projects data, however, has grown largely out of my own observations of this and other work in the Basin over the last 20 years and from prolonged arguments and occasionally civil conversations with Steve Germick, Joe Crary, Dave Doyel, Mark Elson, Jeff Clark, Owen Lindauer, Glen Rice, and Richard Ciolek-Torrello. Underlying all of this, of course, are the results of more than a century of archaeological survey by the Forest Service and a wide variety of permittees, contractors, volunteers, students, and others that has resulted in the recording of well over 2,000 sites in the area and the yet-to-be-fully-reported location of several thousand more. The above-named parties will be pleased to know, however, that I do not blame any of them for this and that I alone am responsible.

CHAPTER SIX

Hohokam and Salado Segmentary Organization:
The Evidence from the Roosevelt Platform Mound Study

Glen E. Rice

Two models of the organization of Salado and Hohokam platform mound complexes are evaluated in this paper drawing largely on data collected as part of the Roosevelt Platform Mound Study (RPMS) in Tonto Basin of central Arizona. A *settlement complex* lies at a scale intermediate between the individual settlement and the regional settlement system (Fish and Fish 1991; Gregory and Nials 1985; Wilcox and Sternberg 1983). Each complex consists of a central site with public architecture (initially ball courts but later platform mounds) surrounded by satellite settlements lacking such facilities. Activities at the ball courts and platform mounds of the primary sites would have included participants from the satellite settlements and integrated 2,000 to 5,000 people into small polities of about 40 km^2 each (Fish and Fish 1991:165).

In current usage, *Salado* refers to an archaeological horizon in the low deserts of the American Southwest that persisted from the late thirteenth century to the middle of the fifteenth century (Lincoln, Chapter 1; Nelson and LeBlanc 1986; Rice n.d. a). The horizon is defined by the appearance of Gila Polychrome in the late phases of the San Carlos, Tonto Basin, Upper Gila, Jornada and Casas Grandes regions of the southwestern United States and northern Mexico (Figure 6.1). At one time researchers applied the term to the late phases of the Hohokam tradition in the Salt, Gila, and Tucson Basins

as well (Haury 1945). The distribution of Gila Polychrome extends well beyond the areas that have commonly been attributed to the Salado unit.

Platform mound complexes occur in the Salt and Gila Basins, the Tucson Basin, the San Pedro Valley, and Tonto Basin. Of these four regions with mounds, only Tonto Basin is assigned to the Salado horizon. My focus on platform mounds necessitates a consideration of data from parts of both the Salado and Hohokam regions. It is not, on the other hand, a complete treatment of the social organization of all variants of the Salado.

Even in Tonto Basin, there was considerable variability in Classic period settlement and, by extension, social organization (Rice and Redman n.d.). At the start of the thirteenth century, populations were associated with two different kinds of settlement. Some resided in *platform mound complexes* on the valley bottom or on the neighboring bajadas. Others, probably immigrants from the surrounding mountains, occupied *primary villages*, a settlement type indigenous to higher elevation areas around the Basin (Redman 1993). In the early fourteenth century, the aggregation of people from platform mound complexes and primary villages into single communities created a third kind of settlement in some parts of Tonto Basin. *Syncretic mound/villages* blended architectural elements of platform mounds with the spatial layout of primary villages.

143

Figure 6.1.
Regions associated with the
Salado horizon and the
distribution of Gila
Polychrome.

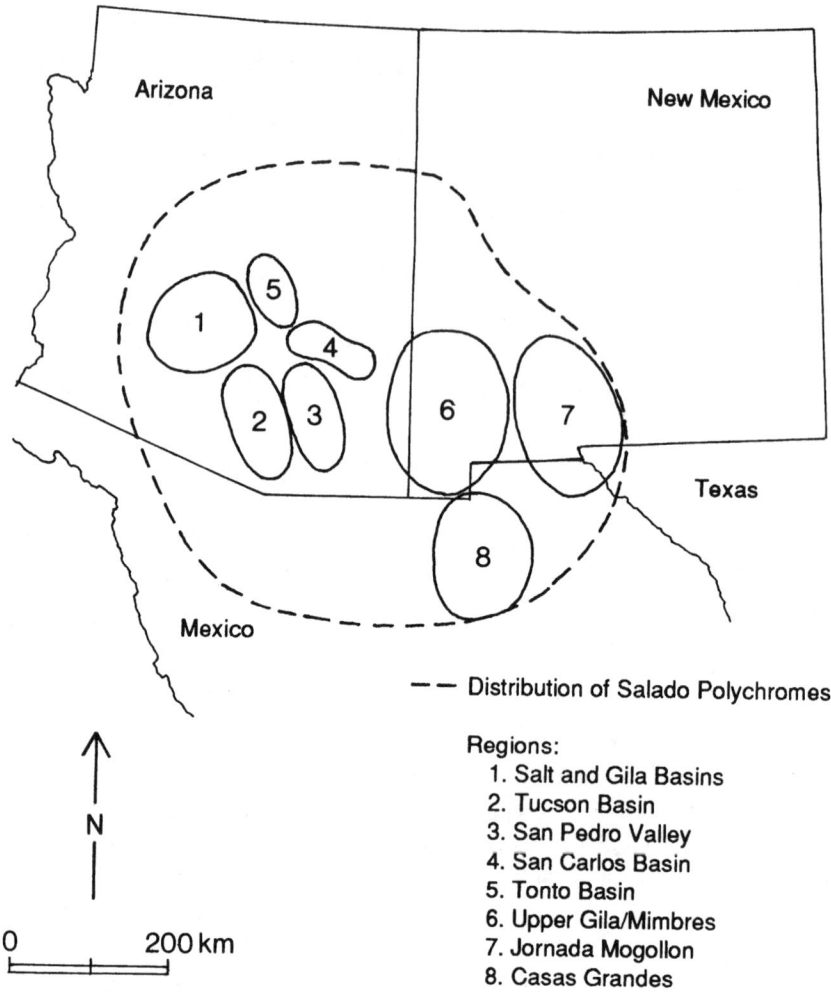

— — Distribution of Salado Polychromes

Regions:
1. Salt and Gila Basins
2. Tucson Basin
3. San Pedro Valley
4. San Carlos Basin
5. Tonto Basin
6. Upper Gila/Mimbres
7. Jornada Mogollon
8. Casas Grandes

Examples of fourteenth century platform mounds in Tonto Basin include Cline Terrace and Bourke's Teocalli (Jacobs 1997; Wood, Chapter 5), each of which was associated with a set of secondary settlements. The Armer Ruin was a syncretic platform mound that served as the center for an extensive multisite complex distributed on both sides of the Salt River. The Schoolhouse Point Mound (Lindauer, Chapter 9) was also a syncretic mound/village, but its population could easily have provided sufficient labor to construct the elevated, platform mound portions of the village. For this reason the Schoolhouse site (at least after 1320) would not have been a central place, and it apparently functioned as a secondary settlement in the Armer complex (Rice and Redman n.d.). In other areas of the Basin, the population continued to live in independent, primary villages without platform mounds, such as that of Tuzigoot-on-Salome (Germick and Crary 1989). Large primary villages also persisted in the area around Globe and Miami (Boggess et al. 1992; Doyel 1978; Wood, Chapter 5).

PLATFORM MOUNDS AS
MANAGERIAL CENTERS

Many researchers attribute the development of the platform mound settlement complexes to the growth of the irrigation canals in the Phoenix and Gila Basins (Doyel 1980; Fish and Fish 1991:97; Grebinger 1976). The first irrigation probably involved little more than ditches to fields on the floodplain and the lowest river terraces.

Where irrigation agriculture was successful, however, growth of the community required extension of the canals to bring additional acreage under cultivation (Woodbury 1961b). With each extension of the canal, it became more difficult to tend all of the fields from the founding settlement and eventually became necessary to establish a new settlement farther down the canal closer to the most distant fields. It is posited that continuing cycles of growth led eventually to sets of historically and socially related settlements strung out along each canal (Doyel 1980). The founding villages (Doyel 1980:59; Grebinger 1976; Wilcox and Sternberg 1983), by virtue of their historic primacy, retained a strong influence over other settlements on the same canal system, which they signaled by retaining control of public facilities such as ball courts (Doyel 1981:59; Grebinger 1976:40; Wilcox and Sternberg 1983). The shared use of a single ceremonial center by the settlements of the same "irrigation community" would clearly facilitate intersettlement cooperation in the maintenance of the canals and distribution of water.

Settlement complexes also occurred in smaller valleys or in stretches of desert where runoff or floodwater agricultural techniques replaced irrigation (Doyel and Elson 1985; Fish et al., eds. 1992:103; Rice 1990a). In these settings, the settlements were frequently dispersed across several neighboring environmental zones (Fish et al., eds. 1992). Such distributions may have helped diversify the risk of agricultural failure (Downum 1993:1; Fish et al., eds. 1992:103) or enhanced some settlements' access to natural food resources and maximized others' access to arable land (Rice 1990a:16). For either alternative, subsistence items could have been exchanged among settlements to balance seasonal and annual fluctuations in food productivity. Leaders residing in settlements with ball courts or in the rooms on platform mounds may have managed the exchange of food across the different microenvironments (Rice 1990a:9) or fostered a sense of extended community by regularly hosting ceremonial and social gatherings in the primary village.

Management of long distance exchange is also recognized as an important factor in the growth of the ball court and platform mound systems. Once in place, even a weak dichotomy between founding and secondary villages on irrigation canals would have proved advantageous for purposes other than managing the irrigation system, setting in motion a positive feedback process that would favor the growth and importance of the central places (Grebinger 1976:40–41; Rice 1990a:24–25). Traders

from outside the region, lacking knowledge of the local area, would find it useful to seek out the most prominent settlements for their transactions. Consequently, they would tend to gravitate to the centers, which would enhance the prestige and local prominence of those settlements. Local leaders, who found it useful to develop stockpiles of trade items in anticipation of future visits from traders would encourage the local production of craft items or procurement of raw materials that could be used for exchange. This would improve the efficiency of the exchange system, which would enhance the managerial importance and prestige of the leaders residing in the centers (Doyel 1981:60; 1991a:252; Grebinger 1976:41; Wilcox and Sternberg 1983).

In some variants of the models, the management of long distance exchange is seen as sufficient for the growth of the system, and the role of irrigation is not mentioned. These models have the advantage of not positing one kind of management (oversight of canals) for areas with irrigation and a different kind (redistribution of subsistence resources) for areas without irrigation. Leaders could increase their influence by controlling access to nonsubsistence items obtained through long distance exchange, such as copper bells, pyrite mirrors, shell trumpets, shell jewelry, obsidian, turquoise, and argillite (McGuire 1985; Teague 1985). It is also possible that the centers were involved in a level of exchange "not accessible to members of the smaller villages" (Doyel 1991a:60). Attempts to monopolize long distance trade would require the stockpiling of materials, and aspiring leaders might have begun managing the craft production as well (Neitzel 1991; Teague 1985). Prestige items such as shell jewelry would have moved down the hierarchy, while subsistence products and craft items would have moved up the hierarchy (McGuire 1985:475–76).

Managerial activities are linked to increasing differences in status. As the system became more centralized in matters having to do with management of the irrigation system, craft production, and long distance exchange, the managers would become more important and capable of demonstrating their importance through the use and display of rare materials (Doyel 1981, 1991a; Grebinger 1976; McGuire 1985; Neitzel 1991:217; Teague 1985; Upham and Rice 1980).

A number of the patterns associated with the development of Hohokam ball court and platform mound settlement complexes are consistent with the expectations of the managerial models, indicating the potential of these models for explaining past events. The Hohokam began using irrigation during the Pioneer period and were constructing relatively long canals by the closing phases of that period (Haury 1976a). Ball courts appeared during the Colonial period, (Doyel 1981:57; Wilcox and Sternberg 1983), satisfying the models' requirements for a weak settlement hierarchy. During the Colonial and Sedentary periods, the ball court system became more centralized, with a decrease in the number of courts and an increased regularity in the spacing of courts (McGuire 1987).

By the middle 1200s, platform mounds had replaced ball courts as the facilities associated with the central places in multisite settlement complexes (Gregory 1991: 167–69). Although initially the rooms on platform mounds were reserved for ceremonial purposes (Rice 1995), by the late thirteenth century residential structures were also being constructed on the platform mounds (Gregory 1987). Only a few families could live in the rooms on the platform mounds, mounds built with assistance from the entire community, while most people lived in ground level rooms in the walled compounds and small room blocks scattered around the mounds (Gregory 1991:167–68; Martin and Plog 1973; Wilcox 1991a:262). The evidence for increased status differentiation in the Classic period is consistent with the expectations of the managerial model.

The volume and intensity of exchange also increased through time. Early in the sequence, settlements with ball courts showed no greater access to items obtained through trade than other communities (Teague 1985). By the Classic period, platform mounds tended to have more marine shell, obsidian, and turquoise than other villages, and some mounds may have had specialists who produced items such as agave knives, axes, or textiles (Neitzel 1991; Teague 1985; Wilcox 1987b).

Test of the Managerial Model

Although managerial models have been discussed in the literature for at least two decades, no data sets collected by modern methods were available to study the organization of exchange, craft production, and food production in single settlement complexes. Researchers (Neitzel 1991; Teague 1985) seeking to test implications about the management of exchange and production of crafts had to compare excavated settlements in different settlement complexes; platform mounds (or ball courts) in one complex were compared to residential compounds (or pithouse villages) in different complexes. The inability to make within-complex comparisons left archaeologists unable to determine whether statistical differences between classes of settlements were expressions of centralized managerial control or consequences of between-complex variation that, due to sampling error, happened to fall in the expected direction. This situation has changed in the past few years with the publication of results from three research projects specifically designed to collect comparative data from platform mounds and residential settlements in the same settlement complexes: the Roosevelt Platform Mound Study (RPMS) (Rice, ed. 1990), the Roosevelt Community Development Study (RCDS) (Doelle, Wallace, Elson, and Craig 1992), and the Northern Tucson Basin Survey (Fish et al., eds. 1992).

Data from Gila phase settlements of the Cline Terrace Complex (Figure 6.2) are used to test implications about the role of platform mounds in managing long distance exchange and craft production. The Cline Terrace platform mound was a settlement of about 47 rooms, of which 16 were located on the elevated surfaces of two platform mounds (Figure 6.3). A massive wall, more than two m wide, enclosed the settlement within a compound measuring 60 m by 130 m. Other settlements in the Cline Terrace complex include three large villages of 35, 50, and 65 rooms and a series of smaller compounds, two-room sites, and field houses distributed along a five km stretch on the east side of Tonto Creek (Jacobs 1997; Oliver and Jacobs, eds 1997).

The intersettlement comparisons use artifact assemblages from screened contexts representing the final occupation of each site. Many rooms in these settlements burned, and the great majority showed evidence of having been rapidly abandoned with little attempt to remove artifacts. For the Cline Terrace site itself, artifact densities are presented for rooms on the elevated platform and for rooms in plazas around the base of the mound. Casa Bandalero, one of the large secondary settlements, is not included in the comparisons because only minor tests were conducted at the site.

Long Distance Exchange

If the platform mounds managed long distant trade and the distribution of the materials to their secondary settlements, central and secondary sites should exhibit different frequencies and densities of materials. There should be more traded commodities at the Cline Terrace platform mound than at the neighboring sites because the mound would be the central location for stockpiling

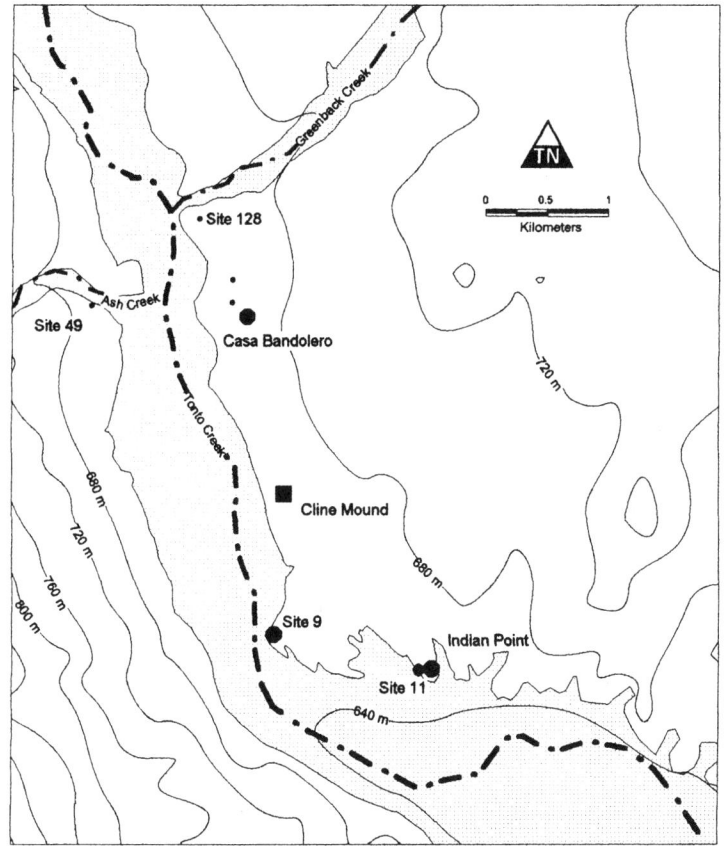

Cline Terrace Settlement Complex
Gila Phase

■ Platform Mound
● Large Settlement
◆ Medium Settlement
· Small Settlement

Figure 6.2.
The Cline Terrace Platform Mound Complex, showing the locations of key sites used in the comparative analysis.

Figure 6.3.
The Cline Terrace Platform Mound, the center of the Cline Terrace Settlement Complex.

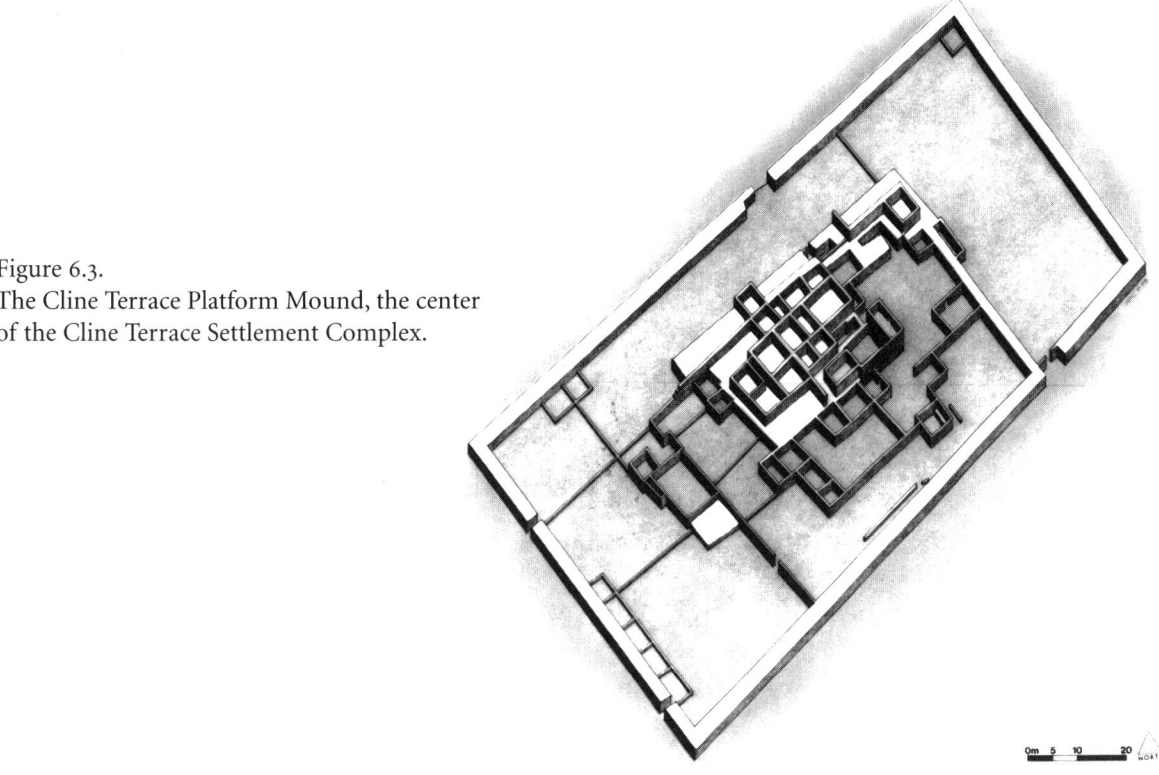

Table 6.1. Distance from the Cline Terrace Mound to Sources of Materials Obtained Through Exchange

Material	Distance	Name of Source
Turquoise	40 km	Cherry Creek
Turquoise	60 km	Globe and Miami
Azurite and Malachite	60 km	Globe and Miami
Hematite	60 km	Young
Obsidian	50 km	Superior
Obsidian	175 km	Flagstaff
Obsidian	> 200 km	Other Sources
Marine Shell	340 km	Gulf of California

the material prior to distribution to the rest of the settlements. Because the thrust of the managerial models is that both the long distance trade and the local redistribution of materials required coordinating the efforts of large numbers of people, these commodities should occur in quantities that would require the transportation efforts of many people.

The settlements of the Cline Terrace Complex obtained marine shell, obsidian, pigments, and turquoise from varying distances beyond their own valley (Table 6.1), and the Cline Terrace platform mound does have more shell, obsidian, and pigment minerals than its neighboring settlements (Table 6.2). This kind of trend has been noted in other comparative studies involving platform mounds (Bayman 1996; Teague 1985) and is consistent with the expectation that mound settlements should have more of a traded commodity. However, the quantities of these traded materials in the platform mound complex are well beneath the levels that would be expected in a system with centralized managerial control. Certain other distributions of materials in the settlements are also inconsistent with managerial control. The differences between the platform mound and the neighboring settlements in the complex have to do with the specialized function of the Cline Terrace Mound settlement, a function pertaining to ceremony and ritual.

Olivella shells (beads) and *Conus* shells (tinklers) comprise most of the shell artifacts recovered from the Cline Terrace platform mound (Table 6.2) and other platform mounds (Bayman 1996; Rice 1995). When these shells are removed from consideration, mound and nonmound settlements have comparable quantities of the remaining categories of shell. Other species of shell, especially *Glycymeris*, which was used to make bracelets and rings, occurred in nearly equal densities at all of the Gila phase settlements. Because all the marine shell species come from one source, it seems unlikely that managerial control would be exercised over a few species and not others.

The quantity of shell is also very low. Less than one kg of shell was recovered from all of the screened excavations at the Cline Terrace Mound, and, based on the sample of room floors, it is likely that only about one-third kg of shell jewelry was actually ever in use at any one time in the settlement. These quantities could have easily been transported into the Basin by a single individual in one trip, and centralized control over such a modest level of effort would do little to improve the efficiency of the exchange. The Cline Terrace platform mound had more *Olivella* beads and *Conus* tinklers, items that were likely used in ceremonial events (see also Rice 1995; Bayman 1996). With this exception, the settlements in the complex all obtained roughly comparable quantities of marine shell artifacts.

If the Cline Terrace platform mound controlled the trade in obsidian, stockpiles of obsidian cores or large flakes should be found there. This is not the case. The obsidian assemblages in two rooms at the Cline Terrace Mound account for the greater abundance of obsidian at the platform mound than at neighboring settlements (Table 6.2). This obsidian occurred mostly as small flakes of the kind generated during the knapping of projectile points or bifaces, and large cores suitable for exchange to other settlements were lacking. Thus, the obsidian procured by the Cline Terrace platform mound was consumed largely within the confines of the settlement itself. Taken together, the assemblages from the two rooms totaled 50 flakes; because even a moderately sized core of obsidian could be reduced to several hundred flakes, this does not constitute a substantially greater level of procurement effort at the mound. The people at the platform mound used more obsidian than the surrounding settlements, certainly, but in quantities that represent the additional efforts of only one or two individuals.

Table 6.2. Comparison of the Density of Artifacts in Rooms at Settlements of the Cline Terrace Complex (Artifacts per Cubic Meter)

| Artifact Category | CLINE MOUND | | SECONDARY SETTLEMENTS | | | |
	On the Mound	Off the Mound	Site 128	Site 9	Indian Point	Site 11
Density per cubic m (highest values in bold):						
All Marine Shell	3.06	.94	.29	.77	2.22	.53
Conus and *Olivella*	1.69	.36	.14	.31	.48	.00
Malachite	7.05	.14	.58	.10	.81	.00
Azurite	3.42	.00	.00	.41	.00	.00
Hematite/Ocher/Limonite	2.09	1.99	.00	.05	.84	.00
Obsidian	1.97	2.16	1.01	1.60	1.32	1.58
Manuports	.56	.96	.44	.62	.79	.00
Agave Knives	.59	.89	.58	.35	.57	.53
Points/Bifaces/Drills	.83	.97	1.16	2.06	.90	.00
Stone Jewelry	.35	.37	.29	.41	.12	.00
Manos	1.01	1.50	2.04	1.13	2.05	1.05
Ceramic Manufacturing Tools	.20	.56	.58	.05	.31	.00
Axes	.12	.21	.00	.36	.53	.00

There is also no evidence that the Cline Terrace platform mound controlled the procurement of pigment minerals. Both the reddish iron-based minerals and the blue minerals found with copper deposits occurred almost exclusively at the platform mound (Table 6.2). Clearly, these items were not traded extensively within the local settlement system. Furthermore, the pigments were obtained from sources only 40 to 60 km from the Cline Terrace area, distances comparable to the obsidian source near the modern town of Superior. Since both the mound and nonmound settlements obtained relatively equal proportions of their obsidian from Superior, it seems likely that all the settlements in the Cline Terrace group could also have procured similar quantities of pigment minerals. Under these conditions, the predominance of pigments at the platform mound has to be interpreted as a functional requirement specific to that settlement. These pigments could have been used to color wooden sticks, rock slabs, tools such as axes and manos, basketry items possibly worn as hats, and even parts of the body. If such preparations took place predominantly at the platform mounds, the necessary coloring materials would only be needed at those locations within the settlement system.

In conclusion, there is no evidence that the Cline Terrace platform mound managed or controlled access to items obtained through long distance exchange. The data demonstrate a specialized function for the mound itself, which resulted in its procuring greater quantities of *Olivella* shell beads, *Conus* shell tinklers, and pigment minerals. The settlement at the platform mound also acquired more obsidian than its neighbors, but it did not develop large stockpiles of the raw material for distribution to the surrounding settlements.

Production and Warehousing of Craft Items

Control by the platform mound of the production of craft items could take one of two progressively more centralized forms. The items might be produced at all the communities and stockpiled at the platform mound for exchange, or both the production and warehousing of items could be concentrated at the platform mounds. The amount of effort expended in the production of crafts should be relatively large, reflecting the requirements of a centralized system and conforming to the expectation that some people were specialized craft producers. Data pertaining to the production of shell jewelry, ceramic vessels, textiles, and projectile points fail to support these implications.

Most marine shell arrived in Tonto Basin as completed pieces of jewelry, but a small local industry produced shell pendants from *Laevicardium* sp., tinklers from

Conus sp., and beads from *Olivella* sp. The *Laevicardium* pendants were produced at the Cline Terrace platform mound and at two of the neighboring sites. All of the production debris from floor contexts in all sites, however, weighs no more than the equivalent of ten whole *Laevicardium* shells; the same contexts yielded only five completed pendants. Artifacts from *Conus* and *Olivella* shells were produced almost exclusively in one room on top of the Cline Terrace platform mound, but only 100 g of such shells were recovered from all of the rooms at the Cline Terrace Mound. A single person could easily transform this quantity of shells into tinklers, beads, and rings in one or two days. Such levels of effort do not qualify as anything close to even a part-time specialization in craft production; an increase in the level of effort by two to three orders of magnitude (i.e., involving hundreds of days of production effort) would make a more convincing case for craft specialists.

Artifacts used in the production of ceramic vessels included polishing stones, lumps of unfired clay, and ceramic anvils (made of stone) used with paddles to shape vessels. Such items were found in particularly high density in some of the ground level rooms at Cline Terrace, and in lower densities in rooms on top of the mound. However, the neighboring settlements at Indian Point also had rooms with comparable densities of the materials used in making pottery, and even the small hamlet (Site 128) in the complex was involved to some degree in ceramic production (Table 6.2). Although it was a major producer of ceramic vessels, the platform mound was not the sole producer nor provider of this commodity to the other settlements in the complex.

There was also little specialization in the production of cotton or textiles. Thirteen spindle whorls were recovered from screened contexts on floors and in middens at the platform mound and two of the neighboring settlements. Cotton occurred at the platform mound and one neighboring settlement, but in well under ten percent of the flotation samples. This level of production is consistent with the local needs of the community, but does not suggest managerial control or production for purposes of exchange.

The production of projectile points has been cited as a craft activity conducted more often at platform mounds than at neighboring settlements (Teague 1984). Lithic anvils used in the bipolar flaking of small nodules of obsidian and particularly important in making projectile points from "apache tears" (Huckell 1981) were found only in the rooms at the Cline Terrace platform mound. The middens at the platform mound also had higher densities of projectile points and bifaces than the middens at neighboring settlements. However, higher densities of projectile points and arrowshaft straighteners were recovered from the floors of secondary settlements than at the platform mound (Table 6.2). This lack of overall directionality in the distribution of projectile points and of implements used to make points does not support the hypothesis of specialized craft production at the platform mound.

The platform mounds, as part of their managerial function, could accumulate stockpiles of utilitarian implements to be used in exchange or displayed as indications of their status. A comparison of the densities of agave knives, manos, polished stone axes, and projectile points (Table 6.2) shows that only agave knives occur in greater density in the rooms at the platform mound. Since agave knives are made with relative ease from tabular pieces of schist or large flakes, it is unlikely that the mounds were specialized locations for the production of these items. Apparently agave was eaten in greater quantities at the platform mound sites than neighboring settlements. Both the Hohokam and Salado baked large batches of agave stems in earthen ovens. Since baked agave turns bitter after a few days, batch preparation suggests that it was meant to be consumed by large groups gathered at the platform mound settlement, such as would have been required during construction events or ceremonial gatherings.

Rooms with stockpiles of agave knives, manos, pestles, metates, and ground stone axes did occur, but they were distributed among four of the five settlements used in the comparison, including the two-room site (Site 128, Figure 6.2). Each room contained hand implements, either manos or agave knives, in numbers that far exceed the potential requirements of any family-size domestic unit that could potentially occupy the space (although these rooms were obviously used for storage rather than residential purposes). Furthermore, there were sufficient numbers of manos and metates in other rooms at each of these sites to satisfy the requirements of those in residence. If these items were stored for trade, nearly every settlement in the Complex participated in such exchange. The implements may have been stockpiled for other purposes, but this does not alter the outcome. The Cline Terrace platform mound did not differ appreciably in economic function from other settlements in the complex.

Redistribution of
Subsistence Resources

Classic period settlements were frequently distributed across neighboring microenvironments (Fish et al., eds. 1992; Rice, ed. 1990). The larger settlements were located in the valley bottoms where irrigation and floodplain agriculture were possible, but other settlements were located on the neighboring bajadas and foothills along the edges of the valleys. In these latter settings, farming could also be practiced but with greater difficulty, using narrow terraces along small streams with enough spring flow to get crops established, or on the sloping surface of the bajada itself using rainfall and runoff techniques. The bajada slopes and foothills were ideal, however, for collecting cacti fruits, cholla buds, and agave stems and were convenient locations from which to stage deer-hunting expeditions into the mountains.

Researchers have posited that platform mounds served as centers that managed the redistribution of subsistence products among settlements of the same complex dispersed in different environments. Two alternate kinds of interdependency have been proposed.

One model recognizes the variation in natural resources between valley bottom and foothill settings and posits specialization of subsistence strategies by microenvironment (Rice, ed. 1990). Settlements in the valley bottoms could focus on the production of agricultural surpluses; settlements in upland locations could augment their limited agricultural productivity with the harvest of valued natural resources such as cactus fruits and agave, which they exchanged with lowland settlements for the balance of their needs in agricultural staples. The addition of high calorie natural plant foods to the diet would avoid the nutritional problems associated with a heavy dependency on maize. Such differences in subsistence should be reflected in the pollen and flotation records and the artifact and feature assemblages of sites in different zones. The expected differences between upland and lowland and environmental zones were not observed in any category of data (Oliver 1997b). Rather, there was considerable uniformity in the pollen, flotation, artifactual, and feature data from settlements in all zones, and the data were consistent with a focal reliance on agriculture in all zones.

The second posited form of interdependency focuses on variation in growing conditions (moisture and temperature) in zones at different elevations (Fish et al., eds.

1992). In winter, temperature inversions keep the valley bottoms cooler and more prone to frost than the upper bajadas. With good winter rains, settlements on the upper bajadas could plant earlier than settlements on the valley bottom. With good summer rains, however, fields in the valley bottoms had the greater chance of success because of access to water from streams. Depending on when the rains arrived, crop failure would sometimes occur on the upper bajadas, other times on the valley bottom, and occasionally in all locations.

Such annual variation in agricultural production could be balanced by exchanging food from the uplands to the valley bottom in years of summer drought, and from the valley bottom to the uplands in years of winter drought. Such exchange seems highly improbable, however, because there was much less arable soil in the uplands than in adjoining lowlands. Moreover, the density of population per hectare of arable land was higher in the uplands than in the lowlands. For a specific part of Tonto Basin, settlements in the uplands had about .5 to .6 ha of arable land per room, compared to values of 1.2 to 1.3 ha per room in contemporary lowland settlements. Upland populations could not have grown enough food to support themselves as well as the much larger lowland populations.

Finally, the hypotheses that the platform mounds managed the redistribution of subsistence resources among settlements in different microenvironments is not supported by some settlement patterns. Platform mounds as well as ball court settlements complexes occasionally fall completely within the upland bajadas (Germick and Crary 1990, Fish et al., eds. 1992). In such cases the central places were associated with dispersed groups of settlements that could not have been functionally specialized or otherwise interdependent on each other for subsistence resources, because they occupied only one microenvironmental zone.

The evidence is that settlements comprising a platform mound (or ball court) complex were economically self sufficient and functionally equivalent. They relied heavily on agriculture and made use of natural resources in roughly comparable ways as a means of diversifying the diet, whatever their location in the landscape. The platform mounds did not manage the redistribution of subsistence resources among settlements because the settlements did not depend on each other for such support.

Centralized Control of Irrigation Districts

The growth of settlement complexes has also been linked to the managerial requirements of irrigation agriculture. The first group to occupy the headgate location for a canal, "by virtue of its primacy … could claim absolute right to all land irrigated by the main canal under its control" (Grebinger 1976:41). As the population grew, the canal would be lengthened to open up new arable land, and additional settlements would be established along the canal. Ball courts in the founding communities would integrate the communities sharing a canal. The population of the secondary settlements on the canals shared a common ancestry with the founding village and returned periodically for ball court-related activities (Grebinger 1976). This model leads to specific expectations about the settlement: ball courts should occur in the settlements at the headgates of each canal and be absent in other settlements of the same canal system. The gradual extension and growth of a canal eventually resulted in the arrangement of multiple sites into a single ball court settlement complex. Since platform mounds had replaced ball courts as central-place facilities by the Classic period, the implication can be extended to the development of platform mound complexes as well.

Doyel (1981:60) provides a more general statement in terms of "primary" villages. Each irrigation community would have a ranking village of larger size with "ceremonial features and elaborated material culture" that set it apart from smaller villages in the same district. The set of settlements sharing the same canal would be integrated through this highest ranked village.

The settlement patterns associated with the canals in the Phoenix and Gila Basins do not conform to the predicted patterns and fail to support the hypothesis that ball court or platform mound complexes integrated the settlements sharing a single canal. Long canals had multiple centers with platform mounds or ball courts, spaced at regular four to five km intervals along the canal; secondary settlements in the complexes were scattered at other points of the canals (Crown 1987; Gregory 1991). At several places in the Phoenix Basin, the prehistoric populations built several canals (from three to five at a time) from the same headgate, and these fanned out and ran roughly parallel to each other across long stretches of terrain. In these settings, the settlements were grouped in clusters, with the long axis of each cluster oriented perpendicular to the canals, and a spacing of four to five km

between clusters (Figure 6.4). Within each cluster were multiple ball court or platform mound centers (Gregory 1991; Howard 1993), sometimes as many as three to five distinct centers, and the number increased with the size of the canal systems. If the platform mounds measure centralization in the irrigation districts, the larger irrigation districts were more decentralized than the smaller districts. Thus, ball court and platform mound settlement complexes did not develop out of a pattern of incremental growth of canal systems, in which the founding villages became the central places in the settlement complexes.

The multisite settlement complexes were undoubtedly instrumental in operating the irrigation districts, not because they provided centralized control of each canal, but because they reduced the scale of the system (Johnson 1978, 1989) to workable proportions. Johnson (1978) makes the points that it is easier to arrive at decisions in small groups than in large groups and there is an upper limit to the size of the group in which consensual decisions can be reached on a regular basis. If the settlement complexes were capable of functioning as units, and the evidence is clear that they did so in constructing ball courts or platform mounds, they may have acted as units in regard to the irrigation canals. Even the largest irrigation districts had no more than a dozen settlement complexes, compared to perhaps scores of settlements and hundreds of courtyard groups (roughly equivalent to households). Reaching group consensus among a dozen or so individuals, each representing one platform mound complex, would be manageable. Consensus would be more difficult in large groups, such as would occur if representation was at the level of the individual settlement or household.

In conclusion, it is highly unlikely that irrigation agriculture was the catalyst for the development of multisite settlement complexes. But on the other hand, without some form of organization similar to that of the ball court or platform mound settlement complexes, the growth of the irrigation system to its eventual scale would not have been possible.

Elites Without Managerial Duties

Platform mounds did not control long distance exchange, craft production, food redistribution, or the flow of water through irrigation canals. The settlements clustered in small territorial units around the platform mounds were not dependent on the mound for some form of centralized economic service. This was not the "glue" that linked dispersed

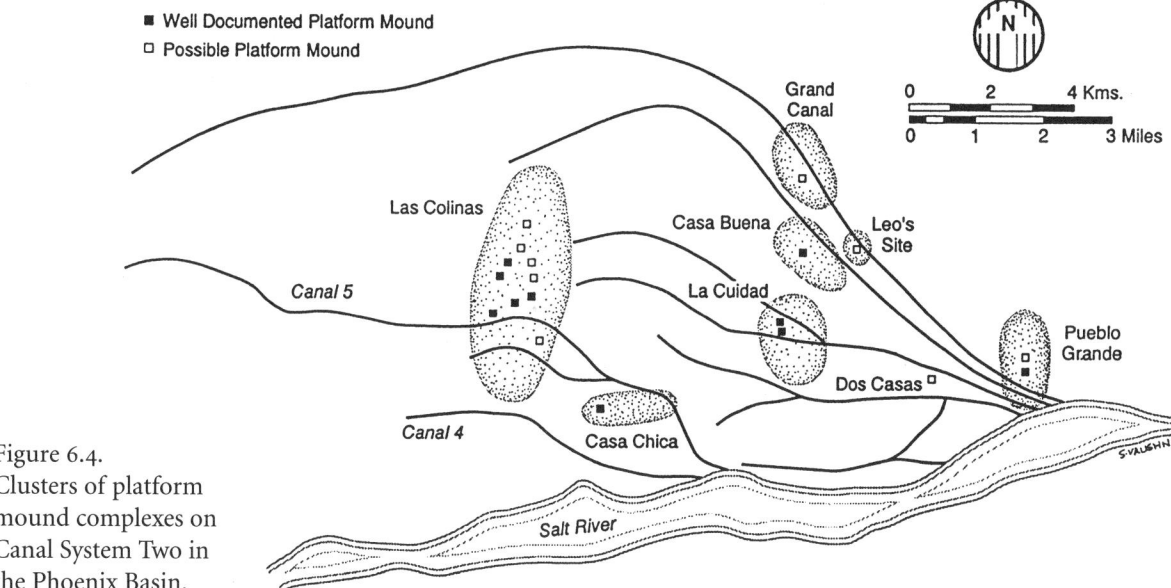

Figure 6.4. Clusters of platform mound complexes on Canal System Two in the Phoenix Basin.

settlements to the central compounds with platform mounds. Moreover, the genesis of multisite complexes with central places was apparently not a product of the incremental growth of the irrigation systems in the Phoenix and Gila Basins; if anything, the growth of the irrigation systems may have depended on the prior existence of the multisite complexes.

Platform mounds did, however, house elites: groups of people with higher status than those residing in the surrounding settlements. These differences were expressed in the more elaborate residential architecture, wealth, and specialized ceremonial duties of those living at the mounds.

Rooms constructed on platform mounds required twelve to 13 times more material than building equivalent rooms at ground level. Although these figures do not translate directly into effort, it is probably safe to say that residential rooms on a platform mound were at least ten times more expensive to construct than residential rooms at ground level. Many platform mound settlements incorporated other forms of elaborate architecture as well, such as massive compound walls or masonry architecture.

The people who lived at the platform mounds also had rare materials and artifacts in quantities as great as or greater than those in other settlements. The mounds had rooms and plazas used for ceremonies. Because artifacts associated with such ceremonies were cached in the residential rooms on the mound, some high status people living at the mounds were very likely ceremonial specialists. Since individual mounds persisted for a century or more, the status of the groups in residence at the mounds extended across generations.

Evidence from the platform mound complexes indicates that ascribed differences occurred in the absence of managerial control of surplus or production, a finding that is at odds with many models of the development of early forms of ranked societies. Nascent elites, these models posit, needed to stimulate the surplus production of subsistence resources that they could divert to fund the construction of public facilities and monuments, or they oversaw the production of crafts to be used in long term exchange for rare materials from distant locations (Adams 1966:45; Johnson 1989:373; Sahlins 1968:26; Service 1962:143). The production of monuments and acquisition of rare objects expressed their status and legitimized differences between them and their subordinates. Elites frequently made themselves indispensable by coordinating economic exchange between different specialized economies occupying different environmental zones (Adams 1966:42; Redman 1978:204; Sahlins 1968:26). These expectations proved not to hold for the populations at the platform mounds.

PLATFORM MOUNDS AS
SEGMENTARY ORGANIZATIONS

Some anthropological models do not posit a necessary relationship between ascribed ranking and economic control. Elites in many segmentary states and societies frequently have little to do with managing economic activities, and a good case can be made that the platform mound complexes were segmentary organizations (Rice 1992) and that relationships between and within complexes were structured by the principle of complementary opposition (Rice n.d. b). Although terms such as *segmentary organizations* and *complementary opposition* derive from ethnographic research, they are used here in ways consistent with archaeological data and archaeological inquiry. While ethnographers apply such concepts to a much wider range of phenomena and constructs than archaeologists, there remains an important area in which their usage overlaps. Both can make significant contributions to the anthropological study of such issues as the development of urban centers, variability in state level societies, and processes of territorial expansion (Evans-Pritchard 1940; Fox 1977; Sahlins 1961; Sanders 1989; Wheatley 1971).

In a segmentary system, the population is divided into parts, or segments, such that all of the parts are alike in structure and function, and larger, more encompassing levels of organization are formed by drawing together equivalent, lower order groups (Sahlins 1961:330). Because archaeologists study distributions of artifacts in space and time, our interests lie in segmentary organizations that have archaeologically recognizable counterparts in space; that is, organizational systems that structure relationships between settlements in a local area or the distributions of facilities and artifacts within a single settlement. The question of whether cognitive divisions and constructs recognized by a population, such as lineages, can be mapped isometrically onto the residential divisions of a society is not easily addressed with archaeological data. As it turns out, this is not an impediment to the archaeological study of segmentary organization, since the segmental organization of a territorial system need not be related to, and is certainly not a consequence of, the organization of cultural constructs such as kinship systems. Evans-Pritchard (1940) found among the Nuer that true lineage membership, based on actual descent, had no relationship to a person's place of residence or territorial allegiance. Ethnographers attribute the development of segmental organizations of territorial units to ecological, technological, and demographic factors, not to kinship (Sahlins 1961). Segmentary organizations also characterize some state level societies, systems in which kinship structure has little or no relationship to political, economic or spatial organizations (Fox 1977:41–43). While the relationship between a society's cultural constructs and their use of territory may be of interest to ethnography, it is not necessary to the archaeological investigation of segmentary settlement systems. Given that there might have been these kinds of settlement systems in the past, the archaeologist seeks to understand how they operated and how they fared through time in comparison to other settlement organizations.

In some segmentary organizations, the segments have the capacity to mass into larger, more inclusive segments in a pattern referred to as complementary opposition. Both ethnographic and archaeological usage of this term refer to situations in which neighboring, primary segments join together for some undertakings in a more inclusive segment, such that the resulting unit continues to constitute a geographical bloc (Sahlins 1961:328–29). The amalgamation process can progress through several cycles, each drawing together neighboring segments of a comparable level of inclusiveness. Because allegiance is based on spatial proximity, each cycle of massing results in a progressively larger territorial unit. The consequence is that segmentary societies, though made up of small units that are independent and self-sufficient in terms of subsistence and economy, can act as large political blocs to face a common external threat or to extend their privileges into new areas (Sahlins 1961:332). Segmentary organizations can have the appearance of big government, but with no centralized leadership and no infrastructure.

Necessary Conditions

A segmentary organization at the settlement level occurs under certain combinations of environmental, demographic, and technological conditions. The use of the landscape must create a long term commitment by a settlement to a particular locality, creating a de facto form of land tenure and territorial control. The situation has to be so dire that a settlement cannot survive just anywhere in the environment, but must control one of a limited number of niches. Second, use of the landscape must foster cooperation between neighboring settlements, a lower order of cooperation with more distant

Figure 6.5.
Irrigation canals and
headgates in the
Phoenix and Gila
Basins (based on
Gregory 1991:171 and
Gregory and Nials
1985).

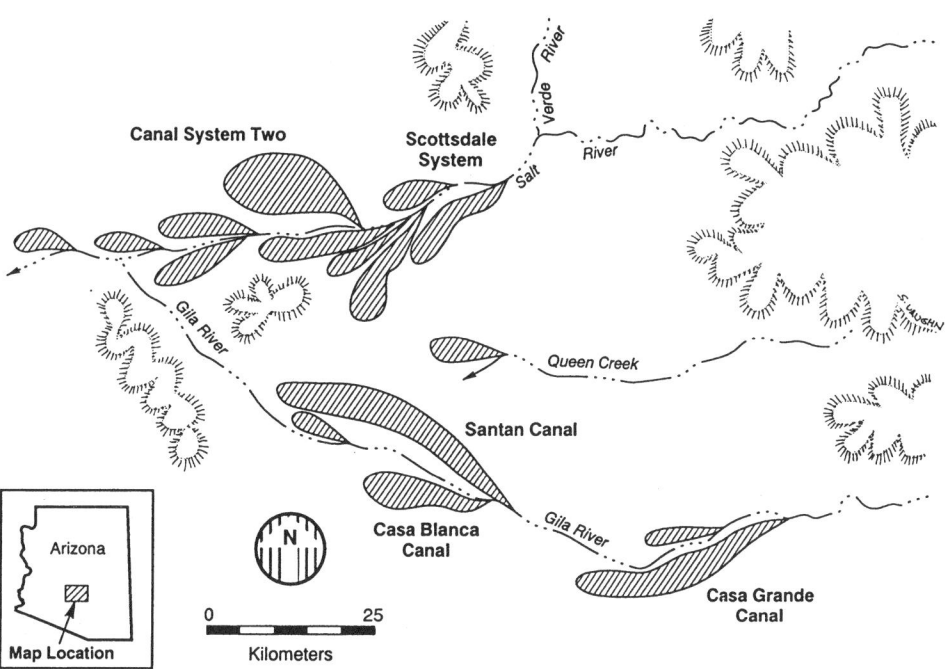

settlements, and so forth until there is essentially no need for cooperation with settlements beyond a given distance. This kind of situation is not particularly common; in many settings, it is the level of competition that is greatest between neighboring settlements and declines with distance. These two ecological conditions are termed the requirements for commitment to territory and for commitment to neighbors and were met in the major valleys of the Sonoran Desert of southern Arizona by the early part of the Hohokam tradition.

Commitment to Territory

For segmentary organizations to be manifested in space, the settlements must depend on a specific locale, and this dependency must persist over the long term (multiple generations). This requires group commitment to a specific territory, changing the question of residence from "with whom shall we live?" to "in which location shall we live?" This kind of situation can develop when production is based on a limited and localized resource (Sahlins 1961:330).

The prehistoric irrigation systems on the Salt and Gila Rivers and the adaptive patterns in the neighboring valleys and basins fostered just such a dependency. Part of the commitment to locale had do to with the fact that once communities had invested labor in constructing a canal, there was a natural desire to retain control over the

use of the facilities and the acreage that could be brought under irrigation. More to the point, there were only a limited number of locations where canal systems could be built (Gregory 1991; Gregory and Niles 1985), so that once a settlement committed to a particular area there were few options for moving on. Canal headgates, especially for canals intended to be used for a number of years, could not be placed at just any location along a river. During the summer, the surface flow ceases in many desert rivers, but water continues to percolate through the gravels in the river beds. This subterranean flow is forced back to the surface in areas where bedrock masses, or "reefs," lie close to the surface (Fish et al., eds. 1992; Gregory 1991). Even in drought years, water flowed at such locations. Bedrock reefs were strategic locations for the headgates of prehistoric canals; ten of 16 canal systems (Figure 6.5) were thus situated (Gregory 1991: 178). The slope of the terrain bordering the river determined the width of the area that could be irrigated, which was narrow along the Gila and wide along the Salt. Intakes could not be located where high ground lay adjacent to the river banks, and canals usually had to terminate where they intersected large tributaries of the main river (Gregory and Niles 1985; Wood et al. 1992).

A settlement situated at a location suitable for a headgate would have had considerable agricultural success but faced the potential threat of being dislodged by a larger and stronger group. Irrigation technology in the Phoenix and Gila Basins created a situation in which settlements competed for access to less than two dozen prime locations, necessitating a commitment to defend particular locations. Territories of this form, incidentally, would not involve a concern for boundaries; only the need to hold onto a very small, advantageous location in and around which a complex of associated settlements could be established.

Irrigation was not as important in other areas; canals were built on a much smaller scale or not at all, and the populations raised crops using a variety of runoff and floodplain strategies. However, even using techniques that required only a temporary access to surface water, the localities that could be reliably farmed were few and widely scattered. Although the specific physiographic and geological characteristics of such localities varied, two general kinds of settings can be described. One strategic type of locality were bedrock "reefs" on small drainages, similar to those that served as good headgate locations on the Salt and Gila Rivers. In smaller valleys, such as the Santa Cruz, such settings were prime locations for floodplain agriculture or small-scale ditch irrigation (Doelle and Wallace 1991; Fish et al., eds. 1992). Because smaller drainages carried less water than either the Salt or Gila River, their surface flow was all the more likely to be limited to the areas of the bedrock reefs during the summer.

Second, floodplain and akchin agriculture could be practiced in certain settings in the foothills and on the bajadas that border the desert valleys and basins. Favorable locations tended to occur where mountain streams exited the foothills and began coursing towards the main stream in the middle of the valley. Usually these side drainages carried water only after heavy rains, and the flow might frequently be too low to actually reach the main drainage. For these reasons, the agricultural use of these secondary catchments was generally restricted to areas in the low foothills and on the upper bajada, close to the mountains. Furthermore, only the streams with relatively large catchment areas in the higher mountains could be counted on to flow regularly, which further reduced the number of suitable locations. Although the sporadic availability of water might appear to make the occupation of such foothill settings tenuous at best, many were occupied continuously from the late Archaic into the Classic period, a span of nearly 2000 years (Fish et al., eds. 1992).

The situation was thus one in which geological and physiographic conditions combined to create a localized and limited distribution of a critical resource—water for agricultural purposes. Areas where agriculture could be practiced reliably were scattered and highly localized; but these settings also remained suitable for long periods of time. Most such niches were occupied early in the prehistoric sequence, some as early as the Late Archaic period when the shift to an intensive reliance on agriculture had only just begun. Even the irrigation systems on the Salt and Gila Rivers had been built to nearly their full extent by about 600 or 700 (Gregory 1991; Howard 1993:297). Settlements were thus committed to specific localities for centuries, and opportunities for establishing settlements in new locations were extremely limited. The mode of production created a situation in which each settlement was committed to a specific segment of space, without which the settlement would cease to exist. Settlements thus functioned as corporate entities with control of specific, though small, territories.

Commitment to Neighbors

The use of irrigation also helped generate conditions necessary for the complementary opposition of segments. The Hohokam practice of several settlements sharing a canal and a common interest in controlling the headgate location created a structured set of priorities for dealing with one's neighbors. The need for cooperation was strongest with one's immediate neighbors on the canal and declined progressively with increasingly distant settlements, a situation that Sahlins (1961:331) terms "segmental sociability." The sharing of a canal created differing levels of priorities; a settlement dealt most often with its immediate neighbors on the canal, with whom it coordinated the use of field systems and feeder canals. It also dealt with more distant settlements on the same canal, settlements that it depended on for the maintenance of the canals, distribution of water, and defense of the headgate. A third level of relationship was to the settlements on other canal systems or beyond the canal system. Relationships with such settlements would be structured by the potential threat such populations might present for control of the headgate.

Although having a close relationship with one's neighbors may appear to be a desirable condition, what makes for good civics and what actually happens in ecological terms scarcely need be the same. In the absence of an overarching, state level organization, a territorial pattern such as that characterized by segmental sociability is actually quite rare. In many environmental settings, the relationship between neighboring groups can be expected to be highly competitive, and the degree of cooperation between settlements might actually improve rather than decline with distance. This was the case in situations where resources had a rather homogeneous but not particularly abundant distribution in the landscape, such that neighboring settlements would find themselves competing for the same resources. Under these more common circumstances, competition for resources was felt less strongly between more distant settlements, and alliances with distant settlements might even prove to be an effective means of handling competition with one's immediate neighbors. As demonstrated by White (1974), this second kind of ecology structured *amity-enmity* relationships among tribal groups across a broad portion of the American Southwest.

The ecology of the irrigation technology generated complementary opposition between segments occupying the same canal network. Abbott (1994) demonstrates that settlements sharing the same canal did in fact tend to cooperate and interact with each other to a greater degree than with other settlements. Those on the same canal system exchanged plain ware ceramic vessels much more regularly than they did with settlements on different canal systems, which, in some cases, were much closer. Economic and social interaction was greater within irrigation communities than between irrigation communities.

The Role of Central Places

One consequence of the definition of a segmentary organization is that we cannot look to economic interdependence as the force that draws segments into a single system or, more specifically, as the force binding secondary settlements and platform mounds into single settlement complexes. By definition, individual segments replicate the other segments and are economically self sufficient and redundant. There can be no structurally based economic specialization or differentiation on which mutual dependence could develop. Having eliminated the possibility that economy or subsistence plays a role in binding segments together, the remaining option is that the cohesion of segments is based on ideational principles. Although this implication is a direct consequence of the definition of segmentary organizations, rather than a generalization of the data, descriptions of extant societies based on segmentary principles comment extensively on the heavy focus on ideology and ritual.

Leadership of extant segmentary societies appears weak and muted, particularly from the perspective of observers who have themselves been members of bureaucratic and/or industrial states (Cunningham 1965; Evans-Pritchard 1940; Sahlins 1961). In tribal societies, the complementary organizing principle is frequently so thoroughly ingrained that the population can mass into large groups for a specific purpose, such as fighting a common enemy, with little or no overt manifestation of leadership positions (Evans-Pritchard 1940). Positions of leadership based on ascription do occur in segmentary states and are often highly revered, but such roles remain firmly embedded in a system of complementary dualism or pluralism. Leaders are always leaders of particular segments, never of the whole, which is one of the essential properties of a segmental organization. Even in cases where the segments are ranked, and the leader of the highest ranked segment is given a title that translates as king, monarch, or emperor, that position remains circumscribed and held in check by the leaders of the complementary segments. Most importantly, the leaders draw only on the economic resources available within their own segments, and even that ability may be circumscribed by lesser leaders (Cunningham 1965; Fox 1977:39–57; Sanders 1989). Regardless of rank, no leader provides overall management of production, exchange, communication, or infrastructural support; such a function would alter the nature of the system to where it would no longer be segmental. As a consequence the authority underlying leadership positions is based primarily on ideology, in the belief in an inherent ranking based on the seniority of segments, access to esoteric knowledge, ordering of the cardinal directions, and so forth (Coe 1965:109–12; Fox 1977:54–57).

These properties of leadership influence the nature and function of central places in segmentary organizations. Central places, when they exist, do not manage long distance trade, redistribution, economic production, or even the allocation of water in irrigation systems. Their role is founded principally, and even wholly, on ideology, and is expressed through the control of ritual and display of prestige items (Fox 1977:56). To this end, a central place has multiple sets of ritual facilities for the independent use of the segments or multiple sets of elite residences for the leaders of the various segments (Fox 1987:25–28; Sanders 1989). The central places also have the artifacts essential to the conduct of ritual and may also be marked by accumulations of prestige items and rare materials as a reflection of status and not for redistribution, control of production, or management of exchange.

If we posit that Classic period platform mounds operated as central places in dispersed settlement systems associated with a segmentary organization, the measurable differences between the platform mounds and other settlements should be found in facilities and materials that are economically unessential. Furthermore, the accumulation of such items at the mound should be sufficient for consumption at the mound settlement itself; unusually large quantities of material would suggest the accumulations of economic capital expected as part of a centrally managed system of production and exchange.

Data from the Cline Terrace Complex are used to test this implication. In the discussion of the managerial model, the platform mound was shown to have somewhat more shell and obsidian, but not quantities that would have required the coordination of large numbers of people to acquire or transform the raw materials into craft items. Nor was there any indication that the platform mound monopolized the production of ceramic vessels, projectile points, or other implements. Rooms at the mound had greater quantities of *Olivella* shells, *Conus* shells, blue and red pigments, and manuports (crystals, fossils, eccentric stones, stone balls, and rubbing stones). Many of these items are used in native Southwestern traditional ceremonies (Rice 1995), but none of them have essential economic or subsistence related functions.

Agave knives occurred in higher densities at the Cline Terrace platform mound, but as previously discussed, this had to do with feeding large groups of people. At the Escalante platform mound, two long rows of hearths on the platform mound also suggest food preparation and consumption in great quantities. Doyel (1981) suggests that the rows of hearths may have been used for preparing saguaro fruit wine, which is consumed among native Southwestern groups in the context of traditional ceremonies.

Platform mounds differed from the surrounding settlements in having more nonessential items and features, consistent with the expectations for a central place in a segmentary organization. Shell tinklers, crystals, eccentric stones, agave knives, and pigments were also used by people living in the neighboring settlements; individuals with key responsibilities for ceremonies at the mound could well have lived in neighboring settlements. Moreover, because of segmental independence, some ceremonies pertaining to individuals or to members of a subsegment could be held at the secondary settlements rather than at the platform mound centers. The nesting of segments within more inclusive segments leads to a repetition of functions at multiple levels of the settlement organization.

Platform Mounds as Clusters of Central Places

Not all segmentary organizations have central places for a network of surrounding settlements (Evans-Pritchard 1940). However, for those segmentary systems that make use of central places, the definition of a segmentary organization leads to specific expectations about the numbers of central places. If one segment in a segmentary settlement complex has a central place, all other segments at a comparable level of inclusiveness in that complex will also have central places. This is a consequence of the definition, which stipulates that a segmentary organization is composed of multiple segments, each of which is comparable in organization to the others.

This expectation can be expressed spatially in one of two forms. The central places for the segments can either be grouped at one location with satellite settlements dispersed in the surrounding territory, or each segment can have a center located in a different place, so that the territorial unit contains multiple central places. The eighth century Mayan center of Copan (Hendon 1991; Sanders 1989) is an example of the former. The core area of Copan includes not one, but several enclaves of elite residences and ceremonial facilities, and additional enclaves are located within an eight km radius of Copan. The largest enclave housed what is called the royal family, and the other enclaves housed the head families of important "lineages." Each enclave was supported by its own following dispersed in small rural settlements scattered throughout the rest of the Copan Basin.

The Antoni princedoms of Timor (Cunningham 1965) in Southeast Asia were segmentary systems with dispersed centers; each of the 17 Antoni princedoms was composed of four to five segments, and each segment had its own central place (a settlement with a sacred rock at which rituals were held) housing the segment leader. The segments were bound together into a single princedom through an elaborate ritual cycle and a commitment, based in ideology, of the four lower ranking segments to defend the highest ranked segment (headed by the "prince") from external enemies.

From an archaeological perspective, it is much easier to identify the first kind of pattern than the second. If the centers for each segment are clustered at a single settlement, that settlement will incorporate multiple, comparable sets of facilities that demarcate central places in that particular system. The association of several such sets of facilities in a single settlement addresses two issues at once: it establishes that the elements are part of a single settlement system and that the settlement system is composed of multiple, complementary parts. When the center for each segment of a single system is located in a spatially distinct settlement, archaeologists must provide an additional argument establishing that the spatially distinct centers operated as part of a single system. Without such an argument, it is not possible to differentiate between a single segmentary system with multiple central places and simply a set of independent systems each with a single center. Fortunately, this is not an issue with platform mound complexes.

In Classic period settlement systems, the platform mounds sites were clusters of central places for two or more segments at a comparable level of inclusiveness. The evidence for this is found in the relationship of *big rooms* to platform mounds; generally there are two or more big rooms at each platform mound. Big rooms are nonresidential structures with floor areas ranging from about 30 to 60 m², providing sufficient space to seat 25 to perhaps 80 people. Many big rooms have assemblages of unusual artifacts generally attributed to ceremonial uses. These kinds of structures also occur in sets of two or more in Preclassic settlements with ball courts (Haury 1976a) and in early Classic settlements prior to the appearance of platform mounds (Craig and Clark 1994; Jacobs 1994a). Generally, they are considered to represent some kind of meeting or council chamber (Haury 1976a: 62). What is of interest to us is that when they occur at a platform mound, it is invariably in multiples. Some platform mounds have as many as six to eight big rooms (Fewkes 1912; Gregory 1988) arranged in groups of two.

Some settlements contained two or more platform mounds, each in turn associated with two or more big rooms. This suggests situations in which two settlement complexes, each with its own mound center, had amalgamated into a more inclusive unit. If the units associated with each big room are arbitrarily referred to as "*minor*" segments, a settlement system with a single platform mound can be thought of as a *segment* (composed of two or more minor segments), and a system with multiple platform mounds as a *major segment* (composed of two or more segments, each composed in turn of several minor segments). Some of the irrigation districts in the Phoenix Basin incorporated several distinct settlement complexes that had amalgamated to the level of a major segment (that is, they contained multiple platform mounds). The settlements of an irrigation district can, in these terms, be thought of as constituting an association of major segments in a *maximal segment.* When operating in concert at this highest level, the settlements of an irrigation district constituted a remarkably large massing of territorial units within the region.

The site plans for several well sampled or completely excavated platform mounds are used to test this implication of a segmentary organization. The Bass Point Mound (Lindauer 1995a) provides a particularly good example of the functional distinctions between the big rooms and the residential rooms at platform mounds (Figure 6.6). This early Classic period platform mound was built shortly after 1280 and abandoned when the rooms were burned prior to 1320. The big rooms (Features 6 and 7) had floor areas of 26 and 35 m² and were situated on top of the platform. These rooms, each large enough to accommodate 25 to 35 adults, are clearly distinguished from the residential rooms by the lack of hearths and by nonutilitarian artifact assemblages (Rice 1995). A small, oval jacal structure (Feature 21) also lacked a hearth and contained an assemblage of items probably used for ritual purposes. Such ancillary structures accompanying clusters of big rooms are known elsewhere as well (Gregory 1988) and may have been used for the preparation of ceremonial items or for retreats.

Three other rooms (Features 2, 3, and 43) on the platform mound were used as residences. Because the rooms at the site had burned, they contained *in situ* assemblages of artifacts associated with their final use. Metates, manos, agave knives, axes, and other utilitarian implements were well represented in the residential rooms on the mound, but were rare or absent in the nonresidential rooms (Figure 6.7). The artifacts in the two big rooms and the associated jacal structure included crystals, eccentrically shaped rocks, fossils, stone balls, elongated smooth stones (called rubbing stones), shell artifacts, and projectile points. Shell artifacts occurred in nearly the same density in both the big rooms and the residential rooms; but the assemblage from the big rooms was much more specialized, consisting of shell tinklers and the burned fragments of a shell trumpet and lacking the bracelets and personal jewelry found in the residential rooms (Rice 1995).

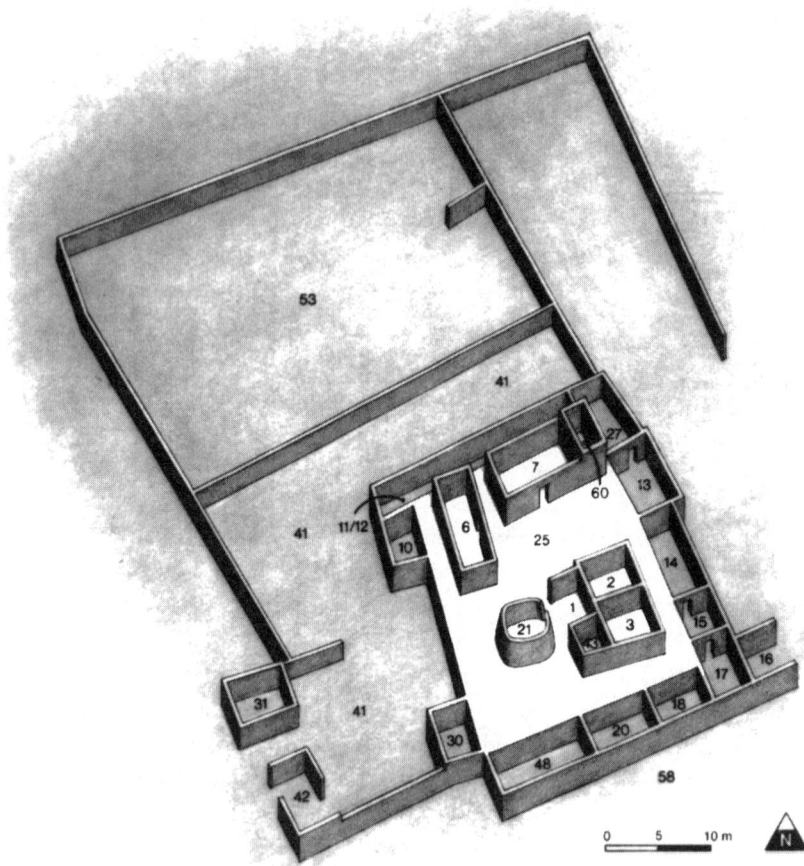

Figure 6.6.
The Bass Point Platform Mound, showing big rooms (Features 6 and 7), a ceremonial room (Feature 21), and alcove (Feature 1) (Rice 1995).

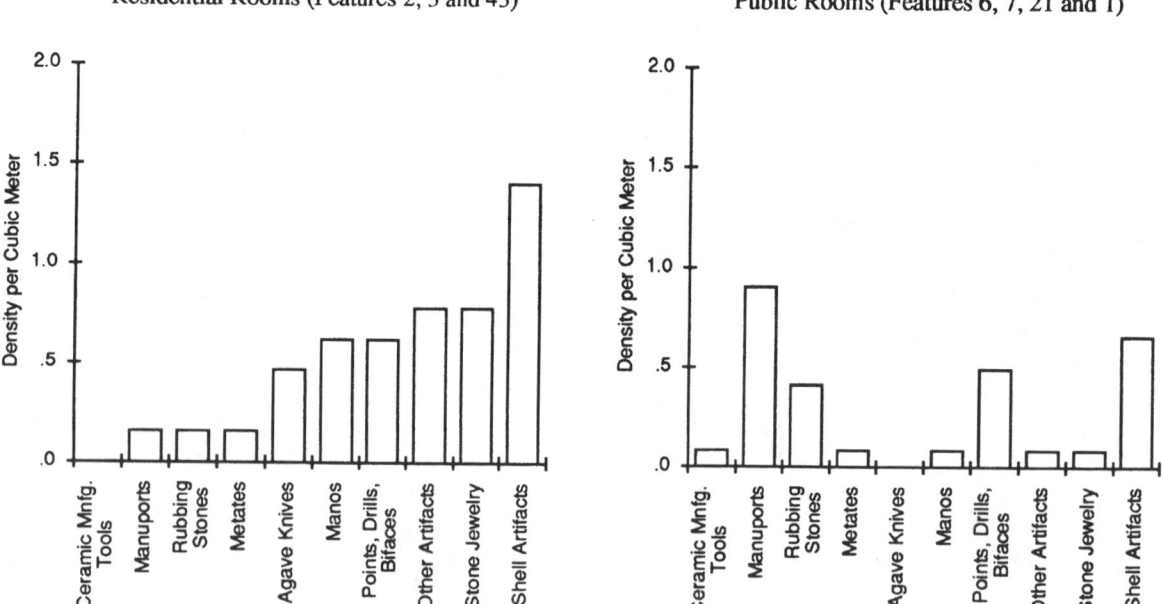

Figure 6.7.   Comparison of artifact assemblages in residential and ceremonial rooms on the Bass Point Mound (Rice 1995:336-337).

Bass Point Mound could not have been built by its inhabitants without serious disregard for subsistence activities. The population of nearby compounds that lacked platform mounds and elaborate architecture likely contributed to the construction of the platform mound and returned at intervals for gatherings in the big rooms on the mound.

In Tonto Basin, the rooms at the Cline Terrace platform mound (Figure 6.3) were configured somewhat differently, but with the same consequence (Jacobs 1997). The residential rooms were clustered into three groups; two in ground level plazas and the third occupied most of the top area of the mound. These room clusters include living quarters, store rooms, utility rooms containing large caches of grinding implements and agave knives, and store rooms that contain assemblages of ceremonial items (caches of pigment minerals, crystals, shell tinklers, eccentric stones). A series of rooms in the outer plazas of the site, including those built against the outer compound wall, may have been used as temporary residences by visitors to the settlement; they lacked prepared floors, storage vessels and food processing implements (Rice 1997).

The four big rooms at Cline Terrace (Figure 6.8, Features 58, 78, 93 and 137) were located around the central plaza of the site, but only the largest of the big rooms (Feature 137) was actually located on the platform. These rooms ranged in area from 35 to 54 m², providing sitting space for about 150 people. Three special store rooms with assemblages of unusual artifacts such as turquoise pendants, carved animal figurines, large knives, obsidian, and pigments were also located around the edges of the same plaza. Additional rooms, such as the one located on the northern extension of the platform (Feature 25) and the tower (Feature 37), were probably associated with the use of the big rooms. The rooms around this central plaza were demonstrably not used for residential purposes; they lacked the necessary food processing and storage facilities. The shell assemblages were also specialized, consisting primarily of tinklers and containers and lacking bracelets, armlets, and pendants (Rice 1997). The people living in the primary and secondary settlements of the Cline Terrace Complex represented an amalgamation of four minor segments, each having the use of a big room at the platform mound.

At the Escalante site (Doyel 1981), the area inside the compound was divided by additional walls into three smaller plaza units, each of which contained storage

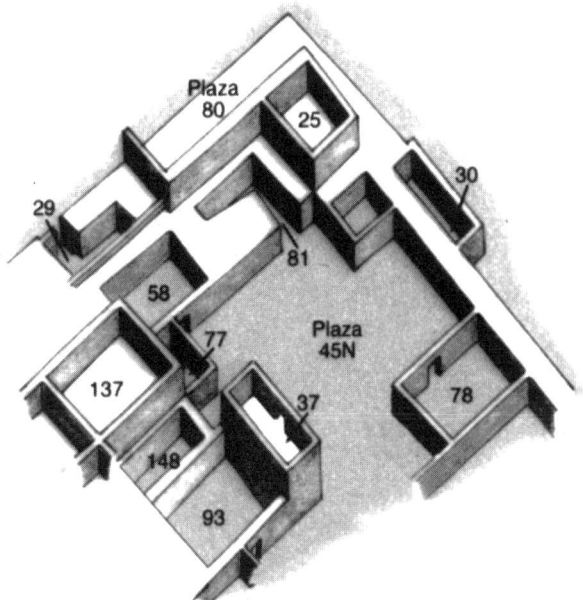

Figure 6.8.   The big rooms (Features 58, 78, 93, and 137), special store rooms and tower (Feature 37) in the central plaza of the Cline Terrace Platform Mound.

rooms, several habitation rooms, and a large ceremonial room. The cluster of rooms on the platform mound constituted a fourth such unit. Doyel (1981:65) comments that "each plaza-room unit, as well as the architecture on top of the platform mound, represents a mirror image of each other such unit."

Compound B at Casa Grande (Fewkes 1912) enclosed two discrete platform mounds of roughly comparable size, and is an example of an amalgamation of segments at two levels of inclusiveness. Two kinds of rooms were present, ones with post-reinforced adobe walls and others with much thicker, solid adobe walls. Fewkes identifies the rooms with solid adobe walls as ceremonial rooms and indicates that one contained a shrine (collections of eccentrically shaped rocks and crystals). Most of the post-reinforced rooms were smaller and used as residences. Using Fewkes' classification, the southern platform mound was associated with four big rooms grouped spatially into two pairs. The northern platform mound was associated with only two big rooms, one north and the other west of the mound. This pattern suggests a grouping of big rooms into two mound segments (four big rooms around the southern mound and two big rooms around the northern mound), and a further amalgamation of two mound segments into a single compound.

Platform mounds functioned as central places in a dispersed settlement system. The patterning in which sev-

eral big rooms were invariably associated with each platform mound, and cases in which multiple platform
mounds occurred in a single settlement, supports the
argument that the platform mounds were actually clusters of multiple centers. This is the pattern that would be
expected for a settlement system based on segmentary
principles of organization. Conversely, these site plans
are not consistent with the expectations of a unitary hierarchy, such as would be expected for a system of centralized administration overseen by a managerial elite.
The duplication of facilities, especially of several platform mounds within the same compound, is not foreseen by such models.

The Massing of Platform Mound Complexes

Having established the lack of centralized control in Classic period settlement organization, it becomes necessary to
demonstrate how segmentary organization could be responsible for the phenomena that have been cited as requiring some form of centralized control. Issues relating to the
internal organization of the settlement complexes have already been addressed. But it remains to be shown how a
segmentary organization could have constructed and operated the extensive Hohokam irrigation systems in the Phoenix and Gila Basins.

Hohokam ball court and platform mound settlements
tended to be spaced at roughly five km intervals along
the longer canals (Crown 1987; Gregory 1991). Settlements at the ends of the canals would seem to have been
at the mercy of those further up the canal, with the settlement at the headgate having the greatest control over the
distribution of water. This problem has led many researchers to conclude that some form of centralized control was
necessary for distributing water and maintaining canals in
an irrigation district (Howard 1993; Nicholas and Feinman
1989; Upham and Rice 1980; Wilcox 1979:105–109), although
others have argued that the canals could have been operated
on a cooperative basis (Bostwick and Downum 1994:379–
86; Haury 1976a; Woodbury 1961b).

A segmentary organization provides a third option,
that the potential use of force assured an equitable distribution of water to all points of the canal (Rice n.d. b).
Settlements at the end of the canal could obtain water if
they were willing to exert force against the settlements at
the head of the canal. For the threat to be effective, the
size of settlements would need to increase with distance
down the canal, such that the settlements at the end of

the canal could match the combined populations of the
settlements between them and the headgate. This potential for opposition within an irrigation district would be
countered by the need to cooperate as a single unit; for
instance, all the settlements of a single canal network
shared a common interest in defending their headgate
against threats from settlements beyond their local system. Furthermore, settlements at prime headgate locations
that allowed (or even recruited) additional settlements to
share their canals stood a better chance of retaining their
location over time than settlements who sought to go it
alone. For these reasons there very probably were cultural
prescriptions limiting the use of full force between settlements in an irrigation district. Less overt displays of power,
such as posting people at regular intervals along the banks
of the canals when water was being delivered, could nonetheless have been effective.

This kind of structural relativity (Sahlins 1961:333)
would characterize relationships at all levels of the settlement system. Although residential groups within a single
settlement might compete with each other over agricultural plots and the local distribution of irrigation water,
they would join forces as a settlement when arguing
against populations farther up the canal for their share
of water. But if some outside group threatened the integrity of the canal, all of the settlements along the same
canal would temporarily set aside their differences and
join forces as a single bloc against their common enemy.

If the platform mound complexes were associated
with a segmentary organization, and if relationships
between settlements on the same canal were structured
in some expression of complementary opposition, we
should expect settlements located at the ends of the canal systems to exhibit the greatest amalgamation of segments. We should also expect to find evidence that
segments were recruited from populations outside the
canal system. The size and number of platform mounds
per settlement, and of big rooms per platform mound,
should tend to be greater in the terminal settlements of
a canal system than in settlements at the headgates.

The settlement pattern on "Canal System Two" in the
Phoenix area exhibits this expected pattern (Figure 6.4).
System Two consisted of four canals with headgates located at a bedrock reef on the Salt River; from this common origin they gradually diverged from each other with
distance from the river. The Classic period population
lived in three *clusters of settlement complexes* distributed
at roughly five km intervals along the system. The settle-

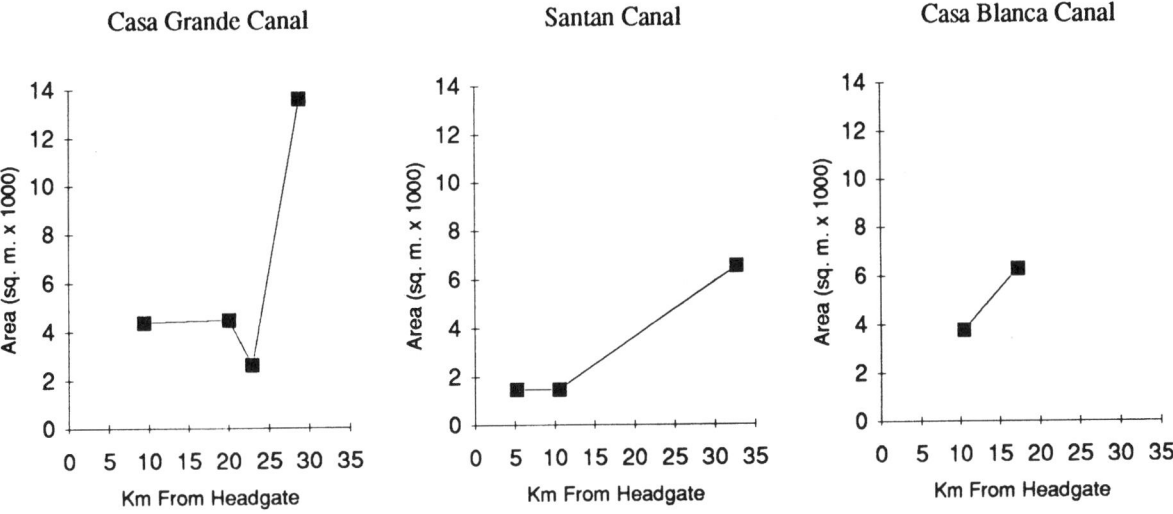

Figure 6.9.   Size of compounds with platform mounds compared to distance from canal headgate.

ment cluster included a number of walled compounds and room blocks, along with an occasional platform mound. The long axis of each cluster was oriented perpendicular to the canals and extended over a distance of several km (Gregory 1991).

The number of platform mounds per settlement cluster increased with distance from the headgates, as shown in Figure 6.4 (Rice n.d. b). Many of these mounds had been destroyed by the early twentieth century, and descriptions of some are vague and subject to multiple interpretations. They might have been large trash mounds, or the remains of room blocks within walled compounds. Counting only the features known to have been mounds, there were no more than two mounds at the headgate, at least three in the middle cluster of settlements, and at least five mounds at the end of the canal. In addition, one of the compounds at Los Colinas enclosed two platform mounds, similar to Compound B at Casa Grande, and was half again larger in area than the main compound at Pueblo Grande (Rice n.d. b).

There is also evidence that the settlement at Las Colinas recruited people from distant locales as one means of insuring that it had the largest concentration of population on Canal System Two. The ceramic assemblage at Las Colinas (Teague 1989:122–23) includes a high percentage of Lower Colorado Buff Ware made in regions that lay between 80

km (Gila Bend area) and 260 km (the lower Colorado River) to the west. One cluster of houses at Las Colinas contained a high concentration of these types, and might have represented people who were native to those more western areas (Teague 1989:122).

Evidence for the massing of large populations at the ends of canals is also found for three irrigation systems on the Gila River (Rice n.d. b). The mounds on these canals suffered less destruction or were documented more accurately by early researchers (e.g., Fewkes 1912) than those along the lower Salt River; as a result it is possible to graph the size of the compounds with platform mounds as a function of the distance from the canal headgates (Figure 6.9). In all three cases, the largest compounds with platform mounds occurred in the settlements at the ends of the canals, consistent with the implication that settlements at the ends of the canals would include more segments than settlements closer to the headgates. On the Casa Grande canal, the final settlement (the Casa Grande Ruin) included two compounds with architecture: Compound B with two platform mounds and Compound A with the multistoried big house also built on a platform (Fewkes 1912). The areas of the two compounds are combined in a single measure for the settlement. Other settlements on the canal lying closer to the headgate contained single platform mounds each; secondary settlements without mounds were also scattered along the course of the canal (Crown 1987). The two compounds with public architecture at Casa Grande had a combined area approximately equal to that of the total of all other platform mound compounds on the canal. On the Santan canal, the platform mound compound in the terminal settlement was greater by a factor of 2.2, and on the Santan canal by a factor of 1.7 (Rice n.d. b).

The massing of segments at the ends of irrigation canals was necessary for the operation of the irrigation system. However, the resulting growth in the size of settlements on the canal systems also had repercussions for populations in adjacent, nonirrigated areas. Platform mound complexes on bajadas or in secondary drainages would need to amalgamate into more inclusive units to match the size of settlements in the irrigated districts. If they remained small, they could be dislodged by forces from the irrigated areas, and because most suitable niches were filled by the Classic period, they could not easily relocate elsewhere. Faced with this prospect, complexes in locations bordering irrigated areas would recruit additional segments. Evidence for responsive massing is found in the desert south of Casa Grande, where the density of population in the McClellan Wash complex increased considerably from the early to the late Classic, apparently by drawing in the populations of the Los Robles and Marana settlement complexes farther south, which were thereafter abandoned (Fish and Fish 1992:103–105).

DISCUSSION

Segmentary Organizations and the Southwest

The ability to mass large groups through complementary opposition gives segmentary organizations considerable military advantage against populations in which effective political organization does not extend beyond the limits of the settlement. They are, for this reason, very effective at moving into and taking control of areas already occupied (Fox 1987; Sahlins 1961:323), leading to Sahlins' infamous characterization of them as "organizations of predatory expansion." Because segmentary organizations are held together largely through a shared ideology, that underpinning of their organization is carried with them as they move into new regions. As long as they are faced with opposition, they tend to remain amalgamated at a high level of segmentary inclusiveness (Fox 1987:23).

The potential for the use of force, with warfare the extreme form, was focal to the ecology of the Hohokam sys-

tem. A balance of power between the settlements on a canal was essential to the operation of the irrigation districts, while the need for all to join against external threats to the headgate held each canal district together. This continuing need to use force to maintain both the internal and external functioning of the irrigation districts contributed substantially to the growth of the platform mound systems; expansion of one irrigation district would lead to a complementary response in neighboring districts.

Such amalgamation also led to responses in neighboring regions where irrigation was not practiced. Platform mound complexes in the stretches of desert bordering the main river valleys (to the extent that they were founded on a similar ideology) would also amalgamate into more inclusive units but in opposition to the massing of segments in the irrigations districts rather than from any ecological requirement inherent in their own adaptation. It is also possible that platform mound-using populations migrated into new areas such as Tonto Basin, although no test has been conducted to determine if such was the case. The absence of ball courts in Tonto Basin indicates there had been no organization of settlements into multisite complexes during the Preclassic; multisite settlement complexes did not make their appearance in Tonto Basin until after 1200. Based on variations in ceramic and architectural styles, the mound complexes at the east end of Tonto Basin appear to be derived from similar traditions in the San Pedro Valley to the southeast, while those in the western Basin resemble mound settlements in the Phoenix Basin to the west.

Once platform mound complexes were established in Tonto Basin, people living in the surrounding mountains, who used neither platform mounds nor great kivas, apparently reacted in one of two different ways. Some populations joined the platform mound settlements in Tonto Basin, which led to the abandonment of areas around Payson and other upland valleys and meadows in the mountain ranges. Other mountain populations remained in their local area and aggregate into large settlements on high hilltops, as occurred in the vicinity of Globe.

The Mogollon populations living at Grasshopper and surrounding pueblos (Longacre et al. 1982), and who integrated their communities through the use of great kivas, formed large settlements, although there is no suggestion of sustained intersettlement organization. The development of the platform mound complexes in Tonto Basin was matched by the aggregation of the

Mogollon population into eleven large pueblos, suggesting that each 100 to 300 room pueblo may have been ready to individually face the forces that might be massed against them by the platform mound communities of the Basin. The response was effective, and the Mogollon populations may have competed with the platform mound complexes for the recruitment of people from the mountain groups (Longacre et al. 1982:112–16). Segmentary organizations did not expand into the Mogollon or other regions in the higher elevations of the Central Mountains because such areas lacked an important criteria for the development of such systems; highly localized resources in the form of canal headgates. The reliance on rainfall agriculture meant that water was equally distributed and difficult to predict. Rather than being committed to the defense of a particular locale, disgruntled members of a settlement could vote with their feet" and walk away to a new location (Jeffrey Dean, personal communication 1997).

Segmentary Organizations and States

Although the platform mound systems were neither urban nor complex, they exhibited two characteristics of early urban centers and states: the mounds functioned as cult centers and as mechanisms for controlling tracts of territory.

The platform mound centers differed from surrounding settlements only with respect to special ceremonial functions and status distinctions such as more elaborate architecture. Fox (1977) describes urban centers in segmentary states in terms applicable to platform mounds. Some urban centers in segmentary states differ from surrounding settlements only in their control of ideology and frequently exhibit none of the other traits traditionally attributed to cities, such as a large population or specialized economic and administrative functions. In an extensive review of the evidence from different parts of the world, Wheatley (1971) argues that the earliest urban centers in all pristine states began as cult centers. Platform mounds qualify as cult centers, and they are the functional equivalent of urban centers in some segmentary states, although on a smaller scale. If the initial distinction between urban and nonurban was based on ideology, rather than on specialized economic and managerial functions, the platform mounds are remarkably good candidates for the predecessors of urban centers.

Related to this is the finding that ascribed differences in ranking occurred in the absence of managerial control of surplus or production at the platform mound complexes. This calls into serious question one of the basic assumption of managerial models. Control of surplus need not drive or be associated with the development of elites. It is difficult to argue that the management of surplus or the redistribution of resources is a necessary condition for the emergence of ceremonial leaders occupying cult centers. The managerial models also equate the appearance of elites with centralization of control and decision making, a relationship not found in segmentary states, which remain decentralized and unspecialized even when elites are elevated to near-deity status (Cunningham 1965; Fox 1987; Fox 1977). Managerial models may account for the development of some instances of complex social organization and urban society, but they fail to cover the full diversity of extant states, a situation that likely holds for past conditions as well.

There are more productive ways of formulating the kind of questions we want to ask about ranking in prehistoric societies. Rather than trying to determine why and under what conditions status differences appeared, an alternate strategy is to take status differentiation (of various kinds) as the starting point, as a trait found in some human groups and not in others, and restate the question in terms of survival (Dunnell 1980); how do groups with ranking, operating within certain environmental and technological conditions, fare compared to populations organized in other ways? The problem inherent in the way the question is posed in managerial models is all the more apparent if early forms of ranking were based on ideology rather than economics. A search for the genesis of ranking necessitates an explanation for the origin of particular religious ideas. Perhaps this kind of question is knowable, but not with archaeological data. However, if ideas had an impact on the distribution of architecture, features and artifacts in the past, archaeologists are well equipped to track the persistence and replacement of those distributions over time.

The platform mound complexes also embody a second characteristic of states: control of territory. People's place of residence determined their membership in a territorial unit and required that they comply with certain basic needs of that unit. For the platform mound complexes, this was driven out of ecological and economic necessity, but the consequences were similar to those attained in state organizations through administrative fiat. Even in the irrigated areas of the Phoenix and Gila Basins, these territories remained remarkably small, often less than a

100 km², but their populations must have loomed large to contemporary populations in surrounding areas where effective political organization did not extend beyond the individual settlement.

The Hohokam use of irrigation did not lead to centralized control, but it created conditions that suppressed competition between neighbors and necessitated a high degree of cooperation, a situation inverting the ecologically more common relationships between competition and cooperation (Rice n.d. b). Although perhaps relatively rare, such conditions undoubtedly occurred in other parts of the world, likely involving different technologies and environments. The recognition of such ecological situations (rather than particular kinds of technology) may bear considerably on the study of early states. The platform mound complexes illustrate that the organization of people into effective political units on a territorial basis can occur in the absence of state organizations or centralized systems of authority. Just as cult centers were the basis for the first cities, commitment to territory may have been necessary for the emergence of states.

The differences between a segmentary organization at a tribal level and one at a state level are almost wholly a matter of scale (Dunnell 1978). Status differences and a basis for land tenure can already exist at the tribal level, as was the case for the platform mound complexes. Systemic growth, occurring in a relatively productive environment and involving perhaps a matter of several centuries, could lead eventually to conditions in which the high status groups in each segment were supported by the economic productivity of large estates; the populace in each segment would be drawn on for military personnel, specialized craftsmen, and agricultural labor. Although a segmentary state might have much more elaborate centers and cover much larger territories, structurally there is little difference between it and an organization like that of the platform mounds complexes.

Segmentary organizations can, under appropriate conditions, develop into segmentary states simply through the process of continuous growth (Chang 1989:160–61). There is, however, a major theoretical question about whether a segmentary state could ever make the transition to a unitary state, the kind of society within which most of us live (Sanders 1989:104; Southall 1956). Southall (1956:250–51) suggests that such a transition is highly improbable, because the similar powers exercised at different levels of inclusiveness in the segmentary system check the development of a centralized bureaucracy at the top. "The monopolization of power at the center and the definition of the territorial lim-

its within which it is exercised, which would transform the segmentary into the unitary state, cannot necessarily occur" (Southall 1956:251).

There is, nonetheless, one way in which such transitions have historically taken place, based again on the use of military power (Sanders 1989:104, Wheatley 1983:13). Occasionally segmentary states conquer a region considerably larger than their own. The control of this region could pass to the leader of a single segment (presumably the highest ranked), who would find it necessary to develop a bureaucracy of administrators to oversee the conquered territory. This would create a new, centralized institution and power base that would eventually overshadow and replace the power of the other segmentary units.

The segmentary state is often seen as a lesser form of the unitary state, but Chang (1989:161) suggests that historically it may have been the more common development. Moreover, rather than viewing one as an aberrant version of the other, it is possible that segmentary states, beginning from relatively simple organizations such as the platform mounds, were necessary for the development of unitary states. The use of force, including war, is a key factor in the operation of most segmentary organizations, and as the basis for massing under complementary opposition, is instrumental in driving the growth of segmentary organizations into larger entities. In a few instances, the continued exercise of warfare can pull a segmentary organization over the threshold to a new organizational form, that of the unitary state. It is likely that other paths led to the formation of early unitary states; but this may well have been the process in many parts of the world (Chang 1989; Fox 1977). The importance of warfare in this process is remarkable.

ACKNOWLEDGMENTS

My thanks to Jeffrey Dean for his valuable comments and suggestions for improving this paper; thanks also to my fellow researchers and colleagues on the Roosevelt Project for their contributions to the success of our research and publications. The drawings of platform mounds used in Figures 6.3, 6.6, and 6.8 are by Glena Cain and were provided by the author. The Roosevelt Platform Mound Study was conducted for the Bureau of Reclamation as a result of modifications to the Roosevelt Dam. Fieldwork for the Roosevelt Platform Mound Study was conducted under the terms of a permit from Tonto National Forest.

CHAPTER SEVEN

Tonto Basin Local Systems:
Implications for Cultural Affiliation and Migration

Mark D. Elson, Miriam T. Stark, and David A. Gregory

Tonto Basin is located in a transitional environmental and cultural zone, lying between the desert-oriented Hohokam to the south and puebloan groups of the plateau and mountain areas to the north and east (Figure 7.1). The archaeology of the Basin is characterized by highly variable architectural remains and ceramic assemblages that contain a multiplicity of wares and types. It is not surprising, then, that the prehistory of Tonto Basin has been interpreted in different ways by different researchers: to some, the Basin was an uninhabited (or empty) niche colonized by groups from the Hohokam or pueblos to the north and east of Tonto Basin (or both); to others, it was a cultural sponge that absorbed complete social systems and traditions from neighboring areas; to still others it was the heartland of the Salado, a migratory but distinctive cultural group who used Tonto Basin as a base from which to spread throughout much of the southern U.S. Southwest. Indeed, Tonto Basin has been included at one time or another as part of nearly every prehistoric culture area that surrounds it.

The variety of architectural forms and ceramic types found in Tonto Basin certainly indicates significant interaction and cultural mixing with neighboring areas. However, few researchers have systematically explored the possibility that an indigenous cultural system developed and persisted in the Basin itself. Our research suggests that prehistoric Tonto Basin populations were neither wholly subsumed by neighboring culture areas nor passive receptors on which cultural imprints of neighboring areas were planted. Instead, the data indicate the presence of an indigenous population that interacted and mixed with neighboring groups (at some times more intensively than others), but who maintained a distinct cultural identity throughout the developmental sequence. Understanding changes in sociocultural systems at local and areal scales, then, is critical to understanding the dynamics of Tonto Basin prehistory and the Salado concept.

The Study Area

Data presented in this paper were recovered primarily from research undertaken by Desert Archaeology, Inc., as part of the Roosevelt Community Development Study (RCD). This study involved the investigation of 27 prehistoric sites along a 6 km continuous stretch of the north bank of the Salt River in the Lower Tonto Basin (Figure 7.2). A variety of site types was investigated, including sites with pithouses, adobe/masonry compounds, masonry room blocks, and platform mounds (Elson, Stark, and Gregory, eds. 1995). The investigated sites ranged in time from the Early Ce-

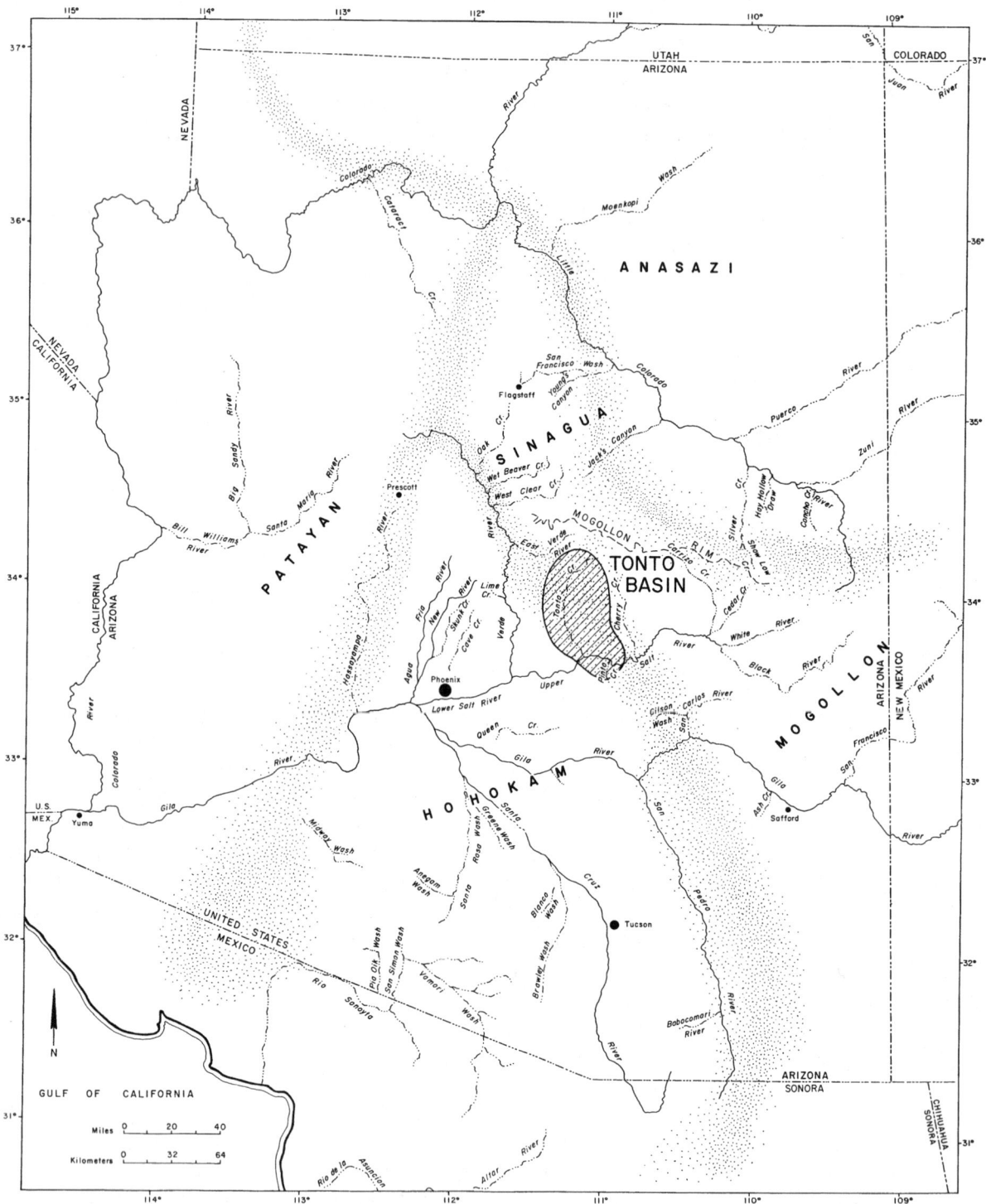

Figure 7.1.   The Tonto Basin and surrounding prehistoric culture areas (as traditionally defined) in Arizona (from Elson and Craig 1992:Figure 1.1).

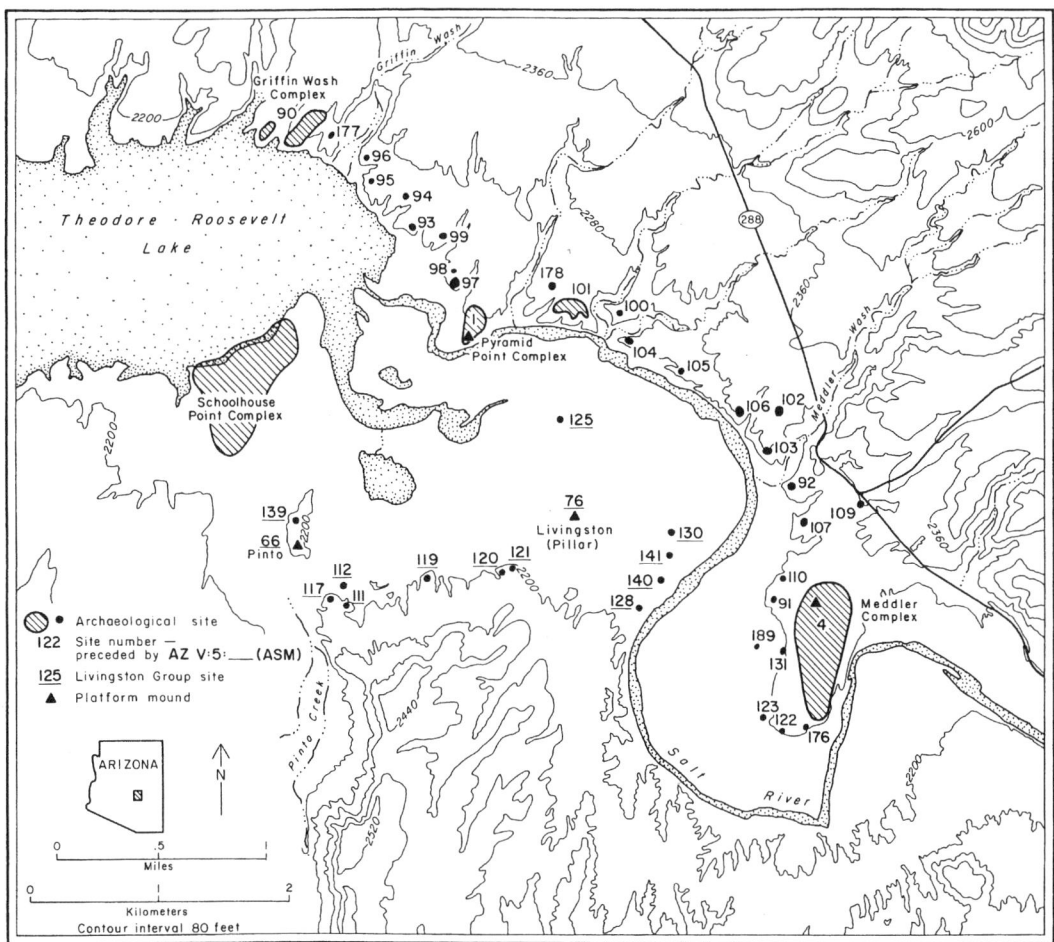

Figure 7.2.   Location of sites in the eastern Tonto Basin. Nonunderlined sites north of the Salt River were investigated by Desert Archaeology. Underlined sites south of the Salt River were investigated by Arizona State University (from Stark and Elson 1995:Figure 1.4).

ramic period (ca. 100–600) to the end of the early Classic period Roosevelt phase (ca. 1250–1350). With few exceptions, settlement in this portion of Tonto Basin ended by the Gila phase of the late Classic period (ca. 1350–1450).

Understanding Local Systems

We view the prehistoric Tonto Basin as a series of *local systems*. Local systems represent social units whose constituent settlements, subsistence regimes, and organizational forms were all closely integrated (Gregory 1995b). They may be seen as the archaeological manifestations of prehistoric communities, in that they are composed of spatially discrete social units that were in regular face-to-

face interaction with one another (Adler 1992; Arensberg and Kimball 1962; Fish and Fish 1991). Local systems contrast with regional and macroregional systems in both geographic scale and in the kinds, frequency, and regularity of social relationships and interactions that each contains. Local systems have an important historical dimension, and are shaped by internal as well as external dynamics. The scale and boundaries of the local system are affected by various environmental factors like topography, access to arable land, and access to water. Boundaries are also shaped by social factors, such as the presence of neighboring local systems. Analysis on the local and intraregional scale is essential to explaining developments in the prehistory of Tonto Basin and therefore for understanding the nature of Salado.

We take as our case study the Eastern Tonto Basin local system. The boundaries of the RCD Study area, and the Livingston (Jacobs 1994a) and Schoolhouse Point (Lindauer 1996a, 1997) study areas investigated by Arizona State University, encompass most sites within this system. This area includes settlements along both sides of the Salt River from the point at which the river enters Tonto Basin to the Griffin Wash/Schoolhouse Point area (Figure 7.2). Between the Gila Butte and Roosevelt phases (ca. 750–1350), the Eastern Tonto Basin local system developed from a single hamlet-level settlement at the Meddler Point site with a few associated farmsteads and other functionally specific loci, into a system containing four principal village and hamlet-level settlements (at Meddler Point, Pinto Point, Schoolhouse Point and Griffin Wash) and a variety of farmsteads and specialized loci (Elson 1996a; Elson, Gregory, and Stark 1995; Gregory 1995b).

The Eastern Tonto Basin local system occupied an approximately 6 km reach along the Salt River. While some nonriverine settlements almost certainly participated in the Meddler system, they were not intensively investigated because of the configurations of the Roosevelt projects areas. All available evidence, however, suggests that the system was primarily riverine in focus (Gregory 1995b). A roughly 3 km break in Roosevelt phase settlement separates the western end of the Meddler system from the large downstream settlement at Armer Ranch and from the larger local system that probably focused on that village.

CRITICAL PERIODS IN THE PREHISTORY OF THE EASTERN TONTO BASIN

RCD investigations identified five critical intervals in the prehistory of the Eastern Tonto Basin. Each marks a turning point in prehistoric settlement and use of this area, and processes involved are crucial for understanding general Tonto Basin prehistory. These include: 1) occupation of Tonto Basin sometime after the first century by an indigenous, pottery making population (Early Ceramic period); 2) migration into Tonto Basin of Hohokam populations from the Phoenix Basin area during the eighth and ninth centuries (Gila Butte phase); 3) the eleventh century reorganization of the Hohokam regional system and the impact of this reorganization on Tonto Basin populations (Sacaton/Ash Creek phase transition); 4) a mid-to-late thirteenth century migration of pueblo-related populations into Tonto Basin and

subsequent construction of platform mounds (Roosevelt phase); and 5) displacement of populations and resulting radical transformation of local settlement systems during the early to mid-fourteenth century (Gila phase).

Early Ceramic Period
Indigenous Populations

The earliest known occupation in the Eastern Tonto Basin occurred during the Early Ceramic period, dated between 100–600 on the basis of radiocarbon age determinations (Elson 1995:Table 2.4). The Early Ceramic occupation is currently known only from a single site, Locus B of the Eagle Ridge site (V:5:104), containing from 30 to 60 pithouses (Figure 7.3; Elson and Lindeman 1994). The unobtrusive nature of these remains strongly suggests that other occupations from this period are present but unrecognized in Tonto Basin. This occupation is highly significant because it represents the first evidence for an indigenous, ceramic-producing population in Tonto Basin prior to the appearance of Hohokam traits and influence in the eighth century.

RCD research indicates that Early Ceramic inhabitants were sophisticated in their subsistence practices and maintained wide-ranging interaction systems. Although gathered and hunted resources were important, and generally more important than in later periods, cultivation of agricultural crops (primarily corn, but also beans and cotton) provided much if not most of the subsistence base. Both local and extrabasin contacts are indicated by ceramic data (Stark 1995a); evidence for long distance interaction comes from a small marine shell assemblage (Vokes 1995).

Although relatively high levels of mobility or seasonal settlement have been suggested for Early Ceramic groups elsewhere (Whittlesey 1995; Whittlesey and Ciolek-Torrello 1994), this may not have been the case for all populations (Haury and Sayles 1947; Wheat 1955). Eagle Ridge inhabitants appear to have been sedentary, with deliberate selection of settlement location for its geomorphic stability and access to large areas of arable land and a reliable water supply (Gregory 1995b). Botanical data also suggest a year-round occupation (Fish 1995e; Miksicek 1995). The fact that most pottery may have been locally made provides additional support for inferring that the Early Ceramic population was largely sedentary (Stark 1995a). Given the number of documented pithouses, the site may have approached hamlet dimensions. This is supported by the presence of a large, circular structure in the approximate center of the settlement that probably functioned in an integrative manner (Figure 7.3).

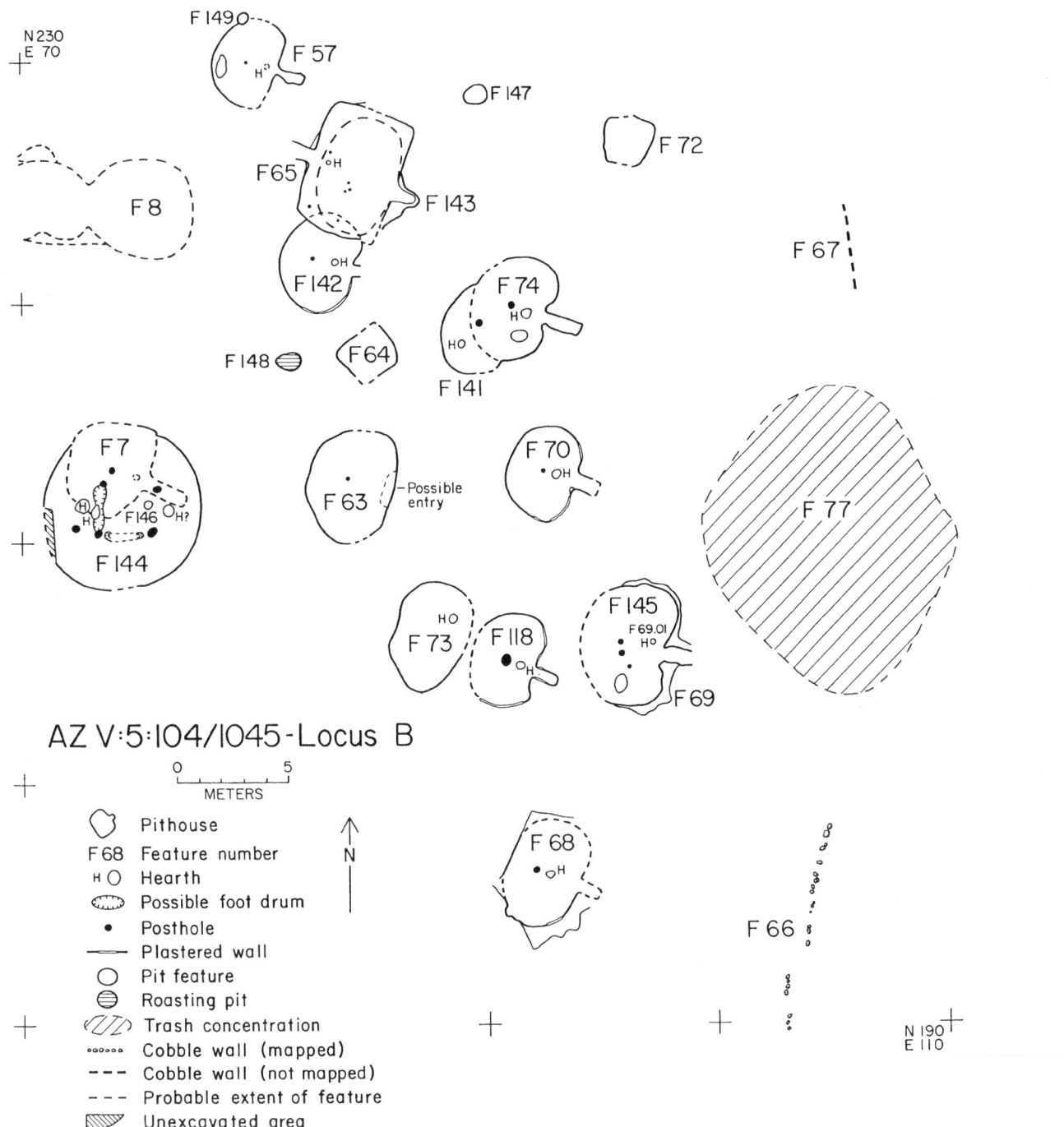

Figure 7.3. The excavated portion of the Early Ceramic period occupation at Locus B of the Eagle Ridge site (AZ V:5:104/1045) (from Elson and Lindeman 1994:Figure 3.25).

The origin of Early Ceramic populations is unknown, but it can be reasonably inferred on the basis of similarities in the ground stone (basin metates) and chipped stone (Cienega and San Pedro style projectile points) assemblages that they developed out of Late Archaic groups known to be present elsewhere in Tonto Basin (Huckell and Vint 1994). Thus, the basin may have been occupied by indigenous groups from the Archaic period onward.

Colonial Period
Hohokam Migration

The RCD data suggest that Hohokam groups first entered the Lower Tonto Basin during the late Snaketown or early Gila Butte phase, sometime between 700 and 800. This supports data gathered by Haury (1932) from the site of Roosevelt 9:6, also in the Lower Tonto Basin. Evidence for migration is based on settlement layout, architectural traits, and artifact assemblages, all of which closely resemble contemporaneous sites in the Phoenix Basin and related areas. The earliest documentation of Hohokam populations comes from the Hedge Apple site (V:5:189), occupied primarily during the first half of the Gila Butte phase. The Meddler Point site (V:5:4) was also initially occupied during this same time or shortly thereafter. A variety of evidence suggests that Hedge Apple was a seasonal settlement that witnessed repeated reoccupation, whereas Meddler Point was probably permanently occupied from the time of its founding (Craig and Clark 1994; Swartz and Randolph 1994a).

Colonial period domestic structures consist predominantly of large, Hohokam-style "houses-in-pits" in contrast to the small ("true") pithouses of the Early Ceramic period. Meddler Point has a Hohokam-like site structure with a central plaza that contained a cremation cemetery and was surrounded by trash mounds and pithouse courtyard groups (Craig and Clark 1994). This layout, which was maintained throughout the nearly 600 year occupation, suggests an intimate knowledge of Hohokam site structure and the proper arrangement of domestic and ritual space (Gregory 1995b:156; Wilcox 1991a:259–62).

The decorated ceramic assemblage also suggests population movement into Tonto Basin. Hohokam Buff Ware ceramics comprise over 20 percent of the total ceramic assemblage and almost 95 percent of the decorated assemblage (Heidke 1995; Wallace 1995a). The high frequency of buff wares is significant when compared to the site of Snaketown where buff wares comprise around 30 percent of the Gila Butte phase ceramic assemblage (Haury 1937).

Given the large size of Snaketown, and the likely presence of ceramic manufacturing activities, the 20 percent buff ware frequency at Hedge Apple is suggestive of population movement rather than long-distance exchange.

Perhaps the strongest evidence for Colonial period population movement comes from the utilitarian plain ware assemblage (Stark, Vint, and Heidke 1995). At Hedge Apple, over 70 percent of the plain wares contain micaceous schist temper. Several factors suggest a nonlocal origin for these wares. First, no raw material sources found within a 30 km radius of the site match the temper composition of the Hedge Apple ceramics. Thirty km is an extremely conservative distance threshold that is ten times higher than previous estimates of distances that potters are willing to travel to procure temper (Arnold 1985; Miksa and Heidke 1995). Second, despite careful monitoring, no micaceous schist chunks (potential raw material for pottery-making) were recovered from the Hedge Apple site or any site in the RCD project area. Finally, a nonlocal origin of the micaceous-tempered ceramics is also supported by paste compositional analyses using inductively coupled plasma mass spectrometry (ICP), which differentiated sherds with micaceous schist temper from those made with locally available stream sands (Stark, Vint, and Heidke 1995).

Possible source zones for the micaceous schist temper lie along the Gila River in the Gila Butte and Santan Mountain areas. This is a known prehistoric temper source area, and sites along the Gila River have very high frequencies of micaceous schist-tempered plain wares (Gregory and Huckleberry 1994; Rafferty 1982). Temper composition in the Hedge Apple ceramics is similar to materials from these areas, which lie 2–3 days' travel from the Eastern Tonto Basin.

Both trade and migration were evaluated as mechanisms for transporting micaceous plain wares into Tonto Basin (Stark, Vint, and Heidke 1995). In traditional small-scale societies, plain ware ceramics circulate in utilitarian exchange spheres (Crown 1991; Doyel 1991a), as do foodstuffs, baskets, and other household goods. Ethnographic data suggest that travel time from point to point in such exchange networks rarely exceeds a day (Stark 1993). Estimates for sizes of prehistoric utilitarian exchange networks offered by Lightfoot (1979), Drennan (1984), and Wilcox (1994) range from approximately 25 to 45 km. Application of these distances to the Hedge Apple site suggests no areas in which micaceous-tempered plain wares might be manufactured for exchange.

Therefore, the Hedge Apple pots seem more likely to have been moved by migrants into the area than to have been traded into Tonto Basin.

Whatever integration of Phoenix Basin migrants and indigenous populations occurred, it was accomplished without obvious strife. Unlike the later Roosevelt phase, also suggested to be a time of population movement into Tonto Basin, little evidence exists for social stress during this period. Therefore, the data suggest that while the Eastern Tonto Basin may have had an indigenous population when Hohokam migrants entered the area, settlement densities were sufficiently low that migrants did not displace or conflict with indigenous groups. Nor did the indigenous groups have any noticeable effect on migrant populations: settlements at Hedge Apple and Meddler Point mirror contemporary settlements in the Phoenix Basin.

The most significant difference between Colonial period Hohokam settlements in the Eastern Tonto Basin and those in the Phoenix Basin is the apparent absence of Hohokam-style ball courts in Tonto Basin. Ball courts are believed to be integrative features, important in maintaining exchange networks and social and ritual interaction (Crown 1991; Wilcox and Sternberg 1983). Explanations for the lack of Tonto Basin courts have ranged from low population densities to the obscuring effect of Roosevelt Lake (Elson 1992a; Wood 1985). Meddler Point is the largest known Preclassic period village in Tonto Basin. If ball courts were part of this system, one should have been present at that site. The intensity of investigation at Meddler was sufficient to rule out the presence of a ball court (Craig and Clark 1994), and alternative explanations must be sought.

Two alternative explanations for the absence of ball courts can be suggested. One is that low population density in Tonto Basin during the Colonial period made local integrative features of this scale unnecessary. This is suggested by the small estimated size of the population at Meddler Point and the low density of Gila Butte phase populations in the Lower Tonto Basin in general (Craig and Clark 1994:176; Doelle 1995a; Gregory 1995b), coupled with a Gila Butte phase ball court at Ranch Creek approximately 50 km southeast of Meddler Point (Wilcox and Sternberg 1983). In this reconstruction, inhabitants of the Lower Basin could easily have made the one or two day trip to Ranch Creek (or to ball courts on the eastern edge of the Phoenix Basin) to participate in the ball court system.

A second scenario suggests that Lower Basin populations simply did not participate in the Hohokam re-

gional system during the Colonial period, since the presence of ball courts has often been used as a key indicator of participation (Crown 1991; Wilcox 1991a). We think this second scenario is unlikely for several reasons. Colonial period inhabitants of Tonto Basin maintained what were apparently strong contacts with the Hohokam core area through exchange of shell, ceramics, and probably perishable materials such as baskets and textiles. Mortuary practices and settlement layout also bear a strong Hohokam imprint (Craig and Clark 1994; Swartz et al. 1995). These markers suggest that the absence of ball courts does not imply a lack of participation in the Hohokam regional system. Given the evidence for migration, it is also likely that webs of social relations linked groups in Tonto Basin with groups in the Phoenix Basin. Periodic trips to those areas, at most a two to three day walk, might have been made for social, ritual, or economic purposes, or to find marriage partners.

Therefore, Colonial period populations in Tonto Basin were likely participants in the larger regional system. Low population density and the presence of nearby courts within a few days' travel appears at present to offer the best explanation for the lack of these features. Doelle's (1995a) regional demographic analysis further supports our stance: his data indicate that other areas in the Hohokam regional system that lacked ball courts, such as the Papaguería, had comparably low population densities.

In summary, the data suggest movement of Hohokam populations into the Eastern Tonto Basin beginning around 700 or 750. The source area of the migrants is unknown, although similarities in utilitarian ceramic temper materials suggest the Gila River portion of the Phoenix Basin as a likely place of origin. The timing of these movements corresponds with the infilling of available niches along the Gila River (Gregory and Huckleberry 1994), which may have been the impetus for small groups to seek irrigable land elsewhere. Given the small size of known Colonial period sites in the Lower Tonto Basin, the scale of movement was probably not large: these may have been extended families or related groups of a similar scale.

Connections between the Eastern Tonto Basin and the Hohokam core area persisted for at least 250 years; contacts weakened through time as the focus of Tonto Basin economic and interaction systems intensified at the local and intraregional level. Although migration from the Hohokam area most likely continued after the Gila Butte phase, it was probably not a frequent occurrence, and population density remained low throughout the 200 years of the Colonial period (Doelle 1995a). Through time, contacts with Cibola White Ware producing groups slowly grew in importance, and by the early Sacaton phase (ca. 950), white ware ceramic types, although still fewer in number than buff wares, made up a substantial proportion of the decorated ceramic assemblage. At some point during the eleventh century, Tonto Basin connections with Hohokam groups were significantly curtailed and interaction shifted toward groups producing white ware ceramics.

The Sacaton/
Ash Creek Phase Transition

The transition between the Sacaton and Ash Creek phases is marked by a shift from a ceramic assemblage dominated by Hohokam Buff Ware to one dominated by Cibola White Ware (Elson 1996b; Elson and Gregory 1995). This involved a significant change in the direction of external interaction, from the southwest to the north and east. In the RCD Study area, this shift is dated at approximately 1025–1050.

The change in interaction networks was related in part to processes in the Phoenix Basin that were associated with the reorganization and geographic retraction of the Hohokam regional system (Crown 1991; Wilcox 1991a). A decrease in Phoenix Basin influence at this time has also been noted in other areas once part of the Hohokam regional system, such as the Tucson Basin (Doelle and Wallace 1991) and the New River area (Doyel and Elson 1985). The realignment of Tonto Basin interaction systems also may be related to the spread of the Chaco system, which reached its greatest extent (extending down to the Mogollon Rim) during the 1000s and early 1100s (Lekson 1991). Therefore, changes in Tonto Basin decorated ceramic assemblages were at least partially the result of external rather than internal factors. However, internal processes, such as increasing population and consequent growth and development of local systems, were also undoubtedly important.

Despite shifts in interaction networks, site structure and architectural construction techniques in Eastern Basin Sedentary period settlements remained unchanged (Elson, Gregory, and Stark 1995). Mortuary practices also did not change: secondary cremation continued, but remains were now interred in white ware rather than buff ware vessels (Swartz et al. 1995). The Sedentary period was thus a time when settlements in the Eastern Tonto Basin became in-

creasingly focused on other Tonto Basin local systems. Not only did the frequency of Phoenix Basin ceramics significantly drop, but the scale of local ceramic manufacture in the RCD Study area increased; for the first time, interaction within Tonto Basin itself became an important factor in the local economy (Stark 1995b). At the same time, interaction also significantly increased between Tonto Basin populations and groups producing Cibola White Ware ceramics.

It is probably no coincidence that the change in ceramic interaction systems corresponds with a change in cotton ubiquity in RCD flotation samples. Cotton ubiquity (i.e., the number of flotation samples with cotton remains) increased from under ten percent during the Colonial period to over 20 percent during the Sedentary period. These figures are sufficiently high to suggest that cotton production expanded significantly at this time (Miksicek 1995:71). Conceivably, Cibola White Ware vessels might have been exchanged for either raw cotton or cotton products, and part of the attraction of Tonto Basin to groups who made white ware ceramics was the availability of this resource (see Adams, Chapter 11). This connection would be particularly important if the Phoenix Basin was no longer a reliable source of cotton.

Little evidence exists for population movement during this time, and both the Ash Creek and following Miami phases appear to be periods of relative stability. Interaction with Hohokam-related populations, while curtailed, still occurred. This is most apparent in the Miami phase, with the introduction of masonry and adobe compound architecture. The Miami phase is difficult to characterize with RCD data because of temporal mixing and the paucity of diagnostic ceramics (Elson 1996b; Rice and Lindauer 1994). However, it may have been the time in which many of the settlements occupied in the succeeding Roosevelt phase were established (Gregory 1995b). RCD data also suggest that little change occurred between the Ash Creek and Miami phases, even though the Miami phase is the traditional start of the Classic period in Tonto Basin (Doyel 1976a). For example, the adoption of masonry compound architecture during the Miami phase involved a continuation of previous architectural traditions (with upright cobbles being added to post-reinforced adobe walls) and spatial organization (pithouse courtyard groups were transposed into courtyard groups within compounds) (Clark 1995a; Gregory 1995b; Sires 1984). Similar architectural changes are evident throughout southern Arizona during this time as part of a larger regional trend. Patterns of stability and local growth were significantly altered during the following Roosevelt phase, when the Eastern Tonto Basin experienced its most intensive occupation.

Roosevelt Phase Transformations

The Roosevelt phase, beginning at approximately 1250, was a time of great change in the Eastern Tonto Basin. Prior to this time, the Eastern Basin contained a relatively stable local system that had evolved gradually from settlements established during the Colonial period. Settlement, subsistence, and economic systems had changed little over five centuries. Principal shifts prior to the Roosevelt phase were in the source area for nonlocal decorated ceramics and the adoption of masonry compound architecture. As argued previously, these transitions did not involve major changes in the structure of the local social or settlement systems. The introduction of very different architectural forms, artifact assemblages, and subsistence practices mark some of the important changes that signal the beginning of the Roosevelt phase.

Changes observed during the Roosevelt phase in the Eastern Tonto Basin may be related to macroregional processes that appear to have acted as catalysts at the local system level. The late thirteenth century has long been recognized as a time of population and settlement displacement in the northern portions of the Southwest (Dean et al. 1985, 1994; Lekson and Cameron 1995; Lindsay 1987). Large areas that had previously witnessed substantial occupation were abandoned, while new settlements were founded in other areas. The effects of increased environmental variability have been suggested as significant factors in these demographic shifts (Dean 1996b:46).

As documented primarily in the northern Southwest, intergroup conflict may also have been widespread between 1250 and 1300 (Wilcox and Haas 1994), possibly in response to deteriorating environmental conditions and subsequent competition for resources. Although conflict was probably low level, newly compiled data suggest that it may have been sufficiently disruptive to provoke a variety of responses by local populations. Movement of populations into defensive locations or construction of fortifications is one response to perceived threat. Another is migration into new areas (Anthony 1990; Cameron, ed. 1995; Clark 1995b). Residential relocations, especially those covering long distances that are not part of a scheduled seasonal round, involve considerable risk. The motives for resettling must outweigh the risk factors before groups decide to move. Motives are based on "pushes" from current settlements and "pulls" into

target destinations (Anthony 1990:899). These must have been particularly strong in long-distance moves (Clark 1995b:371–72).

Therefore, during the mid-to-late thirteenth century, two factors—environmental stress and intergroup conflict—probably played a major role (as "push" factors) in relatively large-scale demographic shifts. Favorable locations ("pull" factors) for migratory groups during this time would include areas with low population densities, dependable water supplies, and ample arable land that were reasonably strife free. Tonto Basin would have been an excellent destination. The Basin is situated immediately below the Mogollon Rim and the Colorado Plateau and close to many pueblo areas known to have experienced shifts in settlement or been depopulated at this time (Dean et al. 1985, 1994). Even during the worst periods of drought, the Salt River and Tonto Creek probably always contained enough water for limited irrigation agriculture (Waters 1994b). Dependable sources of water and available arable land were probably the primary factors in the selection of Tonto Basin by migrant groups. Because immigration generally takes place in areas where migrants have previous contacts (Anthony 1990; Cameron, ed. 1995), established connections between Cibola White Ware producers and Tonto Basin populations may have provided additional incentives for groups to move into Tonto Basin.

Migration of Puebloan Groups into the Tonto Basin

We suggest that environmental and social stress encouraged small numbers of northern pueblo groups to migrate into the Eastern Tonto Basin during the early Roosevelt phase. The idea of migration as a factor in Classic period Tonto Basin prehistory is not new. It was introduced by Gladwin and Gladwin (1935) and has been championed by others (Ciolek-Torrello and Whittlesey 1994; Germick and Crary 1992; Haury 1945; Reid 1989; Whittlesey and Ciolek-Torrello 1992; Whittlesey and Reid 1982), but it has always been an unsubstantiated and somewhat controversial hypothesis. The RCD research has produced the first large body of archaeological data that lends substantive support for this interpretation. This is also the first time that the effects of migrant groups on a local Tonto Basin system can be examined in detail.

Migration can be defined as a residential relocation of more than a day's journey that is not part of a scheduled round or cycle of movement (Clark 1995b:370). This excludes relocations within most local settlement systems or cyclical movements of groups that bring them in close contact with other nonlocal groups on a regular basis. Migration was undoubtedly a common occurrence in prehistory, but migration events are difficult to detect archaeologically; the problem is particularly acute when single households or small groups move over relatively short distances in culturally homogenous areas. Rapid acculturation processes also mask the remains of migratory groups in the archaeological record. However, in regions already populated, like the Classic period prehistoric Southwest, migratory groups must have crossed boundaries that are potentially detectable in the material record. Such boundaries can be defined by subsistence strategy, artifact technology, architecture, and/or larger ideological and exchange systems (Clark 1995a, 1995b; Stark, Clark, and Elson 1995a).

In areas occupied by local groups, the nature of social interactions (i.e., whether cooperative or hostile) between locals and newcomers must be considered. If local populations are displaced by migrant groups, chain reactions of movements could result that would affect settlement patterns at a macroregional scale. However, if population influxes do not displace local inhabitants, "islands" of migrants may be visible in a "sea" of local tradition, and a much higher degree of variability would be expected in the overall settlement pattern, site structure, and material culture assemblage (Clark 1995b:370–73). This last scenario is evident in Roosevelt phase settlement patterns.

Perhaps the most important evidence for migration is the relatively rapid introduction of a distinctive architectural tradition (room blocks constructed out of coursed cobble masonry) that involved an organization of domestic space not found in the indigenous tradition of masonry compound or pithouse architecture. Several sites (or site components) in the Eastern Tonto Basin probably represent intrusive pueblo populations: Loci A and C of the Griffin Wash site (V:5:90) in the RCD project area and Saguaro Muerto (V:5:128) in the Arizona State University Livingston project area (Figure 7.4; Lindauer 1994; Swartz and Randolph 1994b). Intrusive groups may also be present at Locus B of Meddler Point (Clark 1995a) and U:8:454 on Schoolhouse Mesa (Lindauer 1997). Movement of small numbers of people, probably representing extended families or similar-sized groups, fits both the archaeological evidence and the demographic data (Clark 1995a, 1995b; Doelle 1995a). The evidence does not support the movement of sub-

stantial numbers of people, as suggested by Whittlesey and Ciolek-Torrello (1992:320) and earlier researchers (Gladwin and Gladwin 1935; Haury 1945).

Loci A and C of Griffin Wash and Saguaro Muerto are situated on the peripheries of their respective settlements (Figure 7.4). One reason for their peripheral locations may be that intrusive groups did not have ready access to prime agricultural land. Land tenure was most likely held by members of an entrenched local population, and probably related to the location of agriculture fields and irrigation canals (see Adler 1996). Meddler Point, for example, is the first and longest occupied settlement in the Eastern Tonto Basin. It is also situated at the best location for canal irrigation in the local system (Gregory 1995b:158–61). The data suggest that immigrant groups were permitted to construct nearby settlements in areas of lower irrigation potential and participate in the local economy without resistance for several generations. We suspect that this coexistence reflects previous social ties between migrants and local inhabitants, established through the multigenerational Cibola White Ware exchange system. Migrants to Griffin Wash, for example, appear to have joined an extant local settlement that contained four or five dispersed masonry compounds (of which only locations and rough sketch maps are available because portions of the site have been submerged by Roosevelt Lake).

Locus A at the Griffin Wash site contrasts with the contemporaneous Locus A at the Meddler Point site in several respects, although both represent hamlets or small villages during the Roosevelt phase with roughly similar populations (Figures 7.5–7.9). Obvious architectural contrasts exist in the organization and use of physical space (Clark 1995a; Stark, Clark, and Elson 1995a). Differences are also present in the frequencies of *Conus* shell tinklers, corrugated ceramics, and White Mountain Red Ware, which are all substantially higher at Griffin Wash (Clark 1995b; Stark 1995b). These patterns may reflect different exchange networks and therefore that the Griffin Wash population is of a different cultural origin than local Tonto Basin groups (Bradley 1996; Stark and Heidke 1995; Vokes 1995). Griffin Wash is also the only site in the RCD project area with evidence for the manufacture of corrugated ceramics, possibly indicative of specialization in this ware. Locus A at Meddler Point, containing a central platform mound and seven dispersed masonry compounds, is more consistent with local traditions and

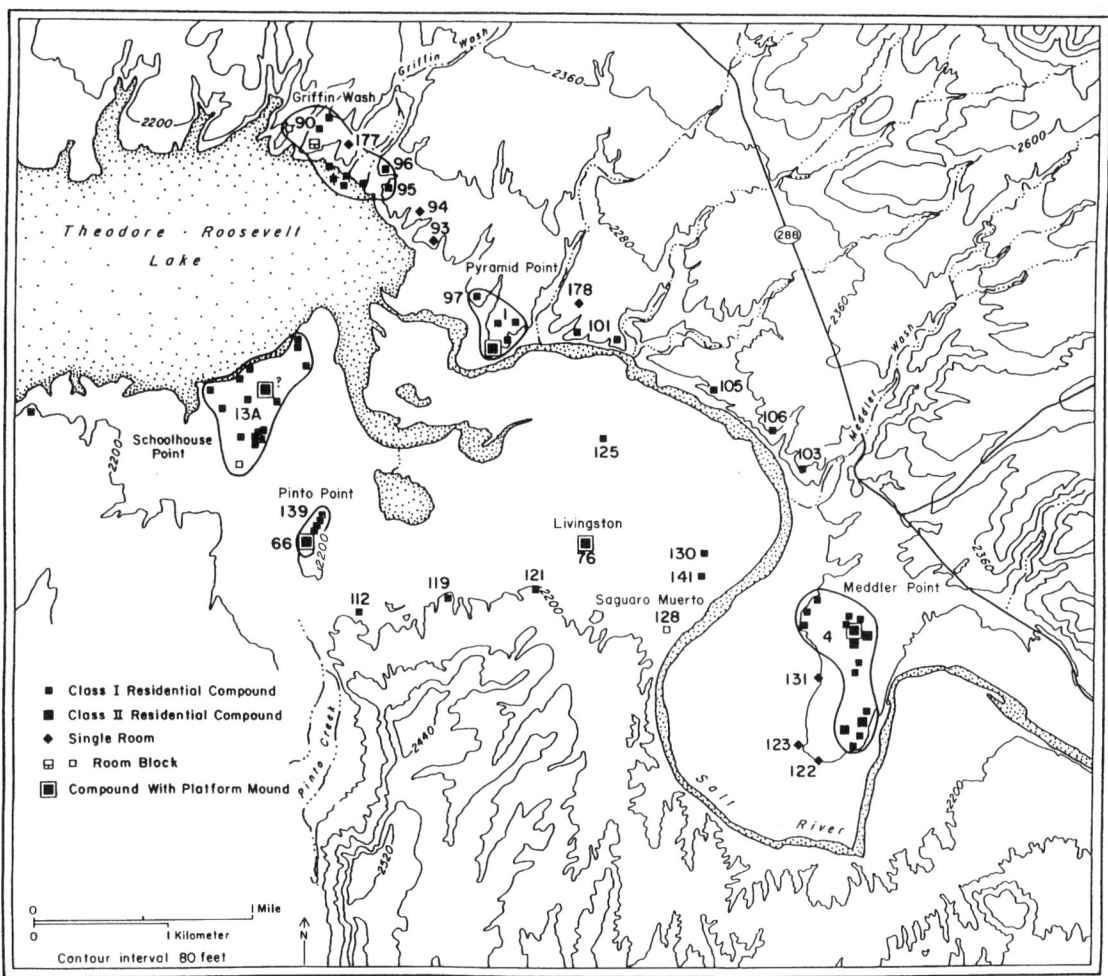

Figure 7.4.   Sites dating to the Roosevelt phase (1150-1350) in the Eastern Tonto Basin (from Clark 1995a:Figure 9.9).

closely resembles groups throughout southern Arizona at this time.

Subsistence remains from Griffin Wash also suggest a culturally distinct population. No mustard pollen was recovered from any analyzed context at the site, even though more samples were analyzed from Griffin Wash than any other RCD site. Mustard pollen was recovered in about 40 percent of the samples from all other Roosevelt phase habitations (Fish 1995e). Differential pollen preservation does not seem to explain these differences because Griffin Wash contained the same range of pollen types that were identified at other RCD sites. This suggests a cultural food preference or perhaps a species unfamiliar to the immigrant group (Gasser and Kwiatkowski 1991). Griffin Wash

also contained some of the highest values for corn pollen yet recovered from southern and central Arizona (Fish 1995e). Rooms believed to have been used primarily for storage had the highest pollen values, but counts were uniformly high across sampled contexts. One possible reason for such high pollen counts is that corn was stored on the cob and unhusked. This pattern differs from storage practices at Meddler Point (and earlier RCD sites) and throughout southern Arizona where available evidence suggests that corn was almost always stored as shelled kernels (Miksicek 1995). Alternatively, corn pollen may have played a greater role in ceremonial practices of the immigrant population, accounting in part for higher recovery rates at Griffin Wash than elsewhere.

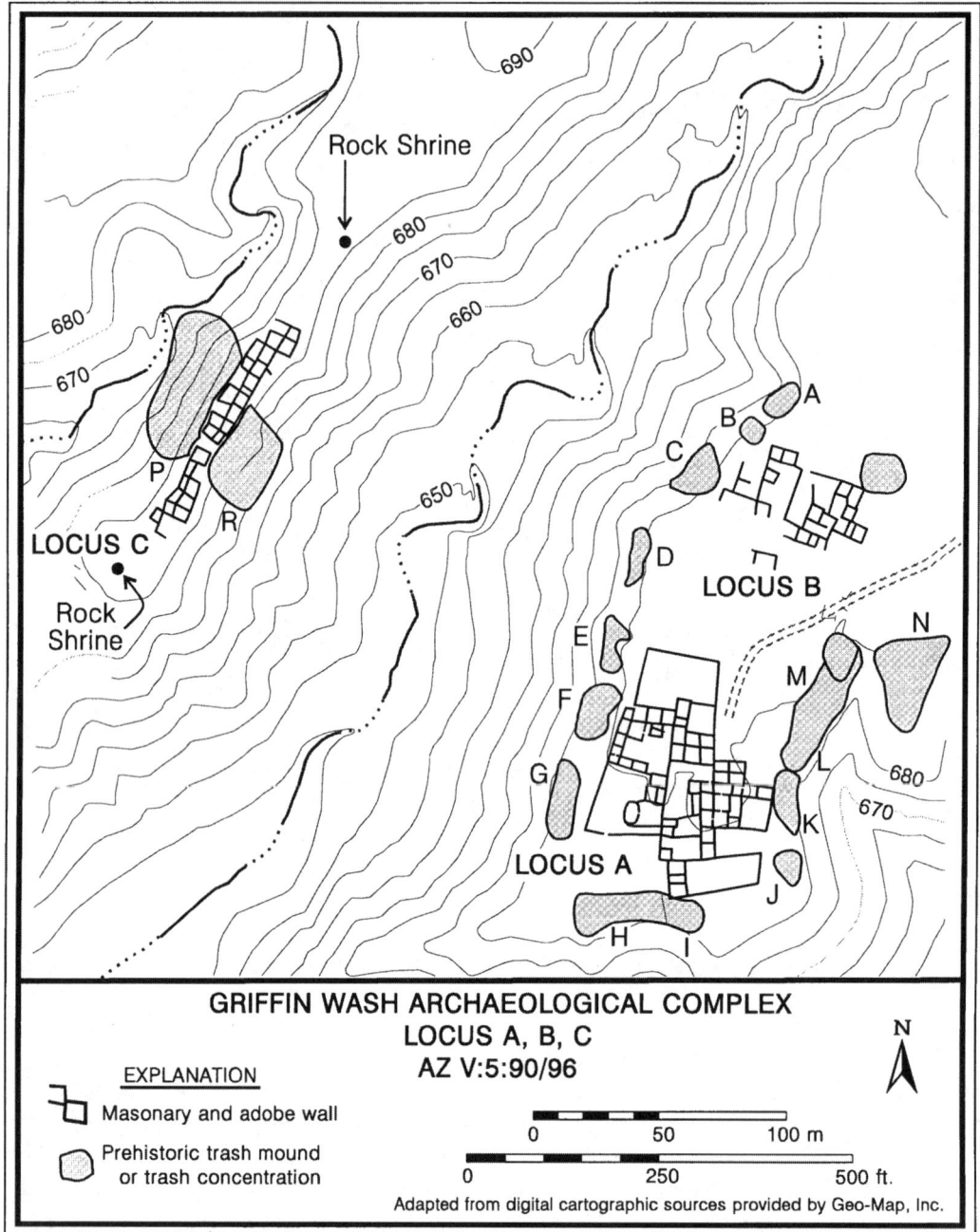

Figure 7.5.   The Griffin Wash site (AZ V:5:90/96) (from Swartz and Randolph 1994a:Figure 9.1).

Figure 7.6.   Architectural reconstruction of Locus A (with Locus C in the background) of the Griffin Wash site (AZ V:5:90/96), facing west. Reconstruction by Ziba Ghassemi (from Stark and Elson 1995:Figure 1.13).

Differences in local and immigrant populations are also suggested by the types of wood species that were used in construction. At Locus A of Griffin Wash, almost 50 percent of the excavated rooms contained a construction wood assemblage that originated at elevations more than 3000 feet higher than the RCD project area, consisting primarily of Douglas-fir, white fir, ponderosa pine, pinyon, and juniper, with little or (primarily) no mesquite (Miksicek 1995). This contrasts markedly with the mesquite-dominated construction wood assemblages of most Roosevelt phase structures. Griffin Wash structures containing this high elevation wood assemblage include both habitation and storage rooms; most do not appear to have any unusual or special function, nor are they significantly larger than other rooms. Although juniper and

pinyon were relatively common in most of the 90 flotation-sampled Roosevelt phase structures, Douglas-fir, white fir, and ponderosa pine were recovered from flotation analysis only from Locus A of Griffin Wash and from a single structure at Meddler Point. The structure with this assemblage at Meddler Point clearly served a specialized function, a point discussed later.

Locus A at Griffin Wash also had the highest ubiquity values of any site in either the RCD or Livingston project areas for agave (100 percent) and cotton (56 percent); in other RCD Roosevelt phase contexts, agave ubiquity averaged 59 percent and cotton 22 percent (Miksicek 1995). High Griffin Wash values suggest the possibility of specialization in these resources, perhaps as a commodity for other subsistence-related exchange. Agave does

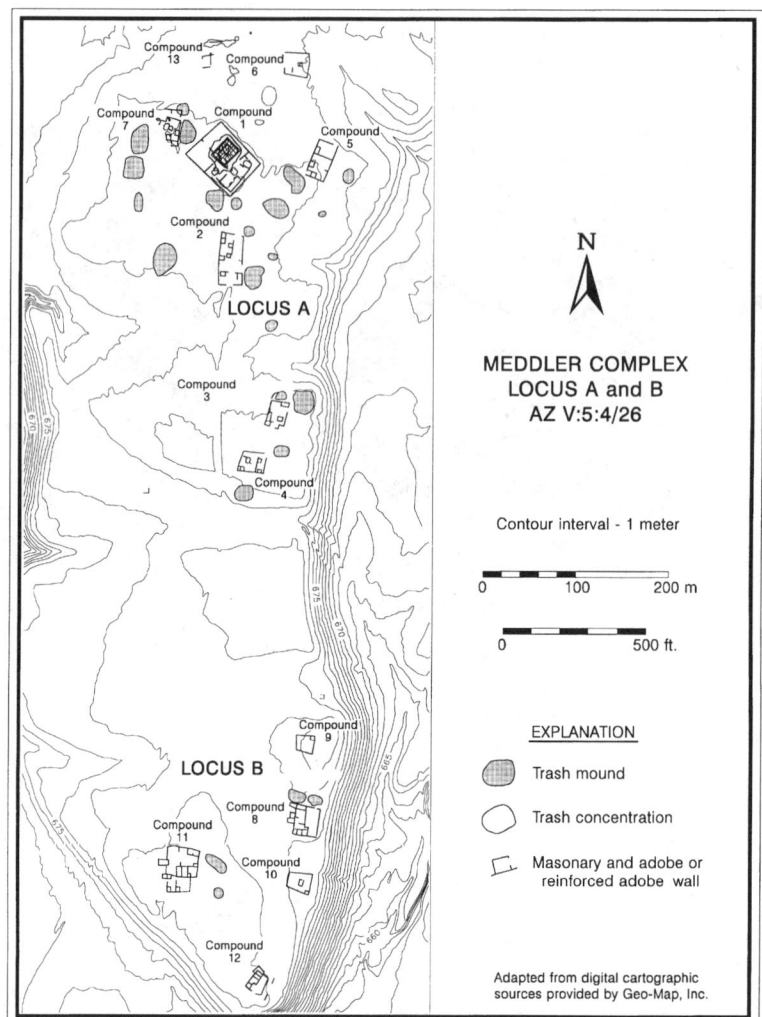

Figure 7.7. The Meddler Point site (AZ V:5:4/26). The platform mound is within Compound 1 in Locus A (from Craig and Clark 1994:Figure 7.1).

not require irrigation, and can be grown in dry or rock-pile field areas not normally cultivated. Griffin Wash inhabitants may have either lacked access to large areas of irrigable land (for reasons having to do with land-tenure or hydrology) or perhaps did not previously practice irrigation farming. Some irrigable land was farmed, however, as indicated by the recovery of cotton, which almost certainly required irrigation water. However, the amount of irrigable land may not have been enough to meet all of the subsistence needs of the larger group, and alternative strategies were employed.

Specialization in utilitarian goods is well documented ethnographically as an alternative means for procuring subsistence resources in conditions of limited agricultural land (Arnold 1985; Kramer 1985; Stark 1991, 1993).

Such specialization (termed *productive specialization*) often compensates for resource deficiencies and fills gaps in a group's livelihood (Brumfiel and Earle 1987). Major differences exist between the organization of productive specialization that involves utilitarian goods (e.g., pottery, basketry, foodstuffs) versus nonutilitarian goods. Surplus accumulation of nonutilitarian or wealth goods through *attached craft specialization* often forms the basis for social stratification. Although attached craft specialization in shell and ceramic manufacture has been claimed for the Classic period Tonto Basin (Hohmann and Kelly 1988), this level of sociopolitical complexity is not supported by RCD data.

Based on the above discussion, we suggest the following reconstruction for the Griffin Wash site: 1) Loci A

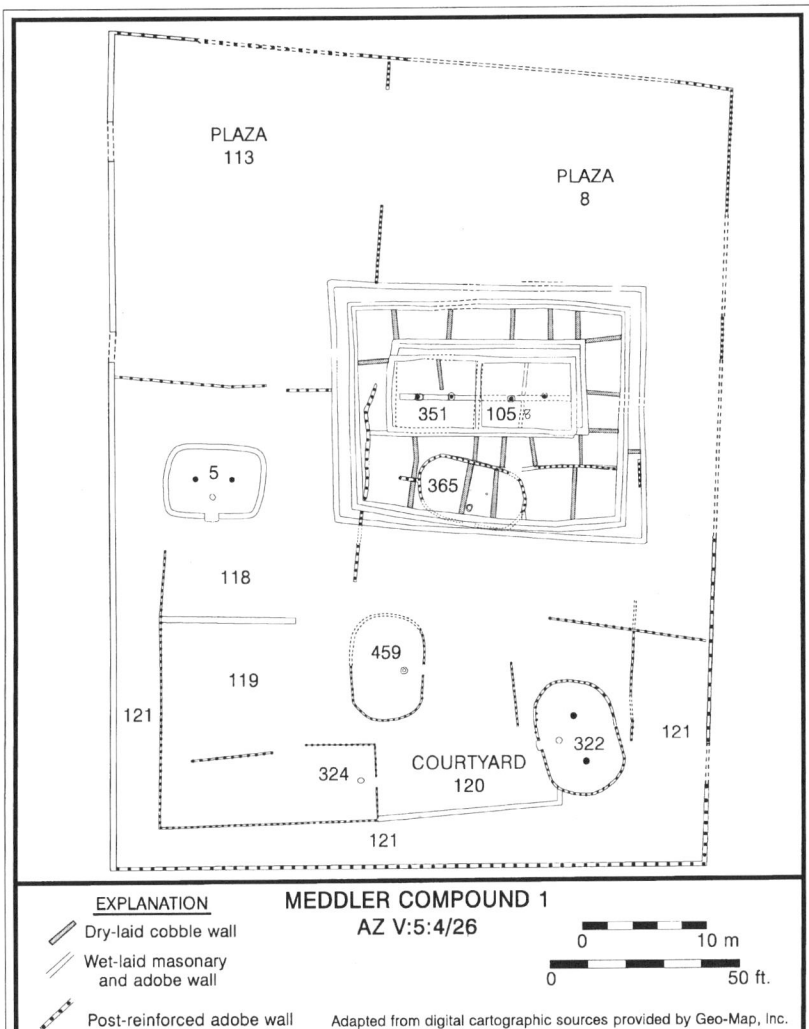

Figure 7.8. *(Left)* Compound 1 at the Meddler Point site (AZ V:5:4/25). Features 105 and 351 are the two rooms on top of the platform mound supported by underlying filled cells. Feature 365 is an earlier pitroom that was filled during mound construction (from Craig and Clark 1994:Figure 7.39).

Figure 7.9. *(Below)* Architectural reconstruction of the platform mound within Compound 1 at Meddler Point site (AZ V:5:4/26), facing east. (Reconstruction by Ziba Ghassemi, from Stark and Elson 1995:Figure 1.10).

PLAZA
113

PLAZA
8

351 105

365

5

118

459

119

121

322

121

324

COURTYARD
120

121

EXPLANATION

Dry-laid cobble wall

Wet-laid masonary
and adobe wall

Post-reinforced adobe wall

MEDDLER COMPOUND 1
AZ V:5:4/26

0   10 m

0   50 ft.

Adapted from digital cartographic sources provided by Geo-Map, Inc.

and C represent the migration of pueblo peoples into Tonto Basin sometime between 1250 and 1275: the immigrants joined a small, dispersed, local settlement on the western periphery of the Meddler local system; 2) the immigrants probably originated in an area in which Cibola White Ware and corrugated ceramics were commonly produced, and may have already been in contact with Tonto Basin inhabitants via ceramic exchange; 3) settlement-specific productive specialization in corrugated ceramics, and possibly cotton and agave, may have been practiced by the immigrants in response to a lack of sufficient irrigable land to meet all subsistence requirements of the increased population.

In summary, data from Griffin Wash provide one of the better supported cases for migration in the prehistoric Southwest. Architectural and ceramic data also suggest that the site of Saguaro Muerto was occupied by a migratory group (Lindauer 1994), although the occupation may represent a different type of adaptation to the local system than that proposed for Griffin Wash. Based on differences in architecture, artifacts, and botanical remains, it is also quite possible that Griffin Wash and Saguaro Muerto represent groups from different source areas.

At present we cannot identify an origin area (or areas) for the Tonto Basin immigrants, except to note that they came from an area with technological traditions that included both Cibola White Ware and corrugated ceramics. We are also aware that there are no precise architectural analogs to Griffin Wash in neighboring pueblo regions, such as the Sierra Ancha, White Mountain, or Mogollon Rim areas. We suggest, however, that the lack of neighboring parallels may reflect acculturation and the mixing of local and immigrant groups in the same architectural complex. Redman (1993) has suggested a similar interpretation for the architecturally anomalous Shoofly Ruin in the nearby Payson Basin. Most importantly, the Griffin Wash settlement represents a completely different conception of physical and social space than that represented by the indigenous architectural tradition. These differences are sufficiently striking to support the inference that its form was strongly influenced by nonlocal groups.

Platform Mounds

Absolute and relative dating suggest that the first platform mounds in the Eastern Tonto Basin were constructed around 1280 (Elson 1995; McCartney et al. 1994). This is more than 150 years later than their initial appearance in the Phoenix Basin, and as much as 50 years or more after the rectangular form of mound became common there (Doelle et al. 1995; Gregory 1987, 1991, 1995b). Unlike mounds in the Phoenix Basin, there is no evidence for a local or long-term developmental sequence of mound construction in Tonto Basin; all excavated mounds indicate relatively rapid construction from a preconceived plan. Discontinuities in the timing of construction, as well as morphological and functional differences, suggest little direct connection between Phoenix and Tonto Basin mounds (Doelle et al. 1995). This separation is supported by the data presented previously on the Sacaton/Ash Creek phase transition, indicating relatively limited contact between the two areas after the eleventh century. We do not suggest a total lack of communication: the "idea" of a platform mound, construction techniques, and perhaps a core ideology were probably derived from the Phoenix Basin. But Tonto Basin platform mounds functioned differently from those in the Phoenix Basin, and therefore were essentially a local adaptation using a similar architectural form (Doelle et al. 1995; Elson 1996a).

The RCD Study identified two types of platform mounds in the Eastern Tonto Basin: the "Meddler" type and the "tower mound" type (Doelle et al. 1995:398–410; Gregory 1995b:169). The Meddler-type mound (Figures 7.7–7.9) is believed to have been constructed largely as a ceremonial facility with an integrative function. It consists of a moderately-sized (approximately 20 m by 25 m by 2 m high) lower level of structural cells and walls that were deliberately filled to support two large rooms on its top. Construction of this feature was relatively rapid, possibly taking less than two years (Craig and Clark 1994). A master plan for the mound is clearly evident by the placement of an initial orienting wall with niches cut for the posts used to support the roofs of the two elevated rooms.

The RCD data do not support intensive occupation of the two rooms on top of the mound or the surrounding compound (Craig 1995; Craig and Clark 1994:194–95; Elson, Gregory, and Stark 1995). The lack of storage facilities and the documentation of private (restricted access) and public areas suggest that the mound functioned primarily as a locus for ceremonial activities that involved both private preparation and public display. Other Meddler-type mounds in the Eastern Tonto Basin include Livingston (the Pillar Mound) and Pinto Point (Figure 7.4). Livingston is most similar to Meddler Point, and on the basis of architec-

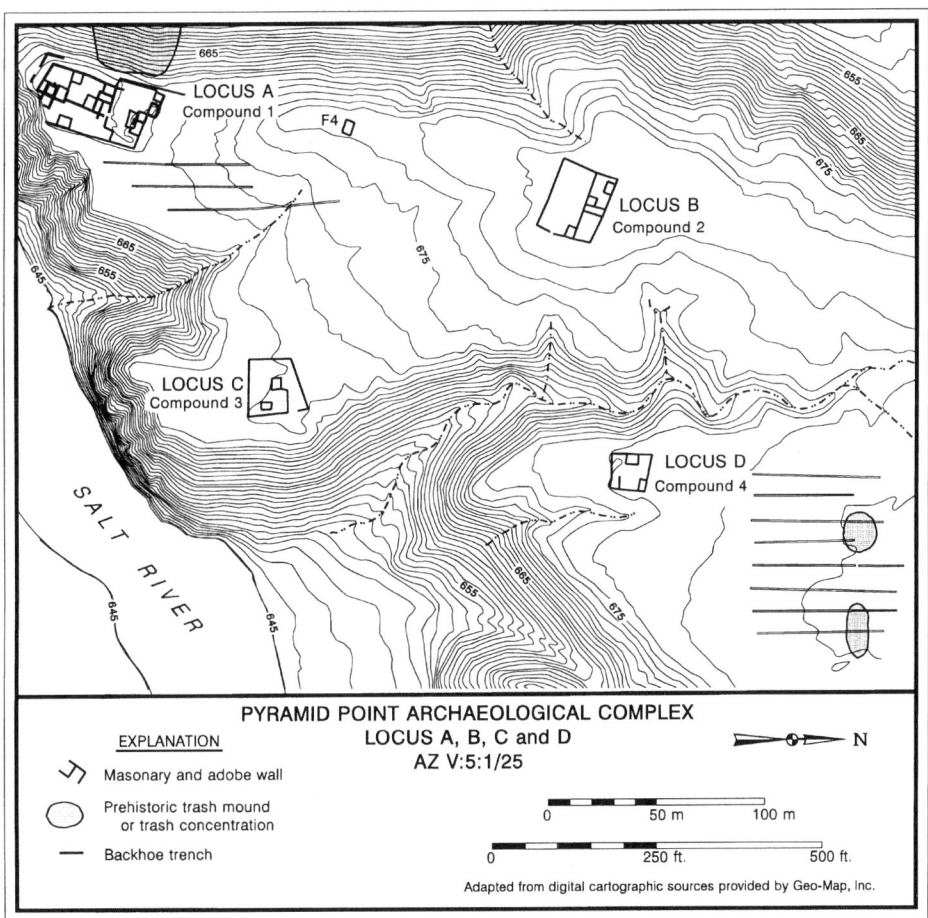

Figure 7.10. The Pyramid Point site (AZ V:5:1/25).

ture, artifact assemblages, and botanical data, is also thought not to have served a residential function (Doelle et al. 1995; Jacobs 1994a). The Pinto Point Mound may have had a residential component in the mound compound, but the rooms on top of the mound are not believed to have been inhabited (Jacobs and Rice 1994b:924).

Defined on the basis of excavations at the Pyramid Point site (Elson 1994a), tower mounds represent morphologically and functionally different types of features (Figures 7.10 and 7.11). In contrast to the Meddler-type, the Pyramid Point tower mound is extremely small; it measures no more than 5.5 m by 8 m by 2 m high. A single 2 m high room was probably constructed on top of the filled-in mound, although the character of this upper room is unknown because of poor preservation.

The mound is contained within a surrounding 15 room masonry compound, which appears to have both residential and ceremonial functions. The small size of the estimated population (10–30 individuals) suggests that residence at the settlement may have been primarily to maintain the mound and its facilities.

The location of the Pyramid Point Mound within the site area and compound (at the very tip of the point), and the location of the site itself on a prominent point in the Eastern Tonto Basin, suggests that the mound served important communication purposes, perhaps as a signal or watchtower (Elson 1994a). Intervisibility is present between the Pyramid Point Mound and every large Roosevelt phase settlement in the Eastern Tonto Basin local system. Unlike the Meddler Point Mound, which

Figure 7.11. Architectural reconstruction of Compound 1 (Locus A) of the Pyramid Point site (AZ V:5:1/25), facing south. The platform mound is the two-story structure at the southern end of the compound. (Reconstruction by Ziba Ghassemi, from Stark and Elson 1995:Figure 1.7).

appears to have been for close public viewing and immediate participation, Pyramid Point was constructed primarily for viewing at a distance, although some types of public or ceremonial activities may have occurred there as well. Tower mounds are not known from other Roosevelt phase contexts in Tonto Basin, although Gila phase examples have been excavated at Cline Terrace and possibly Rye Creek Ruin and are suspected to be present at a number of other sites (Doelle et al. 1995).

Integration in the
Eastern Tonto Basin Local System

Meddler-type platform mounds in the Eastern Tonto Basin may have integrated groups in the local system through public participation in communal and ceremonial events. These types of activities probably linked people within the Meddler Point settlement itself, as well as groups from different settlements, such as Meddler and Griffin Wash. It has been suggested that platform mounds in the Phoenix Basin and related areas served this function, particularly in their earlier nonresidential forms (Crown 1990; Gregory 1991; Wilcox 1991a). In the Phoenix Basin, mounds are consistently present in Classic period settlements and regularly spaced along irrigation canals (Gregory and Nials 1985). Construction and maintenance of these systems required organization and labor. The pressing question for the Eastern Tonto Basin is: why did a need develop for integrative facilities at this point in time?

We suggest three interrelated reasons to explain the need for integration during the Roosevelt phase. All are equally important, and we do not suggest that any one by itself played a larger role than the others. Instead, these factors functioned together to produce, at least briefly, a cohesive local system. These factors are the presence of diverse cultural groups, the need to coordinate irrigation systems and provide access to arable land to supply food for an expanding population, and the need for rapid communication, possibly for defense against external threats.

As noted above, several settlements in the Roosevelt phase Eastern Tonto Basin local system probably included immigrant pueblo groups. While a minority, these groups still represented a significant number of people. This may also have been the first time in Tonto Basin prehistory when different groups coresided within a limited area. Prior to this time, particularly during the Colonial period migrations, population was low enough that unsettled land was available, and the entire Eastern

basin may have been linked through kin ties. Much of the population resided in a single local settlement, that of Meddler Point and its associated farmsteads and field houses (Gregory 1995b).

Integration of immigrant groups would have been beneficial to both parties. The local population would have benefited from increased labor to construct and maintain irrigation systems and to bolster defense against real or perceived threats. Skills of the immigrant group, particularly in craft manufacture, could also have been valuable. Benefits to the immigrant population are obvious and fundamental to the rationale for migration in the first place. Moving from an environmentally (and possibly socially) fragile region into an already land-tenured system that lacked kinship relationships required integration with the local population to ensure a permanent place of residence and dependable food supply.

That the Meddler Point site may have integrated diverse cultural groups is suggested by the dual nature of its mound and compound (Figures 7.7–7.9). The mound contained two rooms on top and two structures (facing each other) in the area of restricted access behind the mound. Perhaps most interesting, one of the two rooms on top of the mound (Feature 351) contained a "high elevation" construction wood assemblage (Douglas-fir, white fir, ponderosa pine, juniper, and no mesquite) identical to that recovered from approximately half of the rooms at Locus A of Griffin Wash. The other room (Feature 105) contained a more typical Roosevelt phase "low elevation" assemblage (mesquite, juniper, pine, creosote, and palo verde). These associations may represent the symbolic integration of two different cultural traditions.

Although the Eastern Tonto Basin probably always had sufficient land and water resources (Waters 1994b), greater coordination and integration of different settlements was probably necessary to feed a larger population. Organizational systems associated with the platform mounds could have provided integrated groups a means for expansion of irrigation systems, and thus increased the amount of land under cultivation (Craig 1995; Craig and Clark 1994:197). This is particularly important if one of the effects of the "Great Drought," starting around 1275, was to make dry-farming less productive or altogether unfeasible in Tonto Basin (Altschul and Van West 1992; Whittlesey and Ciolek-Torrello 1992; see Van West et al., Chapter 2). The Roosevelt phase was also the first time that hamlet or village-level settlements developed away from Meddler Point (at Griffin

Wash, Pinto Point, and Schoolhouse Point), suggesting that the local system was becoming increasingly complex and segmented. Integrative methods were probably necessary to provide labor and organization for various other subsistence and community-related tasks.

The final reason for integration may have been a need for increased intersettlement communication, possibly for defense from real or perceived threats. As noted previously, the period between 1250 and 1300 was a time of increasing intergroup conflict in the northern Southwest (Wilcox and Haas 1994). Prior to the Roosevelt phase, there is very little evidence from the Eastern Tonto Basin for any form of conflict, except for the occasional burned structure (which may or may not represent conflict). Although the data are admittedly equivocal and alternative explanations are possible, this appears to change during the Roosevelt phase. For the first time since the Early Ceramic period, sites are located in defensive locations (e.g., Griffin Wash Locus C) and there is widespread burning of structures, many with floor assemblages. Full-standing compound walls were also built around many settlements, and three adult males were found "sprawled" on the floors of two burned rooms at U:8:221, a small Roosevelt phase compound (Shelley and Ciolek-Torrello 1994).

The construction of the Pyramid Point platform mound, visible from all settlements in the Eastern Tonto Basin, is believed to indicate a concern with communication, with the mound functioning as a tower to facilitate this process. Given relatively close spacing of settlements in the Eastern Tonto Basin (all of which could have been reached on foot within one or two hours), this type of communication was only necessary if a quick response was needed. The threat of conflict is the most obvious possibility, and ethnographic examples of the use of signaling for defensive purposes are common (Di Peso et al. 1974b; Ellis 1991). Although other ethnographic reasons for long- or intermediate-distance communication are known (Ellis 1991:64), the presence of perceived threat is the most likely reason to require rapid notification and response. The Pyramid Point tower may have been particularly important in connecting Griffin Wash and Meddler Point, the only two large settlements that are not intervisible. Griffin Wash is situated on the far western edge of the local system, and may have served as a defensive buffer against threats originating from this direction, particularly from the nearby Armer Ranch local system (Elson, Gregory, and Stark 1995; Gregory 1995b). This may be similar to the manner in which the immigrant Tewa

(at Hano Village) functioned for the Hopi (Connelly 1979; Dozier 1966). The need to organize labor for maintenance of irrigation systems, particularly after destructive floods, is another possibility. Similar prehistoric communication systems based on intervisibility have been documented in the Kayenta, Chaco Canyon, Mesa Verde, and Gallina areas (Dean 1996a; Dean et al. 1978; Ellis 1991; Haas and Creamer 1993; Hayes and Windes 1975; Wilcox and Haas 1994).

In summary, the need for integration during the Roosevelt phase is suggested to have developed because of three primary factors: the presence of diverse cultural groups, organization of irrigation and subsistence related tasks, and communication. Construction and use of platform mounds facilitated integration, probably through ceremonial and communal activities. The mounds may have served as monumental symbols of a new ideological system, although the origin and nature of this system are currently unclear. This period of integration was relatively short-lived, however, lasting no more than 50 years (1275–1325) and possibly less.

Gila Phase Abandonment and Reorganization

The RCD Study area was largely abandoned during the late Roosevelt phase: a lack of Fourmile Polychrome and recovery of only a few sherds of Gila Polychrome suggest abandonment sometime around 1325. The reasons for abandonment are not entirely clear, although we suggest that environmental factors, particularly a series of very wet years with the potential for increased flooding (Craig 1995; Craig and Clark 1994:197; Masse 1991:220–21; Waters 1994b), and the continued presence of conflict, were important factors. Increasing conflict is suggested by the newly aggregated form of the Schoolhouse Point settlement (Lindauer 1996a), the fact that almost all Roosevelt phase structures are burned, and as mortuary data from the Cline Terrace platform mound (Jacobs 1997) and Tapia Del Cerrito (Rice 1985). Platform mounds and their associated activities failed as integrative mechanisms in the RCD area, and the system collapsed after functioning for only 50 years. In this sense, the Roosevelt phase in the Eastern Tonto Basin represents a short-lived experiment in social organization.

The Schoolhouse Point settlement reached its largest extent during the Gila phase, and small populations were present at Pinto Point and a few small compounds on Schoolhouse Mesa (Jacobs 1994a; Lindauer 1996a, 1997). However, the total number of Gila phase rooms could not have accommodated the estimated Roosevelt phase population of the Eastern Basin, suggesting that the majority of inhabitants left the area (Doelle 1995a). These groups may have moved northwest to the Tonto Arm of the Basin, where large Gila phase populations are known, or out of the Basin entirely to the Globe-Miami area or to the northeast to such settlements as Granite Basin Ruin, Grasshopper, Q-Ranch, or Kinishba. All of these sites lie within 50 km of the Eastern Basin, at most a two day walk. It is also during this time that indications of a regional cult appear, as represented by the distribution and iconography of Gila Polychrome ceramics (Crown 1994). Because the RCD project area did not contain definable Gila phase components, we discuss this period no further and turn to several specific problems in Tonto Basin prehistory.

ISSUES OF SCALE AND COMPLEXITY IN THE CLASSIC PERIOD TONTO BASIN

The late prehistoric period witnessed a reorganization of local populations throughout the greater Southwest. Some areas were abandoned, while others felt the pressure of newly-arrived populations (Dean et al. 1994). In regions that experienced continued occupation, formerly more dispersed populations aggregated into large settlements along major drainage systems. During the twelfth through fourteenth centuries, Tonto Basin was one link in a chain of geographically disjunct districts where local sequences all took sharp turns (Lekson et al. 1992). Reasons suggested for these changes generally include four types of factors: environmental stress, shifts in agricultural technology, demographic pressure, and the need for defense (Cordell et al. 1994:109–13). The emphasis accorded to each factor varies with the geographic region and time period. Models of aggregation and sociopolitical organization in Tonto Basin have also relied on these factors to explain early Classic period sociopolitical organization and settlement shifts.

Competing Models of Sociopolitical Organization

The archaeological record of Tonto Basin indicates that major organizational shifts characterized the transition to the Roosevelt phase (Gregory 1995b; Rice 1990b; Wood 1992). There is general agreement among researchers that settlement systems of the thirteenth and fourteenth centu-

ries were more extensive and more complex than those of earlier intervals. However, in identifying factors responsible for early Classic period changes in Tonto Basin, researchers have often been biased by their own particular geographic referents. For example, one group has looked southwestward to the Phoenix Basin because of similarities between the two areas in environment, settlement system morphology, platform mound architecture, and subsistence (Hohmann 1992a; Hohmann and Kelley 1988; Wood 1989; Wood and McAllister 1984a). Another group has looked to the north and east to embrace models based on puebloan (particularly Hopi) ethnography (Ciolek-Torrello and Whittlesey 1994; Whittlesey and Ciolek-Torrello 1992). Findings from the RCD Study, however, suggest that similarities between Tonto Basin and these areas, while real, tend to mask more fundamental and important differences. Identification of both similarities and differences between the Tonto Basin and neighboring regions requires documentation of local developments. Such work strengthens support for a model of indigenous development in which interaction—rather than domination or simple emulation—characterized Classic period dynamics in Tonto Basin.

Broadly grouped, three basic models have been proposed for the Classic period Tonto Basin. The first is a model of egalitarian social organization derived from historic puebloan ethnography (Ciolek-Torrello and Whittlesey 1994; Ciolek-Torrello et al. 1994; Whittlesey and Ciolek-Torrello 1992). In this framework, Roosevelt phase platform mound communities developed in response to social and economic stress brought on by immigration and climatic fluctuations. Social integration was ceremonially-based and emphasized horizontal (rather than hierarchical) organizational forms such as clans and sodalities. The second model postulates macroregional systems with managerial elites, in which Tonto Basin was one link in a pan-Southwestern system of alliances between competing polities (Plog 1979, 1983; Upham 1982). Parts of this model are also subsumed under the Salado macroregion proposed by Wilcox (1994; Wilcox and Sternberg 1983). The third model hinges on the operation of redistributive chiefdoms, and asserts that Classic period settlement patterns indicate the presence of competing polities within Tonto Basin, entities whose centers controlled the distribution of goods. Settlements were organized into a regional (i.e., Basin-wide) hierarchy, in which upland (nonriverine) settlements were tied to riverine villages through exchange relations (e.g., Rice 1990c; Wood and McAllister 1984a).

Therefore, Classic period Tonto Basin groups have been modeled as egalitarian tribal societies, simple chiefdoms, and possibly even complex chiefdoms. However, none of these models is without major flaws, and all suffer from the fact that they were developed in the absence of sufficient Tonto Basin data. For example, the pueblo-based egalitarian model glosses over subtleties of status and rank in puebloan societies (Brandt 1994:10–12; Levy 1992; Parsons 1939; Schlegel 1992). Moreover, current dialogue regarding the utility and implications of the term "egalitarian" (Boehm 1993; Flanagan 1989; Price and Feinman 1995) calls into question the basic assumptions regarding sociopolitical organization that form the foundation of this model.

The macroregional systems model is also problematic. It reflects a narrow understanding of both the source models (i.e., world systems theory and alliance theory; McGuire et al. 1993:240–42; Upham et al. 1994:192) and of how traditional economic systems operate. The greatest problem with some of these models is their weak linkages between theoretical constructs (alliance relationships, managerial elites) and archaeological patterning. For example, we still do not know enough about exchange systems to distinguish periodic trading from a "well-developed exchange network" (Lightfoot and Jewett 1984) in the archaeological record. Nor can we distinguish between patterning produced by centralized ceramic production and that generated by elite control of wealth goods at large prehistoric settlements. Furthermore, this level of complexity, involving economic centralization and managerial control, is difficult to support with archaeological data recovered from Tonto Basin and the greater Southwest.

The redistributive chiefdom model was founded on a skewed site distribution created by uneven survey coverage of Tonto Basin. Thus, large multicomponent sites were emphasized and often assumed to be very late (Gila phase) in the occupation. Roosevelt Project excavations suggest that many of the platform mounds were short-lived and occupied only during the Roosevelt phase; furthermore, some of the mounds lacked substantial associated populations. Equally troublesome is the dilution of the term 'chiefdom', which now encompasses a broad range of diverse social forms. The models for so-called 'redistributive chiefdoms' (Fried 1967; Sahlins and Service 1960) have become so numerous and diverse as to render the concept nearly meaningless in its application to the prehistoric Tonto Basin (Yoffee and Sherratt 1993).

Archaeological research through the Roosevelt Lake projects has provided a strong empirical basis for evaluating competing models of sociopolitical organization in the Classic period Tonto Basin. Results from the RCD Study provide data for refinement and evaluation of previous models.

Scale and Integration in the Classic Period Tonto Basin

Any model of Classic period sociopolitical complexity must address the related issues of scale and integration (Blanton et al. 1981). Throughout the Tonto Basin developmental sequence, the extended family household was probably the basic social unit (Gregory 1995b). Although the scale of the local system changed through time (with a dramatic increase during the Roosevelt phase), there are reasons to suspect that the effective social unit remained stable throughout the sequence.

Understanding sociopolitical structure in Tonto Basin requires examination of degrees of interaction between, and integration within, local systems during this time. One measure of interaction between local systems lies in RCD analyses of utilitarian pottery circulation, which suggests productive specialization but widespread distribution (Stark and Heidke 1995). Another expression of local system interaction involved construction of public architecture. Subsistence systems, dependent on canal irrigation networks that crosscut settlement boundaries, must also have generated interaction within local systems. Settlements in local systems, then, participated in various relations of interdependence.

Our data also suggest that regional systems, each of which involved multiple local systems, were less internally cohesive than local systems. Ties that linked local systems together to form a Basin-wide network symbolized shared interests and beliefs, perhaps best exemplified through the local construction of platform mounds; however, these probably were not kinship oriented as were local systems. The social cohesiveness of regional systems probably fluctuated throughout each phase of the developmental sequence. Various factors—environmental stress (Dean 1996b; Dean et al. 1985, 1994), religious cults (Adams 1991; Crown 1994), charismatic leaders (Clark and Blake 1994), or the threat of interregional aggression (Wilcox and Haas 1994)—alternately accentuated or weakened bonds that tied local systems together at the regional level. That these bonds were ultimately fragile is suggested by the relatively short span of many Roosevelt phase platform mound settlements.

None of the proposed models for Classic period sociopolitical organization fits settlement patterns in the RCD Study area very well. The egalitarian model precludes consideration of social distinctions among groups and within settlements, despite clear evidence that the construction of irrigation canals and platform mounds required group organization and leadership. Residents of mound villages, for example, were probably more intimately involved in platform mound activities than those in outlying settlements, and may have enjoyed some form of higher status or at least greater access to more valuable goods (Bayman 1994; Elson 1996a; Jacobs and Rice 1994b). The macroregional systems model assumes too much control in the hands of elites, particularly in the realm of a subsistence economy. And the redistributive chiefdom model assumes that heightened levels of social interaction (particularly in terms of increased trade and increased population movement [Rice 1990c:38–39]) inevitably lead to sociopolitical complexity. Here again the issue of scale arises: the replacement of kin ties with nonkin ties in defining positions of authority that Rice (1990c:35) describes are more common (but by no means ubiquitous) in state societies than they are in societies found throughout the prehistoric Southwest.

Findings from the RCD Study suggest that several factors limited development of very high levels of Classic period complexity in Tonto Basin. These included low population size (even during its peak in the Classic period); limits to agricultural growth that were imposed by the potential agricultural productivity of the Basin; and limits on control of the production and circulation of high-value goods (Craig 1995; Stark 1995b; Van West et al., Chapter 2; Waters 1994b; see Doelle Chapter 4 and Rice Chapter 6). Unlike Casas Grandes or, on a different scale, Phoenix Basin settlements, Tonto Basin villages apparently never manufactured items for export on a large-scale (Wood 1985). The identification of granaries suggests involvement in surplus storage, but little convincing evidence exists for highly centralized control over storage facilities by Roosevelt phase groups: Granaries were associated with both platform mound and non-platform mound sites, including some very small sites. The identification of productive specialization indicates a considerable degree of horizontal integration, but no evidence was found for hierarchical control over the production and distribution of these utilitarian (and low-value) commodities.

Surplus labor, surplus foods, and monopoly over high-value goods are all preconditions for sociocultural complex-

ity (Kipp and Schortman 1989). Complex societies, which already have an entrenched system of social ranking or stratification, often seek to gain control over aspects of the utilitarian economy through tribute payments, indentured servitude, and attached specialization. However, specialization in the production of utilitarian and subsistence goods, seen during the early Classic period in Tonto Basin, rarely leads to development of political or power relationships (Brumfiel and Earle 1987:6). The absence of centralized control over the production of valuable commodities may have been one reason why Roosevelt phase sociopolitical organization did not reach a very high level of complexity.

To argue that elite control was not formally institutionalized during the early Classic period is not to argue against the existence of relations of inequality. Viewed cross-culturally, mound-building peoples tend to exhibit some form of social ranking with designated leaders in inherited positions (Elson 1996a; Trigger 1990). However, the degree of control and the basis of authority varies widely among these groups. If Southwest ethnography is any guide to interpreting the past, status distinctions may have centered on roles in the ritual system (Brandt 1994; Levy 1992). Ritual specialists among historic Piman and Puebloan groups, for example, had restricted access to ceremonial artifacts and sacred knowledge, both of which were the foundation of their power (Brandt 1994:15). Exotic artifact assemblages from ceremonial rooms have been documented at several platform mound sites in Tonto Basin, including Pyramid Point (Elson 1994a) and Cline Terrace (Jacobs 1997). Whether access to these ceremonial rooms and their contents was restricted remains unclear, and more work is required on hierarchy in Southwestern ritual systems. Hierarchy and egalitarianism, as Flanagan (1989) and Feinman (1992) point out, can and do coexist in a single social system.

Entrepreneurial activity by status seeking individuals (or groups of individuals) is not restricted to highly complex societies (Clark and Blake 1994). We suggest that one logical outcome of increased horizontal integration during the Roosevelt phase would have been the emergence of such individuals, perhaps along descent group lines, who sought power and privilege through ritual means. Platform mound construction may be the physical manifestation of this process, possibly accounting for the relatively short duration of individual Roosevelt phase mounds (Elson 1996a). In the early Classic period Tonto Basin, however, constraints on resources likely prevented the development of enduring positions of rank and status. Findings from the RCD Study clearly demonstrate the lack of sustainability of these organizational structures during the Roosevelt phase. Even the most ambitious individuals or groups in Tonto Basin society were ultimately unsuccessful in their quest to institutionalize power. By the early to middle fourteenth century, the Salt Arm of the Tonto Basin was almost completely abandoned.

THE SALADO CONCEPT

Understanding the scale and integration of social units in the early Classic period Tonto Basin is essential for evaluating the "Salado" concept. The term Salado was initially defined by the Gladwins and others (Gladwin 1957; Gladwin and Gladwin 1935; Schmidt 1928) to refer to the pueblo-building culture of Tonto Basin that used black-on-white and polychrome pottery. The Salado were seen as a migratory pueblo group from the Little Colorado region who entered an uninhabited Tonto Basin sometime in the twelfth century. The importance of Tonto Basin in early theories of Southwestern culture history derives from the claims of Gladwin and Gladwin (1935) and Haury (1945) that Salado people used the Basin as a base to influence (and even truncate) Hohokam development in the Phoenix Basin and much of southeastern Arizona. The Classic period Tonto Basin was viewed as pivotal, then, not so much because of its internal developments, but because it was an origin area for populations whose subsequent migrations profoundly affected the Hohokam heartland (Haury 1945; Hayden 1957).

Since then, Salado has been defined in a number of different ways: as a prehistoric people (indigenous to Tonto Basin, Hohokam or Mogollon-derived, or some sort of hybrid), a geographic culture area in central Arizona, a macroregional interaction sphere, or a regional religious or ideological cult. Salado has become synonymous with the distribution of Salado polychrome (Roosevelt Red Ware) ceramics, particularly Gila Polychrome. However, a few other traits, such as inhumation burial and masonry and adobe compound architecture, are sometimes included in the definition (Crown 1994; Doyel 1992; Doyel and Haury 1976; Hohmann and Kelley 1988; Nelson and LeBlanc 1986; Wilcox 1994; Wood 1992).

Tonto Basin is still commonly referred to as the Salado "heartland" (Hohmann 1992a; Wood 1992), even though frequencies of Salado polychromes within the basin are not substantially different, and in fact, often lower, than those in neighboring areas.

The term Salado (in one of its various manifestations) has now been applied to a very heterogeneous, and often confusing, mixture of peoples and cultural traditions that extends from Arizona to Texas and southward into Chihuahua to the site of Casas Grandes. The definition and meaning of Salado thus remain problematic, and little consensus exists among archaeologists concerning its usage. For these reasons, in the RCD Study we opted not to adopt any previous definitions of Salado, nor to add yet another definition to the general terminological morass.

However, the RCD data strongly suggest that processes occurring in the Roosevelt phase Tonto Basin, traditionally seen as the beginning of the Salado culture, resemble those occurring elsewhere in the Southwest at this time. These include immigration of nonlocal groups, population aggregation, increasing integration and social complexity, and, in some areas, the construction of platform mounds. Our data further suggest that in Tonto Basin these processes were interrelated and may represent a local response to widespread social and environmental stress. For these reasons, we believe that Salado is most appropriately viewed as a regional manifestation (confined to the southern and central Southwest) of processes that affected the Southwest on a grand scale. This argues that Salado should not be defined as the local culture of the Classic period Tonto Basin, nor as the culture of a migratory pueblo people.

Therefore, the RCD data lend support to the concept of Salado as a regional horizon, and possibly a religious or ideological cult as defined by Crown (1994), that was individually interpreted and expressed at the local system level. The Katsina Cult (Adams 1991) may represent a response to similar social and environmental stresses in the northern Southwest. The start of the Salado horizon is currently unclear. Does it begin during the Roosevelt phase with the integrative ideology associated with the platform mounds (but with Pinto, not Gila, Polychrome) as we have suggested above for the Eastern Tonto Basin? Or is the Roosevelt phase a precursor of the Salado horizon, which begins with the production of Gila Polychrome and the reorganization and aggregation of settlements in the following Gila phase? The resolution of this problem awaits future research.

CONCLUSION

The primary goal of this chapter has been to bring together findings of the RCD Study to reconstruct the developmental sequence of the Eastern Tonto Basin. This reconstruction illuminates aspects of Tonto Basin prehistory in general and documents the inception and development of a local Tonto Basin system over a period of 1200 years. Most importantly, our research underscores the need to examine local internal processes of development before reaching conclusions of regional scale. As we have noted previously, our view of Tonto Basin as a series of local systems has important implications not only for reconstructing the prehistory of this area, but for understanding Salado.

Archaeologists have spent much time and energy debating how Tonto Basin fits into defined culture areas of the prehistoric Southwest. Were the inhabitants Mogollon, Hohokam, Anasazi, Salado, Sinagua, all of the above, or something else? In many ways, this represents a belief that if Tonto Basin inhabitants could be appropriately labeled, that label was sufficient for understanding Tonto Basin prehistory. We argue, based on our data, that this line of investigation is limiting and explains little about the prehistoric occupation of this fascinating area. Our findings illustrate the intensity of interaction between people in Tonto Basin and those in neighboring regions and the processes of migration and coresidence. However, our research also demonstrates the presence of a dynamic and evolving indigenous population, one not easily or productively dealt with in terms of existing cultural-historical classifications.

CHAPTER EIGHT

Salado Social Dynamics Networks and Alliances in Tonto Basin

Arleyn W. Simon and David Jacobs

Dｕｒｉｎｇ ｔｈｅ Cｌａｓｓｉｃ ｐｅｒｉｏｄ, ｂｅｔｗｅｅｎ 1200 ａｎｄ 1450, the prehistoric inhabitants of central Arizona built both platform mounds and compound-walled villages. The considerable variations in architecture, site layout, and artifact assemblages (Nelson and LeBlanc 1986; Rice, ed. 1990) have perplexed archaeologists for decades resulting in a number of models to explain the inconsistencies apparent across the Salado area (Rice 1990a, b, c). One explanation has focused on migration (Haury 1958), but such models have been thought to require the complete replacement of the architectural and artifact assemblages. For many sites, these conditions have not been met, and the model has not been supported for all areas. Some models focused on elaborate social complexity and the development of a managerial elite that controlled the accumulation of surplus within a redistribution system (Braun and Plog 1982; McGuire 1985); others have insisted that the prehistoric social organization was strictly egalitarian. Evidence has not supported interpretations of either high level social complexity or the absence of status recognition.

The social dynamics of platform mound complexes undoubtedly lie somewhere between the extremes of high level complexity and strict egalitarianism (Redman 1992; Rice, ed. 1990; Rice et al. 1992). The Salado phenomenon and development of the platform mounds were in large part driven by the reactions of local populations to the influx of migrants and the social mechanisms used to maintain and assure control of their lands and resources. One of the primary goals of the authors' research for the Roosevelt Platform Mound Study (RPMS) (Redman 1992; Rice 1992; Rice, ed. 1990), has been to determine whether there was a systemic reality to the associations among platform mound and compound sites.

Arizona State University archaeologists have excavated a number of platform mound complexes and examined both the architecture and the artifact assemblages (Rice 1992; Rice, ed. 1990). Ceramics are the most abundant artifact class (Simon, ed. 1997; Simon et al. 1992; Simon and Redman 1990) and are used in this study to examine intrasite and intersite relationships. Variations in the architecture and the artifact assemblages (Redman 1992; Rice 1990c, 1992) are viewed as significant indicators of past functional parameters and social influences. These variations are also indirect indicators of social ties within each platform mound complex and the surrounding areas (Simon and Ravesloot 1995). Through analysis of ceramics and architecture, we explore patterns of intersite similarities and differences and use these results to elucidate prehistoric social dynamics and community relationships among Classic period platform mound complexes of Tonto Basin.

REGIONAL PERSPECTIVES:
METONYMS AND STRONG ANALYTICAL CASES

Archaeological sites and their assemblages are the physical expressions of past social interactions. Space is socially constructed, contested, and expressed in different ways by the various participants (Rodman 1992:647, 652). The regional relationships between multiple localities (Rodman 1992:644) are developed through the blending of experience in one place with events there and in other places. Each locality is a setting for social action and evokes meanings and experiences for that and similar places. In archaeological studies, it is important to examine evidence for past social structure from a number of perspectives and different scales.

There is a long history of selection of particular sites for investigating specific archaeological problems. The prehistoric record is relevant for addressing certain questions of prehistory, provided that formation-process variability is controlled (Montgomery and Reid 1990:88–89; Schiffer 1987). Strong analytic cases are often chosen as those individual settlements that have large samples of data for which natural and cultural formation processes have been controlled (Reid and Whittlesey 1982:18). Weak analytic cases are those with small numbers of sample data that may have been distorted by natural and cultural causes, including multiple occupation or vandalism.

Study of the variety of large and small sites, including those with long occupation sequences, in a region is crucial for developing interpretations of past social dynamics. The quality of information gathered from sites must be weighed, but the larger perspective of social interaction among prehistoric settlements is only obtainable through analysis of many cases that include diverse examples. Variation in the archaeological record has been overlooked as an outgrowth of the core definitions developed during the formative and normative years of American archaeology. Now sufficient data have been gathered to test models with more dynamic parameters and explain variation as part of the usual human milieu.

As the discipline of anthropology has matured and more field work has been completed, there have been changes in theoretical and research orientations. Both social anthropology and archaeology have moved away from the normative approach that focused on the definition of core areas (Moore 1994). Initially, intensive studies of single sites provided a wealth of information, but over time these were enthroned as metonyms (Rodman 1992:640), single locations that inappropriately become the interpretation for whole regions. Such sites may have been the first strong analytic cases, but now there are many others that together represent the range of variation in the Classic period occupation of the study area and provide evidence of regional social dynamics.

It is obvious that the "norm" for most societies includes considerable variation in language, in marriage partners, traditions, and material culture (Moore 1994:931). Several studies have identified multilingual intermarriage across ethnic boundaries contributing to cultural variation (Albers 1993; Owen 1965). Different types of interethnic social organization have been identified (Sharrock 1974:96) including alliances, intermarriage and polyethnic coresidence, with fused ethnicity (combinations of different cultural traditions and their languages). We recognize the extensive mixing of ethnicities that took place in historic times and that prehistoric social interactions were at least as dynamic as those documented in historic times.

Models of social organization that encompass variation in the archaeological record are appropriate well before the Classic period. The result of these analyses indicate contrasting ceramic traditions, an amalgamation of production methods, and adoption of local materials over time. Interpretations of these contrasts and similarities in ceramic traditions are used to examine intraregional and intrabasin scales of social networks and alliances.

ALLIANCES AND NETWORKS

Alliances and networks figure prominently in most social interactions (Albers 1993; Ortiz 1972; Rodman 1992; Titiev 1944), but most of these are effected on the personal level, either through kin ties, or ceremonial and other social ties. In this discussion, social networks consist of personal interactions between members of the same community and with members of other communities. Informal networks are not bound by descent groups or kin ties, but may include a variety of other social contacts or common activities that involve the participants. Multiple networks may coexist and commonly overlap with each other locally and at a distance. Alliances are close associations for a common objective or mutual benefit and operate above the level of descent groups (Graburn 1971:213–14) but often emphasize the separateness and equality of social groups and the bonds between them. Alliances may be effected through exogamous marriage rules whereby bonds are established by the exchange of marriage partners. While networks operate informally, primarily through personal contact brought about by proximity or common activities, alliances imply purposeful, or obligatory, bonds between different groups. In theory, an alliance recognizes the participating groups as equally powerful. Among Southwestern cultural groups, ethnographic examples indicate that such equality is rare, or at least only apparent on the surface.

The identification of social bonds among prehistoric settlements is a challenge (Adams 1991:190–91; Braun and Plog 1982; Rautmann 1993; Wobst 1974), yet it can result in the recovery of some relatively intangible aspects of the past. Although the specific details are not obtainable, it is possible to ascertain the degree of commonality in ceramic and other artifact assemblages among features within a site or among various site assemblages. Technological and stylistic traditions in ceramics, architecture, and other aspects of the material record indicate continuity and commonality within the local area, or discontinuity and diversity in the cultural influences. In archaeological studies (Rice et al. 1992), the issues revolve around modeling the social dynamics that held the platform mound communities together, identifying characteristics of the site assemblages, and evaluating the appropriateness of the models through analysis of the site assemblages.

Despite population concentration in cultural core areas, no area of the prehistoric Southwest existed in isolation. Prior to the abandonment of the San Juan Basin, intrusive pottery in site collections from the central Arizona river valleys and deserts indicates contact, at least indirectly through down-the-line exchange, among populations of Anasazi, Hohokam, and Mogollon. Relatively high frequencies of intrusive ceramics from the Colorado Plateau in sites in Tonto Basin (Hensler 1994; Lindauer and Simon 1995; Simon 1996a, 1997) indicate extensive contact with peoples to the north. It is important to note, however, that the majority of the Salado polychromes were made in Tonto Basin (Burton et al. 1994; Lindauer and Simon 1995; Simon 1997; Simon, ed. 1997) as were the majority of the undecorated ceramics. Certainly, there were influences from other culture areas as well (Nelson and LeBlanc 1986; Rice, ed. 1990), especially the Hohokam area in the Phoenix Basin (Wood 1987).

The routes connecting different areas functioned as cultural corridors (Hensler 1994; Wood, Chapter 5), that facilitated the exchange of information as well as goods by means of social contacts established through trade

partnerships, intermarriage, and ceremonial ties among adjacent communities located along these routes (Zedeño 1994). In the archaeological record, the presence of intrusive materials, such as nonlocal decorated ceramics or obsidian, are evidence of down-the-line exchange among individuals or direct procurement, which require both social and physical passage through others' territories. Access to raw materials and goods inevitably involved social contact through networks of association and alliances by establishing social bonds through marriage or other social or ceremonial affiliations.

During the Classic period large areas of the Colorado Plateau were abandoned, and groups from the Four Corners and Tusayan-Kayenta areas moved to the south and east. Evidence of these migrations, forced by deteriorating environmental conditions and failed resource bases, is widely recognized at archaeological sites along the Upper Little Colorado and in the eastern Arizona mountains. For example, the Maverick Mountain component at the Point of Pines Ruin is interpreted as a major incursion by Anasazi people into the White Mountains (Haury 1958). Grasshopper Pueblo is an example of habitation by local Mogollon and migrant Anasazi populations (Haury 1986; Reid 1989).

However, local populations of the central Arizona lands into which these immigrants moved were faced with an influx of people and had to deflect these groups, be displaced, or allow them to share their land and resources. At various locations, the outcome may have included any or all of these scenarios, all of which are centered on the issue of access to, and control of land and resources. The first two outcomes require total control by either the local people or the immigrants, with the other group displaced or driven out of the area. The last option requires mediation of access to and control of land and resources by two or more groups sharing the same area.

COOPERATION OR CONFLICT

Informal networks of social ties, if not kin ties, linked communities throughout much of central Arizona (Burton et al. 1994; Hensler 1994; Simon and Ravesloot 1995), a pattern no doubt typical of much of the Greater Southwest. In times of subsistence stress, which was pervasive on the Colorado Plateau in the early Classic period, these cultural corridors probably funneled movements of displaced groups, as well as materials and information, into more favorable subsistence locations. The modes of social interaction in place among local populations were probably not sufficient to cope with direct influxes of large numbers of outsiders. These pressures forced further expansion and elaboration of the existing social system to cope with the increased size and diversity of the population and to contain conflict. Changes in social organization that allowed integration of nonkin groups and that mediated potential and imminent disputes over prime agricultural land and access to water and wild resources were necessary if the local populations were to maintain control of the subsistence base.

The abandonment of much of the Anasazi region on the Colorado Plateau and migration of populations to locales along the upper Little Colorado River and locations farther south (notably Grasshopper Pueblo and Point of Pines) is well documented in the archaeological record. Until recently, less emphasis was placed on the impacts of these population movements on the local populations and their subsequent reactions. These situations are not unique to the Classic period or to central Arizona and the resulting confrontations have only a few possible outcomes; 1) the local people can expel the migrants, 2) the local people can be ousted by the migrants, 3) the two groups can live in conflict, or 4) the two groups can live cooperatively. Various social strategies are used in these outcomes, ranging from warfare or raiding to competition or selective inclusion.

Given the relatively high frequencies of intrusive ceramics from the Colorado Plateau recovered from sites in Tonto Basin (Hensler 1994; Lindauer and Simon 1995, 1996; Simon 1997), western Pueblo ethnographies, among others, are appropriate as sources for modeling community interactions in the past. Connelly (1979) noted that clusters of settlements form communities on the Hopi mesas and that the social bonds among these villages are orchestrated through ceremonial participation. The level of ceremonial participation, control in scheduling activities, and access to prime agricultural land and resources is justified by sequence of arrival. In this organizational scheme, there are original mother villages, secondary colony villages, and tertiary satellite villages.

The first, or *mother* village, is often the longest occupied and may have a limited population (Connelly 1979), with some two and three story structures present. This village has custody of the major ceremonies, handling scheduling and participation. Inhabitants of this village

also control and manage access to land, water, and residence areas.

A second *colony* village houses surplus population that is necessary for the successful performance of the ceremonies (Connelly 1979). Inhabitants of this village are dependent on the mother village for initiations into the religious societies. The villages are bound together through ceremonial obligation. The physical and social distance of the colony village protects the ceremonial rights and status of the first village.

A third type of village may form a *satellite* (Connelly 1979) whose inhabitants' presence is allowed in exchange for their role as guards of the other villages. The guard village may be composed of outsiders or even another language group. The warrior role is without prestige, but the bilingual skills of these villagers facilitate their service as interpreters and buffers. In return they are allowed to settle in the area and gain access to the socioreligious activities of the larger community. Through this mutual agreement, outsiders are accommodated, although kept at a physical and social distance.

Connelly (1979:542) noted times of warfare and pressure from outside groups in which the surplus population of colony and satellite villages was allowed to settle within the mother community. The aggregation of the extended community enhanced protection from hostilities advanced by outside groups. However, internal pressures and competitive religious ceremonies and groupings led to fission in the community (Connelly 1979:542; Simmons 1979) and the ousting or departure of various groups.

An ethnographic example of competition for agricultural lands occurred in northern Mexico where the Tarahumara interacted with chabochis (non-Indians) when nonagricultural pursuits (mining) by the non-Indians failed (Merrill 1983:295). The two groups resided next to each other, but lived in separate settlements. The relations between the two groups were superficial with most contacts between them confined to the economic sphere. Each group held a negative view of the other, intermarriage was discouraged, and few friendships developed. There was conflict where the chabochis displaced the Tarahumara from the better agricultural land.

Among the Tarahumara (Merrill 1983:290–91), the basis of social organization is the nuclear family, but groups of extended families joined each other during part of the year and at other times scattered to farm dispersed family-owned plots. The population tends crops between the planting and harvesting seasons (Merrill 1983:291). In the off season, they travel to population centers to sell or trade items such as medicinal plants, textiles, and baskets and to obtain other goods through work as laborers while sharing in the residents' resources of food and other goods.

Communal gatherings sponsored by one or more households provide the social interaction for both men and women (Merrill 1983:293), bringing bilateral kin groups and potential exogamous marriage partners together. The sponsors of these social gatherings decide who is invited (Merrill 1983:293), but various neighbors' guest lists overlap to some extent, which results in a general network of household-centered interaction across the area. The motivation for hosting the gathering is usually to obtain assistance with planting maize or to stage a ritual, and alcohol is offered to compensate the visitors for their help. The gatherings feature home brewed maize beer made in quantities of ten to more than 100 gallons. Within this social context, community affairs are discussed, interpersonal conflicts expressed, and marriages arranged.

MULTIPLE ETHNIC INTERACTIONS

We can infer that social dynamics in the past were at least as intricate as those documented in the historic period and that prehistoric society was often equally heterogeneous. Ethnographic studies (Albers 1993; Moore 1994:931; Rodman 1992) have highlighted the diverse elements in nearly all societies. Many types of interethnic social organizations exist that are based on alliances, polyethnic coresidence, and fused ethnicity. It is obvious that variations in language, marriage partners, traditions, and material culture are normal rather than exceptions.

The characterization of Salado ethnic identity and measurement of social complexity are difficult archaeological issues. Rice et al. (1992) have stressed that a biocultural approach is needed to address the issue of ethnicity in an archaeological context. Different variables may be used to investigate interregional relationships and similarities; these variables include genetic affinity, material culture traditions, social organization, and ideological participation.

Whittlesey and Reid (1982) argue that groups traditionally designated as Sinagua, Salado, and other central mountain peoples are more closely related to Mogollon Pueblo than to Hohokam. They state that the low proportions of Hohokam decorated ceramics in Tonto Basin indicate that these were obtained through trade

rather than a Hohokam presence. They note that the distribution of corrugated ceramics is unusually uneven in both temporal and spatial settings, but that these ceramics are often part of the heterogeneous assemblages they term Mogollon. However, genetic distance studies of human remains (Rice et al. 1992) indicate that the population of Tonto Basin is a combination of people from the Hohokam areas to the west and the Mogollon regions to the east.

Material culture traditions expressed in assemblages of ceramics, other artifacts, and architecture indicate that Hohokam and Mogollon influences are present along with the local indigenous traditions. Analysis of the RPMS ceramic collection (Lindauer and Simon 1996; Simon 1994a, 1994b, 1994c, 1994d, 1994e, 1997; ed. 1997; Simon and Lindauer 1997) shows that the indigenous ceramic traditions, including plain ware and Salado Red, are maintained throughout the Classic period, in the presence of intrusive decorated types and the development of Salado polychrome ceramics. Ceramic composition indicates shifts in the production of certain wares from the Sierra Ancha and the slopes of the Mogollon Rim to Tonto Basin. Salado Red and plain corrugated are two cases in point, with Salado Red more common at sites along Tonto Creek and plain corrugated more common at sites along the Salt River. These markedly different wares are indicative of the different ceramic traditions and their different cultural origins that became major elements of the Salado ceramic assemblages (Simon et al. 1992; Stark and Heidke 1994).

VALIDATION OF SOCIAL ORDER

Economies and social organizations of prestate societies are usually based on a generalized form of reciprocity of goods and services (Redman 1991:279–80), which at some point changes to an asymmetrical arrangement, with surplus on one side and unequal exchange on the other. Emergent forms of social complexity are based on group interdependence and those who enhance the legitimacy of the new social order. In egalitarian societies, prestige may be acquired by as many individuals as there are age and sex classifications (Fried 1967; Redman 1991:277; Service 1962, 1975), but in ranked societies there is limited access to status, which is based on birth order, family, economic factors, or access to special knowledge. In stratified societies, differential relationships become institutionalized.

The mechanisms of social relations are based on group interdependence (Redman 1991:279). Factors in the balance of interdependence may include productive specialization, exchange of goods, and control of new knowledge. Increased emphasis on the scales and intensities of these factors allow certain groups to exert influence or control over others provided they have a sufficient support base among the population. A convincing ideology asserts and validates an otherwise unfair allocation of power and resources and diverts conflict from those who hold the advantage (Redman 1991:279). Some elements of the belief system are made public to foster participation, but other rituals are performed in seclusion (Brandt 1980). Selective access to special knowledge provides the means by which group membership is controlled and by which certain groups elevate their position of power. The interdependencies among groups with growing asymmetries can be tracked through the growth, maintenance, and retraction of their belief systems (Redman 1991:280).

Religion is one of the major organizing mechanisms of societies (Lessa and Vogt 1972:1–2) as it incorporates social, political, economic, and cosmological knowledge into an integrated whole that explains and justifies social organization and order in the society and the larger world. Religious practices are expressions of political ideas (Bauer 1996:327; Friedrich 1989:301) including strategies, tactics, and practical symbols for promoting, perpetuating, and changing social order. The ritual calendar is tied directly to the agricultural calendar (Bauer 1996:328), and rituals focus on the powers of reproduction. Those who control access to resources, land, and labor often have the ability to schedule, lead, and participate in ceremonies (Bauer 1996:334). The mythology that is reified through ritual performances provides the context in which social order is defined. Through ceremony, basic social relationships are expressed and current arrangements are endorsed. Ceremonies provide the access to natural and universal forces and integrate these within broader social processes.

RANKED LINEAGES

The contemporaneous presence of both platform mounds and compound walled settlements in Tonto Basin is evidence of functional differences among sites (Rice et al. 1992). Further, more elaborate treatment of certain individuals at the platform mounds and certain compounds indicates differences in status within lineages (Rice et al. 1992; Simon and Ravesloot 1995). Although changes in environment may have been a prime factor in the movements of people during the Classic period, the nature of group relationships must be looked at to determine causal factors (Redman 1991:291) for the integrating mechanism that bridges social divisions and organizes society.

Based on biological and cultural evidence, the Classic period population of Tonto Basin was heterogeneous. Differences in architecture, artifact assemblages, and mortuary treatment indicate a degree of social differentiation among these settlements. Analogy to ethnographic examples among the Hopi, Zuni, and Pima is used to model social organization based on ranked segmentary lineages (Rice et al. 1992; Rice, Chapter 6). Moiety systems (Adams 1991:121) may have been an earlier social mechanism for integrating large populations into villages based on segmentary lineages. Ranking provides the mechanism for assigning status within and among kin groups based on seniority ("elder brother"). Ranking of clans and phratries is related to sequence of arrival, which in turn determines access to agricultural land and resources. This mechanism maintains continuity in social relationships and allows flexibility to restructure power and authority. Although kin groups are largely autonomous and self sufficient, under certain conditions these groups can amalgamate into larger social units. Rapid social change is possible in these situations.

Not only does a ranked segmentary lineage model explain the mechanism of partitioning and ordering groups within the society, it explains the flexibility whereby new groups (migrants) can be included in the social structure, albeit at its lowest ranks. The political and economic framework of the society is manipulated within the rankings of the lineages and explained through ideology. The ranking of the clans and phratries is associated with certain cardinal directions and iconography of the belief system, but pragmatically is based on the arrival sequence and access to prime agricultural lands and resources. The ranking of social units is corroborated through the ideational system; the differential access to land, resources, and ritual knowledge reifies the central beliefs.

MECHANISMS OF SOCIAL MEDIATION

Religious ideology serves integrative functions for groups and individuals (Lessa and Vogt 1972:1–2) and explains and expresses the belief system of the society as well as the sacred or supernatural power that stands behind social values. Religion maintains the basic beliefs and manages tensions and anxieties, thus providing defensive functions by providing ways to manage threats to societal values. In the case of Classic period social dynamics, and the Salado phenomenon in particular, the crisis caused by migrant population inrush, the resultant need of resident populations to keep control of their lands and resources, and the stresses on migrant populations who have deserted their lands and ancestors, results in the development of a religious cult.

Tonto Basin and much of central Arizona are resource rich, based on a diverse resource base and access to many ecozones within a short distance (Rice 1990c:32–33). The various populations that inhabited central Arizona in the Classic period followed cultural corridors into Tonto Basin and other riverine areas. Economic activities, the circulation of goods and services, along boundaries allows the opening of barriers between groups (Barth 1963, 1967). Regional systems, such as Chaco and Hohokam (Crown and Judge 1991:306), are defined in terms of economic interaction and are marked by stylistic unity that is greater within the concentrated core than outside of it. However, the central Arizona settlements, particularly Salado platform mound complexes, exhibit considerable diversity of style throughout the region.

Regional cults are based on ideology and iconography and are mechanisms of social mediation. Crown (1994:214–15) notes that regional cults characteristically are focused on earth, fertility and the relationships of the local community and these natural forces. Symbols of earth and fertility (Crown 1994:215) include icons of the sun, Venus, stars, flowers, sky, clouds, lightning, precipitation, and wind. Shrines are often established in different ecozones and pilgrimages are made to the peripheries of regional territory. Regional cults can cooccur with death cults and political cults but function to unite rather than divide people.

The wide distribution and acceptance of the "Southwestern Regional Cult" (Crown 1994:211–14) was brought about by the direct interaction of different populations following abandonment of the San Juan Basin and migration to already populated areas in the mountains and along the river valleys. Participation in the cult was signaled by the presence of Pinedale style pottery, particularly Salado polychrome vessels. Crown (1994:211–12) identifies the Pinedale style as a true horizon style that crosscuts many of the ceramic wares of the Southwest, and symbolizes an ideology that allows participation by diverse groups over a broad area.

Crown (1994:218) points out that although the imagery (masks and parrots, in particular) on pottery is new, this is not their first appearance. The icons were previously present in the culture and were part of a unified belief system. The flower world complex and use of masks have been documented among both Piman speakers and pueblos (Crown 1994:225) but are absent among Yuman speakers. Crown (1994:222) suggests that various forms based on Mimbres imagery coalesced into the later Southwestern Regional Cult in the late 1200s, but additionally claims that it is unlikely there was a direct evolution of the Mimbres cult of the dead into the Southwestern Regional Cult.

REGIONAL CULTS AND COMMUNITY INTERACTION

The Katsina Cult is an example of a regional cult that developed and spread throughout much of the Southwest during this period. Adams (1991:22) points to the east (Mimbres/Jornada) and southeast (Casas Grandes) for the origins of the Katsina Cult and tracks its spread from the Upper Little Colorado region in the late 1200s or 1300s through the Salado of central Arizona into the Hohokam area, in the fourteenth century. Adams (1991:96) recognizes an early style (Fourmile), marked by bird and parrot motifs and symmetrical layouts that have curvilinear interlocks, and a classic late style (Pinedale) that maintains these elements but has asymmetric layouts in centered designs. Masked figures and mythological beings appear on pottery after 1325.

In pueblo society, the different elements (social, political, ritual, and economic) are interrelated and must all be orchestrated to achieve stability. Although pueblo culture maintains its balance through adaptive change and cooperative behavior (Adams 1991:150), there are also elements of conflict and retribution. The development of the Katsina Cult enhanced the secret knowledge of the leadership as the major basis of authority (Adams 1991:155); it functioned as a social mechanism for the integration of immigrant and indigenous people because it crosscut existing public rituals and allowed all males to participate regardless of kinship. The religious leaders (Adams 1991:158–59) are also the political leaders who construct and maintain communal projects, distribute community food stores, and trade ritual knowledge with other villages. Membership in the warrior society, which protects the village from internal and external threats (Adams 1991:156), is separate from the Katsina society.

In the Classic period, new integrative systems were needed by village leaders to integrate diverse populations (Adams 1991:126). Ceremonies that involve the community demand cooperation and allow individuals to become essential elements of the whole. Rituals become more integrative as parts of them are made accessible to the public, for example, by performing these in an enclosed plaza where they can be viewed (Adams 1991:109). Rectangular ceremonial rooms in room blocks were probably nonpublic ritual staging areas (Adams 1991:125). Private ceremonies allowed ritual knowledge to be controlled by religious leaders, public ceremonies involved all segments of a village in cooperative and integrative activities. Integration is achieved and maintained through ceremonial cooperation focused on ritual performances based on central beliefs of the afterlife, ancestors becoming cloud people, rain and fertility.

Adams (1991:103) suggests that after 1300 there was a new social dynamic in the form of ritual specialization and the development of distinctive iconography. The change in design conventions to asymmetric layouts is the key to the development of mask styles. Architectural forms change with the use of rectangular ceremonial rooms and enclosed plazas rather than round kivas. The shoe pot form, piki stones, and rectangular ceramic vessels are part of this complex (Adams 1991:103). Gila and Tonto Polychromes are seen as products of the interaction between northern and southern groups as a result of population shifts (Adams 1991:98–100). The manufacture and exchange of Salado polychrome united different ethnic groups into "Salado Culture" (Adams 1991:131) and provided the economic and symbolic means to link the Salado regional system (Adams 1991:131).

MOTIF AND DESIGN IN ICONOGRAPHY

Motifs on pottery vessels, as well as other media such as murals, textiles, and wooden artifacts, are recognized as icons of prehistoric ideologies (Adams 1991; Crown 1994; Pauketat and Emerson 1991). The symbolism displayed on pottery must be highly visible and understandable to the community members to assure widespread participation (Pauketat and Emerson 1991:919–20). Broadly painted designs make the icons visible at a distance and signal the owner's participation in the belief system. The relatively homogeneous style, as it reoccurs on pottery, would have had use in calendrical rites, community fo-

cused ceremonies concerning agricultural productivity and fertility (Emerson 1989:47). The vessels may have served as containers for consumable solid or liquid products that were amassed and distributed as part of communal gatherings.

A variety of ideological interpretations and social negotiations are mediated in ritual activities (Bloch 1989; Pauketat and Emerson 1991:920). Ideologies are dynamic entities that express the values and belief system in ceremonies and transfer these through ritual objects. The few with ritual and cosmological knowledge act as mediators between the community and the uncontrolled forces of the natural world. Ideology is perpetuated and spread to the larger community through ceremonies sponsored by those with religious and political power, which ensures their continued success (Pauketat and Emerson 1991:920–22).

We interpret the regional ideology as an ancestor worship cult that evolved to categorize immigrants as kin and to allow the participation of nonkin as peripheral relatives. The boldness and visibility of icons becomes part of the survival strategy to promote the symbols of the belief system and encourage all to participate. Motifs and icons that may have been secret (e.g., kiva murals) became public and used on pottery and other media. The sharing of certain icons acts as an integrative mechanism to pull in the other members of the extended community. But there is still a secretive component, in which a select few control ritual knowledge and store ceremonial items in places with restricted access. Ideology and iconography are used to maintain the belief system, legitimize power and status, and to ensure concurrent control of calendrical rites and access to land and resources.

SALADO POLYCHROME

Several researchers have noted the commonalities between Classic Mimbres ceramic style and that of the later Salado polychromes (Crown 1994:221; LeBlanc and Khalil 1976; Nelson and LeBlanc 1986:13), although there are still unanswered questions related to the temporal gap between the two and influence from the development of Casas Grandes. Mimbres phase pottery (1000–1150) is most often associated with large pueblos in the Mimbres Valley (Gilman et al. 1994:695–96) and is generally recognized as a mortuary ware, with over 50 percent of the burials being accompanied by a Classic Mimbres Black-on-white bowl. Based on compositional analysis and comparison of frequencies among sites, Gilman et al. (1994:695, 706) propose that the production and distribution of Mimbres decorated ceramics were not centralized or controlled, but that it was produced in a number of different settlements both in the valley and at its periphery.

There are similarities in the motifs and design layouts between Mimbres and the later Salado polychromes (Crown 1994:221). On hemispherical bowls (LeBlanc and Khalil 1976), the design zone is separated from the rim by one or more concentric bands located below the rim, but the design zone on flared rim bowls is on the rim and concentric bands are located below the design. Mimbres style motifs and layouts drop out of use and then reappear as icons associated with the Pinedale style, indicating the spread of a regional cult (Crown 1994:221). Whereas the earlier Mimbres ceramics are primarily associated with mortuary assemblages, the later Salado polychromes are found in a broad range of contexts, used essentially as a plain ware with a painted interior.

The Pinedale style symbolism, expressed through shared icons related to the agricultural calendar, was general enough to integrate diverse ethnicities in different farming environments without offending or excluding others. This iconography is widespread and is repeated on Salado polychrome and in other media. The Pinedale style (Crown 1994:212) represents spiritual continuity in the belief system across much of the Southwest. Crown (1994:169–70) states that Salado polychrome imagery represents a narrow set of themes that are part of a unified belief system focused on imagery of water and sun, weather and fertility.

LIFELINE:
LINK TO MIMBRES

Pinto Polychrome is distinguished from Gila and Tonto Polychrome on the basis of design; the latter have a lifeline (a broad framing line including a line break) just below the interior rim of bowls. Lifelines also are present on jars, usually around the neck of the vessel. The percentage of ceramics with lifelines is greater for Tonto Polychrome (71 percent) than Gila Polychrome (59 percent), with none present on Pinto Polychrome (Crown 1994:74).

Shafer and Brewington (1995:17–20) describe the appearance of a framing line on Mimbres Black-on-white pottery, documenting a shift from designs suspended from a broad line below the interior bowl rim in Late

Style II (ca. 970–1020) and multiple, fine framing lines in Style II/III (ca. 970–1020) to unattached broad rim and bottom framing lines in the Middle Style III (ca. 1060 to 1110), with the most common framing scheme two wide lines. The sequence of these Mimbres design styles includes numerous exceptions where combinations occur (Shafer and Brewington 1995:17).

Salado polychrome design styles are equally complex, although a general sequence of style changes is apparent in the comparison of Pinto, Gila, and Tonto Polychrome (Crown 1994:88–89, Figure 5.43). Jars, more often than bowls, offer the opportunity for designs both above and below lifelines (Crown 1994:90, Table 5.1).

INTERLOCKING AND
ASYMMETRICAL SCROLLS

Salado polychrome style contains many examples of dualism where motifs and design elements are placed opposite each other, or twinned (Figures 8.1 and 8.2, particularly Figure 8.2a and 8.2b). Scrolls (Figure 8.1c) appear early in the ceramic traditions of the Hohokam and others. Haury (1936:24) claims that the scroll, as well as life forms and layout, on Mimbres pottery was borrowed from the Hohokam. The early scrolls may represent a whole social unit that has two components, visually represented by positive and negative space.

The earliest transformation from scroll to interlocking scroll in Hohokam design seems to reflect an awareness of the distinctness and separability of the two components of the society. Pre-Gila phase interlocking scrolls, on some Cibola White Wares and other types, are symmetrical and of similar size, although they were differentiated visually (i.e., one solid and the other hatched).

The shift to asymmetrical designs in the Gila phase is significant both in iconography and for its social implications (Figures 8.3 and 8.4; compare Figure 8.3a to Figures 8.3f and 8.3h). Asymmetry is a distinguishing feature of Gila and Tonto Polychrome motifs and layout. The design elements are not always balanced in size and elaboration. Crown (1994:172–73) recorded a high proportion of design "errors" (74 percent) defined as deliberate inconsistencies; for example, different elaboration of dual or twinned motifs (e.g., Figure 8.4d, f, g). Interlocking scrolls on some Salado polychrome vessels are asymmetrical (Figure 8.3f and 8.3h) in size and elaboration (Crown 1994:140).

Figure 8.1.   Vessels associated with
Burial 17 from the Cline Terrace Mound
(Roosevelt 5:10), Arizona State Museum,
Gila Pueblo numbers in parentheses:
(a) Gila Polychrome bowl (GP11282);
(b) Gila Polychrome bowl (GP11283);
(c) Tonto Polychrome jar (GP11286);
(d) Tonto Polychrome parrot effigy jar
(GP11287); (e) Salado Red jar (GP11288);
(f) Salado Red bowl (GP11265).

Figure 8.2.   Additional vessels
associated with Burial 17 from the
Cline Terrace Mound (Roosevelt
5:10), Arizona State Museum, Gila
Pueblo numbers in parentheses:
(a) Gila Polychrome bowl
(GP11285); (b) Gila Polychrome
bowl (GP11281); (c) Tonto Polychrome bowl (GP11284).

Figure 8.3. Vessels from the Cline Terrace Mound (Roosevelt 5:10), Arizona State Museum, illustrating the variation in styles and symmetrical and asymmetrical designs within a multiple burial feature: (a) from Burial 12, upper individual, an additional bowl of Sikyatki Polychrome (GP11270) was not available for illustration; (b-h) from Burial 12, lower individual. Vessel listing with Gila Pueblo numbers in parentheses: (a) Gila Polychrome bowl (GP11269); (b) Salado White-on-red jar (GP11252); (c) Gila Polychrome bowl (GP11259); (d) Gila Polychrome bowl (GP11264); (e) Gila Polychrome bowl (GP11255); (f) Gila Polychrome bowl (GP11253); (g) Gila Polychrome bowl (GP11254); (h) Gila Polychrome bowl (GP11262).

Figure 8.4.
Additional vessels associated with Burial 12, lower individual, from the Cline Terrace Mound (Roosevelt 5:10), Arizona State Museum. Vessel listing with Gila Pueblo numbers in parentheses:
(a) Tonto Polychrome jar (GP11268); (b) Gila Polychrome bowl (GP11257-X-1); (c) Gila Polychrome bowl (GP11261); (d) Tonto Polychrome jar (GP11266); (e) Gila Polychrome bowl (GP11257-X-2); (f) Gila Polychrome bowl (GP11265); (g) Tonto Polychrome jar (GP11267); (h) Gila Polychrome bowl (GP11258); (i) Gila Polychrome bowl (GP11262).

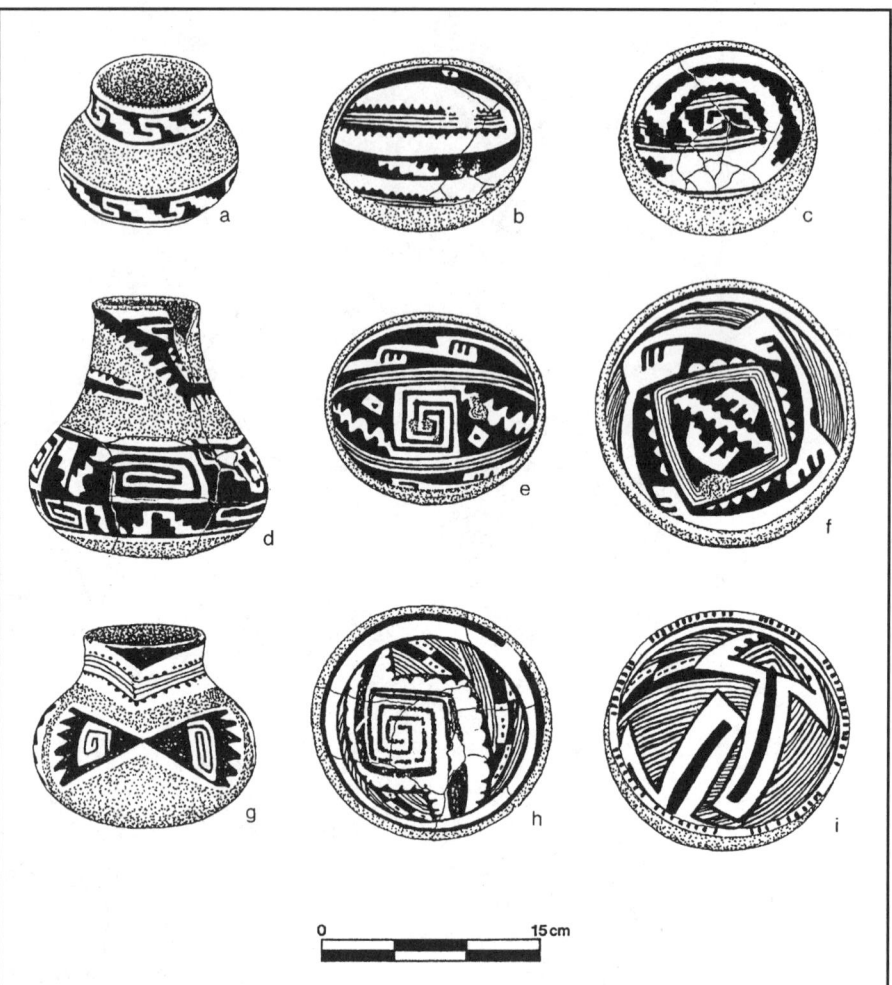

The asymmetries of Gila phase ceramic motifs developed from this earlier social differentiation and coincided with the final expression of the platform mound complexes. Asymmetrical interlocking scrolls on Salado polychrome signify social asymmetries and validate their presence, where in earlier times only social difference was acknowledged through symmetrical designs.

ASSOCIATIONS OF INDIVIDUALS

Most social interaction takes place on a personal level, consequently, analysis of burial assemblages is one of the most relevant and revealing ways to learn about past social organization. Simon and Ravesloot (1995) and others (Whittlesey 1978) have proposed that burial accompaniments are not just personal possessions, but may include gifts that signify social obligations to the deceased. This interpretation is supported by ethnographic examples, such as that provided by Titiev (1944:195–96) (Table 8.1), regarding important life stages and gifts of garments made for the boy, or girl, by their father or grandfather. He notes many instances in which these garments are essential to the afterlife and that the person would be buried in these if they should pass on at that age. In adolescence and adulthood, these garments (Table 8.1), and presumably other accompaniments, may be provided by those recognizing ceremonial ties to the individual. Thus, both the contributions of consanguineal kin and ceremonial relations may be reflected in the material record.

Table 8.1. Clothing Items Related to Important Stages of Hopi Life

First 20 Days of Life	
Baby Boy	*Baby Girl*
Black, or black and grey	Striped horizontally and vertically
cotton blanket	blanket-like garment
Made by father, grandfather	Made by father, grandfather

Prior to Katsina Initiation	
Boy Child (8 or 9 years)	*Girl Child (8 or 9 years)*
Black (later indigo blue)	Black natural wool
G-string like garment	Dress-like garment
Two concentric circle design at ends	Blue stripe along upper edge
For Snake or Flute dance	Regular wear
* worn if died, otherwise naked in afterlife	
Made by father, grandfather	Made by father, grandfather

After Katsina Initiation	
Adolescent Boy	*Adolescent Girl*
Dance Skirt	Garment
* worn if died before maturity	Worn to first dance after completion
Made by father or ceremonial father	Made by grandfather

Other Occasions	
Tribal Initiation	*Adult Woman (Adolescence and on)*
Garment converted to dance kilt	Manta, left shoulder bare
	Worn everyday

Mature Man (35-40 years)	*Bridal Robes*
Garment between G-string and kilt	Marriage
All blue, three parallel black stripes at ends	First Niman dance after Wedding
Two stripes at center	* essential for happiness in the afterlife
Worn for daily activities, rehearsals	
*worn in the other world	
Made by himself	

(based on Titiev 1944:195-96)
*garments essential to the afterlife

Table 8.2. General Order of Hopi Social Attachments to Relatives and Marriage Rules

Order	Relationship	Marriage Rules
1	One's parents, brothers and sisters	incest taboo
2	Mother's sisters and their children	incest taboo
3	Other members of own household	incest taboo
4	Father's household	incest taboo
5	Other members of own clan	tolerated
6	Other members of own phratry	tolerated
7	Other members of father's clan-phratry	tolerated
8	Ceremonial father's clan-phratry	preferred
9	Doctor father's clan-phratry	preferred

(based on Titiev 1944:13-14)

In Titiev's (1944) study of Old Oraibi, he notes that the natal household is the core unit of the society. From birth to maturation, an individual accumulates expanding spheres of associations (Connelly 1979; Titiev 1944:13–14) (Table 8.2). In childhood, this is generally restricted to members of the maternal household and the father's household. Marriage is not allowed with consanguineal kin, establishing a rule of exogamy. In adolescence, an individual is initiated into religious societies, thus expanding the sphere of associates (Table 8.2). Operational kin ties are extended to members of clan-phratries (Connelly 1979), thus expanding the boundaries of exogamy beyond these associations. In adulthood, marriage is preferred with a member of the clan-phratry of a ceremonial parent (Connelly 1979; Titiev 1944), thus establishing bonds through marriage alliances. These preferred partners provide a mechanism to further reinforce the ceremonial cooperation that binds puebloan society together (Lamphere 1983; Ortiz 1972).

An example of a social network was recognized from the interpretation of the ceramic burial accompaniments of a Roosevelt phase cemetery at V:5:119 (Simon and Ravesloot 1995), in the Livingston area of Tonto Basin. In this instance, a young woman (Feature 18) had been interred with a large number of vessels. Acid extraction ICP analysis of ceramics (Burton and Simon 1993) from these features and surrounding residential contexts identified a pattern in the distribution of compositional groups (Simon and Ravesloot 1995:121, Table 4). The set of vessels with the young woman represented nearly all of the compositional groups. The few vessel accompaniments with other individuals were assigned to some of these groups. The vessels with the young woman represent the common tie of the cemetery and indicate that her role in the community was distinguished by considerable social status and obligations from others (Simon and Ravesloot 1995:Table 2).

In an expansion of this study (Lindauer and Simon 1995; Simon 1994b; Simon and Ravesloot 1995), we found that certain compositional units were associated with young children and infants. These same units were commonly associated with adults as well. But other compositional units were almost exclusive to adults. Our interpretation of this finding was that the more common units found with all age groups signify the core social unit, whereas other compositional units may signify broader social bonds, including ceremonial affiliations.

A comparison of Roosevelt phase cemeteries at V:5:119 and the Schoolhouse Point Mound (U:8:24) found that this pattern was consistent, but that the common compositional units were site specific (Simon and Ravesloot 1995:121, Table 4). These associations of compositional units persisted into the later Gila phase at Schoolhouse Point Mound, although in this later instance, another compositional unit marked by Salado polychrome ceramics is associated with certain individuals of all age groups.

The emphasis on kin ties and ceremonial networks within the settlements supports the interpretation that socioceremonial structure was the major organizing principle of these prehistoric villages (Connelly 1979; Lamphere 1983; Ortiz 1972). It follows that economic and subsistence activities were structured within this context (Connelly 1979; Titiev 1944).

SALADO POLYCHROME AND ARCHITECTURE AT THE CLINE TERRACE MOUND

Both Crown (1994:212) and Adams (1991) conclude that there was a strong interaction between the producers of Salado polychrome and Hopi Yellow Ware based on the presence of all four layout/design styles (i.e., Pinedale, Roosevelt, Gila, and Tusayan-Kayenta) in both of these wares, but absent from contemporaneous White Mountain Red Ware. These differences may have stemmed from stronger economic, ancestral, or linguistic ties between Hopi and Salado populations (Crown 1994:212). It has been suggested (Crown 1994:213) that Kayenta-Tusayan immigrants produced unusual pottery to provide an economic service to local villages that controlled agricultural land.

There is considerable evidence for local manufacture of various pottery types at sites in Tonto Basin, including Salado polychrome, which would argue that outsiders may have contributed significantly to the diversification of ceramic technology (Simon 1994a; Simon et al. 1992; Stark and Heidke 1994) but that they were not solely responsible for the manufacture of decorated and other ceramics. Aside from the interpretation of a regional cult, it is difficult to characterize such interactions, but one technique is to categorize burial assemblages by wares that cooccur because these assemblages are important indicators of social networks (Simon and Ravesloot 1995; Tainter 1978; Whittlesey 1978).

The RPMS recovered only a few intact Gila phase burials from the platform mound sites because previous excavation and vandalism had targeted these features at the large sites. Fortunately, a large number of vessels obtained by Gila Pueblo in the 1930s are curated at the Arizona State Museum. These collections are important sources for comparative burial accompaniment and ceramic studies (Ravesloot 1994a:69), providing data on the number of burials and general trends in the variability of ceramic mortuary accompaniments. Our discussion focuses on the ceramic burial accompaniments from the Cline Terrace Mound (U:4:33), cataloged in the Gila Pueblo collection as Roosevelt 5:10. Many of these vessels are illustrated in Crown (1994), but Roosevelt 5:10 is referred to as Angler's Inn.

Nine Gila phase burials were recovered by RPMS excavation on the elevated plazas of the Cline Terrace Mound, with 20 additional burials recovered from the ground level plaza areas of the site. A group of six burials was recovered from elevated Plaza 67 near the southwest corner of the mound (Loendorf 1997). Among these, an adult (Feature 105, male?) and an infant (Feature 109) were buried together. Feature 105 was accompanied by a Tonto Polychrome jar, a Gila Polychrome bowl, fragments of an azurite and ocher-coated wooden bow, and three projectile points. A red/plain jar was placed near the infant. Feature 158, an adult, was accompanied by two red/smudged bowls and two Salado Red

bowls. Feature 66, a three-six year old child, had one Salado Red jar, but Feature 125, an adult male, had only a shell bracelet fragment. Burial Feature 90, the lower of two individuals recovered from elevated Plaza 88 at the northwestern end of the mound was accompanied by a Salado Red jar, whereas the upper individual (Feature 89) had no ceramic accompaniments.

These burials are significant in that they are Gila phase burials on top of the mound and the ceramic accompaniments are similar to many of the features from this site in the Gila Pueblo collection. Features 90, 158, and 66 indicate that not all had decorated ceramic accompaniments; therefore, those burials in the Gila Pueblo collection that have plain and Salado Red vessels, but no decorated ceramics, are not necessarily restricted to the Roosevelt phase. It is also of note that none of the burials recovered by RPMS from the top of the Cline Terrace Mound had Hopi Yellow Ware grave goods, although a few fragmentary Hopi Yellow Ware vessels were recovered from some elevated plazas and rooms on the mound (Simon 1997).

The Gila Pueblo vessel collection from the Cline Terrace Mound (Roosevelt 5:10) includes portions of burial assemblages from 67 burial pits associated with at least 74 individuals. Salado polychrome totals 79 percent of the decorated vessels in this burial collection (Simon 1996) and is the dominant decorated ware. Unfortunately, Gila Pueblo records do not indicate age, sex, or stature of the individuals or the locations where burials were obtained in the site. Loendorf (1997:13.29) notes that, compared to undisturbed burials recovered during RPMS excavations, the Gila Pueblo collection from the Cline Terrace Mound may be biased toward decorated ceramics and that other artifact classes (e.g., ceramic disks, quartz crystals, pigments, painted sticks) may be underrepresented.

Despite the unknown quality of the Gila Pueblo collection, it documents associations of ceramic vessels with particular burial features. Several features had multiple burials (i.e., more than one individual was interred in the same feature) with the individual at the bottom receiving the largest number of grave goods (Table 8.4). This practice is consistent with the treatment of other Salado burial populations excavated by the RPMS in Tonto Basin (Loendorf 1996a, 1997). Because the Gila Pueblo collection from the Cline Terrace Mound is a relatively large collection of Gila phase burials, it provides data with which to evaluate the Salado polychrome/Hopi Yellow Ware connection.

Table 8.3. Burial Vessels From The Cline Terrace Mound (Roosevelt 5:10), Gila Pueblo Collection, Arizona State Museum, Grouped By Similar Assemblages (Boxes Highlight Particular Sets of Ceramic Types In Common Among Subgroups Of Burial Features)

Feature	Ceramic Type Frequencies																											Subtotals			
	Gila Red	Salt Red	Gila Red Smudged	Gila/Salt Smudged	Salt Red Smudged	Tonto Plain	Unident. Plain	Tonto Corr.	Unident. Corr.	Reserve Corr.	Salado Red	Salado W/r	Roosevelt B/w	Tularosa B/w	Pinto Poly.	Gila Poly.	Tonto Poly.	Pinedale B/r	Pinedale Poly.	Cedar Creek Poly.	Unident. Poly.	San Carlos R/Br	Awatovi B/y	Bidahochi Poly.	Jeddito B/or	Jeddito B/y	Sikyatki Poly.	Total	Undecorated	Corrugated	Decorated
2											1					2	3				1							7		1	6
17											2					5	2											9		2	7
34	1										1					8	4											14	1	1	12
43											1					4	2				2							9		1	8
58											3					11	2											16		3	13
12L											1	1				13	3				1							19		2	17
20																2	1											3			3
35														1		2	1				3							7			7
45																4	1											5			5
48																5	1											6			6
10U																1												1			1
12U																1											1	2			2
25		1														2										1		4	1		3
31											1					5					1					1		8		1	7
36											1					4					2					1		8		1	7
60	1															4					1					1		7	1		6
19	1										2			1		1					1							6	1	2	3
23											1					1												2		1	1
64						1	1			1	1					7												11	2	2	7
11	1														1													2	1		1
21								1								1					1							3		1	2
63	1		1													1												3	2		1
9																2							1					3			3
13																1								1				2			2
10L																1			1									2			2
18																1												1			1
26																1		1										2			2
57																1												1			1
61																2												2			2
3											2														1			3		2	1
7											1														1			2		1	1
8			1								1											1						3	1	1	1
65																						1				1		2			2
4	1	1									3		1															6	2	3	1
16	1										2		1															4	1	2	1
24				1							1									1								3	1	1	1
5	1	1									1																	3	2	1	
15			1								2																	3	1	2	
28					1						2																	3	1	2	
28U	2		1		1						2																	6	4	2	
33	1		1	1							2																	5	3	2	
37			1								3																	4	1	3	
39					1						6																	7	1	6	
41			1								2																	3	1	2	
42	1										1																	2	1	1	
49				1							2																	3	1	2	
50	2										3																	5	2	3	
52			2								3																	5	2	3	
54			1								1																	2	1	1	
56L		1			1						1																	3	2	1	
59		1	1								1																	3	2	1	
66M	1		1	7							5																	14	9	5	
66L	6		3	1							5	1																16	10	6	
28L											3										1							4		3	1
14											1																	1		1	
22											1																	1		1	
29											1																	1		1	
30											1																	1		1	
32											2																	2		2	
38											1																	1		1	
46											2																	2		2	
47											2																	2		2	
53											1				1						2							3		3	
56M											1																	1		1	
62											1																	1		1	
66U											3																	3		3	
67											2																	2		2	
6	2																						1					3	2		1
40			1																							1		2	1		1
1			1					1	1																			3	3		
27									1																			1	1		
44			1																									1	1		
51	1																											1	1		
55	1	1																										2	2		
Total	25	4	18	10	3	4	6	1	0	1	90	2	2	2	1	92	21	1	1	1	16	2	1	1	2	5	1	313	70	94	149
Percent	8.0	1.3	5.8	3.2	1.0	1.3	1.9	0.3	0.0	0.3	28.8	0.6	0.6	0.6	0.3	29.4	6.7	0.3	0.3	0.3	5.1	0.6	0.3	0.3	0.6	1.6	0.3	100.0	22.4	30.0	47.6

note: U = upper individual, M = middle individual, L = lower individual of a multiple interment

Table 8.4. Vessels from Multiple Burials at the Cline Terrace Mound (Roosevelt 5:10), Gila Pueblo Collection, Arizona State Museum

Feature	Gila Red	Salt Red	Gila Red Smudged	Gila/Salt Smudged	Salt Red Smudged	Tonto Plain	Unident. Plain	Tonto Corr.	Unident. Corr.	Reserve Corr.	Salado Red	Salado W/R	Roosevelt B/W	Tularosa B/W	Pinto Poly.	Gila Poly.	Tonto Poly.	Pinedale B/R	Pinedale Poly.	Cedar Creek Poly.	Unident. Poly.	San Carlos R/Br	Awatovi B/Y	Bidahochi Poly.	Jeddito B/O	Jeddito B/Y	Sikyatki Poly.	Total	Undecorated	Corrugated	Decorated
10U																	1											1			1
10L																1					1							2	0	0	2
12U																1										1		2	0	0	2
12L											1	1				13	3				1							19	0	2	17
28							1				2																	3	1	2	0
28U	2	1					1				2																	6	4	2	0
28L											3								1									4	0	3	1
56M											1																	1	0	1	0
56L		1					1				1																	3	2	1	0
66U											3																	3	0	3	0
66M	1		1		7						5																	14	9	5	0
66L	6	3	1								5	1																16	10	6	0

note: U = upper individual, M = middle individual, L= lower individual
Boxes highlight particular sets of ceramic types shared by subgroups of burial features

The cooccurrences of Salado polychrome, including Gila and Tonto Polychrome, and Hopi Yellow Ware in the Gila Pueblo collection from the Cline Terrace Mound suggest a social distinction between local networks represented by Salado polychrome and outside networks represented by Hopi Yellow Ware (Hensler 1994), perhaps representing the integrative influence of a regional cult (Crown 1994). In the Cline Terrace Mound collection (Table 8.3), Gila Polychrome vessels are associated with 29 individuals, Tonto Polychrome vessels with eleven individuals, and Hopi Yellow Ware with nine individuals. Tonto Polychrome is not found with individuals associated with Hopi Yellow Ware, but Gila Polychrome is associated with either Tonto Polychrome or Hopi Yellow Ware. Hopi Yellow Ware is found without Gila Polychrome, but is sometimes associated with Salado Red ceramics. In a few cases, Gila Polychrome was found without Tonto Polychrome, Hopi Yellow Ware, or Salado Red.

Some motifs on Salado polychromes are repeated on single vessels but also are repeated among associated vessels. The presence of particular motifs depends on the vessel types that are associated with the same feature. For instance, Crown (1994:160–61, Figure 9.30) interprets the double terrace as the bonding of two terraces (clouds). This motif often occurs as a repeated design on vessels and as the only motif other than a life-line (for example,

Figure 8.1a). The double terrace does not occur on Gila Polychrome associated with Hopi Yellow Ware, but does occur on Gila and Tonto Polychromes that were placed together in the absence of Hopi Yellow Ware.

Generally, the Gila Polychrome associated with the Hopi Yellow Ware do not have some of the motifs (such as the stepped terrace diamond) that were probably important in the regional cult and that occur on Gila Polychrome associated with Tonto Polychrome. The stepped terrace diamond motif is on one of the Hopi Yellow Ware associated with a Gila Polychrome. Most Gila Polychrome associated with Hopi Yellow Ware have interlocking symmetrical motifs (Figure 8.3a), but the Hopi Yellow Ware vessels have some asymmetrical interlocking motifs.

The multiple individual burial features in the Gila Pueblo collection offer the opportunity to observe relative status between the Salado polychrome and Hopi Yellow Ware vessels. Burial Feature 12 (Figures 8.3 and 8.4) has the requisite wares and also contained multiple individuals. The lowest individual, who would have the highest rank (Loendorf 1997; Simon and Ravesloot 1995), does not have Hopi Yellow Ware among vessel accompaniments, but has Gila and Tonto Polychrome. In this case, the lowest individual had the largest number of burial accompaniments (Table 8.4), including 13 Gila Polychrome bowls and three

Tonto Polychrome jars. The upper individual had a single Gila Polychrome bowl and one Sikyatki Polychrome jar. None of the other multiple burials in the Gila Pueblo collection or the RPMS collection have Hopi Yellow Wares associated with the lowest individual. These ceramic distributions indicate the strength of the outside network, but the lowest individuals in multiple burials have the most vessels and these are locally produced rather than intrusive. The motifs on the vessels associated with these burials suggest further relationships that crosscut ceramic ware and style categories.

The Cline Terrace Mound burial collections suggest that the local inhabitants (i.e., those people associated with locally produced red wares, Salado Red, and Gila and Tonto Polychrome ceramics) maintained control of the platform mound even though there was a significant outside influence from northern individuals (i.e., those associated with Gila Polychrome and nonlocal Hopi Yellow Ware burial accompaniments). This evidence reverses the common notion that intrusive decorated vessels indicate greater prestige because of the greater cost involved in obtaining them. The emphasis in the burial assemblages on locally produced ceramics corroborates the prevailing sociopolitical relationships where prestige is derived from local control of access to land, resources, and ritual knowledge. The lesser prestige burial assemblages containing nonlocal decorated wares indicate that individuals with outside ties were allowed to participate but were excluded from the highest ranked roles.

ARCHITECTURAL ASYMMETRY

The architecture of platform mounds has ideological and social ramifications. The changes in the configuration and arrangement of rooms and plazas reflects integrative concerns (Adams 1991:109,125). These architectural transformations are responses to the changing social needs to integrate unrelated members of the community. Platform mounds are public architecture, although they have a limited residential component that was occupied by those with differential access to land, resources, and ritual knowledge. The arrangement of plazas facilitates participation by residents of surrounding settlements, allowing them to become essential elements of the whole. However, access is restricted to the innermost areas where ritual performances are prepared (cf. Adams 19921:126; Jacobs 1992, 1997).

There are both ceramic and architectural manifestations of a ranked social organization with two unequal social units at the Cline Terrace platform mound. The differentiation between the two social components stems back to the Preclassic period, but the asymmetry between the two occurs in the late Classic period and is associated with the development of platform architecture and the integrative, but ranked, ceremonial organization of the society.

The asymmetries reflected in some of the ceramic interlocking motifs are also present in the architecture at the Cline Terrace Mound expressed as unusual L-shaped rooms (Figure 8.5). The interlock of Feature 29, an L-shaped room that opens onto outer Plaza 14, is formed by the room space and the adjacent L-shape of the filled cell. The interlock of Feature 81, an L-shaped room that opens onto inner plaza 45/96, is formed by the room space and the L-shape of the adjacent filled cell.

Each of these interlocks are formed by positive and negative space, the mound fill and the space of the room, the elevated surface of the mound fill and the ground level surface of the L-shaped room. The two sets of interlocks are arranged opposite each other on either side of the mound dividing wall, repeating the inner and outer facing opposition of these rooms. The two L-shaped rooms are faced with gypsum slabs, similar to the exterior of the mound. This provides another contrast between the light (white) walls of the rooms and the dark (black) fill of the mound cells. As units of positive and negative space, the interlock formed by Feature 81 is larger than the one facing the exterior plaza formed by Feature 29. Within each unit, the mound cell portions of the interlock are larger than the L-shaped rooms, lending asymmetry to the architectural motifs.

These architectural oppositions of interlocking L-shaped rooms in black and white, positive and negative, large and small, mirror the motifs and color schemes used on much of the Gila and Tonto Polychrome pottery. Both the polychrome ceramic motifs and architectural structures represent asymmetrical interlocking units, which are physical manifestations of a ranked duality that characterized Salado social organization. In both ceramic design and architecture of the platform mound there is an expression of two parts that have distinct visual representations. The manifestations of this duality began as visually balanced, black or white, solid or hatched. Then asymmetrical layouts become prevalent in the Classic period in a time of population movement

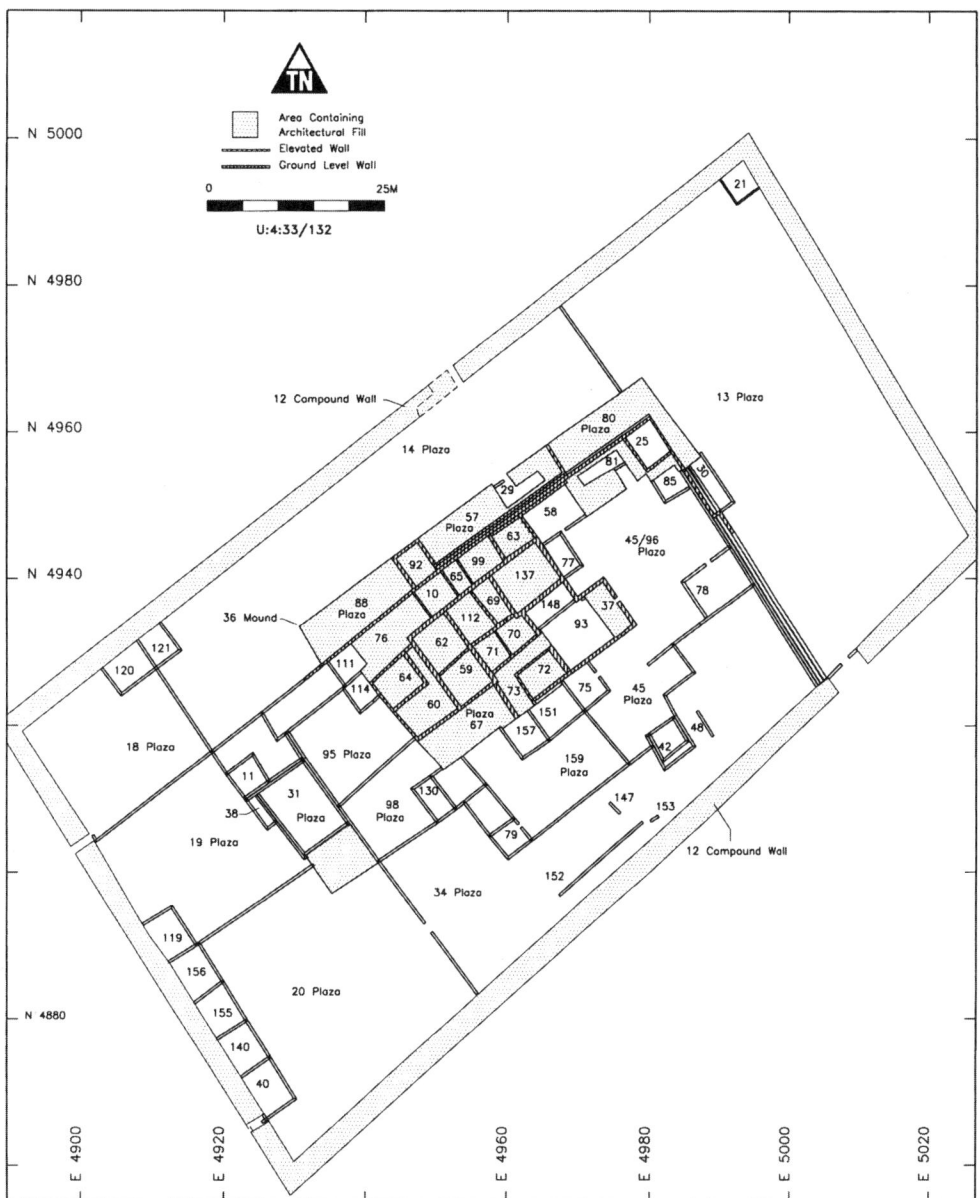

Figure 8.5.   Plan view of the Cline Terrace Mound (U:4:33) illustrating locations of the ground level rooms and areas of architectural fill that form the raised surfaces and rooms of the mound.

where there were imbalances in access to land and resources. The need to maintain and assert control of land and resources is the motivating force behind the ranking of society, and this asymmetry is validated though ceramic and architectural iconography and the organization of integrative communal activities.

Some Salado polychrome motifs are noted for asymmetries in shape, elaborations, or size (Crown 1994:140). The motifs, such as serpents, reflect the emphasis on icons related to water and weather control that are used to ensure fertility. Salado polychromes become the dominant decorated ware, integrating the red-slipped and black smudged surfaces of the local undecorated red wares and Salado Red. The use of white slip as a decorative field ties them to the black-on-white and the Salado White-on-red decorative traditions.

The duality and asymmetry exhibited in the decorated ceramics and the platform mound architecture are physical symbols of the imbalance of power within the platform mound community. The ceremonial leaders would have been able to motivate others from the surrounding residential sites to provide labor for the construction and maintainence of the platform mounds in return for participatory roles in the calendrical rites regularly performed at these specialized structures. Communal activities and related feasting provided the cohesion to pull the extended community together. The ideology would have been perceived to influence the weather and success of agricultural pursuits. Communal feasting and ritual performances provided the mechanisms by which food and materials were shared among the community members, and in return, they were all allowed, in varying degrees, to participate in the calendrical rites and obtain the associated benefits.

Associations Among Settlements

The sites in Tonto Basin consist of compounds of various sizes that were organized into communities focused on the platform mounds (Figures 8.6 and 8.7). Several different contemporaneous platform mounds were present during the Roosevelt and Gila phases. The frequencies of various ceramic classes vary between the Tonto and Salt Arms of the Basin, but the local smooth undecorated ceramics comprise the bulk of the collections at all platform mound complexes. These plain or red-slipped vessels continue to be associated with Gila and Tonto Polychrome ceramics in Gila phase floor as-

semblages at both the Cline Terrace Mound and the Schoolhouse Point Mound. However, some of the compound sites exhibit unusually high proportions of plain corrugated ceramics that indicate Mogollon traditions. These sites also exhibit distinctive architectural styles with linear blocks of contiguous rooms (Elson et al., Chapter 7; Lindauer, Chapter 9).

When decorated ceramics are considered, it is apparent that sites located along the Salt Arm of Tonto Basin, particularly Schoolhouse Point Mound, have high proportions of intrusive ceramics from the Colorado Plateau and the White Mountains. The comparatively high frequencies of Cibola White Ware and White Mountain Red Ware are not maintained in contemporaneous sites on the Tonto Arm. The Cline Terrace Mound has higher proportions of Salado Red and Salado polychrome and low frequencies of intrusive ceramics from the east and north. The Cline Terrace Mound also has higher frequencies of Hopi Yellow Ware ceramics. These differences indicate that the Cline Terrace complex had stronger ties to the Hopi area and that the Schoolhouse Point Complex had stronger ties to areas to the northeast.

There is evidence of ceramic production, including that of Salado polychromes, at both the Cline Terrace and Schoolhouse Point platform mound complexes. The proportion of Salado polychrome among decorated ceramics is higher for the Cline Terrace Complex (92 percent) than for the Schoolhouse Point Complex (69 percent) (Simon 1996). At both platform mound complexes, the dominant ceramic classes on Gila phase room floors and in burials include local undecorated ceramics, Salado Red, and Salado polychrome. Based on the contexts of these ceramic artifacts, we assert that the local population of the area maintained control of the social and religious organization of the platform mound complexes (Lindauer and Simon 1996; Simon 1997). The local religious leaders were able to enhance and legitimize the social order through control of participation in the religious ceremonies conducted at the platform mounds.

The religious and community leaders gained control of the agricultural ceremonial sequence to legitimize their positions through the scheduling of calendrical rites (Bauer 1996), which are performed at regular established intervals, regardless of the immediate needs of the people, and provide generalized benefits for everyone. These leaders controlled the inclusion and expulsion of peripheral groups and used the ideology to organize ritual, allowing roles and positions for new groups within the social structure. The

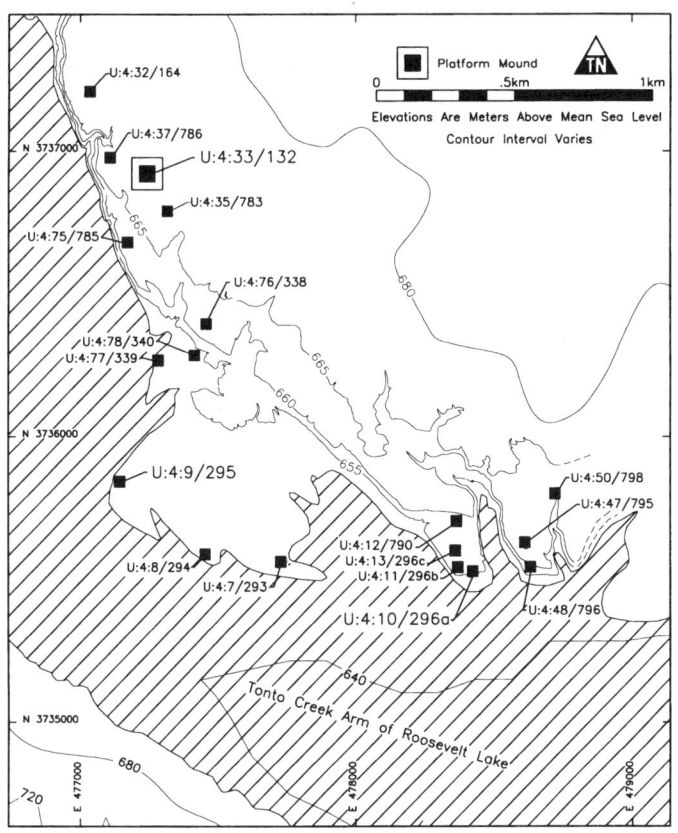

Figure 8.6. *(Left)* The Cline Terrace Complex showing the grouping of sites, particularly the large compounds of U:4:9 and U:4:10 around the Cline Terrace Mound (U:4:33).

Figure 8.7. *(Below)* The Pinto Creek Complex including sites in the Schoolhouse and Livingston groups. The Schoolhouse Point Mound (U:8:24) has several nearby compounds, including U:8:454, which shows similarities in linear block architecture and high proportions of corrugated ceramics to V:5:128 in the Livingston group.

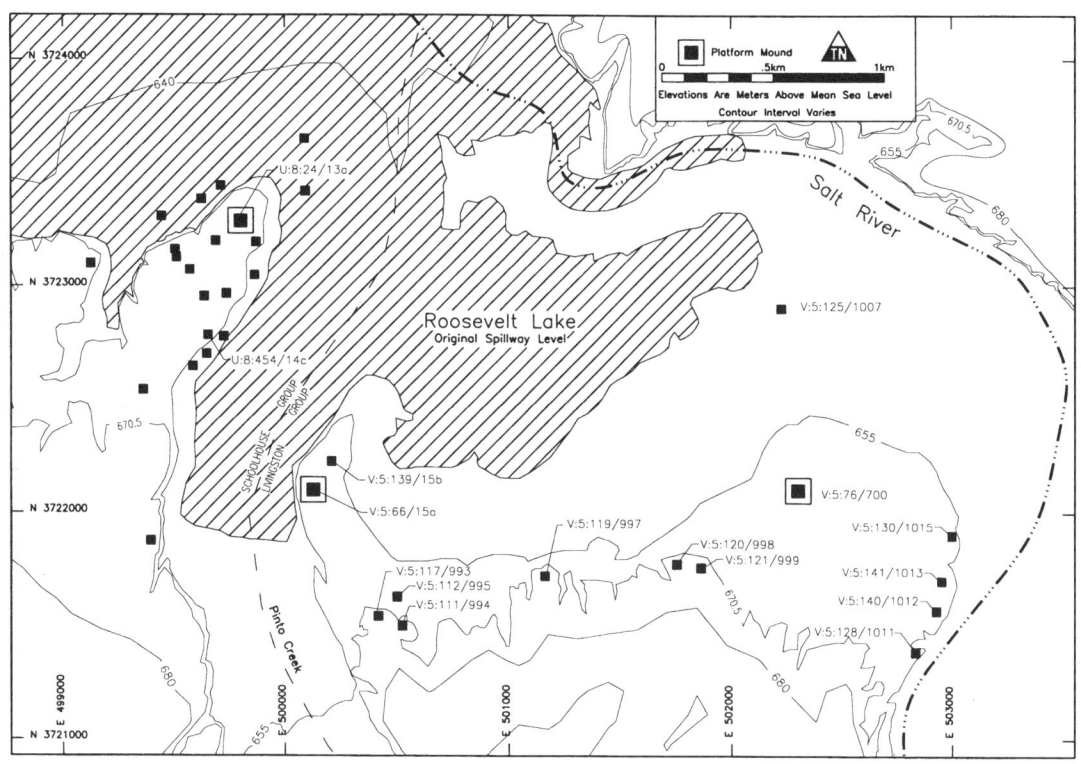

Regional Cult allowed the integration of immigrant populations through membership in the ceremonial societies, based on ritual and social bonds other than consanguineal kin relationships. The immigrant populations who intruded into the area were allowed to settle at the peripheries of the prime agricultural land. Their villages served as social and physical buffers between the platform mound complexes and the outer areas.

With these implications in mind, we now turn to the associations between settlements (Simon 1994a). The platform mounds and settlements in the Livingston area at the eastern end of Tonto Basin (Figure 8.7) provide an example of associations within a platform mound community. The proportions of major ceramic classes were used to order the sites from the Livingston area (Table 8.5). Because these sites are physiographically defined within the area bounded by the Salt River and Pinto Creek, one might expect proximity to contribute to social interaction (Simon 1994a, 1994d), but it is not the only factor.

The first group of sites is relatively early in the temporal sequence and is marked by the high frequency of undecorated pottery (Table 8.5). These sites predate the first platform mound in the area and indicate the presence of a local population whose ceramic assemblages were dominated by smooth-finished, undecorated wares.

This analysis identified a group of three compound sites likely to have been associated with the early platform mound of V:5:76 (Table 8.5). These compounds exhibit considerable architectural variation, yet share undecorated ceramic traditions and had access to a similar set of intrusive decorated types (Simon 1994a, 1994c). These sites are located along the base of the bajada and shared an emphasis on agave, although other domestic and wild foods were used.

The remaining sites are located closer to the riparian zone and terraces amenable to farming corn and cotton (Figure 8.7, Table 8.5). These sites date to the late Roosevelt phase, but there are marked contrasts in their ceramic assemblages. Two compound sites and the Pinto Point Mound (V:5:66) share an emphasis on smooth undecorated ceramics. But V:5:128 and V:5:130 (Figure 8.7) also have large proportions of corrugated ceramics. V:5:128 has distinct architecture marked by linear blocks of rectangular rooms, and is similar to U:8:454 near Schoolhouse Point Mound. Analysis of ceramics from floor contexts indicates that these rooms served domestic and storage purposes (Simon 1994d).

However, analysis of floor assemblages at the platform mounds indicated that some rooms were special purpose chambers (Simon 1994d). Rooms in the northern and western parts of the mounds, in particular, had suites of red slipped and decorated bowls indicating an emphasis on serving, rather than a more diverse suite of domestic activities. These distributions indicate feasting (Blitz 1993; Lindauer and Simon 1996) as part of communal activities in the large enclosed plazas.

These distributions of ceramics support the interpretation of the platform mounds as locations of ceremonies and broader community activities (Jacobs 1992). Large enclosed plaza areas surround the relatively small elevated rooms. Although the mounds had residents, they were few in number. The large enclosed plazas are of sufficient size to host community-wide gatherings; that is, ones attended by the inhabitants of several villages who contributed materially and socially to the communal gatherings. The numerous bowls, including some of large size (Lindauer and Simon 1995, 1996), support the interpretation that communal feasts were part of the ritual integrative activities at these structures.

The archaeological evidence from the Livingston area supports a model of a multisettlement community (Simon 1994a). The socioreligious core would have been the platform mound with other colony and satellite villages in the area.

During the Gila phase, the platform mounds became larger and more impressive. The Cline Terrace Mound (Figure 8.5) is an elaboration of the architectural elements embodied in the earlier Pinto Point Mound. Analysis of ceramics and other features from floor contexts (Simon 1997) indicates that the site was used primarily for food preparation and serving but not large scale storage. The amount of open plaza space is very large compared to rooms and enclosed areas (Jacobs 1997).

The ceramic analysis indicates that decorated wares have an uneven distribution in the site suggesting a social division. The northwestern rooms and southern plaza have higher proportions of Gila Polychrome. In contrast, the southeastern rooms and northern plaza have higher proportions of Tonto Polychrome and the presence of yellow ware. A theme of dualism is expressed in the interlocking L-shaped rooms that is repeated in the mound architecture and the interlocking elements painted on the Salado polychrome pottery.

The resident population at the Cline Terrace Mound was too small to have constructed the site alone (Jacobs

Table 8.5. Ceramic Class Totals and Percentages of Three Major Ceramic Groups and Selected Ratios for the Livingston Sites (Boxes highlight similarities in ceramic class proportions and ratios)

Site Number	Red/Plain	Red/Smudged	Plain/Smudged	Plain/Plain	Plain Corr	Salado Red	Fine Corr	Decorated	Count Percent	Undecorated	Corrugated	Decorated	Corrugated:Smooth	Red:Plain	Smudged:Plain
Group 1 Sites															
V:5:111/994	9	17	152	248	1	14	1	10	452	426	16	10			
	2.0	3.8	33.6	54.9	0.2	3.1	0.2	2.2	0.6	94.3	3.5	2.2	0.04	0.06	0.40
V:5:117/993		1	12	24					37	37	0	0			
		2.7	32.4	64.9					0.0	100.0	0.0	0.0	0.00	0.03	0.35
V:5:140/1012	7	3	83	602	8			7	710	695	8	7			
	1.0	0.4	11.7	84.8	1.1			1.0	0.9	97.9	1.1	1.0	0.01	0.01	0.12
Group 2 Sites															
V:5:128/1011	321	263	3262	4043	6060	774	36	388	15147	7889	6870	388			
	2.1	1.7	21.5	26.7	40.0	5.1	0.2	2.6	20.0	52.0	45.3	2.6	0.47	0.07	0.45
V:5:130/1015	444	121	265	662	967	170	23	324	2976	1492	1160	324			
	14.9	4.1	8.9	22.2	32.5	5.7	0.8	10.9	3.9	50.1	39.0	10.9	0.44	0.38	0.26
Group 3 Sites															
V:5:66/15a	4971	2736	3012	5455	1135	1114	245	1852	20520	16174	2494	1852			
	24.2	13.3	14.7	26.6	5.5	5.4	1.2	9.0	27.1	78.8	12.1	9.0	0.13	0.48	0.36
V:5:139/15b	1568	997	1922	2977	137	598	172	940	9311	7464	907	940			
	16.8	10.7	20.6	32.0	1.5	6.4	1.8	10.1	12.3	80.1	9.7	10.1	0.11	0.34	0.39
V:5:125/1007	22	18	34	52	5	18	2	13	164	126	25	13			
	13.4	11.0	20.7	31.7	3.0	11.0	1.2	7.9	0.2	76.8	15.2	7.9	0.17	0.32	0.41
Group 4 Sites															
V:5:76/700	287	120	732	1365	151	170	63	598	3486	2504	384	598			
	8.2	3.4	21.0	39.2	4.3	4.9	1.8	17.2	4.6	71.8	11.0	17.2	0.13	0.16	0.34
V:5:112/995	1585	490	4628	5460	713	851	66	788	14581	12163	1630	788			
	10.9	3.4	31.7	37.4	4.9	5.8	0.5	5.4	19.3	83.4	11.2	5.4	0.12	0.17	0.42
V:5:119/997	467	402	745	1781	172	113	39	285	4004	3395	324	285			
	11.7	10.0	18.6	44.5	4.3	2.8	1.0	7.1	5.3	84.8	8.1	7.1	0.09	0.26	0.34
V:5:121/999	444	178	890	1303	178	573	19	385	3970	2815	770	385			
	11.2	4.5	22.4	32.8	4.5	14.4	0.5	9.7	5.2	70.9	19.4	9.7	0.21	0.22	0.38
Group 5 Site															
V:5:141/1013	146	49	11	42	20	34	3	63	368	248	57	63			
	39.7	13.3	3.0	11.4	5.4	9.2	0.8	17.1	0.5	67.4	15.4	17.1	0.19	0.79	0.24
Group 6 Site															
V:5:120/998			2						2	2	0	0			
			100.0						0.0	100.0	0.0	0.0	0.00	0.00	1.00
Count	10271	5395	15750	24014	9547	4429	669	5653	75728	55430	14645	5653			
Percent	13.6	7.1	20.8	31.7	12.6	5.8	0.9	7.5	100.0	73.2	19.3	7.5	0.21	0.28	0.38

1997). There are at least two large compounds (U:4:10 and U:4:9) near the mound (Figure 8.6) that could have provided the larger population needed to build and maintain this structure. These villagers would have come to the platform mound to participate in ceremonies.

One of the last occupied mounds in Tonto Basin is at Schoolhouse Point (Figure 8.8). The architectural plan of this mound differs from the Cline Terrace Mound. In addition, its resident population was large enough to have constructed it (Lindauer 1996c). Storage of food was a major activity (Lindauer 1992), and a group of central store rooms provided protected space for granaries and large ollas. Clusters of elevated rooms were built around the central storage area. Analysis of ceramics from floor assemblages (Lindauer and Simon 1995) indicate that certain rooms may have functioned in a ritual capacity rather than being domestic space. Significantly, these rooms are located at the north, east, and south areas of the mound. Such a room on the west was not identified, but several of these rooms were not excavated.

The compounds surrounding the Schoolhouse Point Mound (Figure 8.7) were occupied during different spans of the mound's history (Lindauer, Chapter 9), but it is not clear that any of the compounds persisted as late as the platform mound. This would suggest that the resident population of the immediate area lived at the mound during the end of its use. In times of warfare and pressure from outsiders (Connelly 1979:542; Simmons 1979), residents of outlying communities were allowed to settle in the main site, but this arrangement did not persist due to internal tension and fission. These processes may explain the multiple spatial and social divisions suggested for the Schoolhouse Point Mound (Lindauer, Chapter 9; Lindauer and Simon 1995; Simon 1994e) and the final dispersal of the remaining inhabitants of the mound.

CONCLUSION

Population movements and migrations figure prominently in the oral traditions of the Hopi. When areas are abandoned, remains of actual ancestors are left behind. The movement away from traditional areas and markers that were important to the agricultural calendar coincides with an increasing emphasis on fertility and generalized calendrical rites to evoke control of the weather patterns through spirit ancestors that are not tied to specific settlements. The weather continues to be controlled by the spirits of those departed (Titiev 1944), a form of generalized ancestor worship.

The mixing of populations resulting from immigration and the need to participate in productive social and subsistence systems drives the increasing emphasis on fertility and reliance on nonkin integrators; that is, social mechanisms that permit cooperation among local and immigrant residents, some of whom may be related through affinal ties. The ideological shift from kin-based ancestor worship, as in the Mimbres example, to a generalized form of ancestor worship, which allows ceremonial ties as well as kin ties, facilitates the integration of diverse populations into a shared ceremonial system. The local, or founding, population orchestrates participation in calendrical rites. The assertion and maintenance of rank order over new additions to the system are controlled through selected membership and assigned ceremonial roles.

The shift from kin integrators to nonkin integrators in social and religious organization was a significant modification that was incorporated into the Regional Cult. Nonkin integrators, such as those in a system of ranked lineages based on mythical common ancestors, facilitated the acceptance of migrating groups into the indigenous population in Tonto Basin. Social networks were anchored in kinship (lineages), but ceremonial bonds of alliance were extended through the ceremonial affiliations.

The social and religious organization that held together the diverse elements of Salado communities was in place prior to the appearance of platform mounds and Salado polychrome. The Classic period platform mounds are the late manifestations of the regional ideology. The ceramic and architectural evidence indicates that multivillage communities focused on the platform mounds, the locations of communal integrative activities. The resident populations at the platform mounds maintained control and scheduling of calendrical rites that were performed at these public architectural facilities. Religious ideology provided the mechanism by which other groups were integrated into the social structure of the larger community, but sufficient physical and social distance was imposed to assure status secondary to that of the original inhabitants.

The development of the platform mounds and the transition from symmetrical to asymmetrical layout and design in architectural plans and in ceramic motifs signaled a developing imbalance in the social structure of Salado society. The iconography of the Regional Cult

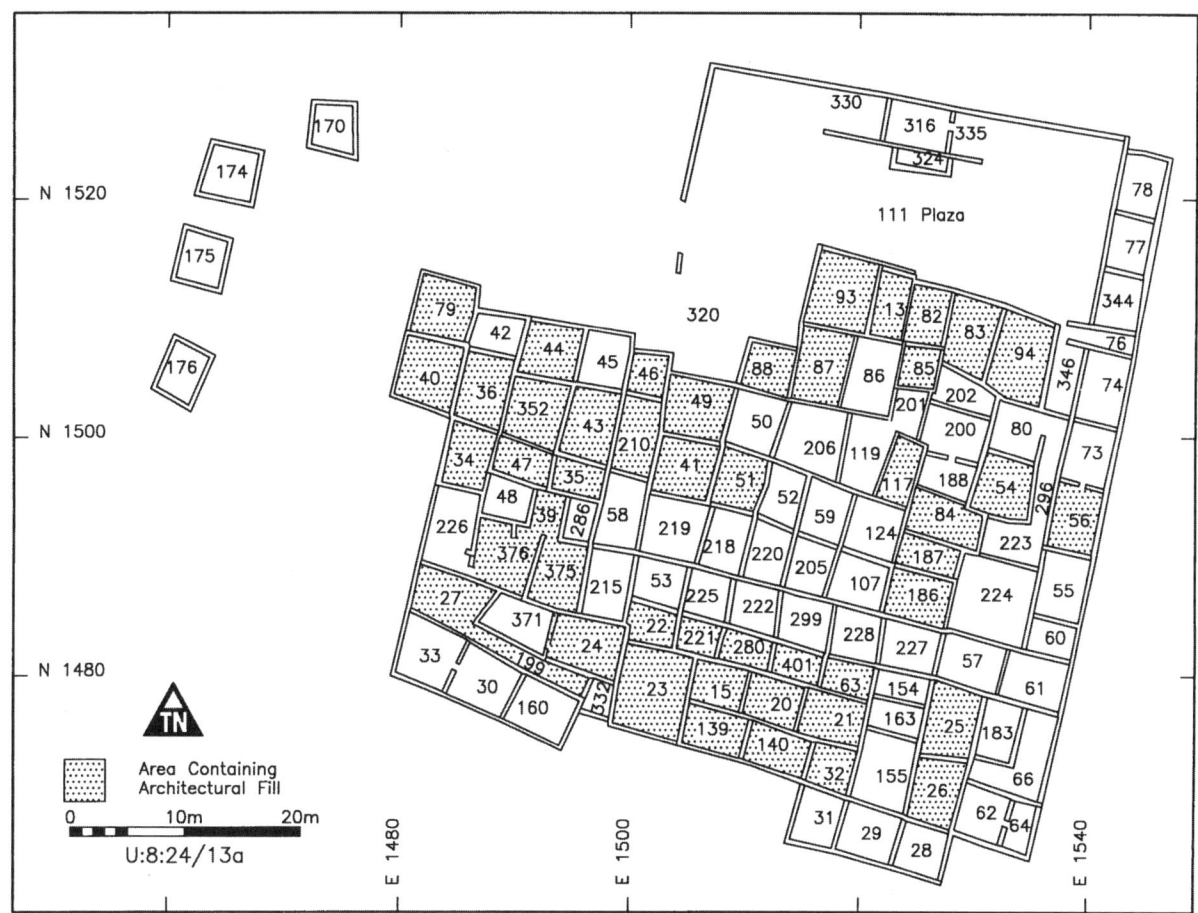

Figure 8.8.   Plan view of the Schoolhouse Point Mound (U:8:24) illustrating locations of the ground level rooms and areas of architectural fill that formed the raised surfaces and rooms of the mound.

signals participation in the communal rites that are the mechanism of integration. Interlocking design elements indicate dualism, where two major segments in the social organization are perceived. The asymmetries are a visual indication of the imbalance of power within the system and authenticate the social order. The privileged few control ritual knowledge and access to prime agricultural lands. The iconography of the architecture and ceramic designs are symbolic confirmation of the cult. The belief system was inclusive and available to most, but acceptance and level of participation were controlled. Ranked status controlled the scale of participation from public performances to secret rites.

Integrative activities conducted at the platform mounds probably included ceremonial performances with atten-

dant communal feasting. Such gatherings would have served to build the cohesion of the system. Participation in the calendrical rites would have been compensation for contributing food and other products necessary for the ceremonies. The platform mound community would have remained viable as long as the inhabitants of the residential sites remained satisfied with their level of ceremonial and social participation and share of subsistence products.

Social distinctions in the Preclassic shift during the Classic period to ranked units that are asymmetrical, but which accommodate the integration of outside groups into a multivillage community focused on platform mounds. Contextual evidence of architecture and ceramic assemblages indicate that the local population maintained and asserted control of the religious ideology and the platform mounds and orchestrated the organization of multiple settlements into platform mound complexes. Integration of the society organized around platform mounds was possible through ranked lineages and ceremonial nonkin ties. Salado polychrome ceramics were decorated with icons that signified participation in the Regional Cult and were not produced as elite symbols of authority (Crown 1994:194–95) but rather were used to promote the Cult and integrate the members of extended multivillage communities into ceremonial participation in the platform mound activities. Architectural design of the platform mounds mirrored the layout of the ceramic designs and signified ceremonial areas for the preparation and performance of calendrical rites.

Around 1350, the Pinedale style, which is recognized across several different wares (Crown 1994:179, Figure 10.1), developed into regionally specific variants. These regional developments of style were products of the relatively stable climatic and environmental conditions that allowed populations to remain largely sedentary and undisturbed by large masses of landless agriculturalists. The social structure that had previously developed to incorporate these diverse groups became more entrenched and rigid. There was a period of aggregation into larger villages and communities. However, worsening climatic and environmental conditions in the late fourteenth and early fifteenth centuries (Waters 1997)

would have jeopardized the validity of the Regional Cult and the platform mound system.

Subsistence stress resulting from increasing population or environmental instability would have necessitated the unburdening of the platform mound communities of the lowest ranked groups. Those groups, who would have been displeased with banishment, would have had to leave the area or displace those who controlled access to the land. In the final result, ideology developed to integrate and unify diverse agricultural populations, but once population movements stabilized, the system became inflexible. The legitimacy of the system was undermined once the climatic conditions changed, contributing to the fission of the platform mound complexes.

Acknowledgments

The thoughtful comments of Jeffrey Dean helped clarify the text and the ideas expressed. Our thanks to Glena Cain for the vessel illustrations, to Lynn Simon for the area and site maps, and to Roosevelt Project archaeologists and colleagues for many stimulating discussions. Part of the research for this paper was conducted for the Bureau of Reclamation as a result of the modifications to the Roosevelt Dam. The field work for the RPMS was conducted under the terms of a permit from the Tonto National Forest.

CHAPTER NINE

A Schoolhouse Point Mesa Perspective on
Salado Community Development

Owen Lindauer

Aɴ ᴜɴᴅᴇʀsᴛᴀɴᴅɪɴɢ ᴏꜰ ᴛʜᴇ ᴅᴇᴠᴇʟᴏᴘᴍᴇɴᴛ ᴀɴᴅ growth of a village allows a characterization of social units and their integration. This paper describes the changing manifestation of a Salado village on Schoolhouse Point Mesa during the Classic period. The shift in residences from multiple, small compounds scattered across the mesa in the Roosevelt phase to a compact, single, large cluster of residences in the Gila phase reflects dramatic social organizational changes at both the village and community scales. Aspects of Salado economy and social relationships are reflected in the arrangement and location of residences that make up a village.

Bounded architectural spaces where people are likely to encounter each other in frequent face-to-face contacts are considered to represent important units of social organization (Arensberg and Kimball 1962). By describing and comparing the size, arrangement, and composition of such architectural spaces, it is possible to infer characteristics of social organization. But the natural landscape also bounds human interactions. Thus, both the cultural and natural landscapes concurrently facilitate or inhibit human interactions. The terms "community," "settlement," or "village" could apply to architectural spaces in a cultural landscape. Although all three terms may be synonymous in some circumstances, communities often are considered as being composed of several

settlements or villages. If settlements and villages are nested within a larger community, a community consists of a large group of people whose face-to-face contacts are less frequent compared with people in villages or settlements but whose interactions are nonetheless circumscribed in a way to separate them from other communities. The differing scale of settlement and social interaction between community and village is recognized by Elson et al. (see Chapter 7) with their terms "interregional systems" and "local systems."

Distinguishing the boundaries of villages or settlements and communities is difficult because most sites contain only traces of walls, features, and associated artifacts that are indirect remains of human interaction. Drawing boundaries around regularly interacting social units is ambiguous even when interaction is observed directly (Barth 1969). In archaeological contexts, the result often is inconsistent unit and subunit community distinction. This has the effect, as observed by Dean (1987:257) for Hohokam villages, of inhibiting the study of community and village structure and organization. But he adds (Dean 1987:259), extensive survey, excavation of large contiguous site areas, derivation of detailed site chronologies, and reconstruction of activities provides a foundation for understanding the social organization of villages and larger communities. The recent extensive excavations on Schoolhouse Point Mesa as part of the

Roosevelt Platform Mound Study (Arizona State University) and in surrounding areas for the Community Development Study (Desert Archaeology, Inc.) and Rural Sites Study (Statistical Research, Inc.) allow a greater degree of chronological control and reconstruction of architecture and activity areas than previously possible.

The structure and arrangement of the village on Schoolhouse Point Mesa is similar to other Tonto Basin villages but differences exist that distinguish it from other villages. Within a few km there are clusters of sites that are contemporary and replicate the scale and composition of the village on Schoolhouse Point Mesa (Figure 9.1). Meddler Point (Craig 1995) and neighboring Pinto Point (Jacobs 1994c) each include a number of sites scattered across a mesa that have been considered a village. Yet those villages were largely abandoned at the end of the Roosevelt phase. By contrast, Schoolhouse Point Mesa was occupied through the Roosevelt and Gila phases of the Classic period. Thus, not only can the Schoolhouse Point Mesa village be compared with the neighboring villages, its occupation into the Gila phase provides a unique opportunity to understand the changing organization of a village. Site survey, intensive and extensive excavation, chronological control from absolute and relative dating techniques, and reconstruction of activities provides the foundation for describing village layout and social organization.

The natural boundedness of Schoolhouse Point Mesa is probably the primary attribute that defines the sites there as a Salado village. The Salt River bounds the northern end of the mesa and major washes bound its eastern and western sides (Figure 9.2). While it is possible that a village could have included sites separated by major washes or rivers, it is more likely that geographically-separated residential sites occupied year-round would have been settlements in a larger community unit rather than a single village. Within the confines of the Schoolhouse Point Mesa and its benches, 19 individual sites have been excavated (Table 9.1) among the clustering of architecture and related features that have been identified from survey information (Figure 9.2, Tables 9.1 and 9.2). The sites are mostly concentrated on the northern end of the mesa within an area of approximately 210 ha (84 acres). Most sites are separated by less than 100 m of open space and are dispersed over the mesa area. The sites range in size and complexity from a platform mound having scores of rooms, to an artifact scatter that lacks architecture.

The natural landscape bounds other nearby sites in similar ways (Figure 9.1) but with some variation. Meddler Point, on the north bank of the Salt River a few km upstream, is a very similar geographic unit that has a number of sites spread across a finger-like mesa and its benches that was recognized as a local system by Elson et al. (Chapter 7). The area of Meddler Point also is comparable, covering about 185 ha (74 acres) (Craig 1995). Another village-sized cluster of sites, although of smaller area, also identified as a local system by Elson et al. (Chapter 7) occurs on Pyramid Point (Figure 9.1). A slightly different topographic landscape characterizes Pinto Creek Wash. Jacobs and Rice (1994a:16) proposed that sites on Pinto Point were a possible village unit, which they call the Pinto Group, whose membership is based on proximity to the Pinto Point Mound (Figure 9.1). Sites of the Pinto Group are located both on and off of Pinto Point Mesa. The Pinto Group of sites covers a slightly larger area than Schoolhouse Point Mesa (Jacobs and Rice 1994a:Figure 1.14) but in it were only nine compounds (six at V:5:139, V:5:66, V:5:112, and V:5:119). A dispersal of residential sites on upper and lower river terraces characterizes the Pillar Group of sites (Jacobs and Rice 1994a:16) that also are distributed across a larger area than Schoolhouse Point Mesa.

It is reasonable to consider the cultural landscape, especially the presence of an integrative site such as a platform mound, as an influence on the boundary of a village. Using proximity to a platform mound site as the criteria for defining a village-scale unit requires marking a boundary by some means. The boundary of a village (Figure 9.1) or local system (Elson et al., Chapter 7, Figure 7.7) will vary somewhat due to differing perceptions of how a site cluster is defined. Jacobs and Rice (1994b:924) distinguished sites they called the Pinto Group on Pinto Point from another group of sites to the east, called the Pillar Group, based on the quantities of obsidian and other types of rare lithic materials. Simon's (1994a:639–40) multivariate analysis of sherd assemblages identified a slightly different grouping of sites. The different groupings should not, however, lead to a rejection of culturally bounded landscapes because there are a variety of reasons why proportions of artifacts vary among a set of sites (due to differences in chronology and function, as well as patterns of interaction, for example). Abbott's (1995) recent analyses of exchange relations from utilitarian pottery at sites along Phoenix area canals indicates that a bounded unit of sites based on proximity did not characterize the pattern of exchanged pottery. Instead, the most intense pottery exchanges crosscut clustered settlement units based on geography.

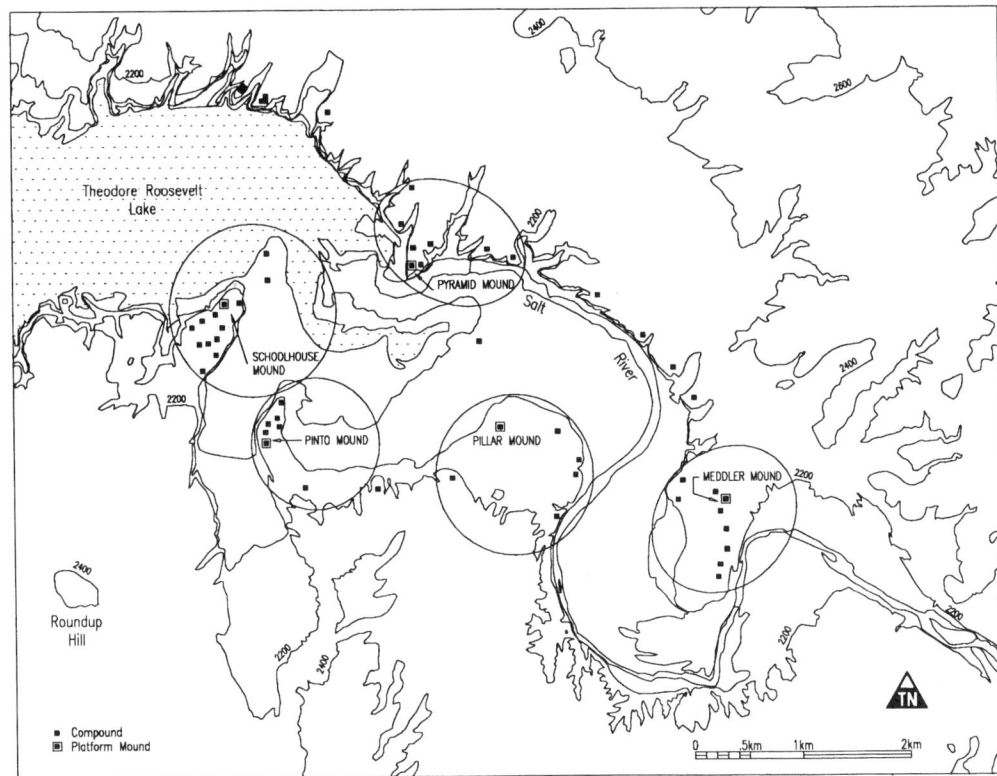

Figure 9.1. Five village-sized clusters of sites on mesas of the Salt River.

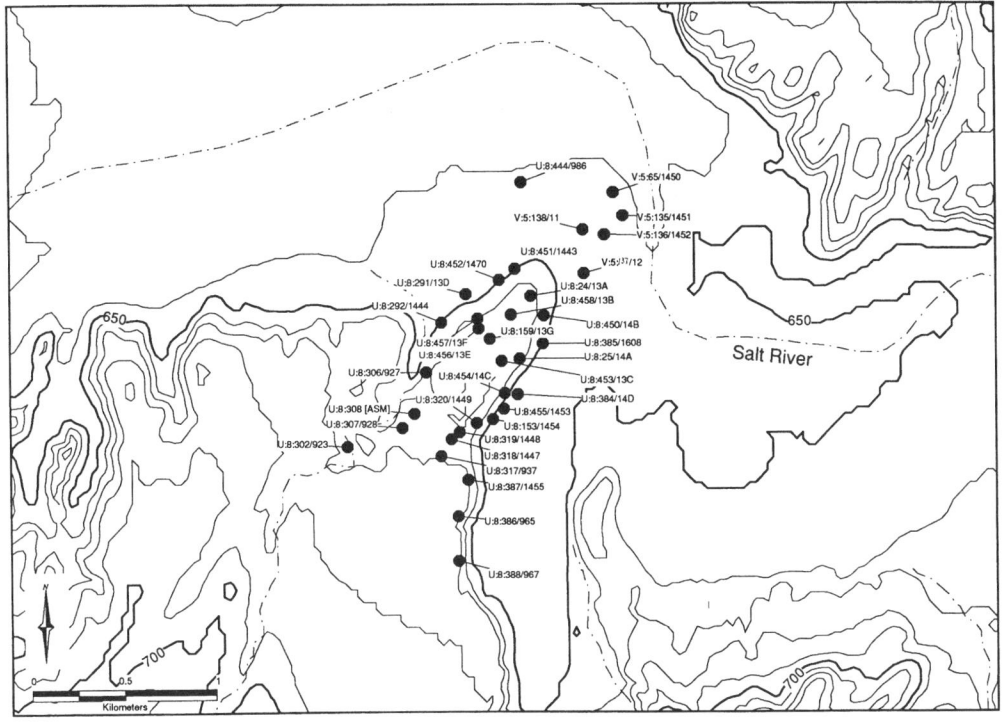

Figure 9.2. Sites on Schoolhouse Point Mesa.

Table 9.1. Data on Sites on Schoolhouse Point Mesa by Time Period

| | Preclassic | | | Roosevelt phase | | | Gila phase | |
| | Pithouses Recorded | Sherds in Middens | Site Type | Rooms (n) | Middens (n) | Roasting Pits (n) | Rooms (n) | Sherds Present |
Site Number								
U:8:24/13a	Yes	Yes	Platform Mound/Compound	14	3	0	92	Yes
U:8:25/14a	Yes	Yes	Compound	14	6	2	0	Yes
U:8:153/1454	No	No	Limited Activity	0	0	1	0	No
U:8:159/13g	No	No	Limited Activity	0	1	0	0	No
U:8:291/13d	No	No	Compound	3	*	1	0	Yes
U:8:318/1447	No	No	Limited Activity	0	0	0	1	Yes
U:8:384/14d	No	No	Limited Activity	0	0	2	0	No
U:8:385/1608	No	No	Room Cluster	5	0	0	0	No
U:8:388/967	No	No	Limited Activity	1	0	0	0	No
U:8:450/14b	No	Yes	Compound	3	5	0	3	Yes
U:8:451/1443	Yes	No	Compound	3	*	*	0	No
U:8:452/1470	No	No	Compound	2	*	*	0	Yes
U:8:453/13c	No	No	Compound	3	1	0	0	No
U:8:454/14c	No	No	Room Block	9	0	0	0	Yes
U:8:456/13e & U:8:457/13f	No	No	Compound	3	2	1	0	No
U:8:458/13b	Yes	Yes	Compound	6	6	1	0	Yes
V:5:137/12	Yes	Yes	Compound	16	2	0	0	Yes
V:5:138/11	No	No	Compound	5	*	0	0	Yes
Totals				87			96	

*Surface traces in area of lake inundation suggest feature was present

Table 9.2. Data on Sites on Schoolhouse Point Mesa Recorded by the CAWCS Survey

Site Number	Probable Site Type	Comment
U:8:292/1444	Room Cluster	2 room pairs, no sherds, probably fieldhouses
U:8:302/923	Limited Activity	Agricultural site, 29 rock piles (.5-.75 m diameter), no sherds, stone ax observed
U:8:306/927	Limited Activity	1 room field house, no sherds
U:8:307/928	Limited Activity	1 room field house, plain and red ware sherds
U:8:308	Limited Activity	1 room field house, red ware sherds
U:8:317/937	Room Cluster	Sherd and lithic scatter, plain, red, R/Buff, B/W sherds, pithouses probably present
U:8:319/1448	Limited Activity	1 room field house, plain and red ware sherds
U:8:320/1449	Limited Activity	2 room field house, no sherds
U:8:386/965	Limited Activity	1 room field house, plain ware sherds
U:8:387/1455	Compound?	Trash area, polygon-shaped masonry enclosure (10 m by 10 m), plain and red ware sherds
U:8:444/986	Limited Activity	1 room field house, no artifacts
V:5:135/1451	Compound?	3 rooms, plain and red ware sherds, ground stone present
V:5:136/1452	Compound?	2 rooms, plain ware sherds
V:5:65/1450	Compound	3 rooms, no artifacts, mounded trash with buff ware sherds to the west

SCALE AND COMPONENTS
OF A SALADO COMMUNITY:
TWO MODELS OF COMMUNITY STRUCTURE

In order to place the Schoolhouse Point Mesa village in a larger context, it is useful to compare the composition and arrangement of sites in two models of community structure from the Hohokam region. Models of community structure define social units and propose means by which those units were integrated. Comparison to Hohokam communities is appropriate because people in both regions relied on farming and collecting wild resources for most of their subsistence, and villages of both regions thrived in the Sonoran Desert at approximately the same time period (ca. 1250 to 1450). Clusters of Hohokam settlements have been described as both *irrigation communities* and *dispersed communities*. Although the components of both types of communities are nearly identical, they differ in arrangement on the landscape and aspects of interconnectiveness.

The concept of irrigation community was proposed by Schroeder (1966) as a set of sites sharing a common canal system, minimally including a large village, several smaller villages, and agriculturally oriented limited activity sites (Crown 1987). Doyel (1981:59–60) and Crown (1987) apply the irrigation community concept to understanding two bands of settlements on opposing sides of the Gila River. Interactions that define a community structure result from reliance on canal irrigation that requires skillful management to regulate the timing and allocation of water, coordinate canal building and maintenance activities, and resolve conflicts related to water allocation (Haury 1976a:149). Each irrigation community had at least one primary village with a platform mound as the locus of decision making, with smaller villages ceremonially and politically related to the primary village (Doyel 1981:60). A variety of agricultural technologies was used in an irrigation community, including canal irrigation, dry farming, and floodwater farming (Crown 1987:153). Crown also indicates that several sites with one platform mound each existed along the irrigation community on the south bank of the middle Gila. The largest village with a platform mound and the one perhaps with oversight over the entire canal system was the primary village, probably the Casa Grande site. Fewkes (1912) mapped and described Casa Grande as a site composed of four compounds and four ruins he called clan houses. This village covered an area of approximately 201.6 ha (81 acres) which closely approximates the village area on Schoolhouse Point Mesa.

The term "dispersed communities," of which an irrigation community is an example, describes widely scattered settlements that are linked together by some form of regular social contact. An alternative form of dispersed community has been identified in the Marana area on the northern edge of the Tucson Basin that extends over much broader area. Fish, Fish, and Madsen (1985; eds. 1992) describe a dispersed community where settlements occur in several environmental zones. The primary village is the site with a platform mound located adjacent to a canal system. Other settlements of the community arrayed perpendicular to the canal extended into the mountain flanks. The community structure centered around risk sharing and subsistence exchange as a result of less dependable irrigation (Fish and Fish 1992:103). The platform mound village also is hypothesized to have been the locus of management decision making for the community. This community grew to encompass 146 km² (56 square miles) during the Classic period. The dispersal area of the primary village is much larger in comparison to the primary village of an irrigation community. Fish et al. (1992a:27–28, Fig. 3.6) estimate that the Marana village area included a platform mound, adjacent compounds, and trash mounds and covered 926 ha (370 acres). This area is almost four and a half times larger than the area identified at Schoolhouse Point Mesa.

Both these community models were proposed by Rice (1990a:12–16) in the preliminary Roosevelt Platform Mound Study research design as alternative organizational strategies for units that he called "platform mound complexes." A platform mound complex is a community including a platform mound, 4 to 20 compounds that are residential sites, agricultural fields, and dense stands of natural plant resources. According to his characterization of the two community models, residential zones will occur only in a valley bottom (the irrigation community) or will crosscut environmental zones from valley bottom to the foothills (the dispersed community). The possible size or nature of a village within a platform mound complex was left as an empirical question that now can be addressed by the investigations conducted on Schoolhouse Point Mesa.

A DESCRIPTION OF THE SALADO VILLAGE ON
SCHOOLHOUSE POINT MESA

The Natural Setting

The natural setting of Schoolhouse Point Mesa probably was an important settlement determinant. It was a landform next to an extensive area of river terraces up and down stream whose rich alluvium and proximity to the Salt River was made very productive with canal irrigation. The mesa itself is composed of two remnant Pleistocene alluvial terraces on the south bank of the Salt River that are high enough above the floodplain that they never flooded. The stable Pleistocene terraces allowed villagers to live conveniently close to the extensive floodplain to the north, east, and west, most of which was probably under cultivation.

Schoolhouse Point Mesa is composed of two Middle to Upper Pleistocene alluvial terraces that occur at differing elevations, above the active alluvial floodplain. Lower Schoolhouse Point Mesa is a terrace of Upper Pleistocene age (T12; Piety and Anderson 1988) that lies 12 to 15 m above the modern stream bed. Upper Schoolhouse Mesa is an alluvial terrace of Middle Pleistocene age (T8) that is about 27 m above the modern stream bed. Both terraces are broad flat areas composed of deposits 3 to 10 m thick of sand and rounded cobbles and boulders. The approximate 15 m elevation difference between the two terraces sloped in many places, allowing easy movement between terraces.

Terraces between Schoolhouse Point Mesa and the river are of Holocene age. Waters' (1994a) river terrace mapping project indicates that Terrace 2 was probably the alluvial surface utilized for irrigation agriculture. It lies only 2 m above the modern stream bed, and it would have been relatively easy to transport water to this surface with prehistoric canal irrigation technology. Prehistoric canals have been recorded a few km east of Schoolhouse Point Mesa (Jacobs 1994d) and it is likely that prehistoric canals extended west of Schoolhouse Point Mesa since several historic irrigated fields were located there (Welch and Ciolek-Torrello 1994:Figure 4.2). Indeed, Welch (1994c:236) indicates that the stretch of Salt River floodplain on the south bank east of Schoolhouse Point to the place where the river emerges from the gorge constriction is the largest and most favorable irrigable context in the lower Tonto Basin.

The soils on Schoolhouse Point Mesa are generally thin, not exceeding 50 cm in thickness, and are a mix of sands and prominent deposits of red smectitic clay. The sands are a mix of materials of volcanic origin (dacite and basalt) and granite (Komorowski 1991:28). Rounded cobbles as large as 60 cm in one dimension are found immediately below the surface soils. Investigation of two agricultural sites in the Grapevine area (Figure 9.1) to the west on the same Pleis-

tocene terrace (T8) suggests that parts of the mesa itself could have been used for sediment and water concentration agriculture (Welch 1994c:234,248–49).

Modern vegetation on Schoolhouse Point Mesa probably is similar to that of the past, although changes have been caused by decades of ranching and recreational activities. Vegetation communities on Schoolhouse Point Mesa include mesquite scrub and mesquite bosque. Shrubs and trees, including cat-claw (Acacia), paloverde (Cercidium floridum, C. microphyllum), creosote (Larrea), and mesquite (Prosopis), dominate the landscape. Other vegetation includes grasses, weeds, and herbaceous perennials, which have been described by Adams and Welch (1994a). They point out that species presence and abundance depends on local weather conditions and amount of domestic pasture. Goose foot (Chenopodium) and pigweed (Amaranthus) occur in scattered locations and are grazed. Other species in the area include thistle (Cirsium), tansy mustard (Descurainia pennata), brittle bush (Encelia farinosa), spurge (Euphorbia), Indian wheat (Plantago), purslane (Portulaca), and globe mallow (Sphaeralcea). A few scattered saguaros (Cereus gigantea) are found along the edges of the upper and lower mesa overlooking the Salt River and Pinto Creek. Prickly pear, cholla (Opuntia), and Christmas cactus (Opuntia leptocaulis) have a patchy distribution across the mesa. Agave (Agave sp.), which was utilized prehistorically, is not present.

The variety in modern fauna corresponds with the variety in fauna identified by bone remains in archaeological sites. That deer were present in low numbers due to the intensity of settlement along the river is confirmed by the low but constant occurrence of deer bones in archaeological contexts. Cottontails and jackrabbits are abundant today and probably were so in the past. A variety of birds inhabit the area, including owls, ravens, hawks, and eagles, whose bones also appear in archaeological contexts. Their scarcity suggests that they probably were utilized for their feathers rather than as food. Reptiles include a variety of lizards, snakes, and turtles, some of which may have been utilized in the past. Carbonized fish bones from middens indicate that fish from the Salt River were a small part of the prehistoric diet.

Village Components: Residential Settlements and Limited Activity Loci

The Schoolhouse Point Mesa village was composed of residential settlements and limited activity loci represented archaeologically as a variety of site types. Comparing and contrasting features among the site types indicates residential and nonresidential (processing, subsistence, ceremonial) functions. The five basic site types on Schoolhouse Mesa are: 1) compound, 2) room block, 3) platform mound, 4) room cluster (Gregory 1995b), and 5) limited activity site. The first four types were residential. Compound, room block, and room cluster sites occurred during the Roosevelt phase, while platform mound and room cluster sites were the residential choices of the Gila phase. Limited activity sites include isolated artifact scatters, trash areas, and roasting pits dating to both the Roosevelt and Gila phases.

A compound site consists of several rooms (usually two to four) built against a compound wall enclosing all the rooms and unroofed areas between the rooms. The amount of enclosed unroofed area varies among compounds and is usually subdivided to form two or more plazas. Adult and subadult inhumations commonly are found in cemeteries beneath the plaza areas. A variety of features, such as pits, hearths, and roasting pits that result from a range of domestic processing and production activities, occur within the compound. Often, a low mounded trash area occurs outside the compound wall. Immediately outside several compounds, large roasting areas indicate large-scale and repeated processing activity. Although all compound sites were residential, only some had large roasting pits. Several compounds are associated with large trash middens, whereas others have little or no trash. Because decorated ceramics collected from these compounds date to the Roosevelt phase (Cibola White Ware [Tularosa, Snowflake, Pinedale Black-on-whites]) St. Johns and Pinedale Black-on-red, and McDonald Corrugated), it is unlikely that some compounds were occupied significantly longer than others. Instead, it is likely the differing amounts of trash, as well as associated features such as roasting pits, probably mark real differences in activity among compounds.

The only room block site on Schoolhouse Point Mesa has rooms arrayed in two linear blocks. It differs from compound sites in that the rooms share a substantial number of common walls and open space between the rooms is not enclosed by compound walls. The arrangement of rooms and open space is thought to indicate that the site was constructed and inhabited by Tonto Basin outsiders (Clark 1995a; Elson et al., Chapter 7) who had been socially integrated locally. This is attested by identical wall construction techniques and other aspects of material culture (Lindauer 1994).

The single platform mound site on Schoolhouse Point has rooms arrayed in linear blocks with a substantial number of common walls. It differs from a room block site in having rooms built both at ground level and on artificially filled platforms. It differs from other Tonto Basin platform mound sites (Meddler Mound, Pinto Point Mound, Pillar Mound, Bass Point Mound, Cline Terrace Mound) by integrating small, room-sized platforms with ground-level rooms and by lacking an enclosing compound wall. Although the platforms at the site are limited to the size of the room they supported, they share architectural attributes (pier post supports, compacted platform fill, buttress walls) with other features in Tonto Basin also called platform mounds (Lindauer 1996b).

A room cluster consists of three to six structures (adobe surface rooms, pit rooms, pithouses) that surround or otherwise define a common exterior space. This definition follows one proposed by Gregory (1995b; also see Germick and Crary 1989:9) but includes pithouses. They are distinguished from compound and room block sites because rooms do not share common walls and compound walls are absent.

At limited activity sites no evidence of habitation was found. Artifact or trash scatters, roasting pits, and agricultural fields are the kinds of limited activity sites recorded for Schoolhouse Point Mesa. Artifact scatters may have been associated with one or more ephemeral structures possibly associated with agricultural fields, while the roasting pits were large-scale processing features. Agricultural fields were indicated by the presence of check dam and rock pile features that served to retain soil and moisture.

RESIDENTIAL CONTINUITY AND CHANGE ON SCHOOLHOUSE POINT MESA

Preclassic Occupation

The first residential sites on Schoolhouse Point Mesa were room cluster, pithouse sites of Preclassic age. Our knowledge of these sites is sketchy because Classic period architecture covers many of them. It is clear from the traces of pithouses and occasional Hohokam red-on-buff sherds in middens from Classic period sites (Tables 9.1 and 9.2) that the Preclassic occupation is substantially less extensive than the Classic period occupation. Few sherds collected by the Roosevelt Platform Mound Study date to the Colonial period (one Gila Butte Red-on-buff and 15 Santa Cruz Red-on-buff). Off the mesa, Colonial period occupation is known for the river terrace (Haury 1932; Swartz and Randolph 1994b) and the Meddler Point area (Craig and Clark 1994:Table:7.8) on the opposite bank of the Salt River, but it seems that Schoolhouse Point Mesa was not extensively settled at this time. Sacaton Red-on-buff, though rare, is the most abundant decorated pottery, which suggests that most pithouses on Schoolhouse Point Mesa date to the Sedentary period.

Pithouse clusters on Pleistocene terraces to the west (Figure 9.1) in the Grapevine area (Shelley and Ciolek-Torrello 1994) and the east on Meddler Point (in Locus A; Craig and Clark 1994) represent Sedentary period farmsteads or hamlets. Evidence from the Grapevine area indicates that pithouse cluster sites were fully agricultural and were occupied intensively and permanently (Ciolek-Torrello et al. 1994:445). At Meddler Point there is evidence for a full-time permanent population from the Colonial period onward. Preclassic settlement on Schoolhouse Point Mesa may have began in the Colonial period, but the quantities of pithouses and sherds encountered indicate the occupation was not as extensive as that documented on Meddler Point. The low quantities of pithouses and Preclassic period sherds (Table 9.1) suggest the Schoolhouse Point Mesa occupation was small scale. Pithouse features were dispersed, and many were ephemeral suggesting seasonal use. By contrast, Craig and Clark (1994:21) recorded many distinct, clustered pithouses (31 definite and 18 possible pithouses) at Locus A at Meddler Point.

Pithouses also are recorded on Pinto Point, just across Pinto Creek to the east. Jacobs (1994c:161) found twelve pithouses and two possible pithouses while trenching the compound area of the Pinto Point Mound (V:5:66). The greater concentration of pithouses there distinguishes the settlement histories of Schoolhouse Point Mesa and Pinto Point. The clustered pithouses on Pinto Point probably reflect year-round sedentism that contrasts with the dispersed pithouses on Schoolhouse Point Mesa, which may have been occupied seasonally (Gilman 1987:553). Both sets of pithouses would have coexisted but the proposed greater residential stability indicated by the pithouse concentration on Pinto Point suggests that its development into a village occurred before that of Schoolhouse Point Mesa. The proximity of both sets of pithouses makes it likely all were part of a single larger community on the south bank of the Salt River that was loosely integrated since ball courts have not been recorded in Tonto Basin.

Classic Period Occupation: Roosevelt Phase Growth of the Dispersed Village

The greatest number and dispersal of sites on Schoolhouse Point Mesa date to the Roosevelt phase of the Classic period. Most are compound sites that indicate year-round residence and a dramatic population increase, which is a pattern that occurred in other areas of Tonto Basin. Accompanying this increase is evidence for differentiation among sites. A two-tiered system of residential sites existed with a single large site (U:8:24) having integrative functions not found at smaller sites. Finally, there is evidence of integrative facilities at some sites that could have accommodated the participation of people from all of the other sites on Schoolhouse Point Mesa.

The Roosevelt phase settlement pattern represents a dramatic change from Preclassic settlement. At least 22 compounds and a room block site are counted on upper and lower Schoolhouse Point Mesa (Figure 9.2, Tables 9.2 and 9.3). These compounds are all associated with trash middens and granaries, which indicates a greater permanency of occupation compared with Preclassic settlement. Continuity between Preclassic and Classic period settlement on Schoolhouse Point Mesa is suggested by the presence of pithouse features underlying five Classic period compounds (Table 9.1). Because pithouses do not underlie all the compounds, the increase was not entirely a product of local growth—people from off of the mesa moved in. There is evidence from site V:5:119 (part of the Pinto Group, Figure 9.1) that, at the transition from the Miami to Roosevelt phase (about 1250), compounds originated as small enclosures containing two or three rooms (Jacobs 1994e:327) arranged like a cluster of pithouses. Evidence from Meddler Point, including tree-ring dates, indicates that compound architecture dates to the late thirteenth century, during the Roosevelt phase (Craig and Clark 1994:176). Although compound sites on Schoolhouse Point Mesa were probably not occupied all at one time, most decorated sherds from these sites date to the Roosevelt phase. The dramatic increase in the number of compound sites is also documented for Roosevelt phase settlements on Meddler Point and the Pinto Point area. Craig and Clark (1994:31) characterize the development of 16 compounds on Meddler Point (13 at V:5:4, two at V:5:91, and one at V:5:110) as a product of steady growth through time. Site growth in the Pinto Group, though not as extensive as at Schoolhouse Point Mesa, includes nine compounds (Jacobs 1994c). Thus, settlement growth on Schoolhouse Point Mesa was part

Table 9.3. Data on Roosevelt Phase Compounds on Schoolhouse Point Mesa

Site Number	Locus	Walled in Area (sq. m)	Rooms (n)	Associated Midden	Associated Roasting Pit	Presence of Oval Pitroom
U:8:24/13a	Fea. 153	378	NR	No	No	No
U:8:24/13a	Fea. 130	903	NR	No	No	No
U:8:24/13a	Premound A	144	2	No	No	No
U:8:24/13a	Premound B	1720	10	No	NR	No
U:8:25/14a	Locus A	500	3	Yes	Yes	Yes
U:8:25/14a	Locus B	420	2	Yes	Yes	Yes
U:8:25/14a	Locus C	500	2	Yes	Yes	Yes
U:8:25/14a	Locus E	—	3	Yes	Yes	No
U:8:25/14a	Locus F	500	4	Yes	Yes	Yes
U:8:291/13d	—	570	3	*	Yes	No
U:8:450/14b	—	405	3	Yes	No	No
U:8:451/1443	—	790	3	*	*	Yes
U:8:452/1470	—	—	2	*	*	No
U:8:453/13c	—	—	3	Yes	No	No
U:8:456/13e & U:8:457/13f	—	—	3	Yes	Yes	Yes
U:8:458/13b	—	—	6	Yes	Yes	No
V:5:137/12	—	1634	16	Yes	No	No
V:5:138/11	—	—	5	*	No	Yes

*Surface traces in area of lake inundation suggest feature was present
NR - None Recorded

of regional population growth in Tonto Basin. The establishment of slightly more compounds on Schoolhouse Point Mesa may have occurred because settlement conditions (perhaps for irrigation agriculture) were more favorable, which, in turn, may be the reason Schoolhouse Point Mesa settlement persisted into the Gila phase.

The first evidence of a two-tiered system of residential compounds occurs during the Roosevelt phase on Meddler Point and the area east of Schoolhouse Point including Pinto Point. Research on Meddler Point identifies a first-tier compound with structures that served to bring people from several compounds together. Two unusually large pit rooms in Compound 1 at Meddler Point are interpreted by Craig and Clark (1994:177) as small-scale, integrative facilities. Although these pithouses could

have functioned as meeting places, perhaps for ceremonies, there is evidence that they functioned as loci of domestic activity. Pit rooms alone did not distinguish this compound, because pit rooms occur in at least two other compounds on Meddler Point (Compounds 4 and 7). The orientation of this compound, rotated 45 degrees from the orientation of surrounding compounds, was a distinguishing factor. Compound 1 was ultimately enlarged to become the largest (ca. 2700 m²) of any compound on Meddler Point and the location of the platform mound.

Differentiation resulting in a two-tiered system of sites is expressed differently east of Pinto Creek where there is a lack of distinct, oval pit rooms in its compounds. Instead, pedestal bases of granaries or large, ringed roasting pits (ca. 10 m in diameter), which suggest a storage or processing facility, distinguish compounds. Pedestals and ringed roasting pits are rare on Meddler Point. The ability to host large feasts may have been the integrative activity that distinguishes these compounds (Rice 1990:9) from those on Meddler Point. Large-scale storage and processing facilities are not concentrated in the same compounds. Instead, compounds with large roasting pits tend not to have granaries (Rice and Redman 1993:59). The first-tier compound site on Pinto Point, V:5:66, ultimately contained a platform mound. Early in its occupation, the compound had a roasting pit, but the investigation of the premound compound did not expose granary pedestals (they occurred within rooms after a platform mound was constructed). We are uncertain whether the original compound was unusually large, but the concentration of pithouses beneath it is similar to Meddler Point (Craig and Clark 1994:180). Once the mound on Pinto Point was constructed, the compound wall enclosed the largest area (ca. 3,770 m²) of any compound on the south bank of the Salt River.

Only subtle evidence exists for a two-tiered system of sites on Schoolhouse Point Mesa. There was no platform mound site during the Roosevelt phase (McCartney and Lindauer 1996) that could have served as a comparable first-tier site. One is located a short distance across Pinto Creek on Pinto Point, which probably drew people from Schoolhouse Point Mesa for ceremonies. Despite the absence of a platform mound, several possible integrative facilities, both in a higher quantity and variety compared with neighboring villages to the east, were spread among residential sites on Schoolhouse Point Mesa. These facilities distinguish the Schoolhouse Point Mesa village from contemporary villages nearby.

Schoolhouse Point Mesa compounds show evidence for the functional distinctions found in compounds just described on Meddler Point and east of Pinto Creek. Oval rooms (Figure 9.3) of the type on Meddler Point that could have been small-scale integrative facilities occur in seven compounds (Table 9.3) — more than twice as many as at Meddler Point. It is unlikely that all the oval rooms were small-scale integrative facilities because all were smaller than the ones on Meddler Point (Table 9.4), had artifacts and hearths typical of habitations, and occurred with rectangular habitation rooms. If oval rooms

Figure 9.3. Oval room (Feature 30) at U:8:25, Schoolhouse Point Mesa.

Table 9.4. Roosevelt Phase Oval Room from Schoolhouse Point Mesa and Meddler Point

Site	Feature Number	Long Dimension (m)	Short Dimension (m)	Wall Construction	Comment
Schoolhouse Point Mesa					
U:8:451/1443	8	4.5	4.3	Rock-reinforced adobe	Metate, jars, hearth
U:8:456/13e	15	7	?	Unknown	Pit room in trench
U:8:25/14a	26	5.45	3	Cobble-masonry	Metate, jars, hearth
U:8:25/14a	30	5.32	4.4	Rock-reinforced adobe	Metate, jars, bowls, hearth
U:8:25/14a	31	5.1	3.4	Cobble-masonry	Jar, hearth
U:8:25/14a	34	3.95	3.55	Cobble-masonry	Metate, hearth
V:5:138/11	2	6.2	4.4	Cobble-masonry	Metate, jar, hearth
Meddler Point					
V:5:4/26	5	7.25	5	Cobble-masonry	Hearth
V:5:4/26	322	8.3	5.75	Rock-reinforced adobe	Hearth
V:5:4/26	459	7.3	5.6	Rock-reinforced adobe	Hearth

represent habitations whose function differed subtly from other rooms, it seems significant that such rooms were absent from the widely dispersed compounds east of Pinto Creek. Perhaps the oval rooms served a rotating, integrative role among the concentration of compounds on Schoolhouse Point Mesa.

Functional distinctions also occur in an unusually large number of compounds with processing or storage facilities larger than a household's. Large roasting pits occur with eight to ten compounds (Table 9.3), more than twice as many compared with the settlements east of Pinto Creek. Granary pedestals, however, are recorded at only two residential sites on Schoolhouse Point Mesa. One is the room block site (U:8:454), where two pedestals occur in one room; the other is in one of the compounds (Premound A and B) that developed into the Schoolhouse Point Mound (Table 9.3).

If there was a first-tier site on Schoolhouse Point Mesa it was probably the compound that was expanded and elaborated in the Gila phase to become the Schoolhouse Point Mound (U:8:24). Four characteristics distinguish this compound: 1) its large walled-in area; 2) its association with an unusually large granary; 3) its location relative to unusually large trash mounds; and 4) its Roosevelt phase cremation cemetery. Excavations at the Schoolhouse Point Mound (McCartney and Lindauer 1996) indicate that it originated

as two, closely spaced compounds during the Roosevelt phase (Table 9.3, Premound A and B). Although many of the walls of these compounds were modified by the architecture of the Gila phase mound, we have a reasonable idea of the extent of the compounds. One of these compounds (Premound B) had the largest enclosed area on the mesa but, as an integrative structure, it is less than half the area enclosed at Pinto Point Mound (3,770 m²) and smaller in area than the Meddler Point Mound (2,700 m²). Its size suggests that it may have functioned as an integrative facility only for Schoolhouse Point Mesa. Near the center of that compound was an unusually large granary pedestal, measuring more than three m in diameter. Evidence from identical smaller features that date to the Gila phase indicate that granaries were semipermanent storage structures for corn and possibly other grains (Lindauer 1996c). The presence of an extra large granary may be an indication of surplus storage, or at least an unusual concentration of food within one compound. Large storage facilities may indicate increased storage time that would have supported year-round sedentism (Gilman 1987:558). The periodic dispersal of stored food may have been a component of feasting, which would account for the three unusually large trash mounds (Features 1, 2, and 116 at U:8:24) at the site. Feasting on meat animals (mainly on deer and rabbits) may also have been important as a means to integrate the inhabitants by reinforcing obligations in the context of larger numbers of people associated with nearby compounds. Densities of meat animal bones from the three large trash mounds were characterized by J. L. Cameron (1996a:Table 14.18) as significantly higher than those of smaller middens from Roosevelt phase compound site U:8:25. The difference in density signals different meat consumption but the low quantity of bone suggests small-scale feasts. The final factor that distinguishes this compound from others on Schoolhouse Point Mesa is its cremation cemetery. Classic period cremation cemeteries are rare; the only others recorded are at the Roosevelt phase platform mounds at Meddler Point (Craig and Clark 1994) and Bass Point (Lindauer 1995a).

Other residential compounds also contained evidence of intercompound integration, mainly as large-scale roasting activity. A roasting pit is defined as a pit that contained sooty soil, fire-cracked rock, and charcoal. Roasting involved heating rocks, placing material to be roasted on the hot rocks, and burying it with more rocks and soil. When cooked, the covering soil and stones were discarded to retrieve the roasted material.

Roasting pits vary in size but fall into small and large size groups (Table 9.5). Small roasting pits are smaller than a m in diameter and 50 cm in depth. They frequently occur in compound plaza areas and occasionally in rooms (see Subfeatures 3.02 and 3.04 at U:8:458, Table 9.5). Large roasting pits occur in the center of roasting areas (Figure 9.4) that are about ten m in diameter (Subfeature 1.01 at U:8:153, Table 9.4). They are two to three m in diameter and approach a m or more in depth. The fill of the central roasting pits is identical to the small roasting pits. This fill also is dispersed in a circular area whose edge is bounded by a ring of cobbles. The combination of a large central pit and a surrounding area of sooty midden suggests repeated roasting activity; the cobble ring suggests a formally bounded aspect to the roasting. If the volume of a roasting pit is a measure of the amount of processed material, and if the volume of small roasting pits in rooms or plazas is a measure of the processing of a single household, the large roasting pit at site U:8:153 would have processed between ca. 18 and 88 times the single household volume. Although we cannot specify the precise magnitude of these large

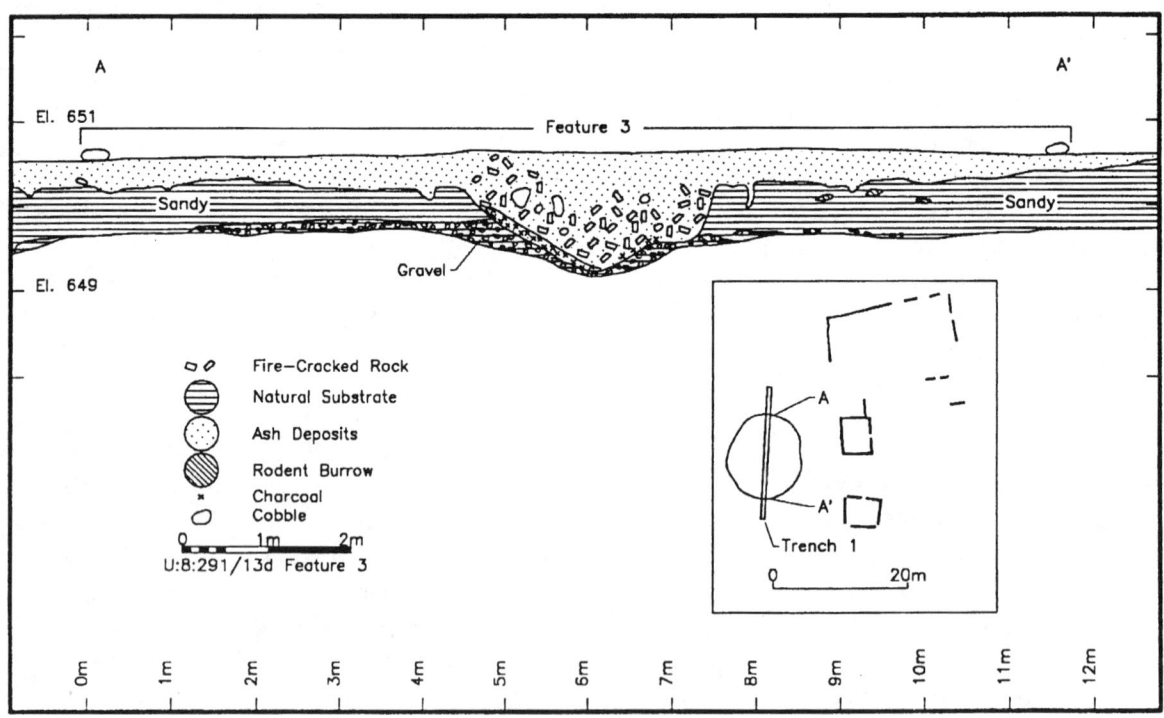

Figure 9.4.   Cross section of large roasting pit at compound U:8:291, view looking east.

Table 9.5. Selected Roasting Pit Dimensions and Volumes from Schoolhouse Point Mesa

Site	Feature/ Subfeature Number	Diameter (m)	Depth (m)	Volume (gal)	Volume (l)
U:8:153/1454	1.01	2.9	0.71	440	1667.6
U:8:318/1447	2.01	1.5	0.82	165	625.4
U:8:458/13b	3.02	0.75	0.35	25	94.8
U:8:458/13b	3.04	0.4	0.22	5	19

roasting pits, their volume indicates processing over and above the needs of the domestic unit. It would have been possible to process enough food for all the residential compounds on Schoolhouse Point Mesa in a single event.

Although the magnitude of roasting activity may have differed between small and large roasting pits, the method of roasting and the material roasted may have been the same. Macrobotanical and pollen evidence indicates residues of corn, agave, and cholla buds in both small and large pits (Table 9.6). Similar wood fuel re-

sources were used as well, indicating that the same kinds of material were processed in similar ways.

The number and dispersal of large roasting pits (Figure 9.5) suggest that large-scale food processing occurred on the mesa, perhaps rotating among compounds. Large-scale food processing probably would have been immediately followed by the sharing of the food among individuals from several different households or, perhaps, different villages that describes a feast. Among modern Southwestern societies, the interhousehold preparation and distribution of food is a regular part of social (i.e., births, deaths, weddings,

Table 9.6. Plants Represented by Macrobotanical and Pollen Remains from Selected Roasting Pits in Tonto Basin

Site	Feature/ Subfeature Number	Roasting Pit Size	Economic Plants	Fuel Wood
U:8:25/14a	46	small	—	Creosote bush
U:8:25/14a	45	small	—	Acacia, Desert Hackberry, Arrowweed
V:5:119/997	3.06	small	corn, cholla	Mesquite
U:8:450/14b	84	small	—	Mesquite, Saltbush type
U:4:33/132	82.04	small	—	Cottonwood/Willow type
U:8:318/1447	2.01	small	—	Mesquite/Paloverde/Acacia type
V:5:66/15a	35.08	small	agave, little barley	Mesquite
U:4:33/132	34.03	small	corn	Mesquite/Paloverde
U:4:33/132	73.06	small	—	Mesquite/Paloverde
U:8:458/13b	3.02	small	—	Mesquite/Paloverde/Acacia type, Jojoba
U:8:384/14d	7	large	—	Mesquite/Paloverde/Acacia type, Cottonwood/Willow type
V:5:66/15a	47	large	corn, agave, cholla buds	Saltbush, Mesquite, Cottonwood/Willow type
U:8:25/14a	6	large	—	Juniper, Mesquite, Cottonwood, Arrowweed
V:5:119/997	5.01	large	corn	Mesquite, Paloverde
U:8:153/1454	1.01	large	—	Mesquite, Paloverde, Cottonwood/Willow type
U:8:291/13d	3	large	agave	Arrowweed
U:3:205/1848	6.01	large	agave, com., cheno-am	Hardwood
U:8:531/106	8	large	cholla	—

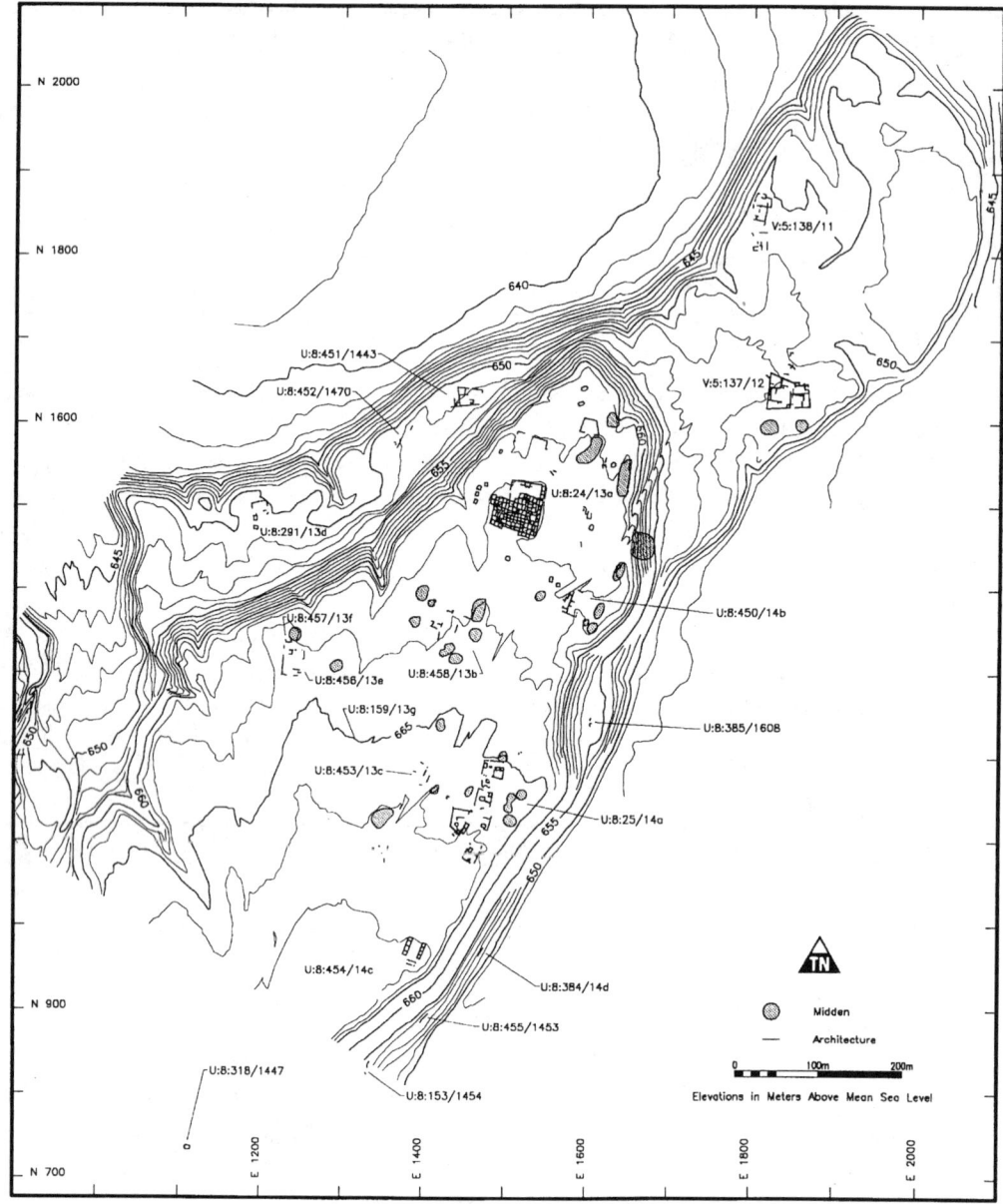

Figure 9.5. Excavated sites, mounded trash, and large roasting features on Schoolhouse Point Mesa.

coming of age) and ceremonial (i.e., rain and fertility dances) events as well as economic work projects (i.e., irrigation canal construction and maintenance). The preparation and distribution of large amounts of food encourages economic and social solidarity and serves to redistribute surpluses at times of need (Ford 1972). Two factors — cost and competition — would have encouraged rotating large-scale roasting among several different compounds. Large-scale roasting probably was followed by a feast that included occupants of neighboring compounds and elsewhere. While hosting the feasts likely diverted time and effort from other activities, there may also have been a competitive aspect to feasting because the host compound would probably gain prestige.

In addition to food preparation or roasting, cultivation may have been an economic aspect that led to interaction or interdependence among Schoolhouse Point Mesa compounds. Limited activity and room cluster sites include field houses and an agricultural field site (Table 9.2). It is likely that most of these sites date to the Roosevelt phase, although we know that one (U:8:318) was occupied during the Gila phase. One- or two-room field house sites are concentrated on the southern portion of upper Schoolhouse Point Mesa (Figure 9.2) and seem to mark the location of fields and perhaps a village boundary. Field houses on the eastern and western edges of the mesa overlook washes that could not have been farmed, which further suggests that agricultural areas were on the mesa top. One archaeological field site in this area is distinct because it is made up of multiple rock piles that retained water and probably encouraged the growth of agave. Site U:8:302, on the southwestern edge of the mesa (Figure 9.2), contained 29 small (about one m in diameter), low rock piles arranged in rows. These piles occur in a flat area on the edge of the upper terrace, which was watered by a wash that drains an extensive area to the south. A larger field containing 82 rock piles was recorded by Neily (1992) as U:8:571, in an identical topographic setting about one km west of the mesa. These observations indicate that the areas on the southern end of Schoolhouse Point Mesa, as well as adjoining upper terraces to the west, served as fields. More extensive fields must have been located on the Holocene terraces next to the river. Although the lake now floods this area, one field house (U:8:444) was recorded there (Figure 9.2). Evidence for river terrace fields downstream is indicated on an 1881 Government Land Office map that shows a quarter-section-sized cultivated field just west of Schoolhouse Point Mesa (in Sections 27 and 28).

A recent analysis of macrobotanical remains from Roosevelt phase compounds on Schoolhouse Point Mesa by Dering (1995b) indicates that the Roosevelt phase agricultural system was diverse and emphasized several codominant cultivated or encouraged plants including corn, cotton, cheno-ams, and agave. Cotton seeds were widely recovered and were the most ubiquitous of the major plant resources, followed by cheno-ams and corn. The widespread occurrence of cotton (recorded in six compounds) suggests that cotton production must have been emphasized perhaps as a trade item. At the Pinto Point Mound, cotton ubiquity in flotation samples was more than twice as high as for sites on Schoolhouse Point Mesa, and the ubiquity of corn and agave was higher. Although contexts from the large compound that lies beneath the Schoolhouse Point Mound were not sampled, the high values for the Pinto Point Mound suggest that these cultigens were concentrated there.

The extensive growth of Schoolhouse Point Mesa is part of a broad process of aggregation that probably involved the construction of canal irrigation systems (Ciolek-Torrello et al. 1994:450) requiring a larger number of cooperating households to build and maintain. The concentration of large trash middens at a few sites and dispersal of large roasting pits among different compounds probably reflect new sets of integrative activities that reinforced household interdependence. Platform mounds are probably also an outcome of the social processes developed to manage and integrate a larger number of households than ever before. While it is likely that multihousehold groups were formed from time to time before the Classic period, they probably were short-lived.

Rice (1992:21) suggests that the multihousehold groups that developed in the Roosevelt phase were corporate descent groups consisting of several lineages (supralineages). He recognized that during the Roosevelt phase several platform mounds were constructed in a three-mile stretch of valley bottom along the Salt River. The mounds (Pinto Point Mound, Pillar Mound, Meddler Point Mound, and Pyramid Point Mound; Figure 9.1) are divided evenly on the north and south sides of the river, and probably each was the "headquarters" of a corporate group such as a lineage. Schoolhouse Point Mesa had a large demographic concentration at the time but lacked a platform mound. Despite the absence of a platform mound, the scattering of large roasting pits and concentrations of trash in mounds indicate that the people of the mesa were integrated by other methods.

The platform mound system may have provided longer term (over the calendar year) and larger scale integration. The virtual collapse of the platform mound system a few generations after it was created, evident by the abandonment of most mounds, indicates platform mound activity was not sustained.

Late Classic Period Occupation: Gila Phase Nucleation, a Process of Social Inclusion and Exclusion

Nearly all sites on Schoolhouse Point Mesa were abandoned during the Gila phase (evidenced by the absence of Gila and Tonto Polychrome sherds) with the notable exception of the Schoolhouse Point Mound (U:8:24) an aggregated village having a few scattered surrounding rooms. If there was a two-tiered system of sites during the Roosevelt phase, it collapsed. Most people on Schoolhouse Point Mesa lived in one village of tightly grouped rooms year-round. The smaller sites, much fewer in number and more widely dispersed, were occupied temporarily. An analysis of architecture at the Schoolhouse Point Mound shows that its platforms were constructed during the Gila phase when the site witnessed its greatest growth (McCartney and Lindauer 1996). Two additional sites have evidence of occupation in the Gila phase. One is at U:8:450, three freestanding rooms that also is the locus of an abandoned Roosevelt phase compound. The other site is a field house with a roasting pit (U:8:318). The remaining compounds of Schoolhouse Point Mesa were abandoned, along with nearly every compound to the east. One compound on Pinto Point (V:5:139) probably was occupied in the Gila phase (Jacobs and Rice 1994a). Limited activity sites (roasting pits, fields, and field houses) on Schoolhouse Point Mesa continued to be used, as evidenced by radiocarbon dates from several large roasting pits.

Aggregation of residence into a single architectural construction on Schoolhouse Point Mesa occurred on a scale unmatched by any of the Roosevelt phase settlements on surrounding terraces. This aggregated settlement, the Schoolhouse Point Mound, could barely have accommodated all inhabitants of the Roosevelt phase residential compounds, at least in terms of number of rooms (Table 9.1). With the wholesale abandonment of surrounding compounds, the Schoolhouse Point Mound did not function as the nucleus of a dispersed village with surrounding residential sites. Instead it represented the massing of people from several compounds into a dense cluster. Several dispersed

Roosevelt phase villages on terraces overlooking the Salt River (east of Pinto Creek, Meddler Point, Pyramid Point, Griffith Wash area) were virtually abandoned at the time the population aggregation occurred on Schoolhouse Point Mesa. We cannot say whether all inhabitants of the Schoolhouse Point Mound originally lived in compounds on Schoolhouse Point Mesa. The pattern of room additions at the mound suggests that some individuals came to live there (possibly from on and off the mesa), while others abandoned their compounds and left. The process of inclusion led to aggregation at the Schoolhouse Point Mound, whereas social exclusion is responsible for the abandonment of many residential sites on this and neighboring mesas.

The Schoolhouse Point Mound functioned as a home village for, at most, 30 households (Lindauer 1996c). The arrangement of rooms, distribution of artifacts, and patterning among burials hints that those domestic groups consisted of several, perhaps four, larger social groupings. Three characteristics imply closer interdependency compared with the Roosevelt phase and distinguish the ways these social groups interacted. First, extensive storage facilities (47 granary pedestals and many large jars) concentrated in about 30 storerooms clustered in the village center suggest an emphasis on the generation and storage of surplus. Second, rooms on elevated platforms surrounded the storerooms and provided both security and the appearance of platform architecture that was, perhaps, an icon for large-scale integrative activity. Perhaps structures on raised platforms were the symbol of integrative activity that persisted while the Roosevelt phase integrative social organization changed. Third is the absence of a compound wall encircling the village, which implies significant change in the organization of personal/private space.

The analysis of the growth of Schoolhouse Point Mound provides insight into the scale of aggregation and, possibly, the source area for some of its population. Wall bonds and abutments indicate that rooms were added in blocks of two or three, suggesting the inclusion of household-sized groups of people. McCartney and Lindauer (1996) indicate that the location of room additions dramatically departs from patterns of Roosevelt phase compound architecture. When the original Roosevelt phase compound was expanded, rooms were added within and outside its boundaries without rebuilding a compound wall. More importantly, for the first time, rooms were built over adult burial pits, indicating a disregard for previous cemetery areas or an ignorance of their existence. Builders from a village off the mesa could have been ignorant of cemetery locations and unintentionally built over them, counter to the custom during the Roosevelt phase. Two Gila phase pit rooms at a site close to the mound (U:8:450) also were built over a Roosevelt phase cemetery.

The way in which some rooms at Schoolhouse Point Mound were filled and converted to platforms for elevated rooms employs Roosevelt phase platform mound engineering and space patterning, but in new ways. Unlike the massive platform constructions at Roosevelt phase mounds (Craig and Clark 1994; Lindauer 1996b), the room-sized platforms of the Schoolhouse Point Mound were roughly the same size and shared walls with adjacent ground-level rooms. Together the ground-level rooms and platforms formed a honeycomb of contiguously constructed walls that provided the engineering strength demanded for walls beneath platforms. The haphazard manner in which room walls connect and the variation in elevated floor elevations indicate that the first platforms at Schoolhouse Point Mound were built in two or three locations simultaneously. In each location, a platform that supported one or two rooms was built next to two or more ground-level rooms, each with evidence of storage facilities. The practice of constructing elevated rooms next to storerooms probably was copied from nearby Roosevelt phase platform mounds—Pinto Point Mound, Pyramid Point Mound, Bass Point Mound. Ultimately, the addition of new platforms led to the encirclement of the storerooms by elevated rooms.

Encircling the storerooms allowed their contents to be secure, if not secret (Gilman 1987:556), from outsiders. Security may have been necessary because the magnitude of stored material is estimated to have been far greater than that at a Roosevelt phase compound (Lindauer 1996c). Assuming that pedestal dimensions correlated to granary size, that all granaries had the same morphology, that they contained corn kernels, and that people relied on corn for 50 percent of their diet, the Schoolhouse Point Mound could have stored between 250 and 391 person-years of food, providing for 1.4 to two years of surplus (with a population of 124). These amounts contrast with the absence of surplus storage associated with a Roosevelt phase compound (occupied by twelve people).

Although a high degree of cooperation must have existed among the mound's inhabitants, social distinctions also existed. Where a degree of social boundedness in the

Roosevelt phase was probably marked by numerous walled compounds across Schoolhouse Point Mesa, such boundedness is absent in the contiguously constructed rooms of the Schoolhouse Point Mound. Gila phase cemeteries at Schoolhouse Point Mound were differentiated in burial location, burial accompaniments, and burial pit type (Loendorf 1996c). Loendorf determined from the position of the human remains and burial accompaniments that some of the individuals were buried together at or about the same time in a single pit or crypt. In other cases, used crypts were reopened and the remains of a new individual added, displacing previous burials in the process.

Crypt burials dating to the Roosevelt phase across Schoolhouse Point Mesa indicate that similar forms of differentiation occurred earlier. The presence of a particular morphological trait in four or five individuals in one Roosevelt phase crypt (Regan et al. 1996) suggests that the individuals in the crypt were genetically related, such as members of an extended family or clan. Independent evidence for such a relationship among individuals lies in similarities in ceramic burial accompaniments (Simon and Ravesloot 1994). Thus, burial crypts in general may have been used by social units whose membership was based on genetic relationships. Roosevelt phase burial crypts in four cemeteries at the Schoolhouse Point Mound site and two other sites (U:8:25 and U:8:450) indicate, on the basis of the variety and quantity of artifacts, that each had at least one burial crypt that was distinctive from other burial facilities in the cemetery. These cemeteries indicate the existence of several social entities, each distinguished by genetic affiliation. The cemetery at U:8:450 is distinguished as having most of its crypts with large, diverse funerary offerings. Other cemeteries have at most one crypt that matched the diversity of funerary offerings. The difference suggests that social ranking existed within and between social entities resident in compounds. Other evidence of social distinctions in the Roosevelt phase, evidenced by alternative burial treatments such as distinct cremation cemeteries and burial in trash middens, may have ended with the Roosevelt phase.

Social distinctions continued to be marked in cemeteries during the Gila phase. Burial crypts at the Schoolhouse Point Mound cluster in several locations in elevated corridor areas and in the South Cemetery. The eight crypts uncovered in the South Cemetery were larger and probably contained more vessels compared with those in the corridors of the Schoolhouse Point Mound. Four of the eight crypts contained painted wooden artifacts that may have been symbols of authority (Loendorf 1996b). The exclusive association of these painted wooden artifacts with the South Cemetery, and the fact that the South Cemetery was too small to have accommodated burials from all the village's social units, suggests that the social units were socially ranked, as postulated by Rice's (1992; Chapter 6) ranked segmentary organization.

The rarity of Gila phase room cluster and limited activity sites contrasts with the abundance of the same documented for the Roosevelt phase. Room cluster sites could have been either temporary or permanent residences. Three Gila phase rooms at U:8:450 probably represent an extension of the permanent residence of the Schoolhouse Point Mound. They are located within 100 m of the mound and were built over, or utilized the remains of, Roosevelt phase architecture. Two rooms intrude burial pits, whereas the third room probably is a remodeled version of an existing room. Each of these rooms contained hearths and similar arrays of domestic artifacts on the floor (mano, metate, Gila and Tonto Polychrome jars), suggesting that they were probably year-round residences.

Temporary residence or field houses dating to the Gila phase indicate continued use of field areas, though probably at a lower intensity. Field house site U:8:318 occurs among a concentration of Roosevelt phase field houses (Figure 9.2) and indicates continuity in land use. The single room at U:8:318 had several Gila phase decorated sherds on its floor, but the unprepared nature of its hearths and the presence of a small roasting pit in its floor suggest that the room was temporarily or seasonally occupied. Processing beyond the needs of a household is suggested by the presence of a second roasting pit on the large end of the small-size class (Table 9.5) directly in front of the room. This pit's volume is about six times the size of roasting pits associated with a single household.

Limited activity sites, especially large roasting pits, document continued large-scale processing activity during the Gila phase on Schoolhouse Point Mesa. Small and large roasting pits from sites on and off of Schoolhouse Point Mesa across Tonto Basin, and the botanical contents of these features are listed in Table 9.6. The figure and table indicate Basin-wide evidence that small- and large-scale roasting pits continued to be used throughout the Classic period and that the same material—corn, agave, and cholla—was processed regardless of the size

of the pit. Thus, the integrative activity centered on large-scale roasting continued in the Gila phase on Schoolhouse Point Mesa as well as elsewhere in Tonto Basin. These data also indicate a trend identified on Schoolhouse Point Mesa for the continued use of a roasting pit at an abandoned Roosevelt phase compound (U:8:291). The two other large roasting pits with Gila phase dates (at U:3:205 and U:8:531) also occur on abandoned Roosevelt phase compounds on the bajada slopes north of the Salt River and in the Tonto Creek area. The dispersal of large roasting pits on Schoolhouse Point Mesa (for both the Roosevelt and Gila phases) probably is related to processing for an entire village, with location shifting in order to spread costs and to allow other social segments to host feasts.

The abandonment of most residential compounds on Schoolhouse Point Mesa and neighboring terraces combined with a reduction in Gila phase field areas (fewer field houses) and processing sites imply integrative activity at a reduced frequency and scale during the Gila phase. The number and location of middens is another indication of change. Large mounded middens generally imply long-term residential stability. When they occur with smaller middens at sites with only a few rooms, they could have resulted from large-scale refuse generating behavior such as feasts. The amount of midden and its distribution across the mesa provides a rough measure of possible integrative activity connected to feasting. During the Roosevelt phase, mounded middens usually occur beside most compounds. Larger Roosevelt phase trash mounds that could have been generated from feasting also occur at the edges of some sites (Figure 9.5). The six trash mounds that surround U:8:458, a Roosevelt phase compound with perhaps six rooms (Table 9.1), is the most unusual instance of midden formation that may be explained by feasting. The dispersal of mounded middens in several areas across the mesa suggests dispersed, possibly large-scale or recurrent feasting activity. Other feasting evidence from mounded middens is equivocal. J. L. Cameron (1995b) indicates that the mounded middens at three compound sites (U:8:450, U:8:453, and U:8:458) apart from those at U:8:24 had unusually high densities of cottontails, artiodactyl, and large mammal bones that could result from periodic feasts, entailing low quantity but out-of-the-ordinary meat processing. The largest of the mounded middens (at U:8:24, U:8:453, U:8:450, and U:8:458) are spatially dispersed, some cooccurring with large roasting pits and others not. By comparison, Gila phase middens occur as refuse areas immediately outside room walls (Lindauer 1997) of the Schoolhouse Point Mound. Because middens associated with the Schoolhouse Point Mound appear to be of appropriate size and location for the duration of occupation, it is likely that feasting activity declined.

The Gila phase aggregation on Schoolhouse Point Mesa is part of a broad process of settlement reorganization that probably left almost the same number of people on the mesa but all living in one location. The abandonment of compounds in surrounding areas indicates that people were excluded (with few exceptions) from living on terraces overlooking the Salt River. A similar process of aggregation and exclusion occurs in the upland area south of Schoolhouse Point Mesa. Crary et al. (1992) document the aggregation process in the uplands in their Las Sierras study area; they recorded 85 Roosevelt phase habitations and only one Gila phase habitation site. Oliver (1994) detected many abandoned Roosevelt phase compounds and a single Gila phase residential site in the upland area along Armer Gulch to the northwest.

DISCUSSION

The dynamic growth and reorganization of the village on Schoolhouse Point Mesa is reflected in other locations in Tonto Basin, particularly, as indicated above, along the Salt River. Growth and reorganization also characterize the settlement pattern for the western end of the Basin along Tonto Creek (Oliver and Jacobs 1997), which suggests that research on Schoolhouse Point Mesa allows an understanding of aspects of Salado economy and power relationships.

Villages in Tonto Basin have always been farming settlements. Elson et al. (Chapter 7) describe some of these early settlements. Investigations of Preclassic period pithouses on Schoolhouse Point Mesa and Pleistocene terraces to the west (Lindauer 1997), suggest that many pithouse settlements could be either seasonally occupied or occupied year-round and that increased sedentism focused on locations near river terraces where floodwater or canal irrigation could have been practiced. The Roosevelt phase of the Classic period brought increased occupational permanence as well as greater numbers of residences. A compound, probably of one or two households, was the basic unit of residence. The scattering of compounds on Schoolhouse Point Mesa, some with in-

tegrative facilities such as circular rooms, large roasting areas, and granary storage facilities, indicates that the inhabitants of those compounds interacted and were perhaps interdependent, forming a larger social unit called a dispersed village that contrasts with an arregated village where residences were attached or very close to each other. The dramatic increase in numbers of residential compounds during the Roosevelt phase took place over a few generations, making it unlikely that the increase was from internal growth. Instead, the Pleistocene terraces overlooking the Salt River became an attractive place to settle due to the stability associated with intensified farming of river terraces and broad-scale climatic changes (Van West and Altschul 1994; Van West et al., Chapter 2). The continuities in artifacts and consistency in compound architecture (as opposed to room blocks) among Roosevelt phase sites suggest that most people relocated from other places within, and a few from outside, Tonto Basin (Elson et al., Chapter 7; Simon and Jacobs, Chapter 8). At the transition of the Roosevelt and Gila phases, sometime between 1300 and 1350, many residences in this dispersed village were abandoned, and a single, large, aggregated village on Schoolhouse Point Mesa came into being. Although the number of people in the dispersed village was equal, or nearly equal, to the aggregated village, the changes in the settlement system described above are marked by large-scale demographic movements within Tonto Basin as well as between the Basin and neighboring regions. After 1350, there were fewer people in the eastern Tonto Basin and many of them lived in the aggregated village at the Schoolhouse Point Mound.

During the Roosevelt phase, villages were complexes of dispersed compounds (Elson et al., Chapter 7). The concentration of several of these "dispersed villages" in an area favorable to canal irrigation (Figure 9.1) suggests that the regional settlement was similar to the Hohokam irrigation community because of the inferred reliance on canal irrigation. Although the Schoolhouse Point Mesa village was dispersed, it was not a dispersed community because habitations, fields, and limited activity sites do not appear to extend beyond the river terraces. The presence of more than one platform mound among villages on the same canal (Pinto Point Mound and Pillar Mound) indicates that the Tonto Basin Roosevelt phase community was a variant of the Hohokam irrigation community model. Although a variety of foods were gathered, cultivated, and harvested, it is likely that canal irrigation was the primary component of the subsistence strategy. Cotton cultivation on river terraces and agave cultivation on Pleistocene terraces overlooking the river led to increased interdependence among households that may partially explain this community pattern.

That interdependence may have been acted out in a number of ways, including small-scale aggregation and the development of sites with integrative functions. In this regard, the Schoolhouse Point Mesa village contained two compounds whose enclosure was two to three times larger than the others (1,600 m^2 or more in area; see Table 9.3) that are not of the same configuration. In Gregory's (1995a:135) analysis of Tonto Basin compounds, he identified these as compounds of intermediate size having enclosed areas of between 800 and 1,800 m^2. He indicates that they result from an aggregation of two or three social entities. Site V:5:137 has an irregular shape that is apparently the result of successive additions of rooms and extensions of the compound wall. This contrasts with the rectangular configuration of the compound at U:8:24 (Premound B), which was built as a single, large compound (McCartney and Lindauer 1996). The former compound results from an aggregation of social entities whereas the latter represents the planned construction of a large enclosure as an integrative activity. The bounding of plaza space can be seen as an investment in nonsubsistence related corporate effort (Rice and Jacobs 1994) such that constructing large compounds could have been an integrative activity unrelated to subsistence that may have integrated people within the dispersed village. Also, this large rectangular compound has evidence of a possible village-scale storage structure. Large rectangular compound walls surrounding the Pillar Mound and Meddler Point Mound and nonhabitation ground-level rooms built against the platforms, suggest that these large compounds were not residential and yet were the locus of integrative activity. Recent estimates of the effort required to build a platform mound suggest that it was not necessary to draft laborers beyond the surrounding irrigation community (Craig and Clark 1994; Lindauer 1996b). Therefore, it is likely integrative activity was village-scale, though the proximity of the Pinto Point Mound to Schoolhouse Point Mesa suggests that platform mounds could become the nucleus for several villages.

Adjustment to changes in the economy probably account for both the growth and changing structure of the village. The rapid growth of the dispersed village combined with increased reliance on irrigation created immediate and new problems that required larger-scale integrative activity. Problems associated with constructing, maintaining, and sharing canals, or perhaps integrating larger numbers of households in dispersed villages (that may have included unrelated kin or migrants), demanded that integrative activity be continuous and occur simultaneously at several social levels. Large rectangular compounds, some with and some without platform mounds, might have developed from a need for integrative facilities catering to different and perhaps overlapping social entities (Rice, Chapter 6). The large compound that precedes the Schoolhouse Point Mound was probably an integrative locus that combined unusually large storage facilities, habitation, and periodic feasting (indicated by unusually large middens). At other large rectangular compounds, the distinction between residential and nonresidential function was blurred. Some compounds with platform mounds were primarily ceremonial precincts (i.e., the Meddler Point Mound and the Pillar Mound), whereas others (i.e., Pyramid Point Mound, Pinto Point Mound, Bass Point Mound) may have combined ceremonial and residential functions. While the unusually large Roosevelt phase rectangular compound on Schoolhouse Point Mesa may have been a locus of village level integration, the nearby platform mound on Pinto Point probably offered another higher or a more regionally inclusive level of social integration.

A variety of processes at the beginning of the Gila phase probably are responsible for aggregation and abandonment on the mesa. Van West et al. (Chapter 2) as well as Waters (1994a) identify erratic stream flow during the Roosevelt-Gila phase transition as a source of stress that may have led to conflicts. The abandonment of all the platform mounds built in the Roosevelt phase in the eastern Tonto Basin (Pinto Point Mound, Meddler Point Mound, Pyramid Point Mound, and Pillar Mound) might be explained by the rejection and collapse of the integrative system symbolized by platform mounds. A similar chain of abandonments and village consolidations is documented on the upper bajada slopes of the eastern Tonto Basin (Oliver 1997b:473), indicating a systematic change for the region. The Gila phase settlement pattern on Schoolhouse Point Mesa is much smaller in scale and less complex. With the aggregation of the dispersed village the irrigation community was replaced by a less integrated dispersed community unit, perhaps one of large-scale that could have included the entire Salt Arm of Tonto Basin.

In several ways, the Schoolhouse Point Mound represents a continuity of processes evident in the Roosevelt phase. Clearly, the large number of habitation rooms indicate the Schoolhouse Point Mound was a residential site composed of several social entities. Large, Roosevelt phase compounds whose rooms and compound walls were added through accretive growth probably represent an earlier, smaller scale manifestation of this process. The Schoolhouse Point Mound also was an enormous storehouse where food surpluses were concentrated and stored securely, perhaps secretly. The construction of platforms served partly to restrict access to storerooms and contributed to their secrecy. This pattern of food storage is documented in the Roosevelt phase Pyramid Point Mound (Elson 1994b) and Bass Point Mound (Lindauer 1995a, 1995b).

The combination of mound architecture, surplus food storage, and aggregated residences made the Schoolhouse Point Mound a large year-round residential village with integrative facilities. The abandonment of residential compounds or other components of earlier village-scale units on neighboring river terraces indicates a fundamental change in the regional community unit. Although other villages on river terraces existed at this time, notably in the Armer area downstream, and probably contained a comparable population, they were more widely separated. Upland villages also existed and were generally of smaller scale with a few exceptions. It is likely that the distance between interacting villages within a community greatly expanded. Competition between villages has been proposed (Rice, Chapter 6) because aggregated settlements in the uplands were established in defensible positions (i.e., rock shelters, hill tops, ridge tops). These positions contrast with the Schoolhouse Point Mound, whose lack of an encircling compound wall made it more approachable. Some upland villages, particularly one on the Basin's south rim (Tonto National Monument; Steen et al. 1962) contain evidence of strong lowland contact. One room in Tonto National Monument's Lower Ruin contained more than 1500 corn cobs (discarded or stored as fuel). Cotton as finished clothing as well as raw bolls was found in both Tonto National Monument's Upper and Lower Ruins. Because cotton and corn could not be grown in great quantity on the steep slopes surrounding these rockshelters, it must have been brought in from villages close to the river

where canal irrigated fields were established. In contrast, Gila phase villages on the Basin's north rim were located in areas where upland farming was possible, allowing these villages to be more independent of villages along the Salt River (Oliver 1997a).

The botanical remains from the Schoolhouse Point Mound suggest that agriculture, probably based on canal irrigation, continued to be the core of the subsistence strategy. A benefit gained by concentrating residence downstream from the confluence of the Salt River and Pinto Creek was the ability to simultaneously monitor two irrigation districts. With the reliance on irrigation, the demands for integrative activity continued. In addition, the large-scale abandonment of compounds removed the demands to solve human problems associated with multiple, closely-spaced, dispersed villages. New problems arose associated with people living in an aggregated settlement and an overreliance on canal irrigation for subsistence. The stream flow reconstruction described by Van West et al. (Chapter 2) as well as work by Waters (1994a) indicate that a succession of drought years were followed by devastating floods that could have rendered the canals inoperable in the mid-fifteenth century. Abandonment of the river-oriented villages probably followed quickly from those events.

Conclusions

The preceding discussion of community development on Schoolhouse Point Mesa is a model for community development in Tonto Basin. It is proposed that the earliest communities in the Basin were dispersed communities composed of pithouses inhabited by people who relied both on wild resources and cultivated foods, some of which were probably grown in irrigated fields. The centers of dispersed communities may have been the locations with the highest densities of pithouses. These were the same locations that provided the best access to irrigated fields. With population growth and platform mound construction in the Roosevelt phase the dispersed community focused on irrigation agriculture and became organized as irrigation communities. Platform mounds and a host of residential compounds were constructed that suggest the expansion of existing canal systems and dividing their control among communities who pooled their efforts to maintain them. The creation of large roasting pits and the development of granaries on Schoolhouse Point Mesa illustrate the importance of large-scale processing and storage of food that became available with intensified irrigation agriculture. Similar features recorded elsewhere in Tonto Basin indicate Basin-wide changes.

Then, by the Gila phase most of Schoolhouse Point Mesa was abandoned, leaving a single large aggregated village that became a unique variant of the irrigation community. While the Roosevelt phase irrigation community was a loosely tied cluster of residential compounds on terraces overlooking arable river land, the Schoolhouse Point Mound was an irrigation community where its occupants lived together in one village location. Both the architectural structure and the storage function of the central rooms indicate increased household interdependence among households than previously. Abandonment and aggregation were processes seen in other parts of Tonto Basin that suggest that the organizational changes observed on Schoolhouse Point Mesa occurred elsewhere. In particular, the Roosevelt phase social organization of Schoolhouse Point Mesa allowed some households to consolidate their hold over productive irrigated lands while excluding others. Both the exclusion and competition (when stream flow became erratic) may explain the large-scale abandonment of residential compounds in the Gila phase. Ultimately, the aggregated community organization of the Schoolhouse Point Mesa could not adapt to the increasingly erratic stream flow of the Salt River.

ACKNOWLEDGMENTS

Research described here was part of the Roosevelt Platform Mound Study, a study of the prehistory of Tonto Basin funded by the Bureau of Reclamation under permit of the Tonto National Forest conducted by Arizona State University. Jeffrey Dean commented and provided editorial suggestions on a draft of this paper. Figures were prepared by Peter McCartney and drafter at the U.S. Bureau of Reclamation under the supervision of Thomas Lincoln. I thank these individuals for their assistance.

CHAPTER TEN

Salado:

The View from the Arizona Mountains

Stephanie M. Whittlesey, Richard S. Ciolek-Torrello, and J. Jefferson Reid

Who were the Salado? This is a mystery that archaeologists have struggled with for more than sixty years. We have come full circle in our understanding of the Salado Culture. Ideas that once were prominent but that were later discarded as old-fashioned have been resurrected and supported with new and stronger evidence. Salado stands as a testament to the intractability of the often mute past and the difficulties encountered when we attempt to make it speak (Reid and Whittlesey 1997:230).

Today, many archaeologists, if not the majority, interpret the prehistory of Tonto Basin Salado in terms of one perspective, that of the Hohokam culture. They treat the Tonto Basin as a northward extension of the Phoenix Basin, to which they apply wholesale the Hohokam culture-historical sequence, organization, and developmental trajectory. In the words of Effland and Macnider (1991:8), "One of the most distinctive expressions of Classic period Hohokam is a group known as the Salado" (also see Wood and McAllister 1982:81). Embedded in this approach is a theoretical construction of sociopolitical complexity and the formation of elites through concentration of power and manipulation of surplus (Rice 1990c).

Our objective is to compare the Salado with the Mogollon of the Arizona mountains north and east of Tonto Basin. In so doing, we provide a counterpoint to the Lower Sonoran Desert perspective that has been applied to the Salado for more than a decade (Effland and Macnider 1991; Macnider and Effland 1989; Rice 1985, 1990c; Wood and McAllister 1982, 1984a). Although it can be claimed that a lack of alternative models is responsible for deference to Phoenix Basin models in explaining Tonto Basin prehistory, most archaeologists actually have ignored alternative models that have existed for many years.

Our perspective is that the Salado phenomenon must be viewed in the context of larger regional processes. We see Tonto Basin as "home to a pluralistic population representing multiple ethnic or cultural affiliations" (Ciolek-Torrello et al. 1994:451). The Roosevelt phase, when the Salado phenomenon began, was "the beginning of a period of major immigration and aggregation in the Tonto Basin sometime in the second half of the thirteenth century" (Ciolek-Torrello et al. 1994:451).

Some aspects of the model we propose have been rediscovered recently by archaeologists who have returned to the Salado migration model, albeit in a much reshaped and more contemporary guise (Stark, Clark, and Elson 1995a). For example, Elson, Gregory, and Stark (1995:452) write, "environmental and social stress encouraged small numbers of pueblo-related groups to migrate into the eastern Tonto Basin during the early portions of the Roosevelt phase." Although we applaud the belated recognition that processes of migration, joint use, and coresidence operated in Tonto Basin, we are saddened that the notion of the Salado as nothing more than the Classic period expression of the Hohokam wasted much time in pointless argument.

Our model is rooted in the original Salado concept (Gladwin and Gladwin 1935) as subsequently modified by Reed (1948, 1950), Pilles (1976), Steen et al. (1962), and others and in a primary question of Grasshopper research at its inception—"to shed considerable light on the movements on Western Pueblo groups and on the origin of the Salado culture" (Thompson 1963:3). Recognizing the extent to which processes of migration and coresidence affected settlement and organizational dynamics in the Grasshopper region (Longacre 1975, 1976; Reid 1973, 1978), Whittlesey and Reid (1982) proposed that similar principles operated in Tonto Basin. Research for the Cholla Project (Reid 1982)—the first sizable contract project in Tonto Basin—indicated that all monothetic cultural labels—Mogollon, Hohokam, or any other—should be discarded and that the multicultural population of Tonto Basin became even more diversified during the late 1200s as displaced Anasazi and Mogollon populations joined established groups (Whittlesey and Reid 1982:80).

The model was refined as new data were collected (Ciolek-Torrello, ed. 1987; Reid 1989), permitting its organizational features to be sketched (Ciolek-Torrello and Whittlesey 1996; Whittlesey and Ciolek-Torrello 1992). Incorrectly known as the "egalitarian model" (Elson, Gregory, and Stark 1995; Lightfoot and Upham 1989), its elements were organization based on membership in kinship groups and sodalities, political authority and decision making vested in ritual authority, and ethnic coresidence requiring large-scale integrative mechanisms. Whittlesey and Ciolek-Torrello (1992; Ciolek-Torrello et al. 1994) also argued that a more realistic appraisal of the constraints and opportunities of Tonto Basin was necessary to balance the prevailing emphasis on its advantageous character (Welch 1994a).

The Salado-as-Hohokam concept emerged in a peculiar context when the trajectory of Southwestern archaeology was changing radically. The notion was born in a paper by Wasley (1966), later published by Doyel (Wasley and Doyel 1980). Wasley's conclusion that the new developments of the Classic period were primarily produced by Mexican influences became subordinate to the idea that the Hohokam alone were responsible, which Doyel (1977, 1981) subsequently expanded. Indigenous development held enormous appeal for archaeologists weary of

traditional models of migration, diffusion, and assimilation as explanations for sociocultural change. "Archaeology as anthropology" was radicalizing the discipline, and the Salado-as-Hohokam notion fit well within this new interpretive framework. Perhaps most significant was the tremendous expansion of contract archaeology, which primarily was Hohokam archaeology associated with the demographic and construction explosion in the Arizona deserts.

No models of Salado prehistory have been tested adequately, for strong archaeological data did not exist until recently. The Cholla Project (Reid 1982), the Miami Wash project (Doyel 1978), and other excavations were small compared to the data base compiled by Bureau of Reclamation-sponsored projects. We return, therefore, to evaluate earlier notions with an extensive data base.

In comparing the Tonto Basin Salado with the mountain Mogollon, we take direction from the themes of *power, economy,* and *ethnicity* that emerged from seminar discussions to discuss subsistence and settlement patterns, social organization, and ethnicity. We consider mountain landscapes first. Tonto Basin is not simply an environmental and physiographic extension of the Phoenix Basin, although it shares many of its Sonoran Desert characteristics. It is viewed more appropriately as part of the central Arizona Transition Zone with which it also shares many attributes. Although most of the mountain zone is agriculturally challenging, there are islands of resource advantage where farming was highly productive. Tonto Basin was such an area, with the unique advantage of a river suitable for irrigation.

We propose that the variable and uneven distribution of resources in the mountain highlands forged an adaptive strategy that was diversified, dispersed, and based on residential mobility throughout much of prehistory. This strategy was altered in particular times and places to involve greater settlement stability and agricultural dependence, as among isolated areas of resource advantage, the village-farming settlements of Tonto Basin, and the late, aggregated mountain pueblos. A key to understanding settlement-subsistence systems is the recognition that the mountains and Tonto Basin alike were focal areas for centuries of joint use and coresidence by people of different ethnic groups (Reid and Whittlesey 1997).

The population of Tonto Basin, as elsewhere in the Transition Zone, was multicultural and multiethnic. Much of the peculiar intractability of the Salado phenomenon stems, we believe, from the fact that the Salado were not one people, but many. The cultural melting pot was the culmination of long-term processes of joint use, immigration, and coresidence by people of varied origins. People closely involved in the Hohokam integrative system certainly occupied Tonto Basin, but they were not alone. The prolonged history of joint use fostered increased immigration during periods of social and environmental stress.

We argue the relevance of three ethnographic analogs to explain economic and social adaptations to mountain landscapes. Western Apache, Hopi, and Eastern Pueblo models explain differing adaptive modes to particular times and places. For most of prehistory, kinship and sodality membership was paramount; land tenure was vested in descent groups, and village-based organization did not develop. Salado social organization took a new direction in the Roosevelt phase, as the need for community-based organizational and integrative systems was necessitated by intensified irrigation agriculture. A key tenet is that throughout prehistory, social and economic organization was oriented toward the management of scarcity. The manipulation of surplus that is the cornerstone of the Hohokam view of Salado is not supportable ethnographically or archaeologically. Under the conditions of late prehistory in Tonto Basin, the emergence of sociopolitical complexity was not a probable developmental trajectory.

Mountain Landscapes

The Mogollon highlands of central Arizona represent a rugged mountain zone that is environmentally diverse and extremely challenging to prehistoric farmers. The growing season is short, with the potential for early and late frosts. Arable soils are limited in extent, and headcutting and erosion are persistent problems (Holbrook and Graves 1982; Reid 1989:69). The mountains are well watered, however, by springs, seeps, permanent streams, and generous although unpredictable precipitation. The advantages for hunter-gatherers are evident. Game and wild plant resources are abundant, and diverse upland and lowland resources are juxtaposed. The distribution and abundance of wild resources vary, however, according to environmental variables that can change yearly, seasonally, and spatially.

Three basic landscapes characterize the Arizona mountains. First are islands of resource advantage, which are upland areas where diverse wild plant and animal resources are combined with exceptional conditions for dry farming. These areas have extensive arable land and reliable water supplies, receiving 46 to 53 cm of rainfall each year and characterized by high water tables, springs, and cienegas—a great attraction during times of drought in surrounding regions. Floodwater farming and small-scale irrigation based on springs and small drainages were relatively productive. Islands include the Forestdale Valley, the Kinishba area, and Point of Pines. The latter was a particularly favorable farming locale, an inland basin characterized by a high water table that was tapped readily with walk-in wells.

Second and most widely distributed are the intervening upland areas between islands of resource advantage, which are characterized by less optimal conditions for farming. These areas were not suited to long-term dependence on farming, but did encourage a mobile hunting-gathering strategy augmented by gardening. Such areas generally are drier than islands of resource advantage and lack surface water, and some are at lower elevations. Floodwater farming on alluvial floodplains and fans, assisted by simple systems for control of runoff, was the gardening practice of choice (Tuggle 1982; Tuggle et al. 1984; Woodbury 1961a). The Grasshopper and Q Ranch regions (Reid 1982, 1989) at the eastern edge of Tonto Basin represent the more typical mountain environment.

Third are lower-elevation basins and canyons characterized by diverse wild plant resources and perennial streams that could be harnessed for agriculture. The largest of these is Tonto Basin. The Basin shares many characteristics with mountain islands of resource advantage. The topographic and vegetative diversity recognized by Doyel (1972, 1976b, 1978) provides a mosaic of upland and riverine resources. The Basin offers a stretch of arable alluvium larger than any other in Welch's (1994b) Circumsonoran uplands, and its physiographic variability provides a variety of agricultural opportunities. Tonto Basin's location between the mountains and the desert, to which it was linked by corridors such as the Salt River and Tonto Creek, was significant economically as well as socially. There is a singular difference from other mountain landscapes, however—a river runs through Tonto Basin. The Salt River, along with Tonto Creek, permitted irrigation agriculture that was not possible in most of the mountains. It is not surprising that Tonto Basin was a magnet for settlement by diverse populations.

These opportunities were balanced, however, by constraints. Precipitation and frost events are highly variable and unpredictable. The Salt River poses management problems for irrigation in its narrow profile, steep gradient, sediment load, and susceptibility to hazardous flooding (Welch 1992, 1994a). Historic records suggest that agriculture was carried out on a relatively small scale, primarily in the Tonto Creek drainage (Davis 1902; Forbes 1916; Greely and Glassford 1891; Welch 1992, 1994a). If a "Sonoran Advantage" (Rice 1990c) existed there, it was modified by disadvantages.

ETHNOGRAPHIC ANALOGS

We have argued the relevance and utility of ethnographic analogy elsewhere (Whittlesey and Ciolek-Torrello 1992), and do not repeat it here. The three models we propose as analogs for the prehistoric settlement, subsistence, and social organizational adaptations to the landscapes discussed here are Western Apache, Hopi, and Eastern Pueblo.

Western Apache

The Western Apache are an appropriate adaptive model for the typical mountain landscape outside islands of resource advantage, explaining well the Mogollon settlement and subsistence system prior to the late 1200s in the Grasshopper and Q Ranch regions (Reid et al. 1996), and much of the Preclassic period occupation of Tonto Basin. Flexibility and mobility in settlement and subsistence were keys to Apache mastery of the unpredictable and variable mountain environment. The amount of wild foods that was incorporated into the diet fluctuated from band to band, with environmental and political conditions, and with agricultural success (Buskirk 1986:197). Goodwin (1935:61) estimates that in prereservation times cultivated foods contributed about one-fourth of the total diet. Some bands farmed much more extensively than others, however, particularly the White Mountain band. Populations remained small through primary dependence on hunting and gathering.

Residential mobility was necessary to exploit seasonally available resources, and population and organization varied along with task groups. Scarcity and resource shortfalls were managed through mobility. Goodwin (1942) illustrates the scope of Western Apache movement across the landscape in exploiting wild resources. Each year, family and task groups ranged from above the Mogollon Rim to the mountains of southeastern Ari-

zona, and raiding parties might foray as far south as Sonora. Larger groups aggregated at gathering areas where the harvest was plentiful and to conduct public ceremonies. Anchoring the system were the farm sites, to which each local group returned yearly. The most permanent houses (*gowa*) were constructed and the most food was stored at the farm sites (Goodwin 1942:160).

Western Apache farming practices offer excellent clues to prehistoric horticulture in the mountains. Although floodwater farming was more typical, farms were irrigated whenever possible. The small main ditches, diversion dams, and feeder ditches used would leave few archaeological traces (Buskirk 1986; Goodwin 1942; Graves 1982b).

Family clusters (Basso 1970:24) were extended families that chose to live together because of blood or economic ties (Goodwin 1942:123). Each household in the cluster lived independently, coming together to cooperate in common tasks. Residence in the family cluster tended to be matrilocal. Local groups composed of family clusters were the basis of society, supporting economic and social enterprises and forming the basis of political leadership (Basso 1983:471; Opler 1983:369). Subsistence activities were organized at the local group level, and directed by the leaders of these groups. The largest unit was the band, composed of local groups.

The matrilineal clan system operated outside of the territorially based bands, local groups, and family clusters. Clans functioned in many areas, but primarily served to create a network of relationships cutting across and integrating bands and local groups (Basso 1983:472). The resulting support mechanism created economic benefits extending beyond simple kinship groups.

Hopi

The Hopi provide the best model for the ways in which upland village farmers structured their social, political, and economic lives. This analog is appropriate for islands of resource advantage and also for the aggregated communities of late Pueblo III-Pueblo IV times in the Mogollon highlands.

Kinship was the basis of land tenure and the source of religious power and social rank. Exogamous, matrilineal clans—ranked according to distance from the prime lineage holding the ritual prerogatives—controlled land, houses, ceremonial knowledge, and the transmission of accompanying rights and responsibilities (Levy 1992:24). Two social strata were based on clans' possession of ritual knowledge and power (Levy 1992:31; Whiteley 1988:65–68).

Settlement and subsistence were predicated on land tenure by kin-based groups and the inequitable distribution of good farmland. Arable land was restricted in extent, and productivity varied according to the amount of runoff received (Bradfield 1971; Forde 1931; Levy 1992). The highest-ranking clans controlled the best land and allocated the best fields to the higher-ranked lineages (Levy 1992:25, 45), creating real economic benefits. High-ranked groups maintained a more dependable food supply and were able to produce cotton, which was traded widely, in all but the driest years (Levy 1992:46).

Group fissioning was the primary mechanism for bringing unbalanced relationships between land and population back to equilibrium (Eggan 1966:125; Levy 1992; Whiteley 1988). In times of drought, residential colonies were established when all of the available well-watered farmland near the village was under cultivation. The lower-ranked clans and lineages were forced to migrate or starve.

Importantly, Levy (1992) discovered that the high-ranking clans had a high infant mortality rate; most were in some danger of dying out (Levy 1992:42–43). Although they controlled the better resources, "they cannot be described as an elite in the sense we usually use the term. There was no economic surplus to speak of," and the high-ranked clans did not manage or redistribute what surplus there was (Levy 1992:156).

Although there have been attempts to argue that the Hopi "class" system was stratified (Brandt 1994), the religious elite exerted extraordinarily little true political authority. The political authority of the village chief was limited to disputes over land ownership and use. His primary role was to ensure the success of the crops and the well-being of the village through exercise of his ceremonial obligations (Titiev 1944:64). The absence of coercive authority is well illustrated in accounts of the Oraibi split (Titiev 1944).

The authority of the leaders was based on fear of the supernatural power they controlled (Whiteley 1988:69, 258). Psychological manipulation, especially fear of group criticism and supernatural repercussions, was the only technique available to compel group action and generally was an effective restriction on radical activity (Adams 1991:150; Titiev 1944:65; Whiteley 1988:128, 215, 268).

Organizations based on principles other than kinship crosscut the community and promoted integration. Clan exogamy and village endogamy constrained the consolidation of hereditary power, and marriage alliances tended to unite households of different rank and prevented the creation of cliques (Levy 1992:68). Although controlled by specific clans and headed by priests from the controlling clan, membership in ceremonial societies was open to everyone, regardless of clan affiliation (Levy 1992:3–4).

Hopi also provides us with an excellent ethnographic example of the extent to which village farmers move across the landscape to join with kin and nonrelatives. The Tewa of the Rio Grande established the village of Hano on First Mesa in 1700. According to traditional history, the Tewa moved as a village to First Mesa at the request of the Walpi village chiefs following the Pueblo Revolt (Dozier 1954; Stanislawski 1983). The history of Oraibi also presents an outstanding example of the instability of organizational principles and the manner in which communities disintegrated and new ones were formed.

Eastern Pueblos

The Eastern Pueblos provide an ethnographic model for interpreting the organizational needs of village irrigation farmers in Tonto Basin. The importance of labor organization in irrigation societies has long been posited (Wittfogel 1957; Wittfogel and Goldfrank 1943). Its role in Rio Grande Pueblo society is illustrated cogently by Dozier (1970:127). Communal effort is required to clear land and build terraced fields, and to construct and maintain irrigation ditches. As a consequence, the Rio Grande Pueblos typically involve the entire adult population in agricultural efforts. Two consequences stem from the need to coordinate labor efforts: land tenure becomes communal, and organizational structures must encompass the entire village. Whereas the Hopi control land by clan and lineage, among the Tanoans land is controlled by extended families. Ownership of property is vested in the sodality leadership, and families are given usufruct rights to village-owned property; the village leaders assign land and houses to individual families (Jorgensen 1980:137).

Control of village sacred and secular organization was invested in nonkinship groups among the Eastern Pueblos. Sodalities, usually dual in nature (moieties), directed and mobilized the labor needed to maintain irrigation systems and coordinated communal subsistence and agricultural pursuits. They also maintained the religious cycle, organized community ceremonies, and directed construction and maintenance of the communal kiva and plaza. Political leadership was invested in the moieties, which controlled the nomination and installation of secular officials. In some villages, these responsibilities alternated between the moieties during the year, and there was an associated dual chieftainship (Dozier 1970:169–70). Sodalities did not, however, regulate marriage or coordinate relationships among kin groups (Jorgensen 1980:190).

Because irrigation provides considerable control over water, ceremonial organization among irrigation societies is directed toward maintaining labor needs rather than ritual appeals for rain (Dozier 1970:128). As Adams (1991) has noted, there is a striking correspondence between the community- and moiety-based organization of the Eastern Pueblo irrigation societies and the weak development of the Katsina Cult, which is especially diluted among the modern Tewa and Tiwa. The Katsina Cult, with its emphasis on bringing rain and fertility to crops, was a less appealing and functional integrative device than among the Hopi (Adams 1991:121).

The principle of duality served as a profound organizing tenet of Eastern Pueblo society, structuring symbolism and ideology as well as organization (Ortiz 1969). There was visible, spatial segregation of moieties by architectural divisions, symbolic division in thought and ideology, and practical division in the ritual, social, and political calendars.

Most important, some coercive authority existed among the Eastern Pueblos. The village chief, who belonged to the sodality that ruled the village, held secular as well as ceremonial power. The chief and associated priests could compel communal duties under threat of physical punishment or banishment with attendant confiscation of houses and land. There was far greater political centralization than among the Western Pueblo (Dozier 1970:129, 132; Jorgensen 1980:155; Ortiz 1969).

Subsistence and Settlement Systems

The adaptive systems that evolved in response to the challenges and opportunities of mountain landscapes remained stable throughout most of prehistory. The key to understanding mountain systems is mobility. Settlements shifted to exploit diverse resources and typically were small and dispersed widely. Subsistence was a mixed strategy combining wild resource collection, hunting, and farming. The uneven distribution of mountain resources conditioned indigenous residents

and their neighbors to the advantages of residential mobility and joint use of islands of resource advantage to solve resource-population imbalances. Population movement was a recurrent response to variables of the natural and social environments and the foundation for managing scarcity and resource shortfalls. Mobility enhanced information exchange, so that groups experiencing hard times knew where good times might be achieved once again. This basic pattern was altered in particular times and places by the unusual characteristics of islands of resource advantage and by the unique suitability of Tonto Basin for irrigation agriculture.

Mountain Mogollon

Mogollon settlement and subsistence systems were a response to the uneven distribution of resources in the mountain landscape (Reid 1989; Reid and Whittlesey 1997). Settlements were distributed unevenly and shifted constantly in response to seasonal variability in resource availability and abundance. There is ample evidence that Plateau and Desert peoples as well as Mogollon used the mountains as a vast resource procurement area. The mountains attracted hunters and those with a taste for pinyon nuts and acorns. People also journeyed there to procure salt, chert, hematite, steatite, argillite, and turquoise, and there is no evidence that access to these resources was controlled or restricted (Lange 1982; Welch and Triadan 1991).

The magnitude of residential mobility within the mountain zone is indicated by Cholla Project research (Reid 1982). Analyses of material remains from sites along the project transect spanning the Little Colorado to the Salt Rivers suggest that, whereas hunting was emphasized in the Q Ranch region and in the Chevelon area above the Mogollon Rim, plant-processing activities dominated in the Tonto-Roosevelt region (Graybill and Reid 1982; Montgomery and Reid 1993; Reid 1982). The use of varied mountain locales on a temporary basis for different aspects of the seasonal round is implied by the paucity of permanent habitation sites. An exploitation zone extending minimally from above the Mogollon Rim to the Salt River is inferred.

By Pueblo II times (900 to 1100), the pattern among typical mountain environments was one of many small, dispersed settlements consisting of pithouses and semisubterranean, cobble and jacal structures ranging from single rooms to small clusters of rooms. These settlements were located near small plots of arable land, and often were associated with check dams and rock-lined terraces (Cart-ledge 1976, 1977; Ciolek-Torrello and Lange 1979; Reid 1989; Tuggle 1982; Tuggle et al. 1984; Wood 1980). Rather than representing a large population, these ubiquitous small sites attest to a mobile exploitative strategy and a long-standing pattern of transient occupation in which settlements were built, soon abandoned, and new settlements constructed nearby (Reid and Tuggle 1988; Tuggle 1982; Whittlesey 1982).

In islands of resource advantage, recurrent occupation and greater residential stability were possible. More extensive farmland and more reliable water sources resulted in settlements that were larger, occupied longer, and occupied recurrently. Islands also drew ethnically diverse populations in greater numbers than other parts of the mountains. The late Pueblo II period Tla Kii Ruin in the Forestdale Valley, for example, is a compact pueblo of 21 rooms and a great kiva that went through at least six building episodes (Haury 1985:34–36). Haury (1985) argues that the distinctive nature of Tla Kii Ruin and the earlier Bear Village in the Forestdale Valley is attributable to a strong Anasazi presence.

A.D. 1200S

In the 1200s, the pattern of mixed subsistence and short-term residential stability that had persisted for centuries in an enormous region of central Arizona gave way to a new pattern of increased aggregation and residential stability reflecting local population growth and increased immigration, as environmental deterioration drove populations from the Colorado Plateau to seek agricultural land in more beneficial climes (Reid 1989). Not all areas were affected in the same ways at the same time, however.

Aggregation clearly was accelerated in islands of resource advantage. The largest Pueblo III period sites of the Grasshopper and Q Ranch regions are minor compared to the contemporaneous, aggregated villages at Forestdale and Point of Pines. In the Forestdale Valley, village size increased to at least 100 rooms by late Pueblo III times (Haury 1985:16). At Point of Pines, Turkey Creek Pueblo, occupied between 1240 and 1300 (Bannister and Robinson 1971; Graves 1984; Lowell 1991), has an estimated 335 rooms, two plazas, and a central great kiva. Much of the accelerated growth in these areas can be attributed to Anasazi migration in response to environmental stresses of the middle 1100s and early 1200s, when the first series of abandonments on the Colorado Plateau occurred (Van West et al., Chapter 2).

Cherry Creek, located between the Q Ranch Plateau and Tonto Basin, represents a microcosm of the region below the Mogollon Rim. The uplands along upper Cherry Creek, including the Vosberg and Pleasant Valley localities, experienced most intensive development during the 1100s and 1200s, when numerous small, probably seasonal settlements were distributed widely near arable land. Middle Cherry Creek near the Sierra Ancha and the Q Ranch Plateau is an intermediate zone with the most environmental diversity. Lower Cherry Creek includes low-elevation areas near the confluence of Cherry Creek and the Salt River. The lower and middle reaches of Cherry Creek are amenable to irrigation agriculture, although the area is considerably smaller than Tonto Basin. Throughout much of its earliest occupational history, settlements there were similar in form and distribution to those in the nearby Tonto Basin. By the 1200s, settlements comparable in type and scale to those of the Roosevelt phase were built along lower and middle Cherry Creek (Wells 1971), and several pueblos were built on high ridges overlooking tributary drainages in the southeastern Sierra Ancha. At least one small platform mound also may have been built there (Richard Lange, personal communication 1995).

The appearance of a complicated settlement system in middle Cherry Creek, consisting of small, medium, and large settlements situated in diverse locations, was coeval with the similar system in Tonto Basin, but 30 to 50 years earlier than in the Q Ranch and Grasshopper regions (Ciolek-Torrello and Lange 1982, 1990). Cliff dwellings built in the 1280s (Ciolek-Torrello and Lange 1990) also were at least 30 years earlier.

Settlement size in more typical upland areas like Grasshopper and Q Ranch remained comparatively small. In the Grasshopper region, there were three settlement clusters around agricultural soil centered on Chodistaas, Grasshopper Spring, and Grasshopper pueblos in the late 1200s. The largest settlement was Chodistaas Pueblo, with 18 rooms and an enclosed plaza (Montgomery 1992; Montgomery and Reid 1990; Reid 1989; Zedeño 1994).

A.D. 1300S

In the 1300s, aggregation on the Grasshopper and Q Ranch plateaus was associated with rapid population growth, an increase in distance between villages, and the occupation of virtually every topographic zone (Tuggle 1970:35, 40). On the Grasshopper Plateau, ten sites have more than 35 rooms and include the 500-room Grasshopper Pueblo, the largest mountain pueblo west of Kinishba Ruin (Reid 1989; Tuggle 1970). Settlements were constructed in high mountain meadows or in the head-water basins of major tributaries of the Salt River, in smaller basins where drainages drop into the canyons at the edges of the plateaus, and along ridges above canyons. The first significant occupation of the cliffs above Canyon, Cibecue, and Cherry Creeks occurs (Ciolek-Torrello and Lange 1979:124), including Canyon Creek Ruin (Haury 1934).

Population dynamics of the Grasshopper region have been studied intensively (Ciolek-Torrello 1978; Graves 1983; Longacre 1975, 1976; Reid 1973, 1989). Construction of the three major room blocks at Grasshopper Pueblo was initiated between 1290 and 1300. The growth of the pueblo describes a logistic curve (Eighmy 1979), accelerating rapidly with the addition of multiple-room construction units (Ciolek-Torrello 1978:80–83, 189–90). A cluster of tree-ring dates for a roofed corridor indicates that the main components of the settlement core were completed by 1320; less than a decade later, one of the plazas was converted into the great kiva. The date of this event corresponds to the time at which logistic growth reached a plateau. Growth in the main room blocks apparently ceased after 1350 (Ciolek-Torrello 1978:80–81).

Longacre (1976) estimates the sizes of founding and peak populations using a simulation program modeling annual population growth and immigration rates. According to Longacre (1976:183), the simulation results indicate that the peak population could only be accounted for by immigration from other settlements. It is unlikely that the hypothetical immigrants derived solely from aggregation of local settlements, given the small number of Pueblo III period habitation sites.

Reid (1973, 1989:85) proposes that as the size of Grasshopper Pueblo stabilized, it began to disperse, first into smaller, less substantially constructed room blocks and later into satellite communities. Many of the older, interior rooms of the main room blocks were abandoned, and others were converted from habitation to nonhabitation functions, signaling a loss of population at the settlement's core (Ciolek-Torrello 1978).

Smaller, satellite pueblos established in the 1300s throughout the Grasshopper Plateau may have absorbed much of the population loss from Grasshopper Pueblo. Graves (1983) argues that Canyon Creek Ruin was established in 1327 after an extended period of stockpiling construction timbers. Its establishment coincided with the point in time when Grasshopper Pueblo reached its peak size. Canyon Creek grew most rapidly between 1330

and 1350, precisely when construction at Grasshopper Pueblo had leveled off. The absence of occupational evidence after 1400 indicates that the entire Grasshopper Plateau was abandoned by this time.

The population dynamics of the Q Ranch Plateau are less well understood, as excavation has been more limited. The Q Ranch Ruin, located in a large, upland basin, was the largest settlement (100 to 200 rooms). Three smaller basins each supported a single pueblo of 20 to 30 rooms and several smaller sites. Cliff dwellings were few and small, although their place in the settlement system was served in part by medium-sized, fortress-type sites situated on high mesa tops (Ciolek-Torrello 1979). The Q Ranch Ruin and several smaller pueblos and cliff dwellings replicate the pattern found on the neighboring Grasshopper Plateau. Site size was considerably smaller, however, as arable land on the more heavily dissected Q Ranch Plateau was broken up into smaller parcels.

By the 1300s, only single, medium-sized pueblos remained on upper Cherry Creek, and these apparently were short lived (Cartledge 1976; Harrill 1967). Population aggregation and the development of settlement complexity also were terminated abruptly in lower Cherry Creek. Abandonment of upper and lower Cherry Creek occurred at the time when populations were beginning to aggregate and expand in the Q Ranch and Grasshopper areas, and were reorganizing in Tonto Basin.

In middle Cherry Creek, there was still greater aggregation as many of the medium-sized pueblos and compounds of the 1200s were abandoned, and the largest settlement, the Granite Basin Ruin, expanded to more than 100 rooms.

Islands of resource advantage maintained their primacy during the 1300s, with population sizes two to four times greater than areas such as Grasshopper and Q Ranch. At Point of Pines, for example, the total number of recorded rooms is nearly 2,000, and the average is 81 rooms per pueblo (Whittlesey 1986). Sites cluster in the Willow Creek drainage within five miles of Point of Pines Pueblo, the largest site with more than 1,000 rooms dating to this period. The 200-room Tundastusa and 800-room Kinishba pueblos represent the largest settlements in the Forestdale and Whiteriver areas, respectively.

Pueblo IV demographic processes and their social and environmental consequences set into motion significant changes in settlement and subsistence patterns. First, higher population density and the presence of immigrant groups increased the competition for resources, especially for scarce agricultural land. The result was an atmosphere of social and economic uncertainty that fostered a concern for defense and protection. The occupation of cliff sites and promontories in the Grasshopper region at this time may reflect such concerns (Reid 1989). The large surface pueblos are located with reference to defensive positioning along the perimeter of the plateau as well as near arable land (Tuggle et al. 1984). Defensive locations also were emphasized in the Q Ranch region, where numerous Pueblo IV settlements were located high atop buttes and in canyons (Ciolek-Torrello 1979). Similarly, nearly one-third of the recorded Pueblo IV sites at Point of Pines are cliff dwellings high above the valley floor along Nantack Ridge (Whittlesey 1986).

Second, the settlement and subsistence strategy that had characterized the Mogollon highlands for centuries was curtailed by population aggregation, depletion of wild food resources (particularly game), greater residential stability, density-induced environmental degradation, and conflict. The result was a transformation to greater maize dependence and its associated consequences. The agricultural expertise of Anasazi dry farmers who came to dwell in increasing numbers among the Mogollon at this time was an important factor in this process (Reid 1994:5; Reid and Whittlesey 1997).

This shift is particularly well demonstrated in the Grasshopper region. Large satellite pueblos were established to bring more distant and smaller areas of arable land under cultivation in an attempt to maintain or increase crop production. Bioarchaeological data from Grasshopper Pueblo indicate that consumption of wild resources decreased (Ezzo 1993:75, 79) as maize dependence increased (Decker 1986). Chronic nutritional stress characterized the subadult population (Hinkes 1983), suggesting that local agriculture was not meeting the needs of the population. It is probable that a reduction in the fallow cycle occurred, with a corresponding depletion in soil fertility. These problems were exacerbated by a 30-year drought beginning in the late 1320s.

Although other management options would have been available, the ultimate response to these processes was fissioning, dispersion, and abandonment (Reid 1989; Reid and Tuggle 1988). Groups gradually left Grasshopper Pueblo to establish new settlements. These probably were permanent habitations, as most arable land close to Grasshopper Pueblo likely already was in cultivation. Emigration of individual households that may have begun as early as 1330 probably peaked around 1350, and

was concluded before 1400. Residential moves were anticipated and planned for, as indicated by stockpiling of construction timbers prior to the actual founding of the Canyon Creek cliff dwelling (Graves 1982a, 1983). Close monitoring of recurrent environmental changes and a short response time for adjusting agricultural shortfalls are apparent (Reid and Graybill 1984).

Regardless of the specific factors that signaled the beginning of abandonment of the mountains, it is clear that agricultural technology was insufficient to support the requirements of a substantial, sedentary population over the long term. A region that for centuries had supported small, relatively mobile populations following a mixed forager-farming strategy could not sustain larger and more stable populations dependent on agriculture (Reid 1989; Welch 1994b).

Tonto Basin Salado

We see clear parallels between Tonto Basin and the Mogollon highlands in adaptive processes. A mixed and dispersed system with considerable residential mobility was practiced throughout Preclassic times, ceasing only in the Pueblo III period (Roosevelt phase) as a response to drought, increased population density, and associated social change (Ciolek-Torrello et al. 1994; Welch 1994b). Its character as an exceptional island of resource advantage marked by an river suitable for irrigation was responsible for many of the apparent differences between Tonto Basin and other areas of the central highlands.

Preclassic Period

The seasonally mobile population lived in small, dispersed settlements and followed a mixed subsistence strategy. The extent to which canal irrigation was practiced in the Lower Basin is not known at present, although the larger, more permanent settlements were situated where irrigation was most feasible. It is clear, however, that existing irrigation systems must have been much smaller than contemporary Phoenix Basin systems due to the narrow terraces and natural barriers of Tonto Basin (Ciolek-Torrello and Whittlesey 1996; Elson, Gregory, and Stark 1995; J. S. Wood et al. 1992).

During the Sedentary period, salubrious climatic conditions (Van West and Altschul 1994) and concomitant population growth resulted in an expansion of settlement onto the higher terraces (Ciolek-Torrello et al. 1994; Wood and McAllister 1984a). Settlement was characterized by small villages concentrated along the Salt

River Arm (Craig and Clark 1994; Elson and Lindeman 1994; Swartz and Randolph 1994a; Vanderpot and Shelley 1994; Vanderpot et al. 1994), and still smaller, seasonally occupied farmsteads distributed more widely throughout the Upper and Lower Tonto Basin and adjacent areas (Ciolek-Torrello 1994; Doyel 1978:207; Elson 1992a; Rice 1985:80, 253).

During the Miami phase, settlement expanded away from the riverine areas into bajada and piedmont zones (Ciolek-Torrello, ed. 1987; Germick and Crary 1989:14; Tagg 1985:144–45; Wood and McAllister 1984a:271, 282). This expansion was made possible by the unusually long period without any severe droughts; population growth may have begun to strain arable land as well (Ciolek-Torrello et al. 1990:20–21; Van West and Altschul 1994; Wood and McAllister 1984a). Curiously, there is relatively little evidence for Miami phase occupation in large areas of the Lower Basin, particularly the Salt River Arm (Ciolek-Torrello et al. 1994; Elson and Craig 1992a; Elson, Gregory, and Stark 1995).

Roosevelt Phase

The Preclassic strategy was altered radically by the appearance of the first Salado villages, consisting of dispersed compounds arranged around a platform mound (Ciolek-Torrello et al. 1994:450). Although aggregated farming villages appeared in the mountains and Tonto Basin at the same time, the advantageous character of the latter was responsible for a larger scale of aggregation. Adjacent mountain areas lacking perennial water supplies experienced a more moderate influx of immigrants who resided in settlements of 20 to 25 rooms. For example, whereas Chodistaas Pueblo is a relatively small compound consisting of two inferred residential and descent groups, the early Classic period complex at Meddler Point consisted of 13 residential compounds and the platform mound (Gregory 1995b:Table 5.10).

Although similar processes operated in the mountains and Tonto Basin, two major factors distinguish them: irrigation agriculture and platform mounds. Tonto Basin clearly was attractive to drought-ridden farmers on the Colorado Plateau seeking better-watered locales. Its physiographic and plant diversity made agricultural and economic diversification possible (Ciolek-Torrello et al. 1994:451–53). Water tables remained high throughout the Roosevelt phase, creating good conditions for irrigation agriculture along the major drainages (Van West et al., Chapter 2), when reliance on dry farming would have proved disastrous (Craig 1995:Figures 8.2 and 8.3; Van West and Altschul 1994:431). Farmers of the Colorado Plateau took advantage of irrigation when it was possible, as evidenced by irrigation ventures along the Little Colorado River (Adams 1989) and the Rio Grande, and Puebloan migrants into Tonto Basin no doubt incorporated irrigation into their agricultural repertoire.

We infer that the appearance of platform mound villages in the late 1200s was associated with the development of large-scale irrigation systems spurred by population immigration and reduced productivity of floodwater and dry-farming methods. Although an association between platform mound communities and irrigation has been posited for some time, there has been little agreement concerning the definition of irrigation-based systems. The locations of site complexes appear to be unequal in potential for different agricultural strategies, and may coincide with natural barriers to irrigation; platform mounds are not well correlated with population aggregations (Elson, Gregory, and Stark 1995; Van West and Altschul 1994; Wood 1985, 1986, 1989:8–13; J.S. Wood et al. 1992).

Nonriverine settlement also expanded in the Roosevelt phase (Ciolek-Torrello 1994; Germick and Crary 1990:14; Wood and McAllister 1984a), paralleling riverine settlement on a smaller scale (Ciolek-Torrello 1994; Gregory 1982; Reid 1982). Puebloan immigrants clearly exploited opportunities for dry farming and farming based on runoff-control technology and exploitation of upland springs. Economic and organizational diversification is well manifested in the middle Cherry Creek area, where a riverine platform mound community was built near large pueblos dependent on dry farming and cliff dwellings in upland canyons.

Gila Phase

Another major change occurred around 1325, when many Roosevelt phase settlements were abandoned, and the platform mound system appears to have fallen into disuse. As elsewhere during Pueblo IV times, the population coalesced into still larger, aggregated settlements, such as Schoolhouse Point. In most cases, Gila phase Salado pueblos are larger settlements than the platform mound communities that they replaced, suggesting amalgamation of several communities (Craig, Elson, and Swartz 1992; Rice and Redman 1993). Some mound villages, such as Cline Terrace, apparently continued to be occupied through the Gila phase (Jacobs 1997). The climatic model posed by Van West and Altschul (1994) indicates that this restructuring was based ultimately on the failure of some irrigation systems, which would have suffered from erosion in the postdrought moisture maximum of the late Roosevelt phase. By contrast, upland farming would have benefited greatly between 1300 and 1320 (Van West and Altschul 1994:431). Reorganization evidently accompanied loss of some of the most productive lands, a phenomenon consistent with ethnographic data that demonstrate fissioning, establishment of new settlements, and restructuring in the face of resource scarcity and loss.

The scale of population growth and aggregation in Tonto Basin and the mountains was the reverse of the previous century. The Roosevelt phase platform mound villages greatly exceed the scale of any settlements in the Grasshopper and Q Ranch areas. Pueblos of more than 100 rooms did not develop in these upland areas until after 1300, during the postdrought precipitation maximum when dry farming would have been most productive. The Grasshopper, Q Ranch, and Granite Basin pueblos are larger than any single, contemporaneous Gila phase site in Tonto Basin. It is likely that the uplands experienced greater levels of immigration from the Plateau during the early 1300s, whereas Tonto Basin population remained stable or was reduced slightly. The largest pueblos were built in the Grasshopper region at the time when most platform mounds and many villages in Tonto Basin were abandoned (Reid and Whittlesey 1997).

The Gila phase socioeconomic system appears to have been highly specialized and vulnerable to climatic unpredictability, given the concentration of population in a few large, riverine settlements, apparent expansion of irrigation, and abandonment of many upland areas (Ciolek-Torrello et al. 1994; Welch 1992, 1994a; Welch and Ciolek-Torrello 1994). In the mountains, population was even more concentrated and dependent on dry farming, fostering a similar instability and fragility. The abandonment of both regions at the end of the fourteenth century is not unexpected, given the pattern of alternating severe flooding and droughts that characterized this period (Van West et al., Chapter 2).

ETHNICITY

Throughout prehistory, the highlands of Arizona were characterized by the joint use of the region's resources by people of different ethnic traditions, and by the coresi-dence of these people at individual settlements (Reid 1989). Plateau and desert dwellers maintained contacts with indigenous people and knowledge of mountain resources and terrain through centuries of joint use, which no doubt facilitated residential moves.

It is unnecessary to look far for ethnographic examples of settled agriculturalists maintaining vast areas for resources procurement and for ritual purposes. A Zuni Atlas (Ferguson and Hart 1985) documents enormous resource exploitation zones that overlap considerably with the territories of neighboring agricultural tribes. Recent research (Zedeño and Lorentzen 1995) interprets a similarly expansive landscape for the Hopi. In the minds of many contemporary Southwestern archaeologists, small-group procurement and movement has replaced managed trade as the primary means of moving commodities across the landscape.

Mountain Mogollon

Because archaeologists examine villages more readily than limited procurement localities, we have more concrete evidence for ethnic coresidence than for joint use among the Mogollon. Bear Village (Haury 1940; Reid 1989), Walnut Creek Village (Morris 1970), Point of Pines (Haury 1958), and the Shoofly Ruin (Redman 1993), among others, mark points in the lengthy tradition of Mogollon people living together with Anasazi and Hohokam. The strongest recent evidence of ethnic movement to the mountains and coresidence comes from the Grasshopper region. During the 1280s, groups of Anasazi moved southward, abandoning the deteriorating Colorado Plateau environment. The contemporaneous Pueblo III period settlements of Chodistaas and Grasshopper Spring Pueblos were occupied by distinct ethnic groups. Chodistaas Pueblo has two room blocks, each consisting of eight domestic rooms and one ceremonial room, linked by an enclosed plaza. The northern and southern room blocks apparently were built by different groups, and one, evidently a Mogollon group having extensive, long-term contacts with Anasazi people, introduced into Chodistaas Pueblo a Plateau-derived ceramic technology that was employed with local materials (Zedeño 1994).

Grasshopper Spring Pueblo is a smaller, multiple-component site consisting of three small room blocks. Two room blocks contemporary with Chodistaas Pueblo include eight domestic rooms and a ceremonial room similar to those at Chodistaas Pueblo. Site layout differs, however, in that there is no enclosed plaza; the two small room blocks are separated by open space. In addition, different hunting technologies were practiced (Lorentzen 1993), firepits were used instead of slab-lined hearths (Lowell 1995), and the use of domestic space differs. The people living at Grasshopper Spring Pueblo may have been Plateau Anasazi people, in contrast to the Anasazi-Mogollon of Chodistaas.

Coresidence continued in the Grasshopper region during the 1300s as indicated by variability in site layouts (Reid and Riggs 1995), and is demonstrated amply at Grasshopper Pueblo. We think that people of the Chodistaas and Grasshopper Spring settlements, already of mixed ethnicity, joined with people living at Grasshopper to found what would become the region's largest settlement (Reid and Whittlesey 1997). Each of three core room blocks forming the initial settlement differed in size and layout. Throughout Grasshopper Pueblo's subsequent history, the integrity of each of the residential units was maintained. The pueblo is viewed most accurately as an aggregate of three "villages," each corresponding in size (120 to 140 rooms) to the next largest settlements in the region (Reid and Riggs 1995; Reid and Tuggle 1988). Each room block is associated with a plaza, each has a distinctive decorated ceramic signature, and bioarchaeological indicators suggest that different lifestyles were maintained. For example, Room Block 1 residents relied more heavily on wild plant foods, whereas maize was used most intensively by residents of Room Block 3 (Ezzo 1993:56).

Strontium isotope ratios of tooth enamel indicate that three of seven analyzed individuals likely were born elsewhere, moving to Grasshopper later in life (Price et al. 1994). Based on bedrock geology, Price et al. (1994:326–27) exclude Kinishba, Point of Pines, and much of the Colorado Plateau as potential origins for these individuals, and they suggest a possible origin in the Little Colorado region or somewhere farther north.

An enclave of Anasazi apparently lived in harmony with the indigenous Mogollon at Grasshopper Pueblo. Although the bulk of the population exhibited the vertical-occipital cranial deformation associated with the Mogollon (Reed 1948; Reid 1989), a small number of lambdoidally deformed individuals, mostly women and children, was found buried among the residential units (Birkby 1973, 1982). One group of Anasazi may have occupied Room Block 5, a small, detached group of rooms north of Room Block 2. The presence there of pit-and-chamber burials, which at Grasshopper Pueblo are associated only with individuals exhibiting lambdoidally deformed skulls, and T-shaped doorways points to a northern origin.

Anasazi males joined the same ceremonial societies to which the majority of Mogollon belonged, with the exception of the warrior (arrow) society. Indeed, the Anasazi residents may have enjoyed somewhat greater personal wealth, to judge by the variety of mortuary accompaniments. That this wealth may have accrued through participation in exchange networks is suggested by a manufacturing room in Room Block 5 with abundant evidence for fabricating turquoise jewelry, stone tools, and ceramic vessels (Triadan 1989).

Mixed ethnicity also is well demonstrated in the Point of Pines region. Rectangular room blocks lacking plazas or courtyards characterize the Pueblo IV sites, only two of which have the central plaza layout that is the Mogollon Pueblo archetype. Three sites exhibit U-shaped or linear layouts more typical of Anasazi settlement patterns (Whittlesey 1986). In the 1280s, a group of Kayenta or Tusayan Anasazi trekked to Point of Pines Pueblo, where they built a block of 70 rooms and a D-shaped, subterranean kiva (Haury 1958). Kayenta-style pottery made with local materials (Maverick Mountain Polychrome), a unique variety of corn, and northern-type architectural features such as T-shaped doorways and banded masonry point to the foreign origin of the enclave. The room block was burned deliberately, the surviving inhabitants fled, and their rooms were remodeled and reoccupied by the indigenous people.

The mixture of cranial deformation types at Point of Pines is especially interesting in light of the documented ethnic coresidence there. Bennett (1973b:10) reports that although vertical-occipital deformation predominated, the number of individuals exhibiting lambdoidal deformation and undeformed skulls was approximately equal, and that lambdoidal deformation was present prior to the Anasazi immigration.

Reid (1989) suggests that the Mogollon great kiva tradition functioned principally to maintain cooperation and harmony among groups of different cultural traditions. If so, the presence of great kivas at a number of mountain sites alone may signal the presence of an ethnically mixed, coresident population. That coresidence was not always harmonious is made clear in the contrast between the successful enclave at Grasshopper Pueblo and the failed Anasazi enclave at Point of Pines.

Tonto Basin Salado

The fact that Tonto Basin was exploited and inhabited by many different people (Ciolek-Torrello 1987; Ciolek-Torrello et al. 1994; Whittlesey and Reid 1982) has been obscured by the dominant desert perspective held by students of its prehistory. The joint use and coresidence that culminated in the Salado phenomenon was rooted as far back as the Early Formative period (Ciolek-Torrello 1995; Deaver and Ciolek-Torrello 1995). Recent excavations at the Eagle Ridge site (Elson and Lindeman 1994) demonstrate an occupation much like that seen at Early Pithouse period Mogollon settlements dating between 200 and 400 (Anyon et al. 1981; Ciolek-Torrello 1995; Haury and Sayles 1947; Martin 1943; Sayles 1945; Wheat 1955). It is unnecessary to define a new culture area to explain Eagle Ridge, as do Elson et al. (1992:284). The most parsimonious explanation is that Eagle Ridge was occupied by people closely related to the Mogollon. The question is whether Eagle Ridge is representative of a culturally homogenous, Basin-wide pattern, or whether joint use of Tonto Basin by different cultural groups began as early as the initial ceramic period. We suspect the latter may be true.

Certainly there is ample evidence for joint use by people of diverse cultural affiliation throughout the Colonial and Sedentary periods. Hohokam groups began to occupy Tonto Basin around 750 and focused on its lower portion, either because the Upper Basin already was occupied or because the greater irrigation potential of the Lower Basin was more attractive (Ciolek-Torrello 1994; Elson et al. 1992; Elson, Gregory, and Stark 1995). Sites along the Salt River Arm appear strongly Hohokam in character, with formal pithouse architecture, courtyard arrangements, and a material culture dominated by Hohokam traits (Elson 1994a; Elson and Lindeman 1994; Elson et al. 1992; Haury 1932; Vanderpot and Shelley 1994; Vanderpot et al. 1994). Settlements remained comparatively small, and ball courts were absent, however, suggesting that the population was not integrated intimately into the Hohokam regional system.

In the Upper Basin, there was an indigenous occupation of a distinctive character. Site structure, architecture, and ceramics differ from typical Hohokam patterns, Hohokam ritual paraphernalia is lacking, and mortuary practices involved primary cremation on a four-post platform (Elson et al. 1992). Similar features characterize recently excavated sites in the Upper Basin near modern Punkin Center

(Michael Lindeman, personal communication 1995), as well as sites near Whiteriver (Halbirt and Dosh 1986) and the Picacho Pass site northeast of Tucson (Greenwald and Ciolek-Torrello 1987), suggesting that this pattern extended throughout much of central Arizona peripheral to the Phoenix Basin.

As suggested sixty years ago by Gladwin and Haury, there was migration into Tonto Basin during the Roosevelt phase (Ciolek-Torrello et al. 1994; Reid and Whittlesey 1997; Whittlesey and Reid 1982). Tonto Basin experienced the effects of the widespread population disjunctions and settlement reorganizations that characterized the mountain and plateau areas of the Southwest in the 1200s and 1300s. The regions that continued to be occupied were those with the most reliable water supplies, among which Tonto Basin was particularly attractive. Water control facilities such as terraces first occurred at this time (Bandelier 1892:388–89). We note that the pattern of Mogollon settlements' shifting to lower-elevation landforms and areas of permanent water supply has been known for many years (Beeson 1966; Danson 1957; Longacre 1962).

There appears to be a distinction between sites identified as room blocks and compounds (Clark 1995a; Crary 1991), although the effects of internal growth on site pattern have not been considered fully. Compared to compounds, room blocks exhibit greater room contiguity, less unroofed space, and fewer isolated rooms, and have an internal focus on courtyards. The pattern of site growth also differs. Whereas room blocks grew by adding new rooms adjacent to existing ones and utilizing common walls, growth in compounds was accomplished by adding new compound units, which often were isolated (Clark 1995a:Figure 9.5). Excavated examples of room block sites include Griffin Wash (Swartz and Randolph 1994b), Locus B at Meddler Point (Craig and Clark 1994), Saguaro Muerto (Lindauer 1994), and possibly U:8:454, a Roosevelt phase site on Schoolhouse Mesa (Lindauer 1997). The most recently excavated example of a large compound site is Locus A of Meddler Point (Craig and Clark 1994).

Other architectural evidence suggesting differing cultural affiliation lies in the varied construction and functions of Roosevelt phase platform mounds. Tonto Basin residents used platform mounds in varied ways, not all of which conformed to Phoenix Basin Hohokam patterns, and many exhibit distinct developmental histories (Whittlesey and Ciolek-Torrello 1992). Some mounds, such as Meddler Point (Craig and Clark 1994), exhibit the archetypal patterns of construction and use that characterize ceremonial mounds in the Phoenix Basin. Others, including the Pillar Mound (Jacobs 1994f) and the Pinto Point Mound (Jacobs 1994c), incorporate unusual architectural details. A few mounds, such as tiny Pyramid Point (Elson 1994a), appear to have functioned differently. The prominent location and single-room construction of the Pyramid Point "mound" suggest that it may have served a communication function (Elson 1994a:294). Doelle et al. (1995) believe it unlikely that Tonto Basin platform mounds represent an emulation of Phoenix Basin forms, either architecturally or organizationally. The platform mound concept clearly was interpreted within the context of already existing organizational systems, and mound diversity implies different organizational systems as well as the potentially differing ethnicity of their builders.

Other unusual architectural features indicating mixed ethnicity include T-shaped doorways, sandstone roof entry collars, and slab-lined hearths suggestive of Anasazi origin at U:8:454 (Lindauer 1997) and other sites. Architectural details that are reminiscent of Chihuahuan patterns are cobble-pedestal wicker granaries (Guevara Sanchez 1986; Sayles 1936) and roof support piers of cobble and adobe (Di Peso et al. 1974b).

Although most Gila phase sites in and near Tonto Basin exhibit room block layouts, such as Schoolhouse Point (Lindauer 1996a), Gila Pueblo, Besh-Ba-Gowah, and others, Cline Terrace is distinct. Its layout is more typical of a platform mound, with fewer contiguous rooms, mound cells, and a massive, enclosing compound wall (Jacobs 1997). Architectural elements foreign to the desert, however, include banded and chinked gypsum masonry, which in some features served as veneer over a cobble-masonry core, and a two-story, tower-like structure. Also distinctive are the cliff dwellings of Tonto National Monument. T-shaped doorways, masonry steps in doorways, and slab-lined hearths are among the architectural elements that suggest an Anasazi presence in these dwellings, which clearly are not typical of the Hohokam.

Ceramic data support the other evidence for ethnic differentiation. Wood and McAllister (1982:90) maintain that: "The Salado ceramic assemblage ... was identical to that recognized as Classic period Hohokam in the Salt-Gila Basin. This assemblage was dominated by sand tempered plain and red wares manufactured by the paddle-and-anvil and hand-molding technique common to all western traditions within the larger Sonoran culture." Whittlesey

and Reid (1982) note that this is simply not the case. Cholla Project data demonstrate a wide range of variability in the proportions of wares among contemporaneous Roosevelt and Gila phase ceramic assemblages. Whereas plain ware and red ware predominate at some sites, others exhibit high frequencies of brown corrugated pottery and Salado Red (Whittlesey and Reid 1982:Table 7.3). The ceramic assemblage of the middle Cherry Creek and southeastern Sierra Ancha areas on the fringes of Tonto Basin clearly falls within the Western or Mogollon Pueblo tradition (Haury 1934:20). Mogollon Brown Ware and Cibola White Ware are the dominant early wares. In later times, brown obliterated corrugated pottery and White Mountain Red Ware are predominate. Although Roosevelt Red Ware is abundant at many sites, it usually is secondary in frequency to White Mountain Red Ware. The strong Mogollon Pueblo flavor of this assemblage is especially significant because of the similarities in architecture, settlement patterns, vegetation, and topography to the adjacent Tonto Basin (Ciolek-Torrello and Lange 1979).

Striking variability exists among collections from recently excavated sites. Some sites exhibit mountain ceramics in high frequencies, particularly in the Salt River Arm and Globe-Miami areas. For example, corrugated ceramics and White Mountain Red Ware are abundant at Griffin Wash (Elson, Gregory, and Stark 1995:453). At Schoolhouse Point, corrugated pottery is 16.8 percent and Salado Red is 5.1 percent of the undecorated ceramic collection (Lindauer 1996d:Table 3.5). By contrast, Cline Terrace produced only 2.4 percent corrugated ceramics and 9.5 percent Salado Red (Jacobs 1995:Table 5.2). At Saguaro Muerto, corrugated pottery is an extremely high 41.2 percent of the undecorated ceramic collection (Lindauer 1994:Table 12.8).

As Ravesloot (1994b:845) notes for a rather typical Roosevelt phase compound, "the standard burial treatments afforded the dead are very similar to those reported at sites throughout central and southern Arizona during the Classic period (Whittlesey 1978; Reid 1989; Hohmann 1992[b]; Mitchell 1992) and ethnographic descriptions of modern pueblo mortuary treatments." Cemetery areas, grave facilities, body disposition, and burial accompaniments are identical to those observed at Grasshopper Pueblo (Reid 1989; Whittlesey 1978), Kinishba Pueblo (Cummings 1940), and Point of Pines (Robinson and Sprague 1965). Examples are found at Schoolhouse Point (Loendorf 1996a); U:8:450, a small residential compound on Schoolhouse Mesa dating primarily to the Roosevelt phase (Loendorf 1997); Mazatzal

House in the upper Tonto Basin (Hartman 1987); and Tapia del Cerrito (U:3:49) along Ash Creek (Hohmann 1985c; Rice 1985).

Bioarchaeological data provide further support. Vertical-occipital deformation, which is associated with Mogollon affiliation (Reed 1948; Reid 1989), predominates among those individuals for whom deformation can be determined (Regan et al. 1996:833; Turner et al. 1994a:830). Dental trait frequencies among Cline Terrace Mound burials (Turner and Regan 1997) and Schoolhouse Point burials (Regan et al. 1996) exhibit more affinity to Mogollon than to Hohokam populations. Further, dental traits exhibit a cline-like regularity on a north-south axis suggestive of gene flow between Mogollon, Hohokam, and Salado (Regan et al. 1996). Regan et al. (1996:829) write, "the apparent clines suggest the Tonto Basin was a corridor of sorts for human migration and gene flow." These observations are appropriate for Roosevelt phase and Gila phase alike (Turner and Regan 1997).

Social Organization

Even though social structure and organization were principal research interests of processual archaeology since the early 1960s, available reconstructions, for the most part, are based on weak and uneven information. Few have had either the context or the patience to build convincing arguments of organizational forms that can be compared. For these and other related reasons, ethnographic analogs provide models for comprehending organizational variability.

Mountain Mogollon

The most complete reconstructions of Mogollon social organization, which we presume to characterize patterns common among upland farmers rather than irrigation agriculturalists, come from the research at Grasshopper Pueblo. Analyses of household and mortuary data indicate that kinship and sodality membership were the twin foundations of Grasshopper society.

Kinship groups were the land-holding and residential units. At base were households—large and small, young and old. Variation in size, composition, and wealth of households reflects stages in the developmental cycle of domestic groups (Ciolek-Torrello 1978,1985; Ciolek-Torrello and Reid 1974; Reid 1973; Reid and Whittlesey 1982). The smallest households were contained within single,

large habitation rooms that provided space for cooking, corn grinding, storage, and manufacturing domestic implements. These households are inferred to represent nuclear families. Larger households probably associated with extended families contained two or more rooms, with at least one smaller room devoted to storage. The largest households were fewest in number, but employed multiple food processing, storage, and manufacturing areas, and resided in large rooms often combined into multiple-story units.

Through time, many of the older, extended households that founded the settlement were replaced gradually by increasing numbers of independent, nuclear households located along the periphery of the main pueblo and in outlying room blocks. As new households were formed on the periphery, older, core domestic areas were abandoned or converted to new uses. These processes affected intramural and extramural space. The great kiva, for example, was constructed within the confines of a former plaza devoted to domestic activities. Some of the oldest households in the pueblo core grew by absorbing abandoned rooms of adjacent households and converting them to storage-manufacturing areas. Food and ceremonial paraphernalia were stored, and stone and bone tools and various ornaments were fabricated in these rooms (Ciolek-Torrello 1978, 1985, 1986). These large residences may represent something similar to ethnographically described "clan houses," where the ritual and storage facilities associated with lineages were housed (Ciolek-Torrello 1978). There were no communal storage facilities beyond those found with individual households, however; none were associated with the great kiva, for example.

Sodalities, which crosscut kin groups, are inferred to have been the integrative and decision-making units (Reid 1989; Reid and Whittlesey 1982). Mortuary data suggest that, although men and women, and younger and older people, were treated differently in death and probably in life as well, status and prestige accrued from participation in restricted sodalities, and the greatest prestige was accorded the leaders of such groups. The emphasis on ceremonial life suggests to us that male religious leaders probably held the strongest role in decision making, with household and kinship groups functioning in matters of social control and discipline.

There is no evidence for the operation of true political authority. Higher social and religious rank evidently was not accompanied by real economic benefits; Ezzo

(1993:81) found that the diets of sodality leaders were the same as those of less prestigious individuals. A significant element reflecting social and economic stress, as well as overt concern with defense, is the presence of an inferred warrior society. It was community-wide, drawing its membership from all sodalities (Reid and Whittlesey 1982).

Three types of ritual structures were present, and are inferred to have integrated households at different levels of organization (Reid and Whittlesey 1982). Three households shared one ceremonial room, a room type containing certain ritual features but lacking the complement of formalized features that identifies kivas. Formal, rectangular kivas with masonry benches, ventilators, and deflectors occur in a ratio of one kiva to six households (Reid and Whittlesey 1982) (cf. Wilshusen's [1989] "corporate kivas"). The entire pueblo, and perhaps the regional community, used the great kiva for ceremonial purposes (cf. Wilshusen's [1989] "community" type of kiva).

Some domestic functions evidently were carried out in the plazas, and we suspect that they also served as ancillary ceremonial features. The plaza or courtyard functioned as the public ritual feature of the Grasshopper region and adjacent areas, whereas in the eastern mountains the great kiva served this function (Reid 1989; Reid and Tuggle 1988; also see Adams 1991:107). In some areas, these structures were not contemporaneous (Adams 1991; Haury 1950b), but elsewhere, such as Grasshopper Pueblo, great kivas and plazas cooccur, although Plaza III precedes construction of the great kiva there. The appearance of small kivas and plazas at Grasshopper Pueblo may coincide with the emergence of the Katsina Cult in this region, although other possibilities exist.

Residential distinctiveness was maintained rather rigidly throughout Grasshopper Pueblo's complicated growth sequence, suggesting that social identity, probably based in kinship, also was preserved. As discussed above, the pueblo remained throughout its history an aggregate of independent "villages." Dietary differences among the room blocks imply land tenure by residential groups, presumably also kinship based. Greater maize use among Room Block 3 residents, for example, may indicate that this unit had more extensive agricultural holdings or more productive land. We note that the autonomous character of residential groups, with signature social and probably religious identities, would have hindered the consolidation of economic and political power in a few households.

Tonto Basin Salado

As expected, given our model of multiple ethnic groups, social organizational forms are not homogenous across Tonto Basin. We suspect that kinship groups maintained corporate functions, possibly including land tenure, much as they did in the mountain communities. The small compounds of the Roosevelt phase apparently reflect corporate groups similar in size and structure to the extended households at Grasshopper Pueblo, but with architectural indicators of a different internal domestic arrangement. Each compound consists of clusters of two or three relatively large rooms (Ciolek-Torrello 1994) comparable in size to those at Grasshopper Pueblo, and with similar functional distinctions such as storage and food processing areas. Mealing bins are not present in Roosevelt phase habitation rooms, however, and slab-lined hearths are rare. Organization of domestic activities also differs. Domestic space among Roosevelt phase settlements was focused on courtyards, and extramural areas were compartmentalized into individual domestic units. By contrast, domestic space at Grasshopper and Chodistaas Pueblos was interior oriented, involving the compartmentalization of interior space and the shared use of extramural space.

Storage facilities apparently were maintained by households, as at Grasshopper Pueblo. Lindauer (1996a) estimates that between 31 and 46 residential or household units occupied Schoolhouse Point, and there are 30 interior, first-story storage rooms.

Exceptions to the general Tonto Basin patterns occur, however. Saguaro Muerto, for example, reflects a domestic arrangement more similar to the small sites in the Grasshopper region. The arrangement of domestic space at Schoolhouse Point also departs from the pattern in Roosevelt phase compounds and achieves greater congruence with the Grasshopper Pueblo pattern.

The construction sequence of Schoolhouse Point (Lindauer 1996a) demonstrates founding by several small core units that may be lineage segments comparable to those founding Chodistaas and Grasshopper Pueblos. Lineages also may have maintained their own ritual facilities and "clan house"-type storage rooms, to judge from the distribution of unusual artifacts (Rice 1996).

Corporate group use of cemeteries in Tonto Basin is indicated by the presence of spatially discrete cemeteries, the repeated use of mortuary facilities over time, and the inclusion of burials of varied ages and both genders in each facility. These patterns occur at U:8:450 (Loendorf 1997), Schoolhouse Point (Loendorf 1996a), Tapia del Cerrito (Hohmann 1985c), and Mazatzal House (Hartman 1987). Bioarchaeological data indicate that the multiple individuals interred in single graves at Schoolhouse Point apparently were closely related (Regan et al. 1996). Developmental abnormalities of the skeleton suggest "that the individuals placed in Burial Locality B were closely related genetically, possibly some type of descent group" (Loendorf 1996c:782).

In comparing ritual organization, we consider small-scale facilities, community facilities, and sodality organization. Small-scale ritual facilities occur in both areas, although the Salado rooms differ in construction and use from those of mountain pueblos. The large, oval rooms found in many residential compounds may represent such ritual structures. These rooms are located centrally, such as the oval rooms in the center of plaza areas in Compounds 4 and 7 at Meddler Point (Craig and Clark 1994) and Griffin Wash (Swartz and Randolph 1994b). The spatial configuration of these rooms—one per compound, inside a large, enclosed plaza rather than a residential courtyard—suggests that they were used by a kinship group larger than the lineage, perhaps the residential groups occupying compounds. These rooms exhibit little evidence of habitation.

By contrast, small-scale ritual rooms of late Pueblo III times in the Grasshopper region were protokivas with a distinctive orientation and placement within the settlement, and they appear to have been associated with lineages or lineage segments (Reid and Montgomery 1993). The ceremonial rooms of the Pueblo IV Grasshopper Pueblo appeared to have maintained similar functions, although their architectural configuration and facilities changed.

Oval rooms may have preceded the development of platform mounds as ritual structures in Tonto Basin. A pair of large, oval, jacal rooms underlies the Roosevelt phase platform mound at Meddler Point (Craig and Clark 1994), reinforcing the ritual nature of such rooms. These oval rooms may represent an older form of ritual structure that has its antecedents in the large oval habitation rooms of the early Classic period in much of central Arizona (Ciolek-Torrello, ed. 1987; Hammack 1969; Neily 1997; Redman 1993).

The most striking difference in ritual organization between the mountain Mogollon and the Salado involves the nature of community facilities. Whereas the Mogollon focused their communal ceremonies on the kiva-plaza com-

plex, the platform mound-plaza complex served community ceremonial requirements of the Salado.

The appearance of platform mounds in Tonto Basin at the height of the Great Drought seems more than coincidental (Ciolek-Torrello et al. 1994; Van West and Altschul 1994). Prior to the Roosevelt phase, the relatively low population density meant that kinship ties were sufficient to integrate communities, coordinate political decision making, and structure land tenure. We maintain that increased immigration during the Great Drought created a climate of social and economic uncertainty that fostered the development of community-based integrative structures (Ciolek-Torrello et al. 1994; Ciolek-Torrello and Whittlesey 1996; Reid and Whittlesey 1997). Resulting sweeping changes in settlement, subsistence, and organization were fueled by environmental and economic stress, development of new agricultural technologies, population growth, and the need for defense (Cordell et al. 1994; Dean 1988a; Reid 1989). The result was a shift to a community-wide organizational system whose structure transcended kinship groups (Ciolek-Torrello and Whittlesey 1996; Ciolek-Torrello et al. 1994; Whittlesey and Ciolek-Torrello 1992). Such a shift did not occur among the Mogollon, who also experienced demographic upheaval, because the accompanying spur of intensification of irrigation agriculture was absent.

The size of the labor force necessary to construct and maintain platform mounds supports the inferred community integrative nature of the platform mound-plaza complex. A relatively large labor force, transcending individual kinship groups such as extended families and lineage segments, is indicated (Craig and Clark 1994). Residents from several settlements must have pooled labor to construct the mounds with small or nonexistent resident populations (Doelle et al. 1995:407; Gregory 1995b). By extension, the integrative function of mounds probably expanded beyond individual settlements to embrace a larger community (Craig and Clark 1994:195). The absence of ceremonial facilities and paraphernalia in "rural" compounds suggests that these widely scattered residential units were integrated with larger site complexes (Ciolek-Torrello 1994).

Platform mounds appear to have served primarily ritual functions, as little evidence for habitation has been found. For example, only specialized structures that do not appear to be habitation rooms occur within the compound surrounding the mound at Meddler Point, and there appears to be strict demarcation of domestic and ceremonial, public and private space (Craig and Clark 1994; Elson, Gregory, and Stark 1995). Although as discussed above, not all mounds followed the Phoenix Basin model, nonconforming platform mounds, such as the Pyramid Point "mound," also seem to have served nonhabitation functions.

As many have noted previously, the absence of kivas large and small in Tonto Basin, Globe-Miami, and adjacent areas stands in stark contrast to prehistoric mountain communities. Their absence during the Gila phase is particularly conspicuous, as Gila phase pueblos otherwise are strikingly similar architecturally to contemporary Mogollon pueblos, representing compact blocks of contiguous, multistoried rooms organized around plazas (Hohmann and Adams 1992; Hohmann and Kelley 1988). Plazas apparently were foci of ritual as well as domestic activity and served as cemeteries, primarily for adults (Hohmann and Kelley 1988:151; Whittlesey 1978). Plazas and kivas have been hypothesized to be associated elements of the Katsina Cult, with kivas housing its esoteric aspects and plazas serving the outdoor, public component of Katsina Cult ceremonies (Adams 1991:83–84). It is possible that kivas have been overlooked, have remained undiscovered due to the low intensity of excavation, or that alternative ritual structures were used for corporate group ceremonies (Hohmann et al. 1992).

We suggest that the lack of kivas indicates the absence of the Katsina Cult in the Tonto Basin and Globe-Miami areas, and its replacement by a village-based type of organization that can be linked to irrigation agriculture. A moiety system may have substituted for the integrative role of the Katsina Cult in large, aggregated villages composed of multiple lineages. Such an organization, with its inherent abilities to amass, organize, and control labor for the purposes of community irrigation, ceremonial, and political functions, would have operated effectively.

The abandonment of the platform mound system and the appearance of nucleated pueblos in the early Gila phase suggests that the ritual systems of the Salado and Mogollon achieved greater congruity. We have little evidence regarding the type of ritual system that replaced the platform mounds in Tonto Basin. The great kiva at Grasshopper Pueblo was constructed at this time, but there is no evidence for such structures in excavated Gila phase settlements. At least one platform mound, at Cline Terrace, continued to be used during the Gila phase. It is possible that the platform mound system became integrated at a larger scale and involved multiple communities.

Evidence for the presence of sodalities in Tonto Basin is mixed. Some artifactual indicators of sodality membership identified in mountain communities are distributed widely in and near Tonto Basin. These include *Glycymeris* bracelets and rings and *Conus* tinklers (Reid and Whittlesey 1982), found at Schoolhouse Point (Loendorf 1996a), Mazatzal House (Hartman 1987), and elsewhere. An inhumation at U:8:450 was accompanied by a cluster of arrow points (Loendorf 1997:16.17–16.18), which at Grasshopper Pueblo signals membership in an inferred warrior or hunting society. Although Loendorf (1997:16.38) acknowledges that these artifacts along with painted wooden staffs and ritual objects "may have symbolized leadership in certain ceremonial societies," he does not recognize the connection with sodality membership at Grasshopper Pueblo.

Bone awls worn as hairpins, an important indicator of sodality membership among the Mogollon (Reid and Whittlesey 1982), are more limited in distribution, however. Although they do not occur among Schoolhouse Mesa burials (Loendorf 1997), four of the five males buried at Mazatzal House had bone awls beside or under the skulls in positions that reflected use as hairpins (Hartman 1987:224). One of these burials also had other accompaniments symbolizing sodality membership, including a shell bracelet, a shell pendant, and two projectile points near the left shoulder.

To consider other organizational features, is there evidence for duality or moiety organization in Tonto Basin? Particular architectural elements may serve as tenuous evidence for a dual social organization. For example, Craig, Elson, and Jacobs (1992:43) note that the Meddler Point settlement consisted of two residential segments containing domestic rooms within compounds separated by 200 m of nonresidential space. This pattern, so evocative of spatially segregated moieties, is reinforced by features of the platform mound. The platform mound contained two rooms on top, each of which had different construction wood species signatures, and there were two oval, jacal structures in the area of restricted access behind the mound. It is possible that each residential cluster was associated with one platform mound room and one jacal room. The two, earlier jacal rooms suggest that the community had a dual division prior to the construction of the platform mound.

More arresting evidence derives from mortuary facilities at U:8:450 (Loendorf 1997). Two spatially discrete plaza cemeteries were present. Grave facilities in the northern cemetery were oriented north-south; most fa-cilities in the southern cemetery were oriented east-west. Most of the inhumations in the latter face east; the northern cemetery facilities were not excavated, so infor-mation concerning head orientation is lacking. The pres-ence of two cemeteries and dual orientation of mortuary facilities certainly suggests a dual organization. The number of interments in this small compound is suffi-ciently high to suggest that residents from other settle-ments may have been buried there (see also Hartman 1987; Hohmann 1985c; Rice 1985).

Economic and craft specialization may have emerged in the ethnically diverse Tonto Basin community as one means of coping with scarcity. Evidence for discrete pro-duction of ceramics within a limited area may indicate this process (Clark 1995b). More convincing evidence is the extremely high ubiquity of cotton and agave at Grif-fin Wash (Elson, Fish, James, and Miksicek 1995). Paren-thetically, these data contradict the notion that the latest groups to arrive in Tonto Basin would have had access only to restricted or poor land, as argued by Elson, Gre-gory, and Stark (1995:454). Given cotton's high water re-quirements, its ubiquity is strong evidence that the Griffin Wash people were not land poor.

The potential for conflict among ethnically diverse social groups competing for scarce resources in a region characterized by environmental degradation and uncer-tainty has not gone unnoticed (Reid 1989; Wilcox and Haas 1994). The inability of integrative systems to cope with the increased competition for land and resources and greater social circumscription, creating reduced resi-dential mobility and ability to disperse farmsites across the landscape, may have induced violence. The Roosevelt Rural Sites Study found three males who appeared to have died violently at the Grapevine Springs site (Van-derpot et al. 1994). They were sprawled on the floors of two nonadjacent rooms that subsequently were burned, and perimortem trauma, including a cranial wound, was observed. Turner et al. (1994b:582) suggest that the evi-dence is consistent with raiding. Similar evidence was found in a room at Tapia del Cerrito (Hohmann 1985c). Craig, Elson, and Wood (1992:30) also note that almost all Roosevelt phase structures were burned.

SUMMARY AND CONCLUDING OBSERVATIONS

In comparing and contrasting Tonto Basin Salado and mountain Mogollon, we have placed the Basin in the

appropriate regional context. Tonto Basin is similar en-vironmentally to other parts of the mountain Transition Zone, although possessing certain characteristics that made it especially attractive for human use. The adaptive strategies that developed in the mountains and Tonto Basin alike were similar throughout much of prehistory. Three variables are most important in understanding prehistoric social, political, and economic organization. First, the diversity of resources, their uneven distribution and variable productivity, and climatic unpredictability fostered an adaptive strategy that was based on residen-tial mobility and diversification and resulted in a system of dispersed, small, and often seasonally occupied settle-ments. Mobility, fissioning, and dispersal of settlements were the primary strategies for resolving resource-popu-lation imbalances. At the same time, the Basin offered diverse agricultural opportunities, including the poten-tial for irrigation agriculture, that did not exist in most other areas of the mountains. These conditions made it possible under particular climatic conditions and popula-tion levels to invest heavily in irrigation. Correspondingly distinct organizational forms developed in response to the social needs of irrigation agriculture.

Second, Tonto Basin, like other parts of the highlands, experienced a long history of joint use and coresidence by multiple ethnic groups who recognized its potential and who were experienced in the value of residential moves in coping with economic uncertainties. Tonto Basin experienced this more intensively than other re-gions by virtue of its peculiar attractiveness. Population increase created ultimately by environmental degrada-tion on the Colorado Plateau and elsewhere affected Tonto Basin like other areas below the Mogollon Rim, and intergroup conflict created by deteriorating envi-ronmental conditions and resource competition played a primary role in organizational and settlement change.

Third, we believe that differences in Mogollon and Salado adaptive strategies can be explained most parsi-moniously by the differential role of irrigation agricul-ture among these groups. Where runoff-control and dry farming predominate, particularly where land is variable in its availability and productivity, land tenure is an important factor in social organization and the basis of economic, social, and ceremonial power (Levy 1992). Among upland farmers, therefore, kinship provided the basic organizational structure, probably served as the foundation for land tenure, and structured social and economic interactions. Sodalities operated as integrative mechanisms and were the basis for political authority. Larger integrative functions were served by the great kivas, which may have developed as a response to the needs of the ethnically diverse mountain communities, and in some areas by plazas. We suspect that the Katsina Cult was embraced by the mountain Mogollon, among whom the emphasis on kinship organization, floodwater farming, and demographic upheaval created favorable conditions for acceptance. Even among extremely large, aggregated highland communities, nonirrigation farming strategies engendered the continuation of an organizational system based on kinship principles, sodalities, and the maintenance of descent group control over land.

By contrast, when the primary agricultural strategy is irrigation on a scale larger than that used by the Hopi or Western Apache in historic times, predictability is increased, uncertainty is reduced, and a mechanism for intensification of production exists. The supply and allocation of water, rather than land tenure, becomes the organizational principle. Community organization by nonkinship-based groups and centralization of decision making tend to occur under these conditions. The Tonto Basin Salado apparently did not participate in the Katsina Cult, and developed community-based organizational and ceremonial systems. The response to social and economic conditions of the Roosevelt phase was the emergence of the platform mound-plaza complex. We suspect that the cooperative aspects of irrigation society and its associated needs for communal labor fostered the development of community-wide integrative mechanisms, that kinship groups were less important parts of the organizational framework, and that groups not based in kinship, perhaps moieties, controlled economic, ceremonial, and political life.

We have viewed the management of scarce resources as the primary factor molding economic and social organization. As Levy (1992:3) contends, "a restricted and tenuous resource base required that Hopi society structure itself on an inequitable distribution of land." Scarcity, not surplus, played the most significant role in mountain prehistory. We have argued (Whittlesey and Ciolek-Torrello 1992) that kinship groups remained important during the Classic period in Tonto Basin precisely because they maintained control of the land. Given the Basin's great diversity in landforms and productivity, ownership of the most productive land would have been as important there as at Hopi, if not more so. The land-controlling descent groups were preserved by removing excess population during times of scarcity. These con-

straints demanded a high degree of cooperation and social integration. Such processes are well demonstrated at Grasshopper Pueblo, where the first, least costly response to shortages of agricultural land and concomitant economic and nutritional stress was fissioning into dispersed communities to bring new land under cultivation. We maintain that similar processes operated in Tonto Basin. Although irrigation reduced productivity and uncertainty, the amount of irrigable land in Tonto Basin is extremely restricted compared to the Phoenix Basin (Ciolek-Torrello and Whittlesey 1996; Elson, Gregory, and Stark 1995) and sensitive to damaging environmental conditions (Welch 1994a). Other types of agriculture probably always remained important over the long term (Van West and Altschul 1994).

Little support for the elite model of social complexity with its foundation of surplus (Rice 1990c) has been found among the platform mound villages. The labor requirements of platform mounds and irrigation systems were met easily by local residents (Craig and Clark 1994; Elson, Gregory, and Stark 1995), and maize surplus remained about the Pueblo ideal, not more, even in the best of years (Craig 1995:242; Lindauer 1996c:849). Evidence for status differentiation also is minimal (Loendorf 1996c:17.18). Significantly, the notion that platform mounds served as elite residences has been abandoned (Jacobs and Rice 1997:18.1; Rice, Chapter 6).

The amalgamated, ethnically diverse communities that emerged in Tonto Basin and the mountains during Pueblo IV times were characterized by elaborations or new developments in ritual organization indicating attempts to maintain equilibrium in socially and economically uncertain times. The time-honored mountain system of dispersed settlements and mixed subsistence efforts was curtailed by a concatenation of factors including greater residential stability, increased population density, and the threat of conflict. The Roosevelt phase communities of Tonto Basin were culturally and ethnically diverse, the population was growing, and the result was competition for agricultural land, water, and other resources. Aggregation, increased investment in irrigation agriculture and upland dry farming, and the emergence of new integrative forms were the responses of the diverse population to these conditions.

It is appropriate to ask, as do other papers in this volume, "Who were the Salado?" We believe that they were no one, and yet they were everyone. The Salado of Tonto Basin were molded by multiple variables of interaction, cultural exchange, and residential mobility acting upon an indigenous population and immigrants in unique ways. The indigenous population—who, we maintain, were essentially Mogollon in character—maintained a long and complicated history of interaction, intermarriage, and exchange with the Hohokam and other people, and, like the Hopi, borrowed those elements of foreign cultural systems that they found useful and discarded the rest. We cannot say that the Salado were Mogollon. We can say that there are many parallels at some Tonto Basin Salado settlements with aspects of Mogollon architecture, social organization, mortuary practices, and subsistence (Reid and Whittlesey 1997).

The Salado also were nonindigenous people who settled in the Basin, forging what was at times a cooperative and multiethnic residential and economic community. The culturally syncretic Salado forged a new pattern in the Roosevelt phase that was unparalleled.

The adage that "what goes around, comes around" has never seemed more appropriate than when applied to the Salado. In acknowledging the role of Gila Pueblo in explaining Tonto Basin prehistory, Elson, Gregory, and Stark (1995:479) write, "the basic processes they proposed to explain the rich and varied remains in the area—migration of both Hohokam and Puebloan groups—indeed appear to have occurred. In this sense, some 60 years later, we have come full circle." Almost two decades have elapsed since these processes were promoted by Whittlesey and Reid (1982) as explanatory models, years during which others traced the spoor of the Salado-as-Hohokam, an ill-conceived idea that flew in the face of established data, across Tonto Basin. Perhaps, as Elliott (1995:216) observes, "disagreement is structurally built into the profession because an original viewpoint is necessary to achieve status." If we can acknowledge without apology the contributions of such pioneer scholars as Gladwin and Haury, it certainly is possible to move forward in developing new, more elegant models of explanation for the Salado phenomenon. To abandon the Salado concept, as some have suggested (Clark 1995b; Elson, Gregory, and Stark 1995), or to view the Salado simply as a regional variant of Hohokam, masks the significant information we can learn about cultural process and evolution. Rather than be daunted by the seeming intractability of the Salado concept, we have before us an opportunity to use it as the vehicle to examine and explain the more subtle dimensions of central Arizona prehistory.

CHAPTER ELEVEN
Salado:
The View from the Colorado Plateau

E. Charles Adams

M<small>Y</small> OBJECTIVE IN THIS CHAPTER IS TO LOOK AT Salado culture from the perspective of more than 25 years' work on the Colorado Plateau, focused recently on the southern Colorado Plateau in the middle part of the Little Colorado River drainage. I focus my observations on environment, population, ritual, and cotton.

It seems only fair that I display my biases with respect to the concept of Salado culture from the outset. I am a nonbeliever. It seems clear to me that recent research has demonstrated that the culture of Tonto Basin, the supposed heartland of the Salado Culture, developed in situ (Elson et al. 1992:284–85). Elson, Gregory, and Stark (1995) have suggested that the indigenous groups in Tonto Basin were influenced by the Hohokam, or that Hohokam migrated into the area around 750–850 (see also Doyel 1978). The key for my purposes is that Salado culture did not develop there. The distinctive nature of "Salado Culture" crystallizes with the Roosevelt Phase (ca. 1250–1350), when card carrying makers of Roosevelt Red Wares (a.k.a. Salado polychromes) joined the indigenous groups. If any points drew consensus at the seminar associated with production of this volume, they are that Roosevelt Red Ware did not originate in Tonto Basin, that they are earlier in the mountains and on the plateau east and north of Tonto Basin, and that their introduction into Tonto Basin was via immigrants from

one or more of these regions to the northeast. However, contacts with the north were established long before that and to understand why groups migrated from the upper Little Colorado River area to Tonto Basin in the late 1200s, we should consider the context of these earlier contacts.

The American Southwest has been dominated by cultural patterns termed Hohokam and Anasazi, desert dwellers and plateau dwellers respectively. These patterns have often masked variability, and this is nowhere truer than in the mountains and basins between the two traditions, the provenance of the Mogollon (Whittlesey and Ciolek-Torrello 1992). To whatever tradition the Tonto Basin people are assigned is really immaterial, for they were strongly influenced at one time or another by the Hohokam and the Anasazi.

The distinctiveness of Tonto Basin prehistory is not unique in the Southwest. Each basin, each region that can be geographically defined can almost certainly be culturally described. The local conditions inevitably give a unique flavor to that area. Elson et al. (1992) describe it as the Central Arizona Tradition. The unique trajectory of Tonto Basin prehistory certainly gives insights into the concept of Salado and how it developed, flourished, and disappeared. The enormous level of recent research in Tonto Basin constrains us to this narrow focus on Salado, yet in terms of "Salado Culture" we are forced to consider the wider issues of the many traditions that shared one thing in common, use of Roosevelt Red Wares. Crown (1994) offers insights into the ritual aspects of this shared ceramics assemblage that may help in understanding not only the concept of Salado Culture, but also why this pottery stopped being manufactured and exchanged.

It is now clear that Roosevelt Red Ware was not extensively traded, but in fact was primarily locally made. Crown (1994:100–101) has shown that two-thirds of the Roosevelt Red Ware vessels were found in mortuary contexts. (Interestingly, Lekson [Chapter 12] notes that almost no Roosevelt Red Ware vessels occur in Casas Grandes burials.) This burial association and the ritual iconography attributed to these vessels by Crown were probably important dynamics to the Roosevelt and Gila phase populations in Tonto Basin, which this paper explores.

A Colorado Plateau Perspective on Tonto Basin Prehistory

As noted by Clark (1995), Cibola White Wares replace Phoenix Basin buff wares before 1100. Later, Little Colorado White Wares appear in the ceramic record of Tonto Basin, although predominantly in the northern portions of the Basin (Elson et al. 1992; Elson, Gregory, and Stark 1995). Early contacts with Tonto Basin by Plateau groups accomplished two tasks. First, the necessary social links between groups in the two areas were established. Second, these contacts involved and probably were focused on exchange. No one has suggested the presence of settlements by Plateau groups prior to 1250 (Stark, Clark, and Elson 1995a), yet contact was persistent after 1050 with Cibola groups (as represented by Cibola White Ware) from the upper Little Colorado River area or Mogollon Mountains seemingly in touch with the Salt River arm of Tonto Basin, and Hopi Buttes/middle Little Colorado River people (as represented by Little Colorado White Wares) in touch with settlements in the Tonto Creek Arm of Tonto Basin.

What was being exchanged? Black-on-white pottery was clearly being exchanged into the Basin. At least for Cibola White Ware, this pottery was clearly superior in its performance characteristics (it was less prone to break during transport) to Hohokam or local counterparts (Reid et al. 1992:214). From Tonto Basin there seem to be two likely exports: agave and cotton. The migrating

Pueblo groups identified by Stark, Clark, and Elson (1995a:230) seemed clearly focused on agave harvesting, if not production. The hearts of the agave were considered delicacies by the Hopi, who traded for them historically from groups in the Verde Valley.

From my perspective, cotton provides the key to initial and sustained contact between the Plateau and Tonto Basin, beginning in the 1050–1100 period. It quite likely involved the introduction and spread of cotton production onto the Plateau. Tonto Basin groups, as growers of cotton in a basin with abundant water, irrigation agriculture, and a lengthy growing season, were in a prime location to exchange cotton and technology for materials from the Plateau whose traces in the archaeological record are ceramics (Adams 1994a; Kent 1957). In fact in neither the Cibola nor the Little Colorado River/Hopi Buttes areas are there indications that groups could, let alone tried, to grow cotton prior to 1250. However, groups in the Canyon de Chelly area, along the Colorado River, and even in Hovenweep, were growing cotton and producing textiles (Kent 1957; Teague 1992b). Later movement of the Kayenta Anasazi into the upper Little Colorado River portion of the Cibola area and points south (Lindsay 1992; Reid et al. 1992), may have been anticipated through cotton exchange dating 100–200 years earlier. As noted by Reed (1958) and others (C. M. Cameron 1995; Stark, Clark, and Elson 1995a), migration into an area must be anticipated by familiarity with the area and its people. Contact between Kayenta and Cibola groups and Cibola and Tonto Basin groups almost certainly involved the exchange of cotton in raw, spun, or textile form.

The post-1100 surge in cotton production on the Plateau (Kent 1983b; Teague 1992b) corresponds with the extensive and apparently continuous movement of ceramics produced by Colorado Plateau groups into Tonto Basin, where conditions were prime for cotton production (Adams 1994a). The continuity of this contact for more than 200 years strongly points to the exchange of a renewable resource, one that could not easily be duplicated on the highlands above the Mogollon Rim or in drainages of the upper Little Colorado River. As noted by Teague (1992a:311), the fabric tradition established by Salado groups is still apparent in fabrics of the pueblos of northern Arizona. The continuity of this fabric tradition is clear evidence of the importance of cotton to groups in both areas, of the exchange of technology of production and manufacture, and of the timing and source of this exchange. Textiles provide undeniable evidence that Salado groups exchanged knowledge of weaving with their Plateau neighbors. This exchange was preceded by contact between the two groups. I argue that this contact was initiated in the late 1000s, was amplified in the late 1200s, and bore fruit in the subsequent generations of textiles woven by Pueblo groups on the Colorado Plateau.

The Roosevelt Phase reflects a major transformation in the prehistory of Tonto Basin. This point can be agreed on by all researchers. Also acceptable to all is that a migration from the north or northeast of the Basin occurred at this time. Finally, these immigrating groups did not enter an empty niche (Gladwin and Gladwin 1935), but joined indigenous groups (Elson, Gregory, and Stark 1995).

Arguments concerning Puebloan ethnicity and immigration have been presented by Stark, Clark, and Elson (1995a) for settlements in the Tonto Basin, particularly the Griffin Wash site. Economic specialization in cotton and agave production has also been documented at Griffin Wash (Elson, Gregory, and Stark 1995). The cause of this specialization can be debated. Whittlesey and Ciolek-Torrello (1992) and others argue that such specialization may have been one means for coping with scarcity, a strategy employed by land-poor people worldwide. My question, then, is why immigrate into Tonto Basin in the first place? If these are indeed Plateau groups from the above or below the Mogollon Rim, and I believe they are, what push or pull factors caused or encouraged them to migrate to Tonto Basin?

What human and environmental dynamics took place in the two areas that prompted or allowed such a movement? The latter half of the 1200s was a time of remarkable change throughout the Southwest (Adams 1991; Cordell 1984; Dean et al. 1985; Dean et al. 1994). Archaeologists are only beginning to understand the complexity and dimensions of this period and the transitions that shook the Pueblo world. There were widespread and massive abandonments of the Four Corners (Fish et al. 1994). The initiation of low-frequency process environmental transformations (Dean et al. 1985) combined with high frequency processes and local conditions to "cause" some of these population movements. But there are two factors to consider. The first, when and why did they leave some areas? The second, which concerns us more here, why and how did they chose to move to a specific location, in this case, Tonto Basin? These are the classic push and pull factors involving human migration (Ahlstrom et al. 1995; Anthony 1990; C. M. Cameron 1995).

An examination of settlement size and room numbers as bases for population in the upper Little Colorado River, Silver Creek, and Grasshopper areas in the late 1200s will be informative (Figure 11.1). According to Mills (1995), during the 1280–1325 period there were probably fewer than 500 rooms occupied in the Silver Creek drainage. Along the same lines, Andrew Duff (personal communication 1995) estimates that the population in the upper reaches of the Little Colorado River from the vicinity of St. Johns to Springerville was also small occupying only about 500 rooms. These surprisingly small populations do not suggest that overpopulation was a primary concern in the upper Little Colorado River or was the push that sent groups to Tonto Basin and elsewhere.

By the same token, settlements below the Mogollon Rim in the late 1200s consist of fairly small pueblos, such as Chodistaas, grouped into clusters around resource-rich areas. There is no indication that overpopulation was a problem given that population increased rapidly at Grasshopper Pueblo after 1300 toward the end of the Roosevelt Phase (Reid 1989).

On the other hand, it is now probable that these low populations are a result, at least in part, of emigration. Carrying capacity does not seem to be causal. In fact, according to the Dean et al. (1985) model and earlier perspectives (Hantman 1978), higher elevations of the upper Little Colorado River, including Silver Creek, were viewed as refuge areas for people abandoning the Four Corners and other areas. To my mind, the pull factor is overriding. Why did people leave their homelands above and below the Mogollon Rim? What attracted them to other areas, including Tonto Basin? I think it is access to resources unavailable in the upper Little Colorado River, most prominently, land with dependable water and a long growing season; that is, land that could grow cotton (Kent 1957).

What is the evidence for, and causes of, migration to Tonto Basin? First of all, contact between the southern Colorado Plateau and Tonto Basin had been established since 1050 (Elson, Gregory, and Stark 1995). This meets the first criterion for a migration, familiarity with the area into which one migrates (Anthony 1990). The second concern is what pushed the Plateau populations into Tonto Basin? I suggest that populations moving above and below the Mogollon Rim from the north could have pushed indigenous groups into nearby areas. A factor pulling populations out of the upper Little Colorado River basin could have been climatic. Streamflow in the

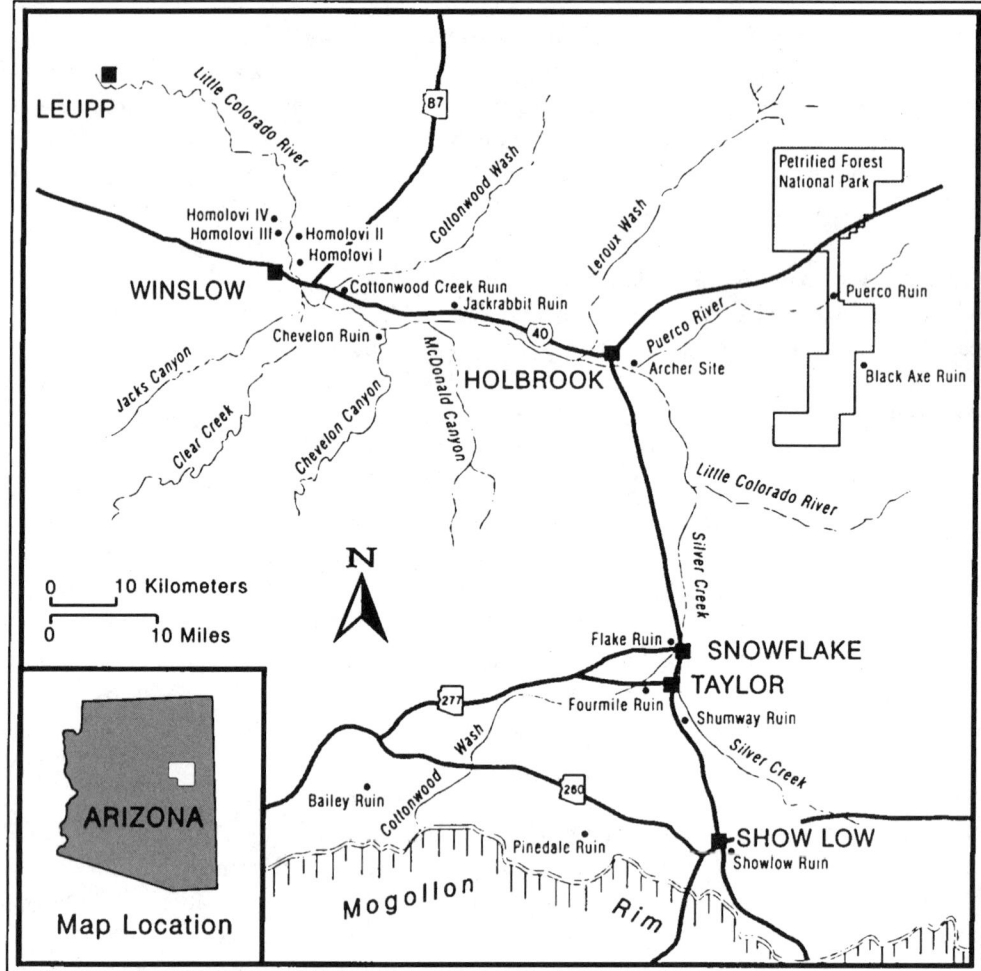

Figure 11.1.
Large pueblos
occupied be-
tween 1275–
1400 in the
middle Little
Colorado and
Silver Creek
areas.

middle Little Colorado River dropped, creating opportunities for farming in the floodplain where none had
existed before (Van West 1996). Such factors were instrumental in drawing populations into the Homol'ovi area
from the upper Little Colorado River about 1280, or
about the time of the Roosevelt phase where a similar
phenomenon occurred in Tonto Basin, except there were
existent populations in the latter area (Altschul and Van
West 1992). Although agricultural productivity using
runoff and floodwater farming would have been hampered by lower precipitation in the late 1200s, the resulting lower streamflows could have encouraged expanded
irrigation farming that supported the pueblo populations (Welch 1992; J. S. Wood et al. 1992). As noted by
Rice (1992:17), the labor potential offered by these new

pueblo groups in the construction of platform mounds
and canals could have offset any problem with the added
population. The initial construction of platform mounds
apparently coincides with the appearance of these new
groups, and the mounds may have been mechanisms to
integrate these diverse populations (Elson, Gregory, and
Stark 1995).

I see every indication that pueblo immigration into
Tonto Basin prompted the events that define the Roosevelt Phase. It seems equally clear that when some of these
groups left the Basin (1300–1330), they returned to their
homelands—the Mogollon Rim and upper Little Colorado River basin. This process of return migration is
common (Anthony 1990). What are perceived as Salado
settlements characterized by Gila and Tonto Poly-

chromes appear at Fourmile Ruin (Johnson 1992), in pueblos along the upper Little Colorado River (Martin and Rinaldo 1960), at Hawikuh (Smith et al. 1966), and in the Acoma area (Dittert 1959). Perhaps not coincidentally, the early 1300s (1300–1340) is a period of change and transformation in the Homol'ovi area related to changes in streamflow and the political dynamics of the arrival of Homol'ovi II from the Hopi Mesas (E. C. Adams 1996). These changing streamflows may also have played a part in the exodus from Tonto Basin and the local reorganization into irrigation districts (Altschul and Van West 1992; Van West and Altschul 1994; J. S. Wood et al. 1992).

With the departure of some of the puebloan component of Tonto Basin, and the absorption of the remaining segments, the Gila phase was launched. This phase is characterized by increased centralization of population into a few, large settlements that were apparently integrated by platform mounds (Rice 1992:21). These mounds were different in planning and scale from their earlier counterparts. In addition to the hypothesized ritual use of platform mounds in the Roosevelt phase is added a residential component in the Gila phase, an indicator of increased organizational complexity (Craig, Elson, and Wood 1992:30). This is not surprising. The Tonto Basin populations added complexity and organization to an existing pattern in an attempt to maintain it. Simply put, the philosophy seems to be, "bigger is better." I suggest this is an attempt to cope with stress (see Rice, Chapter 6; Whittlesey et al., Chapter 10). The pueblo populations left because the pattern that had attracted them into the Basin in the first place had changed. From my perspective, this successful adaptation during the Roosevelt phase involved more favorable farming conditions, probably a favorable carrying capacity (obviously dependent on the first), and a previously established social relationship as suggested by a 200-year history of contact measured through ceramics.

The Gila phase witnessed the aggregation of several settlements into one large pueblo, perhaps based on an irrigation community, along the lines of the Hohokam (Rice 1992; J. S. Wood et al. 1992). Perhaps this was a temporary, successful political adaptation to a labor intensive enterprise, canal irrigation. Gila phase communities were well-integrated, but I agree with Whittlesey and Ciolek-Torrello (1992:324) in believing that the communities were over-specialized. Their increased reliance on irrigation agriculture to cope with a variable climate and

perhaps a high population reduced their flexibility (Rose 1994; Van West and Altschul 1994). Ultimately, when such a specialized adaptation occurs, it is doomed to failure, even in as environmentally-diverse an area as Tonto Basin. Time and again in the Southwest instances of social complexity were ultimately terminated by just that process (Fish et al. 1994). Chaco Canyon is only the most spectacular example. In a marginal environment, specialization is maladaptive.

Perhaps it is the very autonomy of pueblo villages, the flexibility of their social units, and the leveling mechanisms built into their social organization that allowed them to persist. Modern pueblos and their historic counterparts were apparently independent, in terms of providing their own subsistence. This does not mean that there were no alliances, no trade, no warfare, no interaction. It only means that subsistence exchange may not have characterized pueblo economy, except in times of surplus (Kohler and Van West 1996). Exchange of food, such as documented by Spielmann (1991) for the eastern pueblos, involved exchange of surplus and for complementary food stuffs (meat for corn).

LESSONS FROM THE MIDDLE LITTLE COLORADO RIVER

Just as the late prehistory of Tonto Basin has been divided into early and late, the Roosevelt and Gila phases, so too has the middle Little Colorado River region. The Tuwiuca phase dates roughly 1260–1330 and the Homol'ovi phase to about 1330–1400 (Gumerman and Skinner 1968; Lange 1996). It seems likely that the remarkable parallels between the two areas are related. A digression is necessary to present a model of migration and development among Pueblo groups along the middle Little Colorado River that should inform us about comparable developments in Tonto Basin. There are, of course, significant and important differences that are considered as they relate. The area occupied by Pueblo groups is along a 20-mile stretch of the Little Colorado River in the vicinity of modern Winslow (Figure 11.1). These pueblos, collectively called the Homol'ovi group, were occupied from about 1260–1400, roughly contemporary with the Roosevelt and Gila phase Tonto Basin. Lange (1996) has developed a six phase occupation. His survey data from a 33 sq mile area around the late pueblos suggest that the region was unoccupied at the time the first pueblos were established, about 1260. As a result, all occupation of the area was by immigrants, which is at variance with Tonto Basin. Nonlocal tree-ring dated ceramics provide the sequence of pueblo occupation and the chronology for the area.

Ceramics and architecture provide strong evidence for the origin of the immigrant groups that occupied this stretch of the river. Homol'ovi II and IV were settled by groups from the Hopi Mesas area based on contemporary settlement layouts, room size, kiva style, and nonlocal ceramics (Adams 1989; Hays-Gilpin et al. 1996). Homol'ovi I and III, on the other hand, were settled by groups from the upper Little Colorado River area, most likely the Silver Creek drainage using the same criteria (Hays-Gilpin et al. 1996).

A ceramic assemblage dominated by traded wares, including Jeddito Black-on-orange, St. Johns Polychrome, Bidahochi Black-on-white, and Kayenta Black-on-white, at Homol'ovi IV suggests occupation between 1260–1280 (Hays-Gilpin et al. 1996). Initial settlements at Homol'ovi I and III, dominated by Pinedale Polychrome, Pinedale Black-on-white, with some Pinto Polychrome and the absence of St. Johns Polychrome, suggest a 1280 beginning date (Hays-Gilpin et al. 1996). The predominance of Jeddito Yellow Ware at Homol'ovi II associated with Fourmile Polychrome and Gila/Tonto Polychrome suggests a post-1325 settlement (E. C. Adams 1996; Hays-Gipin et al. 1996).

Kolbe (1991) and Van West (1996) have reconstructed streamflow in the Little Colorado River using the Salt/Gila and Verde Rivers tree-ring records. Kolbe has also evaluated the aggregation/degradation cycle of the river from about 1260–1350. Not surprisingly, these records closely parallel reconstructions of agricultural potential for Tonto Basin by Van West and Altschul (1994) and use the same Salt/Gila River database to reconstruct streamflows (Graybill 1989; Rose 1994). The presence of bedrock through the upper portion of the Homol'ovi section of the Little Colorado River and the very wide floodplain, up to 4 km, made this an ideal area for floodplain agriculture. The characteristics of the two floodplains, therefore, are slightly different.

Lower streamflow in the late 1200s and again in the mid-1300s suggests to Van West (1996) that the Little Colorado River would have provided an optimum farming opportunity with less risk of flooding due to lower streamflows. This sequence was interrupted in the 1300–1330 period with a wet phase having enhanced streamflow and flood potential.

Serious flooding events paralleling those in the Salt/Gila drainages for the 1350s and 1380s are also suggested for the middle Little Colorado River (Graybill 1989; Van West 1996).

So what does the archaeological record tell us about the pueblo occupation of the middle Little Colorado River? First, unlike Tonto Basin, this stretch of the Little Colorado River was unoccupied. Second, when groups moved into the area, they did so rapidly and in great numbers. Third, streamflow and fluctuations played a big part in making the area attractive. Fourth, cotton was grown extensively.

Cotton ubiquity increases from 25 percent in the late 1200s to 57 percent in the middle 1300s (K. R. Adams 1996; Miksicek 1989, 1991). In pace with these increases are larger settlements providing larger labor pools. These would have been necessary to divert water into fields. The size of the floodplain and the appearance and growth of five settlements along its banks between 1250–1300, and especially after 1280, parallels remarkably the growth and settlement of Tonto Basin. The equal spacing of the settlements, nearly identical to Hohokam irrigation communities in the Phoenix Basin and Tonto Basin platform mound communities, suggests that dependence on the floodplain was only possible through irrigation (Fish and Fish 1994). Thus, timing, settlement size, spacing, and total population all point to irrigation as the most likely mechanism for watering thirsty plants on the floodplain.

Flood events archaeologically dated to the early 1300s at Homol'ovi III and to the 1350–1390 period at Homol'ovi I, underscore the dangers of farming on the river. The correlation of these events to periods of high streamflow modeled from the tree-ring record is significant (Van West 1996:29). The unpredictability of the middle Little Colorado River floodplain for irrigation agriculture during the post-1330 period parallels that of Tonto Basin. The reorganization of settlement, interaction, and land use in both areas during this period, therefore, is probably not accidental. In the Little Colorado River the width of the floodplain allowed groups to diversify their agricultural strategy by placing fields at distances ranging up to 2 km from the river (Lange 1996). For example, remnants of archaeological materials associated with agriculture along margins of the existing floodplain dating to the early 1300s suggests this was the strategy employed during periods of high streamflow. The post-1330 period characterized by Jeddito Yellow Ware pottery suggests an even more diversified agricultural strategy. Field houses and artifact scatters ranging to over 5 km from the river indicate attempts to cope with the less predictable water flow and environment of the middle Little Colorado River and the highest populations of the pueblo period. The dynamics of interaction among the pueblos, especially after the arrival of Homol'ovi II, suggests that the middle Little Colorado River was contested ground, primarily for its ability to grow cotton (E. C. Adams 1996).

PARALLELS IN TONTO BASIN

So what bearing does this brief prehistory of the Homol'ovi pueblos have on the Salado period (Roosevelt and Gila phases) of Tonto Basin? From my perspective, the parallels are striking. Both areas witnessed influxes of Pueblo populations, both areas probably initiated or expanded irrigation systems as a result of population influx, neither area witnessed violence at the outset of this settlement, population sources for both areas were the uplands of the Mogollon Rim, cotton production was a focus of Pueblo groups in both areas, and the dates and sequence of events are almost identical. Both areas may have seen Pueblo populations before 1280, but the major influx was about 1280. Both were drawn or pulled to these areas as a result of favorable "climatic conditions," that is, lower streamflow allowed increased floodplain agriculture augmented by irrigation. Finally, both areas had to reorganize their agricultural strategies between 1300 and 1330 due to increased streamflows and again after 1330 to cope with extreme rainfall and streamflow variability. In other words, similar processes may have been driving the settlement of both areas.

A HISTORY OF SALADO DISPERSAL

Let us revisit the distribution and dissemination of Salado polychromes. Crown (1994) using INAA techniques and Burton et al. (1994) using ICP acid-extraction are enabling us to clarify the picture of the origin and dispersal of groups that manufactured Roosevelt Red Wares. Early Pinto Polychromes found in pueblos along the Salt and Gila Rivers from Tonto Basin through the Globe/Miami area to Safford have ceramic signatures suggesting origin above or below the Mogollon Rim near the headwaters of the Little Colorado River. This com-

ports with Crown's (1994) observation that the earliest styles on Salado polychromes are most similar to Hopi and White Mountain Red Ware traditions above the rim. Crown (1994:208–209) observes that there is a relationship between the earliest appearance of Roosevelt Red Wares and immigration of Tusayan-Kayenta groups, even into southeastern Arizona.

Thus Salado culture is in fact the product of immigrant groups from the Mogollon Rim. But why did they disperse into various drainages from the Tonto on the northwest into the international Four Corners on the southeast? I discuss this below. We do know from the various ceramic characterizations that after establishing themselves, the Pinto Polychrome tradition of these early groups gave way to locally made Pinto and Gila Polychromes. Both Crown and I argue that not only were people moving into these areas, but ritual traditions were being established. The addition of these ritual systems, which evolved over the following 150 years, fostered the aggregated settlements that begin appearing with Salado polychromes at about 1280–1300.

Why did people move out of the mountains into the major drainages? General environmental models would have us believe that groups were moving into the mountains because during the Great Drought these were refuge areas for agricultural populations. Perhaps this model is wrong, or, too simplistic. Water tables were dropping and perhaps provided opportunities for agriculture in some areas where it was difficult before (Altschul and Van West 1992). I have argued this for the Homol'ovi area. But I have also argued for an incentive for the establishment of the Homol'ovi pueblos—cotton. Could this incentive apply to those settlements along the upper Gila River, and perhaps elsewhere? Elson, Gregory, and Stark (1995) note that cotton has high ubiquity values at Roosevelt phase settlements with pueblo-like features, suggesting specialization. Kent (1983b) and Teague (1992a, 1992b) have noted that pueblo textile designs from about 1250–1450 took on style and structure similar to that of their neighbors to the south, the Salado and Hohokam. This unity in textile designs could be related to the spread of "Salado Culture." Textiles are critical components of ritual. Textiles are traditionally woven in the kivas in modern pueblos. Textiles are depicted in detail in kiva murals as essential elements of ritual paraphernalia (Smith 1952). What I am suggesting is a linkage. The expansion of prehistoric ritual and the areas selected for settlement are connected.

Thus Pinto Polychrome-bearing groups moved from the Mogollon Rim to settle along the upper Salt and Gila Rivers to produce cotton. (At the same time groups moved out of the Silver Creek drainage to settle along the middle Little Colorado River area, founding the Homol'ovi group, for the same reason.) This cotton was exchanged back to the homeland as well as being used locally. In Tonto Basin this system was in place until about 1300 or as late as 1330, when the system changed. Many of the Roosevelt Phase communities were abandoned and burned (Craig, Elson, and Wood 1992:30). The return to wet and unpredictable conditions (1310–1340) may have imperiled the irrigation communities and caused at least some of the puebloans to return to their homeland (Craig, Elson, and Wood 1992:30; Van West and Altschul 1994). At the very least, pueblo groups lost their distinctiveness. They may simply have returned to the homeland (Johnson 1992) by choice because the river shifted and cotton production was no longer viable.

Most likely, it is a combination of the two. Some puebloan groups stayed, some left. The Roosevelt phase with its northern orientation is replaced by the Gila phase representing a reorganization of the entire system. Platform mounds take on a residential as well as ceremonial role (Craig, Elson, and Wood 1992:30). The aggregation of Tonto Basin communities has been related to increased need to control the expanding irrigation system developed during this phase, a period when conditions would make irrigation agriculture most productive (Ciolek-Torrello 1994:678). Expanded irrigation could also have enhanced the production of cotton for exchange to the Mogollon Rim communities. This may be particularly significant because it is early in the Gila phase that the supply of cotton from the Homol'ovi area to Mogollon Rim communities was terminated, or in the 1330s (E. C. Adams 1996).

Where did the Tonto Basin people go?—above the Mogollon Rim to Zuni and Acoma (Dittert 1959; Smith et al. 1966). There is a clear record of Gila Polychrome-bearing groups arriving in the upper Little Colorado River basin and points east as early as the mid-1300s, for example at Fourmile Ruin (Johnson 1992). A later influx appears at Zuni (Hawikuh and Kechipawan) and Acoma after 1400. Some of these are almost certainly from Tonto Basin; however, it is likely that other "Salado" groups arrived in these areas as well. The groups along the Gila River are undoubtedly represented, and perhaps groups from southwestern New Mexico appeared in the Acoma region. But, as noted earlier, some Salado polychrome-producing groups could have ended up in Casas Grandes, if it indeed survived the end of "Salado Culture." Much more ceramic characterization is needed to explore and explain these possibilities.

RITUAL AND THE ROLE OF COTTON

What is it about cotton that makes it such a valuable commodity and why did the value increase in the later 1200s? Cotton is a strong, lightweight, durable fiber that is relatively easy to grow, harvest, and process (Kent 1957; Teague 1992b). Textiles worldwide are important conveyers of information about the wearer, such as wealth and status. From my perspective, cotton's most important new role in prehistoric Pueblo society was its key role in ritual. Among the Hopi today, cotton is used in all articles of dress associated with ritual, including kilts, sashes, and belts (Kent 1983a). It is also a key ingredient in prayer feather making. Clouds are symbolized with unspun cotton when interred with the dead. Textiles nearly identical to modern ones are depicted in murals in kiva walls dating to about 1400 from Hopi to the Rio Grande (Smith 1952). I have proposed that in order to cope with emigrants, aggregation, and concomitant change in the social fabric of pueblo society, it was necessary to amplify the role of ritual (E. C. Adams 1991, 1996).

Crown (1994) has suggested a broader ritual system associated with the Salado polychromes, which she terms the Southwestern Regional Cult. In contrast, I have proposed a Plateau-oriented Katsina Cult derived from elements appearing during the 1200s in a broad region ranging from northern Mexico to the Mogollon Mountains to the southern and western Colorado Plateau (Adams 1991). Many of our arguments are similar and derived from the same database. My central concern was not with the broader regional cult of the period, but with the specific phenomenon of the Katsina Cult. Crown has chosen to emphasize imagery and style in arguing for the presence and subject matter of the Southwestern Cult, which she characterizes as an earth/fertility cult rather than an ancestor/death cult, which characterized the Mimbres tradition. The Katsina Cult incorporates both earth/fertility and ancestor/death aspects. I would argue that style and iconography, while useful, are only the tip of the iceberg in understanding the role regional cults play within a society. The fact that 67 percent of Salado polychromes appear in mortuary contexts suggests to me that ancestor/death ritual may indeed play a role in the Southwestern Cult, regardless of the variability in these mortuary practices (Crown 1994:221–22).

The more significant aspects to my arguments concerning the appearance of the Katsina Cult had to do with why, when, and how it was accomplished. It is at least as interesting and important to know the answers to these questions than to know the specific subject matter of the iconography of the associated ceramics. Why did this imagery appear in the early 1300s? Why does masked imagery become so prevalent in the ceramic and kiva mural traditions of southern Plateau groups and only southern Plateau groups at this time? How do these relate to changes in community and village structure? For the purposes of a Colorado Plateau perspective on Tonto Basin and the Salado in general, what is the relationship between regional cults and the events that led to the appearance of Salado "culture?"

The argument for common origins for the Katsina Cult and the Southwestern Cult in the upper Little Colorado River/Mogollon Rim area in the 1280–1325 period is significant (Adams 1991; Crown 1994). Crown (1994), Reid et al. (1992), and White and Burton (1992) have argued that Pinto Polychrome developed first just below the Mogollon Rim and the upper Little Colorado River region sometime after 1280. Reid et al. (1992:212–15) explain the development of Pinto Polychrome as a technological innovation resulting from the switch to local production of pottery due to lack of access to Cibola White Ware ceramics. The spread of the tradition was due to the buildup of population in fuel-scarce environments. This technological explanation does not account for the specific contexts and spread of later Salado polychromes; for example, in northern Sonora where a polychrome tradition already existed. A ritual expression for Salado polychrome use is the most parsimonious.

Nevertheless, as with the Katsina Cult, the appearance and spread of Pinto, Gila, and Tonto Polychromes is associated with pueblo-like developments and aggregation, often involving plaza-oriented settlements, outside the Hohokam area. As with my arguments for the Katsina Cult, I agree with Crown (1994:214–15) that the Southwestern Cult ritual system brought to these communities mechanisms for integrating divergent groups. Promoting village harmony in the face of immigration would certainly be essential. Nevertheless, one must keep in mind the likelihood that the immigrants were almost

certainly known through previous trade relationships or similar processes. In Tonto Basin, apparently ethnic coresidence occurred on a limited basis when Pueblo groups moved in (Stark, Clark, and Elson 1995a). Extensive burning of settlements at the close of the Roosevelt phase could be interpreted as evidence that integration between groups had not been achieved, a theory also proposed by Haury (1958) to explain the burning of room blocks occupied by a Kayenta Anasazi enclave at the Point of Pines Pueblo dated about 1300. This could point to the failure of the regional cult to accomplish its goals of integration, or may suggest that the cult was not operative in Tonto Basin.

I disagree with Crown (1994:217–21) in her comparison of the Southwestern Cult to the Katsina Cult. I see clear divergence between the two cults by the early 1300s. For example, the Katsina Cult is associated with large pueblos having enclosed plazas, kivas, death/ancestor worship, and new modes of food processing, especially piki (Adams 1991). Its iconography includes rock art, ceramics, and kiva murals (Adams 1991). Although it shares its roots in the Pinedale style with the Southwestern Cult, it clearly diverges in its expression of anthropomorphs, or katsinas, in all of these media from the Southwestern Cult. Exchange seems to be an essential component of the economies of these large pueblos, especially in ceramics. This exchange, especially the possibility of directed exchange of Jeddito Yellow Ware ceramics, could be related to attempts to control access to preciosities. Another aspect of control is secrecy. The planning of katsina ceremonies is focused in kivas. This enhanced control of ritual knowledge may have enabled those in power to integrate larger villages and perhaps to operate such village-wide enterprises as irrigation systems (see Rice, Chapter 6; Whittlesey et al., Chapter 10).

In contrast, the Southwestern Cult is associated with pueblos, but in communities that are organized differently from those on the Plateau. Its emphasis, according to Crown (1994), is on fertility and the earth to the exclusion of ancestors and death. Ceramics are locally produced. There is no association with kivas and the attendant secret ritual. Thus, the power base of the Southwestern Cult may be more diffuse and less successful in maintaining aggregated settlements in the long run.

The two cults have in common the purpose of ensuring community continuity through integration and cooperation and the reduction of conflict. This was accomplished in a more violent fashion in the Katsina Cult involving worship of the dead or ancestors and the control of more power within the community (E. C. Adams 1996). I also agree that they have a common root, whatever one chooses to call it. For example, Hill's (1992) concept of the Flower World has precedence in time, as does Mimbres imagery which is closely linked to the dead and afterlife (Brody 1977; Moulard 1984). The development of both cults in the Mogollon Rim/upper Little Colorado River area at the same time suggests that similar roots and purposes were operative.

There is a clear contrast between the early "formative" stages of the two cults between about 1280 and 1325, and their more formalized expressions after 1325. This is best understood with the Katsina Cult, but developments in Tonto Basin suggest that a similar transformation occurred in the Southwestern Cult. Changes in ceramics also suggest these developments in both areas.

On the Colorado Plateau, the pre-1325 Katsina Cult seems closer to Crown's Southwestern Cult. I characterize it as the early Katsina Cult, strongly associated with the appearance of the Pinedale style (Adams 1991). It was visible in the numerous small to medium pueblos along the drainages of the Little Colorado River from the Homol'ovi area to the Silver Creek, upper Little Colorado River, and Zuni areas. Katsina icons, if they appear at all, occur infrequently on Pinedale-style ceramics of local manufacture. Enclosed plazas may not exist or are small and incorporated into the pueblo room blocks. When large plazas occur, they are often made of coursed adobe or adobe bricks (Gann 1996; Johnson 1992), and are attached to earlier masonry components. They occur initially only in the largest pueblos, as public, integrative constructs. It is in the larger plazas that kivas are constructed separately from the room blocks. Ritual deposits are relatively isolated and small in comparison to their later counterparts.

After 1325, the Katsina Cult becomes a much more formalized and power-laden ritual system. This is best expressed at Homol'ovi II, a 1200-room, 40-kiva pueblo, dating about 1330–1400. Homol'ovi II was constructed on an organized plan around three large, enclosed plazas. It is surrounded with rock art bearing katsina images, contains kivas with murals, and has numerous Jeddito Yellow Ware vessels having katsina faces (E. C. Adams 1996). Homol'ovi II also has numerous other distinctive qualities. There is considerable evidence of violence in the community (E. C. Adams 1996), extensive ritual deposits in kivas and rooms (Walker 1995), and a ubiquity

of Jeddito Yellow Ware pottery, manufactured at Hopi Mesa villages, comprising almost 90 percent of decorated ceramics (Hays 1991; Hays-Gilpin et al. 1996). At the same time that Homol'ovi II was established, Jeddito Yellow Ware replaced local ceramics at Homol'ovi I, and probably at Chevelon Ruin, Cottonwood Creek Ruin, and Jackrabbit Ruin, more than 30 km east (Adams et al. 1993). It is also during this period that Jeddito Yellow Ware appeared at selected pueblos in the upper Little Colorado and Tonto Basin. These patterns all point to more highly organized, ritually-derived communities seizing control or enhancing access to rare or ritually-significant commodities, in this case, cotton (E. C. Adams 1996). At Homol'ovi II there is clear evidence that this new integrative structure was the Katsina Cult (E. C. Adams 1991, 1996). The sudden appearance of Jeddito Yellow Ware at selected pueblos in farflung areas may indicate directed exchange, for example, to Table Rock Pueblo near Springerville, Rye Creek Ruin in the upper Tonto Basin, and even Pottery Mound near the Rio Grande (Haury 1930; Hibben 1975; Martin and Rinaldo 1960). At both Homol'ovi II and Pottery Mound, the katsina ritual system and associated religious leaders were correlated with the appearance of yellow ware. The katsina ritual system allowed control of access to ritual knowledge through the use of kivas for storing ritual objects, for planning ritual activities, and for performing some rituals. These patterns are true of the Hopi ritual system today, where control of ritual through ceremonies is linked to better agricultural land and increased power and control within the pueblo community and results in social stratification (Levy 1992). The association of human remains with many ritual deposits at Homol'ovi II strongly hints of ancestor worship, control of witchcraft, and even warfare in achieving community integration and perhaps in controlling nearby pueblos.

The Southwestern Cult, as described by Crown (1994), also changed after about 1325, with the appearance of Gila and Tonto Polychromes. The cult becomes much more regionally expressed. It is associated with communities from the Jornada and Casas Grandes areas on the east to the Verde Valley on the west. I would argue that it is mutually exclusive of both the Hohokam ritual system and the katsina ritual system. Nevertheless, the elaboration of platform mounds, the greater focus on irrigation, more aggregated settlements, and indications of violence with burning of Roosevelt phase settlements all suggest that the Southwestern Cult was changing too. Indications of ritual structures with restricted access in Roosevelt and Gila phase platform mound settlements and the appearance of Salado polychromes in mortuary deposits may indicate the Southwestern Cult had the capability of unique, local expressions. Certainly, the association of Salado polychromes with a dazzling array of settlement types each producing their own pottery would support this perception. The local production of the Roosevelt Red Wares indicates a different focus from katsina ritual and associated Jeddito Yellow Wares.

As noted earlier, the movement to Tonto Basin by Mogollon Rim groups and to the middle Little Colorado River by upper Little Colorado River/Silver Creek groups in the late 1200s was to gain access to cotton, a much coveted and increasingly necessary component to developing ritual systems, namely the Southwestern Cult. This was made possible by a combination of events including population movements (immigration into the Mogollon Rim and upper Little Colorado River areas) and reduced streamflow making the Tonto Basin and middle Little Colorado River areas more suitable for irrigation farming. These changes were shortlived because streamflows increased during the 1300–1330 period. The correlation of changed streamflows with the reorganization of the local system in the early 1300s suggests a relationship. This relationship underscores the probable importance of streamflows in the Tonto Creek and the Salt Rivers in determining the quantity and quality of arable land in their respective floodplains (Altschul and Van West 1992; Van West and Altschul 1994) and, as a result, the need to adjust subsistence strategies for survival by local residents. In Tonto Basin, Roosevelt phase settlements were burned. Platform mounds took on residential as well as ritual uses. This is reflected in construction of the Gila phase communities and the integration of remaining pueblo groups in Tonto Basin into aggregated Gila phase settlements. In the middle Little Colorado River, reorganization takes a slightly different form. The arrival of Homol'ovi II is signaled in existing settlements with the sudden and total change from the Winslow Orange Wares made from local clay to Jeddito Yellow Ware ceramics traded from Hopi Mesa communities. This transition marked the shift to a northern focus for exchange.

It seems probable that the elaboration of both ritual systems occurred away from the Mogollon Rim area. The Katsina Cult florescence occurred in the Hopi area and the Southwestern Cult, in more localized expressions, in the upper Salt and Gila drainages and, ultimately, per-

haps in the Jornada, southwest New Mexico, and Casas Grandes regions (Nelson and LeBlanc 1986). This is certainly suggested in the distinctively Chihuahuan style of the latest Salado polychromes (Crown 1994:190). The florescence of cotton textile styles from northern Mexico to the southern Plateau is the best evidence of the role of cotton in the process (Kent 1983b; Teague 1992a, 1992b).

Summary and Conclusions

A lot of ground has been covered in this paper. I have attempted to present a lot of ideas. Not being part of the group that excavated in Tonto Basin, I offer speculative ideas about economic, political, and ritual links to groups to the north. I summarize these ideas below.

The location and earliest appearance of Roosevelt Red Wares outside their heartland in the Mogollon Rim country occurs in the Tonto Basin, Globe-Miami, and Gila River/Safford areas (Burton et al. 1994; Crown 1994; White and Burton 1992). Immigrants from above and below the Mogollon Rim settled in these riverine communities between 1280–1300. The areas first settled provided access to new agricultural areas that could have enhanced local resources near the Rim. But as noted, food resources seemed not to be scarce and distance of transport would seem prohibitive. One commodity that was not locally available on the Mogollon Rim was cotton. Contact between Mogollon Rim and riverine settlements along the upper Salt and Gila Rivers, almost certainly involving exchange of cotton, had been established by the 1000s. Ritual elaboration resulting in increased demand for cotton combined with changes in the river systems above and below the Rim where cotton could be grown were the twin push and pull factors causing the immigration into the upper Salt and Gila drainages and into the middle Little Colorado River during the late 1200s.

Reductions in streamflow through the upper Salt/Gila River system made irrigation not only more practical, but almost mandatory to grow adequate food surpluses. Arrival of groups from the Rim provided a much needed labor pool and permitted increased production of and access to cotton. The appearance of weaving traditions on the Plateau identical to their Saladoan counterparts by the fourteenth century underscores the importance and exchange of cotton.

Increased need for cotton may have been partly population-based, but was primarily ritually-derived. The appearance of the Southwestern Cult and associated Katsina Cult in the very Mogollon Rim area that was the source of the immigrating populations strongly suggests a connection. The ritual systems enhanced community integration and ultimately enabled settlement and community size to increase, almost certainly derived in part from Colorado Plateau immigrants. Later katsina iconography on kiva murals implies that the demand for cotton lay partly in clothing worn by katsina dancers. Cotton clothing and textiles also have traditionally been used in Old and New World contexts to assert ethnicity, status, and power. The ritual basis to power in modern Pueblo communities (Levy 1992) and cotton's clear association with ritual elaboration in kiva murals suggests that ethnicity, status, or power were involved in the apparent increase in its production and exchange, perhaps replacing more traditional textiles in ritual contexts. Examples of similar processes of increased cotton production in the Homol'ovi area of the Little Colorado River underline the importance of the role of cotton in ritual on the Colorado Plateau during this same transitional period (K. R. Adams 1996; Miksicek 1991).

More evolved and formalized forms of the Southwestern Cult and the Katsina Cult are associated with late Classic (post-1325) developments away from the Mogollon Rim. For the Southwestern Cult this is manifested in Gila/Tonto Polychrome pottery. For the Katsina Cult it is manifested in Jeddito Yellow Ware, especially Sikyatki Polychrome.

The ebb and flow of influence of the Southwestern Cult as it grew and integrated divergent groups throughout the Salado region shifted from north to south. The Phoenix Basin was apparently peripheral to this cult until after 1350. After 1350 the tie seems to be economic rather than ritual. The depth and stability of Hohokam ritual in the Phoenix Basin based on ball courts and later platform mounds evidently prevented penetration by the Southwestern Cult (Crown 1994:223–25). It seems likely that the concept of regional system, so ably espoused by Wilcox (1991a), should get its due in thinking about the relationships between these regions. From an economic standpoint, involving cotton, the Hohokam were apparently involved in the exchange of cotton after 1350. At least Jeddito Yellow Ware and late Roosevelt Red Ware, signaling post-1330 exchange, appear in Phoenix Basin sites. This coincides with the restructuring of settlement in Tonto Basin and perhaps was due to the inability of Tonto Basin communities to devote enough land to cotton, or to an increased need, system-wide through ritual elaboration, that could not be met locally.

It would seem that Casas Grandes became increasingly influential in ritual and even economic matters as the "Salado Culture" evolved. These influences from the south show up clearly in many ways that I have documented for the Katsina Cult among the pueblos after 1350, including abundant use of abstract parrots and other birds on polychrome pottery and kiva murals, piki stones, and shoe or slipper pots (Adams 1991:99–101). The collapse of Hohokam and Casas Grandes around 1450 caused the withdrawal of remnant Salado groups into the (primarily western) pueblo world. Among Western Pueblos (Hopi, Zuni, and Acoma), cotton production was then dominated by the Hopis until well into the 1600s.

ACKNOWLEDGMENTS

I would like to express my appreciation to the Bureau of Reclamation for inviting me to the Salado Seminar at the Amerind Foundation. Although I was unable to attend the actual Seminar, the sharing of information from fellow participants and their helpful comments substantially improved the present version of this paper from the one presented at the seminar. Jeffrey Dean, who organized the seminar, helped get me copies of all the seminar papers and in general provided support and encouragement. In particular I want to thank Mark Elson for his patience and generally good counsel on a far-ranging list of subjects. Vince LaMotta also made many useful observations. In addition to Vince, I want to especially thank Bill Walker for taking my thinking about ritual into directions I had never fathomed. I should absolve all the aforementioned from guilt by association from the actual content of this paper, which is my own creation. Finally, I want to dedicate this paper to Jenny and Nathan Adams who, through much hardship, have nevertheless provided clear and bright light to my life. Thank you!

CHAPTER TWELVE

Salado in Chihuahua

Stephen H. Lekson

Salado has hit hard times: the grand, imperial Salado of yesteryear is a derided memory, and the new candidate Salado-in-the-Tonto seems a paltry replacement. No longer a torrent of highland warriors, sweeping over cringing desert dwellers, Salado has been reduced to a recreation area. We've dammed it with a slight raise of Lake Roosevelt—this newer smaller Salado is confined and contained within Tonto Basin. The waters rise and the mighty fall.

Yet still we speak of a larger Salado, akin in size if not panache to that vanished ur-Salado. Its emblem is pottery. Nelson and LeBlanc (1986:6–10) distilled Salado down to its essence (or, to its lowest common denominator): Gila Polychrome. Then Crown (1994:203–209) shifted Gila Polychrome away from a people and toward a program—religious, artistic, symbolic, whatever. The Salado question, when asked outside Tonto Basin, becomes the Gila Polychrome question.

Gila Polychrome spills far beyond the banks of Lake Roosevelt—our Salado *must be* more than Tonto—but it is a liquid rarer and more evanescent than Gladwin's raging flood. Less a deluge than a dew, Salado falls across the southern mountains and deserts, twinkles briefly, and transpires.

This chapter examines the archaeology of "Salado in Chihuahua" or, more accurately, Gila Polychrome in the Chihuahuan desert. Chihuahuan discussions of this remarkable pottery customarily focus on quantity: how much and what proportion is Gila Polychrome of the larger ceramic assemblage. How much Gila Polychrome is enough? That is difficult to say: how much is enough for *what*? I will, of course, add my two (per)cents to discussions of "how much" and "what" but first, let us have facts. There is a firmness in the facts, as scattered research gives us to see those facts. So facts first: then let us strive to finish the work we are in, and worry later about "how much" and "what."

Facts are framed by *contexts* and *horizons*. By "context" I mean the role of Gila Polychrome, both as part of a larger ceramic assemblage and as a remarkable and much remarked artifact. By "horizon," I mean broad ceramic distributions with chronological implications. When we understand the range of contexts and horizons embracing Gila Polychrome, we may better restate and perhaps even answer those nagging quantity/quality questions.

SETTING THE STAGE

Throughout most of the Chihuahuan Salado region, the centuries preceding Gila Polychrome's glittery entrance were marked by small, simple pithouse villages with honest brown ware pottery. Between 700 and 1000, many of those simple sites sported locally made red-on-brown decorated pottery; and between 1000 and 1150, local decorated red-on-brown types were joined by Mimbres Black-on-white, a type found in small quantities from the San Pedro River on the west to the Pecos on the east, and from Elephant Butte on the north to La Junta on the south (cf. Lekson 1986b). Mimbres Black-on-white is well-dated from its centers of production (large masonry pueblos, exceptions to that general Chihuahuan pattern of small pithouse villages) on the Mimbres and Gila rivers, from 1000 to about 1130 or 1150. Red-on-brown pottery is a horizon, as that term is used here, and Mimbres marks another.

The archaeology of the Chihuahuan desert becomes difficult to read between the end of Mimbres Black-on-white (about 1150) and the beginnings of home-grown Chihuahuan polychrome traditions (about 1300). All over the southern Southwest, pithouses (or, in the exceptional Mimbres case, stone pueblos) were replaced by above-ground adobe structures. That shift from pithouse to "pueblo" should render sites more visible: after all, "pueblos" stick up. But easily recognized ceramic horizon-markers for this century-and-a-half, from 1150 to 1300, are inconveniently absent. Brown ware traditions continued, and a variety of new undecorated types appear (e.g., a horizon of smudged-polished-interior bowls and red slipped wares; Doyel 1993b:58; Lekson 1987) but those eye-catching intrusives are rare indeed: Chupadero Black-on-white and St. Johns Polychrome appear in very small quantities in the eastern Chihuahuan desert; Tularosa Black-on-white and St. Johns Polychrome are present at some central and northern thirteenth century sites; and late Hohokam and Tucson Basin decorated types mark the western ranges. But over most of the northern Chihuahuan area, the archaeology of the late twelfth and thirteenth centuries is just plain hard to see. Perhaps previous exchange patterns were disrupted; or painted pottery had lost its ideological load; or—mirable dictu—no one was home. Is the post-Mimbres horizon hard to see or is there simply nothing to see? Depopulations happened from time to time in the old Southwest.

Then, after 150 years of ceramic obscurity, the Chihuahuan desert is graced by an explosion of local polychromes (the Casas Grandes series) and one of the highest profile, easily recognized, surveyor-friendly types in the Southwestern panoply: Gila Polychrome. The dating of Gila Polychrome has been a matter of vast past debate, discussed elsewhere in this volume; its appearance can now be placed at or around 1300 without fear of violent censure. Overlaying an explosion of local fourteenth century polychrome types, the ubiquitous Gila Polychrome identifies the horizon, and defines the once-and-future phenomenon called Salado.

DESERT HORIZONS

Saladoan Chihuahua is limited, in so far as I know it, to the northernmost corner of that vast desert (and related grasslands and uplands; Brown and Lowe 1980) or, very roughly, extreme southeastern Arizona, southern New Mexico, and northwesternmost Chihuahua (Figure 12.1). Southeastern Arizona includes small portions of Sonoran Desert (particularly in the Safford Valley), and I ask the reader's pardon for my small incursion into others territories in this volume. When "Chihuahuan Desert" is used here, it means only this small northern corner of the larger Chihuahuan Desert. Archaeologically, Chihuahuan Salado encompasses the Jornada, Mimbres, Upper Gila, Animas, and Casas Grandes districts. Recent archaeological summaries of this area include, for the southern Southwest, Doyel (1993b) and Fish and Fish (1994a); for southeastern Arizona, Whittlesey et al. (1994); for southern New Mexico, LeBlanc and Whalen (1980) and Lekson (1992a); for Chihuahua, Phillips (1989) and Minnis and Whalen (1993).

Chihuahua is a desert, but it hasn't many dates. Of its several districts, only the Mimbres is even middling well dated, with slightly more than 500 tree-ring dates. The chronology of Casas Grandes—the next-best-dated district—rests on only 53 noncutting tree-ring dates, interpreted in a wonderful variety of ways (see Dean and Ravesloot 1993 for a review). The Jornada district has radiocarbon dates, but very few tree-ring dates (Robinson and Cameron 1991). The rest of Chihuahua is a chronometric desert—practically dateless, buried under the shifting sands of nonchronometric time. (All dates in this chapter—chronometric, relative, conjectural, or stark wild guesses—are AD or CE.)

Absent absolute dates, we must rely on pottery and, specifically, on intrusive pottery well dated at its place of origin. Salado polychromes were not the first exotic potsherds sown broadcast over the desert. Other, earlier decorated types spread, in small quantities, from Pecos to San Pedro. These widespread, low-frequency types—like Mimbres Black-on-white—mark temporal (if not

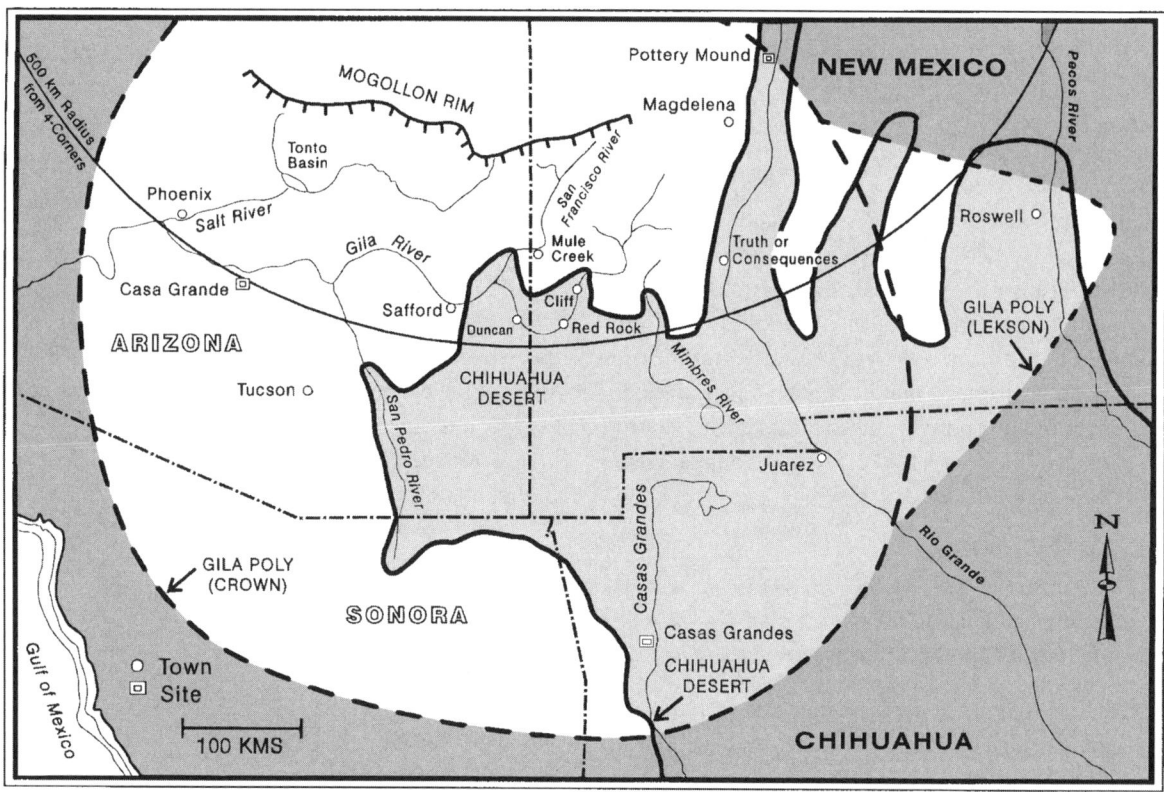

Figure 12.1.   Southwest area map.

cultural or cultic) horizons. By midcentury, the sequence of Chihuahuan horizons was understood, roughly, as:

Mimbres Black-on-white =
    twelfth and thirteenth centuries
Chihuahua polychromes =
    late thirteenth and fourteenth centuries
Salado polychromes =
    fourteenth and early fifteenth centuries

The 1970s saw two chronological studies of signal importance to pan-Chihuahuan systematics: the redating of the Mimbres sequence (Anyon et al. 1981) and the misdating of Casas Grandes (Di Peso 1974a). The new Mimbres chronology pushed Mimbres Black-on-white back to the eleventh century. Di Peso's Casas Grandes chro-

nology pushed the Chihuahua polychromes back almost as far. The old Mimbres-Chihuahua-Salado sequence was temporarily temporally wrecked:

Mimbres Black-on-white =
    eleventh and early twelfth centuries
Salado and Chihuahuan polychromes =
    eleventh to early fourteenth centuries

The recent work of Dean and Ravesloot (1993) restores Casas Grandes (and its hostage Salado polychromes) to the fourteenth century and later. Di Peso (1974a) had dated Casas Grandes from 1060 to 1340. Since all the datable intrusive pottery types at Casas Grandes fell in the fourteenth century, Di Peso's dating met with much criticism (reviewed in Dean and Ravesloot 1993). Reanalysis of the tree-ring samples corrected Di Peso's dating, and reconciled the Casas Grandes ceramic assemblage with the dating of its constituent types elsewhere in the Southwest, "the Paquimé phase was a fourteenth-century phenomenon whose inception can be placed very near 1300 (Dean and Ravesloot 1993:97). Archaeologists returned, with relief, to the old familiar horizon formula: Mimbres-Chihuahua-Salado (e.g., LeBlanc and Whalen 1980).

But we really can't go home again. Mimbres is older now than it was then, and our best dates for Salado-in-Chihuahua are also, of course, our best dates for the Chihuahua polychromes—that is, *both* Salado and Medio period Chihuahua polychromes are fourteenth century (see, for example, Carlson 1982:Table 2). So the formula now becomes:

Mimbres Black-on-white =
    eleventh and very early twelfth centuries
Chihuahua and Salado polychromes =
    fourteenth and fifteenth centuries

… leaving a ugly, obvious gap in the thirteenth century. The reality of that gap is, perhaps, the principal issue in later Chihuahuan prehistory. Who was home in Chihuahua in the thirteenth century? Was anybody there?

At its eastern, western, and northern extremes, there was no thirteenth century gap: Jornada Mogollon has the early El Paso phase, the Safford region has the Bylas phase, and the northern rim has Tularosa: all three fill thirteenth century voids. Since these decorated thirteenth century types *do* appear along the eastern, western, and northern margins, they *should* appear elsewhere. Why? Because earlier and later ceramic horizon markers marked those same larger territories. That is, Mimbres and Casas/Salado types covered the turf, so thirteenth century types should too—if they behaved in archaeologically convenient ways. The formula should be (and, in some portions of the Chihuahuan Desert, is):

Mimbres Black-on-white =
    eleventh and early twelfth centuries
Chupadero Black-on-white (east) and/or Tularosa
Black-on-white (north and west) and/or St. Johns
Polychrome =
    late twelfth and thirteenth century
Salado and Chihuahua polychromes =
    fourteenth and fifteenth centuries

These, then, are (or should be) the ceramic horizons of the northern Chihuahua Desert. The following sections apply these real and ideal horizons to various districts in the Chihuahuan Desert with special claims on Gila Polychrome.

GILA IN CHIHUAHUA

Gila Polychrome's distribution in the Chihuahuan Desert has been mapped several times, most recently by Crown (1994:Figure 1.1). The only amendment I would make to Crown's map would be the extension of Gila Polychrome's range east to Roswell (e.g., at Bloom Mound; Kelley 1984:475) to incorporate the areas of the El Paso and Lincoln phases (Figure 12.1).

How much? The proportions of Gila Polychrome at Chihuahua sites were generally quite low—between one and four percent of the total ceramic assemblage (Nelson and LeBlanc 1986:Table 1.2)—but the type appears to be made locally over most if not all of the districts in which it is found (Crown 1994:21–31). That conundrum reflects the singular nature of Gila Polychrome: rare yet ubiquitous, distinctive yet local. Its high visibility and remarkable distribution explains, in part, Gila Polychrome's particular fascination.

Intriguingly, most of the Gila Polychrome bowls from the Chihuahuan Desert are commonly of an uncommon form: most have flared rims (I include Crown's 1994:Figure 4.3, "recurved"; and Di Peso et al.'s 1974d:Figure 4.6, "everted rim" as "flared rim" forms). Gila Polychrome at Casas Grandes and the Cliff Valley Ormand site are almost entirely flared-rimmed (Di Peso et al. 1974f:152; Harlow 1968 "Cliff Polychrome"). Escondida Polychrome was a "copy" of Gila Polychrome made in the Casas Grandes area; about 70 percent of the Escondida Polychrome bowls at Casas Grandes had this rim form (Di Peso et al. 1974d:228). Everted, flared, or recurved forms are far less common in Gila Polychrome from all other regions: indeed, flared-rim bowls (recurved) constitute only 17 percent of Crown's (1994:Table 4.5) total sample of 448 Gila Polychrome bowls.

Gila Polychrome is everywhere, in small amounts, in the Chihuahuan Desert but three areas have special claims (Figure 12.1): first, the upper Gila River; second, Casas Grandes; third, a band of sites running from Safford, Arizona across the "International Four Corners" to Casas Grandes. Each of these areas is discussed in turn.

The Upper Gila

The Upper Gila River is segmented into several distinct valleys, separated by narrow gorges (Figure 12.1). From up- to down-stream these are the Cliff, Redrock, Duncan, and Safford valleys. The upper Gila (as an archaeological district) can also be stretched without rupture to encircle several Salado sites on the Mimbres River and Mule Creek (Figure 12.1). The archaeology of the Cliff Valley is relatively well known (Lekson 1990); that of the Redrock Valley less so (Lekson 1978). The Duncan Valley—a key area, where important "dotted lines" cross on many archaeological maps—is virtually unknown; archaeological research is limited to spotty survey and excavations at two Early Pithouse sites (interesting, but irrelevant for the present discussion). The Safford Valley, on the margin between Chihuahuan and Sonoran Deserts, had limited but provocative early research (summarized in Brown 1973, 1974) and an encouraging burst of recent work (e.g., Crary, Neily, Kinkade, and Germick 1994; Woodson 1994). For this chapter, I annex the Mimbres Valley to the Upper Gila (something I've always wanted to do); the Mimbres is probably the best researched district in the region (e.g., for periods of interest to this paper: Creel 1993, 1996; LeBlanc 1980a; Nelson and LeBlanc 1986; Ravesloot 1979).

Salado in the Cliff, Redrock, and Mimbres areas has been called "Cliff phase" (Nelson and LeBlanc 1986). The Cliff Valley and Duck Creek (a Salado-magnet tributary of the Gila), host six to eight large adobe pueblos with significant amounts of Gila Polychrome (among many other types), including the famous but unreported site of Kwilleylekia. Despite archaeological investigations beginning in the 1920s with Kidder and the Cosgroves, Cliff Valley Salado remains poorly reported. The Cliff phase itself was actually defined at sites in the Mimbres Valley, thought to represent colonists from Cliff (Nelson and LeBlanc 1986).

Figure 12.2 summarizes Cliff Valley Salado sites. Other Cliff phase sites include three excavated in the Mimbres Valley (Nelson and LeBlanc 1986) and a single, large Cliff phase site called the Dutch Ruin (LA 8706) in the Redrock Valley (with an important, unstudied whole vessel collection at the Johnson-Humrickhouse Museum in Coshocton, Ohio). Two large Cliff phase pueblos are known from the Mule Creek area, about 35 km northwest of Cliff (Ben A. Nelson, personal communication 1994). Several sizable adobe pueblo ruins with Gila Polychrome are reported from the Duncan Valley, but size and assemblage have not been defined. There is at least one large pueblo with Gila Polychrome in the San Francisco River Valley, near Alma (James A. Neely, personal communication 1993).

Salado in the Safford Valley is termed the Safford phase (Crary, Neily, Kinkade, and Germick 1994). Stone masonry is far more common in Safford phase pueblos than in Cliff phase pueblos, but the ground plans are comparable, "room blocks with large walled plazas and possibly rectangular kivas" (Crary, Neily, Kinkade, and Germick 1994:10). Although no comprehensive survey has yet been made of the Safford Valley, it is clear that there were at least six very large Safford phase pueblos.

GILA CONTEXTS

Gila and Tonto Polychromes are, inevitably, minor types at Cliff phase sites; they constitute between one and seven percent of ceramic assemblages. Gila and Tonto Polychromes constitute about 6.5 percent of the assemblage from the Cliff phase Dinwiddie site (Mills and Mills 1972;47; not to be confused with the nearby Mangas phase Dinwiddie site); about twelve percent of controlled surface collections at the Dutch Ruin in the Redrock Valley (Lekson 1978:Tables 13, 15); about one percent of the sherds from the five-room Cliff phase Villareal II site (Lekson 1978:Table 1); six percent of the sherds from Willow Creek (Fitting 1973:Appendix A, Table 3d); and a little more than four percent at the Ormand site (Harlow 1968:Table 1).

Proportions of sherd assemblages are (probably) important, but what of vessels? Crown's (1994) whole vessel data serve as a baseline for Salado contexts in this and other sections of this chapter. Crown analyzed contexts of 718 whole vessels from all parts of the Salado polychrome region (Crown 1994:100–101, Tables 6.3, 6.4). About two-thirds of Salado polychromes in this sample came from burial contexts; almost 90 percent of those burial offerings were from inhumations (opposed to cremations). Crown notes that most Salado polychrome vessels were manufactured for normal quotidian use, despite final deposition in burials, and she notes a possible "shift in the use of Salado polychrome vessels at the end of the sequence and that perhaps their earlier function in burial contexts had been replaced by other types of pottery" (Crown 1994:101).

Gila Polychrome vessels in the Safford and Cliff Valleys were usually found, not in burials, but in living rooms (i.e., rooms with hearths), typically a jar and perhaps a bowl with several non-decorated vessels, either on floors or (quite often) in what the excavators defined as roof

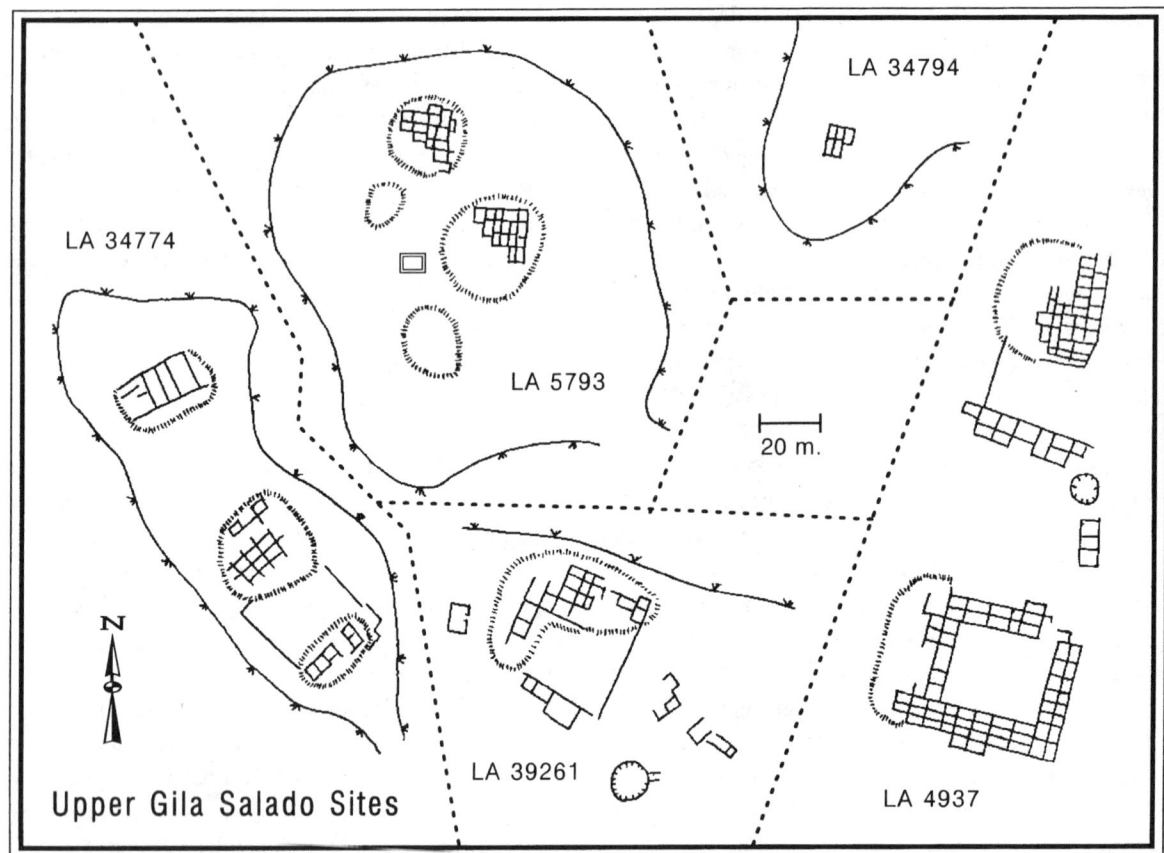

Figure 12.2.   Upper Gila Salado sites.

fall. Most rooms with hearths had Gila or Tonto Poly-chrome vessels among their assemblages. And most Gila Polychrome vessels at Safford and Cliff phase sites were recovered from living rooms. Indeed, in one case a Gila Polychrome bowl was set into the floor as part of a meal-ing bin (Mills and Mills 1978:149).

Cremation with discrete burial areas or cemeteries appears to be typical for adults in the Safford, Cliff and southeastern Arizona Animas phases. In Safford and Cliff phases, cremations were usually buried in jars, of-ten with inverted covering bowls or plates. In Safford and probably the other Upper Gila areas, infant burials were typically subfloor inhumations, often with associated pottery, and, uniquely, these child burial offerings were often Gila Polychrome.

At the Safford phase Buena Vista site (a.k.a. Pueblo Viejo and the Curtis site), one room block produced 38 subfloor burials of infants or children (27 had pottery offerings, of which eleven were Gila or Tonto Polychrome vessels; Brown 1973:Table 20; see also Mills and Mills 1978:97, 175). Typical burial for adults at Buena Vista was cremation placed in jars with covering bowls (Mills and Mills 1978:66–67). Forty-one cremations were excavated from one cemetery area, none with Gila Polychrome (these burials may predate the Gila horizon; Mills and Mills 1978:68–77, 130).

The Ormand site (Dittert 1966) was the only reported Cliff phase site (in distinction to Safford phase) to pro-duce burials; these were found in two cremation areas, one (badly disturbed) that produced 70 cremations and a second from which 35 cremations were excavated. Each cremation was contained in two vessels, a jar covered by an inverted bowl. Only ten of 70 cremation vessels were painted and only a very few of those were Salado polychrome types (Dittert 1966:32).

In neither Safford or Cliff phase sites was Gila Polychrome a major element of adult burial furniture. Instead, Gila and Tonto Polychrome are usually found in living rooms. This pattern stands in marked contrast to Crown's data on more than 700 Gila Polychrome vessels, most of which were from inhumation burials.

GILA HORIZONS

Both the Cliff and Redrock Valleys had long Mimbres Mogollon sequences; but, following the Mimbres phase (1000–1150), they both appear, ceramically, to be all-but-abandoned until the Cliff phase (1300–1450) (Lekson 1990). The dramatic clarity of Cliff phase Salado is in part due to the (apparent) 150-year gap between Mimbres and Salado. Intriguingly, there are two enigmatic tree-ring dates, obtained without documentation, of 1243cG from a Cliff Valley Salado site (Figure 12.2); it is difficult to assess these dates, but they may have important implications for the thirteenth century "gap." Despite ill-fated attempts to fill the gap between Mimbres and Cliff phases (Lekson and Klinger 1973), there does not appear, ceramically, to be any significant occupation of the Cliff and Redrock Valleys between Mimbres and Cliff phases. The 1243 dates invite further research; but for now, the Cliff and Redrock valleys appear effectively vacant in the thirteenth century.

A temporal unit called the Black Mountain phase (1180–1300) at least partially fills the Mimbres Valley sequence between the Mimbres and Cliff phases. In LeBlanc's (1980a) original discussions, the Black Mountain phase was considered a local expression of the Casas Grandes regional system, which LeBlanc (1980b) at that time dated to 1130–1300. The recent redating of Casas Grandes negates the Casas connection. The boundary between Mimbres and Black Mountain phases was originally interpreted as a major cultural disjuncture, with nearly complete population replacement (LeBlanc 1980a; but cf. Nelson and LeBlanc 1986:247). Recent excavations at the Old Town site suggest far more continuity than discontinuity between the two phases (Creel 1996; Lekson 1992a, 1992b).

Certainly, the Black Mountain phase saw the virtual abandonment of the upper and middle Mimbres Valley and

a shift in settlement location out into the deserts of the Deming Plain. The Black Mountain phase was more than just a change in settlement location: it probably represents a decrease in total Mimbres Valley population, although not nearly as dramatic a decrease as indicated by Blake et al. (1986; see Lekson 1992b). In sum, the Black Mountain phase probably represents an immediate post-Mimbres readjustment, with shifts in building technology, ceramic decoration, and site location—but with strong continuity, at reduced levels, from preceding Mimbres populations. They changed clothes—and houses and pottery (as they had done at several points in preceding prehistory)—but they may well have been the same people. Continuity eliminates the unpleasant necessity of eradicating several thousands of ancient Mimbreños.

In fact, the problematic Black Mountain phase in the Mimbres Valley could and probably should be combined with the early El Paso phase, its close neighbor to the south and east (Lekson 1992a:19–20, 88–89). The two share ceramic assemblages, architectural patterns, and a proclivity for inhospitable desert settings. Black Mountain plus early El Paso phases could answer the thorny question of where the Mimbres "went" without cataclysmic drops in total population required by the received Mimbres Valley sequence (Lekson 1992b). But this solution requires us to declare legally dead the old division between Mimbres and Jornada Mogollon—a move some feel is long overdue: it's ripe.

It would be pleasant to link Mimbres and El Paso phases, since the early El Paso phase is our best current candidate for pre-Casas Grandes. If a sequence could be constructed that runs Mimbres–Black Mountain/El Paso–Casas Grandes, Mimbres connects with Casas Grandes—and Salado.

There are tantalizing hints at linkage, through time and space, between Mimbres and Salado. Crown notes intriguing but chronologically problematic ties between Mimbres traditions and Salado polychromes (Crown 1994:221–22; see also LeBlanc and Khalil 1976:297). It may be useful to consider the survival of Mimbres icons and motifs in other media (e.g., rock art; Schaafsma 1980, 1992) during the thirteenth century gap, and their reappearance on pottery in the fourteenth century.

It appears that Cliff phase sites pop up in vacant places. Recognizing its emptiness, the Cliff Valley was identified as a "possible region of [Salado] colonization" by the participants of the 1967 Salado Red Ware Conference (Lindsay and Jennings 1968:4). Nelson and LeBlanc

(1986:246) suggest that "the Cliff area became overpopulated at ca. AD 1300 and some of its population moved eastward to inhabit the Mimbres Valley." In both places, the Cliff phase is seen as an intrusion into largely or wholly depopulated valleys. The Mimbres Valley passes the buck back to Cliff, but where did those Cliff Valley populations originate? This, despite a great deal of unpublished field research, remains obscure; I return to this topic in the conclusions of this paper.

The Safford Valley, in contrast, apparently was continuously occupied, without the gaps and/or depopulations evident in other areas in the Chihuahuan Desert — but with remarkably evident cultural discontinuities. In keeping with its Sonoran Desert environment, the Safford Valley began as part of the Hohokam sphere. Early horizons were marked by red-on-buff ceramics, and ball courts, palettes, and other Hohokam trumpery. The winds changed, and Mimbres Black-on-white was common at twelfth century sites (the Eden phase of Crary, Neily, Kincaid, and Germick 1994). By the late twelfth and early thirteenth centuries, while nearby valleys remained within the old Hohokam sphere (e.g., the San Pedro Valley; Doelle 1995c), the Safford Valley declined to build platform mounds and shifted even more toward puebloan spheres, with Tularosa and Pinedale black-on-whites and St. Johns Polychrome commonly found at Bylas phase sites (Brown 1973; Crary, Neily, Kinkade, and Germick 1994).

In the late thirteenth or early fourteenth centuries, the Safford Valley (and nearby valleys, such as the San Pedro and Cliff valleys) received dramatic immigrations of Pueblo groups (San Pedro: Doelle 1995; Safford: Woodson 1994; Cliff: discussed above). Gila Polychrome was common at these fourteenth century sites — so common, in fact, that the Safford Valley was once nominated for the ever-elusive ur-Salado homeland (Brown 1973:7, citing Charlie Steen).

To summarize: the uppermost Gila (Cliff, Redrock, and the Mimbres) appear to have thirteenth century gaps when they were either dramatically underpopulated or vacant while the Safford Valley sequence was remarkable for "shifts" (ceramic? cultural?) from Hohokam, to Mimbres, to Pueblo, to Salado — but it was never vacant. The Safford Valley was never empty and (at least long ago) never dull.

CASAS GRANDES

Casas Grandes is the 800-pound gorilla of Chihuahuan archaeology, big then and bigger now. Casas Grandes was the largest site of its time, and *Casas Grandes* is the largest site report of its time — probably the largest non-CRM report in the history of Southwestern archaeology (eight oversize volumes: Di Peso 1974a and Di Peso et al. 1974b-f). Casas Grandes and its excavator, Charles Di Peso, cast a long shadow.

Excavations at Casas Grandes produced significant amounts of Gila and Tonto Polychromes and Escondida Polychrome ("imitation Gila Polychrome," Gila and Tonto clones on local pastes; Di Peso et al. 1974d:226–42). Di Peso excavated about one-fifth of Casas Grandes and found 57 Gila Polychrome vessels, three Tonto Polychrome vessels, and 63 Escondida Polychrome vessels — 123 vessels out of a total vessel assemblage of 915 (Di Peso et al. 1974d:77, 240–42; 1974f:148). Di Peso claimed, given his original but incorrect eleventh century dating of Casas Grandes, that the Gila Polychrome originated at Casas Grandes and then spread north to the various suggested Salado home-away-from-homelands (Di Peso 1976a). Historically and substantively, Casas Grandes has a big stake in the archaeology of Gila Polychrome and, therefore, Salado.

Compositional analyses of sherds from Casas Grandes, in particular, suggests that Gila Polychrome was made at Casas Grandes or, more accurately, on the same pastes as Casas Grandes plain wares (Di Peso et al. 1974f:148–50). A more extensive geographic sample of Gila Polychrome led to less specific sourcing: Crown's analysis concludes that Gila Polychrome at Casas Grandes was made in the larger Upper Gila-Casas Grandes area, and possibly at Casas Grandes itself (Crown 1994:27–28). Di Peso argued that Gila Polychrome was actually made at Casas Grandes; Crown's analysis suggests only that Gila Polychrome from Chihuahua forms a group distinct from other Salado polychrome regions (e.g., Hohokam, Tonto, Mogollon Rim). Note that Crown's interpretation does not rule out import *into* Casas Grandes of Gila Polychrome produced at some other desert district (for example, the Upper Gila) — or vice versa. But note, also, that Escondida Polychrome (the local Gila clone) was almost certainly made at Casas Grandes or its near vicinity (Di Peso et al. 1974d:226–42). Certainly, they were making Escondida at Casas Grandes; possibly or probably they were making Gila Polychrome there, too, or in Casas Grandes' immediate area. An important point, however, concerns sample size; Di Peso's analysis included fewer than twenty sherds of both Gila Polychrome and plain ware (inferred from Di Peso et al. 1974f:150; no counts are given here or in Di Peso 1976a) and Crown's analysis included only six sherds of Gila Polychrome from Casas Grandes itself (Crown 1993:Table 3.1). Any conclusions remain, as always, tentative.

Despite the impressive collection of whole vessels and the strong possibility of local manufacture, Gila, Tonto, and Escondida Polychromes, together, make up slightly less than four percent of the total sherd assemblage — compared, for example, to 11.6 percent Ramos Polychrome (the principal decorated type at Casas Grandes) (Di Peso et al. 1974d:226, 1974f:251). Four percent, of course, is far more Gila Polychrome than at many other Chihuahuan sites confidently called "Salado."

CASAS CONTEXTS

Black-on-white and polychrome vessels were remarkable for their shifting formal roles in desert assemblages. Mimbres Black-on-white, the most widely distributed and conspicuous black-on-white type in the Chihuahuan Desert before 1300, was almost exclusively of bowl form. Anyon and LeBlanc (1984:Table 9.7) note that over 90 percent of Mimbres Black-on-white sherds at large sites in the Mimbres Valley were from bowls. As noted above, Mimbres Black-on-white ceased to be made about 1150 and, thereafter, over much of the Chihuahuan Desert, painted bowls were rare or absent. Black-on-white painted decoration, in sites that can be confidently dated from 1150 to 1300, was confined almost exclusively to jars (in the east, Chupadero Black-on-white; in the west, Tularosa Black-on-white). Most bowls and jars, during this (and later) period, were plain, textured, or red-slipped; but painted decoration shifts from bowl interior in Mimbres Black-on-white to jar exterior in Tularosa and Chupadero Black-on-whites. This remarkable switch should be the subject of heated research or, at least, speculation. But it is not.

During the late twelfth and thirteenth century in the Chihuahuan Desert, painted decorated vessels were mainly (but not exclusively) jars. Fourteenth century Casas Grandes ceramics continued that trend: the Chihuahua polychrome series was predominately jar forms. By sherd count, the Chihuahua polychromes at Casas Grandes were 72 percent jars (Ramos Polychrome, the signature type of Casas Grandes, was 86 percent jars). Gila Polychrome at Casas Grandes, on the other hand, is 85 percent bowls. Proportionately, Gila Polychrome complements Chihuahua

polychrome jars — but, of course, Gila, Tonto, and Escondida Polychromes constitute only four percent of the total sherd assemblage at Casas Grandes.

What does four percent mean? More than you might think. Gila-Tonto-Escondida Polychrome bowl sherds constitute one-fifth of all bowl sherds (painted, plain, textured, whatever) and about one-half of all painted decorated bowl sherds (Di Peso et al. 1974d:Table 649:6). Gila-Tonto-Escondida Polychrome bowl sherds far outnumber bowl sherds from any other painted decorated type at Casas Grandes. It is fair to say that Gila Polychrome and its related types were the most important types of painted bowls at Casas Grandes.

It would be nice to think that painted decoration on pottery meant or conveyed something more than nondecorated, textured, or slipped pottery — see, for example, Crown's (1994) monograph on Salado polychrome pottery. If painted decorated pottery functioned, symbolically at least, differently from nonpainted pottery, perhaps we should reconsider Gila Polychrome's four percent presence at Casas Grandes.

Context provides some clues. Gila Polychrome was everywhere at Casas Grandes, but *not* in burials. Recall that almost two-thirds of the vessels in Crown's (1994:103) Salado polychrome study were recovered from "mortuary contexts." Pottery was a common grave offering at Casas Grandes, but only one of almost 450 buried individuals at Casas was accompanied by a Gila Polychrome vessel (Ravesloot 1988:44; Di Peso et al. 1974f:153), and only five single or multiple burials were accompanied by Escondida Polychrome (Di Peso et al. 1974f:240–42). Gila, Tonto, and Escondida Polychromes were *not* a major part of burial ritual at Casas Grandes.

In fact, half of the Gila Polychrome at Casas Grandes came from a single room, Room 18–8, in the form of 49 bowls (plus one Tonto Polychrome bowl and one Springerville Polychrome bowl), all extraordinarily similar in shape and size. The 49 Gila Polychrome bowls in Room 18–8 were remarkably, uniformly large. Rim diameters ranged from 26 to 34 cm (mean=31.6 cm, sd=2.1). (The rim diameters of the associated Tonto and Springerville Polychrome bowls were 36.2 cm and 34.0 cm, respectively). This range was much tighter than the range of bowl rim diameters of the seven Gila Polychrome bowls found in other contexts at Casas Grandes, from 14.5 to 30 cm (mean=23.6, sd=6.5, t=3.1) (Di Peso et al. 1974f:152–53), and much larger than the average bowl rim diameters of other types at Casas. Escondida Polychrome, for example, had a mean rim diameter of 15.8 cm (sd=4.2, n=25) and Ramos bowls averaged 14.7 cm in diameter (sd=4.4, n=53 excluding a single Ramos bowl with the astonishing diameter of 54 cm). Other types range from 14 to 19 cm in diameter, with only Carretas and Huerigos Polychromes (at about 26 cm) approaching the large size of the Gila Polychrome bowls from Room 18–8.

Crown (1994:Table 4.9) provides measurements of maximum diameter (not rim diameter) for Gila Polychrome and other Salado polychrome bowls. She divides bowl forms into three size categories: small (mean maximum diameter of about 14–19 cm), medium (26–29 cm) and large (35–36 cm). The bowls from Room 18–8 are simple restricted forms with everted rims, and the difference between rim diameter and maximum diameter appears to be about 2cm; that is, the average maximum diameter on Room 18–8 bowls is about 34 cm. The Room 18–8 bowls would be "large" bowls in Crown's classification, a relatively rare form—only about six percent of the 399 Gila Polychrome bowls in Crown's (1994:Table 4.6) sample. Crown (1994:Figure 4.1, Table 4.9) notes that bowls from the Chihuahuan Desert are generally larger than bowls from the Hohokam, Tonto Basin, and Mogollon Rim regions. Comparison of pooled data from Crown's Chihuahuan polychrome bowls suggests that the Room 18–8 assemblage is remarkable even when compared to its own region, which averaged 24.4 cm (sd=7.4, n=85, t=8.4).

Room 18–8 and adjoining Room 15–8 were particularly notable, even at this extraordinary site (Di Peso et al. 1974b:424–28, 437–39). Di Peso called them "warehouses" and, on some level, that term is correct. Rooms 15–8 and 18–8 had large shelves and half-story ground floors (interpreted by Di Peso as slave quarters), greatly increasing floor area, perhaps for storage. A staggering trove of materials was, in fact, stored: 90 percent of Casas Grandes' marine shell, 90 percent of the copper and malachite ore, and about 50 percent of all the ricolite (Di Peso et al. 1974d:405, 1974e:188–89, 467–68).

Marine shell, in its astonishing quantity, has been discussed by others (Bradley 1993; Di Peso et al. 1974d). Copper artifacts are much rarer and of contested provenance: Di Peso suggested that copper was crafted at Casas Grandes (Di Peso et al. 1974d; see also Hosler 1994), but others suggest that these artifacts were actually made in West Mexico and traded to Casas. In either case, the number, variety, and quality of copper artifacts at Casas is truly remarkable, both for the Southwest and for the majority of Greater Mesoamerica.

Ricolite (and its related mineral, chrysotile asbestos) is notable both for its origin and use. Shell came from the west; copper came from the south; ricolite came from the north. Ricolite at Casas Grandes was chemically sourced to the Redrock, New Mexico quarries, 270 kms to the north (Di Peso et al. 1974f:188). Presumably, this material reached Casas Grandes via the Cliff phase Dutch Ruin, which is only a few kms from the quarries.

Ricolite was used for a variety of ornaments, ceremonial axes, and effigies, but most was shaped to produce small (22 x 13 x 6 cm) rectangular, four-legged stools (similar to that pictured on a Mimbres Black-on-white bowl; Lekson 1993:Figure 13). Most stools were found in Room 15–8; fragments of one stool each had fallen into the fill of adjacent Rooms 20–8 and 25–8. The bulk of the ricolite in Rooms 15–8 and 18–8 was unworked. The total weight of ricolite, worked and unworked, at Casas Grandes was about 117 kg; compared to 40 kg of copper and 1.2 kg of turquoise (Di Peso et al. 1974f:187–89). After shell, there was far more ricolite than any other nonceramic material imported to Casas Grandes.

Recall that Room 18–8 also contained the Gila Polychrome bowl assemblage. The association of Redrock ricolite and fifty Gila and Tonto Polychrome bowls could be coincidental: bulk exotic materials from a range of source areas were stored in Rooms 15–8 and 18–8. Contextually, it is possible to suggest that Gila Polychrome in Room 18–8 was stored with and treated like a bulk imported commodity.

Alternatively, the association of Gila Polychrome and Redrock ricolite might suggest a common source. Comparison of the bowls from Room 18–8, which have *not* been compositionally sourced, and the Dutch Ruin collections would be very interesting. Crown's (1994:27–28) analysis suggested that Gila Polychrome was made in the Chihuahuan Desert, and Di Peso was emphatically definite about Gila Polychrome's production at Casas (Di Peso et al. 1974f:148–50). However, neither analysis apparently included the bowls from Room 18–8. Absent chemical analysis, it is tempting to consider the implications if the bowls stored in Room 18–8 were indeed imported, as was so much of the astonishing contents of Rooms 5–8 and 18–8. The unique context of the Room 18–8 Gila Polychrome—stored with bulk imported goods—may reopen the question of the origins of at least some of the Gila Polychrome at Casas Grandes.

Eight Gila and two Tonto Polychrome vessels were found in contexts other than Room 18–8. Only one was with a burial (Burial 13-CP; although there is some confusion about this association, cf. Di Peso et al. 1974f:153,409–10). The other Salado vessels were found in plaza fill (three vessels), scattered through multiple rooms' fill (two vessels), in single room fill and floor associations (two), and in general test trenches (two vessels) (Di Peso et al. 1974f:152–54). Examination of artifact inventories from those contexts disclosed no obvious, unusual associations (Di Peso et al. 1974a:658,757). Gila Polychrome at Casas Grandes was remarkable for its absence from burials, and for its concentration in storage contexts with bulk imported good.

Casas Horizons

What comes before Casas Grandes? Presently, we have no secure immediately pre-fourteenth century contexts from the site. (Several much earlier pit structures were discovered in plaza excavations, but these date centuries before Casas Grandes.) Di Peso defined the Buena Fe phase (his dates: 1060–1205) as a "pre-Casas" or "early Casas" candidate, but the Buena Fe phase evaporates on architectural, ceramic, and chronometric grounds. Architecturally, Di Peso suggested that the "compound" form (such as Unit 11 and the first story walls of several multistoried rooms) were Buena Fe phase; while some of this construction clearly predates later building (the first stories, for example, necessarily precede the second and third stories, if only by minutes), there is no stratigraphic superimposition of pueblo over compound and, thus, little reason to believe that Di Peso's "Buena Fe phase" structures date before the fourteenth century. Indeed, Casas Grandes was an exceptionally large, complex site with surprisingly little evidence for large-scale rebuilding—a fact of as yet unexamined significance. Architecturally, the city has no history.

Ceramically, it emerges similarly *de novo*. It is all but impossible to find an assemblage of more than 100 sherds from Casas Grandes that does not include some Gila Polychrome (Di Peso et al. 1974b, 1974c); that is, there are no good candidates, of any size, for pre-fourteenth century ceramic assemblages.

Dates are always a problem at Casas Grandes. There are pre-thirteenth century tree-ring dates: many, uncorrected, and fewer after Dean and Ravesloot's reanalysis. Chronometrically, almost all of the revised thirteenth century tree-ring dates—that might represent the elusive "pre-Casas" horizon—come rooms which also have

fourteenth century dates (Dean and Ravesloot 1993:Table 6.2, Figure 6.4). The best chronometric (if not ceramic or architectural) candidate for mid- to late-thirteenth century construction at Casas Grandes is Unit 16, around Room 23–16 (a *very* interesting cardinal room), where several of Di Peso's proposed "Buena Fe phase" rooms have latest tree-ring dates of 1239, 1243, 1272, and 1319 (Dean and Ravesloot 1993:Table 6.2; Di Peso et al. 1974c: Figure 140–5). Perhaps this is the elusive thirteenth century core of Casas Grandes; perhaps not.

Reliable pre-Casas data come primarily from the Convento site (CHIH:D:9:2), a small pithouse and pueblo site about 5 kms north of Casas Grandes. The Convento site had a large array of undated local brown wares and red-on-brown types and 320 intrusive sherds, of which two-thirds were Mimbres Classic Black-on-white or Mimbres Polychrome; the other intrusive sherds were mostly Mimbres Boldface and Reserve Black-on-whites, with two possible sherds of Tularosa Black-on-white and three of a Galisteo Black-on-white (Di Peso et al. 1974f:Figure 138–8). The Mimbres and Reserve types date to the eleventh and very early twelfth centuries; the numerically rare Tularosa and Galisteo Black-on-white types could date to the thirteenth and fourteenth centuries. Mimbres and Tularosa should not coexist, and, on balance, the intrusive ceramics appear to place most, if not all, of the Convento site no later than the early twelfth century.

(Another scenario can be offered: Mimbres Black-on-white may have lasted longer—perhaps into the late twelfth or early thirteenth century, to live alongside Tularosa and Galisteo types—on the fringes of its eleventh century distribution. Post-Mimbres Mimbres pottery may occur on the east edges of the old Mimbres world (Margaret Nelson, personal communication 1995); perhaps Mimbres survived its lawful lifespan to the south as well. If so: farewell, thirteenth century gap. But this scenario is offered only as an interesting possibility; it currently lacks evidential support, at least in Chihuahuan contexts.)

Pre-Casas contexts, such as the Convento site, appear to predate 1150, while Casas Grandes itself apparently postdates 1300 (or, perhaps, 1250; see above and Dean and Ravesloot 1993). The Casas Grandes sequence, revised by redating and reanalysis, shows a thirteenth century gap, the same middle-aged spread that plagues much Chihuahuan Salado archaeology. Very small amounts of Chupadero Black-on-white, the key intrusive thirteenth and fourteenth century white ware in the northern Chihuahuan Desert, are present, but only on sites with Chihuahua polychromes (Michael Whalen, personal communication 1995)—that is (based on the dating of those polychrome types at Casas Grandes and elsewhere), in fourteenth century associations.

There are, as I write, no well defined thirteenth century "pre-Casas" assemblages, sites, or components in the Casas Grandes area. Ongoing work by Michael Whalen and Paul Minnis should clarify this situation. I use the word "clarify" rather than "rectify" because I believe that the thirteenth century gap may well be real.

Whether that gap is real or not, there was a lot of Gila Polychrome at Casas Grandes, and much of it was found in provocative contexts. Casas Grandes itself was, without question, the major Chihuahuan player during Salado times. Its role in the Salado story must have been huge. But what role? As we reconstruct this antique drama, Tonto Basin dominates stage center, while the Phoenix Basin holds down stage left. Casas Grandes sits up stage right, obscured behind drapes, drops, tormentors, and teasers. It's on stage, partly hidden. But when that classic show moves to newer archaeological media, the Salado story must be modified to fit your screen, truncated to video proportions. Casas Grandes (hero? villain? comic relief?) simply disappears, not so much bowdlerized as reformatted away. Casas Grandes doesn't fit on modern, smaller Salado screens. And that is, perhaps, the unkindest cut of all: Casas Grandes's part may well have been the principal role—and now all its conquests, glories, triumphs, spoils, are shrunk to this little measure. We may restore Casas Grandes to some of its antique glory in the final scenes of this chapter.

THE CASA–CASAS CORRIDOR

The third Chihuahua area with a special claim on Gila Polychrome is a strip of archaeological districts running northwest-southeast across southeastern Arizona and the "bootheel" of southwestern New Mexico (Figure 12.1). Some spectacular fourteenth century sites—real phase-makers—are located in this zone (e.g., the Kuykendall site [Mills and Mills 1969]). I term this the "Casa–Casas Corridor," referring to the desert's twin towers, Casa Grande (Arizona) and Casas Grandes (Chihuahua). Casa Grande (Arizona) is well within the Sonoran Desert and so, for the moment, beyond my reach. (But we will meet the singular Casa Grande again.)

The Chihuahuan portion of the Casa–Casas Corridor begins east of the San Pedro River and continues southeast through the Basin-and-Range country of southeastern Arizona, the New Mexico "bootheel" and northwestern Chihuahua—specifically, from northwest to southeast: the Sulphur Springs, San Bernardino, Animas, Carretas, San Pedro (Chihuahua), and Casas Grandes Valleys (Figure 12.1). Since these areas are currently the subject of research by John Douglas (San Bernardino), Paul Minnis and Michael Whalen (Carretas, San Pedro, Casas Grandes), and Anne Woosley (Sulphur Springs), my remarks are premature; but fools rush in.

CORRIDOR CONTEXTS

For information on contexts of Gila Polychrome in the Casa–Casas Corridor, we rely primarily on the Mills' oeuvre (Mills and Mills 1969, 1971, 1972) and a smattering of other reports (McCluney 1965a, 1965b; Kidder et al. 1948). Jack and Vera Mills were outstanding avocational archaeologists in southeastern Arizona. They excavated more Salado rooms and sites in the Chihuahuan portion of the Casa–Casas corridor than any other person or institution. Their reports are rich in data, but less systematic than we might wish, so my remarks are necessarily even more impressionistic than the rest of this chapter.

As in the Upper Gila and at Casas Grandes, most of the Gila Polychrome (and related types) at excavated sites came, one or two vessels at a time, from living rooms. Burial patterns in the corridor vary from west to east, but Gila Polychrome was a common offering or accompaniment. In southeastern Arizona, cremations appear in (primary) "extended pit" cemeteries and in smaller round (secondary) pits, the latter often associated with masses of "crushed" pottery placed on the ground surface above the pits. This pattern, of small secondary pits covered by a mass of pottery, appears in the plaza of the Pendelton Ruin in southwestern New Mexico, along with four inhumations outside the room block and two infants found, apparently unburied, within rooms (Kidder et al. 1948:130). Other New Mexico Animas phase sites lack burials, but the important Joyce Well site (McCluney 1965a) produced 28 subfloor inhumations, some with associated pottery. Gila Polychrome was a common but not predominant burial offering (where data are available). At the Kuykendall site in southeastern Arizona, more than one hundred cremations were excavated: about 60 percent had pottery and half of those were Gila or Tonto Polychrome vessels.

CORRIDOR HORIZONS

In most of the corridor (and particularly the Animas area), there appears to be a long history of pithouse settlement, with intrusive(?) Mimbres Black-on-white (among other types) marking the final pithouse horizon, presumably ending about 1150. In each of these valleys, many large adobe pueblo sites follow; these were marked by Gila Polychrome (among other types), and presumably postdate 1300. The thirteenth century gap between Mimbres and Chihuahua/Salado, could be suggested for every corridor district, but arguments for continuity from the twelfth through the fourteenth century have been made in the Sulphur Springs (Johnson and Thompson 1963) and San Bernardino Valleys (Douglas 1987). Those arguments are based principally on a few absolute dates (unfortunately, not tree-ring dates) and are not, in my opinion, conclusive. But ongoing research by John Douglas and Anne Woosley may provide gap-bridging data.

In the relatively well researched Animas Valley (summarized in Lekson 1992a:22–23, 88–89, 112–13), early arguments for continuity no longer persuade. The Animas Valley sequence (Kidder et al. 1948; Findlow and DeAtley 1976) reflected the old series of Mimbres-Chihuahua-Salado horizons. That sequence has now been invalidated by the dating of Mimbres and redating of Casas Grandes. In its substantial literature (including radiocarbon and obsidian dates, summarized in Lekson 1992a), there are no archaeological complexes in the Animas region of southwestern New Mexico that appear to date between the Mimbres and Salado/Chihuahua horizons. That is, there appears to be a thirteenth century gap.

CONTEXTS CONTEXTUALIZED

Salado sites often have remarkable whole-artifact floor assemblages; that was a particular charm for early excavators. At these sites, Gila and Tonto Polychromes are part of standard living room assemblage, with a jar and/or a bowl found along with a few other decorated, textured, or plain vessels on the floors of rooms with firepits. (In one case, a Salado polychrome bowl was built into a mealing bin.) At most sites with floor assemblages, Gila Polychrome and Tonto Polychrome do not appear to be used or discarded in any extraordinary fashion. They were not, so to speak, a big deal.

Except at Casas Grandes; Gila and Tonto Polychrome vessels (opposed to sherds) were rare in room contexts at the great Chihuahuan center. Only a few vessels appear in floor assemblages like those at other Chihuahua Salado sites (i.e., one vessel in a set of half a dozen vessels), although Casas Grandes has many impressive floor assemblages of whole artifacts. Most Gila Polychrome vessels at Casas Grandes were stored in "warehouse" rooms along with other bulk imported materials. I know of no comparable context in any other Chihuahua Salado site.

Burial contexts are intriguingly variable. To the west, adult cremations are found in jars (often in Gila or Tonto Polychrome vessels) with inverted "covering" bowls, while infants were buried below room floors, again with Salado vessels or sherds. Gila and Tonto Polychrome were important elements of burial ritual in western Chihuahuan Salado sites. In the Cliff Valley (and, perhaps, other geographically intermediate areas), adult burials were cremations in pottery vessels, but only a very few were Gila or Tonto Polychrome. In the eastern Animas and Casas Grandes areas, adult burials were mostly subfloor inhumations, with pottery but not Salado polychromes.

Crown (1994:100) noted that Salado polychrome vessels in her sample came primarily from mortuary contexts. That pattern does not hold in the Upper Gila or Casas Grandes areas. Gila Polychrome functioned differently in the west (Arizona Salado) and the east (Casas Grandes): whatever Salado polychromes meant in the Sonoran Desert, they meant something else in Chihuahua.

HORIZONS EXPANDED

The Safford Valley and the Mimbres Valley have continuous sequences; that is, each has a series of sequential phases from early pithouse horizons through the Salado horizon. Cultural discontinuities (radical changes in material culture, immigrations, and other unpleasantries) were remarkably evident in the later prehistories of both, accompanied by population decline, especially during the middle to late twelfth century (Blake et al. 1986; Crary, Neily, Kincaid, and Germick 1994). But neither valley appears to have had glaring gaps.

Cultural discontinuities were such that the Mimbres Valley sequence was originally interpreted as interrupted, with actual demographic breaks between Mimbres and Black Mountain phases, and Black Mountain and Cliff phases (LeBlanc 1980a; Nelson and LeBlanc 1986). But the gaps in the Mimbres sequence are so very short, it is difficult to imagine how they could be validated archaeologically, and intriguing continuities between Mimbres and Black Mountain phases (at least) are emerging from recent work at the Old Town site (Creel 1996). The later prehistory of the Mimbres Valley was marked by a shift in site location downstream, south into the desert. Thus Cliff phase sites in the Mimbres appear in an effectively depopulated upper and middle Valley: the "break" between Mimbres and Salado, in the *upper* Mimbres Valley at least, is real.

Over much (most?) of the Chihuahuan Desert later implicated by the Salado horizon, there appears to have been a thirteenth century gap between Mimbres and Salado. In the Arizona Animas area, Douglas (1987) makes a case for continuity, as did earlier researchers in the New Mexico Animas area before him (Findlow and DeAtley 1976); but I find the arguments and evidence unconvincing.

In the Casas Grandes region, Di Peso presented an elaborate, continuous sequence of three periods encompassing ten phases (Di Peso 1974a). Today, it is difficult to see evidence for more than four chronological stages in the Casas Grandes data: pre-Mimbres pithouse, Mimbres pithouse and pueblo, Chihuahua/Salado pueblos, and Spanish colonization. At Casas Grandes, too, there appears to be a thirteenth century gap.

Thus, a thirteenth century gap can be suggested for the central, portions of the Saladoan Chihuahuan Desert: in the upper Gila, in the Animas region of southwesternmost New Mexico and southeasternmost Arizona, and in the Casas Grandes region. There is, in this central zone, a north-south gradient of archaeological knowledge: the upper Gila is reasonably well known; the Animas region is known, but less well; and Casas Grandes—with a single, spectacular, eponymous exception—is practically terra incognita. The thirteenth century gap may be only a gap in knowledge in the Casas Grandes region, but it appears to be real in the upper Gila and the Animas (at least, the New Mexico Animas; apologies to Douglas [1987]). If the gap is real in those better-known areas, it may well be real at Casas Grandes, too.

Is the thirteenth century gap authentic or illusory? Would we find more (or any) contexts, components, and sites that dated to the thirteenth century if we looked harder? That is a possible and customary hope in under-researched areas: we enter new regions on a quest for continuity and search until we find it (or incontrovertibly disprove it). In the words of the venerable Real Mesoamerican Archaeologist, we want to get the "whole sequence."

Nature abhors a vacuum only slightly more than archaeologists abhor a gap in the sequence. A gap is simply proof that more research is necessary. The absence, for example, of whole Pecos stages on Black Mesa and Cedar Mesa came as something of a shock. But why should we assume continuity? People move; the center shifts. Horizon gaps are the taxonomic signal of large-scale regional abandonments. Large-scale regional abandonments were in the repertoire of Southwestern peoples (C. M. Cameron 1995). The Four Corners area was abandoned by 1300 and a century and a half later, the Casa–Casas corridor saw depopulation on similar or even larger scales. That southern sucking sound, heard in the late fifteenth or early sixteenth century, was the sound of people leaving Casas Grandes (and going— where?). The Casas Grandes region was certainly depopulated in the sixteenth century, and I see no logical reason why it could not have been depopulated in the thirteenth.

There are few landscapes in the subpolar post-Pleistocene world that were completely (happily?) devoid of humans for an entire century. Surely the Casas Grandes and Animas areas were not completely empty in the thirteenth century; but there is little evidence for populations of significant size, and no evidence for populations sufficient for the remarkable fourteenth century urban developments at Casas Grandes. More research *is* necessary, but I suspect that we have looked enough to reach preliminary conclusions: people may have been around the Chihuahuan Salado area in the thirteenth century, but far too thin on the ground, I fear, to fuel Casas Grandes and the remarkable sites of the Casa–Casas Corridor during the fourteenth century Salado horizon.

GILA PEOPLE, GILA PIETY, GILA POLITY

Three competing (but not entirely exclusive) models of Gila Polychrome in the Chihuahuan Desert are currently in play: 1) ethnicity, 2) cult, and 3) interaction. Was Salado a people, a piety, or a polity? In parts of the Chihuahua Desert, Gila and Tonto Polychromes may have signaled all three at once. In other parts of this region, they may have been "none of the above." Salado in the Upper Gila requires immigration (Gila = people); Salado at Casas Grandes may not. Salado pottery in urn cremations in the Safford and Animas areas looks like ritual; Salado polychrome stacked up in a warehouse at Casas Grandes looks like commerce. Salado interaction at Gila Pueblo simply cannot be the same dynamic that brought a bowl of Gila Polychrome to Bloom Mound (near Roswell, New Mexico).

GILA PEOPLE:
MIGRATIONS AND OTHER HEADACHES

Salado, in its original formulation, was not simply polychrome pottery but an ethnic group or a people. And, originally, those people were on the move: the old Salado fled enemies in the Tularosa country, arriving in the Mogollon uplands just in time to collide with an influx of Kayenta refugees. Ideas and peoples mingled and stewed, and then Salado came roaring out of the mountains into the Phoenix Basin, messing up/with the Hohokam (Gladwin 1957:248–55, 291–95). That sensational old view of Salado fell out of favor in Arizona, but it lies dormant—like some arid-adapted seed—in the Chihuahuan Desert.

Certainly, people were moving through the southern Southwest in the late thirteenth and fourteenth centuries (Lekson and Cameron 1995; Lindsay 1987). Crown (1994) argues the origins of Salado polychromes through the migration of Tusayan-Kayenta people into the Mogollon uplands of central Arizona. That much of the old Salado epic survives. However, Crown (1994:209) concludes:

> . . . there is no indisputable evidence that the Salado polychromes remained the product of any distinct ethnic group. The pottery may have spread initially in association with the population movements of this time period, but it then seems to have dispersed beyond the immigrant population, becoming the most widely manufactured type in southwestern prehistory.

After its synthesis/genesis in the Mogollon uplands, Salado ceased being a people and became, instead, a cult. The Salado people's services were no longer required in the Hohokam region, and they have been expunged from Sonoran prehistory. But in the Chihuahuan Desert, Salado remains something rather like a people—that is, a group that moved into depopulated or unpopulated areas. The appearance of large adobe pueblos in the Cliff and upper Mimbres Valleys, for example, requires massive immigration presumably of people.

Of course, in the late thirteenth and early fourteenth centuries, that kind of coming-and-going was happening all over the Southwest. Anybody who was anybody was migrating. Bandelier wrote novels about migrations; Hewett, Gladwin, and Haury made migrations the prime movers of Southwestern prehistory. One of Gladwin's finest chapter titles (in a career filled with superb titles and epigrams) was "Gathering of the Clans"—the old boys really liked the biblical sweep of peoples on the march. That was *history*, with people and incidents and drama.

But when science arrived in the 1960s, New Archaeology dismissed migrations as mere chronicle. Ethnic movements were at best mythic and at worst, just-so stories. Today, migration is reemerging as a legitimate if battered research topic (e.g., C. M. Cameron 1995) but there remains a great deal of residual antipathy towards peoples moving from point A to point B, causing epochal events C, D, and E. Salado suffers from our reluctance to retrace the routes of old Gladwinian marches.

In the fabled Four Corners area, the late thirteenth century saw the final abandonment of the Mesa Verde and Kayenta regions. Populations numbering in the several tens of thousands from the Mesa Verde region (Lipe 1995) and ten thousand or less from the Kayenta district (Jeffrey S. Dean, personal communication 1995) moved out of the Four Corners and headed southeast toward the Rio Grande and south toward the Mogollon uplands. The explosive emigrations from the Four Corners were absorbed, like so many subatomic particles, by the considerable mass of existing thirteenth century Puebloan populations that occupied an arc from the northern Rio Grande, south and west through the Acoma-Zuni-Mogollon uplands, and back north along the Little Colorado River to the Hopi district.

As many as forty thousand people were displaced at a time when, according to Dean et al. (1994:73—bravely going where angels fear to tread—estimate the total Southwestern regional population was less than 150,000. If our estimates of Kayenta and Mesa Verde population are correct, this was an epic, even catastrophic demographic displacement: about one-fifth to one-quarter of the region's population moved from 100 km (Navajo National Monument to Hopi) to almost 500 km (Mesa Verde to the southernmost Galisteo Black-on-white sites near Truth or Consequences, New Mexico).

A radius of about 500 km seems to have been the absolute outer limit. The maximum penetration of identifiable Four Corners population was more-or-less due south, at Mesa Verde sites near Magdalena and Truth or Consequences, New Mexico and at Kayenta/Tusayan sites in the San Pedro and Safford Valleys of southern Arizona. Sites at the outermost edges of the 500 km radius, having in some way successfully penetrated beyond the mass of population in the Rio Grande, Tularosa, Little Colorado and Hopi arc, are surprising visible in the non-Anasazi contexts beyond. Galisteo Black-on-white sites in the Santa Fe region are problematic against the background of Santa Fe Black-on-white, but Galisteo sites stick out like the proverbial sore thumb farther south, at Magdalena and near Truth-or-Consequences (Lekson 1986a). Similarly, Kayenta and Tusayan material culture, overwhelmed and obscured along the Little Colorado, is clearly visible at Point of Pines, Goat Hill, and Reeve Ruin (Lindsay 1987; Woodson 1994). Yet to reach Magdalena and Goat Hill, Four Corners peoples had to pass through densely populated regions, where we seek in vain their archaeological traces. Those farthest sites, where the pattern is so very clear, do not represent 30,000 people. Indeed, "smoking gun" or "sore thumb" cases cannot number more than a dozen sites in New Mexico and Arizona and, while some of these de novo sites are large, the majority of the displaced Four Corners persons must have found new homes with existing villagers in the Pueblo arc, trading group identity for residential security.

"Migration" was the conclusion reached by the 1967 Salado Red Ware Conference: Salado in the upper Gila, at least, represented a migration into the Chihuahuan Desert from the north. Thirteenth century Tusayan migrations into Point of Pines, the lower San Pedro Valley, and the Safford Valley (Lindsay 1987, Woodson 1994) support the plausibility and possibility of a "Salado" immigration into Cliff (but Maverick Mountain Polychrome, a Tusayan signature, is scarce in the Upper Gila). In this scenario, the Kayenta-Tusayan exodus of the late thirteenth century caused a cascade of movements south into the Mogollon uplands (e.g., Point of Pines), ultimately spilling over into the adjacent Sonoran (San Pedro, Safford) and Chihuahuan (Cliff, Redrock) Deserts.

Compare the Kayenta/Tusayan trajectory to the Mesa Verde: A case (disputable, of course) can be made for a more-or-less continuous dispersal of Mesa Verde populations throughout the eastern arc of the cone, from the Galisteo Basin, through Acoma and—attenuated, but remarkably visible—to the southernmost sites in west central New Mexico. This represents a "scatter" from the Four Corners over about 40 or 50 degrees. Kayenta/Tusayan "outermost" sites, on the contrary, are almost entirely due south of the Four Corners, from Safford to the Tucson Basin—a restricted arc of only 15 or so degrees, when measured from the Four Corners. Another 20 or 30 degrees west from the Tusayan sites of the San Pedro Valley brings the 500 km arc through the Hohokam heartland, and back to the original Salado question.

There were major differences between the Phoenix Basin and the upper Rio Grande that probably shielded the former more than the latter from the radiation of Four Corners peoples. The Upper Rio Grande, prior to the thirteenth century migrations was not densely populated; before 1250, sites were comparatively few and small (C. M. Cameron 1995). In contrast, the Phoenix Basin had been densely occupied for a very long time (Doyel 1991a). The "mass" to be penetrated was greater, the distance longer, and the "particles" (fewer than 10,000 Kayenta compared to 30,000 Mesa Verde) fewer in number. The differences in these dimensions, facetious but nevertheless real, may help us to conceptualize the differences at the receiving end of the thirteenth century migrations. The Northern Rio Grande and the Plateau's margins, from the Verde to the Upper Gila were swamped; the Phoenix Basin was not. In this framework, Tonto Basin was simply one small segment in a chain of ethnic reactions and relations.

GILA PIETIES: LARGE-SCALE CERAMIC DISTRIBUTIONS AND THE MEANING OF LIFE

Crown (1994) proposed a Southwestern Cult, identified by Gila Polychrome (a theme developed by Crary, Germick, and Doyel 1994, among others). The Southwestern Cult crystallized when immigrants from the Kayenta-Tusayan region moved into the Mogollon uplands (Crown 1994:223). In the late thirteenth and fourteenth centuries, the Cult spread through the southern Southwest. Crown suggests that the dissemination of the Cult, initially through small-scale conversions, was "open to all who chose to participate" and that adoption of the Cult was not socially or politically structured. That is, individuals or small social units were converted. Initially, at least, the pottery was "personal or family-sized serving and eating vessels" (Crown 1994:223). Later, the scale of conversion expanded. Salado vessels became "large storage jars or communal bowls, probably used in association with village feasting" (Crown 1994:224).

The Gila Polychrome bowls from Room 18–8 at Casas Grandes were, indeed, quite large (about 32 cm diameter), but the Gila and Escondida Polychrome bowls from other contexts at Casas Grandes are much smaller (comparable to Crown's small bowls). At Casas Grandes, Gila Polychrome and allied types occurred as both large and small bowls. Gila Polychrome at Casas Grandes was markedly different in context from other Salado sites: as noted above, Gila Polychrome is almost absent in burials, and, in Room 18–8, it appears to be a warehoused commodity. Neither of these circumstances support ritual use, but neither deny such use, either.

The compelling fact supporting Crown's cult model is the remarkably large distribution of tiny amounts of locally made Gila Polychrome. After dismissing ethnic, status, and elite exchange models, there is not much left but ritual to explain that singular situation (Crown 1994:191–209). Several Southwestern types cover almost as much territory as Gila Polychrome: St. Johns Polychrome, for example, but it is presumed to have been made in east-central Arizona and traded out. The frightening thing about Gila Polychrome is that everyone made it, everywhere: it was, apparently, locally produced, in small quantities, over most of its range.

Perhaps that is not unprecedented in the Chihuahuan Desert. Other pottery types apparently were locally made in small quantities over large areas, although none so large an area as Gila Polychrome. At least two high-profile Chihuahua decorated types—Mimbres Black-on-White and Ramos Polychrome—had clear centers of production, but were also locally made far outside those centers. Mimbres Black-on-white was made over a wide range, from Safford to the Upper Gila to the Rio Grande (Garrett 1991; James et al. 1995; Bart Olinger, personal communication 1994). Ramos Polychrome, too, had "localized production sites" even in areas of low frequency, although the center of its production was clearly Casas Grandes (Woosley and Olinger 1993:123–25). No Chihuahua pottery type (and few Southwestern types) has been studied as thoroughly as Gila Polychrome, so it is certainly possible that the pattern of low-frequency local production over a huge area may not be unique to Gila Polychrome. While the possibility of widespread local production of Mimbres and Ramos does not negate Crown's argument for a cult marked by Gila Polychrome, it suggests that mechanisms for local production of widespread types may not have been limited to Gila Polychrome, at least in the Chihuahuan Desert.

Stylistic and iconologic homogeneity is important to the cult model, and Gila Polychrome is sufficiently similar across its range to support Crown's arguments. However, there are intriguing regional differences in style and form between the Phoenix Basin and Casas Grandes. Crown, defines a series of styles, and states that "the Gila Style shows

clear evidence of influence from the Hohokam [Phoenix Basin] area and a clinal distribution with increasing distance from this area" (Crown 1994:197). Escondida style was also significantly clinal. Escondida style (named for Escondida Polychrome) was found at Chihuahua Salado sites and especially at Casas Grandes, but not to the west. Thus the eastern Escondida style was a spatial counterpart to the western Gila style on Salado polychromes.

Crown notes that there are no consistent contexts or associated artifacts and features to support Gila-as-cult-marker (Crown 1994:198–203). Nowhere is that variation more evident than in the Chihuahuan Salado horizon sites. In central and southeastern Arizona, Gila and related polychromes were conspicuous elements in burial ritual, while at Casas Grandes they were conspicuous only by their absence from burials. Instead, they were treated like an imported commodity. If Gila Polychrome had ritual implications, the vessels in Room 18–8 at Casas Grandes suggest a different ritual context than any Crown suggests (1994:201–202).

The iconographic and ceramic correlates of Crown's Southwestern Cult arose from an earlier horizon of Pinedale style, which she posits for the cult's entire range, apparently including Casas Grandes (Crown 1994:178–79, Figure 10.1). It is difficult to reconcile the Pinedale style (Carlson 1970:91–94 108–109; Crown 1994:79–82 excluding her "Stage 5") with any pre-Salado pottery types of the Casas Grandes region or with any Chihuahua-Salado horizon types, save perhaps Escondida Polychrome (Di Peso et al. 1974d). If a Pinedale horizon was the necessary substrate of a Gila Polychrome Southwestern Cult, Casas Grandes and most of the Chihuahua were non-starters.

SALADO AND THE PEERLESS POLITIES

David Wilcox, at least as early as 1983, proposed a Salado linkage of the Hohokam core and Casas Grandes, akin to my Casa–Casas Corridor:

> The Salado phenomenon that crystallized about 1300 is interpreted as the wide-spread adoption of a new ideology that temporarily facilitated the economic articulation of a series of small-scale regional systems from the Phoenix Basin Hohokam on the west to Casas Grandes on the southeast [Wilcox and Sternberg 1983:255].

The linkage of Classic period Hohokam and Casas Grandes has been developed further by Wilcox (1991b, 1994, 1994b) and others (Dittert 1966; Doyel 1993b; Lekson 1987; McGuire 1991; Minnis 1989). The "articulation of a series of small-scale regional systems" was taken one step further by Minnis (1989), who suggested a specific model of "peer-polity interaction." Peer-polity interaction describes a pattern of conjoining social entities of roughly comparable scale. "If the Paquimé system is at a similar scale to others in the prehistoric Southwest, then peer polity interaction models could well prove fruitful" (Minnis 1989:302). The definition of peers in peer-polity interaction is critical: "peer" means "equal" or it means nothing. And it is hard to find a peer for Casas Grandes.

Minnis, after casting glances at Chaco Canyon, saw two megapeers in the ancient Southwest: Casas Grandes and the Phoenix Basin (1989:302–303). Local districts between those two (my Casas–Casas Corridor) were either subsumed by one or the other of the Big Boys, or fell through the net to archaeological oblivion.

Douglas (1995), liberating the Animas phase from the repressive taxonomic domination of Casas Grandes, argues the autonomy and power of small-scale social systems caught between two larger peers. But he need not have worried: the megapeer poles at either end of the Corridor have been shrinking. Classic Hohokam polities have recently been reduced to rather modest sizes (Fish 1996a; Fish and Fish 1994b) and, more importantly for this paper, the Casas Grandes polity in the International Four Corners is shrinking fast.

Di Peso drove Casas Grandes from an unknown site to the blue chip prime mover of Southwestern prehistory. Its stock took a plunge with the Dean-Ravesloot redating, and today the bottom has fallen out of the Casas Grandes market, with the continuing devaluation of Di Peso. Nowhere is this rise-and-fall more evident than in the expansion and reduction of the Casas Grandes "regional system." Early, expansive views of the Casas Grandes region (e.g., Di Peso 1974a, Schaafsma 1979) were large indeed, on the order of 200,000 sq km or, for reference, a circle with a radius of about 250 km. Minnis' 1989 reformulation used a 130 km radius around Casas Grandes as the sphere of "Paquimé's power." And more recently, Minnis and Whalen (1993:43) propose "that the core or nucleus of the [Casas Grandes] regional system appears to have encompassed a relatively small area within 30 km of Paquimé." From 250 to 130 to 30 km: a

polity on that tiny scale would have peers galore: it would be dwarfed, for example, by the Animas phase. Something's wrong here—unregulated downsizing has gone too far, too fast.

Casas Grandes' incredible shrinking act is all the more remarkable given the evidence of the Animas phase Joyce Well site, 130 km north of Casas Grandes (McCluney 1965a; Lekson 1992). Joyce Well is one of the few excavated Animas phase pueblos in southwestern New Mexico. In addition to a great deal of Chihuahua and Salado polychromes, Joyce Well had a Casas Grandes I-shaped ball court and Casas Grandes style raised firepits, otherwise unique (in excavated and reported sites) to Casas Grandes (and one other Animas phase site, Box Canyon; McCluney 1965b:29). Douglas, to preserve Animas phase independence, dismisses Joyce Well as a late Casas Grandes "site intrusion" (Douglas 1995:247), but that special pleading fails to persuade. Intriguingly, Joyce Well defined Minnis' (1989) original 130 km radius for the Casas Grandes region, but it now falls well beyond the limits the leaner, meaner 30 km Casas Grandes region (Minnis and Whalen 1993). I'm perplexed; you should be perplexed, too.

Wilcox (1991b, 1994, 1994b), never modest in his territorial visions, sees Casas Grandes as the regional center of a zoned hegemony: its local system mirrors the distribution of I-shaped ball courts, a second zone extends in a 300 kms radius to include sites with Chihuahua polychromes (and local copies, such as Babocomari Polychrome in south-central Arizona; Wilcox 1991b:149); and a third outermost penumbra incorporating the range of Gila Polychrome and El Paso Polychrome. The farthest distribution of copper bells and macaws in the Southwest mark "the limits of the Paquimé macroeconomy" (Wilcox 1991b:149) With macaw feather sashes in southeastern Utah, that would be a region on the grand old scale.

Viva Wilcox!

Minimally, Casas Grandes was the greatest Pueblo site of its time and place. It was much larger than contemporary Classic period Hohokam centers—if we accept the reductionist position of Fish and Fish (Fish 1996a; Fish and Fish 1994b) (I reserve Casa Grande for further, imminent discussion). Although some might challenge my use of the term "Pueblo" for Casas Grandes, few could deny Casas Grandes' fourteenth century primacy. Its region—defined, for me at least, minimally by the radius to the Joyce Well site—appears to have been hugely larger than any other "polity" of its time. Casas Grandes had no rival in the post-Chaco Pueblo world. It was a polity without a peer.

Di Peso, Casas Grandes' Svengali, tried hard to find a peer companion by arranging a May-December romance with Chaco Canyon. The linkage of Casas Grandes and Chaco captured the imagination of prehistorians (LeBlanc 1986, 1989; McGuire 1986, 1989). The shocking revelation of Casa's tender age annulled Di Peso's proposal, and the subject was no longer discussed in polite society. Attention shifted to more suitable candidates, polities more of-an-age with Casas Grandes: the Classic period Hohokam of the Phoenix Basin (Doyel 1991a, McGuire 1991, Minnis 1989; Wilcox and Sternberg 1983).

Taken in the aggregate, perhaps, the Phoenix Basin was a suitable match for Casas Grandes, but there is doubt that the Phoenix Basin ever took itself in the aggregate (Fish 1996a; Fish and Fish 1994b). There was no Phoenix first-among-equals to hold it all together. Or was there? Casa Grande, which lies almost outside the Phoenix Basin, may be a unique site in the Hohokam region.

Casa Grande does not look like other Hohokam sites of its time. It sits in a Hohokam compound, in the middle of a large Hohokam settlement; but Casa Grande itself was a massive-walled, monumentally constructed, four- or five-story terraced building. There are reports of a few Classic period two-story structures in the Phoenix Basin (David Wilcox, personal communication 1994); House I at Los Muertos, for example, has impressively thick walls. But there currently is no structure in the Phoenix Basin that comes close to Casa Grande. The roof technology alone brands it as unique (Wilcox and Shenk 1977:137ff; Wilcox and Sternberg 1983:15–16); the sequence of construction, planned and built as a single operation, is like nothing else in the Hohokam architectural repertoire, save perhaps canals. Casa Grande was something different.

Hohokam archaeologists have tried to defuse Casa Grande, to bring it safely into the Hohokam fold, by minimizing its spectacular preservation (Wilcox and Shenk 1977:163–64), by promoting other candidate "Great Houses" (David Wilcox personal communication 1994; Doyel 1991a:254), or by transforming this four-story adobe build-

ing into a platform mound (Gregory 1987:197; Wilcox and Sternberg 1983:37). Those attempts to normalize Casa Grande seem strained to someone standing outside the Hohokam tradition. Even without that magnificent tin roof, Casa Grande is remarkable, outstanding in the rather flat field of Hohokam archaeology.

Why take a glorious anomaly like Casa Grande and explain it away? Something that appears unique may really be unique, or it may simply as an accident of preservation. Wilcox asked that important question: "Is the Casa Grande's state of preservation evidence of its prehistoric importance?" (Wilcox and Shenk 1977:163). I would answer: in this case, as at Chaco and Casas Grandes, yes. *Ceteris paribus*, preservation does tell us something about labor investment, scale, and monumentality. Big, massive, monumentally constructed things preserve better than things that aren't big, massive, and monumental. There's only one Casa Grande (the other candidates were not close to Casa Grande's scale and magnitude); there's only been one Casa Grande for at least a century, and maybe for six centuries.

I believe that the preponderance of the evidence shows that Casa Grande was remarkably, importantly different from other Classic period Hohokam sites, just as Chaco and Casas Grandes were different from their regional milieus. The fact that Casa, Casas, and Chaco all emerged from definable regional traditions, that they can be "normalized" by appeals to historically similar forms, does not negate their singularity.

Our understanding of Chaco comes from increasing precision in defining differences between the Canyon and its region, particularly its massive, monumental (and thus spectacularly preserved) architecture. And so, too, for Casa and Casas Grandes: nowhere else in the southern Southwest do we find four standing stories of massive adobe walls. That fact alone should direct our attention to Casas Grandes and Casa Grande as a very small set—a useful corrective exercise. McGuire (1991:371–72) named them the two "power centers of the Salado system." I agree, and I would go further: if they are a set of two, there is not much question of which was larger and which was smaller. Casa Grande is a reduced version of Casas Grandes, a similarity remarked upon early in the history of Southwestern archaeology (by Kidder [1924], for example, and Di Peso et al. 1974b:216; but see Wilcox and Shenk [1977] for a vigorous denial). I suggest that Casa Grande and Casas Grandes are so similar in time, construction, and associations that it is no longer possible to dismiss Casa Grande as a metastasized platform mound: the two Big Houses were a duo, a pair, a set, the twin pillars of the Salado world.

If the Senate had restrained itself on that angry May Monday in 1846, repudiating Polk's border incident and refusing a war of conquest, the premier city of the desert Southwest would be Chihuahua, not Phoenix. Archaeology, of course, would be very different. Archaeologists working outward from Chihuahua would first investigate the obvious center at Paquimé, and later attend to the Salt-Gila and Plateau hinterlands. In this alternate history, they would have little trouble defining center and periphery, and the relative roles of Casas Grandes and Casa Grande. Hohokam archaeologists: can you say "outlier"? I knew you could . . . .

CHAPTER THIRTEEN

In Pursuit of Salado in the Sonoran Desert

David E. Doyel

THE HOHOKAM CLASSIC PERIOD (1100–1450+) IN THE
Sonoran Desert in southern Arizona is closely associated
with the Salado culture concept (Gladwin 1957; Gladwin
and Gladwin 1935; Haury 1945; Willey 1966). Recent research
has shown, however, that traits once identified as "Salado"
were widely distributed by the early Classic period (1100–
1250) prior to the advent of the Salado horizon in the late
thirteenth and fourteenth centuries. Pursuit of Salado in the
Sonoran Desert requires consideration of multiple factors
including the temporal and spatial distributions of multiple
traits, cultural influences emanating from both sides of the
International Border, the development of platform
mounds, the origins of Salado polychrome pottery, and
interregional interaction. As a point of departure, three
statements from the first Salado Conference (Doyel and
Haury 1976) are cited:

> If we say that Salado is a fiction, then we had better
> begin to ask ourselves whether Kayenta or Mesa Verde or
> Chaco are not fictions also [Haury 1976c:125].

> Perhaps one of the problems inherent in the Salado
> definition resides in the development of its classificatory
> system, wherein the final result is a compiled and some-
> what contrived trait list. We must begin to think in
> terms of multiple occupancy in so-called specific culture

areas and we must do this in terms of not only space but
also time [Di Peso 1976b:126].

> I believe that we can profit from a consideration of
> emerging archaeological patterns which might have
> roots in a variety of other patterns—a syncretism and
> integration of ideas to respond to the limitations of a
> region and the background of the people [Dittert
> 1976:127].

I suggest that these statements, while divergent in the
context of 1976, can be integrated into a conception of
Salado culture based on space, time, and history. This
task requires separating "Salado culture" from the more
inclusive concept of the "Gila horizon," a historically related but distinct phenomenon. In this paper, I first summarize cultural attributes from the southern Southwest
and northwestern Mexico to show that traits once used
to define Salado were actually widespread after 1100. As
a focal point for definitions of Salado, the prehistory of
the Phoenix Basin is then summarized with reference to
platform mounds, a trait shared by the Hohokam and
Salado. These topics lead to discussions of ideology and
interaction. Finally, a Salado culture is outlined relative
to broader events occurring late in the prehistory of the
southern Southwest.

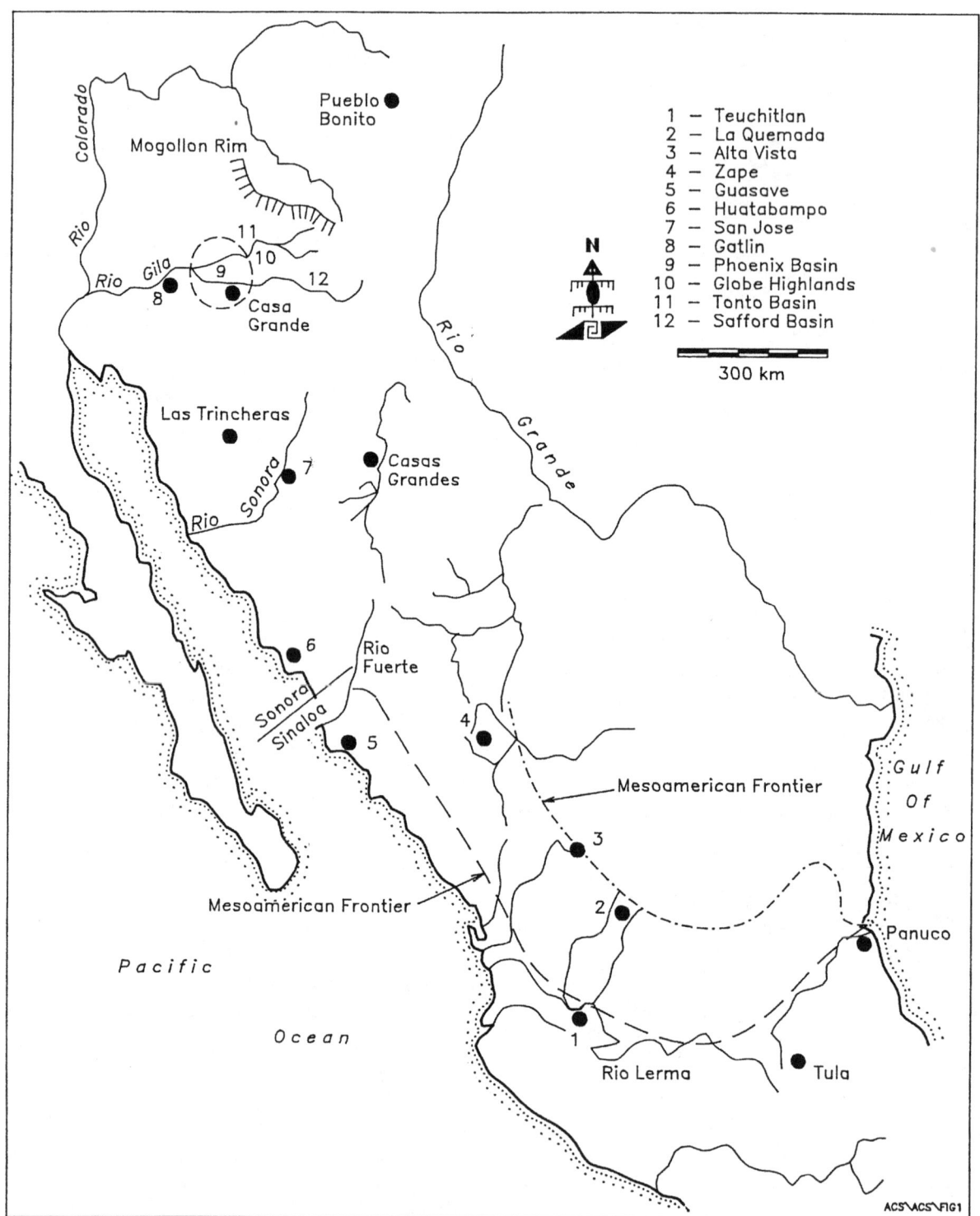

Figure 13.1.   Archaeological sites and localities in northwestern Mexico and the southwestern United States (for Mesoamerican Frontier dates see Braniff C. 1993:67, Figure 5.1).

The Sonoran Desert extends from the Mogollon Rim in Arizona to southern Sonora, Mexico, a distance of 1,200 km that includes 300,000 km^2 (Figure 13.1). Elevation in this basin and range country is under 1,200 m. Annual precipitation is between 200 and 350 mm, with hot, moist summers and mild winters. Supplemental moisture was often necessary for successful farming (Fish and Nabhan 1991:35). Agricultural strategies were adapted to local topographic and hydrological regimes (Doyel 1993a; Masse 1991). Native vegetation, including mesquite and cacti, and large and small mammals (deer, rabbits, and mice), reptiles, and birds, were utilized for subsistence, tools, weapons, and utensils, and for ritual purposes (Gasser and Kwiatkowski 1991; Szuter 1991).

Here and There in the South and West: Cultural Dynamics in Northwestern Mexico and the Southern Southwest

Pursuit of Salado in the Sonoran Desert requires ignoring the international border. Influences on early formative cultures in southern Arizona emanated from the northwestern coast of Mexico and from an east-west band across Durango into Zacatecas (Figure 13.1). Peripheral Mesoamerican polities and traditions more similar to the Southwest, such as Loma San Gabriel (Kelley 1971, 1993:230), were present by 600–900. No geographic boundary separated the Southwest from the Mesoamerican high cultures (Kelley 1974:20; Porter-Weaver 1981:384). Interaction among the residents was facilitated by related languages (Di Peso 1974a; Wilcox 1986). Regarding distances, Hermosillo, Sonora; Casas Grandes, Chihuahua; and Chaco Canyon, New Mexico; are all about 500 km from the modern town of Coolidge adjacent to Casa Grande Ruins in southern Arizona. Averaging 40 km a day, a trip from Coolidge to one of the above destinations would require 12 days. Bioarchaeological evidence in the form of cultural modification (notching and polishing) of dentition on burials at sites in the Phoenix area and in Tonto Basin (Regan et al. 1996) suggests the presence of individuals from Mexico. Some people may have traveled even greater distances, as the practice of tooth polishing is best known from the Valley of Mexico (Christy Turner, personal communication, 1997).

Settlement systems of the Teuchitlan tradition (200–1000) in Jalisco included monumental architecture, circular platforms, hydraulic agriculture, shaft tombs, clay figurines, craft specialization, and trade. Urbanization was underway by 700 with the largest settlement containing 3,000 ha of ceremonial buildings, ball courts, obsidian workshops, terraced gardens, a habitation zone

with 1,000 platform-courtyard complexes, pseudo-cloisonne vessels, turquoise, marine shell, and Thin Orange pottery. Likely organized as states, this tradition underwent reorganization late in the Mesoamerican Classic period (Weigand 1993:232).

The Huatabampo tradition (700–1000?), located between the Rio Mayo and the Rio Fuerte in southern Sonora and northern Sinaloa, may have shared its northern border with Trincheras. Sites contain dispersed dwellings, plazas, trash mounds, and cemeteries with inhumation burials. Caches of offerings are present as are polished red wares and clay figurines. Shell jewelry may have been exported in exchange for obsidian and turquoise. Subsistence was based on marine resources and agriculture. Trade with northern Chihuahua is evident (Ekholm 1942; McGuire and Villalpando 1989:164–65; Phillips 1989:386). A Postclassic occupation (1000–1350) existed in the coastal states of Jalisco, Nayarit, and Sinola that may have affected the residents of the Sonoran Desert to the north (Meighan 1974).

Mesoamerican-related centers including Alta Vista and La Quemada existed in southern Durango and western Zacatecas by 600 (Nelson 1997). The Southwest, and the Phoenix Basin in particular, received influences from these traditions. For example, ceramics of the Chalchihuites tradition between 500–900 had banded and quartered designs; negative painting, interlocking scrolls, cross-hatch and terrace motifs; zoomorphic and tripod shapes; and buff and red ware, all of which were present in the Phoenix Basin by 700 (Haury 1976a; Kelley 1971). Citing similarities in village plans, ceremonialism, and ceramics, Kelley (1966:102) refers to the "Mesoamerican acculturation of the Hohokam." The later phases of Chalchihuites (900–1350) produced distinctive white-on-red ceramics stylistically similar to textured red ware in Tonto Basin, the Globe Highlands, and the White Mountains. This horizon style seems to have bypassed Casas Grandes (Kelley 1974:23).

Directly relevant to the topic at hand are the Trincheras, Rio Sonora, and Casas Grandes traditions of northwestern Mexico. Located in the northeastern edge of the Sonoran Desert, the Safford Basin and Globe Highlands are also addressed, as these areas were involved in Salado cultural developments. Chronologies are illustrated in Figure 13.2.

Trincheras

The Trincheras tradition (800–1400) was centered along the Rio Conception in north-central Sonora. If traveling 40 km a day (Tarahumara runners can double this aver-

Year	Casas Grandes Basin	Trincheras	Rio Sonora	Tucson Basin	Phoenix Basin	Globe Highlands	Safford Basin
1500 —	Robles				Bachi		
1450 —		Phase 5	Period 4				
1400 —	Diablo				Polvoron		
1350 —							
1300 —	Paquime	Phase 4	Period 3	Tucson	Civano	Gila	Safford
1250 —							
1200 —	Buena Fe		Period 2		Soho	Roosevelt	Bylas
1150 —				Tanque Verde			
1100 —					Santan	Miami	Eden
1050 —			Period 1				
1000 —							
950 —	Perros Bravos	Phase 3		Rincon	Sacaton	Sacaton	Two Dog - Encinas

ACS\SR88\FIG2

Figure 13.2.   Cultural chronologies in northwestern Mexico and the southwestern United States.

age), it would require eight days to go from Casa Grande Ruins, Arizona, to the Rio Conception Basin in Sonora. The Trincheras tradition parallels the Hohokam. A pit house period was involved in shell production and trade, and irrigation may have been present by 800 (Johnson 1966; McGuire and Villalpando 1989:166; Phillips 1989: 390). Braniff's work in the Rio San Miguel (in Phillips 1989:391) recorded hamlets with trash mounds and *cerros de trincheras* (hill top sites). Terraced *trincheras* were used for habitation, agriculture, and may have had ideological associations (Downum et al. 1994:292). Trincheras Purple-on-red pottery, which can also be red-on-brown, exhibits parallels to Hohokam and Mogollon wares; several polychrome wares were also made (Doyel 1977; Withers 1973). Polished red ware and marine shell manufacturing debris are common. Cremation and inhumation burials are present (McGuire and Villalpando 1989:167). Trincheras and Hohokam rock art share stylistic similarities (Lindauer and Zaslow 1994; Schaafsma 1980). Classic period trade wares include Chihuahua and Salado polychromes.

Cerros de trincheras were constructed in Sonora between 1200 and 1400. Some sites cover 0.5 km² and single hills contain 50 terraces. The site of Las Trincheras has a courtyard and platform on top. Other compounds (or *corrales*) may represent public architecture. The distri-

butions of *trincheras* and platform mounds overlap along the Santa Cruz River in southern Arizona (Fish and Fish 1994a). The Tucson Basin *trincheras* may have been depopulated by 1300 (Downum et al. 1994:292). Relationships, if any, among the *trincheras* and hilltop sites north of the Phoenix Basin (Spoerl and Gumerman 1984) remain problematic.

Rio Sonora

The Rio Sonora tradition (1000–1450), thought to resemble Mogollon, was located between Cananea on the north and the Rio Fuerte on the south (Doolittle 1988; Pailes 1972, 1984). If our traveler from Casa Grande Ruins, Arizona wanted to visit the coastal town of Guaymas about half way to the Rio Fuerte, it would take 16 days each way. A survey by Doolittle (1988:39) recorded 162 late settlements in the Rio Sonora Valley that contained 1,289 houses. Textured brown and Playas Red wares were present by 1200 at about the time when stone and adobe surface structures and compounds replaced pit houses (McGuire and Villalpando 1989:169). Site locations along streams reflect an emphasis on farming that included irrigation (Phillips 1989:388), although defensive sites were present in the Rio Sonora (Pailes 1984).

Several Casas Grandes-type ball courts (Whalen and Minnis 1996) are present; the San Jose site has a stone platform, ball court, and plaza, while a court at La Mora is T-shaped (Pailes 1984). Large villages cover 25 ha and contain up to 200 structures (Doolittle 1988:39). Although the presence of "statelets" has been suggested (Doolittle 1988; Riley 1987), McGuire and Villalpando (1989:170) opine that the Rio Sonora compounds "are of middling size and organizational complexity." Associated trade wares are Chihuahua and Salado polychromes. Worked marine shell is common (Braniff 1986).

Casas Grandes

The Casas Grandes tradition (700–1450), located in northwestern Chihuahua, is relevant here because of postulated (but unsubstantiated) Salado migrations there and postulated domination (also unsubstantiated) of the Phoenix Basin Hohokam by the primary center of Casas Grandes (Paquimé) (Gladwin 1957; Lekson, Chapter 12). By 1150, a pit house horizon similar to Mogollon was replaced by clusters of surface structures built around small plazas (Di Peso 1974a; Phillips 1989:383). Mimbres Black-on-white and copper artifacts were present. By the Medio period (1275–1400) Paquimé covered 36 ha, contained 2,000 rooms, and had a population of 4,700 (Di Peso 1974a; Phillips 1989:382). Architecture included multistoried puddled adobe structures, colonnades, large plazas, ceremonial mounds, and ball courts. The "enormous wealth accumulation" at Paquimé was controlled by a small group (Minnis and Whalen 1993:37).

The Medio period settlement system included Paquimé and several secondary centers. Distributions of macaw pens and public architecture suggest that the core system had a radius of 30 km. Chihuahua (Casas Grandes) polychromes were distributed far beyond this core. Minnis and Whalen (1993:37, 42) conclude that, through economic interaction, the influence of Casas Grandes was felt throughout the southern Southwest. This influence extended west into Sonora and south to the Rio Carmen. Houses in this area were made of coursed adobe with T-shaped doorways and raised hearths. Trails and hilltop fire beacons linked settlements (Di Peso 1974a; Phillips 1989:383). Influence to the north extended into the Chihuahuan Desert zone of the southern Southwest where it is known as the Black Mountain and/or Animas phases (Creel 1994; LeBlanc 1983:163; 1989).

Di Peso (1976a) argued that Gila Polychrome was locally manufactured at Paquimé by 1060. Recent analysis indicates that Salado wares there were more similar to other Salado wares than to local wares. Also, Ramos Polychrome from the southern Southwest has different chemical signatures than pots made at Paquimé (Woosley and Olinger 1993). Fifty percent of the 23,122 sherds of Salado polychrome at Paquimé was from a single storeroom, indicating that the ware was not generally available. The date range for Gila Polychrome there is strongest between 1340 and 1385 (Dean and Ravesloot 1993:98).

Safford Basin

The Safford Basin is defined as that segment of the Gila River east of the town of Safford to the Mescal Mountains on the west, which includes the San Carlos and San Simon rivers. The town of Safford is 180 km from the modern town of Coolidge adjacent to Casa Grande Ruins. Early Formative (1–750) sites share traits with the San Simon tradition of southeastern Arizona, the Hohokam to the west, and the Mogollon to the east and north (Black and Green 1994; Crary, Neily, Kinkade, and Germick 1994; Di Peso 1979; Doyel 1993b). Early pit house sites are associated with brown and red ware ceramics, while Mogollon textured types, Cibola White Ware, and Snaketown Red-on-buff are present late in the period (Gregory 1994). Late Formative (750–1100) sites include villages and dispersed clusters of pithouses. Ditch irrigation was present near San Carlos by the ninth century (Mitchell 1986). Late Formative (Gila Butte through Sacaton phase) sites near Ranch Creek east of Globe (Brandes 1957) include villages with ball courts. Intrusion of Phoenix Basin Hohokam, probably emanating from the Gila River area, was likely (Crary, Neily, Kinkade, and Germick 1994; Doyel 1991a).

Two Dog-Encinas phase (1000 and 1100) sites contain stone palettes, cremation burials, irrigation systems, and ball courts, indicating participation in the Hohokam interaction sphere (Crary, Neily, Kinkade, and Germick 1994; Sayles 1945). While villages were present, most sites were small hamlets containing dispersed clusters of pithouses. Ceramics are plain and red wares; locally produced decorated types include Encinas Red-on-brown and Sacaton Red-on-buff. Neck banded and corrugated pottery is associated, along with Mimbres, Reserve, Puerco, Black Mesa, Sosi Black-on-whites, and Wingate Black-on-red.

Eden phase (1100 to 1200) sites consist of clusters of pit rooms that face open courtyards while larger more compact villages may be present (i.e., Buena Vista). Pit rooms were constructed with basal stones or coursed adobe walls. Urn cremations placed in cemeteries and flexed and extended inhumations are present. Ceramics are dominated by plain, red, and textured wares. Decorated types include Encinas Red-on-brown and Santan Red-on-buff. Interaction shifted away from the Phoenix Basin and Sulphur Springs areas and toward to the Mimbres and Upper Gila areas (Crary, Neily, Kinkade, and Germick 1994).

Bylas phase (1175–1300) sites are clusters of room blocks and/or compounds. Extensive nonirrigated agricultural systems, including ditch, rock pile, waffle gardens, and check dams, are associated with Bylas phase and later sites (Crary, Neily, Kinkade, and Germick 1994; Neely 1997). Compounds associated with single story architecture and black-on-white pottery and structural mounds with polychrome pottery are present between Cutter and San Carlos (Gladwin 1957; Hohmann and Kelley 1988; Johnson and Wasley 1966). The presence of earlier Hohokam pottery suggests continuity in site location. Cremations were put in jars, covered by bowls with "kill" holes present, and then placed in discrete cemeteries. A variety of textured wares are present. San Carlos Red-on-brown is the local decorated ware. A local obliterated corrugated type with a fugitive red slip and faint design (Thatcher White-on-red) is present. Cibola White Ware, White Mountain Red Ware, and Chihuahua and/or Animas trade wares increased. Tularosa Black-on-white and St. Johns Bichrome and Polychrome were present after 1250.

Around 1275, sites containing masonry rooms facing interior plazas were built on hill tops. Slab lined hearths and a deflector/entry box complex were associated. A D-shaped kiva was present in the plaza at Goat Hill (CC:1:28[ASM]) that included an altar, vent shaft, a circular clay-lined hearth, a foot drum-sipapu complex, and loom holes. Ceramics include Pinedale wares, Maverick Mountain wares, Tucson bichromes and polychromes, and Pinto Polychrome (Woodson 1995). Goat Hill and similar sites seem to represent intrusions of Tsegi phase Anasazi (Di Peso 1958; Lindsay 1987).

Safford phase (1300–1450) architecture consists of adobe and stone room blocks with and without plazas or enclosing walls (Crary, Neily, Kinkade, and Germick 1994). Public architecture includes large plazas and rectangular great kivas (e.g., Buena Vista-Curtis and Marijilda sites). Small "late Mogollon" kivas (e.g., Spear Ranch site) present were similar to those at Point of Pines and the San Pedro River areas (Brown 1973; Di Peso 1958; Mills and Mills 1978). West of San Carlos, multistoried pueblos of adobe and stone enclosed by walls are associated with Gila Polychrome

(Gladwin 1957). No platform mounds are known for the Safford Basin, but early historic period site reports may include descriptions of platforms (Crary, Neily, Kinkade, and Germick 1994).

Urn cremations and extended inhumations were present, and infants were buried below room floors (Brown 1973; Mills and Mills 1978). Unburied bodies and burned rooms were found. Corrugated pottery, including Tusayan-affinis types, increased, but San Carlos Red-on-brown, White Mountain Red Ware, and Cibola White Ware decreased. El Paso and Ramos Polychromes and Playas Red are present. Local production of Gila Polychrome dominated decorated assemblages. Intrusions of different groups resulting in a merging of Little Colorado, Point of Pines, and White Mountain populations with the Safford tradition has been proposed (Crary, Neily, Kinkade, and Germick 1994).

Globe Highlands

The Globe Highlands encompass the mountains surrounding Globe-Miami, south to the Dripping Springs Mountains, and north along Pinal Creek to Tonto Basin. While early ceramic period occupations were present in the Tonto and Safford basins and at Point of Pines (Elson 1996a; Elson and Craig 1992; Haury 1989), similar occupations have not been identified in the Globe Highlands. Ceramic-period sites date to the Late Formative Snaketown through Sacaton phases (800–1100) (Doyel 1978). Villages and hamlets containing pit houses and extensive middens are present along the drainages (Doyel and Hoffman 1997). Classic period sites along Miami Wash had underlying pithouses indicating some continuity in site location (Doyel 1978). Trade pottery indicates interaction with the Phoenix Basin, Point of Pines, Safford, and Cibola areas.

The Miami phase (1100–1200/1250) consists of hamlets of stone and adobe pit rooms with or without enclosing walls (Doyel 1976a, 1976b, 1978). Extended burials are associated with polished red wares and Cibola White Ware. No local decorated or corrugated pottery is associated, but local Gila Red ware is present.

The Roosevelt and Gila phases (1200/1250–1450) shared characteristics with the Mogollon, Sinagua, Anasazi, and Hohokam. Sites consist of cobble and adobe architecture, enclosed plazas and compounds, and terraces. The Roosevelt phase is similar to the Bylas phase except that it lacks locally-made decorated pottery and may show a preference for inhumation over cremation burial. No Roosevelt phase components have been excavated and/or reported in the area, although such components are known to be present under later Gila phase pueblos (Emil Haury, personal communication 1976). Excavations in progress (Doyel and Hoffman 1997) north of Globe recently uncovered Roosevelt phase compound and room block sites containing Cibola White Ware, White Mountain Red Ware, Salado Red Ware, and Salado polychrome. Massive multistoried Gila phase sites (200+ rooms) include Gila Pueblo, Bead Mountain, and Besh-Ba-Gowah (Doyel 1978; Gladwin 1957; Hohman and Kelley 1988; Vickery 1939). A Gila phase platform mound community is located along Pinal Creek north of Globe, and features similar to platforms may exist near Miami (Joe Crary, personal communication 1996). Plain, polished, textured, and polychrome wares are present.

Changes in Roosevelt and Gila phase culture have been attributed to immigrations of Western Anasazi (Plog 1979) into Tonto Basin, and inferentially, the Globe Highlands (Elson 1996a; Gladwin 1957). Interpreting the transitions among the Late Formative, Miami, and Salado occupations remains problematic. The presence of immigrant populations, as postulated for the Tonto and Safford basins (Elson 1996a; Crary, Neily, Kinkade, and Germick 1994), has not been carefully studied for the Globe Highlands. But given the paucity of Roosevelt phase settlements, formation of the large Gila phase pueblos may include immigrants from Tonto Basin.

CULTURAL DYNAMICS IN THE SOUTHERN SOUTHWEST AND NORTHWESTERN MEXICO

One goal of this review is to demonstrate that processes of regional cultural development were occurring across northwestern Mexico and southern Arizona by 1200 (Figure 13.3). Distributions of selected attributes across this zone are provided in Table 13.1. Some qualifications are necessary to interpret this table. Ceramic dates are used in the absence of tree-ring dates. Less secure dates are shown with a question mark. When a trait is not common it is listed as atypical; for example, platform mounds in Trincheras and intensive irrigation in Papaguería. The presence of some traits is uncertain; for example, no multistoried architecture has been excavated in the Rio Sonora but some believe that it was present (Doolittle 1988). Other attributes, such as site hierarchies

and worked marine shell, were deleted as these traits were shared by all the regional traditions inventoried.

Inspection of this table prompts a number of generalizations:

(1). The earliest ball courts were clustered in and around the Phoenix Basin.
(2). For southern Arizona, compounds, platforms, and plazas appear earliest in the Phoenix Basin.
(3). Both cremation and extended burial were practiced in most areas.
(4). Irrigation was practiced to some degree in all areas.
(5). Salado polychrome was nearly ubiquitous.
(6). Chihuahua Polychromes was centered in northwestern Mexico and was rare in the Sonoran Desert in southern Arizona.

It is apparent that interacting regional traditions existed across the Sonoran Desert by 1200. Characteristics once thought to be uniquely "Salado" were, in fact, shared by multiple traditions, i.e., plazas, compounds, polished red ware, worked shell, extended burials, etc. The trait distributions do not point to single center or source area. Some appear earlier in the Phoenix Basin than in northwestern Mexico, which suggests a leadership role for this region. These data reinforce Gumerman's (1993:7) observation on Southwest-Mesoamerican interaction, that the question is no longer, "Was there interaction," but rather, "What was its nature, scale, intensity, duration, direction, and social, economic, and ideological context?"

The development of coursed adobe architecture remains a critical research issue. The earliest known in the Southwest is from several rooms (B9 and B11) at Old Town in the Mimbres Valley that may date to 900 (Creel 1995). Coursed adobe is present in Chaco Canyon in northern New Mexico, Casas Grandes in northern Chihuahua, and Gila Bend in southwestern Arizona by 1150 (C. M. Cameron 1996; Doyel et al. 1984; Wasley and Johnson 1965). Once developed, this technology spread quickly. C. M. Cameron (1996) suggests that coursed adobe took on symbolic properties that were incorporated into native world view. The fact that coursed adobe was first used by the Phoenix Basin Hohokam to construct platform mounds is consistent with this view. The origin and development of compound architecture, also usually made of adobe, remains problematic, and may be a key to sorting out some cultural dynamics, if researchers can agree on a definition of a compound.

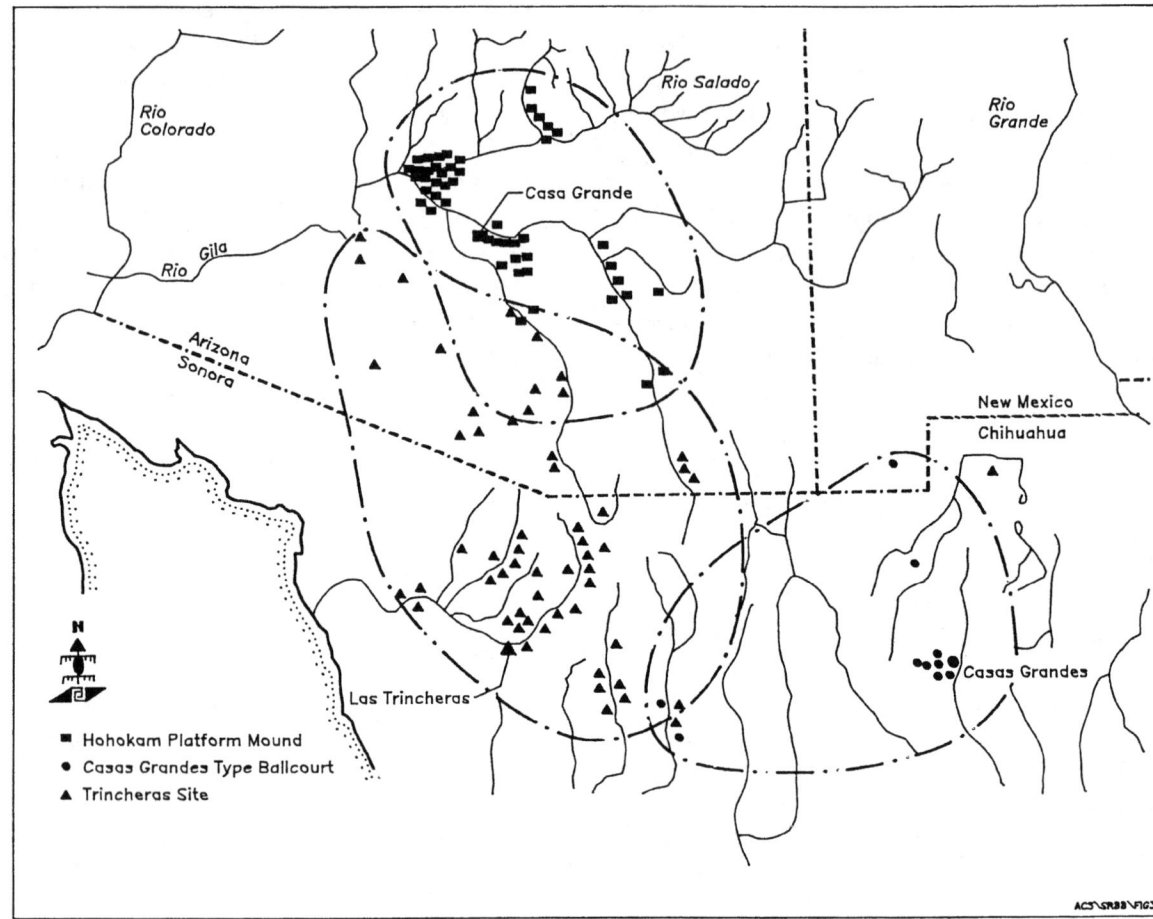

Figure 13.3.   Cultural traditions in the Sonoran Desert zone (modified from Fish and Fish 1994).

Table 13.1.   Selected Attributes of Sonoran Desert Settlements after A.D. 1100

Trait/Area	Rio Sonora	Trincheras	Papagueria	Gila Bend	Phoenix Basin	Tucson Basin	Lower San Pedro	Tonto-Globe	Safford Basin
Ball courts	1200	?	no	800	800	800?*	900?	no	900+?
Compounds	1200	yes	1200+*	1200*	1100+	1200+	1200+	1150+	yes
Platform mounds	1200+	yes*	1100+**	1000*	800	1200+	1250+	1275+	**
Multistoried rooms	1300?	no	no	no	1300+	no?	no?	1300+	yes
Coursed adobe	1200	?	yes	1050+	1050+	yes	yes	yes	yes
Walled plazas	?	?	?	yes*	1150+?	1200	1250+	yes	yes
Extended burial	?	yes	yes?	yes	yes	yes	?	yes	yes
Cremation	?	?	?	yes	yes	yes	?	yes*	yes
Irrigation	yes	yes	yes*	yes	yes	yes	yes	yes	yes
Salado polychrome	yes	yes	yes	trace	yes	yes	yes	yes	yes
Chihuahua polychrome	yes	yes	no	no	trace	trace	trace	trace?	trace
Polished red ware	yes	yes	yes	yes	yes	yes	yes	yes	yes

*atypical **rare

The Southern Distribution
of Salado Polychrome

The *cerros de trincheras* of Papaguería can no longer be seen as barriers to the distribution of Salado polychrome (Haury 1950:8). Multiple sites are known to contain this pottery (Doelle and Wallace 1988:240), and villages near Organ Pipe National Monument (e.g., Lost City, the Reservoir site) have up to 10 percent Salado polychrome (Rankin 1995). It was also "common" in Sonora (McGuire and Villalpando 1989:167).

Some years ago I inspected the Gila Pueblo survey collections from Sonora and Chihuahua (Sayles 1936a, 1936b) housed at the Arizona State Museum (ASM). This significant collection shows that Salado polychrome (Gila-Tonto) extends south to Caborca and Hermosillo, and west to the Gulf of California. Salado and Chihuahua polychromes cooccur near Caborca (e.g., SON E:12:1 and SON E:12:2 [ASM]). Red Mesa Black-on-white, Wingate and St. Johns Polychrome, and Salado and Chihuahua polychromes cooccur at SON F:11:5 (ASM). Salado and Chihuahua polychromes and White Mountain Red Ware are found near Hermosillo (SON J:4:8 [ASM]). Mimbres and Chupadero Black-on-white and White Mountain Red Ware occur with El Paso, Tucson, Salado, and Chihuahua polychromes in ASM survey quads CHI B, C, and D.

These widespread distributions must be studied further to identify travel routes and to measure participation in interregional exchange systems. The fact remains that Salado polychrome was distributed from central Sonora, to the Four Corners region of the American Southwest, and from Gila Bend on the west to the plains of Texas on the east. This distribution, combined with multiple production centers and local stylistic variations (Crown 1994), indicates that Salado polychrome cannot be ascribed to a single center or "culture."

Cultural Dynamics
in the Phoenix Basin

Three large time periods are present in the Hohokam cultural sequence in the Phoenix Basin: the Early Formative (1–800; Red Mountain through Sweetwater phases), the Late Formative (800–1075; Snaketown through Sacaton phases), and the Classic (1075/1100–1450; Santan through Polvoron phases). Early Formative Phoenix Basin villages reflect their heritage of developing near the Mesoamerican periphery (e.g., plazas, polished red and brown ware, clay figurines, worked shell, stylistic elements, etc.). Early Formative populations in the Phoenix

Basin were in a favorable position to serve as cultural mediators between the cultures to the north and south (Doyel 1991a; Pailes 1990).

Canal irrigation and sedentary villages were in place by the Gila Butte horizon. Site hierarchies included villages with and without ball courts and villages with multiple courts. Large villages exhibited a concentric site structure with mounds and ball courts surrounding a central plaza, a pattern found at Cashion, Gatlin, Grewe, Snaketown, and other sites. Villages with public architecture were evenly spaced along the rivers, a pattern that survived into the Classic period (Doyel 1987, Doyel et al. 1997, Gregory 1991; Masse 1981; Wilcox 1991a). Population estimates for Late Formative villages range between 300 (Wilcox 1991a:262) and 2,000 (Haury 1976a:356). Increasing numbers of discrete cemeteries indicate population segmentation that required greater integration. Cremation rituals were more elaborate. Construction of ball courts and capped mounds reflects growing emphasis on ceremonialism. A platform, copper bells, and macaw remains at the Gatlin site (Wasley 1960) hint at ceremonialism emanating from northwestern Mesoamerica. Other Mesoamerican elements added in the Late Formative include formal village plans; ball courts; platform mounds; worked shell; turquoise mosaic; copper bells; pyrites-encrusted, and stone-backed mirrors (Doyel 1991a; Haury 1976a, Kelley 1966). This cultural elaboration suggests the emergence of positions of power and authority (Bayman 1994; Doyel 1996).

Increasing integration of irrigation networks in the Classic period resulted in some towns becoming more dominant (e.g., Pueblo Grande, Mesa Grande, Casa Grande, Los Muertos, and Pueblo Viejo). Continuity in village location at some sites and not others was likely due to environmental and historical factors (Gregory 1991). Central site precincts contained platforms, towers, and great houses surrounded by walled compounds, large "trash" mounds, and, in cases, ball courts. Large central compounds containing public buildings and residential areas surrounded by smaller compounds and house groups gave way to farmsteads, canals, and fields. Population of the larger towns may have averaged around 600 (Wilcox 1991a:263), but many were smaller.

Platform Mounds
in the Phoenix Basin

Platform mounds were constructed for 500 years in the Phoenix Basin. Other platforms occur throughout south-central Arizona including those in Tonto Basin. Platforms are more common and had a longer history in the Phoenix Basin, but historical connections between Hohokam and other platform mounds merit discussion.

Construction in the Phoenix Basin peaked in the Soho phase (1200–1300) when 42 sites had a total of 64 platforms (Doelle et al. 1995). One site—Las Colinas—appears to have had as many as ten platforms while multiple platforms were present at other sites (Gregory 1987; Gregory et al. 1988). Thirteen multistoried structures (great houses?) and seven towers (Doelle et al. 1995:390) were constructed either in the late Soho phase or the early Civano phase. Few, if any, platforms were built in the Civano phase (1300–1400) in the Phoenix Basin. Platforms were built after 1250 in Tonto Basin, the San Pedro and Santa Cruz river valleys, and Papaguería. Small platforms and *casitas grandes* such as Brady Wash (Ciolek-Torrello et al. 1988), Jackrabbit Ruin (Scantling 1940), and Coyote Hills (Dart et al. 1990), were constructed around the edges of the Phoenix Basin in the late Classic period. Similarities in form suggest that the concept of platforms moved out from the Phoenix Basin to other populations who built platform mounds to suit their purposes.

The largest platforms, such as Pueblo Grande and Las Colinas, contained between 15,000 and 20,000 m³ of fill. A platform's size seems to correspond to the size of its associated community. Turney (1929) estimated the Pueblo Grande site to be two miles north-south by one mile east-west. I estimate that 100 people working one month a year for 20 years could gather the fill for the Pueblo Grande platform, for a total of 230 person years (one person working for 230 years). In contrast, the smaller Escalante platform (1,900 m³) was built within a community that contained fewer than 100 people (Doyel 1981:21). If half the people contributed labor it would have taken 38 days (7.25 person years) to fill the Escalante platform, or roughly three percent that of Pueblo Grande. Most platforms located on the basin edge (e.g., Brady Wash) or in surrounding areas (Papaguería, San Pedro) were even smaller. For example, the average volume of 12 platforms along the San Pedro River was only 272 m³—one person could have built one in a year (Doelle et al. 1995:423)!

For comparison, Monk's Mound near St. Louis, Missouri, the largest Precolumbian artificial platform north of Mexico, contains 500,000 m³ of fill. The platform-pyramid at the Olmec site of La Venta contained 4,700,000 m³ and required 1,000 men 100 days for eight periods (3,050 person years) to

complete (Heizer 1960). These comparisons place the modest efforts of the Hohokam within a continental context. Something less than state-level polities is suggested. Yet the single-most achievement of the Hohokam was their canal systems, which rivaled anything in the New World (Doolittle 1990). A high degree of interaction and organization, minimally on an intradrainage level (e.g., the lower Salt River Valley, the Middle Gila River Valley, etc.) must have been in place to produce these remarkable systems (Rice, Chapter 6).

The Meaning of Mounds

Harold Gladwin (Gladwin et al. 1937:259) speculated that Hohokam mounds were related to the "grandiose idea of building pyramids." Museum exhibits unfortunately describe platforms as "tells," which contradicts the concept of a platform. Bandelier, Cushing, Fewkes, and Hayden all recognized that platform mounds were purposefully constructed architectural features not to be confused with Old World tells that represent hundreds, if not thousands, of years of sequential occupations. In contrast, Haury (1945) claimed that the Classic period platforms were the collapsed remains of multistoried "great houses" that he referred to as (Salado) "house mounds," a position he never relinquished in the face of mounting evidence to the contrary (Haury 1987:251). Cushing (in Haury 1945:8) described platforms as "great temples" or "priest's temples" that were located near the village center. The presence of shrines and ceremonial rooms convinced Fewkes (1912) that platforms were "temples used for ceremonial purposes." As Fewkes (1912:152) summarized, "An American feudal system developed in the Gila-Salado Basin, marked by the erection of buildings belonging to some chief, around which were clustered small huts in which the common people lived . . . nothing like this [existed] among the Pueblos or even probably among the cliff dwellers, but such a condition existed in Mexico before the days of the advent of the European conquerors."

Based on work at Casa Grande, Gladwin (1928; Gladwin and Gladwin 1935) proclaimed that the Sonoran Desert had been peacefully invaded by puebloan Salado people from Tonto Basin. The Salado, and not the Hohokam, had constructed the great houses and made the polychrome pottery. Variation in architecture and other remains was therefore not due to priestly and commoner classes but to the presence of a different people. With this pronouncement, the "Salado invasion" became the ruling hypothesis for the next 50 years (Willey 1966). This model overlooked the fact that coursed adobe architecture, extended burials, platform mounds, and other traits predated Salado polychrome by 100 years.

Based on excavations at Pueblo Grande, Halseth (1943, 1947) stated that platforms were "community buildings" used as elevated granaries to protect stored food from a rising water table. They were not "living quarters." This view ignored the rooms on the mound that contained fire hearths and artifact arrays and also ignored the platforms along the Gila River where waterlogging was not a problem (Hayden 1957:194).

Haury only became convinced of a Mesoamerica source for the Late Formative platforms after he witnessed excavations at the Gatlin platform and personally excavated Mound 16 at Snaketown (Haury 1976a). This is an odd slice of history, as he had earlier championed the position that ball courts were southern and had identified other items of Mesoamerican origin in Hohokam sites (Gladwin et al. 1937). He had also described the "west Mexican trait complex" in Papaguería that consisted of unsmudged red ware, overlap manos, modeled spindle whorls, *comales*, and possibly platform mounds and adobe architecture (Di Peso 1958:16; Haury 1950:17).

Wasley (Wasley and Doyel 1980) broke from the status quo by claiming that Classic period Phoenix Basin architecture resembled features in northern Mexico more than anything definitively "Salado." Wasley (1960) also suggested that the large Classic period platforms were historically related to the earlier platforms of the Late Formative period. This work initiated a new era of investigations that continues to the present.

A Sequence of Platform Mounds in the Phoenix Basin

Based on the limited available evidence, a developmental sequence that links the small platforms of the Late Formative period with the massive structures of the Soho phase can be proposed. Mounds at Snaketown, Gatlin, Mound 8 at Las Colinas, Escalante, and Pueblo Grande provide data for this general outline.

Early examples of capped platforms are two Snaketown phase mounds (39 and 40) at Snaketown. These mounds were trash-filled and capped with caliche-rich soil (Haury 1976a:93). Between 1000 and 1100, constructed platforms at Snaketown (Mound 16), Gatlin, and Las Colinas (Mound 8) began as small, oval-shaped, slope-sided features under 15 m in diameter and one m high (Figure 13.5); they were built in areas that showed little prior use. Post holes ringing the mounds indicate

that the platforms were surrounded by palisades, which suggests exclusivity. Compare, for example, that 500 people could have stood around the large ball court adjacent to Mound 16 at Snaketown. The mound floors and steps had repeated coatings of plaster. Each mound had at least one structure outside the palisade that may have been part of platform choreography.

Some Sacaton phase platforms were renovated in the Santan phase (1075–1200). Mound 16 at Snaketown did not exhibit Santan phase construction, which is why we know of its existence. The Gatlin platform was abandoned before 1200, which is why we know of its existence. Both Gatlin and Mound 8 at Las Colinas exhibit multiple building episodes containing post-reinforced adobe walls (Gregory 1987; Wasley 1960). Ancillary structures located near the platforms were connected by walls. Little is known about Santan phase platforms as the evidence remains concealed inside the massive mounds of later phases.

The addition of structures to the platforms at Gatlin and Mound 8 indicates a change. They became temples, similar in appearance, but not in scale, to temple mounds of Mesoamerica and the southeastern United States. Round structures in Mesoamerica were associated with Quetzalcoatl (Porter-Weaver 1981:386). The presence of shell trumpets and other items may support this association for the Late Formative Hohokam platforms, which would question Di Peso's (1968) assertion of Tezcatlipoca dominance. Hayden (1957:192) thought that the Santan phase was a time of dramatic and perhaps violent changes in lifestyles. Haury (1976a:93) stated that the "religious fervor" that had stimulated construction of Mound 16 seemed to have faded, but the opposite appears likely. Platforms became increasingly prominent, but Snaketown was not a player in the following rounds.

New technologies were developed in the Soho phase (1200–1300) to increase the size of platforms. Massive exterior caliche-adobe walls several m thick were first erected, usually in rectangular patterns. The interior space created was then filled with trash or clean soil that encased existing platforms. Stone or wood was sometimes embedded in walls. Vertical exposures were usually two or three m high but may have approached six or seven m in cases. Many massive-wall platforms without complex internal sequences, such as Escalante, were constructed. Multiple floors in the platforms at Pueblo Grande (Hayden 1957:44), Compound B at Casa Grande (Fewkes 1912), and Escalante (Doyel 1974) reveal continuity in practices with the Late Formative platforms.

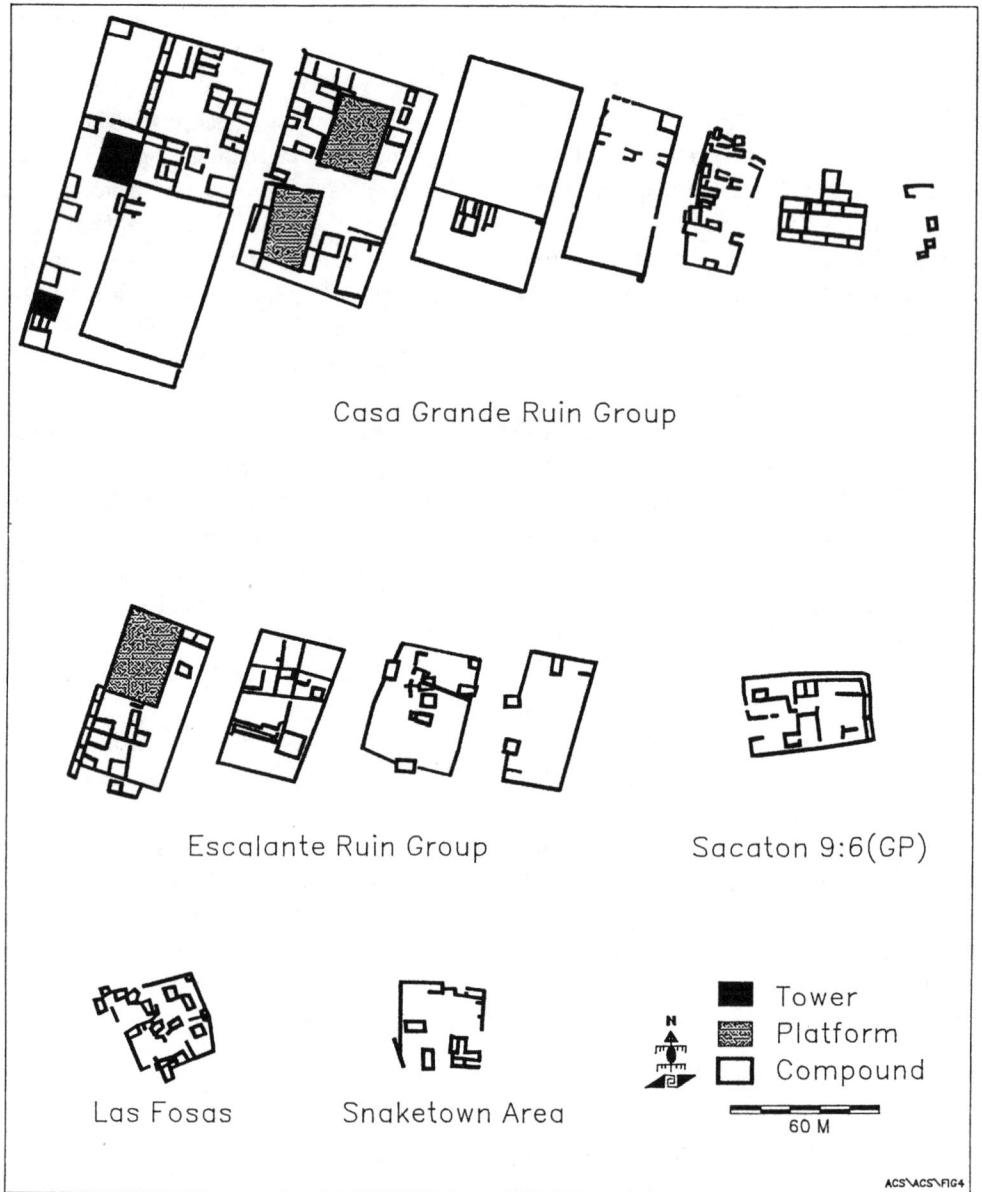

Casa Grande Ruin Group

Escalante Ruin Group

Sacaton 9:6(GP)

Las Fosas

Snaketown Area

■ Tower
▨ Platform
□ Compound

60 M

Figure 13.4. Classic period architecture in the middle Gila River Basin.

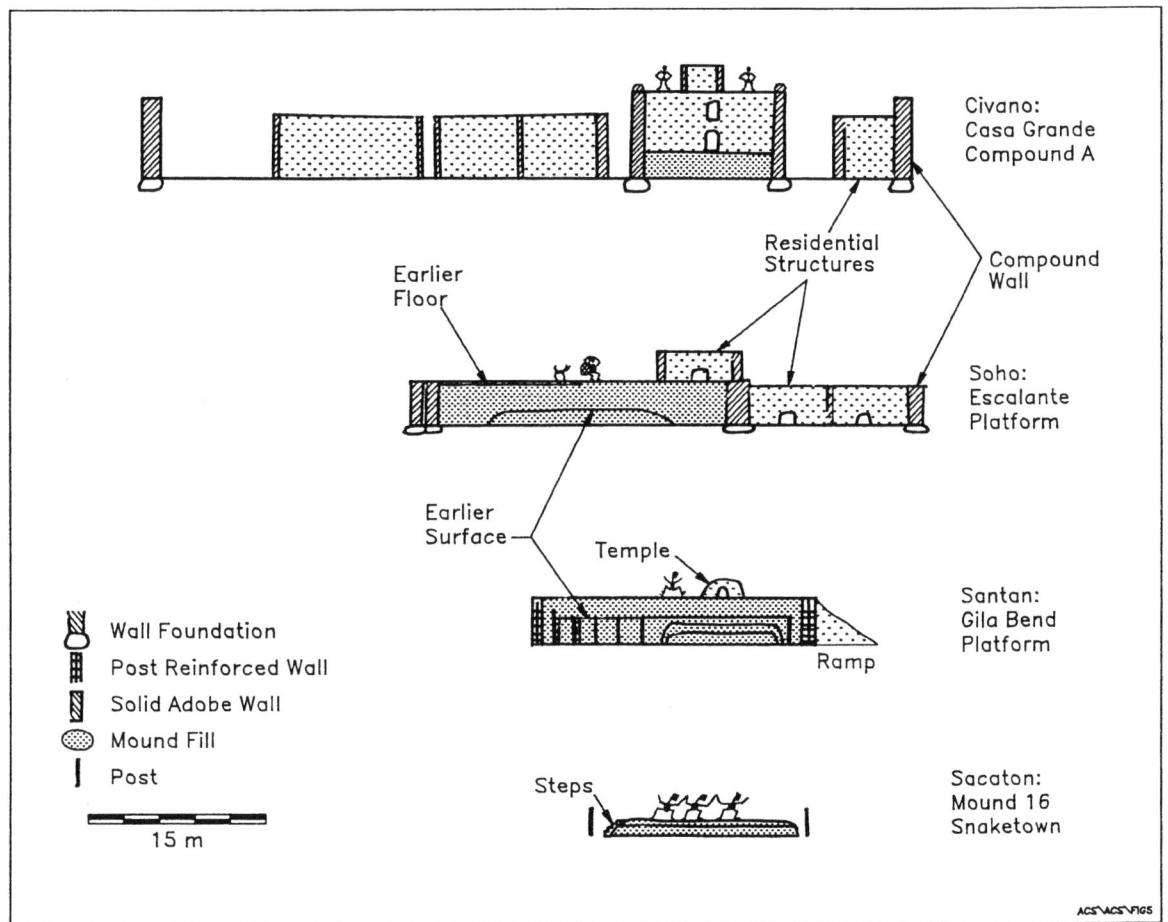

Figure 13.5. Developmental sequence of platform mounds in the middle Gila River Basin.

Even in the presence of the massive wall technology, the first features built on these platforms were simple houses made of wood and adobe like those of earlier phases (Doyel 1974). The small number of structures relative to available space indicates that platforms continued to serve as temples. Ceremonial rooms in excess of 50 m² were located in adjacent plazas and occurred in patterned arrangements near platforms, further suggesting continuity with earlier phases (Doyel 1974; Gregory et al. 1988; Howard 1992a).

To underscore their power, sanctity, and/or exclusivity, the temple mounds were surrounded by walled compounds constructed with massive wall technology. These features seem to have developed from the earlier palisaded forms. Compound walls stood two to three m high. It is possible

that the compound-cum-temple mound may represent an extension of the sacred enclosure concept prominent in Mesoamerica. Regardless, extensive communication must have occurred among the builders regarding shared concepts of architecture, related features, and choreography, (Gregory et al. 1988:48). This formal complex likely expressed the dominant symbolic structure or cosmology of Hohokam society.

Replacement of the temple structures with massive-wall rooms in the Civano phase signals new functions for the platforms. Some Civano phase platforms contained many rooms and plazas. The Pueblo Grande platform contained up to 60 rooms (Hayden 1957). Specialized rooms, such as storage, habitation, and ceremonial rooms, show patterned distributions at Escalante (Doyel

1974, 1981), and similar patterns probably exist at other sites. For the first time people were actually living on top of the platforms (Doelle et al. 1995; Doyel 1974). Since platforms were initially constructed for ritual purposes, these occupants may have been accorded ritual power. Howard (1992a) suggests that some platforms remained more involved in ritual and less involved in residential functions. There is no *a priori* reason to suspect that all mounds served the same functions, and some larger villages may have constructed different mounds for different purposes. By 1300, however, some families had either promoted themselves or were promoted to the highly visible status of mound dwellers.

Built by 1320 (Andresen 1985), the Casa Grande was the culmination of the massive-wall technology. The basal floor was a filled platform two m high. This four-story edifice likely functioned as a tower, residence, storage facility, and as an astronomical observatory (Wilcox and Shenk 1977). A labor force of 100 could have constructed the great house in three months, or 24 people could have built it in one year. Elsewhere, multistoried structures were built on the Pueblo Grande platform that made it appear as several small great houses on top of the huge platform (Doyel 1991b:11). While 13 great houses may have existed (Doelle et al. 1995), these features are not present in all communities, which suggests local and/or regional hierarchies.

Cultural Implications
of Mounds

Between 1000 and 1400, Hohokam platforms underwent changes in function. The ceremonial platforms of the Late Formative period were transformed into temple mounds by the Santan phase. Construction of the massive Soho phase platforms was associated with ritual elaboration. Still later, some platforms were converted into habitation features, presumably for elite families. Throughout, the importance of platforms was underscored by their central locations within their communities. These Soho and Civano models were emulated by other populations surrounding the Phoenix Basin.

Between 1050–1200, platforms replaced ball courts as the major form of public architecture (other than irrigation systems). Courts and platforms coexisted as parts of Hohokam ceremonial life, as ball courts and platforms were constructed with patterned relationships at some sites (Gregory 1987). At other villages, however, ball courts were defaced and destroyed (La Ciudad, Las Co-

linas, Pueblo Grande), and Ball Court 2 at Gatlin was never completed (Wasley and Johnson 1965). Ball courts and platform mounds may have represented competing forces within Hohokam society, with the outcome that platforms became dominant after 1200. This shift seems to have been from one of community-wide participation in ritual (ball courts) to more exclusive performances (platforms), although public rituals likely occurred in large plazas.

Powerful symbols were associated with the platforms. Astronomical devices (windows, doors, niches) were strategically placed in these features. Pits thought to be associated with the preparation of saguaro wine, historically associated with rain-making, were associated with platforms at Escalante and Mound 8 at Las Colinas. (Doyel 1974, 1991a; Haury 1976a Underhill 1946). This elaboration suggests investment of power in the platforms and the growing importance of leadership roles. By 1300, the priests/leaders of the Phoenix Basin had created monuments to what Fewkes (1912:152) called an "expression of abstract power" or what I refer to as "power architecture." The commanding presence of the platforms and great houses must have been impressive to the average villager, to visiting traders, and to competitors. Plastered elevations were brightly painted with symbols and icons (see Doyel 1991b:11). For example, a serpent was painted on an exterior wall of a house on the platform at Pueblo Grande (Bostwick and Downum 1994) and designs were present on a building at Casa Grande (Andresen 1983). Like Chacoan great houses, many of which were also elevated, these monuments were built to impress, and indeed must have been effective, for a while.

A tradition of power relations was in place in the Phoenix Basin by the Late Formative period. Classic period platforms and great houses represent the physical remains of social arrangements related to the expression of power between 1050 and 1400. Scalar variation in the expression of power was different. Communities of differing sizes could be expected to express power differently. For example, Escalante was a single platform village wherein most daily interaction could have occurred face-to-face. In contrast, across the Gila River, the Casa Grande community integrated multiple villages with platforms (Crown 1987). *A priori*, one might expect scalar differences in expressions of power between these communities, i.e., a community of fewer than 100 versus a dispersed community of several thousand. Use of power by leaders could also have differed. Feinman (1991) states that in Mesoamerica leaders used different strategies, such as trade in prestige items, the control of production or ceremonialism, or the use of force to keep power.

ICONS AND IDEOLOGY:
THE SERPENT COMETH

Three major ideological systems present in the Phoenix Basin correspond to the three major time periods. First, a fertility and/or ancestor cult was in place by the Sweetwater phase of the Early Formative period. It was an integrated ideology, with polished red ware, unique clay figurines, and worked marine shell available even to those located on the edges of the Phoenix Basin (Doyel and McDonnell 1997). Other Mesoamerican concepts are represented by stylistic icons including the interlocking scroll and world-quarters motifs. This ideological system provided horizontal integration as the new village-farming economy spread across the Phoenix Basin.

By the Snaketown/Gila Butte phase this ideology underwent transformation with the addition of new elements, including use of water and serpent symbolism designs on pottery, textiles, and rock art; an explosion of worked shell; ornate stone palettes and carved stone censors; stone mirrors identical to those associated with Tezcatlipoca at Chichen Itza and Kaminaljuyu (Kidder et al. 1946); elaborate cremation burials; ball courts; mounds; and possible use of hallucinogenic plants, fermented agave drink, and blood-letting (Doyel 1991a; Feinman 1991; Haury 1976a). Named the "Rainbow Way" (Doyel 1994), this ideology was central to Hohokam social integration for several centuries prior to 1050. A central point here is that connections existed with Mesoamerica well before the rise of Paquimé and Salado polychrome pottery.

By 1075, the old icons were rejected, as seen in shifts away from cremation burial, a revival of polished red ware pottery, adoption of coursed adobe architecture, growth of platform mounds, and depopulation of some ancestral villages (e.g., Snaketown, Grewe, Poston Butte, Cashion, Gatlin). The dominance of straight and wavy designs in early Classic pottery indicates continued use of water and serpent symbolism (Figure 13.6). Frogs and birds, also water symbols, continued as conspicuous elements of Classic period iconography. By 1300, serpents were the most common designs on Salado polychrome in the southern Southwest (Crown 1994:146). Examples

of Hohokam Buff Ware and Salado polychrome serpent/water designs illustrated here are from Snaketown and platform mound sites in the Tonto Basin and the Phoenix Basin (Doyel et al. 1995; Haury 1976a; Jacobs 1994a). In the Phoenix Basin, the emphasis on water and serpent symbolism connected the earlier Rainbow Way to the ideology of Salado polychrome. This ware seems to have represented a fourteenth century equivalent of Late Formative buff ware; its presence signaled participation in a larger interaction sphere and/or ideology (Crown 1994; Doyel 1993b).

Competing ideologies may have existed among the Hohokam. Variation in Classic period mortuary practices—cremation versus inhumation—combined with differences in burial goods—red ware versus polychrome—may be due to competing ideologies (Doyel 1981). The use of serpent symbolism in the Gila horizon may also illustrate a historical continuum into the ethnohistoric period in the form of Snake dances among the Pueblos and the reverence shown snakes among the O'odham (Fewkes 1894; Schaafsma 1994; Underhill 1946).

Salado Polychrome

Gila Polychrome has been viewed as a development out of Pinto Polychrome with influence from the Tusayan-Kayenta and Jeddito styles (Carlson 1970; Gladwin 1957; Haury 1945). The Pinto bichrome and Polychrome wares of the Roosevelt phase in Tonto Basin are clearly related to the Tularosa and Pinedale styles as seen on White Mountain Red Wares (Zedeño 1994). With this background, Crary et al. (1996) suggest that Gila Polychrome actually emerged from a Tsegi phase ceramic tradition strongly influenced by Winslow Orange and Jeddito Yellow ware technologies and design styles. Stylistic antecedents can be found in Tusayan White Ware. For example, the nearly ubiquitous "life line" present below the rim on Gila Polychrome is found on Tusayan Black-on-white and is common on late thirteenth century Winslow Orange and Jeddito Yellow Wares (Smith 1971). Manufacture of Gila Polychrome appears to have been concentrated near the southern range of the western Anasazi in the interconnected basins in the Tonto-Globe and Safford areas (Crary et al. 1996).

To the south, Salado polychrome has an uneven distribution across the Phoenix Basin. Wasley (Wasley and Doyel 1980:345) reported that it was rare, but more work has shown that this ware was common at some sites. Salado polychrome comprised ten percent of the pottery and 85 percent of the decorated assemblage at Escalante.

Gila Butte

Santa Cruz

Sacaton

Red-on-buff from Snaketown

Casa Grande Red-on-buff
Los Muertos

Gila Polychrome
Kinishba

Gila Polychrome
Pueblo Blanco

Gila Polychrome
Escalante

Gila Polychrome
Tonto Basin

Tonto Polychrome
Los Muertos

Figure 13.6.   Serpent designs on Hohokam and Salado pottery in Arizona.

It was common at Pueblo Grande and Las Colinas but rare at Casa Grande Ruins (Doyel 1981:34, 1993c; Haury 1945; Wasley and Doyel 1980:339). Much of this pottery looks imported but local copies may have been made. Abbot and Schaller (1992) have questioned local production of Salado polychrome in the Salt River Valley. While Crown and Bishop (Crown 1994) have identified multiple production areas for Gila Polychrome in the southern Southwest, production in the Phoenix Basin remains problematic.

Miksa (1995) analyzed eleven thin sections of Gila Polychrome, including six sherds from Pueblo Blanco in the lower Salt River Valley and five sherds from the Escalante Ruin in the middle Gila. Four of five sherds from Escalante have temper from the Inspiration Petrofacies that includes the Superstition Mountains and the Globe Highlands. Three sherds from Pueblo Blanco were also assigned to the Inspiration Petrofacies, while three others were assigned to petrofacies closer to the lower Salt River valley. In total, seven reflected the Inspiration petrofacies while four had other tempers (McDowell Mountains?). If these results survive additional analysis—and much more is needed—they would suggest importation of Salado polychrome into the Phoenix Basin from the Superstition Mountain-Globe areas *and* possible production in the eastern Salt River Valley.

Introduced here is the concept of the "Corona effect." This has to do with fads and bandwagons, both common themes in the ancient Southwest and among Southwestern archaeologists. The Corona effect derives from a Mexican beer that has not been shown to be of superior quality, yet is a beverage of choice. Hundreds of thousands of Corona bottles embossed with "Hecho en Mexico" are distributed across this zone. While unclear, its popularity may be symbolic of exotic places and sunshine. This analogy might apply to the distributions of some Salado polychrome, perhaps not the same symbolism but faddish just the same!

Economics

The Hohokam interaction sphere extended beyond the Sonoran Desert to encompass 73,000 km² (45,000 mi²) from Flagstaff in the north to Mimbres on the east, the international border to the south and Gila Bend on the west. Commerce throughout this region included movement of prestige items, ornaments, and utilitarian products (Doyel 1991c). Ethnography informs us that the Tohono O'odham traded cactus seeds, syrup, and fruit,

agave cakes and fiber, wild gourd, peppers, acorns, sleeping mats, baskets, dried meat, buckskin, pigments, and salt to the Akimel O'odham for corn and wheat (Underhill 1939:103). Similarly active systems probably operated in prehistory (Doyel 1991a, 1993c; Riley 1986).

Exotic minerals found in Hohokam sites (e.g., ocher, copper minerals, limonite, galena, serpentine, soap stone, asbestos, turquoise) came from source areas outside the Phoenix Basin (Doyel 1991c). Argillite was used to produce rings, pendants, beads, nose and lip plugs, overlay, and carved effigy vessels. Source areas include the upper Agua Fria and upper Tonto Basin (Doyel 1991c; Elson and Craig 1992b). Steatite quarries were located northeast of Tonto Basin on sites that contained red-on-buff pottery and shell (Lange 1982). Black Mesa Black-on-white was the most common Late Formative trade ware in the Phoenix Basin (Doyel 1993c), which indicates active trade with the Tusayan-Kayenta region. Trade in obsidian involving numerous source areas increased dramatically in the Classic period (Bayman 1994; Doyel 1996, Mitchell and Shackley 1995).

A zone of active interaction existed between the Verde Valley east to Point of Pines where rare resources were acquired (Doyel 1991c). Trade routes passed through the area to Cibola. Shell bracelets, a stone mirror, and platform mounds were found at Pueblo Bonito (Haury 1976a:321). Turquoise beads from Snaketown may have come from a source near Cerrillos, New Mexico (Nelson 1981:383). The Hohokam and Chaco interaction spheres may have overlapped along the Little Colorado River, which may have facilitated exchange of Hohokam shell and cotton for Cerillos turquoise. Copper bells at Hohokam platform mound sites indicate continued links with northwestern Mexico (Nelson 1981:403). The presence of copper bells in the Gatlin platform (Wasley 1960:259) and in a Chacoan kiva at Bis sa'ani (Breternitz et al. 1982:443), both dating to the early 1100s, suggests a similarity in offertory behavior that is indeed intriguing.

Pottery types common in Tonto Basin and elsewhere between 1100 and 1250 (e.g., McDonald Corrugated, St. Johns Polychrome, Tularosa Black-on-white) are rare in the Phoenix Basin (Doyel 1991c). Did the ascendancy of the Salado impact established interregional trade structures? The Phoenix Basin Hohokam held a monopoly on cotton until the early Classic period. With Tonto Basin as a closer source, and with Phoenix Basin populations undergoing reorganization after 1075, a major trade link was broken. Trade patterns shifted with the development of regional population clusters after 1300 (Little Colorado, San Pedro, Tucson Basin, Safford Valley, etc.) that may have created opportunities for "entrepreneurial expansion" (Wood 1989). The Tonto Basin Salado may have been geographically positioned to exert an important role in interregional trade. This situation changed later in the Classic period, as more trade wares are present at Pueblo Grande after 1275 than in any other phase (Doyel 1993c). These data suggest an increase in long distance trade, perhaps indicating that the trade problem had been resolved (see Adams, Chapter 11).

Few pottery sherds (and no vessels) from northwestern Mexico are present in the Phoenix Basin (Doyel 1993c). It would seem that the Chihuahua polychromes amounted to little more than curiosities. There is little direct evidence of Casas Grandes-Phoenix Basin interaction, although Doolittle (1993) suggests that the Casas Grandes irrigation systems may have emulated those of the Hohokam.

FROM TONTO TO TULA: PROCESS, HISTORY, AND CHANGE

Numerous models account for interregional organizational change in the Classic period. The proposition that organized trading groups (*puchteca*) entered the Southwest (Di Peso 1974a) and effected change among local systems continues to suffer from a lack of unambiguous evidence. World systems theory has limited application because the region was never economically or politically as integrated as the model implies. Peer polity interaction provides a midrange perspective for studying relations among regional populations but provides no clear structure for the study of culture processes (McGuire et al. 1994). But around 1100, it would seem that the Chaco Anasazi and the Hohokam had few peers. For decades the processual school ignored issues of interregional organization and the reality that important changes could not be explained using the preferred closed-system evolutionary approach. More synthetic models are needed that consider historical processes. As Di Peso (1968, 1974a) postulated, economics and competition were important organizing forces in the Southwest. Unlike Di Peso, however, who viewed significant change as a result of external causes, archaeologists should be looking to identify internal dynamics in local economies, ideologies, and organization in the evolution of Southwestern culture.

Interpretation of the Classic period (and Salado) will require better understanding of the historical processes and cultural trajectories of the Late Formative period (800–1100) across the Southwest. This earlier period witnessed increasing organizational complexity, new power relations, settlement hierarchies, integrative mechanisms, and economic networks. Regional populations were on intensification cycles, including the Hohokam, Chaco, Mimbres, and perhaps the societies in northwestern Mexico. The reorganization of these systems between 1075 and 1150 created power vacuums that provided opportunities for new social arrangements. Did any new regional systems or polities emerge to fill this void?. At present, no regional polity has been identified, which leaves the twelfth century without a driving force or power center(s) (Braniff 1986; Doyel 1993b; but see Lekson 1997 for an alternative).

Thinking about "the really big picture" of interaction, cultural dynamics in Postclassic (900–1200) Mesoamerica may ultimately question a completely Southwestern based model for the region. For example, residential compounds at Tula share similarities with those in the southern Southwest (Diehl 1983:Plates 12, 71). In both areas rooms were made of adobe, rubble, and stone, and were organized into walled compounds. Similarity exists between the small, high-necked Gila Red ware jars that proliferate early in the Hohokam Classic period and that of plumbate and polished red wares at Tula (compare Diehl 1983:Plates 14, 38, and 44; with Doyel 1981:Figure 5, and Haury 1945:Figures 57 and 58). Some pottery designs at Tula are similar to the parallel, wavy (water and/or serpent?) patterns on Casa Grande Red-on-buff and contemporary wares (Diehl 1983:48, Plate 36). Combined with the Toltec passion for cotton and turquoise (Diehl 1983:117, 120), these similarities are intriguing. This does not necessarily imply migrations of Toltec from 1,000 miles away (Ferdon 1955; Di Peso 1974a), but future research may reveal a widespread horizon of shared technology and stylistic elements that encompassed northwestern Mexico and the southern Southwest in the thirteenth century.

In Pursuit of Salado

In 1976, two general views of Salado were outlined, termed the "northern" and "southern" models (Doyel and Haury 1976). Neither model was serviceable at the 1995 seminar as the focus was on new fieldwork. "Really big picture" perspectives, such as presented by Di Peso

(1974a), received much less attention. In 1995, two perspectives were discussed, including "Salado Chico" (a geographically restricted regional culture) and "Salado Grande" (a widespread cultural pattern or interaction sphere). Like the 1976 conference, it again became apparent that most data still derive from the opposite ends of the distribution of Salado polychrome and that new data from the vast middle zone to which the appellation "Salado" has been rather uncritically applied remain missing.

Nonetheless, several general observations can be offered. Cultural trajectories in Tonto Basin, the Globe Highlands, and the Safford Basin reflect the influences of geography, ecology, and history. Located at the edge of the Sonoran Desert, geography insured that these people would be exposed to different cultural forces than their neighbors to the north and south. Their ecological niche was unique, situated in the Transition Zone between the lowlands to the south and the plateaus to the north. Preceeding Late Formative occupations to the north and south originated from different traditions, adaptive areas, and backgrounds. The Tonto-Globe Salado were "people in–between," which is reflected in their history (Doyel 1972, 1976b; Hohmann 1992).

Late Formative Hohokam and/or related systems were present in the Tonto, Globe, and Safford areas (Elson et al., eds. 1995; Haury 1932; Mitchell 1996). The presence of ball court communities provides historical depth and suggests occupation on a broad scale by a southern desert tradition. Through trade and interaction these groups introduced new concepts, such as cremation burial and ball courts, to their neighbors (Doyel 1991a). With the reorganization of the Hohokam and Chacoan interaction spheres between 1075 and 1150, these local traditions began to accept other characteristics and perhaps other people. This process accelerated in the early Classic (1100–1200/1250) resulting in the poorly documented Miami/Hardt, Eden, and Santan phases. Lack of knowledge of this critical period undermines attempts to model historical trajectories and limits evaluations of subsequent events, such as migrations, system reorganization, etc.

While on the subject of chronology, I had hoped that the Roosevelt projects would provide new, if indirect, perspectives on dating the development of platforms in the Phoenix Basin. The Classic period in the Sonoran Desert remains poorly dated relative to the north. How do the *ca.* 1280 dates for the inception of platforms in Tonto Basin speak to the Phoenix Basin? Were phases of

platform development correlated between regions, or can lag be identified? Research in the Phoenix Basin (e.g., Pueblo Grande) suggests that compounds may date to the Civano rather than the Soho phase. One certainty, however, is that platforms and the associated ideology had much greater time depth in the Phoenix Basin. Synthesis of the Roosevelt projects data will hopefully address the chronology and cultural sequence within an interregional framework.

After 1250, expressions of power through platform mounds was a short-term experiment in the Tonto-Globe areas (Crary, Neily, Kinkade, and Germick 1994; Elson et al., eds. 1995). Investigations of the Tonto platforms indicate that variation was the rule and that not all communities had similar histories. Current views about the Tonto mound system (i.e., Jacobs and Rice 1997) reflect discussions about the organization of the Chacoan culture insofar as the focus is on regional centers, community structure, ritual landscapes, and shared power (Doyel, ed. 1992; Doyel et al. 1984; Marshall et al. 1982). In the long run, however, neither the Tonto Basin Salado nor Chaco were able to develop the stability necessary for long-term success. Tonto Basin also lacked the safety net of the "Sonoran advantage," which reached its full potential only in the Phoenix Basin (Doyel 1992). It was a boom and bust situation that did not last.

Around 1300, the Phoenix Basin Hohokam received Salado polychrome pottery, but interestingly they did not receive much of the distinctive Salado Red Ware or the corrugated pottery. Aspects of ideology were widely shared, such as niche and bench burials and associated offerings such as painted wands. In the Phoenix Basin, Salado polychrome may have been more closely associated with the late Classic period collapse than with the Civano phase, as this pottery is strongly associated with late Classic components (Abbott 1994). It may have served more as a symbol of a new (post-mound) ideology than it did as a symbol to bolster the old Civano power structure. The shift from preplanned compounds to individual house groups in the late Classic (1375+) argues for the disintegration of the Civano phase organizational system.

Population for the Phoenix Basin has been estimated at 24,000 (Wilcox 1991a:263), 60,000 (Haury 1976a), and between 53,000 to 133,000 (Fish et al., eds. 1992:100). Doelle (1995a) recently down-sized the Phoenix Basin estimate to 15,000 and Tonto Basin to between 3,000 and 5,000. While the latter estimates are too conservative, the relative differences point to the demographic dominance of the Phoenix Basin. It is unlikely that Phoenix Basin populations would welcome several thousand additional people between 1250 and 1350, especially if they were experiencing their own internal challenges (Fink 1991; Gregory 1991; Mitchell 1994). Regardless, the archaeological pattern documented in Tonto Basin cannot account for the Phoenix Basin sequence, and vice-versa.

In the larger view, both Hohokam and Salado were players in something much larger that involved the reorganization of populations across the Southwest and northwestern Mexico. To separate Hohokam from Salado, it will be necessary to decouple the elements: platform mounds, compounds, extended burials, ceramics, especially Salado polychrome, and other attributes associated with the Salado concept (Gladwin 1957; Haury 1945). The historical developments and spatial distributions of these traits must be traced independently. By 1200, numerous populations were sharing technologies and style trends as they had done for hundreds of years, which is why Di Peso (1976b:126) referred to the Salado trait list as "rather contrived." Once the elements are decoupled it will be possible to define a "Salado region" (Salado Chico) for the Tonto Basin, Globe Highlands, and probably the Safford Basin, with the recognition that subregional differences did exist (Plog 1979:109), for example, recognized 11 variants of Western Anasazi. The new definition of Salado must shed the baggage of older concepts that combined a culture area with widespread migrations and interaction spheres. Salado (Chico) should be used like other culture-unit terms (e.g., Hohokam, Sinagua) that focus on time, space, and form (Wood 1992, Chapter 5).

It is counterproductive to identify all fourteenth century manifestations in the southern Southwest as Salado. One alternative, "Southern Pueblo" (Nelson and LeBlanc 1986:13), is not serviceable as such terms imply a unitary ethnic affiliation when variation is apparent. Some sites may represent descendants of the Encinas phase or remnant populations from the Safford Basin, while other sites may represent post-Mimbres occupations. Salado polychrome in the southern Southwest is usually present as an overlay on local wares, indicating that there is no single ceramic assemblage for "Salado Grande" (Franklin 1980:117–27).

The *Gila horizon* is associated with the massive reorganization that occurred in the southern Southwest around 1300. It recognizes a time of widespread interaction but does not apply cultural affiliations to any specific sites or areas. In contrast to the Gila horizon, the term *Gila phase* (1300–1400/1450) should be restricted to Tonto-Globe where the strongest pattern emerged, just as the Civano and Safford phases are used for this time period in the Phoenix and Safford basins, respectively. These phases were all part of the Gila horizon. This approach is similar to that used for the almost equally widespread St. Johns Polychrome ware (Carlson 1970); it suggests a brief temporal and spatial horizon of widespread interaction, yet a "St. Johns culture" has not been suggested. The "Salado interaction sphere" (and/or the Salado alliance?, Crown 1994) would focus on the socioeconomic and political dynamics of the Gila horizon.

What happened to the people collectively known as Salado after 1450? Where did they go? After their travels to the south along the mountainous zone of the Arizona-New Mexico border, some went to Zuni where they buried their cremated dead in Gila Polychrome vessels (Smith et al. 1966). Others probably regrouped as composite tribes prior to and early in the Protohistoric period. This latter process would account for the presence of highly specific traits considered "puebloan" among historic O'odham (Di Peso 1958; Hayden 1987; Teague 1993). Since some groups called Salado did not make the *sine-qua-non* of Saladoness—Salado polychrome pottery—they will be harder to track. Many unanswered questions will provide intellectual and practical challenges for the next generation of archaeologists interested in pursuing the mystery of Salado.

Acknowledgments

My appreciation goes to Jeffrey Dean for his patience and leadership and for editing this unwieldy volume, and to Tom Lincoln of the Bureau of Reclamation and Anne Woosley of the Amerind Foundation for inviting me to participate in the seminar. Thanks also to my colleagues for the stimulating conversation and enjoyable experience. This paper is dedicated to my compadre J. Charles Kelley.

CHAPTER FOURTEEN

Social Dynamics in the Tonto Basin

Charles L. Redman

Acommentary on a volume such as this can take many forms. These chapters are excellent and have been very informative for me. The discussion that follows is stimulated by the papers, but does not attempt to critique or supplement any of them. Rather, I seek to put this endeavor in the broader perspective of its potential lasting contribution to our discipline. All too often, scientists produce well reasoned important works that receive only limited distribution and fail to have the impact that they deserve. In being concerned about impact, one must first consider the audience one is oriented toward and then the nature of contributions that audience would appreciate. There is no question that everything we say will be of great interest to immediate colleagues who are specialists concerned with related sets of data because our data may provide supplementary or comparative case studies. The chapters in this volume reflect enormous, creative research in a very important region of the American Southwest. A second, overlapping, set of specialists are those concerned with the ideas generated from those data because they may prove to be useful in reinterpreting the cultures they investigate. For these readers, my comments are hardly necessary, since they already have a firm grasp of the kinds of things we have done and why they are important.

There is also the potential for this book to be appreciated by a broader audience of readers, especially those who are interested in archaeological project reports and the reconstruction of regional prehistories. Members of this audience are eclectic, ranging from the educated public to colleagues who conduct their own research in other parts of the world, but retain an interest in the bigger picture. These are the readers that I am anxious to reach with my comments. In fact, it is a subset of these—authors of general syntheses, textbooks, and theoretical treatises—that I am most anxious to stimulate into further consideration of the contributions of this volume. The work in the Roosevelt Lake basin during the past ten years has been of an intensity and creativity that should be a significant part of the rewriting of archaeology and prehistory.

Beyond this professional readership, I do believe that we have an obligation to write for the public and there is much in this volume that would be of interest to the general public. Questions that I think are of special interest to the public:

1. To have a name for these people.
2. What is special about these people, e.g., technological ingenuity, ceremonialism, unique settlements.
3. What happened to these people? This could either end with their abandonment of the area as most Park Service visitor center texts do, or it could suggest who their descendants became.

With these objectives and audiences in mind, I want to review some of the stimulating issues that have been brought up here. We should consider each, and whether it will lead somewhere, and what still needs to be done.

For these ideas to be effectively communicated to the public, we would have to reach a consensus on what we think and it would have to have understandable referents. My opinion is that we do not waste energy on this approach for this volume. Yet, I believe for the larger project, it would be irresponsible if we did not service this audience.

For the scholarly audience, we must document what we found in a way that can be used in the future for re-analysis and comparative interpretations. I believe the lengthy research reports suitably cover this approach. By the way, I think site maps with features identified are our greatest contribution. I also think that we should put extra energy into being sure we have worked out the chronology as well as we can. Right now all of this is clearest in our minds, and later scholars will not be able to do as good a job as we can.

Another point I want to make clear is that, for the long-term significance of our projects, I believe the clear and concise representation of our data in chronologically meaningful units is our greatest contribution. I expect that our graphs, analyses, and interpretations will have a much shorter period of interest. However, it is on the basis of our analyses that the "value and impact" of our projects will be judged. Although I feel most of our analyses will be overturned or soon forgotten, it is in them that the success of the project will be measured. Hence, the most important audience for this book and for our projects are those interested in our ideas. Text book authors will be interested in our maps and in the best, that is, most lasting of our ideas. The rest of what I say, then, is to suggest some directions for identifying ideas that might have lasting significance!

SEVEN DOMAINS OF INQUIRY REFLECTED IN THE PREVIOUS CHAPTERS

The Salado Concept

I would love to see us agree that the term Salado represents something real in the past, especially if it were specific people or a specific belief system. However, if what we are going to do is like what has been done before—debate it and come up with the conclusion that it may represent many different things—then let's dispatch and move on!

Population Estimation

This is a fundamental calculation for many analyses that follow, and hence, it must be done, but I believe it is one of the areas where it is difficult to escape ambiguous conclusions. I have seen archaeologists swing between wanting to have more or fewer people in their regions. I grew up in an era of bigger is better, but now it seems at least for the Southwest, that fewer is better. As Carla van West has said, several lines of evidence seem to converge, and should give us all confidence, but each of these approaches does have a variety of inputs that can be manipulated. Yet, these are the data of the past and we must work with them, and they do offer their own special potential.

However, at some point I think the absolute numbers we come up with will be forgotten, overturned, and, like Bill Doelle, I would rather deal with the pattern of growth and decline. An interesting article by three demographers (Whitmore et al. 1990) summarizes archaeological and historical data from four major regions of the world. They believe that the pattern of population change in each region can be best conceptualized as "millennial long waves of change" where each successive cycle is shorter than the one before, but has a greater amplitude.

I should admit that I am seriously disappointed by the low population estimates proposed in this book. However, I am the first to tell you that the material residues at even the large sites in the Tonto Basin are not very abundant and may in themselves confirm the absence of dense aggregations of people. My disappointment comes from the fact that I consider one of the prime drivers of social complexity to be as a means of adjusting to increasingly large aggregates of people. Another unanticipated implication of lower estimates of prehistoric populations in the Southwest, and New World in general, is our understanding of the impact of the Spanish contact. Current estimates put a precontact hemispherical population at 54 million (Denevan 1992). He then suggests that by a century after contact that number has fallen by anywhere from 75 to 90 percent, depending on the region. If the current trend toward low population estimates hold true, then I expect the precontact numbers to fall by a factor of between two and four. This would imply that the population decline following European contact was far less than previously claimed, albeit still significant.

Significance of Irrigation

Just like the case for population estimates, I think we need to have a better understanding of the significance of irrigation before we can go further with other ideas. There have been suggestions that the Salado had more than one kind of water control mechanism, and I am happy for that, but the central issue is canals—how large they were, what it took to keep them operating, and how important they were in promoting an integration of society. I also want to know more about their role in the everyday life of the people. Some overall modeling would be useful, especially if it incorporated guiding concepts such as managing food resources in a scarce environment, risk minimization, conservatism in the face of change, etc. My understanding based on the ideas put forth in the preceding chapters is that Tonto Basin was attractive to immigrants from neighboring regions because of the potential of its canal irrigation, perhaps not as the primary means of production, but as a key to an acceptable minimax alternative.

I think the really promising area to consider is a thorough explication of the irrigation district concept brought up by Wood and others. Although we are not certain of the topography below lake level, we can do a good job of predicting major constraints on canals and relating specific settlements to them. We have a unique database with complete coverage of major areas, and we must play it out. I also would look to these districts as major units within any pattern of social dynamics. It would be nice if they each held about enough people for a stable breeding population (c. 500) and could be endogamous; or, if not, what were the nature of exogamous linkages.

Specialization of Production, Concentration of Storage, and Mechanisms of Redistribution

This is a major set of interpretive domains that I have always felt had great potential, but received little attention of their own. In the chapters here, they were largely discussed "in the service" of social organizational issues. These subjects have figured large in our previous thinking, and other archaeologists working in the region expect us to make some major statements about them. As for specialization, we do have goods that require special skills and exotic materials to produce. However, my own reaction is that full-time specialists did not exist in Tonto Basin and producing these special goods may have been one of the means of achieving favored status (life near or on the platform mound). The working of certain materials (or knowledge of it) may have been restricted to people of elevated statuses; however, our archaeological evidence indicates that these same people also conducted the full range of domestic pursuits, casting some doubt on their characterization as "specialists." The point here is that I see production of specialized goods, and concentration of storage as possibly being important mechanisms for reaffirming extant status but probably not as the original source of differentiation.

Role of Climate and/or the Environment

The characteristics of the environment and changing climate have always had strong interpretive appeal to Southwestern archaeologists. I, like others, am seduced by the precision of the runoff charts derived from tree-ring data (Nails et al. 1989). Information like this may hold the answer to numerous specific events of the past, but I want to keep it in perspective. I fear that climatic determinism lurks nearby. It is not enough to say that these forces would only act when enough people were present—that is still quite deterministic. The amazing thing about society is what people have done with a given environment and how they have reacted in the face of a changing climate. What we need to know is how people react and create new adjustments given the resources at their command. We, as a species, are extraordinarily inventive and opportunistic! This has been especially true in the Southwest. Ingenious is not sufficient to describe the Salado, we must add resilient, flexible, and enduring. I am a bit lost by hearing that low rainfall is good and high rainfall is bad in the Southwest! What proportion of their food came from fields fed by canals versus all of the other sources of food that would benefit from excess rainfall (is there such a thing)? Perhaps canals were only there to cover shortfalls in particularly low precipitation years. How did people deal with these issues?

Scott Wood briefly brought up something that interests me a great deal, but has not been examined in these chapters. It has to do with potential human impacts on the environment. If I had my choice, I would recommend that the whole volume focus on it, but I know better. It was mentioned for the uplands, and I am sure it was relevant in a broader context as well, but so far the analyses and interpretation done on material from Tonto

Basin have not emphasized this perspective; hence, a synthetic volume would have trouble pursuing this.

Of the possible domains of inquiry that I suggest above, environment and climate change is the first that I think could be a winner, but only if it is treated in a sufficiently broad context. I fear the general audience, in particular, would be very receptive to definitive climatic or environmental explanations, but I worry about being the one to put them forward.

This brings me to the last two domains of inquiry, that are quite general, but I believe hold the greatest potential for making a lasting contribution (or at least a contribution that is widely recognized even if it fades quickly).

Theory of Migration

I am increasingly convinced of the relative mobility of prehistoric peoples of the Southwest. I accept that in certain locations sedentism may have lasted a long time, but perhaps even in those locations the people were more mobile than generally thought. In Tonto Basin, there appears to be some real coming and going as well as shifting about. There are some methodologically important questions like site duration that we need to deal with for other interpretations that would also inform on questions of mobility.

But this also brings up a series of interesting interpretive questions for me. When do small scale, short-term movements of people become migrations? I am reasonably certain that some people from Payson came down into Tonto Basin on a regular basis and perhaps vice versa. I also expect that by 1300 virtually all the people from that area had moved down or elsewhere, but when was the migration? Or, was it even a migration or just movements within a regional settlement system? Another key question is what migrates? Is it people, families, villages, societies, ideas, materials, or food? We can begin to address these questions with the material remains, but we should be ready for more than one answer. Another fascinating line of inquiry would be to model details of how "migrants" were received and acculturated in the new region and society. Elson suggested that we could productively think of them as buffers, while Lekson thought that the situations between migrants and recipient societies were "negotiated." If we could talk about and document what makes people move, what makes it a migration versus a settlement rotation, and how people are acculturated we would be onto something really important!

Getting back to questions on a more general level, where do ethnic groups fit in? One might wonder whether there were ethnic groups in prehistory at all? Are they only a development of industrialized or state-level societies. Our goal should be to present some fundamentally interesting ideas and at the same time use them to clear up long-standing puzzles in the archaeological record.

Social Dynamics

This is the central interpretive issue that overlaps with most of the other subjects described above. It is the big question, and I think it can bring together most of the chapters of this book. Several of the chapters indicate that the Salado of Tonto Basin developed an "irrigation society," suggesting that the landscape played a particularly important role in social organization. In a society that relies on irrigation is it the configuration of land between tributaries of the river that binds people together in social and political units? It clearly is a factor, but I am skeptical that it is the entire story. If not, what is the primary mechanism of ordering individuals and households?

Having emphasized the role of productive strategies and the possible role of an ideology of legitimization already, it is now necessary to entertain other key processes such as competition, cooperation, and acculturation. These too, have to be central to any explanation of social dynamics. This brings us to what is probably the pivotal point of my commentary, and that is that social dynamics touch virtually every aspect of society and require that we look at it from many lines of evidence. Although I do not yet know whether they have answered all of the questions, Rice and Simon's efforts at an integrated conceptual approach are on the right track. I am fascinated by any attempt that looks at the social enterprise as a coherent system and examines so many material correlates, and I welcome other attempts, as well.

The key for this (and I believe for migration as well) is that we are dealing with domains that affect all aspects of society and must be examined in the light of veritably every category of evidence we have. I am a strong believer that we must look at our problems in a regional context because some processes may only become clear at that scale. Given the incredible intensity with which we all have examined Tonto Basin, I believe that our unique contribution of our projects will derive from an analysis of intrabasin dynamics.

Contextualism and the Conjunctive Approach

This brings me to what I think may be our greatest challenge. The scale and intensity of the combined Roosevelt Projects presents us with the opportunity to use the most diverse set of information to confront issues that clearly had something to do with each other. This is a relatively small place with a relatively short duration of substantial settlement. Virtually all the sites are relevant. We must bring the diverse lines of information reflected in the chapters in this book to bear on one or two key issues of interest to all of us and to the profession. This mixture of a rich descriptive reconstruction of the culture history of Tonto Basin's Salado culture with the scientific application of diverse lines of evidence to illuminate underlying principles of social dynamics might be characterized as a marriage of Taylor's (1948) conjunctive approach and British contextualism. How well can this be done? Have we accomplished it? This volume is an initial test of that proposition and takes us quite far down that path.

CHAPTER FIFTEEN

Salado at the End of the Twentieth Century

Ben A. Nelson

Southwestern archaeologists have spent significant energy during this century deliberating about Salado, and while much of the debate has been merely definitional, the persistence of concern suggests the existence of important issues. Does the term denote a people, a migration, an invasion, a culture, a polity, a cult, an ideology, a style? Is the term Salado of any utility? Data relevant to these questions, as well as more sophisticated ones, are at hand as a result of the intensive work that many of the contributors to this volume have recently conducted in Tonto Basin, once thought to be the "heartland" of the Salado. I summarize the findings of each paper only insofar as necessary to respond to the authors' contentions, while attempting to concentrate on the advances that the papers collectively represent.

The Gladwins, and many others who have used the term Salado, invoked the concept in an attempt to explain changes that they saw in a particular area ca. 1300, in their case the Phoenix Basin. They sought to account for ceramic and mortuary styles that appeared foreign to the region; seeing stylistic relationships to similar phenomena elsewhere, they inferred migration, in accordance with early twentieth century archaeological practice. Some scholars held to that explanation through the middle third of the century and applied it to other regions, but those who came of age a little later found fault with it, not only because prevailing theory told us to look for other causes, but because we could demonstrate empirically that some Salado traits appeared before the supposed arrival of the Salado people.

Several authors in this volume take positions on the notion of Salado, identifying themselves as believers or nonbelievers; the detractors seem to be under the impression that those of us who have used the term take it to represent some sort of ethnic, linguistic, or political entity. I have not spoken to anyone for at least twenty years who thought that such was the case, and it seems significant that the term is now completely rejected in the Phoenix Basin, where it was originally associated with that meaning. But why does the term survive in the zone along the base of the Mogollon Rim, and out into the Basin-and-Range Province associated with the Chihuahuan desert? Apparently it has some utility there. I suggest that many archaeologists find the term useful because they feel a need to connote something that happened in their study area, and that seems to be paralleled in others. That generalized phenomenon seems to consist of community change in association with the arrival of Salado polychrome pottery.

Tonto Basin is one of a dozen or more places in southeastern Arizona, southwestern New Mexico, and northwestern Chihuahua that were occupied during the thirteenth and fourteenth centuries by concentrations of Salado candidates, i.e., people using Salado polychromes and often some form of compound architecture, and in some places other features, e.g., platform mounds. It is now clear that each of those places has its own dynamic of development, with an identity expressed in local styles, and that the unity of Gila Polychrome, while real, is a relatively small part of the material culture picture in each place. In few of those places do we have the fine-grained data on occupational history that would allow full assessment of the onset of the local Salado pattern, if that is what we wish to call it; Tonto Basin is by far the richest case study in terms of documenting changing material culture and community development processes.

COMMENTS ON CHAPTERS

Adams (Chapter 11) suggests that ritual became so important as a basis for social integration during the fourteenth century that places were selected for occupation because of their suitability for ritually related production. As evidence for increased ritual activity, he cites the water and fertility symbols of the Southwestern Cult, noted by Crown (1994), as well as the Katsina Cult symbolism brought out in his own work (Adams 1991). Because Tonto Basin is a particularly good place to grow cotton, as evidenced by the high ubiquity of cotton seeds and other plant parts in flotation samples, Adams proposes that the Basin may have been colonized by Plateau peoples or others who produced cotton for ritual use. This is an intriguing proposition, in that it suggests that people settled regions for what amount to ideological reasons. I am a little uncomfortable with the idea that archaeologists can reliably measure the importance of ritual as an integrative mechanism. My discomfort stems partly from a general sense that ritual was probably important throughout Southwestern prehistory, and could manifest itself (or not) in so many different ways. Apart from that, there is evidence of Salado peoples moving into and out of other valleys where cotton production may not have been so feasible; mobility seems to be one of the general characteristics of occupations during the Salado period.

Doelle (Chapter 4) provides a much-needed characterization of the demographic context of the Tonto Basin occupation, tracking changes in local populations in numerous areas throughout southern and central Arizona. One can always ask for more or quibble at length with the assumptions and measurement strategies, but it seems that the most serious problem is how to control for area-to-area variation in the proportion of population residing in large vs. small sites. Nevertheless, working with data that exist seems far preferable to ignoring demographic questions. Doelle shows that the occupation of Tonto Basin is part of the general Colonial period expansion of the Hohokam pattern, and asks how the Phoenix Basin was able to export population at this time. He notes that the Tonto Basin occupation is relatively small relative to those of some of the other areas populated by the Hohokam. Looking at the numbers closely, the number of migrants involved—as opposed to total occupants—seems small indeed; it is truly amazing that one can talk seriously and plausibly about demographic processes with such good resolution.

Doyel's "pursuit" of the Salado throughout the Sonoran and Upper Chihuahuan Deserts (Chapter 13) provides a summary of all of the candidates for Saladohood, and generates a table that summarizes certain patterns on a grand scale. The main accomplishment of this paper, in my mind, is to confirm that any search for a Salado people, per se, is bound to turn up empty-handed, for reasons noted above. I am still not sure, by the end of the paper, who the Salado were, or who Doyel thinks they were. Doyel enumerates several Mesoamerican derived traits that are found in Hohokam sites, and suggests that "this cultural elaboration suggests the emergence of positions of power and authority"; elsewhere he notes that many of those traits appeared prior to the Salado time level. References to Mesoamerican derived elements are always interesting, but the Salado phenomenon is not consistently associated with anything Mesoamerican. In fact, one of the interesting properties of the group of occupations that Doyel summarizes is that, while all share Salado polychromes, their use of potentially Mesoamerican derived elements, such as platform mounds and copper bells, appears highly variable. Doyel rightly points out that such patterns may imply the presence of competing ideologies within what archaeologists perceive as single traditions. I must note that, having excavated Mesoamerican sites with temples, the platform mounds of the Hohokam or Salado appear to me to be remarkably un-Mesoamerican. The same is true of ball courts of course, and yet as Wilcox (1986) infers, that does not mean that the *idea* of ball courts was not derived from Mesoamerica.

Elson, Stark, and Gregory (Chapter 7) discuss evidence for changing cultural affiliation and migration in Tonto

Basin. This is one of the papers that demonstrates the dramatic growth of knowledge about Tonto Basin in particular and the Salado phenomenon in general. They make a case for migration into Tonto Basin, first by Hohokam peoples ca. 700–800, and later by Puebloan groups, ca. 1250. The evidence—primarily ceramic and architectural in both cases, but strongly reinforced by other differences—is compelling. Two especially significant features of their modeling of the later migration process have broad applicability in the Southwest and perhaps elsewhere. First, the pathways for migration were foreshadowed by ceramic exchange; before the Puebloan migrants arrived, the ceramic exchange connections of Tonto Basin shifted from the Hohokam to the Cibola region. People apparently acted upon connections that had been expressed and maintained through exchange. This finding is similar to that of Hegmon et al. (1998) in the Mimbres area, where ceramic interaction patterns change markedly following the Classic Mimbres "collapse." Second, in Tonto Basin, the migrants settled into the peripheries of existing communities. Considering the implications of these phenomena for social and political organization, Elson et al. find it difficult to accept any of the models that have been proposed, which include egalitarian, managerial, and redistributive formulations. Rather, they seem to suggest, Tonto Basin had a more subtle kind of complexity, incorporating aspects of egalitarianism and inequality. They reject the notion that Salado was a local culture, and view it instead as a regional horizon, linking common processes that are variably manifested.

Lekson's paper (Chapter 12) covers both more and less ground than the title implies. The "data" discussed in this paper exceed considerably the actual information that archaeologists command, while dismissing things that we do know, and the conclusions go yet further. However, like many another Lekson paper, this one raises some interesting questions. The paper begins by looking at the various occupations in the northern Chihuahuan Desert, which includes parts of southwestern New Mexico and southeastern Arizona. Commenting adequately on this part of the paper would require a detailed discussion, most of which fortunately has already been written (Nelson and Anyon 1996). Lekson is quite correct in asserting that a Mimbres through Salado continuity can be found in the northern Chihuahuan Desert—though it is by realizing that the discontinuities are illusions created by shifting populations within the Mimbres Mogollon

region, as well as looking outside to places like the Jornada area, that such continuity is best observed.

Lekson further argues that there is "no one home" in Chihuahua in the 1200s, a conclusion that can be reached only by conflating the Black Mountain and Animas phases, where evidence is available, and applying that misconstrual to Chihuahua, where archaeological coverage is much thinner. This suggestion ignores: 1) Chihuahuan pottery in association with Mimbres pottery in the Mimbres Valley and the Black Range; 2) Chihuahuan pottery with Reserve wares and without Mimbres Black-on-white or Gila Polychrome in the Mimbres Valley and the Cliff area; 3) later, Chihuahuan pottery with Salado polychromes and without Mimbres and Reserve; 4) associated patterning in the varieties of Playas textured, Reserve corrugated, and obliterated-corrugated wares. As the terms "short-term sedentism" (Nelson and LeBlanc 1986) and "fallow valleys" (Nelson and Anyon 1996) are intended to imply, these sequential associations, with the whole sequence not present in any one place, imply regional population continuity coupled with relatively frequent shifts of local populations from valley to valley. As suggested by Douglas (1995:244), "'phase contemporaneity' may obscure a complex pattern of sequential use and abandonment within the Animas phase time span." There is no thirteenth century gap in the U.S. part of the northern Chihuahuan Desert, and no reason to assume one to the south.

Perhaps the most significant issue discussed in Lekson's paper is the possibility, raised previously by a number of scholars, that Paquimé and Casa Grande were poles of a single sphere. This idea makes sense given what we now know about chronology, though the commonalities of massive adobe architecture and Salado polychromes seem thin threads upon which to hang a political connection, as Lekson implies when suggesting that Casa Grande was an "outlier" to Paquimé. Casa Grande certainly is not a structural replica of Paquimé in the way that Chacoan outliers are replicas of Chaco Canyon great houses; rather, it is overwhelmingly Hohokam in structure except for the massiveness of the one building. Yet, formal recognition of a "Casa-Casas corridor," may be important in terms of documenting the breakup, ca. 1300, of patterns known up to that point as Anasazi, Mogollon, and Hohokam. More comparative work needs to be done, and it should encompass areas within a 250 km radius of Paquimé in all directions as well as the Paquimé-Casa Grande line. I am not sure how addition of another term, as opposed to simply calling this sphere Salado, adds clarity, but if that makes the idea more palatable to people, so be it.

Lincoln (Chapter 1) traces the history of the Salado concept, pointing out among other things that it was Schmidt rather than the Gladwins who first gave us the concept of Salado. I confess guilt in this error of attribution. Lincoln shows how the changing conceptions of Salado are linked with wider paradigm shifts in archaeology, and he insists that the older work remains valuable, grounded as it is in nearly the same set of facts that we ourselves are attempting to explain. Yet, the shifting paradigms add dimensions to the explanation, as we are currently seeing with the emphasis on ideology. Southwestern archaeologists owe a debt to Lincoln for his role in constructing a request for proposal for the massive Lake Roosevelt project. The specifications for the project accommodated a range of theoretical positions and encouraged scholars to place priority on problem orientation.

Lindauer's paper (Chapter 9) is another testimony to the advances in knowledge of Salado archaeology that have resulted from the Roosevelt Archaeological Project. Taking the Schoolhouse Point sequence as a case study, he traces changes in configurations of Tonto Basin settlements through time. The temporal control in this discussion, as well as the precision with which different kinds of features, structures, and their distributions can be characterized, are truly remarkable. Reading this discussion, one gets the feeling of a community in constant motion. Using models of Hohokam community, Lindauer describes the transition from dispersed village to irrigation community to large aggregated village. Suggestions are made as to how platform mounds and other special features, such as oval rooms and granaries, indicate increasing utilization of integrative facilities within this dynamic context. The fact that the settlement pattern remains dispersed until near the abandonment, at which time a rather sudden nucleation occurs, may reveal something about social tensions within the region as a whole.

Ravesloot and Regan (Chapter 3) summarize the bioarchaeological evidence from the recently excavated Tonto Basin sites, evaluating a number of propositions about the health, mortuary practices, and genetic relationships of the occupants. Based on pathologies, they characterize the health status of the population as good relative to other Southwestern populations, and are unable to find evidence for differential health according to

social status. The unusual crypts in which some residents are buried might be considered elite facilities, given the relative rarity of this type of treatment within Tonto Basin. However, Ravesloot and Regan reject that interpretation because people of all ages and sexes are represented and there is evidence of biological affiliation among the occupants of single tombs. These valuable observations notwithstanding, I wonder if it could not be the case that higher-status lineages, as opposed to individuals, would be thus treated. The authors refer to Turner's studies of biological affinity to make the point that Tonto Basin populations appear to be of mixed origin. For Ravesloot and Regan, this patterning raises questions about the biological reality of Salado; however, if we take mobility and accommodation of immigrants to be hallmarks of the Salado pattern, biological mixing would be a logical consequence.

Rice (Chapter 6) systematically evaluates models of complexity that emphasize the political-economic roles of elites as managers and manipulators of economic commodities. He searches for evidence of concentrations of rare resources, such as shell, obsidian, and pigments at platform mounds, looking for patterns consistent with either control of exchange or production. He also looks for evidence of redistributive exchange of surplus products and for indications that irrigation control was a basis of social power. Without enumerating the whole series of tests that Rice conducts, I wish to say that the bridging arguments are very well crafted. While some of the tests do show unusual frequencies of items in association with the platform mounds, contextual and scalar considerations lead Rice to conclude that such anomalies are more indicative of control of ritual than of the economy. He then turns to a model of social organization that decouples political leadership from economic power, i.e., the African model of segmentary organization. Rice finds the replication of facilities connected with power to be especially telling of the poor fit of unitary-hierarchy models to the Tonto Basin context, and is also impressed with the "massing" of numerous social units without any clear evidence of centralization. These characteristics, and others that he discusses, accord well with aspects of the segmentary-organization model. This chapter is a valuable contribution, not only to the description of Tonto Basin patterning, but to archaeologists' efforts to understand Southwestern patterns that seem to include large scale aggregates with minimal hierarchy.

Simon and Jacobs (Chapter 8) discuss the kinds of social networks that are likely to have existed among the

Salado and the roles that material goods may have played maintaining those networks. As is the case with several other papers, much attention is focused on immigration. The ceramics provide telling evidence of interaction patterns; one of their particularly interesting insights concerns the association of local pottery with highest-status individuals in the crypt burials, which implies that control of exchange was not, in the case of ceramics, a basis of power. Another interesting argument concerns the relationship between interlocking, asymmetric elements of ceramic decoration and similar patterns in the L-shaped rooms that are repeated in platform mound architecture. Simon and Jacobs argue that the appearance of these parallel stylistic asymmetries late in the prehistoric sequence is tied to the onset of asymmetric or unequal social relations. While this argument seems somewhat far fetched, it is worthy of further exploration.

Whittlesey, Ciolek-Torrello, and Reid (Chapter 10) offer a Mountain Mogollon perspective, opening with the statement that most modeling of organization and change in Tonto Basin has been colored by a Hohokam orientation. In their view, that orientation has blinded researchers to the processes of migration and ethnic coresidence and caused them to search for kinds of complexity that are not germane to the region. The authors see the mountain region as one where migration, joint use of lands, and ethnic coresidence were long-established practices, and Tonto Basin as one of a number of areas that had specific subsistence-related advantages. As a result, a variety of peoples were drawn to Tonto Basin, and the sequence of developments there paralleled that of other mountain locales such as Grasshopper, but differed from them in ways relatable to the particular mix of ecological characteristics of Tonto Basin. The land-use strategies of selected Southwestern populations provide productive analogies for the various contrasting adaptations. For example, they argue that the viability of irrigation encourages centralized integrative strategies, as in the Eastern Pueblos, because the focus is on water control, while in areas that cannot be irrigated, crosscutting sodalities are more likely, as in the Western Pueblos. Hence the absence of kiva facilities in Tonto Basin. These are intriguing arguments that definitely add depth and color to the interpretation of the record. However, it does not seem necessary or accurate to paint the scholars working in Tonto Basin as untutored provincials.

Van West, Ciolek-Torrello, Welch, Altschul, Adams, Shelley, and Homburg (Chapter 2) provide an elegant characterization of the biotic resources, climatic conditions, and human subsistence strategies of Tonto Basin. They consider that the environment of 900–1300 was not drastically different from that of today, though its occupants experienced some pronounced fluctuations of conditions. Since the majority of the reconstruction in this chapter is both highly plausible to me and outside my areas of expertise, I do not comment on it in detail. Van West et al. are the only authors in the group to tackle the question of what happened to the populations that departed Tonto Basin. Since we cannot identify their destination, the question is difficult to address; however, the authors suggest that many of the inhabitants may have elected to return to their Plateau homelands after failing to become fully integrated into the mixed Mogollon-Hohokam culture. While interesting, this notion would not seem to account for a very large percentage of the population, since those who can be clearly discerned as immigrants constitute only a few room blocks. One suspects that the dispersal of people from Tonto Basin took families and lineages in a variety of directions.

Wood (Chapter 5) provides an extremely useful overview of geographic variability and settlement history, ranging well beyond the Roosevelt Archaeological Project limits. He first concentrates on Tonto Basin itself, providing a classification of the landscape from a human use perspective, discussing variants of settlement form and then their distributions across the geographic categories and through time. Wood emphasizes that human occupation of the Uplands does not occur throughout the period that the Lowlands are occupied, and he considers the use of the Uplands to be one of the keys to understanding Tonto Basin prehistory, even suggesting that platform mounds may be integrative devices to help cope with the "landless labor" that flows back into Tonto Basin when the uplands occupation ends. To contextualize the Tonto Basin patterns, he also sketches the settlement histories of several surrounding localities, including the Lower Verde, Payson, Globe, Sierra Ancha, Q Ranch-Vosberg, and Cherry Creek. These sketches allow characterization of the distributional limits of features such as ball courts and ceramic styles such as Salado Red, while also revealing some of the nearby places from which migrants to Tonto Basin might have originated.

Wood is skeptical about the notion that Puebloan— which he seems to equate with Plateau or Anasazi— peoples were responsible for the influx of population into Tonto Basin, and in fact eschews the term *pueblo* in reference to the late room block style of architecture that represents the final stages of occupation. The term *caseron*, which he prefers instead, does not add much clarity, and is easily confused with great house in the mind of the Spanish-speaking reader. The more important issue, however, is what this last preabandonment transformation of architecture might represent in terms of the cultural identity of arriving populations. Wood makes the telling point that none of the excavated sites in Tonto Basin contain obvious Anasazi characteristics such as mealing bins or kivas, features that are seen in intrusive Anasazi sites of the Point of Pines and Safford areas.

CONCLUSION

The decades leading up to and following 1300 were clearly dynamic times in the southern Southwest. The authors of this volume, whether they look in depth at the occupational history of a particular valley, or scan a wider horizon, provide evidence of mixing and change, of blurring and blending of traditions, and of the movement of peoples. The Gladwins and Haury inferred that migration was an important process during this period, but the migration that we perceive is not the kind that they envisioned, which involved wholesale movements of peoples. The Salado were not a people. The migrants have no clear source, perhaps because they come from multiple sources, following lines of kinship and alliance that had been established on lineage, rather than ethnic, levels. There was not one migration. A shared ideology, expressed in the carefully replicated symbolism of Gila Polychrome and no doubt in other media, probably permitted the detachment of social segments from troubled communities and their reattachment elsewhere. Local experiments in sociopolitical complexity—i.e., the scale, hierarchy, and nature of integrative mechanisms—are also evident. There was no one form of Salado social organization.

The majority of the authors seem to be more or less comfortable using Salado to refer to the remains reflecting these phenomena and not overly concerned about the taxonomic status or precise definition of the term. Salado is a fuzzy set, an initial classificatory handle; Salado horizon seems fittingly noncommittal. Its apparent slipperiness derives in part from the actual disintegration of historical patterns that preceded the centuries in which the Salado lived and in part from the variable strategies and identities of Salado actors. As the contributors to this volume demonstrate, understanding the changes will require application of systemic, ideational, and actor-based perspectives and far more field data than we now possess. This volume demonstrates that real progress can be made.

Bibliography

Abbott, David R.

1994   *Hohokam Social Structure and Irrigation
       Management: The Ceramic Evidence from the
       Central Phoenix Basin.* Ph.D. dissertation,
       Department of Anthropology, Arizona State
       University, Tempe.

1995   Recognizing the Limitations of a Settlement-
       Pattern Approach for Building Models of
       Social Organization. Paper presented at the
       60th Annual Meeting of the Society for
       American Archaeology, Minneapolis.

Abbott, David R. (editor)

1994   *Pueblo Grande Project,* Vol. 3: *Ceramics and
       the Production and Exchange of Pottery in the
       Central Phoenix Basin.* Soil Systems Publica-
       tions in Archaeology No. 20. Phoenix.

Abbott, David R., and David M. Schaller

1992   Exploring the Production and Social Signifi-
       cance of Salado Polychrome at Central Phoe-
       nix Basin Hohokam Sites. In *Proceedings of the
       Second Salado Conference Globe, AZ 1992,*
       edited by Richard C. Lange and Stephen Ger-
       mick, pp. 248–57. Arizona Archaeological
       Society Occasional Paper. Phoenix.

Ackerly, Neal W.

1989   Paleohydrodynamic Impacts on Hohokam
       Irrigation Systems. In *Prehistoric Agricultural
       Activities on the Lehi-Mesa Terrace: Perspec-
       tives on Hohokam Irrigation Cycles,* edited by
       Neal W. Ackerly and T. Kathleen Henderson,
       pp. 46–83. Northland Research, Inc., Flagstaff.

Acsadi, Gyorgy, and Janos Nemeskeri

1970   *History of Human Life Span and Mortality.*
       Akademiai Kiado, Budapest.

Adams, E. Charles

1989   Homol'ovi III: A Pueblo Hamlet in the
       Middle Little Colorado River Valley. *Kiva*
       54:217–30.

1991   *The Origin and Development of the Pueblo
       Katsina Cult.* The University of Arizona
       Press, Tucson.

1996   Understanding Aggregation in the Ho-
       mol'ovi Pueblos: Scalar Stress and Social
       Power. In *River of Change: Prehistory of the
       Middle Little Colorado River Valley, Arizona,*
       edited by E. Charles Adams, pp. 1–14. Ari-
       zona State Museum Archaeological Series
       No. 185. The University of Arizona, Tucson.

Adams, E. Charles, Miriam T. Stark, and
Deborah S. Dosh

1993   Ceramic Distribution and Exchange: Jeddito
       Yellow Ware and Implications for Social Com-
       plexity. *Journal of Field Archaeology* 20:3–21.

Adams, Karen R.

1994a Synthesis of Archaeobotanical and Ecologi-
       cal Data. In *The Roosevelt Rural Sites Study,*

Vol. 3: *Changing Land Use in the Tonto Basin,* edited by Richard Ciolek-Torrello and John R. Welch, pp. 297–309. Statistical Research Technical Series No. 28. Tucson.

1994b   Macrobotanical Analyses. In *The Roosevelt Rural Sites Study,* Vol. 3: *Changing Land Use in the Tonto Basin,* edited by Richard Ciolek-Torrello and John R. Welch, pp. 167–87. Statistical Research Technical Series No. 28. Tucson.

1996   Archaeobotany of the Middle Little Colorado River. In *River of Change: Prehistory of the Middle Little Colorado River Valley, Arizona,* edited by E. Charles Adams, pp. 163–86. Arizona State Museum Archaeological Series No. 185. The University of Arizona, Tucson.

Adams, Karen R., and John R. Welch

1994a   Tonto Basin Plant Geography and Ecology. In *Roosevelt Rural Sites Study,* Vol. 3: *Changing Land Use in the Tonto Basin,* edited by Richard Ciolek-Torrello and John R. Welch, pp. 121–34. Statistical Research Technical Series No. 28. Tucson.

1994b   Tonto Basin Ethnobotany. In *The Roosevelt Rural Sites Study,* Vol. 3: *Changing Land Use in the Tonto Basin,* edited by Richard Ciolek-Torrello and John R. Welch, pp. 135–66. Statistical Research Technical Series No. 28. Tucson.

Adams, Robert McC.

1966   *The Evolution of Urban Society: Early Mesopotamia and Prehispanic Mexico.* Aldine, Chicago.

Adler, Michael A.

1992   Fathoming the Scale of Anasazi Communities. Paper presented at the 3rd Southwest Symposium, Tucson.

1996   Land Tenure, Archaeology, and the Ancestral Pueblo Social Landscape. *Journal of Anthropological Archaeology* 15:337–72.

Adovasio, James M., and Rhonda L. Andrews

1987   A Final Report on the Examination of a Prehistoric Mummy and Associated Artifacts from TIN Cave, AR-03–12–06–104, Arizona. University of Pittsburgh. Ms. on file, Tonto National Forest, Phoenix.

Ahlstrom, Richard V. N., Carla R. Van West, and Jeffrey S. Dean

1995   Environmental and Chronological Factors in the Mesa Verde-Northern Rio Grande Migration. *Journal of Anthropological Archaeology* 14:125–42.

Albers, Patricia C.

1993   Symbiosis, Merger, and War: Contrasting Forms of Intertribal Relationship Among Historic Plains Indians. In *The Political Economy of North American Indians,* edited by John H. Moore, pp. 94–132. University of Oklahoma Press, Norman.

Altschul, Jeffrey H.

1996   From North to South: Shifting Sociopolitical Alliances During the Formative Period in the San Pedro Valley. In *Prehistory of the Borderlands: Recent Research in the Archaeology of Northern Mexico and the Southern Southwest,* edited by John Carpenter and Guadalupe Sanchez, pp. 57–69. Arizona State Museum Archaeological Series 186. The University of Arizona, Tucson.

Altschul, Jeffrey H., and Cesar A. Quijada

1996   Cultural Evolution and the Prehistory of the San Pedro Valley. Ms. on file, Statistical Research, Inc., Tucson.

Altschul, Jeffrey H., Cesar A. Quijada, and Robert A. Heckman

1996   Villa Verde and the Late Classic Period Along the San Pedro River. In *Papers of the 9th Mogollon Conference,* edited by Stephanie M. Whittlesey, in preparation. Ms. on file, Statistical Research, Inc., Tucson.

Altschul, Jeffrey H., and Carla R. Van West

1992   Agricultural Productivity Estimates for the Tonto Basin, A.D. 740–1370. In *Proceedings of the Second Salado Conference Globe, AZ 1992,* edited by Richard C. Lange and Stephen Germick, pp. 172–82. Arizona Archaeological Society Occasional Paper. Phoenix.

Anderson, Larry W., and Lucille A. Piety

1987   Surficial Geological Map of the Tonto Basin. In *Seismotectonic Investigation for Theodore Roosevelt Dam, Salt River Project, Arizona,* by L. W. Anderson, L. A. Piety, and T. C. LaForge, Plate 1. Seismotectonic Report 87–5. U.S. Bureau of Reclamation, Engineering and Research Center, Seismotectonic Section, Denver.

Andresen, John

1983   Hohokam Murals at the Clan House, Casa Grande Ruins National Monument. *The Kiva* 48:267–78.

1985   Pottery and Architecture at Compound F, Casa Grande Ruins National Monument. In *Proceedings of the 1983 Hohokam Symposium,* edited by Alfred E. Dittert, Jr., and Donald E. Dove, pp. 595–640. Arizona Archaeological Society Occasional Paper No. 2. Phoenix.

Anthony, David W.
1990   Migration in Archeology: The Baby and the Bathwater. *American Anthropologist* 92:895–914.

Anyon, Roger, Patricia A. Gilman, and Steven A. LeBlanc
1981   A Reevaluation of the Mogollon-Mimbres Archaeological Sequence. *The Kiva* 46:209–26.

Anyon, Roger, and Steven A. LeBlanc
1984   *The Galaz Ruin: A Prehistoric Mimbres Village in Southwestern New Mexico.* University of New Mexico Press, Albuquerque.

Arensberg, Conrad M., and Solon T. Kimball
1962   *Culture and Community.* Harcourt, Brace, and World, Chicago.

Arnold, Dean E.
1985   *Ceramic Theory and Cultural Process.* Cambridge University Press, Cambridge.

Ayres, Y. S., and D. W. Westcot
1989   *Water Quality for Agriculture.* FAO Irrigation and Drainage Paper No. 29. Food and Agricultural Organization of the United Nations, Rome.

Bahr, Donald, Juan Smith, William Smith Allison, and Julian Hayden
1994   *The Short, Swift Time of the Gods on Earth: The Hohokam Chronicles.* University of California Press, Berkeley.

Baker, Frederick, Sarah Taylor, and Julian Thomas
1990   Writing the Past in the Present: An Introductory Dialogue. In *Writing the Past in the Present*, edited by Frederick Baker and Julian Thomas, pp. 1–11. Saint David's University College, Lampeter, Wales.

Baker, Marc
1996   Modern Vegetation of the Tonto Basin. In *Environment and Subsistence in the Classic Period Tonto Basin, Roosevelt Platform Mound Study* (Draft), edited by Katherine A. Spielmann. Roosevelt Monograph Series No. 10. Arizona State University Anthropological Field Studies No. 39. Tempe.

Bandelier, Adolf F.
1892   *Final Report of Investigations Among the Indians of the Southwestern United States Carried on Mainly in the Years 1880 to 1885, Part II.* Papers of the Archaeological Institute of America, American Series, Vol. 4. John Wilson and Son, Cambridge, England.

Bannister, Bryant, John W. Hannah, and William J. Robinson
1970   *Tree-Ring Dates from New Mexico M–N, S, Z: Southwestern New Mexico Area.* Laboratory of Tree-Ring Research, The University of Arizona, Tucson.

Bannister, Bryant, and William J. Robinson
1971   *Tree-Ring Dates from Arizona U-W: Gila-Salt Rivers Area.* Laboratory of Tree-Ring Research, The University of Arizona, Tucson.

Barnes, Ethne
1988   Inhumations Recovered from Casa Buena: Skeletal Analysis. In *Excavations at Casa Buena: Changing Hohokam Land Use Along the Squaw Peak Parkway*, Vol. 2, edited by Jerry B. Howard, pp. 619–91. Soil Systems Publications in Archaeology No. 10. Phoenix.

Barsch, Dietrich, and Chester F. Royse
1971   A Model for Development of Terraces and Pediment-Terraces in the Southwestern United States of America. *Zeitschrift für Geomorphologie* 16:54–75.

Barth, Fredrik
1963   *The Role of the Entrepreneur in Social Change in Northern Norway.* Universitetsforlanget, Bergen.

1967   Economic Spheres in Darfur. In *Themes in Economic Anthropology*, edited by Raymond Firth, pp. 149–74. Tavistock, London.

1969   *Ethnic Groups and Boundaries: The Social Organization of Cultural Differences.* George Allen and Unwin, London.

Bassett, Everett J., and Karen A. Atwell
1985   Osteological Data on the Ash Creek Populations. In *Studies of the Hohokam and Salado of the Tonto Basin*, edited by Glen E. Rice, pp. 221–36. Office of Cultural Resource Management Report No. 63. Arizona State University, Tempe.

Basso, Keith H.
1970   *The Cibecue Apache.* Holt, Rinehart, and Winston, New York.

1983   Western Apache. In *Southwest*, edited by Alfonso Ortiz, pp. 462–88. Handbook of North American Indians, Vol. 10, William C. Sturtevant, general editor. Smithsonian Institution, Washington, D.C.

Bauer, Brian S.
1996   Legitimization of the State in Inca Myth and Ritual. *American Anthropologist* 98:327–37.

Bayham, Frank E., and Pamela Hatch
1985   Hohokam and Salado Animal Utilization in the Tonto Basin. In *Studies in the Hohokam and Salado of the Tonto Basin*, edited by Glen E. Rice, pp. 191–209. Office of Cultural Resource Management Report No. 63. Arizona State University, Tempe.

Bayman, James M.
1994   *Craft Production and Political Economy at the*

Marana Platform Mound Community. Ph.D dissertation, Department of Anthropology, Arizona State University, Tempe.

1996   Shell Ornament Consumption in a Classic Hohokam Platform Mound Community Center. *Journal of Field Archaeology* 23:403–20.

Beckwith, Kim E.

1988   Intrusive Ceramic Wares and Types. In *The 1982–1984 Excavations at Las Colinas,* Vol. 4: *Material Culture,* edited by Lynn S. Teague, pp. 199–256. Arizona State Museum Archaeological Series No. 162. The University of Arizona, Tucson.

Beeson, William J.

1966   *Archaeological Survey Near St. Johns, Arizona: A Methodological Study.* Ph.D dissertation, Department of Anthropology, The University of Arizona, Tucson.

Benfer, Robert A.

1968   *An Analysis of a Prehistoric Skeletal Population, Casas Grandes, Chihuahua, Mexico.* Ph.D dissertation, Department of Anthropology, University of Texas, Austin.

Bennett, Kenneth A.

1973a   On the Estimation of Some Demographic Characteristics on a Prehistoric Population from the American Southwest. *American Journal of Physical Anthropology* 39:223–32.

1973b   *The Indians of Point of Pines, Arizona: A Comparative Study of Their Physical Characteristics.* Anthropological Papers of The University of Arizona No. 23. The University of Arizona Press, Tucson.

Berry, David R.

1985a   Aspects of Paleodemography at Grasshopper Pueblo, Arizona. In *Health and Disease in the Prehistoric Southwest,* edited by Charles F. Merbs and Robert J. Miller, pp. 43–64. Arizona State University Anthropological Research Papers No. 34. Tempe.

1985b   Dental Paleopathology of Grasshopper Pueblo, Arizona. In *Health and Disease in the Prehistoric Southwest,* edited by Charles F. Merbs and Robert J. Miller, pp. 253–74. Arizona State University Anthropological Research Papers No. 34. Tempe.

Billewicz, W. Z., and I. A. McGregor

1982   A Birth-to-Maturity Longitudinal Study of Heights and Weights in Two West African (Gambian) Villages, 1951–1975. *Annual of Human Biology* 4:309–20.

Binford, Lewis R.

1962   Archaeology as Anthropology. *American Antiquity* 28:217–25.

1965   Archaeological Systematics and the Study of Culture Process. *American Antiquity* 31:203–10.

1968   Archaeological Perspectives. In *New Perspectives in Archaeology,* edited by Sally R. Binford and Lewis R. Binford, pp. 5–32. Aldine, Chicago.

1971   Mortuary Practices: Their Study and Their Potential. In *Approaches to the Social Dimensions of Mortuary Practices,* edited by James A. Brown, pp. 6–29. Memoirs of the Society for American Archaeology No. 25.

Binford, Lewis R. (editor)

1977   *For Theory Building in Archaeology.* Academic Press, New York.

Birkby, Walter H.

1973   *Discontinuous Morphological Traits of the Skull as Population Markers in the Prehistoric Southwest.* Ph.D dissertation, Department of Anthropology, The University of Arizona, Tucson.

1982   Bio-Social Interpretations from Cranial Non-Metric Traits of the Grasshopper Pueblo Skeletal Remains. In *Multidisciplinary Research at Grasshopper Pueblo, Arizona,* edited by William A. Longacre, Sally J. Holbrook, and Michael W. Graves, pp. 36–41. Anthropological Papers of The University of Arizona No. 40. The University of Arizona Press, Tucson.

Black, Andrew, and Margerie Green (editors)

1994   *San Carlos Reservoir Cultural Resources Survey.* Archaeological Consulting Services Cultural Resources Report No. 87. Tempe.

Blake, Michael, Stephen A. LeBlanc, and Paul E. Minnis

1986   Changing Settlement and Population in the Mimbres Valley, SW New Mexico. *Journal of Field Archaeology* 13:439–64.

Blanton, Richard E., Stephen A. Kowalewski, Gary Feinman, and Jill Appel

1981   *Ancient Mesoamerica: A Comparison of Change in Three Regions.* Cambridge University Press, Cambridge.

Blitz, John H.

1993   Big Pots for Big Shots: Feasting and Storage in a Mississippian Community. *American Antiquity* 58:80–96.

Bloch, Maurice

1989   From Cognition to Ideology. In *Ritual, History, and Power: Selected Papers in Anthropol-*

ogy, edited by Maurice Bloch, pp. 106–36. Athlone Press, London.

Boehm, Christopher

1993   Egalitarian Behavior and Reverse Dominance Hierarchy. *Current Anthropology* 34:227–54.

Boggess, Doug, Norma Ajeman, Catherine Gilman, and Linda Bozarth

1992   Incorporating Site Vandalism: An Assessment of Pinal Pueblo. In *Proceedings of the Second Salado Conference Globe, AZ 1992,* edited by Richard C. Lange and Stephen Germick, pp. 183–90. Arizona Archaeological Society Occasional Paper. Phoenix.

Bohrer, Vorsila L.

1962   Nature and Interpretation of Ethnobotanic Material from Tonto National Monument. In *Archeological Studies at Tonto National Monument, Arizona,* by Charlie R. Steen, Lloyd M. Pierson, Vorsila L. Bohrer, and Kate Peck Kent, pp. 75–114. Southwestern Monuments Association Technical Series, Vol. 2. Globe, Arizona.

Bolton, Herbert E.

1948   *Kino's Historical Memoir of Pimería Alta.* 2 vols. University of California Press, Berkeley and Los Angeles.

Bostwick, Todd W., and Christian E. Downum (editors)

1994   *Archaeology of the Pueblo Grande Platform Mound and Surrounding Features,* Vol. 2: *Features in the Central Precinct of the Pueblo Grande Community.* Pueblo Grande Museum Anthropological Papers No. 1. Phoenix.

Bozarth, Steven

1994   Pollen and Phytolith Analysis. In *The Roosevelt Rural Sites Study,* Vol. 3: *Changing Land Use in the Tonto Basin,* edited by Richard Ciolek-Torrello and John R. Welch, pp. 189–222. Statistical Research Technical Series No. 28. Tucson.

Bradfield, Maitland

1971   *The Changing Pattern of Hopi Agriculture.* Royal Anthropological Institute Occasional Paper No. 30. Royal Anthropological Institute of Great Britain and Ireland, London.

Bradley, Ronna J.

1993   Marine Shell Exchange in Northwest Mexico and in the Southwest. In *The American Southwest and Mesoamerica: Systems of Prehistoric Exchange,* edited by Jonathon E. Ericson and Timothy G. Baugh, pp. 121–51. Plenum, New York.

1996   Networks of Shell Ornament Exchange: A Critical Assessment of Prestige Economics in the North American Southwest. Paper presented at the 7th Southwest Symposium, Tempe.

Brand, Donald D.

1943   The Chihuahua Culture Area. *New Mexico Anthropologist* 6–7(3):115–58.

Brandes, Raymond

1957   An Archaeological Survey Within Gila County. Ms. on file, Arizona State Museum, Tucson.

Brandt, Elizabeth A.

1980   On Secrecy and Control of Knowledge: Taos Pueblo. In *Secrecy, A Cross-Cultural Perspective,* edited by Stanton K. Tefft, pp. 123–46. Human Sciences Press, New York.

1994   Egalitarianism, Hierarchy, and Centralization in the Pueblos. In *The Ancient Southwestern Community,* edited by W. H. Wills and Robert D. Leonard, pp. 9–23. University of New Mexico Press, Albuquerque.

Braniff C., Beatriz

1986   Ojo de Agua, Sonora, and Casas Grandes, Chihuahua: A Suggested Chronology. In *Ripples in the Chichimec Sea: New Considerations of Southwestern-Mesoamerican Interactions,* edited by Frances Joan Mathien and Randall H. McGuire, pp. 70–80. Southern Illinois University Press, Carbondale.

1993   The Mesoamerican Northern Frontier and the Gran Chichimeca. In *Culture and Contact: Charles C. Di Peso's Gran Chichimeca,* edited by Anne I. Woosley and John C. Ravesloot, pp. 65–82. University of New Mexico Press, Albuquerque.

Braun, David P., and Stephen Plog

1982   Evolution of "Tribal" Social Networks: Theory and Prehistoric North American Evidence. *American Antiquity* 47:504–25.

Breternitz, Cory Dale, David E. Doyel, and Michael P. Marshall (editors)

1982   *Bis Sa'ani: A Late Bonito Phase Community on Escavada Wash, Northwest New Mexico.* Navajo Nation Papers in Anthropology No. 14. Window Rock, Arizona.

Broderick, J. Howard

1974   *Tonto Basin Area Soil Resource Inventory.* USDA Forest Service, Southwestern Region, Phoenix.

Brody, J. J.

1977   *Mimbres Painted Pottery.* University of New Mexico Press, Albuquerque.

Brothwell, Donald R.

1971   Paleodemography. In *Biological Aspects of Demography*, edited by William Brass, pp. 111–30. Symposia of the Society for the Study of Human Biology, Vol. 10. Taylor and Francis, London.

Brown, David E. (editor)

1994   *Biotic Communities: Southwestern United States and Northwestern Mexico.* University of Utah Press, Salt Lake City.

Brown, David E., and Charles H. Lowe

1980   *Biotic Communities of the Southwest.* (Map) General Technical Report RM-78. USDA Forest Service Rocky Mountain Forest and Range Experiment Station, Fort Collins, Colorado.

Brown, James A.

1971   The Dimensions of Status in the Burials at Spiro. In *Approaches to the Social Dimensions of Mortuary Practices*, edited by James A. Brown, pp. 92–112. Society for American Archaeology Memoir No. 25.

Brown, Jeffrey L.

1973   *The Origin and Nature of Salado: Evidence from the Safford Valley, Arizona.* Ph.D dissertation, Department of Anthropology, The University of Arizona, Tucson.

1974   Pueblo Viejo Sites and Their Relationship to Western Pueblo Culture. *The Artifact* 12(2):i–53.

Brumfiel, Elizabeth, and Timothy K. Earle

1987   Specialization, Exchange and Complex Societies: An Introduction. In *Specialization, Exchange and Complex Societies*, edited by Elizabeth Brumfiel and Timothy K. Earle, pp. 1–9. Cambridge University Press, Cambridge.

Brunson, Judy L.

1989   *The Social Organization of the Los Muertos Hohokam: A Reanalysis of Cushing's Hemenway Expedition Data.* Ph.D dissertation, Department of Anthropology, Arizona State University, Tempe.

Bryan, Kirk

1925   Dates of Channel Trenching (Arroyo-Cutting) in the Arid Southwest. *Science* 62:338–44.

1928   Changes in Plant Associations by Changes in Ground Water Level. *Ecology* 9:474–78.

1940   Erosion in the Valleys of the Southwest. *New Mexico Quarterly Review* 10:227–32.

Burrus, Ernest J., S.J.

1971   *Kino and Manje: Explorers of Sonora and Arizona.* Sources and Studies for the History of the Americas No. 10. Jesuit Historical Institute, Rome, Italy, and St. Louis.

Burton, James H., and Arleyn W. Simon

1993   Acid Extraction as a Simple and Inexpensive Method for Compositional Characterization of Archaeological Ceramics. *American Antiquity* 58:45–59.

Burton, James H., Arleyn W. Simon, and David R. Abbott

1994   Interregional Connections in the Development and Distribution of Salado Polychromes in Central Arizona. Paper presented at the 59th Annual Meeting of the Society for American Archaeology, Anaheim.

Buskirk, Winfred

1986   *The Western Apache: Living with the Land Before 1950.* University of Oklahoma Press, Norman.

Cable, John S., and David E. Doyel

1985   The Pueblo Patricio Sequence: Its Implications for the Study of Hohokam Origins, Pioneer Period Site Structure and Processes of Sedentism. In *City of Phoenix, Archaeology of the Original Townsite, Block 24-East*, edited by John S. Cable, Kathleen S. Hoffman, David E. Doyel, and Frank Ritz, pp. 211–70. Soil Systems Publications in Archaeology No. 8. Phoenix.

Cairns, Kellie M.

1994   Faunal Analysis. In *The Roosevelt Rural Sites Study*, Vol. 2: *Prehistoric Rural Settlements in the Tonto Basin*, edited by Richard Ciolek-Torrello, Steven D. Shelley, and Su Benaron, pp. 535–49. Statistical Research Technical Series No. 28. Tucson.

Cameron, Catherine M.

1995   Migration and the Movement of Southwestern Peoples. *Journal of Anthropological Archaeology* 14:104–24.

1996   Coursed Adobe Architecture, Style, and Social Boundaries in the American Southwest. Ms. on file, Archaeological Consulting Services, Ltd., Tempe.

Cameron, Catherine M. (editor)

1995   Special Issue: Migration and the Movement of Southwestern Peoples. *Journal of Anthropological Archaeology* 14(2).

Cameron, Judi L.

1994   Archaeofaunal Remains from the Livingston Area. In *Archaeology of the Salado in the Livingston Area of Tonto Basin, Roosevelt Platform Mound Study: Report on the Livingston Management Group, Pinto Creek Complex*, by David Jacobs, pp. 883–913. Roosevelt Monograph Series No. 3. Arizona State University Anthropological Field Studies No. 32. Tempe.

1995a Faunal Remains from the Bass Point Mound. In *Where the Rivers Converge, Roosevelt Platform Mound Study: Report on the Rock Island Complex,* by Owen Lindauer, pp. 385–99. Roosevelt Monograph Series No. 4. Arizona State University Anthropological Field Studies No. 33. Tempe.

1995b Faunal Remains from Schoolhouse Mesa Sites. Ms. on file, Office of Cultural Resource Management, Department of Anthropology, Arizona State University, Tempe.

1996a Faunal Remains from the Schoolhouse Point Mound, U:8:24/13a. In *The Place of the Storehouses, Roosevelt Platform Mound Study: Report on the Schoolhouse Point Mound, Pinto Creek Complex,* by Owen Lindauer, pp. 649–79. Roosevelt Monograph Series No. 6. Arizona State University Anthropological Field Studies No. 35. Tempe.

1996b Faunal Resource Use in the Prehistoric Tonto Basin. In *Environment and Subsistence in the Classic Period Tonto Basin, Roosevelt Platform Mound Study* (Draft), edited by Katherine A. Spielmann. Roosevelt Monograph Series No. 10. Arizona State University Anthropological Field Studies No. 39. Tempe.

1997a Faunal Remains from U:4:33/132, the Cline Terrace Mound. In *A Salado Platform Mound on Tonto Creek, Roosevelt Platform Mound Study: Report on the Cline Terrace Mound, Cline Terrace Complex,* by David Jacobs, pp. 553–76. Roosevelt Monograph Series No. 7. Arizona State University Anthropological Field Studies No. 36. Tempe.

1997b Faunal Remains from the Schoolhouse Point Mesa Sites. In *The Archaeology of Schoolhouse Point Mesa, Roosevelt Platform Mound Study: Report on the Schoolhouse Point Mesa Sites, Pinto Creek Complex,* by Owen Lindauer, pp. 507–47. Roosevelt Monograph Series No. 8. Arizona State University Anthropological Field Studies No. 37. Tempe.

1997c Faunal Remains from the Uplands Complex Sites. In *Classic Period Settlement in the Uplands of Tonto Basin, Roosevelt Platform Mound Study: Report on the Uplands Complex*, by Theodore J. Oliver, pp. 457–60. Roosevelt Monograph Series No. 5. Arizona State University Anthropological Field Studies No. 34. Tempe.

Carlson, Roy L.

1970 *White Mountain Redware: A Pottery Tradition of East-Central Arizona and Western New Mexico.* Anthropological Papers of the University of Arizona No. 19. The University of Arizona Press, Tucson.

1982 The Polychrome Complexes. In *Southwestern Ceramics: A Comparative Review*, edited by Albert H. Schroeder, pp. 201–34. The Arizona Archaeologist No. 15. Arizona Archaeological Society, Phoenix.

Cartledge, Thomas R.

1976 Prehistory in Vosberg Valley, Central Arizona. *The Kiva* 42:95–104.

1977 *Human Ecology and Changing Patterns of Co-Residence in the Vosberg Locality, Tonto National Forest, Central Arizona.* Cultural Resources Report No. 17. USDA Forest Service, Southwestern Region, Albuquerque.

Caywood, Louis R., and Edward H. Spicer

1935 *Tuzigoot, the Excavation and Repair of a Ruin on the Verde River Near Clarkdale, Arizona.* National Park Service, Field Division of Education, Berkeley.

Chang, K. C.

1989 Ancient China and its Anthropological Significance. In *Archaeological Thought in America*, edited by C. C. Lamberg-Karlovsky, pp. 155–66. Cambridge University Press, Cambridge.

Chapman, Richard C., William Gossett, and Cye Gossett

1985 *Class II Cultural Resources Survey of the Upper Gila Water Supply Study Area.* Ms. on file, Bureau of Reclamation, Phoenix.

Chenhall, Robert G.

1972 *Random Sampling in an Archaeological Survey.* Ph.D dissertation, Department of Anthropology, Arizona State University, Tempe.

Ciolek-Torrello, Richard S.

1978 *A Statistical Analysis of Activity Organization, Grasshopper Pueblo, Arizona.* Ph.D dissertation, Department of Anthropology, The University of Arizona, Tucson.

1979 Late Mogollon Settlement in Central Arizona. Paper presented at the 44th Annual Meeting of the Society for American Archaeology, Vancouver.

1984 *Archaeological Investigations Along State Route 87, Gila County, Arizona.* Museum of Northern Arizona, Flagstaff.

1985 A Typology of Room Function at Grasshopper Pueblo, Arizona. *Journal of Field Archaeology* 12:42–63.

1986   Room Function and Households at Grasshopper Pueblo. In *Mogollon Variability*, edited by Charlotte Benson and Steadman Upham, pp. 107–19. New Mexico State University Occasional Papers No. 15. Las Cruces.

1987   Cultural Affiliation. In *Archaeology of the Mazatzal Piedmont, Central Arizona*, edited by Richard S. Ciolek-Torrello, pp. 356–69. Museum of Northern Arizona Research Paper No. 33. Flagstaff.

1988   Conclusions. In *Hohokam Settlement Along the Slopes of the Picacho Mountains*, Vol. 6: *Synthesis and Conclusions*, edited by Richard Ciolek-Torrello and David R. Wilcox, pp. 300–314. Museum of Northern Arizona Research Paper No. 36. Flagstaff.

1994   Some Thoughts on Rural Settlement and Subsistence. In *The Roosevelt Rural Sites Study*, Vol. 2: *Prehistoric Rural Settlements in the Tonto Basin*, edited by Richard Ciolek-Torrello, Steven D. Shelley, and Su Benaron, pp. 669–87. Statistical Research Technical Series No. 28. Tucson.

1995   The Houghton Road Site, the Agua Caliente Phase, and the Transition to Sedentism in the Tucson Basin. *Kiva* 60:531–74.

Ciolek-Torrello, Richard S. (editor)

1987   *Archaeology of the Mazatzal Piedmont, Central Arizona*, Vols. 1 and 2. Museum of Northern Arizona Research Paper No. 33. Flagstaff.

Ciolek-Torrello, Richard S., and Richard C. Lange

1979   The Q Ranch Region. In *An Archaeological Survey of the Cholla-Saguaro Transmission Line Corridor*, edited by Lynn S. Teague and Linda Mayro, pp. 109–74. Arizona State Museum Archaeological Series No. 135, Vol. 1. The University of Arizona, Tucson.

1982   Archaeology of the Sierra Ancha: A Synthesis of the Gila Pueblo Survey. In *Cholla Project Archaeology*, Vol. 1: *Introduction and Special Studies*, edited by J. Jefferson Reid, pp. 95–126. Arizona State Museum Archaeological Series No. 161. The University of Arizona, Tucson.

1990   The Gila Pueblo Survey of the Southeastern Sierra Ancha. *Kiva* 55:127–54.

Ciolek-Torrello, Richard S., and J. Jefferson Reid

1974   Change in Household Size at Grasshopper. *The Kiva* 40:39–47.

Ciolek-Torrello, Richard S., Steven D. Shelley, Jeffrey H. Altschul, and John R. Welch

1990   *The Roosevelt Rural Sites Study*, Vol. 1: *Research Design*. Statistical Research Technical Series No. 28. Tucson.

Ciolek-Torrello, Richard, Steven D. Shelley, and Su Benaron (editors)

1994   *The Roosevelt Rural Sites Study*, Vol. 2: *Prehistoric Rural Settlements in the Tonto Basin*. Statistical Research Technical Series No. 28. Tucson.

Ciolek-Torrello, Richard, and John R. Welch (editors)

1994   *The Roosevelt Rural Sites Study*, Vol. 3: *Changing Land Use in the Tonto Basin*. Statistical Research Technical Series No. 28. Tucson.

Ciolek-Torrello, Richard, and Stephanie M. Whittlesey

1994   Summary and Conclusions. In *The Roosevelt Rural Sites Study*, Vol. 3: *Changing Land Use in the Tonto Basin*, edited by Richard Ciolek-Torrello and John R. Welch, pp. 473–92. Statistical Research Technical Series No. 28. Tucson.

1996   Complexity Revisited: A New Look at the Archaeology of Central Arizona. In *Debating Complexity: Proceedings of the 26th Annual Conference of the Archaeological Association of the University of Calgary*, edited by D. A. Meyer, P. C. Dawson, and D. T. Hanna, pp. 312–25. Reprint on file, Statistical Research, Inc., Tucson.

Ciolek-Torrello, Richard, Stephanie M. Whittlesey, and John R. Welch

1994   A Synthetic Model of Prehistoric Land Use. In *The Roosevelt Rural Sites Study*, Vol. 3: *Changing Land Use in the Tonto Basin*, edited by Richard Ciolek-Torrello and John R. Welch, pp. 437–72. Statistical Research Technical Series No. 28. Tucson.

Ciolek-Torrello, Richard and David R. Wilcox (editors)

1988   *Hohokam Settlement Along the Slopes of the Picacho Mountains: Synthesis and Conclusions*. Museum of Northern Arizona Research Paper No. 35, Vol. 6. Flagstaff.

Clark, Jeffery J.

1995a   Domestic Architecture in the Early Classic Period. In *The Roosevelt Community Development Study: New Perspectives on Tonto Basin Prehistory*, edited by Mark D. Elson, Miriam T. Stark, and David A. Gregory, pp. 251–305. Center for Desert Archaeology Anthropological Papers No. 15. Tucson.

1995b   The Role of Migration in Social Change. In *The Roosevelt Community Development Study: New Perspectives on Tonto Basin Prehistory*, edited by Mark D. Elson, Miriam T. Stark, and David A. Gregory, pp. 369–84.

Center for Desert Archaeology Anthropological Papers No. 15. Tucson.

Clark, John E., and Michael Blake
1994   The Power of Prestige: Competitive Generosity and the Emergence of Rank Societies in Lowland Mesoamerica. In *Factional Competition and Political Development in the New World*, edited by Elizabeth M. Brumfiel and John W. Fox, pp. 17–30. Cambridge University Press, Cambridge.

Coe, Michael D.
1965   A Model of Ancient Community Structure in the Maya Lowlands. *Southwestern Journal of Anthropology* 21:97–114.

Colton, Harold S.
1965   *Check List of Southwestern Pottery Types.* Museum of Northern Arizona Ceramics Series No.2, rev. Northern Arizona Society of Science and Art, Flagstaff.

Connelly, John C.
1979   Hopi Social Organization. In *Southwest*, edited by Alfonso Ortiz, pp. 539–53. Handbook of North American Indians, Vol. 9, William C. Sturtevant, general editor. Smithsonian Institution, Washington, D.C.

Cooke, Ronald U., and Richard W. Reeves
1976   *Arroyos and Environmental Change in the American Southwest.* Oxford University Press, Oxford.

Cordell, Linda S.
1984   *Prehistory of the Southwest.* Academic Press, New York.

Cordell, Linda S., David E. Doyel, and Keith W. Kintigh
1994   Processes of Aggregation in the Prehistoric Southwest. In *Themes in Southwest Prehistory*, edited by George J. Gumerman, pp. 109–34. School of American Research Press, Santa Fe.

Cordell, Linda S., and George J. Gumerman (editors)
1989   *Dynamics of Southwest Prehistory.* Smithsonian Institution Press, Washington, D.C.

Cordell, Linda S., Steadman Upham, and Sharon L. Brock
1987   Obscuring Cultural Patterns in the Archaeological Record: A Discussion from Southwestern Archaeology. *American Antiquity* 52:565–77.

Corruccini, Robert S.
1972   The Biological Relationships of Some Prehistoric and Historic Pueblo Populations. *American Journal of Physical Anthropology* 37:373–88.

1983   Pathologies Relative to Subsistence and Settlement at Casas Grandes. *American Antiquity* 48:509–10.

Cosgrove, Hattie S., and C. Burton Cosgrove
1932   *The Swarts Ruin: A Typical Mimbres Site in Southwestern New Mexico.* Papers of the Peabody Museum of American Archaeology and Ethnology Vol. 15, No. 1. Harvard University, Cambridge.

Craig, Douglas B.
1989   *Archaeological Testing at Honey Bee Village, AZ BB:9:88 (ASM).* Institute for American Research Technical Report No. 89–6. Tucson.

1995   The Social Consequences of Irrigation Agriculture: A Perspective from Meddler Point. In *The Roosevelt Community Development Study: New Perspectives on Tonto Basin Prehistory,* edited by Mark D. Elson, Miriam T. Stark, and David A. Gregory, pp. 227–49. Center for Desert Archaeology Anthropological Papers No. 15. Tucson.

Craig, Douglas B., and Jeffery J. Clark
1994   The Meddler Point Site, AZ V:5:4/26 (ASM/TNF). In *The Roosevelt Community Development Study, Meddler Point, Pyramid Point, and Griffin Wash Sites,* by Mark D. Elson, Deborah L. Swartz, Douglas B. Craig, and Jeffery J. Clark, pp. 1–198. Center for Desert Archaeology Anthropological Papers No. 13, Vol. 2. Tucson.

Craig, Douglas B., and William H. Doelle
1990   *Interpretive Plan for Rye Creek Ruin.* Desert Archaeology Technical Report No. 90–5. Tucson.

Craig, Douglas B., Mark D. Elson, and David Jacobs
1992   Architectural Variability in the Tonto Basin: A Roosevelt Phase Perspective. *Proceedings of the Second Salado Conference Globe, AZ 1992,* edited by Richard C. Lange and Stephen Germick, pp. 38–49. Arizona Archaeological Society Occasional Paper. Phoenix.

Craig, Douglas B., Mark D. Elson, and Deborah L. Swartz
1992   *Roosevelt Community Development Project Phase 2 Summary and Phase 3 Work Plan.* Desert Archaeology, Inc., Tucson.

Craig, Douglas B., Mark D. Elson, and J. Scott Wood
1992   The Growth and Development of a Platform Mound Community in the Eastern Tonto Basin. In *Proceedings of the Second Salado Conference Globe, AZ 1992,* edited by Richard C. Lange and Stephen Germick, pp. 22–30. Arizona Archaeological Society Occasional Paper. Phoenix.

Craig, Douglas B., and Henry D. Wallace
  1987   *Prehistoric Settlement in the Cañada del Oro Valley, Arizona: The Rancho Vistoso Survey Project.* Institute for American Research Anthropological Papers No. 8. Tucson.

Crary, Joseph S.
  1991   An Archaeological Survey of the Lower Verde Area: A Preliminary Report. Paper presented at the 64th Annual Pecos Conference, Nuevo Casas Grandes, Chihuahua, Mexico.

Crary, Joseph S., and Stephen Germick
  1992   Late Classic Period Cultural and Subsistence Patterns of the Upper Pinal Creek Drainage. Ms. on file, Tonto National Forest, Phoenix.

Crary, Joseph, Stephen Germick, and David E. Doyel
  1994   Exploring the Gila Horizon. Paper presented at the 8th Mogollon Conference, El Paso.

  1995   Exploring the Gila Horizon. Paper presented at the 8th Mogollon Conference, El Paso, 1994 (revised). Ms. on file, Tonto National Forest. Phoenix.

  1996   Exploring the Gila Horizon. Paper presented at the 8th Mogollon Conference, El Paso, 1994 (rerevised). Ms. on file, Archaeological Consulting Services, Ltd., Tempe.

Crary, Joseph S., Stephen Germick, and Michael Golio
  1992   Las Sierras and Los Alamos: A Comparative Study of Classic Period Upland and Riverine Community Patterns in the Tonto-Globe Region of Central Arizona. In *Proceedings of the Second Salado Conference Globe, AZ 1992*, edited by Richard C. Lange and Stephen Germick, pp. 149–60. Arizona Archaeological Society Occasional Paper. Phoenix.

Crary, Joseph S., Robert B. Neily, Gay M. Kinkade, and Stephen Germick
  1994   Late Prehistoric Regional Dynamics: A View from the Safford Basin of Arizona. Paper presented at the 8th Mogollon Conference, El Paso.

Creel, Darrell
  1993   Status Report on Excavations at the Old Town Site (LA 1113), Luna County, New Mexico, Summer 1993. Report submitted to the USDI Bureau of Land Management, Santa Fe.

  1994   Interpreting the End of the Mimbres Classic. Paper presented at the Arizona Archaeological Council Meeting, Tucson.

  1995   Status Report on Excavations at the Old Town Site (LA 1113), Luna County, New Mexico, Summer 1994. Texas Archaeological Research Laboratory, Austin.

  1996   Environmental Variation and Prehistoric Culture in the Mimbres Area. Paper presented at the 61st Annual Meeting of the Society for American Archaeology, New Orleans.

Crown, Patricia L.
  1987   Classic Period Hohokam Settlement and Land Use in the Casa Grande Ruins Area, Arizona. *Journal of Field Archaeology* 14:147–62.

  1990   The Hohokam of the American Southwest. *Journal of World Prehistory* 4:223–55.

  1991   The Role of Exchange and Interaction in Salt-Gila Basin Hohokam Prehistory. In *Exploring the Hohokam: Prehistoric Desert Peoples of the American Southwest*, edited by George J. Gumerman, pp. 383–416. University of New Mexico Press, Albuquerque.

  1994   *Ceramics and Ideology: Salado Polychrome Pottery.* University of New Mexico Press, Albuquerque.

Crown, Patricia L., and W. James Judge (editors)
  1991   *Chaco and Hohokam: Prehistoric Regional Systems in the American Southwest.* School of American Research Press, Santa Fe.

Cummings, Byron
  1940   *Kinishba: A Prehistoric Pueblo of the Great Pueblo Period.* Hohokam Museums Association and University of Arizona Press, Tucson.

Cunningham, C. E.
  1965   Order and Change in an Atoni Diarchy. *Southwestern Journal of Anthropology* 21:359–82.

Czaplicki, Jon S., and John C. Ravesloot
  1989   *Hohokam Archaeology Along Phase B of the Tucson Aqueduct, Central Arizona Project.* Arizona State Museum Archaeological Series No. 178. The University of Arizona, Tucson.

Danforth, Marie Elaine, Della Collins Cook, and Stanley G. Knick III
  1994   The Human Remains from Carter Ranch Pueblo, Arizona: Health in Isolation. *American Antiquity* 59:88–101.

Daniel, T. M.
  1981   An Immunochemist's View of the Epidemiology of Tuberculosis. In *Prehistoric Tuberculosis in the Americas*, edited by Jane E. Buikstra, pp. 35–48. Northwestern University Archeological Program, Evanston, Illinois.

Danson, Edward Bridge
  1957   *An Archaeological Survey of West Central New Mexico and East Central Arizona.* Papers

of the Peabody Museum of American Archaeology and Ethnology Vol.44, No. 1. Harvard University, Cambridge.

Dart, Allen, James Holmlund, and Henry D. Wallace

1990   *Ancient Hohokam Communities in Southern Arizona: The Coyote Mountains Archaeological District in the Altar Valley.* Center for Desert Archaeology Technical Report No. 90–3. Tucson.

Dart, Allen, Stephen H. Lekson, and Henry D. Wallace

1989   *Historic Properties Management Plan for the U.S. Army Corps of Engineers Painted Rock Reservoir Project, Southwestern Arizona.* Institute for American Research Technical Report No. 88–6. Tucson.

Davis, Arthur P.

1902   *Water Storage on Salt River, Arizona.* U.S. Geological Survey Water-Supply Paper No. 73. U.S. Government Printing Office, Washington, D.C.

Dean, Jeffrey S.

1969   *Chronological Analysis of Tsegi Phase Sites in Northeastern Arizona.* Papers of the Laboratory of Tree-Ring Research No. 3. The University of Arizona Press, Tucson.

1987   Thoughts on Hohokam Settlement Behavior: Comments on "The Hohokam Village." In *The Hohokam Village: Site Structure and Organization,* edited by David E. Doyel, pp. 253–62. Southwestern and Rocky Mountain Division of the American Association for the Advancement of Science, Glenwood Springs, Colorado.

1988a   A Model of Anasazi Behavioral Adaptation. In *The Anasazi in a Changing Environment,* edited by George J. Gumerman, pp. 25–44. Cambridge University Press, Cambridge.

1988b   Dendrochronology and Paleoenvironmental Reconstruction on the Colorado Plateaus. In *The Anasazi in a Changing Environment,* edited by George J. Gumerman, pp. 119–67. Cambridge University Press, Cambridge.

1994   Environmental Change and/or Human Impact: The Case of the Colorado Plateau. Paper presented at the 1994 Southwest Symposium, Arizona State University, Tempe.

1996a   Kayenta Anasazi Settlement Transformations in Northeastern Arizona, A.D. 1150 to 1350. In *The Prehistoric Pueblo World, A.D. 1150–1350,* edited by Michael A. Adler, pp. 29–47. The University of Arizona Press, Tucson.

1996b   Demography, Environment, and Subsistence Stress. In *Evolving Complexity and Environ-*

mental Risk in the Prehistoric Southwest, edited by Joseph A. Tainter and Bonnie Bagley Tainter, pp. 25–56. Santa Fe Institute Studies in the Sciences of Complexity, Proceedings Volume 24. Addison-Wesley, Reading, Massachusetts.

Dean, Jeffrey S., William H. Doelle, and Janet D. Orcutt

1994   Adaptive Stress, Environment, and Demography. In *Themes in Southwest Prehistory,* edited by George J. Gumerman, pp. 53–86. School of American Research Press, Santa Fe.

Dean, Jeffrey S., Robert C. Euler, George J. Gumerman, Fred Plog, Richard H. Hevly, and Thor N. V. Karlstrom

1985   Human Behavior, Demography, and Paleoenvironment on the Colorado Plateaus. *American Antiquity* 50:537–54.

Dean, Jeffrey S., and Gary S. Funkhouser

1995   Dendroclimatic Reconstructions for the Southern Colorado Plateau. In *Climate Change in the Four Corners and Adjacent Regions: Implications for Environmental Restoration and Land-Use Planning,* edited by W. J. Waugh, pp. 85–104. U.S. Department of Energy, Grand Junction Projects Office, Grand Junction, Colorado.

Dean, Jeffrey S., Alexander J. Lindsay, Jr., and William J. Robinson

1978   Prehistoric Settlement in Long House Valley, Northeastern Arizona. In *Investigations of the Southwestern Anthropological Research Group: An Experiment in Archeological Co-operation: The Proceedings of the 1976 Conference,* edited by Robert C. Euler and George J. Gumerman, pp. 25–44. Museum of Northern Arizona, Flagstaff.

Dean, Jeffrey S., and John C. Ravesloot

1993   The Chronology of Cultural Interaction in the Gran Chichimeca. In *Culture and Contact: Charles C. Di Peso's Gran Chichimeca,* edited by Anne I. Woosley and John C. Ravesloot, pp. 83–103. University of New Mexico Press, Albuquerque.

Deaver, William L., and Richard Ciolek-Torrello

1995   Early Formative Period Chronology for the Tucson Basin. *Kiva* 60:481–529.

Decker, Kenneth A.

1986   Isotopic and Chemical Reconstruction of Diet and its Biological and Social Dimensions at Grasshopper Pueblo, Arizona. Paper presented at the 51st Annual Meeting of the Society for American Archaeology, New Orleans.

Denevan, William M.

1992   The Pristine Myth: The Landscape of the Americas in 1492. *Annals of the Association of American Geographers* 82(3):369–85.

Dering, J. Phil

1994   Plant Remains from Six Roosevelt and Gila Phase Sites. In *Archaeology of the Salado in the Livingston Area of Tonto Basin, Roosevelt Platform Mound Study: Report on the Livingston Management Group, Pinto Creek Complex,* by David Jacobs, pp. 867–82. Roosevelt Monograph Series No. 3. Arizona State University Anthropological Field Studies No. 32. Tempe.

1995a   Plant Remains From Bass Point Mound, A Classic Period Site in the Tonto Basin. In *Where the Rivers Converge, Roosevelt Platform Mound Study: Report on the Rock Island Complex,* by Owen Lindauer, pp. 359–73. Roosevelt Monograph Series No. 4. Arizona State University Anthropological Field Studies No. 33. Tempe.

1995b   Macrobotanical Remains from the Schoolhouse Mesa Sites. Ms. on file, Office of Cultural Resource Management, Department of Anthropology, Arizona State University, Tempe.

1996a   Plant Remains from the Schoolhouse Point Mound, U:8:24/13a. In *The Place of the Storehouses, Roosevelt Platform Mound Study: Report on the Schoolhouse Point Mound, Pinto Creek Complex,* by Owen Lindauer, pp. 623–39. Roosevelt Monograph Series No. 6. Arizona State University Anthropological Field Studies No. 35. Tempe.

1996b   Macrobotanical Remains from Classic Period Farming Villages in the Tonto Basin. In *Environment and Subsistence in the Classic Period Tonto Basin, Roosevelt Platform Mound Study* (Draft), edited by Katherine A. Spielmann. Roosevelt Monograph Series No. 10. Arizona State University Anthropological Field Studies No. 39. Tempe.

1997a   Plant Remains from U:4:33/132, the Cline Terrace Mound. In *A Salado Platform Mound on Tonto Creek, Roosevelt Platform Mound Study: Report on the Cline Terrace Mound, Cline Terrace Complex,* by David Jacobs, pp. 529–44. Roosevelt Monograph Series No. 7. Arizona State University Anthropological Field Studies No. 36. Tempe.

1997b   Plant Remains from the Schoolhouse Point Mesa Sites. In *The Archaeology of Schoolhouse Point Mesa, Roosevelt Platform Mound Study: Report on the Schoolhouse Point Mesa Sites, Schoolhouse Management Group, Pinto Creek Complex,* by Owen Lindauer, pp. 491–501. Roosevelt Monograph Series No. 8. Arizona State University Anthropological Field Studies No. 37. Tempe.

1997c   Plant Remains from the Uplands Complex Sites. In *Classic Period Settlement in the Uplands of Tonto Basin, Roosevelt Platform Mound Study: Report on the Uplands Complex,* by Theodore J. Oliver, pp. 443–55. Roosevelt Monograph Series No. 5. Arizona State University Anthropological Field Studies No. 34. Tempe.

Diehl, Richard A.

1983   *Tula: The Toltec Capital of Ancient Mexico.* Thames and Hudson, London.

Di Peso, Charles C.

1958   *The Reeve Ruin of Southeastern Arizona: A Study of a Prehistoric Western Pueblo Migration Into the Middle San Pedro Valley.* The Amerind Foundation Series No. 8. Dragoon, Arizona.

1968   Casas Grandes and the Gran Chichimeca. *El Palacio* 75(4):45–61.

1974a   *Casas Grandes: A Fallen Trading Center of the Gran Chichimeca.* Vols. 1–3. The Amerind Foundation Series No. 9. Northland Press, Flagstaff.

1974b   *Casas Grandes: A Fallen Trading Center of the Gran Chichimeca,* Vol. 2: *Medio Period.* Amerind Foundation Series No. 9. Northland Press, Flagstaff.

1976a   Gila Polychrome in the Casas Grandes Region. *The Kiva* 42:57–63.

1976b   Comments on Papers. *The Kiva* 42:126.

1979   Prehistory: O'otam. In *Southwest,* edited by Alfonso Ortiz, pp. 366–79. Handbook of North American Indians, Vol. 9, William C. Sturtevant, general editor. Smithsonian Institution, Washington, D.C.

Di Peso, Charles C., John B. Rinaldo, and Gloria J. Fenner

1974a   *Casas Grandes: A Fallen Trading Center of the Gran Chichimeca,* Vols. 4–8. The Amerind Foundation Series No. 9. Northland Press, Flagstaff.

1974b   *Casas Grandes: A Fallen Trading Center of the Gran Chichimeca,* Vol. 4: *Dating and Architecture.* The Amerind Foundation Series No. 9. Northland Press, Flagstaff.

1974c *Casas Grandes: A Fallen Trading Center of the Gran Chichimeca*, Vol. 5: *Architecture*. The Amerind Foundation Series No. 9. Northland Press, Flagstaff.

1974d *Casas Grandes: A Fallen Trading Center of the Gran Chichimeca*, Vol. 6: *Ceramics and Shell*. The Amerind Foundation Series No. 9. Northland Press, Flagstaff.

1974e *Casas Grandes: A Fallen Trading Center of the Gran Chichimeca*, Vol. 7: *Stone and Metal*. The Amerind Foundation Series No. 9. Northland Press, Flagstaff.

1974f *Casas Grandes: A Fallen Trading Center of the Gran Chichimeca*, Vol. 8: *Bone-Economy-Burials*. The Amerind Foundation Series No. 9. Northland Press, Flagstaff.

Dittert, Alfred E., Jr.

1959 *Culture Change in the Cebolleta Mesa Region, Central Western New Mexico*. Ph.D dissertation, Department of Anthropology, University of Arizona, Tucson.

1976 Comments on Papers. *The Kiva* 42:126–27.

Dittert, Alfred E., Jr. (editor)

1966 The Cliff Highway Salvage Project. *Lab Note* No. 40, Laboratory of Anthropology, Santa Fe.

Doelle, William H.

1981 The Gila Pima in the Late Seventeenth Century. In *The Protohistoric Period in the North American Southwest, A.D. 1450–1700*, edited by David R. Wilcox and W. Bruce Masse, pp. 57–70. Arizona State University Anthropological Research Papers No. 24. Tempe.

1984 The Tucson Basin During the Protohistoric Period. *The Kiva* 49:195–211.

1992 Demographic Change and the Adoption of Wheat by the Gila River Pima. Paper presented at the Chacmool Conference, Calgary, Alberta.

1995a Tonto Basin Demography in a Regional Perspective. In *The Roosevelt Community Development Study: New Perspectives on Tonto Basin Prehistory*, edited by Mark D. Elson, Miriam T. Stark, and David A. Gregory, pp. 201–26. Center for Desert Archaeology Anthropological Papers No. 15. Tucson.

1995b A Method for Estimating Regional Population. In *The Roosevelt Community Development Study: New Perspectives on Tonto Basin Prehistory*, edited by Mark D. Elson, Miriam T. Stark, and David A. Gregory, pp. 513–36. Center for Desert Archaeology Anthropological Papers No. 15. Tucson.

1995c The Centuries Before Coronado: The Classic Period on the San Pedro River. *Archaeology in Tucson* 9(2):1–6.

Doelle, William H., and Douglas B. Craig

1992 Prehistoric Demography in the Tonto Basin. In *Research Design for the Roosevelt Community Development Study*, by William H. Doelle, Henry D. Wallace, Mark D. Elson, and Douglas B. Craig, pp. 81–88. Center for Desert Archaeology Anthropological Papers No. 12. Tucson.

Doelle, William H., David A. Gregory, and Henry D. Wallace

1995 Classic Period Platform Mound Systems in Southern Arizona. In *The Roosevelt Community Development Study: New Perspectives on Tonto Basin Prehistory*, edited by Mark D. Elson, Miriam T. Stark, and David A. Gregory, pp. 385–440. Center for Desert Archaeology Anthropological Papers No. 15. Tucson.

Doelle, William H., and Henry D. Wallace

1990 The Transition to History in Pimería Alta. In *Perspectives on Southwestern Prehistory*, edited by Paul E. Minnis and Charles L. Redman, pp. 239–57. Westview Press, Boulder.

1991 The Changing Role of the Tucson Basin in the Hohokam Regional System. In *Exploring the Hohokam: Prehistoric Desert Peoples of the American Southwest*, edited by George J. Gumerman, pp. 279–345. University of New Mexico Press, Albuquerque.

Doelle, William H., Henry D. Wallace, and Douglas B. Craig

1992 A Framework for Studying Prehistoric Communities. In *Research Design for the Roosevelt Community Development Study*, by William H. Doelle, Henry D. Wallace, Mark D. Elson, and Douglas B. Craig, pp. 121–37. Center for Desert Archaeology Anthropological Papers No. 12. Tucson.

Doelle, William H., Henry D. Wallace, Mark D. Elson, and Douglas B. Craig

1992 *Research Design for the Roosevelt Community Development Study*. Center for Desert Archaeology Anthropological Papers No. 12. Tucson.

Donaldson, Marcia

1996 Botanical Remains. In *Archeological Investigations at the Upper Ruin, Tonto National Monument*, Pt. I: *Salvage Excavations at the Upper Ruin, AZ U:8:48 (ASM)—1995*, by Gregory L. Fox, pp. 119–56. Western Archeological and Conservation Center Publications in Anthropology No. 70. U.S. National Park Service, Tucson.

Doolittle, William E.

1988   *Prehistoric Occupance in the Valley of Sonora, Mexico.* Anthropological Papers of the University of Arizona No. 48. The University of Arizona Press, Tucson.

1990   *Canal Irrigation in Prehistoric Mexico: The Sequence of Technological Change.* University of Texas Press, Austin.

1993   Canal Irrigation at Casas Grandes: A Technological and Developmental Assessment of Its Origins. In *Culture and Contact: Charles C. Di Peso's Gran Chichimeca*, edited by Anne I. Woosley and John C. Ravesloot, pp. 133–52. University of New Mexico Press, Albuquerque.

Douglas, John E.

1987   Late Prehistoric Archaeological Remains in the San Bernardino Valley, Southeastern Arizona. *The Kiva* 53:35–51.

1995   Autonomy and Regional Systems in the Late Prehistoric Southern Southwest. *American Antiquity* 60:240–57.

Douglass, Andrew Ellicott

1929   The Secret of the Southwest Solved by Talkative Tree Rings. *National Geographic Magazine* 54:737–70.

Downum, Christian E.

1993   *Between Desert and River: Hohokam Settlement and Land Use in the Los Robles Community.* Anthropological Papers of the University of Arizona No. 57. The University of Arizona Press, Tucson.

Downum, Christian E., and Todd W. Bostwick

1993   *Archaeology of the Pueblo Grande Platform Mound and Surrounding Features*, Vol. 1: *Introduction to the Archival Project and History of Archaeological Research.* Pueblo Grande Museum Anthropological Papers No. 1. Phoenix.

Downum, Christian E., Paul R. Fish, and Suzanne K. Fish

1994   Refining the Role of *Cerros de Trincheras* in Southern Arizona Settlement. *Kiva* 59:271–96.

Doyel, David E.

1972   *Cultural and Ecological Aspects of Salado Prehistory.* Master's thesis, California State University, Chico.

1974   *Excavations in the Escalante Ruin Group, Southern Arizona.* Arizona State Museum Archaeological Series No. 37. The University of Arizona, Tucson.

1976a   Revised Phase System for the Globe-Miami and Tonto Basin Areas, Central Arizona. *The Kiva* 41:241–66.

1976b   Salado Cultural Development in the Tonto Basin and Globe-Miami Areas, Central Arizona. *The Kiva* 42:5–16.

1976c   Classic Period Hohokam in the Gila River Basin, Arizona. *The Kiva* 42:27–37.

1977a   *Classic Period Hohokam in the Escalante Ruin Group.* Ph.D dissertation, Department of Anthropology, The University of Arizona, Tucson.

1977b   *Excavations in the Middle Santa Cruz River Valley, Southeastern Arizona.* Arizona State Museum Contributions to Highway Salvage Archaeology in Arizona No. 44. The University of Arizona, Tucson.

1978   *The Miami Wash Project: Hohokam and Salado in the Globe-Miami Area, Central Arizona.* Arizona State Museum Contribution to Highway Salvage Archaeology in Arizona No. 52. The University of Arizona, Tucson.

1980   Hohokam Social Organization and the Sedentary to Classic Transition. In *Current Issues in Hohokam Prehistory: Proceedings of a Symposium,* edited by David Doyel and Fred Plog, pp. 23–40. Arizona State University Anthropological Research Papers No. 23. Tempe.

1981   *Late Hohokam Prehistory in Southern Arizona.* Contributions to Archaeology No. 2. Gila Press, Scottsdale.

1991a   Hohokam Cultural Evolution in the Phoenix Basin. In *Exploring the Hohokam: Prehistoric Desert Peoples of the American Southwest,* edited by George J. Gumerman, pp. 231–78. University of New Mexico Press, Albuquerque.

1991b   The Hohokam: Ancient Dwellers of the Arizona Desert. In *The Hohokam: Ancient People of the Desert,* edited by David Grant Noble, pp. 5–17. School of American Research Press, Santa Fe.

1991c   Hohokam Exchange and Interaction. In *Chaco and Hohokam: Prehistoric Regional Systems in the American Southwest,* edited by Patricia L. Crown and W. James Judge, pp. 226–52. School of American Research Press, Santa Fe.

1992   On Models and Methods: Comments on the History of Archaeological Research in the Southern Southwest. In *Proceedings of the Second Salado Conference Globe, AZ 1992,*

edited by Richard C. Lange and Stephen
Germick, pp. 345–51. Arizona Archaeological
Society Occasional Paper. Phoenix.

1993a   Prehistoric Non-Irrigated Agriculture in
Arizona: A Context for Study. Estrella Cultural Research and Arizona State Preservation Office, Arizona State Parks, Phoenix.

1993b   Interpreting Prehistoric Cultural Diversity in
the Arizona Desert. In *Culture and Contact:
Charles C. Di Peso's Gran Chichimeca*, edited
by Anne I. Woosley and John C. Ravesloot,
pp. 39–64. University of New Mexico Press,
Albuquerque.

1993c   On Rivers and Boundaries in the Phoenix
Basin, Arizona. *Kiva* 58:455–74.

1994   Charles Corradino Di Peso: Expanding the
Frontiers of New World Prehistory. *American Antiquity* 59:9–20.

1996   Resource Mobilization and Hohokam Society: Analysis of Obsidian Artifacts from the
Gatlin Site, Arizona. *Kiva* 62:45–60.

Doyel, David E. (editor)

1987   *The Hohokam Village: Site Structure and
Organization.* Southwestern and Rocky
Mountain Division of the American Association for the Advancement of Science, Glenwood Springs, Colorado.

1992   *Anasazi Regional Organization and the Chaco
System.* Maxwell Museum of Anthropology
Papers No. 5. Albuquerque.

Doyel, David E., Andrew Black, and Barbara Macnider
(editors)

1995   *Archaeological Excavations at Pueblo Blanco:
The MCDOT Alma School Road Project.*
Archaeological Consulting Services Cultural
Resources Report No. 90. Tempe.

Doyel, David E., Cory D. Breternitz, and Michael P. Marshall

1984   Chacoan Community Structure, Bis Sa'ani
Pueblo, and the Chaco Halo. In *Recent Research on Chaco Prehistory*, edited by W.
James Judge and John D. Schelberg, pp. 37–
54. Reports of the Chaco Center No. 8. National Park Service, Albuquerque.

Doyel, David E., Joseph Crary, Gina Gage, and
Karolyn Jensen

1995   *A Class One Overview for the Proposed San
Carlos Irrigation Project Joint Works Rehabili-
tation.* Archaeological Consulting Services
Cultural Resources Report No. 91. Tempe.

Doyel, David E., and Mark D. Elson (editors)

1985   *Hohokam Settlement and Economic Systems*

in the Central New River Drainage, Arizona.
Soil Systems Publications in Archaeology
No. 4. Phoenix.

Doyel, David E., Suzanne K. Fish, and Paul R. Fish
(editors)

1997   *The Hohokam Village Revisited.* American
Association for the Advancement of Science.
In prep.

Doyel, David E., and Emil W. Haury (editors)

1976   The 1976 Salado Conference. *The Kiva* 42(1).

Doyel, David E., and Theresa Hoffman (editors)

1997   Settlement History of the Globe Highlands.
Archaeological Consulting Services, Ltd.,
Tempe. In prep.

Doyel, David E., and Mac McDonnell

1997   Locus of Production of Lower Verde Ceram-
ics. In *Archaeological Excavations at AZ
U:6:87, U:6:105, and U:6:253 (ASM) on the
Fort McDowell Mohave-Apache Indian Com-
munity, Maricopa County, Arizona*, edited by
Theresa Hoffman and Amy Phillips. Ar-
chaeological Consulting Services Cultural
Resources Report No. 99. Tempe.

Dozier, Edward P.

1954   *The Hopi-Tewa of Arizona.* Publications in
American Archaeology and Ethnology Vol.
44, pp. 259–376. University of California,
Berkeley.

1966   *Hano: A Tewa Indian Community in Arizona.*
Holt, Rinehart, and Winston, New York.

1970   *The Pueblo Indians of North America.* Holt,
Rinehart, and Winston, New York.

Drennan, Robert D.

1984   Long-Distance Transport Costs in Pre-
Hispanic Mesoamerica. *American Anthropologist* 86:105–12.

Dunnell, Robert C.

1978   Archaeological Potential of Anthropological
and Scientific Models of Function. In *Archaeological Essays in Honor of Irving B. Rouse*, edited
by Robert C. Dunnell and Edwin S. Hall, Jr.,
pp. 41–73. Mouton, The Hague.

1980   Evolutionary Theory and Archaeology. In
Advances in Archaeology Method and Theory,
Vol. 3, edited by Michael B. Schiffer, pp. 35–
99. Academic Press, New York.

1982   Americanist Archaeological Literature: 1981.
American Journal of Archaeology 85:509–29.

Effland, Richard W., Jr.

1988   A Examination of Hohokam Mortuary
Practices from Casa Buena. In *Excavations at
Casa Buena: Changing Hohokam Land Use*

Along the Squaw Peak Parkway, edited by
Jerry B. Howard, pp. 693–794. Soil Systems
Publications in Archaeology No. 11. Phoenix.

Effland, Richard W., Jr., and Barbara S. Macnider

1991   *An Overview of the Cultural Heritage of the
Tonto National Forest.* Archaeological Con-
sulting Services Cultural Resources Report
No. 49. Tempe.

Eggan, Fred R.

1950   *Social Organization of the Western Pueblos.*
University of Chicago Press, Chicago.

1966   *The American Indian: Perspectives for the
Study of Social Change.* Aldine, Chicago.

Eighmy, Jeffrey L.

1979   Logistic Trends in Southwest Population
Growth. In *Transformations: Mathematical
Approaches to Culture Change*, edited by
Colin Renfrew and Kenneth L. Cooke, pp.
205–20. Academic Press, New York.

Ekholm, Gordon F.

1942   *Excavations at Guasave, Sinaloa, Mexico.*
Anthropological Papers of the American
Museum of Natural History Vol. 38, pp. 123–
39. New York.

Elliott, Melinda

1995   *Great Excavations.* School of American Research Press, Santa Fe.

Ellis, Andrea H.

1991   Towers of the Gallina Area and Greater
Southwest. In *Puebloan Past and Present:
Papers in Honor of Stewart Peckham*, edited
by Meliha S. Duran and David T. Kirkpat-
rick, pp. 57–70. Papers of the Archaeological
Society of New Mexico No. 17. Albuquerque.

Ellis, Florence Hawley

1968   An Interpretation of Prehistoric Death Cus-
toms in Terms of Modern Southwestern
Parallels. In *Collected Papers in Honor of
Lyndon Lane Hargrave*, edited by Albert H.
Schroeder, pp. 57–76. Papers of the Archaeological Society of New Mexico No. 1. Museum of New Mexico Press, Santa Fe.

El-Najjar, Mahmoud Y.

1974   *The People of Canyon de Chelly: A Study of
Their Biology and Culture.* Ph.D dissertation,
Department of Anthropology, Arizona State
University, Tempe.

1978   Southwestern Physical Anthropology: Do
the Cultural and Biological Parameters
Correspond? *American Journal of Physical
Anthropology* 48:151–58.

1979   Human Treponematosis and Tuberculosis:
Evidence from the New World. *American
Journal of Physical Anthropology* 51:599–618.

El-Najjar, Mahmoud Y., Dennis J. Ryan,
Christy G. Turner II, and Betsy Lozoff

1976   The Etiology of Porotic Hyperostosis
Among the Prehistoric and Historic Anasazi
Indians of the Southwestern United States.
American Journal of Physical Anthropology
44:477–88.

Elson, Mark D.

1992a   Settlement, Subsistence, and Cultural
Affiliation Within the Upper Tonto Basin.
In *The Rye Creek Project: Archaeology in
the Upper Tonto Basin*, Vol. 3: *Synthesis and
Conclusions*, by Mark D. Elson and Dou-
glas B. Craig, pp. 119–53. Center for Desert
Archaeology Anthropological Papers No.
11. Tucson.

1992b   Contact or Colonization: The Origins of the
Tonto Basin Salado Culture. Paper presented
at the 25th Chacmool Conference, Calgary.

1994a   The Pyramid Point Site, AZ V:5:1/25 (ASM/
TNF). In *The Roosevelt Community Development Study: Meddler Point, Pyramid Point,
and Griffin Wash Sites*, by Mark D. Elson,
Deborah L. Swartz, Douglas B. Craig, and
Jeffery J. Clark, pp. 199–295. Center for Desert Archaeology Anthropological Papers No.
13, Vol. 2. Tucson.

1994b   Pyramid Point Mound: Integration in the
Tonto Basin. Paper presented at the 59th
Annual Meeting of the Society for American
Archaeology, Anaheim.

1995   Assessment of Chronometric Methods and
Dates. In *The Roosevelt Community Develop-
ment Study: New Perspectives on Tonto Basin
Prehistory*, edited by Mark D. Elson, Miriam
T. Stark, and David A. Gregory, pp. 39–60.
Center for Desert Archaeology Anthropo-
logical Papers No. 15. Tucson.

1996a   *An Ethnographic Perspective on Prehistoric
Platform Mounds of the Tonto Basin, Central
Arizona.* Ph.D dissertation, Department of
Anthropology, The University of Arizona,
Tucson.

1996b   A Revised Chronology and Phase Sequence
for the Lower Tonto Basin of Central Arizona. *Kiva* 62:117–47.

Elson, Mark D., and Jeffery J. Clark

1994   *The Roosevelt Community Development
Study: Paleobotanical and Osteological Analy-*

ses. Center for Desert Archaeology Anthropological Papers No. 14, Vol. 3. Tucson.

Elson, Mark D., and Douglas B. Craig

1992a   *The Rye Creek Project: Archaeology in the Upper Tonto Basin.* Center for Desert Archaeology Anthropological Papers No. 11. Tucson.

1992b   *The Rye Creek Project: Archaeology in the Upper Tonto Basin,* Vol. 1: *Introduction and Site Descriptions.* Center for Desert Archaeology Anthropological Papers No. 11. Tucson.

1992c   *The Rye Creek Project: Archaeology in the Upper Tonto Basin,* Vol. 3: *Synthesis and Conclusions.* Center for Desert Archaeology Anthropological Papers No. 11. Tucson.

Elson, Mark D., Suzanne K. Fish, Steven R. James, and Charles H. Miksicek

1995   Prehistoric Subsistence in the Roosevelt Community Development Study Area. In *The Roosevelt Community Development Study: Paleobotanical and Osteological Analyses,* edited by Mark D. Elson and Jeffery J. Clark, pp. 217–60. Center for Desert Archaeology Anthropological Papers No. 14, Vol. 3. Tucson.

Elson, Mark D., and David A. Gregory

1995   Tonto Basin Chronology and Phase Sequence. In *The Roosevelt Community Development Study: New Perspectives on Tonto Basin Prehistory,* edited by Mark D. Elson, Miriam T. Stark, and David A. Gregory, pp. 61–77. Center for Desert Archaeology Anthropological Papers No. 15. Tucson.

Elson, Mark D., David A. Gregory, and Miriam T. Stark

1995   New Perspectives on Tonto Basin Prehistory. In *The Roosevelt Community Development Study: New Perspectives on Tonto Basin Prehistory,* edited by Mark D. Elson, Miriam T. Stark, and David A. Gregory, pp. 441–79. Center for Desert Archaeology Anthropological Papers No. 15. Tucson.

Elson, Mark D., and Michael Lindeman

1994   The Eagle Ridge Site, AZ V:5:104/1045 (ASM/TNF). In *The Roosevelt Community Development Study: Introduction and Small Sites,* by Mark D. Elson and Deborah L. Swartz, pp. 23–116. Center for Desert Archaeology Anthropological Papers No. 13, Vol. 1. Tucson.

Elson, Mark D., Miriam T. Stark, and David A. Gregory (editors)

1995   *The Roosevelt Community Development Study: New Perspectives on Tonto Basin Pre-*

history. Center for Desert Archaeology Anthropological Papers No. 15. Tucson.

Elson, Mark D., Miriam T. Stark, and James M. Heidke

1992   Prelude to Salado: Preclassic Period Settlement in the Upper Tonto Basin. In *Proceedings of the Second Salado Conference Globe, AZ 1992,* edited by Richard C. Lange and Stephen Germick, pp. 274–85. Arizona Archaeological Society Occasional Paper. Phoenix.

Elson, Mark D., and Deborah L. Swartz

1994   *The Roosevelt Community Development Study: Introduction and Small Sites.* Center for Desert Archaeology Anthropological Papers No. 13, Vol. 1. Tucson.

Ely, Lisa L., Jim E. O'Connor, and Victor R. Baker

1988   Paleoflood Hydrology of the Salt and Verde Rivers, Central Arizona. Eighth Annual USCOLD Lecture, Ms. on file, Statistical Research, Inc., The University of Arizona, Tucson.

Emerson, Thomas E.

1989   Water, Serpents, and the Underworld: An Exploration into Cahokia Symbolism. In *The Southeastern Ceremonial Complex: Artifacts and Analysis,* edited by Patricia K. Galloway, pp. 45–92. University of Nebraska Press, Lincoln.

Erickson, Clark L.

1992   Prehistoric Landscape Management in the Andean Highlands: Raised Field Agriculture and its Environmental Impact. *Population and Environment* 13:285–300.

Evans-Pritchard, E. E.

1940   *The Nuer: A Description of the Modes of Livelihood and Political Institutions of a Nilotic People.* Clarendon Press, Oxford.

Eveleth, Phyllis B., and J. M. Tanner

1976   *Worldwide Variation in Human Growth.* 2nd ed. Cambridge University Press, Cambridge.

Ezzo, Joseph A.

1993   *Human Adaptation at Grasshopper Pueblo, Arizona: Social and Ecological Perspectives.* International Monographs in Prehistory, Archaeological Series No. 4. Ann Arbor.

Feinman, Gary M.

1991   Hohokam Archaeology in the Eighties: An Outside View. In *Exploring the Hohokam: Prehistoric Desert Peoples of the American Southwest,* edited by George J. Gumerman, pp. 461–83. University of New Mexico Press, Albuquerque.

1992   An Outside Perspective on Chaco Canyon.

In *Anasazi Regional Organization and the Chaco System*, edited by David E. Doyel, pp. 177–82. Maxwell Museum of Anthropology Anthropological Papers No. 5. Albuquerque.

Ferdon, Edwin N.

1955   A *Trial Survey of Mexican-Southwestern Architectural Parallels*. School of American Research Monographs No. 21. Santa Fe.

Ferguson, Cheryl

1980   Analysis of Skeletal Remains. In *Tijeras Canyon: Analyses of the Past*, edited by Linda S. Cordell, pp. 121–48. Maxwell Museum and University of New Mexico Press, Albuquerque.

Ferguson, T. J., and E. Richard Hart

1985   *A Zuni Atlas*. University of Oklahoma Press, Norman.

Fewkes, Jesse Walter

1894   The Snake Ceremonials at Walpi. *Journal of American Ethnology and Archaeology* No. 4. Boston.

1895   Archaeological Expedition to Arizona in 1895. Seventeenth Annual Report, Pt. II, Bureau of American Ethnology, Washington, D.C.

1912   *Casa Grande, Arizona*. Twenty-Eighth Annual Report of the Bureau of American Ethnology, 1906–1907, pp. 25–179. Washington, D.C.

Findlow, Frank J., and Suzanne P. DeAtley

1976   Prehistoric Land Use Patterns in the Animas Valley: A First Approximation. *Anthropology UCLA* 6:1–57.

Fink, T. Michael

1985   Tuberculosis and Anemia in a Pueblo II-III (ca. 900–1300) Anasazi Child from New Mexico. In *Health and Disease in the Prehistoric Southwest*, edited by Charles F. Merbs and Robert J. Miller, pp. 359–79. Arizona State University Anthropological Research Papers No. 34. Tempe.

1989   The Human Skeletal Remains from the Grand Canal Ruins, AZ T:12:14 (ASU) and AZ T:12:16 (ASU). In *Archaeological Investigations at the Grand Canal Ruins: A Classic Period Site in Phoenix, Arizona*, edited by Douglas R. Mitchell, pp. 619–704. Soil Systems Publications in Archaeology No. 12. Phoenix.

1991   Prehistoric Irrigation Canals and Their Possible Impact on Hohokam Health. In *Prehistoric Irrigation in Arizona: Symposium 1988*, edited by Cory Dale Breternitz, pp. 61–88. Soil Systems Publications in Archaeology No. 17. Phoenix.

Fink, T. Michael, and Charles F. Merbs

1991   Paleonutrition and Paleopathology of the Salt River Hohokam: A Search for Correlates. *Kiva* 56:293–318.

Fish, Paul R., and Suzanne K. Fish

1991   Hohokam Political and Social Organization. In *Exploring the Hohokam: Prehistoric Desert Peoples of the American Southwest*, edited by George J. Gumerman, pp. 151–75. University of New Mexico Press, Albuquerque.

1994a   Southwest and Northwest: Recent Research at the Juncture of the United States and Mexico. *Journal of Archaeological Research* 2:3–44.

1994b   How Complex Were the Southwestern Great Towns' Polities? Paper presented at the Advanced Seminar "Great Towns and Regional Polities: Cultural Evolution in the U.S. Southwest and Southeast," Amerind Foundation, Dragoon.

Fish, Paul R., Suzanne K. Fish, George J. Gumerman, and J. Jefferson Reid

1994   Toward an Explanation for Southwestern "Abandonments." In *Themes in Southwest Prehistory*, edited by George J. Gumerman, pp. 135–63. School of American Research Press, Santa Fe.

Fish, Suzanne K.

1994   Pollen Results from the Livingston Management Group. In *Archaeology of the Salado in the Livingston Area of Tonto Basin, Roosevelt Platform Mound Study: Report on the Livingston Management Group, Pinto Creek Complex*, by David Jacobs, pp. 851–66. Roosevelt Monograph Series No. 3. Arizona State University Anthropological Field Studies No. 32. Tempe.

1995a   Pollen Results from Bass Point Mound, U:8:23/177. In *Where the Rivers Converge, Roosevelt Platform Mound Study: Report on the Rock Island Complex*, by Owen Lindauer, pp. 375–83. Roosevelt Monograph Series No. 4. Arizona State University Anthropological Field Studies No. 33. Tempe.

1995b   Pollen Results from Roosevelt Community Development Study Sites. In *The Roosevelt Community Development Study: Paleobotanical and Osteological Analyses*, edited by Mark D. Elson and Jeffery J. Clark, pp.1–42. Center for Desert Archaeology Anthropological Papers No. 14, Vol. 3. Tucson.

1996a   Pollen Results from Schoolhouse Mound, U:8:24/13a. In *The Place of the Storehouses, Roosevelt Platform Mound Study: Report on the Schoolhouse Point Mound, Pinto Creek Complex,* by Owen Lindauer, pp. 641–48. Roosevelt Monograph Series No. 6. Arizona State University Anthropological Field Studies No. 35. Tempe.

1996b   Pollen Summary of the Roosevelt Platform Mound Study. In *Environment and Subsistence in the Classic Period Tonto Basin, Roosevelt Platform Mound Study* (Draft), edited by Katherine A. Spielmann. Roosevelt Monograph Series No. 10. Arizona State University Anthropological Field Studies No. 39. Tempe.

1997a   Pollen Results from U:4:33/132, the Cline Terrace Mound. In *A Salado Platform Mound on Tonto Creek, Roosevelt Platform Mound Study: Report on the Cline Terrace Mound, Cline Terrace Complex,* by David Jacobs, pp. 545–52. Roosevelt Monograph Series No. 7. Arizona State University Anthropological Field Studies No. 36. Tempe.

1997b   Pollen Results from the Schoolhouse Point Mesa. In *The Archaeology of Schoolhouse Point Mesa, Roosevelt Platform Mound Study: Report on the Schoolhouse Point Sites, Pinto Creek Complex,* by Owen Lindauer, pp. 483–89. Roosevelt Monograph Series No. 8. Arizona State University Anthropological Field Studies No. 37. Tempe.

1997c   Pollen Results from the Uplands Complex Sites. In *Classic Period Settlement in the Uplands of Tonto Basin, Roosevelt Platform Mound Study: Report on the Uplands Complex*, by Theodore J. Oliver, pp. 431–42. Roosevelt Monograph Series No. 5. Arizona State University Anthropological Field Studies No. 34. Tempe.

Fish, Suzanne K., and Paul R. Fish

1992a   Prehistoric Landscapes of the Sonoran Desert Hohokam. *Population and Environment* 13:269–83.

1992b   The Marana Community in Comparative Context. In *The Marana Community in the Hohokam World,* edited by Suzanne K. Fish, Paul R. Fish, and John H. Madsen, pp. 97–106. Anthropological Papers of The University of Arizona No. 56. The University of Arizona Press, Tucson.

1994   Multisite Communities as Measures of Hohokam Aggregation. In *The Ancient Southwestern Community,* edited by W. H. Wills and Robert D. Leonard, pp. 119–30. University of New Mexico Press, Albuquerque.

Fish, Suzanne K., Paul R. Fish, and John H. Madsen

1985   A Preliminary Analysis of Hohokam Settlement and Agriculture in the Northern Tucson Basin. In *Proceedings of the 1983 Hohokam Symposium,* edited by Alfred E. Dittert, Jr., and Donald E. Dove, pp. 75–100. Arizona Archaeological Society Occasional Papers No. 2. Phoenix.

1992a   Evolution and Structure of the Classic Period Marana Community. In *The Marana Community in the Hohokam World,* edited by Suzanne K. Fish, Paul R. Fish, and John H. Madsen, pp. 20–40. Anthropological Papers of The University of Arizona No. 56. The University of Arizona Press, Tucson.

1992b   Evidence for Large-Scale Agave Cultivation in the Marana Community. In *The Marana Community in the Hohokam World,* edited by Suzanne K. Fish, Paul R. Fish, and John H. Madsen, pp. 73–87. Anthropological Papers of The University of Arizona No. 56. The University of Arizona Press, Tucson.

Fish, Suzanne K., Paul R. Fish, and John H. Madsen (editors)

1992   *The Marana Community in the Hohokam World.* Anthropological Papers of The University of Arizona No. 56. The University of Arizona Press, Tucson.

Fish, Suzanne K., Paul R. Fish, Charles H. Miksicek, and John H. Madsen

1985   Prehistoric Agave Cultivation in Southern Arizona. *Desert Plants* 7(2):107–12.

Fish, Suzanne K., and Gary P. Nabhan

1991   Desert as Context: The Hohokam Environment. In *Exploring the Hohokam, Prehistoric Desert Peoples of the American Southwest,* edited by George J. Gumerman, pp. 29–60. University of New Mexico Press, Albuquerque.

Fitting, James E.

1973   *Four Archaeological Sites in the Big Burro Mountains of New Mexico.* COAS Monograph No. 1. Center of Anthropological Study, Las Cruces, New Mexico.

Flanagan, James G.

1989   Hierarchy in Simple "Egalitarian" Societies. *Annual Reviews in Anthropology* 18:245–66.

Flannery, Kent V.

1972   The Cultural Evolution of Civilizations. *Annual Review of Ecology and Systematics* 3:399–426.

Forbes, R. D.
1916   Extensive Land Classification of the Tonto National Forest. Ms. on file, Tonto National Forest, Phoenix.

Ford, Richard I.
1972   An Ecological Perspective on the Eastern Pueblos. In *New Perspectives on the Pueblos*, edited by Alfonso Ortiz, pp. 1–17. University of New Mexico Press, Albuquerque.

1983   Inter-Indian Exchange in the Southwest. In *Southwest*, edited by Alfonso Ortiz, pp. 711–22. Handbook of North American Indians, Vol. 10, William C. Sturtevant, general editor. Smithsonian Institution, Washington, D.C.

Forde, C. Daryll
1931   Hopi Agriculture and Land Ownership. *The Journal of the Royal Anthropological Institute of Great Britain and Ireland* 61:357–99.

Fox, Gregory L.
1996   *Archeological Investigations at the Upper Ruin, Tonto National Monument, Pt. I: Salvage Excavations at the Upper Ruin, AZ U:8:48 (ASM)—1995*. Western Archeological and Conservation Center Publications in Anthropology No. 70. U.S. National Park Service, Tucson.

Fox, John W.
1987   *Maya Postclassic State Formation: Segmentary Lineage Migration in Advancing Frontiers*. Cambridge University Press, Cambridge.

Fox, Richard G.
1977   *Urban Anthropology, Cities in Their Cultural Settings*. Prentice-Hall, Englewood Cliffs, New Jersey.

Fradkin, Philip L.
1984   *A River No More: The Colorado River and the West*. The University of Arizona Press, Tucson.

Franklin, Hayward H.
1980   *Excavation at the Second Canyon Ruin, San Pedro Valley, Arizona*. Arizona State Museum Contributions to Highway Salvage Archaeology in Arizona No. 60. The University of Arizona, Tucson.

Franklin, Hayward H., and W. Bruce Masse
1976   The San Pedro Salado: A Case for Prehistoric Migration. *The Kiva* 42:47–55.

Fried, Morton H.
1967   *The Evolution of Political Society: An Essay in Political Anthropology*. Random House, New York.

Friedrich, Paul
1989   Language, Ideology, and Political Economy. *American Anthropologist* 91:295–312.

Gann, Douglas W.
1996   The Use of Adobe Brick Architecture in the Homol'ovi Region. In *River of Change: Prehistory of the Middle Little Colorado River Valley, Arizona*, edited by E. Charles Adams, pp. 93–105. Arizona State Museum Archaeological Series No. 185. The University of Arizona, Tucson.

Garrett, Elizabeth M.
1991   Petrographic Analysis of Selected Sherds from the Cuchillo Site. In *The Cuchillo Negro Archaeological Project: On the Periphery of the Mimbres-Mogollon*, edited by Jeanne A. Schutt, Richard C. Chapman, and June-el Piper, pp. 2–1–2–28. University of New Mexico Office of Contract Archaeology, Albuquerque.

Gasser Robert E., and Scott M. Kwiatkowski
1991   Food for Thought: Recognizing Patterns in Hohokam Subsistence. In *Exploring the Hohokam: Prehistoric Desert Peoples of the American Southwest*, edited by George J. Gumerman, pp. 417–59. University of New Mexico Press, Albuquerque.

Genovés, Santiago
1967   Proportionality of the Long Bones and Their Relation to Stature Among Mesoamericans. *American Journal of Physical Anthropology* 26:67–78.

1970   Estimation of Age and Mortality. In *Science in Archaeology: A Survey of Progress and Research*, revised and enlarged edition, edited by Don Brothwell and Eric S. Higgs, pp. 440–52. Praeger, New York.

Germick, Stephen, and Joseph S. Crary
1989   *Prehistoric Adaptations in the Bajada-Upland Areas of the Tonto Basin: Examples from the A-Cross Road and Henderson Mesa Surveys, Tonto National Forest*. Cultural Resources Inventory Report No. 89–240. Tonto National Forest, Phoenix.

1990   *Prehistoric Settlement and Adaptations in the East Piedmont of the Mazatzal Mountains*. Cultural Resources Inventory Report No. 90–200. Tonto National Forest, Phoenix.

1992   From Shadow to Substance: An Alternative Perspective on the Roosevelt Phase. In *Proceedings of the Second Salado Conference Globe, AZ 1992*, edited by Richard C. Lange and Stephen Germick, pp. 286–304. Arizona Archaeological Society Occasional Paper. Phoenix.

Gill, George W.
1985   Cultural Implications of Artificially Modified Human Remains from Northwestern Mexico. In *The Archaeology of West and Northwest Mesoamerica,* edited by Michael S. Foster and Phil C. Weigand, pp. 193–215. Westview Press, Boulder.

Gilman, Patricia A.
1987   Architecture as Artifact: Pit Structures and Pueblos in the American Southwest. *American Antiquity* 52:538–64.
1997   Wandering Villagers: Pit Structures, Mobility, and Agriculture in Southeastern Arizona. *Arizona State University Anthropological Research Papers* No. 49. Tempe.

Gilman, Patricia A, Veletta Canouts, and Ronald L. Bishop
1994   The Production and Distribution of Classic Mimbres Black-on-White Pottery. *American Antiquity* 59:695–709.

Gladwin, Harold S.
1928   *Excavations at Casa Grande, Arizona February 12—May 1, 1927.* Southwest Museum Papers No. 2. Los Angeles.
1957   *A History of the Ancient Southwest.* Bond-Wheelwright, Portland, Maine.

Gladwin, Harold S., Emil W. Haury, E. B. Sayles, and Nora Gladwin
1937   *Excavations at Snaketown: Material Culture.* Medallion Papers No. 25. Gila Pueblo, Globe, Arizona.

Gladwin, Winifred, and Harold S. Gladwin
1930   *Some Southwestern Pottery Types: Series I.* Medallion Papers No. 8. Gila Pueblo, Globe, Arizona.
1935   *The Eastern Range of the Red-on-Buff Culture.* Medallion Papers No. 16. Gila Pueblo, Globe, Arizona.

Goldstein, Lynne
1981   One-Dimensional Archaeology and Multidimensional People: Spatial Organization and Mortuary Analysis. In *The Archaeology of Death,* edited by Robert Chapman, Ian Kinnes, and Klavs Randsborg, pp. 53–69. Cambridge University Press, Cambridge.

Goodwin, Grenville
1935   The Social Divisions and Economic Life of the Western Apache. *American Anthropologist* 39:394–407.
1942   *The Social Organization of the Western Apache.* University of Arizona Press, Tucson.

Graburn, Nelson
1971   Alliance and Descent. In *Readings in Kinship and Social Structure,* edited by Nelson Graburn, pp. 213–14. Harper and Row, New York.

Graves, Michael W.
1982a   Anomalous Tree-Ring Dates and the Sequence of Room Construction at Canyon Creek Ruin, East-Central Arizona. *The Kiva* 47:107–131.
1982b   pache Adaptation to the Mountains. In *Cholla Project Archaeology,* Vol. 3: *The Q Ranch Region,* edited by J. Jefferson Reid, pp. 193–215. Arizona State Museum Archaeological Series No. 161. The University of Arizona, Tucson.
1983   Growth and Aggregation at Canyon Creek Ruin: Implications for Evolutionary Change in East-Central Arizona. *American Antiquity* 48:290–315.
1984   Temporal Variation Among White Mountain Redware Design Styles. *The Kiva* 50:3–24.

Graves, Michael W., Sally J. Holbrook, and William A. Longacre
1982   Aggregation and Abandonment at Grasshopper Pueblo: Evolutionary Trends in the Late Prehistory of East-Central Arizona. In *Multidisciplinary Research at Grasshopper Pueblo, Arizona,* edited by William A. Longacre, Sally J. Holbrook, and Michael W. Graves, pp. 110–22. Anthropological Papers of The University of Arizona No. 40. The University of Arizona Press, Tucson.

Graybill, Donald A.
1989   The Reconstruction of Prehistoric Salt River Streamflow. In *The 1982–1984 Excavations at Las Colinas,* Vol. 5: *Environment and Subsistence,* by Donald A. Graybill, David A. Gregory, Fred L. Nials, Suzanne K. Fish, Charles H. Miksicek, Robert E. Gasser, and Christine R. Szuter, pp. 25–38. Arizona State Museum Archaeological Series No. 162. The University of Arizona, Tucson.

Graybill, Donald A., and J. Jefferson Reid
1982   A Cluster Analysis of Chipped Stone Tools. In *Cholla Project Archaeology,* Vol. 1: *Introduction and Special Studies,* edited by J. Jefferson Reid, pp. 47–50. Arizona State Museum Archaeological Series No. 161. The University of Arizona, Tucson.

Grebinger, Paul F.
1976   Salado Perspectives from the Middle Santa Cruz Valley. *The Kiva* 42:39–46.

Greely, Adolphus W., and William A. Glassford
1891   *Climate of Arizona with Particular Reference to Questions of Water Storage in the Arid*

Region. U.S. Government Printing Office, Washington, D.C.

Greenleaf, J. Cameron

1975   The Fortified Hill Site Near Gila Bend, Arizona. *The Kiva* 40:213–82.

Greenwald, David H., and Richard Ciolek-Torrello

1987   The Picacho Pass Site, NA 18,030. In *Hohokam Settlement Along the Slopes of the Picacho Mountains, Picacho Area Sites*, edited by Richard Ciolek-Torrello, pp. 130–216. Museum of Northern Arizona Research Paper No. 35, Vol. 3. Flagstaff.

Gregory, David A.

1982   Upper Devore Wash Survey. In *Cholla Project Archaeology* Vol. 4: *The Tonto-Roosevelt Region*, edited by J. Jefferson Reid, pp. 174–257. Arizona State Museum Archaeological Series No. 161. The University of Arizona, Tucson.

1987   The Morphology of Platform Mounds and the Structure of Classic Period Hohokam Sites. In *The Hohokam Village: Site Structure and Organization*, edited by David E. Doyel, pp. 183–210. Southwestern and Rocky Mountain Division of the American Association for the Advancement of Science, Glenwood Springs, Colorado.

1991   Form and Variation in Hohokam Settlement Patterns. In *Chaco and Hohokam: Prehistoric Regional Systems in the American Southwest*, edited by Patricia L. Crown and W. James Judge, pp. 159–94. School of American Research Press, Santa Fe.

1994   Prehistoric Ceramic Variability. In *San Carlos Reservoir Cultural Resources Survey*, edited by Andrew Black and Margerie Green, pp. 43–51. Archaeological Consulting Services Cultural Resources Report No. 87. Tempe.

1995a   A Chronological Framework for the Prehistory of the Safford Basin. In *The San Carlos Reservoir Cultural Resources Survey*, edited by Andrew T. Black and Margerie Green, pp. 123–48. Archaeological Consulting Services Cultural Resources Report No. 87. Tempe.

1995b   Prehistoric Settlement Patterns in the Eastern Tonto Basin. In *The Roosevelt Community Development Study: New Perspectives on Tonto Basin Prehistory*, edited by Mark D. Elson, Miriam T. Stark, and David A. Gregory, pp. 127–84. Center for Desert Archaeology Anthropological Papers No. 15. Tucson.

1998   *The Early Agricultural Occupation at Los Pozos, AZ AA:12:91 (ASM).* Center for Desert Archaeology Anthropological Papers No. 21. Tucson.

Gregory, David A. (editor)

1988   *The 1982–1984 Excavations at Las Colinas: The Mound 8 Precinct.* Arizona State Museum Archaeological Series No. 162, Vol. 3. The University of Arizona, Tucson.

Gregory, David A., and Gary Huckleberry

1994   *An Archaeological Survey in the Blackwater Area*, Vol. 1: *The History of Human Settlement in the Blackwater Area.* Archaeological Consulting Services Cultural Resources Report No. 86. Tempe.

Gregory, David A., and Fred L. Nials

1985   Observations Concerning the Distribution of Classic Period Hohokam Platform Mounds. In *Proceedings of the 1983 Hohokam Symposium,* edited by Alfred E. Dittert, Jr., and Donald E. Dove, pp. 373–88. Arizona Archaeological Society Occasional Paper No. 2. Phoenix.

Grissino-Mayer, Henri D.

1994   A 2129-Year Reconstruction of Precipitation for Northwestern New Mexico, USA. In *Tree-Rings, Environment and Humanity: Proceedings of the International Conference, Tucson, Arizona, 17–21 May 1994,* edited by Jeffrey S. Dean, David M. Meko, and Thomas W. Swetnam, pp. 191–204. Radiocarbon, Tucson.

Grossman, Frederick E.

1873   The Pima Indians of Arizona. In *Annual Report, 1871,* pp. 407–19. Smithsonian Institution, Washington, D.C.

Guevara Sanchez, Arturo

1986   *Arqueologia del Area de las Cuarenta Casas, Chihuahua.* Instituto Nacional de Antropologia y Historia, Mexico.

Gumerman, George J.

1993   On the Acquisition of Archaeological Knowledge: The American Southwest and Northwestern Mexico. In *Culture and Contact: Charles C. Di Peso's Gran Chichimeca,* edited by Anne I. Woosley and John C. Ravesloot, pp. 3–10. University of New Mexico Press, Albuquerque.

Gumerman, George J. (editor)

1991   *Exploring the Hohokam: Prehistoric Desert Peoples of the American Southwest.* The University of New Mexico Press, Albuquerque.

Gumerman, George J., and S. Alan Skinner

1968   A Synthesis of the Prehistory of the Central Little Colorado Valley, Arizona. *American Antiquity* 33:185–99.

Haas, Jonathan
  1971 The Ushklish Ruin: A Preliminary Report on Excavations in a Colonial Hohokam Site in the Tonto Basin, Central Arizona. *Arizona Highway Salvage Preliminary Report.* Arizona State Museum, The University of Arizona, Tucson.

Haas, Jonathan, and Winifred Creamer
  1993 *Stress and Warfare Among the Kayenta Anasazi of the Thirteenth Century A.D.* Fieldiana, Anthropology, New Series, No. 21. Field Museum of Natural History, Chicago.

Halbirt, Carl D., and Steven G. Dosh
  1986 *The Late Mogollon Pit House Occupation of the Whiteriver Region, Gila and Navajo Counties, Arizona.* Museum of Northern Arizona, Flagstaff.

Halbirt, Carl D., and Robert E. Gasser
  1987 Archaeobotanical Analyses. In *Archaeology of the Mazatzal Piedmont, Central Arizona,* edited by Richard Ciolek-Torrello, pp. 282–327. Museum of Northern Arizona Research Paper No. 33, Vol. 1. Flagstaff.

Halseth, Odd
  1943 Pueblo Grande. *Arizona Highways.* August: 16–19.
  1947 *Arizona's 1500 Years of Irrigation History.* Pueblo Grande Museum, Phoenix.

Halstead, Paul, and John O'Shea (editors)
  1989 *Bad Year Economics: Cultural Responses to Risk and Uncertainty.* Cambridge University Press, Cambridge.

Hammack, Laurens C.
  1969 Highway Salvage Excavations in the Upper Tonto Basin, Arizona. *The Kiva* 34:132–75.

Hanna, B. L.
  1962 The Biological Relationships Among Indian Groups of the Southwest. *American Journal of Physical Anthropology* 20:499–508.

Hantman, Jeffrey L.
  1978 Models for the Explanation of Changing Settlement on the Little Colorado Planning Unit. In *An Analytical Approach to Cultural Resource Management: The Little Colorado Planning Unit,* edited by Fred Plog, pp. 168–86. Arizona State University Anthropological Research Papers No. 13. Tempe.

Harlow, Francis H.
  1968 Fourteenth Century Painted Pottery From Near Cliff, New Mexico. Ms. on file, Laboratory of Anthropology, Santa Fe.

Harrill, Bruce G.
  1967 Prehistoric Burials Near Young, Arizona. *The Kiva* 33:54–59.

Hartman, Dana
  1987 Burial Analysis. In *Archaeology of the Mazatzal Piedmont, Central Arizona,* edited by Richard Ciolek-Torrello, pp. 216–40. Museum of Northern Arizona Research Paper No. 33, Vol. 1. Flagstaff.

Hassan, Fekri A.
  1981 *Demographic Archaeology.* Academic Press, New York.

Hastings, James Rodney, and Raymond M. Turner
  1965 *The Changing Mile: An Ecological Study of Vegetation Change with Time in the Lower Mile of an Arid and Semiarid Region.* The University of Arizona Press, Tucson.

Haury, Emil W.
  1930 A Report on Excavations at the Rye Creek Ruin, Gila County, Arizona. Ms. on file, Arizona State Museum, The University of Arizona, Tucson.
  1932 *Roosevelt 9:6: A Hohokam Site of the Colonial Period.* Medallion Papers No. 11. Gila Pueblo, Globe, Arizona.
  1934 *The Canyon Creek Ruin and the Cliff Dwellings of the Sierra Ancha.* Medallion Papers No. 14. Gila Pueblo, Globe, Arizona.
  1936 *Some Southwestern Pottery Types, Series IV.* Medallion Papers No. 14. Gila Pueblo, Globe, Arizona.
  1937 Pottery Types at Snaketown. In *Excavations at Snaketown: Material Culture,* by Harold S. Gladwin, Emil W. Haury, E. B. Sayles, and Nora Gladwin, pp. 169–29. Medallion Papers No. 25. Gila Pueblo, Globe, Arizona.
  1940 *Excavations in the Forestdale Valley, East-Central Arizona.* University of Arizona Bulletin Vol. 11, No. 4. Social Science Bulletin No. 12. Tucson.
  1945 *The Excavation of Los Muertos and Neighboring Ruins in the Salt River Valley, Southern Arizona.* Papers of the Peabody Museum of American Archaeology and Ethnology Vol. 24, No. 1. Harvard University, Cambridge.
  1950a *The Stratigraphy and Archaeology of Ventana Cave.* University of Arizona Press, Tucson.
  1950b A Sequence of Great Kivas in the Forestdale Valley, Arizona. In *For the Dean: Essays in Anthropology in Honor of Byron Cummings on his Eighty-Ninth Birthday, September 20, 1950,* edited by Erik K. Reed and Dale S. King, pp. 29–39. Hohokam Museums Association, Tucson, and Southwest Monuments Association, Santa Fe.

1958   Evidence at Point of Pines for a Prehistoric Migration from Northern Arizona. In *Migrations in New World Culture History*, edited by Raymond H. Thompson, pp. 1–6. Social Science Bulletin No. 27. The University of Arizona, Tucson.

1976a   *The Hohokam, Desert Farmers and Craftsmen: Excavations at Snaketown, 1964–1965.* The University of Arizona Press, Tucson.

1976b   Salado: The View from Point of Pines. *The Kiva* 42:81–84.

1976c   Comments on Papers. *The Kiva* 42:125–27.

1985   Tla Kii Ruin, Forestdale's Oldest Pueblo. In *Mogollon Culture in the Forestdale Valley, East-Central Arizona*, by Emil W. Haury, pp. 1–133. The University of Arizona Press, Tucson.

1986   Thoughts after Sixty Years as a Southwestern Archaeologist. In *Emil W. Haury's Prehistory of the American Southwest*, edited by J. Jefferson Reid and David E. Doyel, pp. 451–56. The University of Arizona Press, Tucson.

1987   Comments on Symposium Papers. In *The Hohokam Village: Site Structure and Organization*, edited by David E. Doyel, pp. 249–52. Southwestern and Rocky Mountain Division of the American Association for the Advancement of Science, Glenwood Springs, Colorado.

1989   *Point of Pines: A History of the University of Arizona Archaeological Field School.* Anthropological Papers of The University of Arizona No. 50. The University of Arizona Press, Tucson.

Haury, Emil W., and E. B. Sayles
1947   *An Early Pit House Village of the Mogollon Culture, Forestdale Valley, Arizona.* Social Science Bulletin No. 16. University of Arizona, Tucson.

Hawley, Florence M.
1932   The Bead Mountain Pueblos of Southern Arizona. *Art and Archaeology* 33:227–36.

Hayden, Julian D.
1957   *Excavations, 1940, at University Indian Ruin.* Southwestern Monuments Association Technical Series Vol. 5. Globe, Arizona.

1987   The Vikita Ceremony of the Papago. *Journal of the Southwest* 29:273–324.

Hayes, Alden C., and Thomas C. Windes
1975   An Anasazi Shrine in Chaco Canyon. In *Collected Papers in Honor of Florence Hawley Ellis*, edited by Theodore R. Frisbie, pp. 143–56. Papers of the Archaeological Society of New Mexico No. 2. Hooper Publishing, Norman, Oklahoma.

Hays, Kelley A.
1991   Ceramics. In *Homol'ovi II: Archaeology of an Ancestral Hopi Village, Arizona*, edited by E. Charles Adams and Kelley A. Hays, pp. 23–48. Anthropological Papers of The University of Arizona No. 55. The University of Arizona Press, Tucson.

Hays-Gilpin, Kelley, Trixi Bubemyre, and Louise Senior
1996   The Rise and Demise of Winslow Orange Ware. In *River of Change: Prehistory of the Middle Little Colorado River Valley, Arizona*, edited by E. Charles Adams, pp. 53–74. Arizona State Museum Archaeological Series No. 185. The University of Arizona, Tucson.

Hegmon, Michelle, Margaret C. Nelson, and Susan M. Roth
1998   Abandonment and Reorganization in the Mimbres Region of the American Southwest. *American Anthropologist* 100:148:162

Heidke, James M.
1995   Overview of the Ceramic Collection. In *The Roosevelt Community Development Study: Ceramic Chronology, Technology, and Economics*, edited by James M. Heidke and Miriam T. Stark, pp. 7–18. Center for Desert Archaeology Anthropological Papers No. 14, Vol. 2. Tucson.

Heidke, James M., and Miriam T. Stark
1995   Ceramic Chronology, Technology, and Economics in the Roosevelt Community Development Study Area. In *The Roosevelt Community Development Study: Ceramic Chronology, Technology, and Economics*, edited by James M. Heidke and Miriam T. Stark, pp. 395–408. Center for Desert Archaeology Anthropological Papers No. 14, Vol. 2. Tucson.

Heizer, Robert
1960   Agriculture and the Theocratic State in Lowland Southeastern Mexico. *American Antiquity* 26:215–22.

Henderson, T. Kathleen
1987a   Ceramics, Dates, and the Growth of the Marana Community. In *Studies in the Hohokam Community of Marana*, edited by Glen E. Rice, pp. 49–78. Arizona State University Anthropological Field Studies No. 15. Tempe.

1987b   *Structure and Organization at La Ciudad.* Arizona State University Anthropological Field Studies No. 18. Tempe.

1993   Perspectives on the Classic Period Occupation of the Santa Cruz Flats. In *Classic Period*

*Occupation on the Santa Cruz Flats: The
Santa Cruz Flats Archaeological Project*, ed-
ited by T. Kathleen Henderson and Richard
J. Martynec, pp. 579–96. Northland Research,
Inc., Flagstaff.

1995   *The Prehistoric Archaeology of Heritage
Square.* Pueblo Grande Museum Anthropological Papers No. 3. Phoenix.

Henderson, T. Kathleen (editor)

1989   *Prehistoric Agricultural Activities on the Lehi-
Mesa Terrace: Excavations at La Cuenca
del Sedimento.* Northland Research, Inc.,
Flagstaff.

Hendon, Julia A.

1991   Status and Power in Classic Maya Society:
An Archaeological Study. *American Anthropologist* 93:894–918.

Hensler, Kathy N.

1994   Social Boundaries Set in Clay: Trade Ware
Patterning in the Tonto Basin of East-Cen-
tral Arizona. Paper presented at the 59th
Annual Meeting of the Society for American
Archaeology, Anaheim.

Hibben, Frank C.

1975   *The Kiva Art of the Anasazi at Pottery
Mound.* K. C. Publishing, Las Vegas.

Hill, James N.

1968   Broken K Pueblo: Patterns of Form and
Function. In *New Perspectives in Archaeology*,
edited by Sally R. Binford and Lewis R. Binford, pp. 103–42. Aldine, Chicago.

1970a   *Broken K Pueblo: Prehistoric Social Organization in the American Southwest.* Anthropological Papers of The University of Arizona
No. 18. The University of Arizona Press,
Tucson.

1970b   Prehistoric Social Organization in the American Southwest: Theory and Method. In *Reconstructing Prehistoric Pueblo Societies*, edited by
William A. Longacre, pp. 11–58. University of
New Mexico Press, Albuquerque.

1971   Research Propositions for Consideration:
Southwestern Anthropological Research
Group. In *The Distribution of Prehistoric
Population Aggregates*, edited by George J.
Gumerman, pp. 55–62. Prescott College
Anthropological Reports No. 1. Prescott,
Arizona.

Hill, Jane

1992   The Flower World of Old Uto-Aztecan.
Journal of Anthropological Research
48(2):117–44.

Hillson, Simon

1986   *Teeth.* Cambridge University Press, Cambridge.

Hinkes, Madeleine J.

1983   *Skeletal Evidence of Stress in Subadults: Trying to Come of Age at Grasshopper Pueblo.*
Ph.D dissertation, Department of Anthropology, The University of Arizona.

Hodder, Ian

1979   Social and Economic Stress and Material
Culture Patterning. *American Antiquity*
44:446–54.

1982   *Symbolic and Structural Archaeology.* Cambridge University Press, Cambridge.

1986   *Reading the Past: Current Approaches to
Interpretation in Archaeology.* Cambridge
University Press, Cambridge.

Hohmann, John W.

1985a   Status and Ranking as Exhibited in Burial
Studies. In *Studies of the Hohokam and Salado of the Tonto Basin*, edited by Glen Rice,
pp. 211–20. Office of Cultural Resource Management Report No. 63. Department of
Anthropology, Arizona State University,
Tempe.

1985b   *Hohokam and Salado Hamlets in the Tonto
Basin: Site Descriptions.* Office of Cultural
Resource Management Report No. 64. De-
partment of Anthropology, Arizona State
University, Tempe.

1985c   Site AZ U:3:49 (ASU). In *Hohokam and
Salado Hamlets in the Tonto Basin: Site De-
scriptions*, by John W. Hohmann, pp. 216–90.
Office of Cultural Resource Management
Report No. 64. Department of Anthropol-
ogy, Arizona State University, Tempe.

1992a   An Overview of Salado Heartland Archaeol-
ogy. In *Proceedings of the Second Salado
Conference Globe, AZ 1992*, edited by Richard
C. Lange and Stephen Germick, pp. 1–16.
Arizona Archaeological Society Occasional
Paper. Phoenix.

1992b   *Through the Mirror of Death: A View of
Prehistoric Social Complexity in Central
Arizona.* Ph.D dissertation, Department of
Anthropology, Arizona State University,
Tempe.

Hohmann, John W., and Christopher D. Adams

1992   Salado Site Configuration and Growth: The
Besh-Ba-Gowah Example. In *Proceedings of
the Second Salado Conference Globe, AZ 1992*,
edited by Richard C. Lange and Stephen
Germick, pp. 109–24. Arizona Archaeological
Society Occasional Paper. Phoenix.

Hohmann, John W., Stephen Germick, and
Christopher D. Adams

1992   Discovery of a Salado Ceremonial Room. In
        *Proceedings of the Second Salado Conference
        Globe, AZ 1992*, edited by Richard C. Lange
        and Stephen Germick, pp. 92–102. Arizona
        Archaeological Society Occasional Paper.
        Phoenix.

Hohmann, John W., and Linda B. Kelley

1988   *Erich F. Schmidt's Investigations of Salado
        Sites in Central Arizona: The Mrs. W. B.
        Thompson Archaeological Expedition of the
        American Museum of Natural History.* Mu-
        seum of Northern Arizona Bulletin No. 56.
        Flagstaff.

Holbrook, Sally J., and Michael W. Graves

1982   Modern Environment of the Grasshopper
        Region. In *Multidisciplinary Research at
        Grasshopper Pueblo, Arizona*, edited by Will-
        iam A. Longacre, Sally J. Holbrook, and
        Michael W. Graves, pp. 5–11. Anthropological
        Papers of The University of Arizona No. 40.
        The University of Arizona Press, Tucson.

Homburg, Jeffrey A.

1994   Soil Fertility of Prehistoric Agricultural
        Fields in the Tonto Basin. In *The Roosevelt
        Rural Sites Study*, Vol. 3: *Changing Land Use
        in the Tonto Basin*, edited by Richard Ciolek-
        Torrello and John R. Welch, pp. 253–95.
        Statistical Research Technical Series No. 28.
        Tucson.

Hooton, Earnest A.

1930   *The Indians of Pecos Pueblo.* Yale University
        Press, New Haven.

Hosler, Dorothy

1994   *The Sounds and Colors of Power: The Sacred
        Metallurgical Technology of Ancient West
        Mexico.* MIT Press, Cambridge.

Hough, Walter

1907   *Antiquities of the Upper Gila and Salt River
        Valleys in Arizona and New Mexico.* Bureau
        of American Ethnology Bulletin 35. Smith-
        sonian Institution, Washington, D.C.

Howard, Jerry B.

1992a   Architecture and Ideology: An Approach to
        the Functional Analysis of Platform
        Mounds. In *Proceedings of the Second Salado
        Conference Globe, AZ 1992*, edited by Richard
        C. Lange and Stephen Germick, pp. 69–77.
        Arizona Archaeological Society Occasional
        Paper. Phoenix.

1992b   Between Dessication and Flood: A Com-
        puter Simulation of Irrigation Agriculture
        and Food Storage During the Hohokam
        Classic Period. Paper prepared for ASM 566,
        Simulation, Modeling and Monte Carlo
        Methods. Department of Anthropology,
        Arizona State University, Tempe.

1993   A Paleohydraulic Approach to Examining
        Agricultural Intensification in Hohokam
        Irrigation Systems. *Research in Economic
        Anthropology*, Supplement 7:263–324.

Howard, Jerry B. (editor)

1988   *Excavations at Casa Buena: Changing Hoho-
        kam Land Use Along the Squaw Peak Parkway.*
        Soil Systems Publications in Archaeology No.
        11. Phoenix.

Howells, William W.

1960   Estimating Population Numbers Through
        Archaeological and Skeletal Remains. In *The
        Application of Quantitative Methods in Ar-
        chaeology*, edited by Robert F. Heizer and
        Sherburne F. Cook, pp. 158–80. Quadrangle
        Books, Chicago.

Hrdlicka, Ales

1931   Catalog of Human Crania in the USNM
        Collections. *United States National Museum
        Proceedings* 78:1–95.

Huckell, Bruce B.

1981   The Las Colinas Flaked Stone Assemblage. In
        *The 1968 Excavations at Mound 8, Las
        Colinas Ruins Group, Phoenix, Arizona*, ed-
        ited by Laurens C. Hammack and Alan P.
        Sullivan, pp. 171–200. Arizona State Museum
        Archaeological Series No. 154. The University
        of Arizona, Tucson.

1990   *Late Preceramic Farmer-Foragers in Southern
        Arizona: A Cultural and Ecological Consider-
        ation of the Spread of Agriculture into the
        Arid Southwestern United States.* Ph.D disser-
        tation, Arid Lands Resource Sciences, The
        University of Arizona, Tucson.

1995   *Of Marshes and Maize: Preceramic Agricul-
        tural Settlements in the Cienega Valley,
        Southeastern Arizona.* Anthropological Pa-
        pers of The University of Arizona No. 59.
        The University of Arizona Press, Tucson.

Huckell, Bruce B., and James M. Vint

1994   *Phase 1 Archaeological Data Recovery Report
        and Phase 2 Data Recovery Proposal for the
        Slate Creek Section, ADOT State Route 188
        Project, Tonto Basin, Arizona.* Center for

Desert Archaeology Technical Report No. 94–4. Tucson.

Huntington, Richard, and Peter Metcalf

1979　*Celebrations of Death.* Cambridge University Press, Cambridge.

Jackson, Earl, and Sallie P. Van Valkenburgh

1954　*Montezuma Castle Archaeology: Excavations.* Southwestern Monuments Association Technical Series Vol. 3, Pt.1. Globe, Arizona.

Jacobs, David F.

1992　Increasing Ceremonial Secrecy at a Salado Platform Mound. In *Developing Perspectives on Tonto Basin Prehistory,* edited by Charles L. Redman, Glen E. Rice, and Kathryn E. Pedrick, pp. 45–60. Roosevelt Monograph Series No. 2. Arizona State University Anthropological Field Studies No. 26. Tempe.

1994a　*Archaeology of the Salado in the Livingston Area of Tonto Basin, Roosevelt Platform Mound Study: Report on the Livingston Management Group, Pinto Creek Complex.* Roosevelt Monograph Series No. 3. Arizona State University Anthropological Field Studies No. 32. Tempe.

1994b　The Architecture and Chronology of V:5:66/15a. In *Archaeology of the Salado in the Livingston Area of Tonto Basin, Roosevelt Platform Mound Study: Report on the Livingston Management Group, Pinto Creek Complex,* by David Jacobs, pp. 249–66. Roosevelt Monograph Series No. 3. Arizona State University Anthropological Field Studies No. 32. Tempe.

1994c　The Excavation and Description of V:5:66/15a. In *Archaeology of the Salado in the Livingston Area of Tonto Basin, Roosevelt Platform Mound Study: Report on the Livingston Management Group, Pinto Creek Complex,* by David Jacobs, pp. 133–48. Roosevelt Monograph Series No. 3. Arizona State University Anthropological Field Studies No. 32. Tempe.

1994d　Sample Excavations at Livingston Sites: V:5:141/1013, V:5:130/1015, V:5:120/998, V:5:125/1007, V:5:139/15b. In *Archaeology of the Salado in the Livingston Area of Tonto Basin, Roosevelt Platform Mound Study: Report on the Livingston Management Group, Pinto Creek Complex,* by David Jacobs, pp. 501–78. Roosevelt Monograph Series No. 3. Arizona State University Anthropological Field Studies No. 32. Tempe.

1994e　V:5:119/997, A Roosevelt Phase Compound. In *Archaeology of the Salado in the Livingston Area of Tonto Basin, Roosevelt Platform Mound Study: Report on the Livingston Management Group, Pinto Creek Complex,* by David Jacobs, pp. 287–334. Roosevelt Monograph Series No. 3. Arizona State University Anthropological Field Studies No. 32. Tempe.

1994f　The Excavation and Description of V:5:76/100. In *Archaeology of the Salado in the Livingston Area of Tonto Basin, Roosevelt Platform Mound Study: Report on the Livingston Management Group, Pinto Creek Complex,* by David Jacobs, pp. 75–118. Roosevelt Monograph Series No. 3. Arizona State University Anthropological Field Studies No. 32. Tempe.

1997a　*A Salado Platform Mound on Tonto Creek, Roosevelt Platform Mound Study: Report on the Cline Terrace Mound, Cline Terrace Complex.* Roosevelt Monograph Series No. 7. Arizona State University Anthropological Field Studies No. 36. Tempe.

1997b　Ground-Level Features at U:4:33/132, the Cline Terrace Mound. In *A Salado Platform Mound on Tonto Creek, Roosevelt Platform Mound Study: Report on the Cline Terrace Mound, Cline Terrace Complex,* by David Jacobs, pp.139–24. Roosevelt Monograph Series No. 7. Arizona State University Anthropological Field Studies No. 36. Tempe.

Jacobs, David, and Glen E. Rice

1994a　The Livingston Site Group. In *Archaeology of the Salado in the Livingston Area of Tonto Basin, Roosevelt Platform Mound Study: Report on the Livingston Management Group, Pinto Creek Complex,* by David Jacobs, pp. 1–20. Roosevelt Monograph Series No. 3. Arizona State University Anthropological Field Studies No. 32. Tempe.

1994b　Summary. In *Archaeology of the Salado in the Livingston Area of Tonto Basin, Roosevelt Platform Mound Study: Report on the Livingston Management Group, Pinto Creek Complex,* by David Jacobs, pp. 923–26. Roosevelt Monograph Series No. 3. Arizona State University Anthropological Field Studies No. 32. Tempe.

1997　The Function of U:4:33/132, the Cline Terrace Mound. In *A Salado Platform Mound on Tonto Creek, Roosevelt Platform Mound Study: Report on the Cline Terrace Mound, Cline Terrace Complex,* by David Jacobs, pp. 577–85. Roosevelt Monograph Series No. 7. Arizona State University Anthropological Field Studies No. 36. Tempe.

James, Steven R.

1995   Hunting and Fishing Patterns at Prehistoric Sites Along the Salt River: The Archaeofaunal Analysis. In *The Roosevelt Community Development Study: Paleobotanical and Osteological Analyses*, edited by Mark D. Elson and Jeffery J. Clark, pp. 85–168. Center for Desert Archaeology Anthropological Papers No. 14, Vol. 3. Tucson.

James, W. D., R. L. Brewington, and H. J. Shafer

1995   Compositional Analysis of American Southwestern Ceramics by Neutron Activation Analysis. *Journal of Radioanalytical and Nuclear Chemistry* 192:109–16.

Jenkins, Carol L.

1981   Patterns of Growth and Malnutrition Among Preschoolers in Belize. *American Journal of Physical Anthropology* 56:169–78.

Jeter, Marvin D.

1978   *The Reno-Park Creek Project: Archaeological Investigations in Tonto Basin, Arizona*. Arizona State Museum Contribution to Highway Salvage Archaeology in Arizona No. 49. The University of Arizona, Tucson.

Johanson, S. R., and S. Horowitz

1986   Estimating Mortality in Skeletal Populations: Influence of the Growth Rate on the Interpretation of Levels and Trends During the Transition to Agriculture. *American Journal of Physical Anthropology* 71:233–50.

Johnson, Alfred E.

1966   Archaeology of Sonora, Mexico. In *Archaeological Frontiers and External Connections*, edited by Gordon F. Ekholm and Gordon R. Willey, pp. 26–37. Handbook of Middle American Indians, Vol. 4, Robert Wauchope, general editor. University of Texas Press, Austin.

Johnson, Alfred E., and Raymond H. Thompson

1963   The Ringo Site, Southeastern Arizona. *American Antiquity* 28:465–81.

Johnson, Alfred E., and William W. Wasley

1966   Archaeological Excavations Near Bylas, Arizona. *The Kiva* 31:205–53.

Johnson, Douglas A.

1992   Adobe Brick Architecture and Salado Ceramics at Fourmile Ruin. In *Proceedings of the Second Salado Conference Globe, AZ 1992*, edited by Richard C. Lange and Stephen Germick, pp. 131–38. Arizona Archaeological Society Occasional Paper. Phoenix.

Johnson, Gregory A.

1978   Information Sources and Development of Decision-Making Organizations. In *Social Archaeology: Beyond Subsistence and Dating*, edited by Charles L. Redman, pp. 87–112. Academic Press, New York.

1989   Dynamics of Southwestern Prehistory: Far Outside—Looking In. In *Dynamics of Southwest Prehistory*, edited by Linda S. Cordell and George J. Gumerman, pp. 371–89. Smithsonian Institution Press, Washington, D.C.

Jorgensen, Joseph G.

1980   *Western Indians*. Freeman, San Francisco.

Karhu, Sandra L., and Julie Amon

1994   Childhood Stress Recorded in the Enamel Defects of the Hohokam of Pueblo Grande. In *The Pueblo Grande Project*, Vol. 6: *The Bioethnography of a Classic Period Hohokam Population*, edited by Dennis P. Van Gerven and Susan Guise Sheridan, pp. 25–46. Soil Systems Publications in Archaeology No. 20. Phoenix.

Karhu, Sandra L., Julie Amon, and Dennis P. Van Gerven

1992   Childhood Stress Patterns Among the Hohokam of Pueblo Grande as Indicated by Enamel Defects. *American Journal of Physical Anthropology Supplement* 14:97–98.

Keck, C. W., R. K. St. John, T. M. Daniel, M. Pantoja, D. Danielson, and W. W. Fox

1973   Tuberculosis in the Yungas Area of Bolivia. *Health Services Reports* 88:499–507.

Kelley, J. Charles

1966   Mesoamerica and the Southwestern United States. In *Archaeological Frontiers and External Connections*, edited by Gordon F. Ekholm and Gordon R. Willey, pp. 95–111. Handbook of Middle American Indians, Vol. 4, Robert Wauchope, general editor. University of Texas Press, Austin.

1971   Archaeology of the Northwestern Frontier: Zacatecas and Durango. In *Archaeology of Northern Mesoamerica*, edited by Gordon F. Ekholm and Ignacio Bernal, pp. 768–801. Handbook of Middle American Indians, Vol. 11, Robert Wauchope, general editor. University of Texas Press, Austin.

1974   Speculations on the Culture History of Northwest Mexico. In *The Archaeology of West Mexico*, edited by Betty Bell, pp. 19–39. Sociedad de Estudios Avanzados del Occidente de Mexico, Ajijic, Jalisco.

1993   Zenith Passage: The View from Chalchihuites. In *Culture and Contact: Charles C. Di Peso's Gran Chichimeca*, edited by

Anne I. Woosley and John C. Ravesloot, pp. 227–50. University of New Mexico Press, Albuquerque.

Kelley, Jane H.
1984   *The Archaeology of the Sierra Blanca Region of Southeastern New Mexico.* University of Michigan Museum of Anthropology, Anthropological Papers No. 74. Ann Arbor.

Kent, Kate Peck
1957   *The Cultivation and Weaving of Cotton in the Prehistoric Southwestern United States.* Transactions of the American Philosophical Society Vol. 47, Pt. 2. Philadelphia.
1983a   *Pueblo Indian Textiles: A Living Tradition.* School of American Research Press, Santa Fe.
1983b   Temporal Shifts in the Structure of Traditional Southwestern Textile Design. In *Structure and Cognition in Art*, edited by Dorothy K. Washburn, pp. 113–37. Cambridge University Press, Cambridge.

Kidder, Alfred Vincent
1916   The Pottery of the Casas Grandes District, Chihuahua. *Holmes Anniversary Volume: Anthropological Essays Presented to William Henry Holmes in Honor of His Seventieth Birthday, December 1, 1916*, edited by F. W. Hodge, pp. 253–68. Washington, D.C.
1924   *An Introduction to the Study of Southwestern Archaeology with a Preliminary Account of the Excavations at Pecos.* Papers of the Phillips Academy Southwest Expedition No. 1. Yale University Press, New Haven.

Kidder, A. V., H. S. Cosgrove, and C. B. Cosgrove
1948   *The Pendleton Ruin, Hidalgo County, New Mexico.* Carnegie Institution of Washington, Contributions to American Archaeology and History No. 50. Washington, D.C.

Kidder, Alfred V., Jesse D. Jennings, and Edwin M. Shook
1946   *Excavations at Kaminaljuyu, Guatemala.* Carnegie Institution of Washington Publication No. 561. Washington, D.C.

Kipp, Rita Smith, and Edward M. Schortman
1989   The Political Impact of Trade in Chiefdoms. *American Anthropologist* 91:370–85.

Kohler, Timothy A.
1992   Prehistoric Human Impact on the Environment in the Upland North American Southwest. *Population and Environment* 13:255–68.

Kohler, Timothy A., and Meredith H. Matthews
1988   Long-Term Anasazi Land Use and Forest Reduction: A Case Study from Southwest Colorado. *American Antiquity* 53:537–64.

Kohler, Timothy A., and Carla R. Van West
1996   The Calculus of Self Interest in the Development of Cooperation: Sociopolitical Development and Risk Among the Northern Anasazi. In *Evolving Complexity and Environmental Risk in the Prehistoric Southwest*, edited by Joseph A. Tainter and Bonnie Bagley Tainter, pp. 169–96. Santa Fe Institute Studies in the Sciences of Complexity, Proceedings Volume 24. Addison-Wesley, Reading, Massachusetts.

Kolbe, Thomas
1991   *Fluvial Changes of the Little Colorado River, Northeast Arizona, and Their Effect on the Settlement Patterns of Homol'ovi III Pueblo, a P-IV Flood-Plain Hamlet.* Master's thesis, Quaternary Studies, Northern Arizona University, Flagstaff.

Komorowski, Jean-Christophe
1991   Geologic Setting of Lower Tonto Basin and Adjacent Areas: A Synthesis Based on Available Information and Recent Reconnaissance Field Work, With Implications for the Roosevelt Platform Mound Study. Ms. on file, Office of Cultural Resource Management, Department of Anthropology, Arizona State University, Tempe.

Kramer, Carol
1985   Ceramic Ethnoarchaeology. *Annual Reviews in Anthropology* 14:77–102.

Lahr, M. M., and J. E. Bowman
1992   Paleopathology of the Kechipawan Site: Health and Disease in a South-Western Pueblo. *Journal of Archaeological Science* 19:639–54.

Lamphere, Louise
1983   Southwestern Ceremonialism. In *Southwest*, edited by Alfonso Ortiz, pp. 743–63. Handbook of North American Indians, Vol. 10, William C. Sturtevant, general editor. Smithsonian Institution, Washington, D.C.

Lange, Charles H., and Carroll L. Riley (editors)
1971   *The Southwestern Journals of Adolph F. Bandelier, 1883–1884*, Vol 2. University of New Mexico Press, Albuquerque.

Lange, Richard C.
1982   Steatite: An Analysis and Assessment of Form and Distribution. In *Cholla Project Archaeology, Vol. 1: Introduction and Special Studies*, edited by J. Jefferson Reid, pp. 167–92. Arizona State Museum Archaeological Series No. 161. The University of Arizona, Tucson.

1996 The Little Colorado River, Farming, and Prehistory in the Homol'ovi Area. In *River of Change: Prehistory of the Middle Little Colorado River Valley, Arizona*, edited by E. Charles Adams, pp. 239–58. Arizona State Museum Archaeological Series No. 185. The University of Arizona, Tucson.

LeBlanc, Steven A.

1980a The Post-Mogollon Periods in Southwestern New Mexico: the Animas/Black Mountain Phase and the Salado Period. In *An Archaeological Synthesis of South-Central and Southwestern New Mexico*, by Steven A. LeBlanc and Michael E. Whalen, pp. 271–316. University of New Mexico Office of Contract Archaeology, Albuquerque.

1980b The Dating of Casas Grandes. *American Antiquity* 45:799–806.

1983 *The Mimbres People*. Thames and Hudson, London.

1986 Aspects of Southwestern Prehistory: A.D. 900–1400. In *Ripples in the Chichimec Sea: New Considerations of Southwestern-Mesoamerican Interactions*, edited by Frances Joan Mathien and Randall H. McGuire, pp. 105–34. Southern Illinois University Press, Carbondale.

1989 Cultural Dynamics in the Southern Mogollon Area. In *Dynamics of Southwest Prehistory*, edited by Linda S. Cordell and George J. Gumerman, pp. 179–207. Smithsonian Institution Press, Washington, D.C.

LeBlanc, Steven A., and Carole Khalil

1976 Flare-Rimmed Bowls: A Sub-Type of Mimbres Classic Black-on-White. *The Kiva* 41:289–298.

LeBlanc, Steven A., and Michael E. Whalen

1980 *An Archaeological Synthesis of South-Central and Southwestern New Mexico*. University of New Mexico Office of Contract Archaeology, Albuquerque.

Lekson, Stephen H.

1978 *Settlement Patterns in the Redrock Valley, Southwestern New Mexico*. Master's thesis, Department of Anthropology, Eastern New Mexico University, Portales.

1986a Mesa Verde-Like Pottery Near T-or-C, New Mexico. *Pottery Southwest* 13(4):1.

1986b The Mimbres Region. In *Mogollon Variability*, edited by Charlotte Benson and Steadman Upham, pp. 147–55. New Mexico State University Museum Occasional Papers No 15. Las Cruces.

1987 The El Paso Phase, Casas Grandes, and Classic Period Hohokam. Paper presented at the 5th Jornada Mogollon Conference, Tularosa.

1990 *Mimbres Archaeology of the Upper Gila, New Mexico*. Anthropological Papers of The University of Arizona No. 53. The University of Arizona Press, Tucson.

1991 Settlement Patterns and the Chaco Region. In *Chaco and Hohokam: Prehistoric Regional Systems in the American Southwest*, edited by Patricia L. Crown and W. James Judge, pp. 31–56. School of American Research Press, Santa Fe.

1992a *Archaeological Overview of Southwestern New Mexico*. Historic Preservation Division, Santa Fe.

1992b The Surface Archaeology of Southwestern New Mexico. *The Artifact* 39(3):1–36.

1993 Chaco, Hohokam, and Mimbres: The Southwest in the 11th and 12th Centuries. *Expedition* 35(1):44–52.

1997 Rewriting Southwestern Prehistory. *Archaeology* 50:52–55.

Lekson, Stephen H., and Catherine M. Cameron

1995 The Abandonment of Chaco Canyon, the Mesa Verde Migrations, and the Reorganization of the Pueblo World. *Journal of Anthropological Archaeology* 14:184–202.

Lekson, Stephen H., Mark D. Elson, and Douglas B. Craig

1992 Previous Research and Culture History. In *Research Design for the Roosevelt Community Development Study*, by William H. Doelle, Henry D. Wallace, Mark D. Elson, and Douglas B. Craig, pp. 19–34. Center for Desert Archaeology Anthropological Papers No. 12. Tucson.

Lekson, Stephen H., and Timothy J. Klinger

1973 Villareal II: Preliminary Notes on an Animas Phase Site in Southwestern New Mexico. *Awanyu* 1(2):33–38.

Leone, Mark P.

1986 Symbolic, Structural, and Critical Archaeology. In *American Archaeology Past and Future: A Celebration of the Society for American Archaeology 1935–1985*, edited by David J. Meltzer, Donald D. Fowler, and Jeremy A. Sabloff, pp. 415–38. Smithsonian Institution Press, Washington, D.C.

Leone, Mark P., Parker B. Potter, Jr., and Paul A. Shackel

1987 Toward a Critical Archaeology. *Current Anthropology* 28:283–302.

Lessa, William A., and Evon Z. Vogt

1972 General Introduction. In *Reader in Com-*

parative Religion: An Anthropological Approach, edited by William A. Lessa and Evon Z. Vogt, pp. 1–6. Harper and Row, New York.

Levy, Jerrold E.

1992   *Orayvi Revisited: Social Stratification in an "Egalitarian" Society.* School of American Research Press, Santa Fe.

Lightfoot, Kent G.

1979   Food Redistribution Among Prehistoric Pueblo Groups. *The Kiva* 44:319–39.

Lightfoot, Kent G., and Roberta A. Jewett

1984   Late Prehistoric Ceramic Distributions in East-Central Arizona: An Examination of Cibola, White Mountain, and Salado Wares. In *Regional Analysis of Prehistoric Ceramic Variation: Contemporary Studies of the Cibola Whitewares*, edited by Alan P. Sullivan and Jeffrey L. Hantman, pp. 36–73. Arizona State University Anthropological Research Papers No. 31. Tempe.

Lightfoot, Kent G., and Steadman Upham

1989   Complex Societies in the Prehistoric American Southwest: A Consideration of the Controversy. In *The Sociopolitical Structure of Prehistoric Southwestern Societies*, edited by Steadman Upham, Kent Lightfoot, and Roberta Jewett, pp. 3–30. Westview Press, Boulder.

Lindauer, Owen

1992   Centralized Storage: Evidence from a Salado Platform Mound. In *Developing Perspectives on Tonto Basin Prehistory*, edited by Charles L. Redman, Glen E. Rice, and Kathryn E. Pedrick, pp. 33–44. Roosevelt Monograph Series No. 2. Arizona State University Anthropological Field Studies No. 26. Tempe.

1994   Site V:5:128/1011, Saguaro Muerto. In *Archaeology of the Salado in the Livingston Area of Tonto Basin, Roosevelt Platform Mound Study: Report on the Livingston Management Group, Pinto Creek Complex,* by David Jacobs, pp. 399–462. Roosevelt Monograph Series No. 3. Arizona State University Anthropological Field Studies No. 32. Tempe.

1995a   *Where the Rivers Converge, Roosevelt Platform Mound Study: Report on the Rock Island Complex.* Roosevelt Monograph Series No. 4. Arizona State University Anthropological Field Studies No. 33. Tempe.

1995b   Bass Point Mound Architecture. In *Where the Rivers Converge, Roosevelt Platform Mound Study: Report on the Rock Island Complex,* by Owen Lindauer, pp. 161–92. Roosevelt Monograph Series No. 4. Arizona State University Anthropological Field Studies No. 33. Tempe.

1996a   *The Place of the Storehouses, Roosevelt Platform Mound Study: Report on the Schoolhouse Point Mound, Pinto Creek Complex.* Roosevelt Monograph Series No. 6. Arizona State University Anthropological Field Studies No. 35. Tempe.

1996b   Room and Platform Mound Architecture at Schoolhouse Point Mound. In *The Place of the Storehouses, Roosevelt Platform Mound Study: Report on the Schoolhouse Point Mound, Pinto Creek Complex,* by Owen Lindauer, pp. 355–82. Roosevelt Monograph Series No. 6. Arizona State University Anthropological Field Studies No. 35. Tempe.

1996c   Understanding the Salado Through Work at Schoolhouse Point Mound, U:8:24/13a. In *The Place of the Storehouses, Roosevelt Platform Mound Study: Report on the Schoolhouse Point Mound, Pinto Creek Complex,* by Owen Lindauer, pp. 841–58. Roosevelt Monograph Series No. 6. Arizona State University Anthropological Field Studies No. 35. Tempe.

1996d   Room Feature Descriptions at the Schoolhouse Point Mound, U:8:24/138. In *The Place of the Storehouses, Roosevelt Platform Mound Study: Report on the Schoolhouse Point Mound, Pinto Creek Complex,* by Owen Lindauer, pp. 57–335. Roosevelt Monograph Series No. 6. Arizona State University Anthropological Field Studies No. 35. Tempe.

1997   *The Archaeology of Schoolhouse Point Mesa, Roosevelt Platform Mound Study: Report on the Schoolhouse Point Mesa Sites, Schoolhouse Management Group, Pinto Creek Complex.* Roosevelt Monograph Series No. 8. Arizona State University Anthropological Field Studies No. 37. Tempe.

Lindauer, Owen, and Arleyn W. Simon

1995   Plain, Red, and Other Ceramic Wares from the Rock Island Complex. In *Where the Rivers Converge, Roosevelt Platform Mound Study: Report on the Rock Island Complex,* by Owen Lindauer, pp. 249–91. Roosevelt Monograph Series No. 4. Arizona State University Anthropological Field Studies No. 33. Tempe.

Lindauer, Owen, and Bert Zaslow
1994   Homologous Style Structures in Hohokam and Trincheras Art. *Kiva* 59:319–44.

Lindsay, Alexander J., Jr.
1987   Anasazi Population Movements to Southeastern Arizona. *American Archeology* 6:190–98.
1992   Tucson Polychrome: History, Dating, Distribution, and Design. In *Proceedings of the Second Salado Conference Globe, AZ 1992,* edited by Richard C. Lange and Stephen Germick, pp. 230–37. Arizona Archaeological Society Occasional Paper. Phoenix.

Lindsay, Alexander J., Jr., and Calvin H. Jennings (editors)
1968   *Salado Red Ware Conference, Ninth Southwestern Ceramic Seminar.* Museum of Northern Arizona Ceramic Series No. 4. Flagstaff.

Lipe, William D.
1995   The Depopulation of the Northern San Juan: Conditions in the Turbulent 1200s. *Journal of Anthropological Archaeology* 14:143–69.

Loendorf, Chris
1996a   Burial Practices at the Schoolhouse Point Mound, U:8:24/13a. In *The Place of the Storehouses, Roosevelt Platform Mound Study: Report on the Schoolhouse Point Mound, Pinto Creek Complex,* by Owen Lindauer, pp. 681–759. Roosevelt Monograph Series No. 6. Arizona State University Anthropological Field Studies No. 35. Tempe.
1996b   Painted Wooden Artifacts from Burials, Schoolhouse Point Mound. In *The Place of the Storehouses, Roosevelt Platform Mound Study: Report on Schoolhouse Point Mound, Pinto Creek Complex,* by Owen Lindauer, pp. 761–65. Roosevelt Monograph Series No. 6. Arizona State University Anthropological Field Studies No. 35. Tempe.
1996c   Quantitative Analysis of the Burial Assemblage from Schoolhouse Point Mound, U:8:24/13a. In *The Place of the Storehouses, Roosevelt Platform Mound Study: Report on Schoolhouse Point Mound, Pinto Creek Complex,* by Owen Lindauer, pp. 767–85. Roosevelt Monograph Series No. 6. Arizona State University Anthropological Field Studies No. 35. Tempe.
1997   Burial Practices at U:4:33/132, the Cline Terrace Mound. In *A Salado Platform Mound on Tonto Creek, Roosevelt Platform Mound Study: Report on the Cline Terrace Mound, Cline Terrace Complex,* by David Jacobs, pp.

465–503. Roosevelt Monograph Series No. 7. Arizona State University Anthropological Field Studies No. 36. Tempe.
1998   Salado Burial Practices and Social Organization. In *The Salado Populations of Tonto Basin: The Roosevelt Archaeology Studies, 1989 to 1998* (Draft), by Christy G. Turner, II, pp. 41–81. Roosevelt Monograph Series No. 13. Arizona State University Anthropological Field Studies No. 41. Tempe.

Loendorf, Chris, Owen Lindauer, and John C. Ravesloot
1995   Burial Features at the Bass Point Mound, U:8:23/177. In *Where the Rivers Converge, Roosevelt Platform Mound Study: Report on the Rock Island Complex,* by Owen Lindauer, pp. 401–14. Roosevelt Monograph Series No. 4. Arizona State University Anthropological Field Studies No. 33. Tempe.

Longacre, William A.
1962   Archaeological Reconnaissance in Eastern Arizona. In *Chapters in the Prehistory of Eastern Arizona I,* by Paul S. Martin, John B. Rinaldo, William A. Longacre, Constance Cronin, Leslie G. Freeman, and James Schoenwetter, pp. 148–67. Fieldiana: Anthropology Vol. 53. Chicago Natural History Museum, Chicago.
1970   *Archaeology as Anthropology: A Case Study.* Anthropological Papers of The University of Arizona No. 17. The University of Arizona Press, Tucson.
1975   Population Dynamics at the Grasshopper Pueblo, Arizona. In *Population Studies in Archaeology and Biological Anthropology: A Symposium,* edited by Alan C. Swedlund, pp. 71–74. Society for American Archaeology Memoir No. 30.
1976   Population Dynamics at the Grasshopper Pueblo, Arizona. In *Demographic Anthropology: Quantitative Approaches,* edited by Ezra B. W. Zubrow, pp. 169–84. University of New Mexico Press, Albuquerque.

Longacre, William A., Sally J. Holbrook, and Michael W. Graves (editors)
1982   *Multidisciplinary Research at Grasshopper Pueblo, Arizona.* Anthropological Papers of The University of Arizona No. 40. The University of Arizona Press, Tucson.

Lorentzen, Leon H.
1993   *From Atlatl to Bow: The Impact of Improved Weapons on Wildlife in the Grasshopper Region.* Master's paper, Department of Anthropology, The University of Arizona, Tucson.

Lowell, Julie C.

1991   *Prehistoric Households at Turkey Creek Pueblo, Arizona.* Anthropological Papers of The University of Arizona No. 54. The University of Arizona Press, Tucson.

1995   Illuminating Fire-Feature Variability in the Grasshopper Region of Arizona. *Kiva* 60:351–69.

Mabry, Jonathan B. (editor)

1998   *Archaeological Investigations of Early Village Sites in the Middle Santa Cruz Valley: Analyses and Syntheses.* Center for Desert Archaeology Anthropological Papers No. 19. Tucson.

Mabry, Jonathan B., Deborah L. Swartz, Helga Wöcherl, Jeffery J. Clark, Gavin H. Archer, and Michael W. Lindeman

1997   *Archaeological Investigations of Early Village Site in the Middle Santa Cruz Valley.* Center for Desert Archaeology Anthropological Papers No. 18. Tucson.

McCartney, Peter H., and Owen Lindauer

1996   The Developmental Sequence and Site Chronology of Schoolhouse Point Mound, U:8:24/13a. In *The Place of the Storehouses, Roosevelt Platform Mound Study: Report on Schoolhouse Point Mound, Pinto Creek Complex,* by Owen Lindauer, pp. 383–417. Roosevelt Monograph Series No. 6. Arizona State University Anthropological Field Studies No. 35. Tempe.

McCartney, Peter H., Owen Lindauer, Glen E. Rice, and John C. Ravesloot

1994   Chronological Methods. In *Archaeology of the Salado in the Livingston Area of Tonto Basin, Roosevelt Platform Mound Study: Report on the Livingston Management Group, Pinto Creek Complex,* by David Jacobs, pp. 21–50. Roosevelt Monograph Series No. 3. Arizona State University Anthropological Field Studies No. 32. Tempe.

McCluney, Eugene B.

1965a   Excavation of the Joyce Well Site. Ms. on file, Laboratory of Anthropology, Santa Fe.

1965b   *Clanton Draw and Box Canyon.* School of American Research Monograph No. 26. Santa Fe.

McGuire, Randall H.

1985   The Role of Shell Exchange in the Explanation of Hohokam Prehistory. In *Proceedings of the 1983 Hohokam Symposium,* edited by Alfred E. Dittert, Jr., and Donald E. Dove, pp. 473–82. Arizona Archaeological Society Occasional Paper No. 2. Phoenix.

1986   Economies and Modes of Production in the Prehistoric Southwestern Periphery. In *Ripples in the Chichimec Sea: New Considerations of Southwestern-Mesoamerican Interactions,* edited by Frances Joan Mathien and Randall H. McGuire, pp. 243–69. Southern Illinois University Press, Carbondale.

1987   A Gila Butte Ballcourt at La Ciudad. In *The Hohokam Community of La Ciudad,* edited by Glen E. Rice, pp. 69–110. Office of Cultural Resource Management Report No. 69. Department of Anthropology, Arizona State University, Tempe.

1989   The Greater Southwest as a Periphery of Mesoamerica. In *Centre and Periphery: Comparative Studies in Archaeology,* edited by Timothy C. Champion, pp. 40–66. Unwin Hyman, London.

1991   On the Outside Looking In: The Concept of Periphery in Hohokam Archaeology. In *Exploring the Hohokam: Prehistoric Desert Peoples of the American Southwest,* edited by George J. Gumerman, pp. 347–82. University of New Mexico Press, Albuquerque.

1992   *A Marxist Archaeology.* Academic Press, New York.

McGuire, Randall H., E. Charles Adams, Ben A. Nelson, and Katherine Spielmann

1994   Drawing the Southwest to Scale: Perspectives on Macroregional Relations. In *Themes in Southwest Prehistory,* edited by George J. Gumerman, pp. 239–66. School of American Research Press, Santa Fe.

McGuire, Randall H., and Maria Elisa Villalpando

1989   Prehistory and the Making of History in Sonora. In *Columbian Consequences: Archaeological and Historical Perspectives on the Spanish Borderlands West,* edited by David Hurst Thomas, pp. 159–78. Smithsonian Institution Press, Washington, D.C.

Macnider, Barbara S., and Richard W. Effland, Jr.

1989   *Cultural Resources Overview: The Tonto National Forest.* Tonto National Forest Cultural Resources Inventory Report No. 88–12–312A. Archaeological Consulting Services Cultural Resources Report No. 51. Phoenix.

McWilliams, Kenneth R.

1974   *Gran Quivira Pueblo and Biological Distance in the U.S. Southwest.* Ph.D dissertation, Department of Anthropology, Arizona State University, Tempe.

Malina, R. M., and J. H. Himes
1971   Patterns of Childhood Mortality and Growth Status in a Rural Zapotec Community. *Annals of Human Biology* 5(6):517–31.

Marshall, Michael P., David E. Doyel, and Cory Dale Breternitz
1982   A Regional Perspective on the Late Bonito Phase. In *Bis Sa'ani: A Late Bonito Phase Community on Escavada Wash, Northwest New Mexico*, edited by Cory Dale Breternitz, David E. Doyel, and Michael P. Marshall, pp. 1227–1240. Navajo Nation Papers in Anthropology No. 14. Window Rock, Arizona.

Martin, Debra L.
1994   Patterns of Diet and Disease: Health Profiles for the Prehistoric Southwest. In *Themes in Southwest Prehistory*, edited by George J. Gumerman, pp. 87–108. School of American Research Press, Santa Fe.

Martin, Debra L., Alan H. Goodman, George J. Armelagos, and Ann L. Magennis
1991   *Black Mesa Anasazi Health: Reconstructing Life from Patterns of Death and Disease.* Southern Illinois University Center for Archaeological Investigations Occasional Paper No. 14. Carbondale.

Martin, Paul S.
1943   *The SU Site, Excavations at a Mogollon Village, Western New Mexico, Second Season, 1941.* Anthropology Series Vol. 32, No. 2. Field Museum of Natural History, Chicago.

Martin, Paul S., and Fred Plog
1973   *The Archaeology of Arizona: A Study of the Southwest Region.* Doubleday/Natural History Press, Garden City, New York.

Martin, Paul S., and John B. Rinaldo
1960   *Table Rock Pueblo.* Fieldiana: Anthropology 51:2. Chicago Natural History Museum. Chicago.

Martorell, Reynaldo
1989   Body Size, Adaptation, and Function. *Human Organization* 48(1):15–20.

Masse, W. Bruce
1981   Prehistoric Irrigation Systems in the Salt River Valley. *Science* 214:408–15.
1991   The Quest for Subsistence Sufficiency and Civilization in the Sonoran Desert. In *Chaco and Hohokam: Prehistoric Regional Systems in the American Southwest*, edited by Patricia L. Crown and W. James Judge, pp. 195–223. School of American Research Press, Santa Fe.

Matthews, W., J. L. Wortman, and J. S. Billings
1893   *The Human Bones of the Hemenway Collection in the United States Army Medical Museum at Washington.* Memoirs of the National Academy of Sciences, Vol. 6, Memoir 7, pp. 141–286.

Mayro, Linda L., Stephanie M. Whittlesey, and J. Jefferson Reid
1976   Observations on the Salado Presence at Grasshopper Pueblo. *The Kiva* 42:27–37.

Meighan, Clement W.
1974   Prehistory of West Mexico. *Science* 184:1254–1261.

Merbs, Charles F.
1992   ABO, MN, and Rh Frequencies Among the Havasupai and Other Southwest Indian Groups. *Kiva* 58:67–88.

Merbs, Charles F., and Judy Brunson
1987   Burial Orientation and Concepts of Afterlife in the American Southwest and Canadian Arctic. Paper presented at the 52nd Annual Meeting of the Society for American Archaeology, Toronto.

Merbs, Charles F., and Ellen M. Vestergaard
1985   The Paleopathology of Sundown, a Prehistoric Site Near Prescott, Arizona. In *Health and Disease in the Prehistoric Southwest*, edited by Charles F. Merbs and Robert J. Miller, pp. 85–103. Arizona State University Anthropological Research Papers No. 34. Tempe.

Merchant, V. L., and D. H. Ubelaker
1977   Skeletal Growth of the Protohistoric Arikara. *American Journal of Physical Anthropology* 46:61–72.

Merriam, C. Hart
1890   *Life-Zones and Crop-Zones of the United States.* U.S. Department of Agriculture, North American Fauna 3. Washington, D.C.
1898   *Life-Zones and Crop-Zones of the United States.* U.S. Department of Agriculture, Division of Biological Survey, Bulletin 10.

Merrill, William L.
1983   Tarahumara Social Organization, Political Organization, and Religion. In *Southwest*, edited by Alfonso Ortiz, pp. 290–305. Handbook of North American Indians, Vol. 10, William C. Sturtevant, general editor. Smithsonian Institution, Washington, D.C.

Micozzi, Marc S., and Marc A. Kelley
1985   Evidence for Pre-Columbian Tuberculosis at the Point of Pines Site, Arizona: Skeletal

Pathology in the Sacro-Iliac Region. In *Health and Disease in the Prehistoric Southwest*, edited by Charles F. Merbs and Robert J. Miller, pp. 347–58. Arizona State University Anthropological Research Papers No. 34. Tempe.

Miksa, Elizabeth J.

1995   Petrographic Analysis of Pottery from Pueblo Blanco. In *Archaeological Excavations at Pueblo Blanco: The MCDOT Alma School Road Project*, edited by David E. Doyel, Andrew Black, and Barbara Macnider, pp. 169–86. Archaeological Consulting Services Cultural Resources Report No. 90. Tempe.

1998   *A Model for Assigning Temper Provenance to Archaeological Ceramics with Case Studies from the American Southwest.* Ph.D Dissertation, Department of Geosciences, The University of Arizona, Tucson.

Miksa, Elizabeth J., and James M. Heidke

1995   Drawing a Line in the Sands: Developing Compositional Models of Sand Temper Resource Procurement Zones for Archaeological Provenance Studies. In *The Roosevelt Community Development Study: Ceramic Chronology, Technology, and Economics*, edited by James M. Heidke and Miriam T. Stark, pp. 133–206. Center for Desert Archaeology Anthropological Papers No. 14, Vol. 2. Tucson.

Miksicek, Charles H.

1989   *Paleobotany of Homol'ovi III.* Ms. on file, Homol'ovi Research Program, Arizona State Museum, The University of Arizona, Tucson.

1991   Paleoethnobotany. In *Homol'ovi II: The Archaeology of an Ancestral Hopi Village*, edited by E. Charles Adams and Kelley A. Hays, pp. 88–102. Anthropological Papers of The University of Arizona No. 55. Tucson.

1995   Temporal Trends in the Eastern Tonto Basin: An Archaeobotanical Perspective. In *The Roosevelt Community Development Study: Paleobotanical and Osteological Analyses*, edited by Mark D. Elson and Jeffery J. Clark, pp. 43–83. Center for Desert Archaeology Anthropological Papers No. 14, Vol. 3. Tucson.

Miller, Robert J.

1981   *Chavez Pass and Biological Relationships in Prehistoric Central Arizona.* Ph.D dissertation, Department of Anthropology, Arizona State University, Tempe.

Mills, Barbara J.

1995   Interpretive Summary. In *Silver Creek Archaeological Research Project: 1995 Field Report*, by Barbara J. Mills, Sarah A. Herr, Eric J. Kaldahl, Joanne M. Newcomb, Susan L. Stinson, and Scott Van Keuren, pp. 90–94. Report submitted to the Apache-Sitgreaves National Forests, Springerville, Arizona.

Mills, Jack P., and Vera M. Mills

1969   *The Kuykendall Site.* El Paso Archaeological Society Special Report No. 6. El Paso.

1971   The Slaughter Ranch Site. *The Artifact* 9(3):23–52.

1972   The Dinwiddie Site. *The Artifact* 10(2):i–50.

1975   The Meredith Ranch Site, VIV Ruin: A Prehistoric Salado Pueblo in the Tonto Basin, Central Arizona. Privately published by Jack and Vera Mills, Elfrida, Arizona.

1978   The Curtis Site: A Prehistoric Village in the Safford Valley. Privately published by Jack and Vera Mills, Elfrida, Arizona.

Minc, Leah D., and Kevin P. Smith

1989   The Spirit of Survival: Cultural Responses to Resource Availability in North Alaska. In *Bad Year Economics: Cultural Responses to Risk and Uncertainty*, edited by Paul Halstead and John O'Shea, pp. 8–39. Cambridge University Press, Cambridge.

Minnis, Paul E.

1989   The Casas Grandes Polity in the International Four Corners. In *The Sociopolitical Structure of Prehistoric Southwestern Societies*, edited by Steadman Upham, Kent G. Lightfoot, and Roberta A. Jewett, pp. 269–305. Westview Press, Boulder.

1996   Notes on Economic Uncertainty and Human Behavior in the Prehistoric North American Southwest. In *Evolving Complexity and Environmental Risk in the Prehistoric Southwest*, edited by Joseph A. Tainter and Bonnie Bagley Tainter, pp. 57–78. Santa Fe Institute Studies in the Sciences of Complexity, Proceedings Volume 24. Addison-Wesley, Reading, Massachusetts.

Minnis, Paul E., and Michael E. Whalen

1993   Casas Grandes: Archaeology in Northern Mexico. *Expedition* 35(1):34–43.

Mitchell, Douglas R.

1986   *Hohokam, Mogollon, and Western Pueblo Settlement Systems in the San Carlos River Valley, Arizona.* Master's thesis, Department of Anthropology, Arizona State University, Tempe.

1992   Burial Practices and Paleodemographic Reconstructions of Pueblo Grande. *Kiva* 58:89–105.

Mitchell, Douglas R. (editor)
1994   *The Pueblo Grande Project,* Vol. 7: *An Analysis of Classic Period Mortuary Patterns.* Soil Systems Publications in Archaeology No. 20. Phoenix.

Mitchell, Douglas R., T. Michael Fink, and Wilma Allen
1989   Disposal of the Dead: Explorations of Mortuary Variability and Social Organization at the Grand Canal Ruins. In *Archaeological Investigations at the Grand Canal Ruins: A Classic Period Site in Phoenix, Arizona*, edited by Douglas R. Mitchell, pp. 705–73. Soil Systems Publications in Archaeology No. 12. Phoenix.

Mitchell, Douglas R., and M. Steven Shackley
1995   Classic Period Hohokam Obsidian Studies in Southern Arizona. *Journal of Field Archaeology* 22:291–304.

Mittler, Diane, and Dennis P. Van Gerven
1994   Porotic Hyperostosis and Diploic Thickening at Pueblo Grande. In *The Pueblo Grande Project,* Vol. 6: *The Bioethnography of a Classic Period Hohokam Population*, edited by Dennis P. Van Gerven and Susan Guise Sheridan, pp. 55–74. Soil Systems Publications in Archaeology No. 20. Phoenix.

Montgomery, Barbara K.
1992   *Understanding the Formation of the Archaeological Record: Ceramic Variability at Chodistaas Pueblo, Arizona.* Ph.D dissertation, Department of Anthropology, The University of Arizona, Tucson.

Montgomery, Barbara K., and J. Jefferson Reid
1990   An Instance of Rapid Ceramic Change in the American Southwest. *American Antiquity* 55:88–97.

1993   The Brown and the Gray: Pots, People, and Population Movement in East-Central Arizona. Paper presented at the Spring Meeting, Arizona Archaeological Council, Flagstaff.

Moore, James A., Alan C. Swedlund, and George J. Armelagos
1975   The Use of Life Tables in Paleodemography. In *Population Studies in Archaeology and Biological Anthropology: A Symposium*, edited by Alan C. Swedlund, pp. 57–70. Memoirs of the Society for American Archaeology No. 30.

Moore, John H.
1994   Putting Anthropology Back Together Again: The Ethnogenetic Critique of Cladistic Theory. *American Anthropologist* 96:925–48.

Morris, Donald H.
1967   Preliminary Report on the First Season's Work at Walnut Creek, Arizona. Ms. on file, Tonto National Forest, Phoenix.

1969a   Red Mountain: An Early Pioneer Period Hohokam Site in the Salt River Valley of Central Arizona. *American Antiquity* 34:40–54.

1969b   A 9th Century Salado (?) Kiva at Walnut Creek, Arizona. *Plateau* 42:1–10.

1970   Walnut Creek Village: A Ninth-Century Hohokam-Anasazi Settlement in the Mountains of Central Arizona. *American Antiquity* 35:49–61.

Moulard, Barbara L.
1984   *Within the Underworld Sky: Mimbres Ceramic Art in Context.* Twelvetrees Press, Pasadena.

Neely, James A.
1997   Foothill Irrigation and Domestic Water Systems of the Safford Valley, Southeastern Arizona. Paper presented at the 62nd Annual Meeting of the Society for American Archaeology, Nashville.

Neily, Robert B.
1992   *Archaeological Survey of the Schoolhouse Point, Cottonwood Wash, and Indian Point Parcels Around Roosevelt Lake, Tonto Basin Ranger District, Tonto National Forest, Gila County, Arizona.* Archaeological Consulting Services Cultural Resources Report No. 70. Tempe.

1997   Roadhouse Ruin: AZ U:2:73/01–167. In *Descriptions of Habitation and Nonagricultural Sites*, edited by Richard Ciolek-Torrello, pp. 133–72. Vanishing River: Landscapes and Lives of the Lower Verde Valley: The Lower Verde Archaeological Project, Vol. 1. SRI Press, Tucson.

Neitzel, Jill
1991   Hohokam Material Culture and Behavior: The Dimensions of Organizational Change. In *Exploring the Hohokam: Prehistoric Desert Peoples of the American Southwest*, edited by George J. Gumerman, pp. 177–230. University of New Mexico Press, Albuquerque.

Nelson, Ben A.
1997   Chronology and Stratigraphy at La Quemada, Zacatecas, Mexico. *Journal of Field Archaeology* 24:85–109.

Nelson, Ben A., and Roger Anyon
1996   Fallow Valleys: Asynchronous Occupations in Southwestern New Mexico. *Kiva* 61:275–94.

Nelson, Ben A., and Steven A. LeBlanc

1986   *Short-Term Sedentism in the American Southwest: The Mimbres Valley Salado.* University of New Mexico Press, Albuquerque.

Nelson, Richard S.

1981   *The Role of a Puchteca System in Hohokam Exchange.* Ph.D dissertation, Department of Anthropology, New York University.

Nials, Fred L., David A. Gregory, and Donald A. Graybill

1989   Salt River Streamflow and Hohokam Irrigation Systems. In *The 1982–1984 Excavations at Las Colinas,* Vol. 5: *Environment and Subsistence,* by Donald A. Graybill, David A. Gregory, Fred L. Nials, Suzanne K. Fish, Charles H. Miksicek, Robert E. Gasser, and Christine R. Szuter, pp. 59–76. Arizona State Museum Archaeological Series No. 162. The University of Arizona, Tucson.

Nicholas, Linda M., and Gary M. Feinman

1989   A Regional Perspective on Hohokam Irrigation in the Lower Salt River Valley, Arizona. In *The Sociopolitical Structure of Prehistoric Southwestern Societies*, edited by Steadman Upham, Kent G. Lightfoot, and Roberta A. Jewett, pp. 199–235. Westview Press, Boulder.

Noss, John F.

1986   The Effects of Non-Stationary Population Growth Rates on Paleodemographic Life Tables (Abstract). *American Journal of Physical Anthropology* 69:247.

Oliver, Theodore J.

1997a   *Classic Period Settlement in the Uplands of Tonto Basin, Roosevelt Platform Mound Study: Report on the Uplands Complex.* Roosevelt Monograph Series No. 5. Arizona State University Anthropological Field Studies No. 34. Tempe.

1997b   Classic Period Subsistence and Settlement in the Uplands of Tonto Basin. In *Classic Period Settlement in the Uplands of Tonto Basin, Roosevelt Platform Mound Study: Report on the Uplands Complex,* by Theodore J. Oliver, pp. 465–76. Roosevelt Monograph Series No. 5. Arizona State University Anthropological Field Studies No. 34. Tempe.

Oliver, Theodore J., and David Jacobs

1997   Changing Patterns of Settlement, Subsistence, and Society on Tonto Creek. In *Salado Residential Settlements on Tonto Creek, Roosevelt Platform Mound Study: Report on the Cline Mesa Sites, Cline Terrace Complex,* by Theodore J. Oliver and David Jacobs, pp.

967–89. Roosevelt Monograph Series No. 9. Arizona State University Anthropological Field Studies No. 38. Tempe.

Oliver, Theodore J., and David Jacobs (editors)

1997   *Salado Residential Settlements on Tonto Creek, Roosevelt Platform Mound Study: Report on the Cline Mesa Sites, Cline Terrace Complex.* Roosevelt Monograph Series No. 9. Arizona State University Anthropological Field Studies No. 38. Tempe.

Opler, Morris E.

1983   The Apachean Culture Pattern and Its Origins. In *Southwest*, edited by Alfonso Ortiz, pp. 368–93. Handbook of North American Indians, Vol. 10, William C. Sturtevant, general editor. Smithsonian Institution, Washington, D.C.

Ortiz, Alfonso

1969   *The Tewa World: Space, Time, Being, and Becoming in a Pueblo Society*. University of Chicago Press, Chicago.

1972   Ritual Drama and the Pueblo World View. In *New Perspectives on the Pueblos*, edited by Alfonso Ortiz, pp. 135–61. University of New Mexico Press, Albuquerque.

O'Shea, John M.

1984   *Mortuary Variability: An Archaeological Investigation.* Academic Press, Orlando.

Owen, Roger C.

1965   The Patrilocal Band: A Linguistically and Culturally Hybrid Social Unit. *American Anthropologist* 67:675–90.

Pailes, Richard A.

1972   *An Archaeological Reconnaissance of Southern Sonora and Reconsideration of the Rio Sonora Culture.* Ph.D dissertation, Southern Illinois University, Carbondale.

1984   Agricultural Development and Trade in the Rio Sonora. In *Prehistoric Agricultural Strategies in the Southwest*, edited by Suzanne K. Fish and Paul R. Fish, pp. 309–25. Arizona State University Anthropological Research Papers No. 33. Tempe.

1990   Elite Formation and Interregional Exchanges in Peripheries. In *Perspectives on Southwestern Prehistory*, edited by Paul E. Minnis and Charles L. Redman, pp. 213–24. Westview Press, Boulder.

Paine, Richard R.

1989   Model Life Tables as a Measure of Bias in the Grasshopper Pueblo Skeletal Series. *American Antiquity* 54:820–24.

1994   Modelling the Effect of Migration on Age-at-Death Distributions: Implications for Paleodemography. *American Journal of Physical Anthropology Supplement* 18:156 (abstract).

Palkovich, Ann M.

1980   *The Arroyo Hondo Skeletal and Mortuary Remains.* Arroyo Hondo Archaeological Series, Vol. 6. School of American Research Press, Santa Fe.

1985   Interpreting Prehistoric Morbidity Incidence and Mortality Risk: Nutritional Stress at Arroyo Hondo Pueblo, New Mexico. In *Health and Disease in the Prehistoric Southwest,* edited by Charles F. Merbs and Robert J. Miller, pp. 128–38. Arizona State University Anthropological Research Papers No. 34. Tempe.

Parsons, Elsie Clews

1923   *Laguna Genealogies.* Anthropological Papers Vol. 19. American Museum of Natural History, New York.

1936   *The Hopi Journal of Alexander M. Stephen,* Pt. II. Columbia University Press, New York.

1939   *Pueblo Indian Religion.* University of Chicago Press, Chicago.

Parsons, Jeffrey R., and Mary H. Parsons

1990   *Maguey Utilization in Highland Central Mexico, an Archaeological Ethnography.* Museum of Anthropology Anthropological Papers No. 82. University of Michigan, Ann Arbor.

Partridge, J., and V. R. Baker

1987   Paleoflood Hydrology of the Salt River, Arizona. *Earth Surface Processes and Landforms* 12:109–25.

Pauketat, Timothy R., and Thomas E. Emerson

1991   The Ideology of Authority and the Power of the Pot. *American Anthropologist* 93:919–41.

Pedrick, Kathryn E.

1992   Introduction. In *Developing Perspectives on Tonto Basin Prehistory,* edited by Charles L. Redman, Glen E. Rice, and Kathryn E. Pedrick, pp.1–4. Roosevelt Monograph Series No. 2. Arizona State University Anthropological Field Studies No. 26. Tempe.

Peterson, Jane D.

1994   Salado Polychrome from Pueblo Grande: Indices of Ceramic Production Systems. In *The Pueblo Grande Project,* Vol. 3: *Ceramics and the Production and Exchange of Pottery in the Central Phoenix Basin,* edited by David

R. Abbott, pp. 371–406. Soil Systems Publications in Archaeology No. 20. Phoenix.

Phillips, David A., Jr.

1989   Prehistory of Chihuahua and Sonora, Mexico. *Journal of World Prehistory* 3:373–401.

Pierson, Lloyd M.

1962   Excavations at the Lower Ruin, Tonto National Monument. In *Archeological Studies at Tonto National Monument, Arizona,* by Charlie R. Steen, Lloyd M. Pierson, Vorsila L. Bohrer, and Kate Peck Kent, pp. 33–69. Southwestern Monuments Association Technical Series Vol. 2. Globe, Arizona.

Piety, Lucy A., and Larry W. Anderson

1988   Distribution, Characteristics, and Estimated Ages of Quaternary (?) Deposits in the Tonto Basin, Central Arizona. *The Field Trip Guidebook to the Tonto Basin, Arizona,* edited by Larry W. Anderson and Lucy A. Piety, pp. 57–78. Friends of the Pleistocene, Rocky Mountain Cell, Denver.

Pilles, Peter J., Jr.

1976   Sinagua and Salado Similarities as Seen from the Verde Valley. *The Kiva* 42:113–24.

Pindborg, J. J.

1982   *Pathology of the Dental Hard Tissues.* W. B. Saunders, Philadelphia.

Plog, Fred T.

1979   Prehistory: Western Anasazi. In *Southwest,* edited by A. Ortiz, pp. 108–30. Handbook of North American Indians, Vol. 9, William C. Sturtevant, general editor. Smithsonian Institution, Washington, D.C.

1983   Political and Economic Alliances on the Colorado Plateaus, A.D. 400–1450. In *Advances in World Archaeology,* Vol. 2, edited by Fred Wendorf and Angela Close, pp. 289–330. Academic Press, New York.

Plog, Fred, George J. Gumerman, Robert C. Euler, Jeffrey S. Dean, Richard H. Hevly, and Thor N. V. Karlstrom

1988   Anasazi Adaptive Strategies: The Model, Predictions, and Results. In *The Anasazi in a Changing Environment,* edited by George J. Gumerman, pp. 230–76. Cambridge University Press, Cambridge.

Porter-Weaver, Muriel

1981   *The Aztecs, Maya, and Their Predecessors.* Academic Press, New York.

Price, T. Douglas, and Gary M. Feinman

1995   Foundations of Prehistoric Social Inequality. In *Foundations of Social Inequality,* edited by

T. Douglas Price and Gary M. Feinman, pp. 3–11. Plenum Press, New York.

Price, T. Douglas, Clark M. Johnson, Joseph A. Ezzo, Jonathon Ericson, and James H. Burton

1994 Residential Mobility in the Prehistoric Southwest United States: A Preliminary Study Using Strontium Isotope Analysis. *Journal of Archaeological Science* 21:315–30.

Rafferty, Kevin

1982 Hohokam Micaceous Schist Mining and Ceramic Craft Specialization: An Example from Gila Butte, Arizona. *Anthropology* 6:199–222.

Rankin, Adrianne

1995 *Archaeological Survey at Organ Pipe Cactus National Monument, Southwestern Arizona* (Draft). National Park Service Western Archaeological and Conservation Center, Tucson.

Rautman, Alison E.

1993 Resource Variability, Risk, and the Structure of Social Networks: An Example from the Prehistoric Southwest. *American Antiquity* 58:403–24.

Ravesloot, John C.

1979 *The Animas Phase: The Post-Classic Occupation of the Mimbres Valley, New Mexico.* Master's thesis, Department of Anthropology, Southern Illinois University, Carbondale.

1988 *Mortuary Practices and Social Differentiation at Casas Grandes, Chihuahua, Mexico.* Anthropological Papers of The University of Arizona No. 49. The University of Arizona Press, Tucson.

1990 Burial Studies: The Cultural Component. In *A Design for Salado Research*, edited by Glen E. Rice, pp. 139–56. Roosevelt Monograph Series No. 1. Arizona State University Anthropological Field Studies No. 22. Tempe.

1992 The Anglo-American Acculturation of the Gila River Pima: The Mortuary Evidence. Paper presented at the 25th Annual Conference on Historical and Underwater Archaeology, Kingston, Jamaica.

1994a Gila Pueblo Collections from the Livingston Sites. In *Archaeology of the Salado in the Livingston Area of Tonto Basin, Roosevelt Platform Mound Study: Report on the Livingston Management Group, Pinto Creek Complex*, by David Jacobs, pp. 69–73. Roosevelt Monograph Series No. 3. Arizona State University Anthropological Field Studies No. 32. Tempe.

1994b Burial Practices in the Livingston Area. In *Archaeology of the Salado in the Livingston Area of Tonto Basin, Roosevelt Platform Mound Study: Report on the Livingston Management Group, Pinto Creek Complex,* by David Jacobs, pp. 833–50. Roosevelt Monograph Series No. 3. Arizona State University Anthropological Field Studies No. 32. Tempe.

Ravesloot, John C., and Chris Loendorf

1996 Table 15.1. Description of Burial Features, U:8:24/13a. In *Burial Practices at the Schoolhouse Point Mound, U:8:24:13a,* by Chris Loendorf, pp. 722–59. In *The Place of the Storehouses, Roosevelt Platform Mound Study: Report on the Schoolhouse Point Mound, Pinto Creek Complex,* by Owen Lindauer, pp. 681–759. Roosevelt Monograph Series No. 6. Arizona State University Anthropological Field Studies No. 35. Tempe.

Redman, Charles L.

1978 *The Rise of Civilization: From Early Farmers to Urban Society in the Ancient Near East.* W. H. Freeman, San Francisco.

1991 The Comparative Context of Social Complexity. In *Chaco and Hohokam: Prehistoric Regional Systems in the American Southwest,* edited by Patricia L. Crown and W. James Judge, pp. 277–92. School of American Research Press, Santa Fe.

1992 Pursuing Southwestern Social Complexity in the 1990s. In *Developing Perspectives on Tonto Basin Prehistory*, edited by Charles L. Redman, Glen E. Rice, and Kathryn E. Pedrick, pp. 5–10. Roosevelt Monograph Series No. 2. Arizona State University Anthropological Field Studies No. 26. Tempe.

1993 *People of the Tonto Rim: Archaeological Discovery in Prehistoric Arizona.* Smithsonian Institution Press, Washington, D.C.

Reed, Erik K.

1948 The Western Pueblo Archaeological Complex. *El Palacio* 55:9–15.

1950 East-Central Arizona Archaeology in Relation to the Western Pueblos. *Southwestern Journal of Anthropology* 6:120–38.

1958 Comment. In *Migrations in New World Culture History*, edited by Raymond H. Thompson, pp. 7–8. Social Science Bulletin No. 27. The University of Arizona, Tucson.

Regan, Marcia H.

n.d. Skeletal Metric Data from the Pima Butte Cemetery, AZ T:16:88.

1988   *Methodological and Nutritional Correlates of Long Bone Growth in Two Southwestern Prehistoric Skeletal Samples.* Master's thesis, Department of Anthropology, Arizona State University, Tempe.

Regan, Marcia H., Christy G. Turner II, and Joel D. Irish

1994   Skeletal and Dental Indicators of Health Among the Salado from Tonto Basin, Arizona. Paper presented at the 59th Annual Meeting of the Society for American Archaeology, Anaheim.

1996   Physical Anthropology of the Schoolhouse Point Mound Site, U:8:24/13a. In *The Place of the Storehouses, Roosevelt Platform Mound Study: Report on Schoolhouse Point Mound, Pinto Creek Complex,* by Owen Lindauer, pp. 749–802. Roosevelt Monograph Series No. 6. Arizona State University Anthropological Field Studies No. 35. Tempe.

Reid, J. Jefferson

1973   *Growth and Response to Stress at Grasshopper Pueblo, Arizona.* Ph.D dissertation, Department of Anthropology, The University of Arizona, Tucson.

1978   Response to Stress at Grasshopper Pueblo. In *Discovering Past Behavior: Experiments in the Archaeology of the American Southwest,* edited by Paul Grebinger, pp. 195–228. Gordon and Breach, New York.

1989   A Grasshopper Perspective on the Mogollon of the Arizona Mountains. In *Dynamics of Southwest Prehistory,* edited by Linda S. Cordell and George J. Gumerman, pp. 65–97. Smithsonian Institution Press, Washington, D.C.

1994   Rethinking Mogollon Pueblo. In *Mogollon VII,* edited by Patrick H. Beckett, pp. 3–7. COAS Publishing and Research, Las Cruces, New Mexico.

Reid, J. Jefferson (editor)

1982   *Cholla Project Archaeology,* Vol. 4: *The Tonto-Roosevelt Region.* Arizona State Museum Archaeological Series No. 161. The University of Arizona, Tucson.

Reid, J. Jefferson, and Donald A. Graybill

1984   Paleoclimate and Human Behavior in the Grasshopper Region, Arizona. Paper presented at the 49th Annual Meeting of the Society for American Archaeology, Portland.

Reid, J. Jefferson, and Barbara K. Montgomery

1993   Rapid Change of Formal Ritual Space in the Grasshopper Region, Arizona. Paper presented at the 58th Annual Meeting of the Society for American Archaeology, St. Louis.

Reid, J. Jefferson, Barbara K. Montgomery, Maria Nieves Zedeño, and Mark A. Neupert

1992   The Origin of Roosevelt Red Ware. In *Proceedings of the Second Salado Conference Globe, AZ 1992,* edited by Richard C. Lange and Stephen Germick, pp. 212–15. Arizona Archaeological Society Occasional Paper. Phoenix.

Reid, J. Jefferson, and Charles R. Riggs, Jr.

1995   Dynamics of Pueblo Architecture. Paper presented at the 60th Annual Meeting of the Society for American Archaeology, Minneapolis.

Reid, J. Jefferson, and H. David Tuggle

1988   Settlement Pattern and System in the Late Prehistory of the Grasshopper Region, Arizona. Ms. on file, Department of Anthropology, The University of Arizona, Tucson.

Reid, J. Jefferson, John R. Welch, Barbara K. Montgomery, and Maria Nieves Zedeño

1996   Demographic Overview of the Late Pueblo III Period in the Mountains of East-Central Arizona. In *The Prehistoric Pueblo World, A.D. 1150–1350,* edited by Michael A. Adler, pp. 73–85. The University of Arizona Press, Tucson.

Reid, J. Jefferson, and Stephanie M. Whittlesey

1982   Households at Grasshopper Pueblo. *American Behavioral Scientist* 25:687–703.

1982   Archaeological Research for the Practical Prehistorian. In *Cholla Project Archaeology,* Vol. 1: *Introduction and Special Studies,* edited by J. Jefferson Reid, pp. 13–26. Arizona State Museum Archaeological Series No. 161. The University of Arizona, Tucson.

Reid, J. Jefferson, and Stephanie M. Whittlesey

1992   New Evidence for Dating Gila Polychrome. In *Proceedings of the Second Salado Conference Globe, AZ 1992,* edited by Richard C. Lange and Stephen Germick, pp. 223–29. Arizona Archaeological Society Occasional Paper. Phoenix.

1997   *The Archaeology of Ancient Arizona.* The University of Arizona Press, Tucson.

Rice, Glen E.

n.d.a   Salado Horizon. In *Archaeology of Prehistoric Native Americans: An Encyclopedia,* edited by Guy Gibbon. Garland Publishing (in press).

n.d.b   War and Water: An Ecological Perspective on Hohokam Irrigation. Ms. on file, Office of Cultural Resource Management, Department of Anthropology, Arizona State University, Tempe.

1987a The Marana Community Complex: A Twelfth Century Hohokam Chiefdom. In *Studies in the Hohokam Community of Marana,* edited by Glen E. Rice, pp. 249–53. Arizona State University Anthropological Field Studies No. 15. Tempe.

1987b *A Spatial Analysis of the Hohokam Community of La Ciudad.* Arizona State University Anthropological Field Studies No. 18. Tempe.

1990a Toward a Study of the Salado of the Tonto Basin. In *A Design for Salado Research,* edited by Glen E. Rice, pp. 1–20. Roosevelt Monograph Series No. 1. Arizona State University Anthropological Field Studies No. 22. Tempe.

1990b An Intellectual History of the Salado Concept. In *A Design for Salado Research,* edited by Glen E. Rice, pp. 21–30. Roosevelt Monograph Series No. 1. Arizona State University Anthropological Field Studies No. 22. Tempe.

1990c Variability in the Development of Classic Period Elites. In *A Design for Salado Research,* edited by Glen E. Rice, pp. 31–40. Roosevelt Monograph Series No. 1. Arizona State University Anthropological Field Studies No. 22. Tempe.

1992 Modeling the Development of Complexity in the Sonoran Desert of Arizona. In *Developing Perspectives on Tonto Basin Prehistory,* edited by Charles L. Redman, Glen E. Rice, and Kathryn E. Pedrick, pp. 11–26. Arizona State University Anthropological Field Studies No. 26. Tempe.

1995 Special Artifacts and Evidence for the Differentiation of Residential and Ritual Rooms at Bass Point Mound. In *Where the Rivers Converge, Roosevelt Platform Mound Study: Report on the Rock Island Complex,* by Owen Lindauer, pp. 331–50. Roosevelt Monograph Series No. 4. Arizona State University Anthropological Field Studies No. 33. Tempe.

1996 The Distribution of Special Artifacts at Schoolhouse Point Mound, U:8:24/13a. In *The Place of the Storehouses, Roosevelt Platform Mound Study: Report on the Schoolhouse Point Mound, Pinto Creek Complex,* by Owen Lindauer, pp. 599–622. Roosevelt Monograph Series No. 6. Arizona State University Anthropological Field Studies No. 35. Tempe.

1997 Special Artifacts and the Uses of Rooms at U:4:33/132, the Cline Terrace Mound. In *A Salado Platform Mound on Tonto Creek,*

Roosevelt Platform Mound Study: Report on the Cline Terrace Mound, Cline Terrace Complex, by David Jacobs, pp.431–54. Roosevelt Monograph Series No. 7. Arizona State University Anthropological Field Studies No. 36. Tempe.

1998 The Bureau of Reclamation Archaeology Projects in Tonto Basin. In *The Synthesis of Tonto Basin Prehistory: The Roosevelt Archaeology Studies, 1989 to 1998* (Draft), by Glen E. Rice, pp. 1–52. Roosevelt Monograph Series No. 12. Arizona State University Anthropological Field Studies No. 41. Tempe.

Rice, Glen (editor)

1985 *Studies in the Hohokam and Salado of the Tonto Basin.* Office of Cultural Resource Management Report No. 63. Arizona State University, Tempe.

1990 *A Design for Salado Research.* Roosevelt Monograph Series No. 1. Arizona State University Anthropological Field Studies No. 22. Tempe.

Rice, Glen E., and David Jacobs

1994 Salado Platform Mounds and Settlement Networks in the Tonto Basin of Central Arizona. Paper presented at the 59th Annual Meeting of the Society for American Archaeology, Anaheim.

1997 The Function of U:4:33/132, the Cline Terrace Mound. In *A Salado Platform Mound on Tonto Creek, Roosevelt Platform Mound Study: Report on the Cline Terrace Mound, Cline Terrace Complex,* edited by David Jacobs, pp. 577–85. Roosevelt Monograph Series No. 7. Arizona State University Anthropological Field Studies No. 32. Tempe.

Rice, Glen E., and Owen Lindauer

1994 Phase Chronology. In *Archaeology of the Salado in the Livingston Area of Tonto Basin, Roosevelt Platform Mound Study: Report on the Livingston Management Group, Pinto Creek Complex,* by David Jacobs, pp. 51–68. Roosevelt Monograph Series No. 3. Arizona State University Anthropological Field Studies No. 32. Tempe.

Rice, Glen E., and Rachel Most (editors)

1984 *Research Issues in the Prehistory of Central Arizona: The Central Arizona Water Control Study,* Vol. 1 (Draft). Office of Cultural Resource Management, Arizona State University, Tempe.

Rice, Glen E., John C. Ravesloot, and Christy G. Turner II

1992 Salado Ethnic Identity and Social Complexity: The Biocultural Approach. Paper presented at the 57th Annual Meeting of the Society for American Archaeology, Pittsburgh.

Rice, Glen E., and Charles L. Redman
n.d. Compounds, Villages and Mounds: The Salado Alternative. In *The Hohokam Village Revisited*, edited by David E. Doyel, Suzanne K. Fish, and Paul R. Fish. American Association for the Advancement of Science (in press).

1993 Platform Mounds of the Arizona Desert: An Experiment in Organizational Complexity. *Expedition* 35(1):53–63.

Riley, Carroll L.
1986 An Overview of the Greater Southwest in the Protohistoric Period. In *Ripples in the Chichimec Sea: New Considerations of Southwestern-Mesoamerican Interactions*, edited by Frances Joan Mathien and Randall H. McGuire, pp. 45–54. Southern Illinois University Press, Carbondale.

1987 *The Frontier People: The Greater Southwest in the Protohistoric Period.* University of New Mexico Press, Albuquerque.

Robinson, William J., and Catherine M. Cameron
1991 *A Directory of Tree-Ring Dated Prehistoric Sites in the American Southwest.* Laboratory of Tree-Ring Research, Tucson.

Robinson, William J., and Roderick Sprague
1965 Disposal of the Dead at Point of Pines, Arizona. *American Antiquity* 30:442–53.

Rodman, Margaret C.
1992 Empowering Place: Multilocality and Multivocality. *American Anthropologist* 94:640–56.

Rogge, A. E., D. Lorne McWatters, Melissa Keane, and Richard P. Emanuel
1995 *Raising Arizona's Dams: Daily Life, Danger, and Discrimination in the Dam Construction Camps of Central Arizona, 1890s–1940s.* The University of Arizona Press, Tucson.

Rose, Martin R.
1994 Long Term Drought Reconstructions for the Lake Roosevelt Region. In *The Roosevelt Rural Sites Study*, Vol. 3: *Changing Land Use in the Tonto Basin*, edited by Richard Ciolek-Torrello and John R. Welch, pp. 311–59. Statistical Research Technical Series No. 28. Tucson.

Royse, Chester F., Michael F. Sheridan, and H. Wesley Peirce
1971 *Geological Guidebook 4—Highways of Arizona, Arizona Highways 87, 88, and 188.* Arizona Bureau of Mines Bulletin No. 184. The University of Arizona, Tucson.

Russell, Frank
1908 The Pima Indians. *Twenty-Sixth Annual Report of the Bureau of American Ethnology, 1904–1905.* Smithsonian Institution, Washington, D.C.

Sahlins, Marshall D.
1961 The Segmentary Lineage: An Organization of Predatory Expansion. *American Anthropologist* 63:322–45.

1968 *Tribesmen.* Prentice-Hall, Englewood.

Sahlins, Marshall D., and Elman R. Service (editors)
1960 *Evolution and Culture.* University of Michigan Press, Ann Arbor.

Sanders, William T.
1989 Household, Lineage, and State at Eighth-Century Copan, Honduras. In *The House of the Bacabs, Copan, Honduras*, edited by David L. Webster, pp. 89–105. Studies in Pre-Columbian Art and Archaeology No. 29. Dumbarton Oaks, Washington, D.C.

Sarrafian, Shahan K.
1983 *Anatomy of the Foot and Ankle: Descriptive, Topographic, Functional.* J. B. Lippincott, Philadelphia.

Sattenspiel, Lisa, and Henry Harpending
1983 Stable Populations and Skeletal Age. *American Antiquity* 48:489–98.

Saxe, Arthur A.
1970 *Social Dimensions of Mortuary Practices.* Ph.D dissertation, Department of Anthropology, University of Michigan, Ann Arbor.

Sayles, E. B.
1936a *Some Southwestern Pottery Types, Series V.* Medallion Papers No. 21. Gila Pueblo, Globe, Arizona.

1936b *An Archaeological Survey of Chihuahua, Mexico.* Medallion Papers No. 22. Gila Pueblo, Globe, Arizona.

1945 *The San Simon Branch, Excavations at Cave Creek and in the San Simon Valley I: Material Culture.* Medallion Papers No. 34. Gila Pueblo, Globe, Arizona.

Scantling, Frederick H.
1940 *Excavations at Jackrabbit Ruin, Papago Indian Reservation, Arizona.* Master's thesis, Department of Anthropology, University of Arizona, Tucson.

Schaafsma, Curtis F.
1979 The "El Paso Phase" and its Relationship to the "Casas Grandes Phenomenon." In *Jornada Mogollon Archaeology*, edited by Patrick H. Beckett and Regge N. Wiseman,

pp. 383–88. Historic Preservation Bureau, Santa Fe.

Schaafsma, Polly

1980   *Indian Rock Art of the Southwest*. University of New Mexico Press, Albuquerque.

1992   *Rock Art in New Mexico*. Museum of New Mexico Press, Santa Fe.

Schaafsma, Polly (editor)

1994   *Kachinas in the Pueblo World*. University of New Mexico Press, Albuquerque.

Schiffer, Michael B.

1987   *Formation Processes of the Archaeological Record*. University of New Mexico Press, Albuquerque.

Schlegel, Alice

1992   African Political Models in the American Southwest: Hopi as an Internal Frontier Society. *American Anthropologist* 94:376–97.

Schmidt, Erich F.

1928   *Time-Relations of Prehistoric Pottery in Southern Arizona*. Anthropological Papers Vol. 30, pp. 245–302. American Museum of Natural History, New York.

Schroeder, Albert H.

1947   Did the Sinagua of the Verde Valley Settle in the Salt River Valley? *Southwestern Journal of Anthropology* 3(3):230–46.

1953   The Problem of Hohokam, Sinagua, and Salado Relations in Southern Arizona. *Plateau* 26:75–83.

1961   An Archaeological Survey of the Painted Rocks Reservoir, Western Arizona. *The Kiva* 27:1–28.

1966   Pattern Diffusion from Mexico into the Southwest After A.D. 600. *American Antiquity* 31:683–704.

Scott, G. Richard

1973   *Dental Morphology: A Genetic Study of American White Families and Variation in Living Southwestern Indians*. Ph.D dissertation, Department of Anthropology, Arizona State University, Tempe.

1981   A Stature Reconstruction of Skeletal Populations. In *Contributions to Gran Quivira Archeology, Gran Quivira National Monument, New Mexico*, by Alden C. Hayes, pp. 129–37. National Park Service Publications in Archeology No. 17. Washington, D.C.

Scott, G. Richard, and Christy G. Turner II

1988   Dental Anthropology. *Annual Review of Anthropology* 17:99–126.

Seltzer, Carl C.

1944   *Racial Prehistory in the Southwest and the Hawikuh Zunis*. Papers of the Peabody Museum of American Archaeology and Ethnology Vol. 23, No. 1. Harvard University, Cambridge.

Service, Elman R.

1962   *Primitive Social Organization*. Random House, New York.

1975   *Origins of the State and Civilization: The Process of Cultural Evolution*. W. W. Norton, New York.

Shafer, Harry J., and Robbie L. Brewington

1995   Microstylistic Changes in Mimbres Black-on-White Pottery: Examples from the NAN Ruin, Grant County, New Mexico. *Kiva* 61:5–29.

Sharrock, Susan R.

1974   Crees, Cree-Assiniboine and Assiniboines: Interethnic Social Organization on the Far Northern Plains. *Ethnohistory* 21:95–122.

Shelley, Steven D., and Richard Ciolek-Torrello

1994   Grapevine Recreation and Stockpile Areas. In *The Roosevelt Rural Sites Study*, Vol. 2: *Prehistoric Rural Settlements in the Tonto Basin*, edited by Richard Ciolek-Torrello, Steven D. Shelley, and Su Benaron, pp. 223–58. Statistical Research Technical Series No. 28. Tucson.

Shipman, Jeffrey H.

1982   *Biological Relationships Among Prehistoric Western Pueblo Indians*. Ph.D dissertation, Department of Anthropology, The University of Arizona, Tucson.

Simmons, Leo W. (editor)

1942   *Sun Chief: The Autobiography of a Hopi Indian*. Yale University Press, New Haven.

Simmons, Marc

1979   History of the Pueblos Since 1821. In *Southwest*, edited by Alfonso Ortiz, pp. 206–23. Handbook of North American Indians, Vol. 9, William C. Sturtevant, general editor. Smithsonian Institution, Washington, D.C.

Simon, Arleyn W.

1994a   Analysis of Plain Ware Ceramic Assemblages. In *Archaeology of the Salado in the Livingston Area of Tonto Basin, Roosevelt Platform Mound Study: Report on the Livingston Management Group, Pinto Creek Complex*, by David Jacobs, pp. 635–46. Roosevelt Monograph Series No. 3. Arizona State University Anthropological Field Studies No. 32. Tempe.

1994b   Compositional Analysis of the Livingston Ceramic Assemblage. In *Archaeology of the Salado in the Livingston Area of Tonto Basin, Roosevelt Platform Mound Study: Report on the Livingston Management Group, Pinto Creek Complex,* by David Jacobs, pp. 647–62. Roosevelt Monograph Series No. 3. Arizona State University Anthropological Field Studies No. 32. Tempe.

1994c   Performance Analysis of the Livingston Ceramic Assemblage. In *Archaeology of the Salado in the Livingston Area of Tonto Basin, Roosevelt Platform Mound Study: Report on the Livingston Management Group, Pinto Creek Complex,* by David Jacobs, pp. 663–80. Roosevelt Monograph Series No. 3. Arizona State University Anthropological Field Studies No. 32. Tempe.

1994d   Ceramic Evidence for Room Function. In *Archaeology of the Salado in the Livingston Area of Tonto Basin, Roosevelt Platform Mound Study: Report on the Livingston Management Group, Pinto Creek Complex,* by David Jacobs, pp. 681–708. Roosevelt Monograph Series No. 3. Arizona State University Anthropological Field Studies No. 32. Tempe.

1994e   A Comparative Study of Ceramics from Household Floor Assemblages and Burial Accompaniments and Implications for Salado Social Organization. Paper presented at the 93rd Annual Meeting of the American Anthropological Association, Atlanta.

1996a   Plain, Red, and Other Ceramic Wares from the Schoolhouse Point Mound, U:8:24/13a. In *The Place of the Storehouses, Roosevelt Platform Mound Study: Report on the Schoolhouse Point Mound, Pinto Creek Complex,* by Owen Lindauer, pp. 419–519. Roosevelt Monograph Series No. 6. Arizona State University Anthropological Field Studies No. 35. Tempe.

1996b   Salado Polychrome, Social Relationships, and Prehistoric Community. Paper presented at the 61st Annual Meeting of the Society for American Archaeology, New Orleans.

1997   Plain, Red, and Other Ceramic Wares from U:4:33/132, the Cline Terrace Mound. In *A Salado Platform Mound on Tonto Creek, Roosevelt Platform Mound Study: Report on the Cline Terrace Mound, Cline Terrace Complex,* by David Jacobs, pp. 291–362. Roosevelt Monograph Series No. 7. Arizona State University Anthropological Field Studies No. 36. Tempe.

Simon, Arleyn W. (editor)

1997   *Salado Ceramics and Social Organization, Roosevelt Platform Mound Study: Prehistoric Interactions in the Tonto Basin* (Draft). Roosevelt Monograph Series No. 11. Arizona State University Anthropological Field Studies No. 40. Tempe.

Simon, Arleyn W., Jean-Christophe Komorowski, and James H. Burton

1992   Patterns of Production and Distribution of Salado Wares as a Measure of Complexity. In *Developing Perspectives on Tonto Basin Prehistory,* edited by Charles L. Redman, Glen E. Rice, and Kathryn E. Pedrick, pp. 61–76. Roosevelt Monograph Series No. 2. Arizona State University Anthropological Field Studies No. 26. Tempe.

Simon, Arleyn W., and Owen Lindauer

1994   Plain, Red, and Other Ceramic Wares from Sites from the Uplands Complex. In *Classic Period Settlement in the Uplands of Tonto Basin, Roosevelt Platform Mound Study: Report on the Uplands Complex,* by Theodore J. Oliver, pp. 349–88. Roosevelt Monograph Series No. 5. Arizona State University Anthropological Field Studies No. 34. Tempe.

Simon, Arleyn W., and John C. Ravesloot

1994   Salado Ceramic Burial Offerings: A Consideration of Gender and Social Organization. Paper presented at the 1994 Southwest Symposium, Arizona State University, Tempe.

1995   Salado Ceramic Burial Offerings: A Consideration of Gender and Social Organization. *Journal of Anthropological Research* 51:103–24.

Simon, Arleyn W., and Charles L. Redman

1990   An Integrated Approach to the Roosevelt Lake Ceramics. In *A Design for Salado Research,* edited by Glen E. Rice, pp. 65–78. Roosevelt Monograph Series No. 1. Arizona State University Anthropological Field Studies No. 22. Tempe.

Simonis, Don E.

1976   Excavation at AZ P:13:29 (ASU), A Small Site in Vosberg Valley, Arizona. Ms. on file, Tonto National Forest, Phoenix.

Sires, Earl W., Jr.

1984   Hohokam Architecture and Site Structure. In *Hohokam Archaeology Along the Salt-Gila Aqueduct, Central Arizona Project,* Vol. 9: *Synthesis and Conclusions,* edited by Lynn S.

Teague and Patricia L. Crown, pp. 115–40. Arizona State Museum Archaeological Series No. 150. The University of Arizona, Tucson.

Smith, Watson

1952   *Kiva Mural Decorations at Awatovi and Kawaika-a, With a Survey of Other Wall Paintings in the Pueblo Southwest.* Papers of the Peabody Museum of American Archaeology and Ethnology Vol. 37. Harvard University, Cambridge.

1971   Painted Ceramics of the Western Mound at Awatovi. Papers of the Peabody Museum of Archaeology and Ethnology No. 38. Harvard University, Cambridge.

Smith, Watson, Richard B. Woodbury, and Nathalie F. S. Woodbury

1966   *The Excavation of Hawikuh by Frederick Webb Hodge: Report of the Hendricks-Hodge Expedition, 1917–1923.* Contributions from the Museum of the American Indian, Heye Foundation Vol. 20. New York.

Southall, Aidan W.

1956   *Alur Society: A Study in Processes and Types of Domination.* Oxford University Press, Oxford.

Speth, John

1988   Do We Need Concepts Like "Mogollon," "Anasazi," and "Hohokam" Today? A Cultural Anthropological Perspective. *The Kiva* 53:201–04.

Spielmann, Katherine A.

1991   Coercion or Cooperation? Plains-Pueblo Interaction in the Protohistoric Period. In *Farmers, Hunters, and Colonists: Interaction Between the Southwest and the Southern Plains,* edited by Katherine A. Spielmann, pp. 36–50. The University of Arizona Press, Tucson.

1994   Subsistence Patterns at the Livingston Sites. In *Archaeology of the Salado in the Livingston Area of Tonto Basin, Roosevelt Platform Mound Study: Report on the Livingston Management Group, Pinto Creek Complex,* by David Jacobs, pp. 915–22. Roosevelt Monograph Series No. 3. Arizona State University Anthropological Field Studies No. 32. Tempe.

1996   Diet and Subsistence in the Classic Period Tonto Basin. In *Environment and Subsistence in the Classic Period Tonto Basin, Roosevelt Platform Mound Study* (Draft), edited by Katherine A. Spielmann. Roosevelt Monograph Series No. 10. Arizona State University Anthropological Field Studies No. 39. Tempe.

1997   Upland Subsistence and the Nature of Upland-Riverine Interaction. In *Classic Period Settlement in the Uplands of Tonto Basin, Roosevelt Platform Mound Study: Report on the Uplands Complex,* by Theodore J. Oliver, pp. 461–63. Roosevelt Monograph Series No. 5. Arizona State University Anthropological Field Studies No. 34. Tempe.

Spoerl, Patricia M., and George J. Gumerman (editors)

1984   *Prehistoric Cultural Development in Central Arizona: Archaeology of the Upper New River Region.* Center for Archaeological Investigations Occasional Paper No. 5. Southern Illinois University, Carbondale.

Spuhler, J. N.

1954   ome Problems in the Physical Anthropology of the American Southwest. *American Anthropologist* 56:604–25.

Stanislawski, Michael B.

1983   Hopi-Tewa. In *Southwest,* edited by Alfonso Ortiz, pp. 587–602. Handbook of North American Indians, Vol. 9, William C. Sturtevant, general editor. Smithsonian Institution, Washington, D.C.

Stark, Miriam T.

1991   Ceramic Production and Community Specialization: A Ceramic Ethnoarchaeological Study. *World Archaeology* 23:64–78.

1993   *Pottery Economics: A Kalinga Ethnoarchaeological Study.* Ph.D dissertation, Department of Anthropology, The University of Arizona, Tucson.

1995a   The Early Ceramic Horizon and Tonto Basin Prehistory. In *The Roosevelt Community Development Study: Ceramic Chronology, Technology, and Economics,* edited by James M. Heidke and Miriam T. Stark, pp. 249–72. Center for Desert Archaeology Anthropological Papers No. 14, Vol. 2. Tucson.

1995b   Commodities and Interaction in the Prehistoric Tonto Basin. In *The Roosevelt Community Development Study: New Perspectives on Tonto Basin Prehistory,* edited by Mark D. Elson, Miriam T. Stark, and David A. Gregory, pp. 307–42. Center for Desert Archaeology Anthropological Papers No. 15. Tucson.

Stark, Miriam T., Jeffery J. Clark, and Mark D. Elson

1995a   Causes and Consequences of Migration in the 13th Century Tonto Basin. *Journal of Anthropological Archaeology* 14:212–46.

1995b   Social Boundaries and Cultural Identity in the Tonto Basin. In *The Roosevelt Commu-*

nity Development Study: New Perspectives on Tonto Basin Prehistory, edited by Mark D. Elson, Miriam T. Stark, and David A. Gregory, pp. 343–68. Center for Desert Archaeology Anthropological Papers No. 15. Tucson.

Stark, Miriam T., and James Heidke

1994   Standardized Theories and Specialized Production: A View from the Tonto Basin. Paper Presented at the 59th Annual Meeting of the Society for American Archaeology, Anaheim.

1995   Early Classic Period Variability in Utilitarian Ceramic Production and Distribution. In The Roosevelt Community Development Study: Ceramic Chronology, Technology, and Economics, edited by James M. Heidke and Miriam T. Stark, pp. 363–94. Center for Desert Archaeology Anthropological Papers No. 14, Vol. 2. Tucson.

Stark, Miriam T., James M. Vint, and James M. Heidke

1995   Compositional Variability in Utilitarian Ceramics at a Colonial Period Site. In The Roosevelt Community Development Study: Ceramic Chronology, Technology, and Economics, edited by James M. Heidke and Miriam T. Stark, pp. 273–96. Center for Desert Archaeology Anthropological Papers No. 14, Vol. 2. Tucson.

Steen, Charlie R.

1962   Excavations at the Upper Ruin, Tonto National Monument. In Archeological Studies at Tonto National Monument, Arizona, by Charlie R. Steen, Lloyd M. Pierson, Vorsila L. Bohrer, and Kate Peck Kent, pp. 1–30. Southwestern Monuments Association Technical Series Vol. 2. Globe, Arizona.

Steen, Charlie R., Lloyd M. Pierson, Vorsila L. Bohrer, and Kate Peck Kent

1962   Archeological Studies at Tonto National Monument, Arizona. Southwestern Monuments Association Technical Series Vol. 2. Globe, Arizona.

Stein, Pat H.

1977   Hohokam-Yuman Interaction at the Palo Verde Hills. Paper presented at the 42nd Annual Meeting of the Society for American Archaeology, New Orleans.

Steward, Julian H.

1955   Theory of Culture Change. University of Illinois Press, Urbana.

Sumner, D. R.

1985   A Probable Case of Prehistoric Tuberculosis from Northeastern Arizona. In Health and Disease in the Prehistoric Southwest, edited by Charles F. Merbs and Robert J. Miller, pp. 340–46. Arizona State University Anthropological Research Papers No. 34. Tempe.

Swartz, Deborah L.

1992   The Deer Creek Site, AZ O:15:52 (ASM). In The Rye Creek Project: Archaeology in the Upper Tonto Basin, Vol. 1: Introduction and Site Descriptions, by Mark D. Elson and Douglas B. Craig, pp. 93–164. Center for Desert Archaeology Anthropological Papers No. 11. Tucson.

Swartz, Deborah L., Penny D. Minturn, and Dana Hartman

1995   The Mortuary Assemblage. In The Roosevelt Community Development Study: Paleobotanical and Osteological Analyses, edited by Mark D. Elson and Jeffery J. Clark, pp. 169–216. Center for Desert Archaeology Anthropological Papers No. 14, Vol. 3. Tucson.

Swartz, Deborah L., and Brenda G. Randolph

1994a   The Hedge Apple Site, AZ V:5:189/1605 (ASM/TNF). In The Roosevelt Community Development Study: Introduction and Small Sites, by Mark D. Elson, and Deborah L. Swartz, pp. 117–40. Center for Desert Archaeology Anthropological Papers No. 13, Vol. 1. Tucson.

1994b   The Griffin Wash Site, AZ V:5:90/96 (ASM/TNF). In The Roosevelt Community Development Study: Meddler Point, Pyramid Point, and Griffin Wash Sites, by Mark D. Elson, Deborah L. Swartz, Douglas B. Craig, and Jeffery J. Clark, pp. 297–415. Center for Desert Archaeology Anthropological Papers No. 13, Vol. 2. Tucson.

Szuter, Christine R.

1989   Spatial and Temporal Intra-Site Variability in the Faunal Assemblage at the Las Colinas Site. In The 1982–1984 Excavations at Las Colinas, Vol. 5: Environment and Subsistence, by Donald A. Graybill, David A. Gregory, Fred L. Nials, Suzanne K. Fish, Charles H. Miksicek, Robert E. Gasser, and Christine R. Szuter, pp. 117–49. Arizona State Museum Archaeological Series No. 162. The University of Arizona, Tucson.

1991   Hunting by Prehistoric Horticulturalists in the American Southwest. Garland Publishing, New York.

Tagg, Martyn D.

1985   Tonto National Monument: An Archeological Survey. Western Archeological and Conservation Center Publications in Anthropology No. 31. U.S. National Park Service, Tucson.

Tainter, Joseph A.

1975　*The Archaeological Study of Social Change: Woodland Systems in West-Central Illinois.* Ph.D dissertation, Department of Anthropology, Northwestern University, Evanston, Illinois.

1978　Mortuary Practices and the Study of Prehistoric Social Systems. In *Advances in Archaeological Method and Theory* Vol. 1, edited by Michael B. Schiffer, pp. 104–41. Academic Press, New York.

Taylor, Walter W.

1948　*A Study of Archeology.* Memoirs of the American Anthropological Association, No. 69. Menasha.

Teague, Lynn S.

1984　Role and Ritual in Hohokam Society. In *Hohokam Archaeology Along the Salt-Gila Aqueduct, Central Arizona Project,* Vol. 9: *Synthesis and Conclusions,* edited by Lynn S. Teague and Patricia L. Crown, pp. 155–85. Arizona State Museum Archaeological Series No. 150. The University of Arizona, Tucson.

1985　The Organization of Hohokam Exchange. In *Proceedings of the 1983 Hohokam Symposium,* edited by Alfred E. Dittert, Jr., and Donald E. Dove, pp. 397–419. Arizona Archaeological Society Occasional Paper No. 2. Phoenix.

1989　Production and Distribution at Las Colinas. In *The 1982–1984 Excavations at Las Colinas,* Vol. 6: *Synthesis and Conclusions,* by Lynn S. Teague and William L. Deaver, pp. 89–132. Arizona State Museum Archaeological Series No. 162. The University of Arizona, Tucson.

1992a　Textiles in Late Prehistory. In *Proceedings of the Second Salado Conference Globe, AZ 1992,* edited by Richard C. Lange and Stephen Germick, pp. 304–11. Arizona Archaeological Society Occasional Paper. Phoenix.

1992b　*The Materials and Technology of Textiles: An Archaeological Perspective.* Ms. on file, Arizona State Museum Library, The University of Arizona, Tucson.

1993　Prehistory and the Traditions of the O'odham and Hopi. *Kiva* 58:435–54.

Teague, Lynn S., and Patricia L. Crown (editors)

1984　*Hohokam Archaeology Along the Salt-Gila Aqueduct, Central Arizona Project,* Vol. 9: *Synthesis and Conclusions.* Arizona State Museum Archaeological Series No. 150. The University of Arizona, Tucson.

Thompson, Raymond H.

1963　Report of Archaeological Excavations by University of Arizona Archaeological Field School, Fort Apache Indian Reservation, June, July, and August, 1963. Ms. on file, Department of Anthropology, The University of Arizona, Tucson.

Titiev, Mischa

1944　*Old Oraibi: A Study of the Hopi Indians of Third Mesa.* Papers of the Peabody Museum of American Archaeology and Ethnology Vol. 22, No. 1. Harvard University, Cambridge. Reprinted 1992 by University of New Mexico Press, Albuquerque.

Triadan, Daniela

1989　*Defining Local Ceramic Production at Grasshopper Pueblo, Arizona.* Master's thesis, Freie Universität, Berlin.

Trigger, Bruce G.

1989　*A History of Archaeological Thought.* Cambridge University Press, Cambridge.

1990　Monumental Architecture: A Thermodynamic Explanation of Symbolic Behavior. *World Archaeology* 22:119–32.

Tuggle, H. David

1970　*Prehistoric Community Relationships in East-Central Arizona.* Ph.D dissertation, Department of Anthropology, The University of Arizona, Tucson.

1982　Settlement Patterns in the Q Ranch Region. In *Cholla Project Archaeology,* Vol. 3: *The Q Ranch Region,* edited by J. Jefferson Reid, pp. 151–75. Arizona State Museum Archaeological Series No. 161. The University of Arizona, Tucson.

Tuggle, H. David, J. Jefferson Reid, and Robert C. Cole, Jr.

1984　Fourteenth Century Mogollon Agriculture in the Grasshopper Region of Arizona. In *Prehistoric Agricultural Strategies in the Southwest,* edited by Suzanne K. Fish and Paul R. Fish, pp. 101–10. Arizona State University Anthropological Research Papers No. 33. Tempe.

Turner, Christy G. II

1979　Dental Anthropological Indications of Agriculture Among the Jomon People of Central Japan. *American Journal of Physical Anthropology* 51:619–36.

1987　Affinity and Dietary Assessment of Hohokam Burials from the Site of La Ciudad, Central Arizona. In *La Ciudad: Specialized Studies in the Economy, Environment, and Culture of La Ciudad,* edited by Jo Ann E.

Kisselburg, Glen E. Rice, and Brenda L. Shears, pp. 215–30. Arizona State University Anthropological Field Studies No. 20. Tempe.

1993   Southwest Indian Teeth. *National Geographic Research and Exploration* 9(1):32–53.

1998   The Salado Dentition: Univariate Comparisons Within the Greater Southwest. In *The Salado Populations of Tonto Basin: The Roosevelt Archaeology Studies, 1989 to 1998* (Draft), by Christy G. Turner, II, pp. 13–39. Roosevelt Monograph Series No. 13. Arizona State University Anthropological Field Studies No. 41. Tempe.

Turner, Christy G. II, Christian R. Nichol, and G. Richard Scott

1991   Scoring Procedures for Key Morphological Traits of the Permanent Dentition: The Arizona State University Dental Anthropology System. In *Advances in Dental Anthropology*, edited by Marc A. Kelley and C. Spencer Larsen, pp. 13–31. Wiley-Liss, New York.

Turner, Christy G. II, and Marcia H. Regan

1997   Physical Anthropology and Human Taphonomy of U:4:33/132, the Cline Terrace Mound. In *A Salado Platform Mound on Tonto Creek, Roosevelt Platform Mound Study: Report on the Cline Terrace Mound, Cline Terrace Complex*, by David Jacobs, pp. 505–28. Roosevelt Monograph Series No. 7. Arizona State University Anthropological Field Studies No. 36. Tempe.

Turner, Christy G. II, Marcia H. Regan, and Joel D. Irish

1990a   Physical Anthropology: Policy and Procedures for Skeletal Excavation and Laboratory Analysis. In *A Laboratory Plan for Salado Research*, by Arleyn W. Simon, pp. 8–3–8–47. Office of Cultural Resource Management, Department of Anthropology, Arizona State University, Tempe.

1990b   The Biology of the Salado Period People. In *A Design for Salado Research*, edited by Glen E. Rice, pp. 131–37. Roosevelt Monograph Series No. 1. Arizona State University Field Studies No. 22. Tempe.

1994a   Physical Anthropology of the Roosevelt Lake Livingston Study Area. In *Archaeology of the Salado in the Livingston Area of Tonto Basin, Roosevelt Platform Mound Study: Report on the Livingston Management Group, Pinto Creek Complex*, by David Jacobs, pp. 819–32. Roosevelt Monograph Series No. 3. Arizona State University Anthropological Field Studies No. 32. Tempe.

1994b   Physical Anthropology and Human Taphonomy. In *The Roosevelt Rural Sites Study*, Vol. 2: *Prehistoric Rural Settlements in the Tonto Basin*, edited by Richard Ciolek-Torrello, Steven D. Shelley, and Su Benaron, pp. 559–83. Statistical Research Technical Series No. 28. Tucson.

Turney, Omar S.

1929   *Prehistoric Irrigation in Arizona*. Arizona State Historian, Phoenix.

Tyler, Hamilton A.

1964   *Pueblo Gods and Myths*. University of Oklahoma Press, Norman.

Ubelaker, Douglas H.

1989   *Human Skeletal Remains: Excavation, Analysis, Interpretation*. Aldine, Chicago.

Underhill, Ruth

1939   *Social Organization of the Papago Indians*. Columbia University Press, New York.

1946   *Papago Indian Religion*. Columbia University Press, New York.

Upham, Steadman

1982   *Polities and Power: An Economic and Political History of the Western Pueblo*. Academic Press, New York.

1986   Imperialists, Isolationists, World Systems, and Political Realities: Perspectives on Mesoamerican-Southwestern Interaction. In *Ripples in the Chichimec Sea: New Considerations of Southwestern-Mesoamerican Interactions*, edited by Frances Joan Mathien and Randall H. McGuire, pp. 205–19. Southern Illinois University Press, Carbondale.

Upham, Steadman, Patricia L. Crown, and Stephen Plog

1994   Alliance Formation and Cultural Identity in the American Southwest. In *Themes in Southwest Prehistory*, edited by George J. Gumerman, pp. 183–210. School of American Research Press, Santa Fe.

Upham, Steadman, and Glen E. Rice

1980   Up the Canal Without a Pattern: Modeling Hohokam Interaction and Exchange. In *Current Issues in Hohokam Prehistory*, edited by David Doyel and Fred Plog, pp. 78–105. Arizona State University Anthropological Research Papers No. 23. Tempe.

Vanderpot, Rein, and Steven D. Shelley

1994   AZ U:8:224/1579 Grapevine Vista Site. In *The Roosevelt Rural Sites Study*, Vol. 2: *Prehistoric Rural Settlements in the Tonto Basin*, edited by Richard Ciolek-Torrello, Steven D. Shelley, and Su Benaron, pp. 259–91. Statistical Research Technical Series No. 28. Tucson.

Vanderpot, Rein, Steven D. Shelley, and Su Benaron
1994   AZ U:8:225/1580 Riser Site. In *The Roosevelt Rural Sites Study,* Vol. 2: *Prehistoric Rural Settlements in the Tonto Basin,* edited by Richard Ciolek-Torrello, Steven D. Shelley, and Su Benaron, pp. 292–337. Statistical Research Technical Series No. 28. Tucson.

Van Gerven, Dennis P., and Susan Guise Sheridan
1994   Life and Death at Pueblo Grande: The De-mographic Context. In *The Pueblo Grande Project,* Vol. 6: *The Bioethnography of a Classic Period Hohokam Population,* edited by Dennis P. Van Gerven and Susan Guise Sheridan, pp. 5–24. Soil Systems Publications in Archaeology No. 20. Phoenix.

Van West, Carla R.
1994   *River, Rain, or Ruin: Intermittent Prehistoric Land Use Along the Middle Little Colorado River.* Statistical Research Technical Series No. 53. Tucson.
1996   Modeling Prehistoric Agricultural Strategies and Human Settlement in the Middle Little Colorado River Valley. In *River of Change: Prehistory of the Middle Little Colorado River Valley, Arizona,* edited by E. Charles Adams, pp. 15–35. Arizona State Museum Archaeological Series No. 185. The University of Arizona, Tucson.

Van West, Carla R., and Jeffrey H. Altschul
1994   Agricultural Productivity and Carrying Capacity in the Tonto Basin. In *The Roosevelt Rural Sites Study,* Vol. 3: *Changing Land Use in the Tonto Basin,* edited by Richard Ciolek-Torrello and John R. Welch, pp. 361–435. Statistical Research Technical Series No. 28. Tucson.
1997   Environmental Variability and Agricultural Economics along the Lower Verde River, A.D. 750–1450. In *Vanishing River: Landscapes and Lives of the Lower Verde Valley, the Lower Verde Archaeological Project,* edited by Stephanie M. Whittlesey, Richard Ciolek-Torrello, and Jeffrey H. Altschul, pp. 337–92. SRI Press, Tucson.

Vickery, Irene
1939   Besh-ba-go-wah. *The Kiva* 4:19–22.

Vivian, R. Gwinn
1965   An Archaeological Survey of the Lower Gila River, Arizona. *The Kiva* 30:95–146.

Vokes, Arthur W.
1995   The Shell Assemblage. In *The Roosevelt Community Development Study: Stone and Shell Artifacts,* edited by Mark D. Elson and Jeffery J. Clark, pp. 151–211. Center for Desert Archaeology Anthropological Papers No. 14, Vol. 1. Tucson.

Wade, William D.
1970   *Skeletal Remains of a Prehistoric Population from the Puerco Valley, Eastern Arizona.* Ph.D dissertation, Department of Anthropology, University of Colorado, Boulder.

Walker, William H.
1995   Ceremonial Trash? In *Expanding Archaeology,* edited by James M. Skibo, William H. Walker, and Axel E. Nielsen, pp. 67–79. University of Utah Press, Salt Lake City.

Wallace, Henry D.
1995a   Decorated Buffware and Brownware Ceramics. In *The Roosevelt Community Development Study: Ceramic Chronology, Technology, and Economics,* edited by James M. Heidke and Miriam T. Stark, pp. 19–84. Center for Desert Archaeology Anthropological Papers No. 14, Vol. 2. Tucson.
1995b   Ceramic Accumulation Rates and Prehistoric Tonto Basin Households. In *The Roosevelt Community Development Study: New Perspectives on Tonto Basin Prehistory,* edited by Mark D. Elson, Miriam T. Stark, and David A. Gregory, pp. 79–126. Center for Desert Archaeology Anthropological Papers No. 15. Tucson.

Wallace, Henry D., and Douglas B. Craig
1988   A Reconsideration of the Tucson Basin Hohokam Chronology. In *Recent Research on Tucson Basin Prehistory: Proceedings of the Second Tucson Basin Conference,* edited by William H. Doelle and Paul R. Fish, pp. 9–29. Institute for American Research Anthropological Papers No. 10. Tucson.

Wallace, Henry D., William H. Doelle, John Murray, Allen Dart, and James Bayman
1998   *Archaeological Survey of the Lower San Pedro Valley.* Center for Desert Archaeology Technical Report No. 97–1. Tucson.

Wallerstein, Immanuel
1974   *The Modern World-System I: Capitalist Agriculture and the Origins of the European World-Economy in the Sixteenth Century.* Academic Press, New York.
1980   *The Modern World-System II: Mercantilism and the Consolidation of the European World-Economy, 1600–1750.* Academic Press, New York.

Wasley, William W.

1957   *The Archaeological Survey of the Arizona State Museum.* Arizona State Museum, The University of Arizona, Tucson.

1960   A Hohokam Platform Mound at the Gatlin Site, Gila Bend, Arizona. *American Antiquity* 26:244–62.

1966   Classic Period Hohokam. Paper presented at the 31st Annual Meeting of the Society for American Archaeology, Reno.

Wasley, William W., and David E. Doyel

1980   Classic Period Hohokam. *The Kiva* 45:337–52.

Wasley, William W., and Alfred E. Johnson

1965   *Salvage Archaeology in Painted Rocks Reservoir, Western Arizona.* Anthropological Papers of The University of Arizona No. 9. The University of Arizona Press, Tucson.

Waters, Jennifer A.

1996   Vertebrate Faunal Remains. In *Archaeological Investigations at the Upper Ruin, Tonto National Monument,* Pt. I: *Salvage Excavations at the Upper Ruin, AZ U:8:48 (ASM)—1985,* by Gregory L. Fox, pp. 85–109. Western Archeological and Conservation Center Publications in Anthropology No. 70. U.S. National Park Service, Tucson.

Waters, Michael R.

1994a   Geoarchaeological Investigations of the Tonto Basin, Arizona. Paper presented at the 59th Annual Meeting of the Society for American Archaeology, Anaheim.

1994b   Geoarchaeological Investigation of the Tonto Basin, Arizona. Ms. on file, Office of Cultural Resource Management, Arizona State University, Tempe.

1996   Geoarchaeological Investigations in the Tonto Basin. In *Environment and Subsistence in the Classic Period Tonto Basin, Roosevelt Platform Mound Study* (Draft), edited by Katherine A. Spielmann. Roosevelt Monograph Series No. 10. Arizona State University Anthropological Field Studies No. 39. Tempe.

1997   Geoarchaeological Investigations in the Tonto Basin. In *Environment and Subsistence in the Classic Period Tonto Basin, Roosevelt Platform Mound Study* (Draft), edited by Katherine A. Spielmann. Roosevelt Monograph Series No. 10. Arizona State University Anthropological Field Studies No. 39. Tempe.

Watson, Patty Jo, Steven A. LeBlanc, and Charles L. Redman

1971   *Explanation in Archaeology: An Explicitly Scientific Approach.* Columbia University Press, New York.

Weaver, David S.

1985   Subsistence and Settlement Patterns at Casas Grandes, Chihuahua, Mexico. In *Health and Disease in the Prehistoric Southwest,* edited by Charles F. Merbs and Robert J. Miller, pp. 119–27. Arizona State University Anthropological Research Papers No. 34. Tempe.

Weigand, Phil C.

1993   Large-Scale Hydraulic Works in Prehistoric Western Mesoamerica. In *Research in Economic Anthropology, Supplement* 7:223–62.

Weiss, Kenneth M.

1973   *Demographic Models for Anthropology.* Memoirs of the Society for American Archaeology No. 27.

Welch, John R.

1992   Irrigation Agriculture in the Tonto Basin. In *Proceedings of the Second Salado Conference Globe, AZ 1992,* edited by Richard C. Lange and Stephen Germick, pp. 161–71. Arizona Archaeological Society Occasional Paper. Phoenix.

1994a   Environmental Influences on Tonto Basin Agricultural Productivity and Sustainability. In *The Roosevelt Rural Sites Study,* Vol. 3: *Changing Land Use in the Tonto Basin,* edited by Richard Ciolek-Torrello and John R. Welch, pp. 19–39. Statistical Research Technical Series No. 28. Tucson.

1994b   Ethnographic Models for Tonto Basin Land Use. In *The Roosevelt Rural Sites Study,* Vol. 3: *Changing Land Use in the Tonto Basin,* edited by Richard Ciolek-Torrello and John R. Welch, pp. 79–120. Statistical Research Technical Series No. 28. Tucson.

1994c   Archaeological Studies of Archaeological Contexts. In *The Roosevelt Rural Sites Study,* Vol. 3: *Changing Land Use in the Tonto Basin,* edited by Richard Ciolek-Torrello and John R. Welch, pp. 223–52. Statistical Research Technical Series No. 28. Tucson.

Welch, John R., and Richard Ciolek-Torrello

1994   Nineteenth- and Twentieth-Century Land Use in the Tonto Basin. In *The Roosevelt Rural Sites Study,* Vol. 3: *Changing Land Use in the Tonto Basin,* edited by Richard Ciolek-Torrello and John R. Welch, pp. 57–78. Statistical Research Technical Series No. 28. Tucson.

Welch, John R., and Daniela Triadan

1991   The Canyon Creek Turquoise Mine, Arizona. *Kiva* 56:145–64.

Wells, Susan J., and Keith M. Anderson
1988   *Archaeological Survey and Architectural Study of Montezuma Castle National Monument.* Western Archaeological and Conservation Center Publications in Anthropology No. 50. USDI National Park Service, Tucson.

Wells, Wesley E.
1971   Prehistoric Settlement Patterns of Lower Cherry Creek. Ms. on file, Department of Anthropology, Arizona State University, Tempe.

Whalen, Michael E., and Paul E. Minnis
1996   Ball Courts and Political Centralization in the Casas Grandes Region. *American Antiquity* 61:732–46.

Wheat, Joe Ben
1955   *Mogollon Culture Prior to A.D. 1000.* American Anthropological Association Memoir No. 82. Menasha, Wisconsin.

Wheatley, Paul
1971   *The Pivot of the Four Quarters: A Preliminary Enquiry into the Origins and Character of the Ancient Chinese City.* Aldine, Chicago.
1983   *Nagara and Commandery: Origins of the Southeast Asian Urban Traditions.* Department of Geography Research Papers Nos. 207–208. University of Chicago.

White, Chris
1974   Lower Colorado River Area Aboriginal Warfare and Alliance Dynamics. In *Antap, California Indian Political and Economic Organization,* edited by Lowell John Bean and Thomas F. King. Ballena Press Anthropological Papers No. 2. Ramona, California.

White, Diane E., and James Burton
1992   Pinto Polychrome: A Clue to the Origin of the Salado Polychromes. In *Proceedings of the Second Salado Conference Globe, AZ 1992,* edited by Richard C. Lange and Stephen Germick, pp. 216–22. Arizona Archaeological Society Occasional Paper. Phoenix.

White, Leslie A.
1942   *The Pueblo of Santa Ana, New Mexico.* Memoirs of the American Anthropological Association No. 60. Menasha, Wisconsin.
1949   *The Science of Culture.* Farrar, Straus, New York.
1959   *The Evolution of Culture.* McGraw-Hill, New York.
1962   *The Pueblo of Sia, New Mexico.* Bureau of American Ethnology Bulletin No. 184. Washington, D.C.

1975   *The Concept of Cultural Systems.* Columbia University Press, New York.

Whitecotton, Joseph W., and Richard A. Pailes
1986   New World Precolumbian World Systems. In *Ripples in the Chichimec Sea: New Perspectives on Southwestern-Mesoamerican Interactions,* edited by Frances Joan Mathien and Randall H. McGuire, pp. 183–204. Southern Illinois University Press, Carbondale.

Whiteley, Peter M.
1988   *Deliberate Acts: Changing Hopi Culture Through the Oraibi Split.* The University of Arizona Press, Tucson.

Whitmore, Thomas M., B. L. Turner II, Douglas L. Johnson, Robert W. Kates, and Thomas R. Gottschang
1990   Long-Term Population Change. In *The Earth as Transformed by Human Action: Global and Regional Changes in the Biosphere Over the Past 300 Years,* edited by B. L. Turner, pp. 25–39. Cambridge University Press, New York.

Whittlesey, Stephanie M.
1978   *Status and Death at Grasshopper Pueblo: Experiments Toward an Archaeological Theory of Correlates.* Ph.D dissertation, Department of Anthropology, The University of Arizona, Tucson.
1982   Examination of Previous Work in the Q Ranch Region: Comparison and Analysis. In *Cholla Project Archaeology,* Vol. 3: *The Q Ranch Region,* edited by J. Jefferson Reid, pp. 123–50. Arizona State Museum Archaeological Series No. 161. The University of Arizona, Tucson.
1986   Pueblo IV Settlement Patterns and Organizational Variability in the Point of Pines Region. Paper presented at the 4th Mogollon Conference, Tucson.
1995   Mogollon, Hohokam, and O'otam: Rethinking the Early Formative Period in Southern Arizona. *Kiva* 60:465–80.

Whittlesey, Stephanie M., and Richard Ciolek-Torrello
1992   A Revolt Against Rampant Elites: Toward an Alternative Paradigm. In *Proceedings of the Second Salado Conference Globe, AZ 1992,* edited by Richard C. Lange and Stephen Germick, pp. 312–24. Arizona Archaeological Society Occasional Paper. Phoenix.
1994   The Archaic-Formative Transition in the Tucson Basin. Paper presented at the 59th Annual Meeting of the Society for American Archaeology, Anaheim.

Whittlesey, Stephanie M., Richard S. Ciolek-Torrello, and Matthew A. Sterner

1994   *Southern Arizona, The Last 12,000 Years.* Statistical Research Technical Series No. 48. Tucson.

Whittlesey, Stephanie M., and J. Jefferson Reid

1982   Cholla Project Perspectives on Salado. In *Cholla Project Archaeology*, Vol. 1: *Introduction and Special Studies*, edited by J. Jefferson Reid, pp. 63–80. Arizona State Museum Archaeological Series No. 161. The University of Arizona, Tucson.

Wilcox, David R.

1979   The Hohokam Regional System. In *An Archaeological Test of Sites in the Gila Butte-Santan Region, South-Central Arizona*, by Glen E. Rice, David R. Wilcox, Kevin Rafferty, and James Schoenwetter, pp. 77–116. Technical Paper No. 3. Arizona State University Anthropological Research Papers No. 18. Tempe.

1986   The Tepiman Connection: A Model of Mesoamerican-Southwestern Interaction. In *Ripples in the Chichimec Sea: New Considerations of Southwestern-Mesoamerican Interactions*, edited by Frances Joan Mathien and Randall H. McGuire, pp. 135–54. Southern Illinois University Press, Carbondale.

1987   *Frank Midvale's Investigation of the Site of La Ciudad.* Arizona State University Anthropological Field Studies No. 19. Tempe.

1991a   Hohokam Social Complexity. In *Chaco and Hohokam: Prehistoric Regional Systems in the American Southwest*, edited by Patricia L. Crown and W. James Judge, pp. 253–76. School of American Research Press, Santa Fe.

1991b   Changing Contexts of Pueblo Adaptations, A.D. 1250–1600. In *Farmers, Hunters, and Colonists: Interaction Between the Southwest and the Southern Plains*, edited by Katherine A. Spielmann, pp. 128–54. The University of Arizona Press, Tucson.

1995   A Processual Model of Charles C. Di Peso's Babocomari Site and Related Systems. In *The Gran Chichimeca: Essays on the Archaeology and Ethnohistory of Northern Mesoamerica*, edited by Jonathan E. Reyman, pp. 281–319. Aldershot, Avebury, United Kingdom.

1998   Macroregional Systems in the North American Southwest and Their Relationships. In *Great Towns and Regional Polities*, edited by Jill Neitzel. University of New Mexico Press, Albuquerque, in press.

Wilcox, David R., and Jonathan Haas

1994   The Scream of the Butterfly: Competition and Conflict in the Prehistoric Southwest. In *Themes in Southwest Prehistory*, edited by George J. Gumerman, pp. 211–38. School of American Research Press, Santa Fe.

Wilcox, David R., Thomas R. McGuire, and Charles Sternberg

1981   *Snaketown Revisited: A Partial Cultural Resource Survey, Analysis of Site Structure and an Ethnohistoric Study of the Proposed Hohokam-Pima National Monument.* Arizona State Museum Archaeological Series No. 155. The University of Arizona, Tucson.

Wilcox, David R., and Lynette O. Shenk

1977   *The Architecture of the Casa Grande and Its Interpretation.* Arizona State Museum Archaeological Series No. 115. The University of Arizona, Tucson.

Wilcox, David R., and Charles Sternberg

1981   *Additional Studies of the Architecture of the Casa Grande and Its Interpretation.* Arizona State Museum Archaeological Series No. 146. The University of Arizona, Tucson.

1983   *Hohokam Ballcourts and Their Interpretation.* Arizona State Museum Archaeological Series No. 160. The University of Arizona, Tucson.

Willey, Gordon R.

1966   *An Introduction to American Archaeology: North and Middle America.* Prentice-Hall, Englewood Cliffs.

Willey, Gordon R., and Philip Phillips

1958   *Method and Theory in American Archaeology.* The University of Chicago Press, Chicago.

Wilshusen, Richard H.

1989   Unstuffing the Estufa: Ritual Floor Features in Anasazi Pit Structures and Pueblo Kivas. In *The Architecture of Social Integration in Prehistoric Pueblos*, edited by William D. Lipe and Michelle Hegmon, pp. 89–111. Crow Canyon Archaeological Center Occasional Papers No. 1. Cortez, Colorado.

Withers, Arnold

1973   *Excavations at Valshni Village, Arizona.* Arizona Archaeological Society, Phoenix.

Wittfogel, Karl A.

1957   *Oriental Despotism: A Comparative Study of Total Power.* Yale University Press, New Haven.

Wittfogel, Karl A., and Esther S. Goldfrank

1943   Some Aspects of Pueblo Mythology and Society. *Journal of American Folklore* 56:17–30.

Wobst, H. Martin

1974   Boundary Conditions for Paleolithic Social Systems: A Simulation Approach. *American Antiquity* 39:147–78.

Wolf, Eric R.

1982   *Europe and the People Without History*. University of California Press, Berkeley.

Wood, J. Scott

1979   Settlement and Reoccupation Along Queen Creek, Central Arizona: An Archeological Survey of the Superior Proposed Base for Exchange (South Half), Globe Ranger District, Tonto National Forest. Cultural Resources Report No. 29. USDA Forest Service Southwestern Region, Albuquerque.

1980   The Gentry Timber Sale: Behavioral Patterning and Predictability in the Upper Cherry Creek Area, Central Arizona. Ms. on file, Tonto National Forest, Phoenix.

1983   *The Salado Tradition of the Tonto National Forest: Ethnic Groups and Boundaries.* Cultural Resources Inventory Report No. 82–100. Tonto National Forest, Phoenix.

1985   The Northeastern Periphery. In *Proceedings of the 1983 Hohokam Symposium*, edited by Alfred E. Dittert, Jr., and Donald E. Dove, pp. 239–62. Arizona Archaeological Society Occasional Paper No. 2. Phoenix.

1986   Vale of Tiers: Tonto Basin in the 14th Century. Paper Presented at the 59th Pecos Conference, Payson.

1987   Checklist of Pottery Types for the Tonto National Forest: An Introduction to the Archaeological Ceramics of Central Arizona. *The Arizona Archaeologist* No. 21. Tonto National Forest Cultural Resources Inventory Report No. 87–01. Phoenix.

1989   *Vale of Tiers, Too: Late Classic Period Salado Settlement Patterns and Organizational Models for Tonto Basin.* Cultural Resource Inventory Report 89–12–280. Tonto National Forest, Phoenix.

1992   Toward a New Definition of Salado: Comments and Discussion on the Second Salado Conference. In *Proceedings of the Second Salado Conference Globe, AZ 1992*, edited by Richard C. Lange and Stephen Germick, pp. 337–44. Arizona Archaeological Society Occasional Paper. Phoenix.

Wood, J. Scott, and John W. Hohmann

1985   Foundation's Edge: The Northeastern Periphery and the Development of the Hoho-kam Classic Period. Paper presented at the 50th Annual Meeting of the Society for American Archaeology, Denver.

Wood, J. Scott, and Linda B. Kelley

1988   *Adolph F. Bandelier's Archaeological Survey of Tonto Basin, Tonto National Forest, Arizona.* National Register of Historic Places, Multiple Property Listing, Washington, D.C.

Wood, J. Scott, and Martin E. McAllister

1980   Foundation and Empire: The Colonization of the Northeastern Hohokam Periphery. In *Current Issues in Hohokam Prehistory*, edited by David Doyel and Fred Plog, pp. 180–99. Arizona State University Anthropological Research Papers No. 23. Tempe.

1982   The Salado Tradition: An Alternative View. In *Cholla Project Archaeology*, Vol. 1: *Introduction and Special Studies*, edited by J. Jefferson Reid, pp. 81–94. Arizona State Museum Archaeological Series No. 161. The University of Arizona, Tucson.

1984a   Second Foundation: Settlement Patterns and Agriculture in the Northeastern Hohokam Periphery Central Arizona. In *Prehistoric Agricultural Strategies in the Southwest*, edited by Suzanne K. Fish and Paul R. Fish, pp. 271–89. Arizona State University Anthropological Research Papers No. 33. Tempe.

1984b   Approaches to the Study of Complexity in Prehistoric Central Arizona. In *Research Issues in the Prehistory of Central Arizona: The Central Arizona Water Control Study*, Vol. 1 (Draft), edited by Glen E. Rice and Rachel Most, pp. 84–103. Arizona State University, Tempe.

Wood, J. Scott, Glen Rice, and David Jacobs

1992   Factors Affecting Prehistoric Salado Irrigation in the Tonto Basin. In *Developing Perspectives on Tonto Basin Prehistory*, edited by Charles L. Redman, Glen E. Rice, and Kathryn E. Pedrick, pp. 27–32. Roosevelt Monograph Series No. 2. Arizona State University Anthropological Field Studies No. 27. Tempe.

Wood, James W., George R. Milner, Henry C. Harpending, and Kenneth M. Weiss

1992   The Osteological Paradox: Problems of Inferring Prehistoric Health from Skeletal Samples. *Current Anthropology* 33:343–70.

Woodbury, Richard B.

1961a   *Prehistoric Agriculture at Point of Pines, Arizona*. Memoirs of the Society for American Archaeology No. 17.

1961b   A Reappraisal of Hohokam Irrigation.
         American Anthropologist 63:550–60.

Woodson, Michael Kyle

1994   The Goat Hill Site. Paper presented at the
         67th Pecos Conference, Mesa Verde.

1995   *The Goat Hill Site: A Western Anasazi Pueblo
         in the Safford Valley of Southeastern Arizona.*
         Master's thesis, University of Texas, Austin.

Woosley, Anne I., and Bart Olinger

1993   The Casas Grandes Ceramic Tradition: Pro-
         duction and Interregional Exchange of Ramos
         Polychrome. In *Culture and Contact: Charles C.
         Di Peso's Gran Chichimeca*, edited by Anne I.
         Woosley and John C. Ravesloot, pp. 105–32.
         University of New Mexico Press, Albuquerque.

Wright, Thomas E.

1991   Corn in Them There Hills: Evidence for Up-
         land Agriculture in the Tonto Basin Region,
         Central Arizona. Paper prepared for ASM 450,
         Bioarchaeology. Department of Anthropology,
         Arizona State University, Tempe.

Yoffee, Norman, and Andrew Sherratt

1993   *Archaeological Theory: Who Sets the Agenda?*
         Cambridge University Press, Cambridge.

Young, Jon N.

1967   *The Salado Culture in Southwestern Prehis-
         tory.* Ph.D dissertation, Department of An-
         thropology, The University of Arizona,
         Tucson.

Zedeño, Maria Nieves

1994a   Defining Material Correlates for Ceramic
         Circulation in the Prehistoric Puebloan
         Southwest. Paper presented at the 59th An-
         nual Meeting of the Society for American
         Archaeology, Anaheim.

1994b   *Sourcing Prehistoric Ceramics at Chodistaas
         Pueblo, Arizona: The Circulation of People
         and Pots in the Grasshopper Region.* Anthro-
         pological Papers of the University of Arizona
         No. 58. The University of Arizona Press,
         Tucson.

Zedeño, Maria Nieves, and Leon H. Lorentzen

1995   Landscape, Land Use, and the History of
         Territory Formation: An Example from the
         Puebloan Southwest. Paper presented at the
         60th Annual Meeting of the Society for
         American Archaeology, Minneapolis.

Contributors

E. Charles Adams, Arizona State Museum,
Tucson, Arizona

Karen R Adams, Statistical Research, Inc.,
Tucson, Arizona

Jeffrey H. Altschul, Statistical Research, Inc.,
Tucson, Arizona

Richard S. Ciolek-Torrello, Statistical Research, Inc.,
Tucson, Arizona

Jeffrey S. Dean, Laboratory of Tree-Ring Research ,
Tucson, Arizona

William H. Doelle, Center for Desert Archaeology,
Tucson, Arizona

David E. Doyel, Estrella Cultural Research,
Phoenix, Arizona

Mark D. Elson, Center for Desert Archaeology,
Tucson, Arizona

David A. Gregory, Center for Desert Archaeology,
Tucson, Arizona

Jeffrey A. Homburg, Statistical Research, Inc.,
Tucson, Arizona

David Jacobs, Arizona State University,
Tempe, Arizona

Stephen H. Lekson, University Museum,
Boulder, Colorado

Thomas R. Lincoln, Bureau of Reclamation,
Phoenix, Arizona

Owen Lindauer, Arizona State University,
Tempe, Arizona

Ben A. Nelson, Arizona State University,
Tempe, Arizona

John C. Ravesloot, Gila River Indian Community,
Sacaton, Arizona

Charles L. Redman, Arizona State University,
Tempe, Arizona

Marcia H. Regan, Arizona State University,
Tempe, Arizona

J. Jefferson Reid, University of Arizona,
Tucson, Arizona

Glen E. Rice, Arizona State University, Tempe, Arizona

Steven D. Shelley, Statistical Research, Inc.,
Tucson, Arizona

Arleyn W. Simon, Arizona State University, Tempe, Arizona

Miriam T. Stark, University of Hawaii, Honolulu, Hawaii

John R. Welch, Statistical Research, Inc., Tucson, Arizona

Carla R. Van West, Statistical Research, Inc., Tucson, Arizona

Stephanie M. Whittlesey, Statistical Research, Inc., Tucson, Arizona

J. Scott Wood, Tonto National Forest, Arizona

Index

Acoma, 267, 270

Adobe, coursed, 301, 302

Agave, 48, 150, 179, 231, 264

Alta Vista, 297

Anasazi: coresidence with Mogollon, 251–52; long bone length, 69, 70; migration, 13, 25, 175–82, 195, 196, 263–64, 265–66, 270, 273, 289–90, 322; Preclassic contact with Tonto Basin, 264; skeletal pathology, 67; stature, 71

Animas phase, 292

Anloni, 158

AR-03-12-06-115H, 114

AR-03-12-06-293, 114

AR-03-12-06-746, 115

Arikara, 68, 69, 70

Armer Gulch Ruin, 118

Armer Ranch Ruin, 122; architecture, 113, 118, 140; irrigation district, 134, 137; population, 101; settlement complex, 120, 121, 144

Arroyo Hondo Pueblo, 67, 71, 75

Ash Creek, 61, 84, 86, 87, 88

Azatlan, 123

Ball courts: absent in Tonto Basin, 173; Casas Grandes-type, 298–99, 302; distribution of, 97, 99, 302; irrigation communities and, 152; management of exchange, 145–46; replaced by platform mounds, 308

Bandelier, Adolph, 18, 101

Bass Point Mound, 47, 113, 159–61, 230, 239

Bead Mountain, 125

Bear Village, 247, 251

Besh-Ba-Gowah, 115, 117, 119, 125, 132, 254

Big Ditch, 99

Bis sa'ani, 311

Black Mesa, 71

Bloom Mound, 288

Bourke's Teocalli, 113, 134, 144

Brady Wash, 304

Buena Vista, 280

Burials: accompaniments, 75–78, 206, 207–10; cremations, 73; distribution of, 302; grave facilities, 74–75, 235; with skull deformations, 252, 255; orientation of, 73; postmortem body treatment, 75; Roosevelt Platform Mound Study sample, 58, 59; Salado polychromes associated with, 76–78, 202–4, 207–10; in upper Gila, 280; variation in, 72–73. *See also* Cemeteries

Canyon Creek Ruin, 248, 249

Carter Ranch Pueblo, 67, 71

Casa Buena, 61, 65, 67, 71

Casa Grande Ruin, 223, 286, 304; architecture, 306; Casas Grandes and, 293, 323; platform mounds, 161, 163–64, 305, 307, 308; Salado polychromes, 311

Casas Grandes, 189, 297; burials, 77, 78, 283; Casa Grande and, 293, 323; dating of, 276, 277–78, 285, 288; dental pathology, 66; depopulation of, 288; Gila Polychrome at, 290–91; irrigation at, 312; life expectancies, 65; regional system, 292; Salado and, 8, 13–14, 16, 18, 20, 274, 299; Salado polychromes at, 282–85, 286; skeletal pathology, 67; stature, 71; warehouses, 284

Caserones, 115, 117–18

Cashion, 303

Cemeteries: corporate use of, 256–57; dual organization in,

compound, 163; dental and skeletal pathology, 67; platform mound, 304, 305, 307, 308
Puerco Valley, 71
Pyramid Point: architecture, 118, 134, 183–85, 186, 189, 254, 258; population, 84; site group, 220

Q Ranch region, 246, 247, 248, 249
Q Ranch Ruin, 127, 187, 248, 251
Q Ranch/Vosberg valleys, 126–28

Ranch Creek, 173
Redington, 99
Redistribution, 151, 188
Reeve Ruin, 290
Regional cults, 199–200. See also Katsina Cult; Southwestern Regional Cult
Ricolite, 284
Rio Sonora tradition, 298–99, 302
Risser Ranch, 124
Roasting pits: Gila phase, 236; Roosevelt phase, 227, 228, 229, 230–33
Rock Ball Court, 97, 100
Rock Island Mound, 113, 134
Roosevelt 9:6, 19, 100, 132, 172
Roosevelt Archaeological Project, xiii–xv, 14–15
Roosevelt phase: burials, 73, 74, 230; climate and streamflow, 44, 51, 53; compounds, 225, 256; cotton, 47, 48, 53; demography/population, 47, 62, 63, 64; 86, 87, 88, 90, 91; integration during, 185–86; irrigation, 47–48, 53; middens, 236; plant and animal remains, 39, 40, 48, 49, 50; Pueblo migration during, 175–82, 265–66; roasting pits, 227, 228, 229, 230–33; settlement, 250; social organization, 256–57; Uplands use, 122; wood use, 41, 48, 50
Round Valley site, 124
Rye Creek Ruin: architecture, 113, 114, 118, 137, 185; burials, 74, 77–78; ceramics, 272; sub-Mogollon Rim Cultural Tradition at, 24

Sacaton 9:6, 306
Sacaton phase, 84, 86, 87, 88, 89, 91
Safford Basin, 298, 299–300, 302
Saguaro Muerto, 25, 134, 253, 256; ceramics, 254; intrusive pueblo population at, 176, 182
Salado: burial patterns, 286, 287; in Casa-Casas corridor, 286–87; chronology of, 4, 7; definition of, 143, 314, 321; dispersal of, 269–70; as ethnic/multiethnic group, 260–61, 289; end of, 314; historic review of, 4, 8–9, 18–24, 57, 190; as Hohokam, 24, 241–42; local vs. regional definitions of, 8; as material culture phenomenon, 78–79; as result of Pueblo migration into Tonto Basin, 263–64; social dynamics, 10–12; textiles and spread of, 269; in Upper Gila, 279–82
Salado Conference, 21
Salado polychromes: in burial contexts, 76–78; dating of, 277; as definer of Salado, 4, 8, 24, 190; designs on, 201, 204, 399; distribution of, 16, 144, 302; function outside Tonto Basin, 14; in Globe Highlands, 301; as indicator of

Southwestern Cult, 8, 15, 199; latest, 273; local manufacture of, 20; in northern Mexico, 298, 299, 303; origin of, 269; in Phoenix Basin, 309, 311, 313; relation to Hopi yellow ware, 206; in Tonto Basin, 195. See also Gila Polychrome; Tonto Polychrome
San Jose site, 298–99
San Pedro River, 93, 99, 302
Santa Cruz phase, 84, 86, 87, 88, 89, 91
Schmidt, Erich F., 18
Schoolhouse Point Mesa, 134; Gila phase on, 86, 120, 186, 234–37; natural setting, 224; oval rooms, 229; Preclassic occupation, 225–26; Roosevelt phase, 226–34; site types, 213, 225; village, 220–23, 224–25, 238
Schoolhouse Point Mound, 137, 138; architecture, 115, 117–18, 216, 217, 225, 254, 256; burials/cemeteries, 74, 76, 77, 206, 235–36, 254, 255, 257; ceramics, 212; compounds, 229, 238; Gila phase at, 140, 234–37, 238–39, 250; middens, 236–37; modified human teeth, 72; population, 51, 60, 62, 63; as secondary settlement, 144; shell, 258; skeletal pathology, 67, 68
Sedentary period: climate and streamflow, 42, 43; in eastern Tonto Basin, 174–75, 226; settlement, 249–50; subsistence, 42
Segmentary organizations, 154–55, 156–59, 162–66, 198
Serpent symbolism, 309, 310
Settlement systems: mountain Mogollon, 246–49; Tonto Basin, 113–20, 249–51
Shell, 148, 149–50, 258
Shoofly Ruin, 124, 182, 251
Sierra Ancha, 47, 53, 126–29
Sinagua, 72
Site 9, 149
Site 11, 149
Site 128, 149, 150
Skeletal remains: age and sex distributions, 58, 60, 62, 64; dental pathology, 66–67; life expectancy/survivorship, 61, 63, 64, 65; long bone lengths, 68–70; nonrepresentativeness of, 58; skeletal pathology, 67–68; stature, 70, 71, 72; teeth modification, 72
Snaketown, 19, 172, 303, 305, 307, 310, 311
Snaketown phase, 41, 85, 88
Social organization: indicated in burials, 73, 74, 75, 78, 258; moiety, 258–59; mountain Mogollon, 255–56; segmentary, 154–59, 162–66; sodalities, 258; Tonto Basin Salado, 187–88, 156–59
SON F:11:5, 303
Southwestern Regional Cult, 24; difference from Katsina Cult, 271, 272–73; as nonkin integrative mechanism, 214, 216; Salado polychromes and, 8, 12, 199, 218, 270, 271, 274, 290
Specialization, 180, 181, 189
Squash, 42, 48
Subsistence: Classic period, 47–52, 53; mountain Mogollon, 246–49; plant and animal remains, 33–40; Preclassic, 33–42, 46–47, 48, 49, 50; Tonto Basin, 249–51
Sundown site, 66
Sycamore Creek, 120